Depression and Anxiety Disorders: Diagnosis and Treatment

Depression and Anxiety Disorders: Diagnosis and Treatment

Edited by Dustin Layton

AMERICAN
MEDICAL PUBLISHERS
www.americanmedicalpublishers.com

American Medical Publishers,
41 Flatbush Avenue,
1st Floor, New York,
NY 11217, USA

Visit us on the World Wide Web at:
www.americanmedicalpublishers.com

ISBN: 978-1-63927-437-6

Cataloging-in-Publication Data

Depression and anxiety disorders : diagnosis and treatment / edited by Dustin Layton.
p. cm.
Includes bibliographical references and index.
ISBN 978-1-63927-437-6
1. Anxiety disorders. 2. Depression, Mental. 3. Neuroses. 4. Manic-depressive illness.
5. Psychiatry. I. Layton, Dustin.
RC531 .A59 2022
616.852 2--dc23

Table of Contents

Preface

A group of mental disorders categorized by significant feelings of anxiety and fear are known as anxiety disorders. Anxiety is an emotion in which a person feels an unpleasant state of inner turmoil. Fear is a feeling caused by perceived danger or threat. These feelings can cause physical symptoms such as a fast heart rate and shakiness. The cause of anxiety disorders is a combination of environmental and genetic factors. It can also be caused due to drugs, stress and medical conditions. Anxiety disorders can be classified into generalized anxiety disorder, specific phobias, social anxiety disorder and panic disorder, etc. Depression is a condition of low mood and aversion to activity, which directly affects a person's thought, behavior, feelings, motivation, and sense of well-being. Depression can be long term as well as short term. It can cause sadness, difficulty in thinking and concentration, a feeling of dejection and hopelessness. Major depressive disorders are generally accompanied by anxiety disorders. This book provides comprehensive insights into anxiety disorder and depression. It is a compilation of chapters that discuss the most vital aspects related to this disorder. This book is a resource guide for experts as well as students.

The researches compiled throughout the book are authentic and of high quality, combining several disciplines and from very diverse regions from around the world. Drawing on the contributions of many researchers from diverse countries, the book's objective is to provide the readers with the latest achievements in the area of research. This book will surely be a source of knowledge to all interested and researching the field.

In the end, I would like to express my deep sense of gratitude to all the authors for meeting the set deadlines in completing and submitting their research chapters. I would also like to thank the publisher for the support offered to us throughout the course of the book. Finally, I extend my sincere thanks to my family for being a constant source of inspiration and encouragement.

Editor

1

Suicidal ideation in primary care patients suffering from panic disorder with or without agoraphobia

Tobias Teismann[1*], Karoline Lukaschek[2,3], Thomas S. Hiller[4], Jörg Breitbart[4], Christian Brettschneider[5], Ulrike Schumacher[6], Jürgen Margraf[1], Jochen Gensichen[2,4] and the Jena Paradies Study Group

Abstract

Background: Suicidal ideation is common in patients suffering from panic disorder. The present study investigated rates of suicidal ideation and risk factors for suicidal ideation in a sample of primary care patients suffering from panic disorder with or without agoraphobia.

Methods: A total of $N = 296$ patients [$n = 215$ (72.6%) women; age: $M = 43.99$, $SD = 13.44$] were investigated. Anxiety severity, anxiety symptoms, avoidance behavior, comorbid depression diagnosis, severity of depression, age, sex, employment status, living situation and frequency of visits at the general practitioner were considered as risk factors of suicidal ideation.

Results: Suicidal ideation was experienced by 25% of the respondents. In a logistic regression analysis, depression diagnosis and depression severity emerged as significant risk factors for suicidal ideation. Anxiety measures were not associated with suicidal ideation.

Conclusion: Suicidal ideation is common in primary care patients suffering from panic disorder with or without agoraphobia. Individuals with greater burden of mental illness in terms of mood disorder comorbidity and depressive symptomatology are especially likely to suffer from suicidal ideation.

Keywords: Suicidal ideation, Panic disorder, Agoraphobia, Primary care

Background

Suicidal ideation is highly prevalent in the general population (8.5%; [1]) and even more in clinical samples (18–32%; [2]). Thinking about suicide is a risk factor for completed suicide [3], and even passive ideation, such as a wish to die, has been identified as a predictor for death by suicide [4]. Since there is a rapid transition from suicidal ideation to plans and attempts [5] early detection of suicidal ideation is essential to initiate timely interventions. A better knowledge of risk factors for suicidal ideation, especially in primary care patients, may therefore help to identify potentially suicidal patients.

One of the strongest risk factors for suicidal ideation and behavior is the presence of a mental disorder, most prominently affective disorders, schizophrenia and substance use disorders [6], but also anxiety disorders [7]. Among anxiety disorders, panic disorder has received a great deal of attention: Using data from the National Institute of Mental Health Epidemiologic Catchment Area (ECA) study, Weissman et al. [8] found that 47% of individuals with panic disorder reported lifetime suicidal ideation. In European community studies lower - but still significant - rates of lifetime suicidal ideation have been found in persons suffering from panic disorder (23.7%: [2]; 15.7%: [9]). In studies on treatment-seeking patients suffering from panic disorder 31% reported having had suicidal thoughts in the past year [10] and 25% in the past week [11] - even after excluding patients suffering from comorbid major depression. Taken together, there is strong evidence that patients suffering

* Correspondence: tobias.teismann@rub.de
[1]Mental Health Research and Treatment Center, Ruhr-Universität Bochum, Massenbergstraße 11, 44787 Bochum, Germany
Full list of author information is available at the end of the article

from panic disorder display heightened risk for suicidal ideation, which underscores the debilitating character of the disorder. Yet, most information concerning suicidal ideation in panic disorder stems from studies on the general population or psychiatric services [7] and may not apply to primary care settings.

The prevalence of anxiety disorders is higher in primary care settings than in the general population [12] and current panic disorder/agoraphobia diagnoses are found in about 4% of primary care patients [13]. Mental health care for panic disorder/agoraphobia is sought and obtained mostly from general practitioners [14]. Yet, suicidal ideation often goes unrecognized in these settings [15], even though almost 50% of patients who died through suicide had seen their general practitioner in the month preceding their death [16] and up to 20% visit a primary care provider within 1 day of their death [17]. In light of these findings, primary care settings have been emphasized as an essential component of effective and comprehensive suicide prevention [18].

Therefore, the first aim of this study was to identify rates of suicidal ideation in primary care patients diagnosed with panic disorder with or without agoraphobia. The second aim was to identify characteristic symptoms that are associated with suicidal ideation and may therefore guide risk assessment in primary care patients. Anxiety severity, anxiety symptoms, agoraphobic avoidance as well as depression diagnosis, depression severity, demographic markers (age, sex, living alone, unemployment) previously shown to be associated with suicidal ideation [19], and frequency of visits at the general practitioner, as an alternative measure of general distress, were considered as potential predictors of suicidal ideation.

Methods

Study design

A cross-sectional study that was nested in a randomized trial comparing a practice team-supported, self-managed exposure program for patients with panic disorder (PD) with or without agoraphobia (AG) in general practices to usual care was conducted [Trial Registration: ISCRTN64669297]. The study was approved by the Ethics Committee of the Friedrich-Schiller-University at the Medical Faculty (Jena, Germany). Details of the study design and recruiting process have been published previously [20]. To be eligible for the trial, patients had to meet the following inclusion criteria: (1) being at least 18 years of age, (2) being diagnosed with PD/AG (ICD-10: F41.0 or F40.01) by a general practioner-led clinical interview, (3) showing a minimum total score on the 'Overall Anxiety and Impairment Scale' (OASIS) of 8 points [21] and at least two positive answers on the panic module of the 'Patient Health Questionnaire' (PHQ; [22]) at the time of inclusion, (4) having sufficient German language skills, (5) having a telephone connection, (5) being able of giving written informed consent to participate in the study. Patients were excluded if they met one or more of the following exclusion criteria according to general practitioner's clinical evaluation: suffering from suicidal tendencies in need of immediate treatment, acute or chronic psychosis, dependence on psychoactive substance(s), or severe physical illness, being pregnant, receiving professional psychotherapeutic treatment for their anxiety disorder at the time of inclusion. Of note, none of the patients screened for the study was excluded due to suicidal tendencies in need of immediate treatment. Data collection occurred between August 2012 and October 2014.

Participants

At baseline, a sample of 419 patients took part in an exhaustive assessment. The full set of questionnaires was completed by 296 patients [$n = 215$ (72.6%) women; age: $M = 43.99$, $SD = 13.44$] and only patients who completed all questionnaires were included in the current analysis. Patients with complete data and patients who completed only a subset of questionnaires did neither differ in sex nor diagnosis. However, patients who completed only a subset of questionnaires were older than patients with complete data, $t(414) = 5.23$, $p < .000$.

Half of the patients were married ($n = 150$; 50.6%), 33.4% were singles ($n = 99$), 11.8% were separated/divorced ($n = 35$) and 4.1% were widowed ($n = 12$). A minority of patients was unemployed ($n = 41$, 13.6%). The vast majority ($n = 231$, 78%) suffered from panic disorder with agoraphobia, and $n = 65$ (22%) from panic disorder without agoraphobia. Fifty-five individuals (18.6%) suffered from a comorbid depressive disorder. Most patients saw their general practitioner on a very regular basis, with $M = 8.76$ ($SD = 8.72$) visits within the last 6 months. All participants were Caucasian.

Measures

Suicidal ideation

Suicidal ideation was measured using the respective item from the Patient Health Questionnaire' (PHQ-9; [22]): "Over the last two weeks, how often have you been bothered by thoughts that you would be better of dead, or of hurting yourself in some way?" Response options range from "not at all", "several days", "more than half the days" to "nearly every day". Response to the PHQ-9-suicide item has recently been shown to be a strong predictor of suicide attempt and suicide death within the following year [23].

Anxiety symptoms

Anxiety Symptoms were measured with the Beck Anxiety Inventory (BAI; [24]). The BAI is a 21-item self-report measure that surveys anxiety symptoms on a 4-point severity scale. It has demonstrated good internal consistency (Cronbach's $\alpha \geq .85$ across clinical and non-clinical samples [25]). The internal consistency for the BAI in the current sample was $\alpha = .91$.

Anxiety severity

The Overall Anxiety Severity and Impairment Scale (OASIS; [26]) is a 5-item self-report measure to assess frequency and intensity of anxiety symptoms, functional impairment related to these symptoms and behavioral avoidance. All items are answered on a 5-point scale ranging from 0 (not at all) to 4 (extreme). The OASIS has a unidimensional factor structure and has been shown to have a good internal consistency (Cronbach's $\alpha = .89$) as well as convergent and divergent validity [21]. Internal consistency was rather modest in the current sample: $\alpha = .67$.

Agoraphobic avoidance

The 'Mobility Inventory' (MI; subscale 'alone'; [27]) was used to assess agoraphobic avoidance behavior across a variety of different situations. All items are answered on a 5-point scale ranging from 1 (never) to 5 (always). The MI-total score has an excellent internal consistency: Cronbach's $\alpha \geq .94$ [27]. Accordingly, internal consistency was good in the present sample: $\alpha = .95$.

Depressive symptoms

Severity of depressive symptoms was measured by the 'Patient Health Questionnaire' (PHQ-[9, 22]). The PHQ-9 assesses the occurrence of nine depressive symptoms within the previous 2 weeks. It has been shown to have good internal consistency: Cronbach's $\alpha \geq .86$ [28]. Internal consistency was $\alpha = .84$ in the present sample. The suicide item was excluded from the PHQ-sum score to avoid overlapping and thus part-whole correlations.

Statistical analyses

We conducted bivariate correlation analyses (Spearman) of all study variables. Then, a logistic regression analysis was performed with suicidal ideation (yes/no) as criterion. Age, sex, current unemployment (yes/no), living status (living alone: yes/no), frequency of visits at the general practitioner, diagnosis of panic disorder with vs. without agoraphobia, comorbid depression disorder (yes/no), depressive symptom severity, anxious symptoms, anxiety severity and avoidance behavior were considered as predictors of suicidal ideation. Derived odds rations (including 95% confidence interval, CI) are presented for each predictor variable. Tolerance in the collinearity statistics was higher than 0.2 for all models, indicating the absence of multicollinearity. All statistical analyses were conducted using the statistical analysis program IBM SPSS Statistics 21 (SPSS Inc., Illinois, Chicago).

Results

Descriptive statistics and correlations

Descriptive statistics for each measure are presented in Table 1. A quarter of the sample (25%; $n = 74$) reported suicidal ideation (i.e., scores > 0 on the PHQ-9 suicide item) within the last 2 weeks: Sixty-one patients (20.5%) indicated suffering from suicidal ideation for "several days" during the last 2 weeks, nine patients (3.1%) indicated that they had suffered from suicidal ideation for "more than half the days" and four patients (1.4%) indicated suffering from suicidal ideation "nearly every day".

As shown in Table 1, suicidal ideation correlates positively with anxiety symptoms, anxiety severity and depression. However, an association with avoidance behavior was not detected.

Risk factors of suicidal ideation

Table 2 shows the results of the logistic regression analysis with suicidal ideation as criterion variable.

Only comorbid depression disorder and depression severity predicted concurrent suicidal ideation. Neither anxiety symptoms nor anxiety severity and avoidance behavior emerged as significant predictors.

Discussion

Results of the present study indicate that suicidal ideation is common in primary care patients suffering from panic disorder with or without agoraphobia. In total, 25% of the patients reported suicidal ideation within the last 2 weeks. This percentage closely approximates those from other studies on patient samples suffering from anxiety disorders [11, 29] and points to the debilitating character of the disorder. In a logistic regression analysis, only comorbid depression diagnosis and depression severity emerged as significant predictors of suicidal

Table 1 Means, standard deviations and correlations of study variables

	M (SD)	PHQ-SI
PHQ-SI	0.31 (0.59)	–
BAI	28.71 (12.33)	.233**
OASIS	12.54 (2.66)	.190**
MI	2.28 (0.83)	.077
PHQ	11.10 (5.25)	.417**

BAI Beck Anxiety Inventory, *MI* Mobility Inventory, *OASIS* Overall Anxiety Severity and Impairment Scale, *PHQ* Patient Health Questionaire, *PHQ-SI* Patient Health Questionaire – Suicide Ideation Item
**= $p < .01$

Table 2 Logistic regression analysis predicting suicidal ideation

	OR (95% CI)	21p
Age	1.01 (.99–1.04)	n.s.
Sex	.83 (.40–1.72)	n.s.
Living alone (yes/no)	1.20 (.64–2.61)	n.s.
Unemployment (yes/no)	.79 (.32–1.96)	n.s.
GP-visits	1.02 (.99–1.06)	n.s.
PD with AG vs. PD without AG	1.07 (.49–2.35)	n.s.
Comorbid depression (yes/no)	2.33 (1.12–4.84)	.023
PHQ	1.22 (1.13–1.32)	.000
BAI	1.01 (.98–1.04)	n.s.
OASIS	1.02 (.90–1.16)	n.s.
MI	.70 (.45–1.07)	n.s.

AG Agoraphobia, *BAI* Beck Anxiety Inventory, *MI* Mobility Inventory, *GP* general practitioner, *OASIS* Overall Anxiety Severity and Impairment Scale, *PD* Panic disorder, *PHQ* Patient Health Questionaire

ideation. Anxiety measures were not associated with suicidal ideation. Furthermore, patients suffering from panic disorder with agoraphobia were not more likely to suffer from suicidal ideation than patients suffering from panic disorder without agoraphobia.

Taken together, the current findings complement previous research that found depression to be the key risk factor for suicidal ideation and behavior within samples of anxiety patients (e.g., [29, 30]). However, the relationship between panic disorder and suicidal ideation and behavior remains a controversial one, as some studies found such an association, even in the absence of coexisting major depression [8]. Furthermore, panic attacks have repeatedly been shown to be associated with imminent suicide risk [31, 32]. Against this background the findings of Yaseen et al. [32] are of particular interest: they report that only fear of dying within a panic attack is prospectively associated with suicide attempts, whereas no other panic attack symptom was associated with subsequent suicidal ideation and behavior.

In terms of clinical implications, the results of the current study highlight the importance of suicide risk assessments in anxiety patients. Though suicide assessments for individuals suffering from depression has received considerable attention within primary care (e.g., [33]), findings point to the additional need for routine suicide risk assessments in patients suffering from panic disorder [29]. Taken together, general practitioners should be encouraged to ask about suicidal ideation in their anxiety patients, particularly in those suffering from comorbid depression.

The strengths of the present investigation are its embedding within the framework of the thoroughly designed Jena-PARADIES study and the use of well-established depression and anxiety instruments. Yet, there are some limitations to the current study. First, the present investigation is a cross-sectional analysis; therefore, conclusions on causality cannot be drawn. Second, suicidal ideation was assessed using a single item self-report measure, instead of a multi-item self-report questionnaire. Single-item assessment are associated with an increased risk of misclassification [34]; at the same time, Simon et al. [23] reported strong evidence for the predictive ability of the PHQ suicide item [23]. Third, most patients reported that suicidal ideation would occur only occasionally. It therefore remains unclear to what extent results generalize to samples with more intensive suicidal thoughts. Finally, the group of predictors used in the study was far from exhaustive. In particular, we did not measure anxiety cognitions or anxiety sensitivity, both variables that have been associated with suicidal ideation [32, 35].

Conclusion

The present study showed that suicidal ideation is not uncommon in primary care patients suffering from panic disorder with or without agoraphobia. Patients particularly affected are those suffering from comorbid mood disorders and depressive symptomatology [29].

Acknowledgements

The authors thank all GPs and patients who participated in this study.

Funding

This trial was funded by the German Federal Ministry of Education and Research (BMBF; grant-number: 01GY1146). The funding source was not involved in the interpretation of the data, in the writing of the report and in the decision to submit the article for publication.

Authors' contributions

TT and KL wrote a first draft of the current manuscript. TSH, JM and JG were responsible for the design and conception of the study. TSH, JB, CB were responsible for the acquisition of data and US for data analysis. All authors were involved in revising the manuscript critically for important intellectual content and all authors gave final approval of the current manuscript version to be published.

Consent for publication

Not applicable.

Competing interests

The authors declare that they have no competing interests. All authors had financial support from BMBF for the submitted work; no financial relationships with any organisations that might have an interest in the submitted work in the previous 3 years; no other relationships or activities that could appear to have influenced the submitted work.

Author details

[1]Mental Health Research and Treatment Center, Ruhr-Universität Bochum, Massenbergstraße 11, 44787 Bochum, Germany. [2]Institute of General Practice and Family Medicine, University Hospital of Ludwig-Maximilians- University Munich, Pettenkoferstr. 10, D-80336 Munich, Germany. [3]Institute of

Epidemiology, Helmholtz Zentrum München, German Research Center for Environmental Health, Ingolstädter Landstraße 1, D-85764 Neuherberg, Germany. [4]Institute of General Practice and Family Medicine, Jena University Hospital, Friedrich-Schiller-Universität, Bachstr. 18, D-07743 Jena, Germany. [5]Department of Health Economics and Health Services Research, Hamburg Center for Health Economics, University Medical Center Hamburg-Eppendorf, Martinistr. 52, D-20246 Hamburg, Germany. [6]Centre for Clinical Studies, Jena University Hospital, Salvador-Allende-Platz 27, D-07747 Jena, Germany.

References

1. Lukaschek K, Engelhardt H, Baumert J, Ladwig KH. No correlation between rates of suicide ideation and completed suicides in Europe: analysis of 49,008 participants (55+) based on the survey of health, ageing and retirement in Europe (SHARE). Eur Psychiatry. 2015;30:874–9.
2. Bernal M, Haro JM, Bernert S, Brugha T, de Graaf R, Bruffaerts R, Lépine JP, de Girolamo G, Vilagut G, Gasquet I, Torres JV, Kovess V, Heider D, Neeleman J, Kessler R, Alonso J. Risk factors for suicidality in Europe: results from the ESEMED study. J Affect Disord. 2007;101:27–34.
3. Brown GK, Beck AT, Steer RA, Grisham JR. Risk factors for suicide in psychiatric outpatients: a 20-year prospective study. J Consult Clin Psychol. 2000;68:371–7.
4. Brown GK, Steer RA, Henriques GR, Beck AT. The internal struggle between the wish to die and the wish to live: a risk factor for suicide. Am J Psychiatry. 2005;162:1977–9.
5. Borges G, Chiu WT, Hwang I, Panchal BN, Ono Y, Sampson NA, Kessler RC, Nock MK. Prevalence, onset , and transitions among suicidal behaviors. In Nock MK, Borges G, Ono Y, editors. Suicide. Global perspectives from the WHO world mental health survey. Cambridge: Cambridge University Press; 2014. p. 65–74.
6. Turecki G, Brent DA. Suicide and suicidal behavior. Lancet. 2016;387:1227–39.
7. Kanwar A, Prokop LJ, Sim LA, Feldstein D, Wang Z, Murad MH. The association between anxiety disorders and suicidal behavior: a systematic review and meta-analysis. Depress Anxiety. 2013;30:917–29.
8. Weisman MM, Klerman GL, Markowith JS, Ouelette R, Phil N. Suicidal ideation and suicide attempts in panic disorder and attacks. N Engl J Med. 1989;321:1209–14.
9. Sareen J, Cox BJ, Afifi TO, de Graaf R, Asmundson GJG, ten Have M, Stein MB. Anxiety disorders and risk for suicidal ideation and suicide attempts. Arch Gen Psychiatry. 2005;62:1249–57.
10. Cox BJ, Direnfeld DM, Swinson RP, Norton GR. Suicidal ideation and suicide attempts in panic disorder and social phobia. Am J Psychiatry. 1994;151: 882–7.
11. Fleet RP, Dupuis G, Marchand A, Burelle D, Arsenault A, Beitman MD. Panic disorder in emergency department chest pain patients. Am J Med. 1996; 101:371–80.
12. Kroenke K, Spitzer RL, Williams JB, Monahan PO, Lowe B. Anxiety disorders in primary care: prevalence, impairment, comorbidity, and detection. Ann Intern Med. 2007;146:317–25.
13. Löwe B, Gräfe K, Zipfel S, Spitzer RL, Herrmann-Lingen C, Witte S, Herzog W. Detecting panic disorder in medical and psychosomatic outpatients: comparative validation of the hospital anxiety and depression scale, the patient health questionnaire, a screening question, and physicians' diagnosis. J Psychosom Res. 2003;55:515–9.
14. Kessler RC, Chiu WT, Jin R, Ruscio AM, Shear K, Walters EE. The epidemiology of panic attacks, panic disorder, and agoraphobia in the National Comorbidity Survey Replication. Arch Gen Psychiatry. 2006;63:415–24.
15. Vannoy SD, Robins LS. Suicide-related discussions with depressed primary care patients in the USA: gender and quality gaps. A mixed methods analysis. BMJ. 2011;1:e000198.
16. Luoma JB, Martin CE, Pearson JL. Contact with mental health and primary care providers before suicide: a review of the evidence. Am J Psychiatry. 2002;169:909–16.
17. Pirkis J, Burgess P. Suicide and recency of health care contacts: a systematic review. Br J Psychiatry. 1998;36:29–35.
18. Bryan CJ, Britton PC. Treating self-directed violence in primary care settings. In: Bryan, CJ, editor. Preventing suicide attempts. A guide to brief treatments across clinical settings. New York: Routledge; 2015. p. 141–57.
19. Nock MK, Borges G, Ono Y. Suicide. Global perspectives from the WHO world mental health survey. Cambridge: Cambridge University Press; 2014.
20. Gensichen J, Hiller TS, Breitbart J, Teismann T, Brettschneider C, Schumacher U, Piwtorak A, König HH, Hoyer H, Schneider N, Schelle M, Blank W, Thiel P, Wensing M, Margraf J. Patient activation for anxiety disorders – study protocol of a cluster randomized controlled trial in primary care [ISRCTN64669297]. Trials. 2015;15:112.
21. Norman SB, Campbell-Sills L, Hitchcock CA, Sullivan S, Rochlin A, Wilkins KC, Stein MB. Psychometrics of a brief measure of anxiety to detect severity and impairment: the overall anxiety severity and impairment scale (OASIS). J Psychiatr Res. 2011;45:262–8.
22. Spitzer RL, Kroenke K, Williams JB. Validation and utility of a self-report version of PRIME-MD: the PHQ primary care study. JAMA. 1999;282:1737–44.
23. Simon GS, Rutter CM, Peterson D, Oliver M, Whiteside U, Operskalski B, Ludman EJ. Do PHQ depression questionnaires completed during outpatient visits predict subsequent suicide attempt or suicide death? Psychiatr Serv. 2013;64:1195–202.
24. Beck AT, Epstein N, Brown G, Steer RA. An inventory for measuring clinical anxiety: psychometric properties. J Consult Clin Psychol. 1988;56:893–7.
25. Margraf J, Ehlers A. Beck-Angstinventar. Göttingen: Hogrefe; 2007.
26. Norman SB, Hami-Cissell S, Means-Christensen AJ, Stein MB. Development and validation of an overall anxiety severity and impairment scale (OASIS). Depress Anxiety. 2006;23:245–9.
27. Chambless DL, Caputo GC, Jasin SE, Gracely EJ, Williams C. The mobility inventory for agoraphobia. Behav Res Ther. 1985;23:35–44.
28. Kroenke K, Spitzer RL, Williams JB. The PHQ-9 – validity of a brief depression severity measure. J Gen Intern Med. 2001;16:606–13.
29. Bomyea J, Lang AJ, Craske MG, Chavira D, Sherbourne CD, Rose RD, Golinell D, Campells-Sills L, Welch SS, Sullivan G, Bystritsky A, Roy-Byrne P, Stein MB. Suicidal ideation and risk factors in primary care patients with anxiety disorders. Psychiatry Res. 2013;30:60–5.
30. Warshaw MG, Massion AO, Peterson LG, Pratt LA, Keller MB. Suicidal behavior in patients with panic disorder: retrospective and prospective data. J Affect Disord. 1995;34:235–47.
31. Fawcett J, Scheftner MD, Fogg L, Clark DC, Young MA, Hedeker D, Dibbons R. Time-related predictors of suicide in major affective disorder. Am J Psychiatry. 1990;147:1189–94.
32. Yaseen ZS, Chartrand H, Mojtabai R, Bolton J, Galynker II. Fear of dying in panic attacks predicts suicide attempts in comorbid depressive illness. Depress Anxiety. 2013;30:930–9.
33. Bruce ML, Ten Have TR, Reynolds CF, Katz II, Schulberg HC, Mulsant BH, Brown GK, McAvay GJ, Pearson JL, Alexopoulos GS. Reducing suicidal ideation and depressive symptoms in depressed older primary care patients: a randomized controlled trial. JAMA. 2004;291:1081–91.
34. Millner AJ, Lee MD, Nock MK. Single-item measurement of suicidal behaviors: validity and consequences of misclassification. PLoS One. 2015; 10(10):e0141606.
35. Valentiner DP, Gutierrez PM, Blacker D. Anxiety measures and their relationship to adolescent suicidal ideation and behavior. J Anxiety Disord. 2002;16:11–32.

2

Anxiety and depression in primary Sjögren's syndrome

Yafei Cui[1,2†], Ling Xia[3†], Lin li[2†], Qian Zhao[2], Shengnan Chen[2] and Zhifeng Gu[1*]

Abstract

Background: Prevalence of anxiety and depression is high in people with Primary Sjögren's syndrome (pSS). However, there are currently no known reported studies about anxiety/depression in pSS patients from China. Our aim was to compare anxiety/depression in pSS patients and healthy controls; to investigate the prevalence of anxiety and/or depression among pSS patients in China; to evaluate its relationship with the disease activity, fatigue, pain, education, ocular surface disease, oral health, swallowing disorders, employment status, European League Against Rheumatism Sjögren's Syndrome Patient Reported Index(ESSPRI) as well as to analyze potential determinants of anxiety and depression.

Methods: In this study, 160 pSS patients and 170 age- and sex- matched healthy controls were included. Participants completed self-administered questionnaires, Hospital Anxiety and Depression Scale (HADS) and so on. Independent samples t-tests, χ^2 analyses and multivariable stepwise logistic regression modeling were used to analyze the data.

Results: We found 33.8% pSS patients were anxiety, and 36.9% had depression, which were significantly higher than controls. And there were significant correlations among education, employment status, disease activity, fatigue, ocular surface disease, ESSPRI, oral health, swallowing disorders and anxiety/depression. Meanwhile, logistic regression analysis revealed that oral health and swallowing disorders were significantly associated with anxiety in pSS patients; as well as fatigue was significantly associated with depression.

Conclusions: The prevalence of depression and anxiety was high in adult pSS patients. Interestingly, oral health and swallowing disorders were the most important predictors of anxiety in pSS patients. Therefore, rheumatologists should pay attention to the potential mental comorbidities while managing patients with pSS and provide the basis for mental health providers in order to identify effective strategies for preventing and treating depression and anxiety among adult pSS patients. Simultaneously, rheumatologists should also focus on the oral health and swallowing disorders in pSS patients.

Keywords: Primary Sjögren's syndrome, Depression, Anxiety, Disease activity

Background

Primary Sjögren's syndrome (pSS) is a systemic rheumatic autoimmune disease characterized by dryness in eyes and mouth [1]. In addition, pSS also may cause extraglandular features, with patients experiencing symptoms of pain, fatigue, anxiety, depression and negatively affect psychological, physical and social functioning [2], which has eventually the potential to impair the health-related quality of life (HR-QoL) [3]. Meanwhile, a significantly higher prevalence of mental health disorders has been consistently demonstrated in pSS patients compared with the general population [4]. As the most frequent subjective symptoms reported, depression and anxiety often have profound impacts on pSS patients' well-being including increased incidence of cardiovascular diseases [4], associated with several psychological disorders [5], working disability [6] and may lead to disease flares. Therefore, depression and anxiety may be useful targets for interventions aimed at improving subjective health and quality of life in individuals with pSS.

* Correspondence: guzf@ntu.edu.cn
†Equal contributors
[1]Department of Rheumatology, Affliated Hospital of Nantong University, 20th Xisi road, 226001 Nantong, People's Republic of China
Full list of author information is available at the end of the article

Anxiety and/or depression may cause a decreased level of physical activity and decreased compliance with therapy, which can lead to worsening of disease and poorer health outcomes. pSS is a chronic debilitating condition that mainly affects the patients emotionally [7]. A common mental health problem among adults with pSS is depression. Depression was more common in patients with pSS than health controls, with a prevalence of 32-45.8% [8]. Generally depression accompanies a number of illnesses characterized by chronic inflammatory response [9]. Depression in pSS patients has been related to continuous fatigue, decreased HR-QoL, loss of work productivity, enhanced levels of physical disability and medical costs [10, 11]. Notably, anxiety was more frequent than depression in pSS. Besides, depressed pSS patients have poorer prognosis, including various complications [3]. The aim of the present study was to investigate the prevalence and characteristics of anxiety and depression in pSS and to examine the relationships between disease activity, fatigue, pain, education, the ocular surface disease, oral health, swallowing disorders, employment status, ESSPRI and anxiety/depression. Moreover, we wished to explore the possible risk factors of anxiety and depression.

Methods

Participants

The study was carried out in the Afliated Hospital of Nantong University from July 2016 to June 2017. pSS patients were outpatients or inpatients and healthy controls were from a population for a checkup. Of 182 patients with pSS were consecutively recruited to join in a single cross-sectional study and 160 (87.91% of the patients) participated in and finished questionnaires finally. We matched them by age and sex to avoid a possible bias. This study was approved by the Ethics Committee of the Afliated Hospital of Nantong University (2017-K003), and all subjects signed an informed consent form. Criteria for inclusion were age 18 years and older; patients conformed to the American College of Rheumatology criteria for pSS [12]. Controls were removed if they shown other systemic diseases. There was no significant demographic difference between the two groups.

Main research tools

Participants finished self-administered questionnaires, Hospital Anxiety and Depression Scale (HADS), Fatigue Severity Scale (FSS), the Visual Analogue Scale (VAS) and so on. Additionally, the European League Against Rheumatism Sjögren's Syndrome Disease Activity Index (ESSDAI) and Patient Reported Index (ESSPRI) were documented in patients.

Demographics and clinical variables

Demographic features contain the following: age, sex, marital status, education level, occupation, yearly per capita income, type of medical insurance, family history of Sjögren's syndrome, disease duration, comorbidity(autoimmune liver disease, blood system disease, cardiovascular disease, kidney disease, lung disease, thyroid disease, myositis, etc), hospitalization(admission to a hospital for treatment due to Primary Sjögren's syndrome ever). Clinical variables of disease duration and medications use were obtained by asking patients or viewing medical records.

Disease activity

EULAR Sjögren's Syndrome Disease Activity Index (ESSDAI) is a clinical index assessed by rheumatologists to measure disease activity in pSS cases. There are 12 weighted fields (organ systems: cutaneous, respiratory, renal, articular, muscular, peripheral nervous system, central nervous system, haematological, glandular, constitutional, lymphadenopathy, biological), with a score ranging form 0-123 [13]. For each question, characteristics of disease activity are divided into three or four levels based on their severity [14]. Scores < 5 suggest "low disease activity"; 5 to 13 represent a "moderate disease activity"; and ≥ 14 indicate a "high disease activity" [15].

Patient reported index

EULAR Sjögren's Syndrome Patient Reported Index (ESSPRI) tests the intensity of symptoms and contains three domains for dryness, pain and fatigue on 0-10 numerical scales then calculating an average of the three scores [16].

Hospital anxiety and depression scale

The Hospital Anxiety and Depression Scale (HADS) were used to measure levels of anxiety and depression, which is a self-assessment scale. Anxiety and depression were assessed respectively using the 7-item subscales, which were scored from 0 to 21 for each subscale. Scores between 0 and 7 suggest "no case"; 8 to 10 represent a "possible case"; and 11 to 21 indicate a "probable case of anxiety/depression". Example items in the anxiety subscale include: "I can sit at ease and feel relaxed," and "Worrying thoughts go through my mind." Example items from the depressive subscale include: "I feel as if I am slowed down," and "I still enjoy things I used to enjoy." These cutoff points have been validated against clinical interviews with sensitivity and specificity approximately 0.80. Studies have reported good internal consistency for both anxiety (0.89) and depression (0.86) [17, 18].

Other related scales

The Ocular Surface Disease Index (OSDI) [19] assesses symptoms of ocular irritation consistent with dry eye disease and their impact on vision-related function. The total OSDI score ranges from 0 to 100, with higher scores indicating more severe symptoms. And it has been validated in Chinese populations [20]; the M.D. Anderson Dysphagia Inventory (MDADI) [21] measures patient's swallowing disorders and the Oral Health Impact Profile 14 (OHIP-14) [22] was used to survey oral distress(score ranges from 0 to 100, with higher scores indicating more severe symptoms).

Data analysis

Data were analyzed using the computer program, SPSS 21. The data were shown as means ± SD for continuous data and as frequencies (%) for categorical data. Variables were used univariate tests (independent samples t-tests and χ^2 tests) of the group difference. Correlation analysis was used for exploration of the relation between two variables. All variables with a significant association with anxiety/depression were entered into a multiple stepwise logistic regression model with the dichotomous anxiety/depression as the dependent variable, to explore the predictors of psychological status. $P < 0.05$(two-tail) was considered statistically significant.

Results

Patient features

22 pSS patients and 16 controls didn't complete the questionnaires, resulting in the admission of 160 pSS patients and 170 healthy subjects with matched age and sex in this study. The mean age of pSS patients was 50. 54 ± 12.22 years and the mean disease duration was 4. 5 years. Demographic, clinical, and laboratory characteristics of pSS patients and controls are shown in Table 1. Anti-SSA antibody and anti-SSB antibody were positive in 85 (81%) and 53 (50.5%), respectively. 55 outpatients did not perform the anti-SSA antibody and antiSSB antibody examination and 57 outpatients did not perform the RF examination. 114 (71.3%) pSS patients showed moderate to high disease activity (ESSDAI ≥5). The score of depression is higher in pSS patients than controls(6.71 ± 4.32 vs 3.87 ± 2.80). And the score of anxiety is higher in pSS patients than controls(6.52 ± 4.06 vs 3. 02 ± 2.78). There was no significant difference in the age, sex, marital status, education level, occupation, income/year between the two groups ($P > 0.05$).

Differences between anxiety/depression and non-anxiety/depression patients

As indicated in Table 2, demographic, clinical and psychological variables were compared between anxiety/depression and non-anxiety/depression pSS patients. Depressed pSS patients had more serious disease activity, higher ESR scores and unemployment rate, lower education level, severer total pain, compared with non-depression patients ($p < 0.05$). However, no similar results were found in anxiety. For age, gender, marital status, disease duration, type of medical insurance, complication, hospitalization and family history, no statistically significant difference was found between the two groups ($P>0.05$). Enhanced pain, physical limitations, and fatigue may be interpreted as increased activity of these diseases.

Correlations among fatigue, disease activity and the HADS-depression/anxiety in pSS patients

As shown in Table 3, we found there were significant correlations among pain, employment status, fatigue, the ocular surface disease, swallowing disorders and oral health were significantly associated with the HADS-depression ($p < 0.05$). In addition, fatigue, disease activity, ESSPRI, employment status, the ocular surface disease, swallowing disorders and oral health were significantly associated with the HADS-anxiety ($p < 0.05$).

Logistic regression analysis for the HADS-anxiety and depression

We used logistic regression analysis to investigate predictors of anxiety and depression, the result revealed oral health(odds ratio = 0.956; $P<0.05$) and swallowing disorders(odds ratio = 1.036; $P<0.05$) were significantly associated with the HADS-anxiety in pSS patients, which means oral health and swallowing disorders were the predictors of anxiety in pSS patients(Table 4). Meanwhile, fatigue(odds ratio = 0.587; $P<0.05$) was significantly accounted for the HADS-depression (Table 5).

Discussion

According to this study, the prevalence of depression and anxiety is 36.9%/33.8% among people with pSS in China and Chinese pSS patients are more likely to suffer from depression and anxiety than healthy people. As far as we know, this is a study chiefly researching the relations between disease activity, fatigue, pain, education, ocular surface disease, oral health, swallowing disorders, employment status, ESSPRI and anxiety/depression in Chinese pSS patients.

Depression patients had higher disease activity scores, higher level of ESR, higher unemployment rate, lower education level, severer total pain, compared with depression patients. One explanation would be that pSS and pain can cause adverse coping ways, work restriction and impaired quality of life, which might in turn bring about a further depressive flare. However, no similar results were found in anxiety. A recent meta-analysis showed that prevalence estimates for depression in pSS range between 8.33 and 75.56% [23]. As reported previously, depression

Table 1 summarizes the demographic and clinical characteristics of the participants in the study

Clinical characteristics	pSS(n = 160)	Controls(n = 170)	t/x^2	p
Age, mean ± sd years	51.09 ± 12.11	50.14 ± 11.22	0.32	0.446
Gender, female, no. (%)	152(95)	162(95.3)	0.02	0.901
Marital status, no. (%)			3.50	0.061
Married	151 (94.4)	167 (98.2)		
Other marital status	9 (5.6)	3 (1.8)		
Education, years	12.19 ± 4.33	12.03 ± 4.62	0.33	0.740
Employment status, no. (%)			1.28	0.259
Employed	71(44.4)	86(50.6)		
Unemployed	89(55.6)	84(49.4)		
Income/person/year, yuan, no. (%)			1.65	0.569
< 15,000 yuan	55 (34.37)	49(28.8)		
15,000-33,000 yuan	49 (30.63)	62(36.5)		
≥ 33,000 yuan	56(35)	59(34.7)		
Type of medical insurance, n (%)			4.33	0.115
With basic medical insurance	146(91.3)	164(96.5)		
Self-pay	13(8.1)	6(3.5)		
Other	1(0.6)	0(0)		
HADS-A, mean ± sd	6.52 ± 4.06	3.02 ± 2.78	9.08	0.000
HADS-D, mean ± sd	6.71 ± 4.32	3.87 ± 2.80	7.05	0.000
Disease duration, mean ± sd years	4.498 ± 5.44	–		–
OSDI, mean ± sd	29.14 ± 25.12	–		–
VAS pain (range 0–10), mean ± sd	2.36 ± 2.65	–		–
ESR, mean ± sd mm/h	30.65 ± 24.13	–		–
RF positivity, yes, no. (%)	51(49.5)	–		–
Hospitalization, yes, n (%)	108(67.5)	–		–
Family history, yes, n (%)	23(14.4)	–		–
Comorbid conditions, yes, n (%)	102(63.75)	–		–
ESSDAI	9.6 ± 7.3	–		–
ESSPRI	4.53 ± 1.95	–		–
FSS	3.89 ± 1.59	1.64 ± 0.89	15.76	0.000
OHIP-14	12.89 ± 11.38	3.41 ± 4.92	9.29	0.000
MDADI	72.33 ± 18.83	–		–
IgG (g/L)	18.93 ± 6.65	–		–
C3 (g/L)	0.81 ± 0.27	–		–
C4 (g/L)	0.18 ± 0.65	–		–
ANA ≥1: 320	96(91.4)	–		–
Anti-SSA ≥ 200 RU/mL	85(81)	–		–
Anti-SSB ≥ 20 RU/mL	53(50.5)	–		–

VAS visual analog scale, *ESR* erythrocyte sedimentation rate, *RF* rheumatoid factor, *HADS* hospital anxiety and depression scale, *HADS-A* hospital anxiety scale, *HADS-D* hospital depression scale, *ESSDAI* EULAR Sjögren's syndrome disease activity index, *ANA* antinuclear antibodies, *IgG* Immunoglobulin G, *C3* complement C3, *C4* complement C4, *OSDI* the ocular surface disease index

in pSS patients is associated with poorer health status, including low quality of life [24], suicide risk [25], increased medical costs [26], lower rate of treatment compliance [27], and even increased mortality. Similarly, Lendrem et al. [28] found that pSS patients complaining any problem in mobility, self-care, daily activities, pain/malaise, and anxiety/depression were higher than normal people. Moreover, Shen et al. [29] reported that pSS may increase

Table 2 Differences between different factors of anxiety/depression and non-anxiety/depression patients

Clinical characteristics	non-anxiety	Anxiety	*p*	non-depression	depression	*p*
Age, mean ± sd years[a]	50.08 ± 11.90	51.44 ± 12.90	0.508	49.69 ± 11.96	51.12 ± 12.68	0.228
Gender, female, no. (%)[b]	100(94.3)	55 (96.3)	0.878	97(96)	55 (93.2)	0.679
Marital status, no. (%)[b]			1.000			0.401
Married	100 (94.3)	51 (94.4)		97 (96)	54 (91.5)	
Other marital status	6 (5.7)	3 (5.6)		4 (4)	5 (8.5)	
Education, years, no. (%)[a]	12.43 ± 4.42	11.72 ± 4.16	0.327	13.00 ± 3.96	10.81 ± 4.62	0.002*
Employment status, no. (%)[b]			0.064			0.049*
Employed	53 (50)	18 (33.3)		51 (50.5)	20 (33.9)	
Unemployed	53 (50)	36 (66.7)		50 (49.5)	39 (66.1)	
Income/person/year, yuan, no. (%)[b]			0.423			0.094
< 15,000 yuan	34 (32.1)	21 (38.9)		31 (30.7)	24 (40.7)	
15,000-33,000 yuan	36 (34)	13 (24.1)		37 (36.6)	12 (20.3)	
≥ 33,000 yuan	36 (34)	20 (37)		33 (32.7)	23 (39)	
Type of medical insurance, n (%)[b]			0.749			0.660
With basic medical insurance	96 (90.6)	50 (92.6)		91 (90.1)	55 (93.2)	
Self-pay	9 (8.5)	4 (7.4)		9 (8.9)	4 (6.8)	
Other	1 (0.9)	0 (0)		1 (1)	0 (0)	
Disease duration, mean ± sd years[a]	4.48 ± 5.61	4.53 ± 5.15	0.957	4.30 ± 4.72	4.83 ± 6.53	0.557
VAS pain (range 0–10), mean ± sd[a]	2.12 ± 2.51	2.83 ± 2.98	0.127	2.35 ± 1.95	3.07 ± 2.99	0.016*
ESR, mean ± sd mm/h[a]	28.10 ± 21.38	35.87 ± 28.47	0.085	27.10 ± 20.04	36.78 ± 29.10	0.027*
OSDI, mean ± sd[a]	25.07 ± 22.40	37.15 ± 28.28	0.008*	23.82 ± 20.81	38.26 ± 29.14	0.001*
RF positivity, yes, no. (%)[b]	29 (46)	22 (55)	0.422	30 (49.2)	21 (50)	1.000
Hospitalization, yes, n (%)[b]	68 (64.2)	40 (74.1)	0.218	68 (67.3)	40 (67.8)	1.000
Family history, yes, n (%)[b]	15 (14.2)	8 (14.8)	1.000	17 (16.8)	6 (10.2)	0.351
Comorbid conditions, yes, n (%)[b]	66 (62.3)	36 (66.7)	0.607	61 (60.4)	41 (69.5)	0.307
ESSDAI[a]	9.16 ± 7.73	10.48 ± 6.37	0.281	8.73 ± 7.35	11.10 ± 7.03	0.047*
IgG (g/L)[a]	19.05 ± 6.72	18.72 ± 6.60	0.806	18.99 ± 6.54	18.84 ± 6.85	0.909
C3 (g/L)[a]	0.80 ± 0.26	0.82 ± 0.28	0.781	0.80 ± 0.24	0.82 ± 0.30	0.632
C4 (g/L)[a]	0.18 ± 0.07	0.17 ± 0.06	0.627	0.18 ± 0.66	0.17 ± 0.06	0.552
ANA ≥1: 320[b]	61 (91)	35 (92.1)	1.000	60 (93.8)	36 (87.8)	0.481
Anti-SSA ≥ 200 RU/mL[b]	54 (80.6)	31 (81.6)	1.000	50 (78.1)	35 (85.4)	0.449
Anti-SSB ≥ 20 RU/mL[b]	32 (47.8)	21 (55.3)	0.544	29 (45.3)	24 (58.5)	0.231

VAS visual analog scale, *ESR* erythrocyte sedimentation rate, *RF* rheumatoid factor, *HADS* hospital anxiety and depression scale, *ESSDAI* EULAR Sjögren's syndrome disease activity index, *ANA* antinuclear antibodies, *IgG* immunoglobulin G, *C3* complement C3, *C4* complement C4, *OSDI* the ocular surface disease index. * = $p<0.05$; [a] = t-tests; [b] = χ^2 analyses

the risk of ensuing newly diagnosed depressive disorder, anxiety disorder that might damage quality of life. Depression was found more common in pSS patients than controls, with a prevalence of 38.3% [30], which is consistent with our findings. However, some other researches made inconsistent conclusions, and need further discussions.

We could not detect a difference in sex because of the small male proportion in this study. There are disputed data whether active disease adds the susceptibility to anxiety/depression. However, we found a positive relationship between disease activity and anxiety/depression. Pain severity were also related to an increased risk of anxiety and depression. This finding supports the opinion of a mutually reinforcing mechanism between pain and depression and indicates the importance of clarifying neurobiological links for the sake of optimizing pain and depression management. pSS affects patients' HR-QoL, mental status and relationships with family [31]. Fatigue is significantly associated with various psychological factors, including depression [32], anxiety [33] in pSS patients.

Patients with pSS usually have characteristic chronic symptoms of ocular and oral dryness. While the

Table 3 Correlations among fatigue, pain, education etc. and the HADS-depression/anxiety in pSS patients

correlative variable	Anxiety		depression	
	r	*p*	r	*p*
OHIP	−0.353	0.000**	−0.228	0.004**
OSDI	−0.228	0.004**	− 0.278	0.000**
FSS	−0.215	0.006**	−0.358	0.000**
Pain	−0.127	0.109	−0.204	0.010**
ESSDAI	−0.086	0.281	−0.157	0.047*
ESSPRI	− 0.169	0.053	−0.268	0.002**
Education	0.078	0.327	0.244	0.002**
Employment status	0.159	0.045*	0.161	0.042*
Swallowing disorders	0.398	0.000**	0.233	0.003**

*$p<0.05$; ** $p<0.01$

pathomechanism of pSS is still unclear, environmental factors are considered to trigger abnormal immunological reactions in people with genetic susceptibility [34]. Ocular and oral dryness were the most frequently symptoms in pSS patients reported by 44 and 39%, respectively [11]. While corticosteroid and immunomodulatory drugs are often ineffective in the treatment of oral and ocular symptoms of pSS. The possible explanation is that manifestations of oral and ocular dryness are vague in the early phase of the disease and usually ignored by patients and clinicians alike [35]. The pSS patients in our study had severer ocular expressions and signs of dry eye and reported severer anxiety and depression. Furthermore, studies show that pSS patients have a decreased salivary flow with high risk of dental caries, enhanced susceptibility to oral candidiasis, tooth loss, severer periodontal destruction, pain during chewing, pararthria, tongue palpitation and angular cheilitis [36–38]. Anxious pSS individuals, because of their avoidant behaviours, often have poorer dental health. Oral dryness in pSS may impair functions such as chewing, talking or swallowing, and lead to a "choking" sensation, which might cause anxiety [39]. Fortunately, Hydroxychloroquine has shown improvement of subjective oral symptoms in patients with pSS. Therefore, it is essential that patients with pSS undergo regular oral examinations and medication therapy.

The amount of saliva in pSS patients was significantly less than controls, and these patients perceived their swallowing to be impaired [40]. Moreover, dysphagia in pSS patients increase with disease severity and anxiety/

Table 4 Result of analysis of forward stepwise ordered logit regression models in anxiety

Predictors	B	S.E.	*P*	OR (95%CI)
OHIP	−0.045	0.019	0.017	0.956(0.921, 0.992)
Swallowing disorders	0.035	0.011	0.002	1.036(1.013, 1.059)

CI confdence interval, *OHIP* oral health impact profile

Table 5 Result of analysis of forward stepwise ordered logit regression models in depression

Predictors	β	S.E.	*P*	OR (95%CI)
FSS	−0.533	0.123	0.000	0.587 (0.461, 0.747)

CI confdence interval, *FSS* Fatigue severity scale

depression, indicating the important for increased recognition and management of dysphagia. Since eating and drinking form an important part of social interaction, dysphagic pSS patients often eat in seclusion because of shame. And they worry choking on their food or develop aspiration pneumonia. Frequent worries can decrease quality of life even more and aggravate the anxiety. Hence, it is important to strengthen the assessment of the swallowing function of the pSS patient. Educational programs might help an early identification of the disease and lessen the emotional burden of patients during the initial course of disease [41]. In addition, lacking of knowledge about pSS may lead to anxiety/depression, so patient education about pSS may relieve anxiety and depression.

The large sample size available for this analysis and systematic investigation of the disease activity in pSS patients were major strengths for this study. However, there are some limitations. Firstly, this study is a single-center research. Secondly, the data analysed were cross-sectional, and thus we were unable to comment on causal relationships. Thirdly, some of the positive findings cannot survive correction for multiple comparisons. Additionally, prospective studies on pSS patients' anxiety and depression should be conducted to support the development of effective interventions to manage their anxiety and depression in the future.

Conclusion

Patients with pSS complained more commonly of anxiety and depression than controls, and oral health and swallowing disorders were greatly relevant to anxiety in pSS patients. Clinicians should focus on the potential mental comorbidities while managing patients with pSS. Simultaneously, rheumatologists should also pay more attention to the oral health and swallowing disorders in pSS patients. Early identification and proper intervention are therefore vital to minimize the negative effect of anxiety and depression on the patient's QoL and outcome of their disease. Accordingly, the findings in our study can be used for prevention and intervention of psychological distress(anxiety and depression) among pSS patients. The findings have significant policy or practical implications. Finally, further studies are indispensable to search potential pathophysiologic pathways that might interpret anxiety and depression in pSS.

Abbreviations
ESSDAI: European League Against Rheumatism Sjögren's Syndrome Disease Activity Index; ESSPRI: European League Against Rheumatism Sjögren's Syndrome Patient Reported Index; FSS: Fatigue severity scale; HADS: Hospital Anxiety and Depression Scale; HR-QoL: Health-related quality of life; MDADI: the M.D. Anderson Dysphagia Inventory; OHIP-14: the Oral Health Impact Profile 14; OSDI: the Ocular Surface Disease Index; pSS: Primary Sjögren's syndrome; VAS: the Visual Analogue Scale

Acknowledgments
We would like to thank ZML and YFX for their great assistance with this study.

Funding
This study was supported by Grants from the Chinese National Natural Science Foundation (Grant no. 81671616, and 81471603); Jiangsu Provincial Commission of Health and Family Planning Foundation (Grant no. H201317 and H201623); Science Foundation of Nantong City (Grant no. MS32015021, MS2201564, MS22016028 and MS22016019); Science and Technology Foundation of Nantong City (Grant no. HS2014071 and HS2016003).

Authors' contributions
YFC and LL searched and investigated the patients according to the inclusion and exclusion criteria. LX analyzed the data and wrote the draft of the paper. QZ and SNC checked the data and polished the manuscript. LX and ZFG gave advice on methodology and revised the paper. All authors contributed to reviewing or revising the paper and read and approved the final manuscript. ZFG is the guarantor of this work and had full access to all the data in the study and takes responsibility for its integrity and the accuracy of the data analysis.

Competing interests
The authors declared that they have no competing interests.

Author details
[1]Department of Rheumatology, Affliated Hospital of Nantong University, 20th Xisi road, 226001 Nantong, People's Republic of China. [2]School of Nursing, Nantong University, 19th Qixiu Road, 226001 Nantong, People's Republic of China. [3]Department of Nursing, Affliated Hospital of Nantong University, 20th Xisi road, Nantong 226001, China.

References
1. Karlsen M, Jakobsen K, Jonsson R, Hammenfors D, Hansen T, Appel S. Expression of toll-like receptors in peripheral blood mononuclear cells of patients with primary Sjögren's syndrome. Scand J Immunol. 2017;85(3): 220–6.
2. Koh JH, Kwok SK, Lee J, et al. Pain, xerostomia, and younger age are major determinants of fatigue in Korean patients with primary Sjogren's syndrome: a cohort study. Scand J Rheumatol. 2017;46(1):49–55.
3. Kotsis K, Voulgari PV, Tsifetaki N, Drosos AA, Carvalho AF, Hyphantis T. Illness perceptions and psychological distress associated with physical health-related quality of life in primary Sjögren's syndrome compared to systemic lupus erythematosus and rheumatoid arthritis. Rheumatol Int. 2014;34(12): 1671–81.
4. Anyfanti P, Pyrpasopoulou A, Triantafyllou A, et al. Association between mental health disorders and sexual dysfunction in patients suffering from rheumatic diseases. J Sex Med. 2014;11(11):2653–60.
5. Lendrem D, Mitchell S, McMeekin P, et al. Health-related utility values of patients with primary Sjogren's syndrome and its predictors. Ann Rheum Dis. 2014;73(7):1362–8.
6. Westhoff G, Dorner T, Zink A. Fatigue and depression predict physician visits and work disability in women with primary Sjogren's syndrome: results from a cohort study. Rheumatology. 2012;51(2):262–9.
7. Van L N, Bossema E R, Van M H, et al. Dealing with emotions when the ability to cry is hampered: emotion processing and regulation in patients with primary Sjögren's syndrome. Clin Exp Rheumatol. 2012;30(4):492–8.
8. Koçer B, Tezcan ME, Batur HZ, et al. Cognition, depression, fatigue, and quality of life in primary Sjögren's syndrome: correlations. Brain Behav. 2016;6(12):e586.
9. Buras A, Waszkiewicz N, Szulc A, Sierakowski S. Monocytic parameters in patients with rheumatologic diseases reflect intensity of depressive disorder. Pol Merkur Lekarski. 2012;33(198):325–9.
10. Inal V, Kitapcioglu G, Karabulut G, Keser G, Kabasakal Y. Evaluation of quality of life in relation to anxiety and depression in primary Sjogren's syndrome. Mod Rheumatol. 2010;20(6):588–97.
11. Segal B, Bowman SJ, Fox PC, et al. Primary Sjogren's syndrome: health experiences and predictors of health quality among patients in the United States. Health Qual Life Out. 2009;7(46):1.
12. Shiboski SC, Shiboski CH, Criswell L, et al. American College of Rheumatology classification criteria for Sjögren's syndrome: a data-driven, expert consensus approach in the Sjögren's international collaborative clinical alliance cohort. Arthritis Care Res. 2012;64(4):475–87.
13. Seror R, Bowman SJ, Brito-Zeron P, et al. EULAR Sjogren's syndrome disease activity index (ESSDAI): a user guide. RMD Open. 2015;1(1):e22.
14. Seror R, Ravaud P, Bowman SJ, et al. EULAR Sjogren's syndrome disease activity index: development of a consensus systemic disease activity index for primary Sjogren's syndrome. Ann Rheum Dis. 2010; 69(6):1103–9.
15. Seror R, Bootsma H, Saraux A, et al. Defining disease activity states and clinically meaningful improvement in primary Sjögren's syndrome with EULAR primary Sjögren's syndrome disease activity (ESSDAI) and patient-reported indexes (ESSPRI). Ann Rheum Dis. 2016;75(2):382–9.
16. Seror R, Ravaud P, Mariette X, et al. EULAR Sjogren's syndrome patient reported index (ESSPRI): development of a consensus patient index for primary Sjogren's syndrome. Ann Rheum Dis. 2011;70(6):968–72.
17. Cordingley L, Prajapati R, Plant D, et al. Impact of psychological factors on subjective disease activity assessments in patients with severe rheumatoid arthritis. Arthrit Care Res. 2014;66(6):861–8.
18. Olsson I, Mykletun A, Dahl AA. The hospital anxiety and depression rating scale: a cross-sectional study of psychometrics and case finding abilities in general practice. BMC Psychiatry. 2005;5:46.
19. Schiffman RM, Christianson MD, Jacobsen G, Hirsch JD, Reis BL. Reliability and validity of the ocular surface disease index. Arch Ophthalmol. 2000; 118(5):615–21.
20. Zhang Y, Lin T, Jiang A, Zhao N, Gong L. Vision-related quality of life and psychological status in Chinese women with Sjogren's syndrome dry eye: a case-control study. BMC Womens Health. 2016;16(1):75.
21. Pierce JL, Tanner K, Merrill RM, Miller KL, Kendall KA, Roy N. Swallowing disorders in Sjögren's syndrome: prevalence, risk factors, and effects on quality of life. Dysphagia. 2016;31(1):49–59.
22. Enger TB, Palm Ø, Garen T, Sandvik L, Jensen JL. Oral distress in primary Sjögren's syndrome: implications for health-related quality of life. Eur J Oral Sci. 2011;119(6):474–80.
23. Cui Y, Li L, Yin R, et al. Depression in primary Sjögren's syndrome: a systematic review and metaanalysis. Psychol Health Med. 2017;23(2):198–209.
24. Morgane M, Cornec D, Chastaing M, et al. Sicca symptoms are associated with similar fatigue, anxiety, depression, and quality-of-life impairments in patients with and without primary Sjögren's syndrome. Joint Bone Spine. 2016;83(6):681–5.
25. Choo C, Diederich J, Song I, Ho R. Cluster analysis reveals risk factors for repeated suicide attempts in a multi-ethnic Asian population. Asian J Psychiatr. 2014;8:38–42.
26. Ho RC, Mak K, Chua AN, Ho CS, Mak A. The effect of severity of depressive disorder on economic burden in a university hospital in Singapore. Expert Rev Pharm Out. 2014;13(4):549–59.
27. Jamilloux Y, Sarabi M, Kerever S, et al. Adherence to online monitoring of patient-reported outcomes by patients with chronic inflammatory diseases: a feasibility study. Lupus. 2015;24(13):1429–36.
28. Lendrem D, Mitchell S, McMeekin P, et al. Health-related utility values of patients with primary Sjögren's syndrome and its predictors. Ann Rheum Dis. 2014;73(7):1362–8.
29. Shen CC, Yang AC, Kuo BI, et al. Risk of psychiatric disorders following primary Sjögren syndrome: a Nationwide population-based retrospective cohort study. J Rheumatol. 2015;42(7):1203–8.

30. Morreale M, Marchione P, Giacomini P, et al. Neurological involvement in primary Sjogren syndrome: a focus on central nervous system. PLoS One. 2014;9(1):e84605.
31. Karageorgas T, Fragioudaki S, Nezos A, Karaiskos D, Moutsopoulos HM, Mavragani CP. Fatigue in primary Sjögren's syndrome: clinical, laboratory, psychometric, and biologic associations. Arthrit Care Res. 2016;68(1):123–31.
32. Ibn Yacoub Y, Rostom S, Laatiris A, Hajjaj-Hassouni N. Primary Sjögren's syndrome in Moroccan patients: characteristics, fatigue and quality of life. Rheumatol Int. 2012;32(9):2637–43.
33. Milin M, Cornec D, Chastaing M, et al. Sicca symptoms are associated with similar fatigue, anxiety, depression, and quality-of-life impairments in patients with and without primary Sjögren's syndrome. Joint Bone Spine. 2016;83(6):681–5.
34. KANG JH, LIN HC. Comorbidities in patients with primary sjogren's syndrome: a registry-based case-control study. J Rheumatol. 2010;37(6): 1188–94.
35. Leung KCM, McMillan AS, Wong MCM, Leung WK, Mok MY, Lau CS. The efficacy of cevimeline hydrochloride in the treatment of xerostomia in Sjogren's syndrome in southern Chinese patients: a randomised double-blind, placebo-controlled crossover study. Clin Rheumatol. 2008;27(4):429–36.
36. Ambrosio LM, Rovai ES, Franca BN, et al. Effects of periodontal treatment on primary sjogren's syndrome symptoms. Braz Oral Res. 2017;31:e8.
37. Lu M, Jheng C, Tsai T, Koo M, Lai N. Increased dental visits in patients prior to diagnosis of primary Sjögren's syndrome: a population-based study in Taiwan. Rheumatol Int. 2014;34(11):1555–61.
38. Olate S, Munoz D, Neumann S, Pozzer L, Cavalieri-Pereira L, de Moraes M. A descriptive study of the oral status in subjects with Sjogren's syndrome. Int J Clin Exp Med. 2014;7(4):1140–4.
39. Rostron J, Rogers S, Longman L, et al. Health-related quality of life in patients with primary Sjögren's syndrome and xerostomia: a comparative study. Gerodontology. 2002;19(1):53–9.
40. Roguspulia NM, Logemann JA. Effects of reduced saliva production on swallowing in patients with Sjögren's syndrome. Dysphagia. 2011;26(3):295–303.
41. Lackner A, Ficjan A, Stradner MH, et al. It's more than dryness and fatigue: the patient perspective on health-related quality of life in primary Sjögren's syndrome - a qualitative study. PLoS One. 2017;12(2):e172056.

3

Prevalence of acute stress disorder among road traffic accident survivors

Wenjie Dai[1,2,3,4], Aizhong Liu[1*], Atipatsa C. Kaminga[1,5], Jing Deng[1], Zhiwei Lai[6], Jianzhou Yang[7] and Shi Wu Wen[1,2,3,4*]

Abstract

Background: Road traffic accident (RTA), an unexpected traumatic event, may not only lead to death and serious physical injuries, but also could put survivors at an increased risk for a wide range of psychiatric disorders, particularly acute stress disorder (ASD). Early assessment of trauma-related psychological responses is important because acute trauma responses in the early post-traumatic period are among the robust predictors of long-term mental health problems. However, estimates of the prevalence of ASD among RTA survivors varied considerably across studies. Therefore, this meta-analysis aimed to identify the pooled prevalence of ASD among RTA survivors.

Methods: A systematic literature search in the databases of PubMed, PsycINFO, PsycARTICLES, Embase and Web of Science was performed from their inception dates to December 2017. Subject headings were used to identify relevant articles, and the search strategy was adjusted across databases. Heterogeneity across studies was evaluated by Cochran's χ^2 test and quantified by the I^2 statistic. Subgroup analyses were performed to identify the pooled prevalence in relation to the country of study, instrument used to identify ASD, age, gender and traumatic brain injury. When significant heterogeneity was observed, the influence of some potential moderators was explored using meta-regression analyses.

Results: Thirteen eligible studies conducted in 8 countries were included. A total of 2989 RTA survivors were assessed, of which 287 were identified with ASD. The overall heterogeneity was high across studies (I^2=96.8%, $P < 0.001$), and the pooled prevalence of ASD among RTA survivors was 15.81% (95% confidence interval: 8.27–25.14%). Subgroup analyses indicated that the prevalence of ASD among RTA survivors differed significantly with regard to the country of study, instrument used to identify ASD, age and gender ($P < 0.05$). Meta-regression analyses showed that mean age of participants and quality assessment score were significant moderators for heterogeneity ($P < 0.05$).

Conclusions: Nearly one-sixth of RTA survivors suffer from ASD, indicating the need for regular assessment of early trauma responses among RTA survivors, as well as the importance of implementing early psychological interventions.

Keywords: Acute stress disorder, Road traffic accident, Prevalence; meta-analysis

* Correspondence: lazroy@live.cn; swwen@ohri.ca
[1]Department of Epidemiology and Health Statistics, Xiangya School of Public Health, Central South University, Changsha, Hunan, China
Full list of author information is available at the end of the article

Background

With the rapid increase in the number of motor vehicles in the past few decades, road traffic accidents (RTA) have become a public health problem [1–3]. According to the latest global status report on road safety by World Health Organization (WHO), more than 1.2 million people die from RTA each year, with millions more sustaining serious injuries and living with long-term adverse health consequences [http://www.who.int/violence_injury_prevention/road_safety_status/2015/en/]. Notably, children and adolescents are more vulnerable to RTA than adults, and the injuries caused by RTA is the leading cause of death among those aged 15 to 19 years and the second leading cause among those aged 10 to 14 years [http://www.who.int/violence_injury_prevention/child/injury/world_report/en/].
Accumulated evidence has shown that RTA, an unexpected traumatic event, may not only lead to death and serious physical injuries, but also could put survivors at an increased risk for a wide range of psychiatric disorders, particularly acute stress disorder (ASD) and post-traumatic stress disorder (PTSD) [4–6].

ASD, an acute trauma response that occurs within four weeks following a traumatic event, was first introduced into the fourth edition of the Diagnostic and Statistical Manual of Mental Disorders (DSM-IV) in 1994 [7]. According to the DSM-IV criteria, ASD is characterized by the symptom clusters of dissociation, intrusion, avoidance, and arousal [7]. The main difference between ASD and PTSD based on the DSM-IV criteria is the former's emphasis on dissociative reactions to the trauma and the duration of the symptoms [8, 9]. Specifically, the ASD diagnosis requires that individuals must experience at least three dissociative symptoms, and PTSD can only be diagnosed from at least four weeks after the trauma, whereas ASD can be diagnosed from two days to four weeks after the trauma. A major reason for the introduction of ASD is to predict trauma-related individuals who would subsequently develop chronic PTSD [10]. In 2013, substantial changes have been made to the diagnosis of ASD with the release of DMS-V. In particular, ASD has been reclassified into Trauma- and Stressor-Related Disorders, and according to the DSM-V criteria, ASD is defined by five symptom clusters namely intrusion, negative mood, dissociation, avoidance, and arousal [11].

RTA is the most persistently common traumatic event in the modern world, and numerous studies have shown that ASD is quite prevalent among RTA survivors [12]. Estimates of the prevalence of ASD among RTA survivors varied considerably across studies, ranging from 1.6 to 41.1% [13–16], which may be mainly associated with the sample characteristics including gender, age, injury severity, and the instruments used to identify ASD [8, 13, 17]. Early assessment of trauma-related psychological responses is important because acute trauma responses in the early post-traumatic period are among the robust predictors of long-term mental health problems [18, 19]. For example, Bryant et al. found that 57% of males and 92% of females who met the criteria of ASD within one month following RTA were diagnosed with PTSD 6 months later [8], and Brewin et al. found that 83% of the victims of violent assaults who were diagnosed with ASD within 1 month following the crime still suffered from PTSD 6 months later [20]. In this regard, a reliable estimate of the pooled prevalence of ASD among RTA survivors is crucial, as it could help the health care providers determine an accurate amount of those who may develop ASD in the early period after RTA, and further estimate the amount of those who would subsequently suffer from long-term mental health problems. However, research interests have mainly focused on PTSD [21–23], and no meta-analysis has synthesized the evidence on the prevalence of ASD among RTA survivors to date. Therefore, this meta-analysis aimed to identify the pooled prevalence of ASD among RTA survivors.

Methods

Search strategy

This meta-analysis was performed according to the Preferred Reporting Items for Systematic Reviews and Meta-Analyses (PRISMA) guidelines (the Additional file 1). A systematic literature search in the databases of PubMed, PsycINFO, PsycARTICLES, Embase and Web of Science was performed from their inception dates to December 2017. Subject headings were used to identify relevant articles, and the search strategy was adjusted across databases. Specifically, for the database of PubMed and Web of science, search terms was: "Stress Disorders, Traumatic, Acute"[Mesh]) AND "Accidents, Traffic"[Mesh]; for the databases of Emabse and PsycARTICLES, search terms was: su(traffic accident) AND su(Acute Stress Disorder); and for the database of PsycINFO, a combination of the subject headings "Acute Stress Disorder" and "Motor Traffic Accidents" was applied. The reference lists of full articles were manually searched for more relevant publications.

Eligibility criteria

Studies were included in this meta-analysis if they meet the following criteria: (1) the study design was observational; (2) the target population focused on or included RTA survivors; (3) the ASD diagnosis was made from two days to four weeks following RTA with specific reference to RTA; (4) the instrument used to identify ASD was based on the DSM-IV criteria with a binary outcome of "yes" or "no";(5) information about the sample size and the prevalence of ASD among RTA survivors was provided; and (6) full article was written in English. Studies were excluded if they were abstracts, case reports, comments, reviews, or book chapters. Furthermore, if repeated data were observed across studies, the study published earlier was included.

Data extraction

Two investigators independently assessed articles for eligibility and extracted relevant data from eligible articles. The primary outcome of this meta-analysis was the prevalence of ASD among RTA survivors, and for the purpose of this study, the following data were extracted: first author, year of publication, country of study, recruitment site, proportion of hospitalized participants, proportion of male participants, mean age of participants, instrument used to identify ASD, trauma-assessment interval, number of RTA survivors with ASD, and sample size. Consistent with previous meta-analyses exploring the post-traumatic stress responses among trauma-related populations [24, 25], the instruments used to identify ASD were categorized into self-report questionnaire and structured interview. Additionally, if available, data on traumatic brain injury (TBI) were extracted to perform subgroup analysis.

Quality assessment

The Loney criteria, which has been widely used to evaluate observational studies estimating the prevalence of a health-related problem [26, 27], was used to assess the quality of the methodology of each eligible article for this meta-analysis. This instrument comprises eight items including (1) random sample or whole population, (2) unbiased sampling frame, (3) adequate sample size, (4) standard measures, (5) outcomes measured by unbiased assessors, (6) adequate response rate and refusers described, (7) confidence intervals (CI) and subgroups analysis, and (8) study subjects described. Each item is assigned a score of 1 point, and studies satisfying one item will be given 1 point. Thus, the total score of this instrument ranges from 0 to 8 points, with more scores indicating higher degree of quality.

Statistical analysis

Statistical analyses were performed using SPSS 20.0 (IBM corp) and the "meta" and "metafor" package of R version 3.4.1. Heterogeneity across studies was evaluated by Cochran's χ^2 test and quantified by the I^2 statistic, with $I^2 \geq 25\%$, $\geq 50\%$, and $\geq 75\%$ indicating low, moderate, and high heterogeneity, respectively [28]. The pooled prevalence of ASD among RTA survivors was combined using Freeman-Tukey double arcsine method by a random effects model if significant heterogeneity was observed across studies ($P \leq 0.10$ and/or $I^2 > 50\%$). Otherwise, a fixed effects model was used [29].

Subgroup analyses were carried out to identify the pooled prevalence according to some categorical study-level characteristics of the eligible studies. These included the country of study, instrument used to identify ASD (self-report questionnaire vs. structured interview), age (child or adolescent vs. adult), gender (male vs. female), and traumatic brain injury (yes vs. no). Differences across categories within each subgroup were compared using chi-square tests.

When significant heterogeneity was observed, mixed-model meta-regression analyses were conducted to explore the influence of some potential moderators on the heterogeneity using the restricted maximum-likelihood estimator method. The moderators tested were proportion of hospitalized participants, proportion of male participants, mean age of participants, instrument used to identify ASD, and quality assessment score of the eligible studies.

Sensitivity analysis was performed not only by serially removing each study, but also excluding low-quality studies to show their corresponding effects on the stability and strength of the pooled results [23, 30]. Publication bias was assessed by the Begg's rank test, and a Begg's funnel plot for asymmetry was presented. All statistical analyses were two-tailed with a significance level of 0.05.

Results

Search results

A total of 225 articles were initially yielded. After excluding duplicates, 148 articles were screened. After reviewing abstract, 33 full articles were further shortlisted for eligibility assessment. Among the 33 full articles, 1 was excluded for not using the instrument based on DSM-IV criteria to identify ASD, 4 were excluded for not reporting a binary outcome of ASD, 3 were excluded for not reporting the prevalence of ASD, and 12 were excluded for repeating data. Finally, a total of 13 eligible articles were included in this meta-analysis (Fig. 1).

Study characteristics

The characteristics of the eligible studies are shown in Table 1. The 13 studies were conducted in 8 countries: Australia, United Kingdom (UK), United States of America (USA), Denmark, Japan, Turkey, South Africa, and Switzerland. A total of 2989 RTA survivors were assessed, of which 287 were identified with ASD. Among the 13 eligible studies, 12 were hospital-based, and 1 was population-based; 5 focused on adults, and 6 focused on children or adolescents; 6 used exclusively self-report questionnaire to identify ASD, 6 used exclusively structured interview, and 1 used both self-report questionnaire and structured interview. Furthermore, ASD was assessed from 2 days to one month after RTA.

The results of the methodological quality assessment of the eligible studies are shown in Table 2. Among the 13 eligible studies, 1 used random sampling method and was considered to have unbiased sampling frame. Additionally,

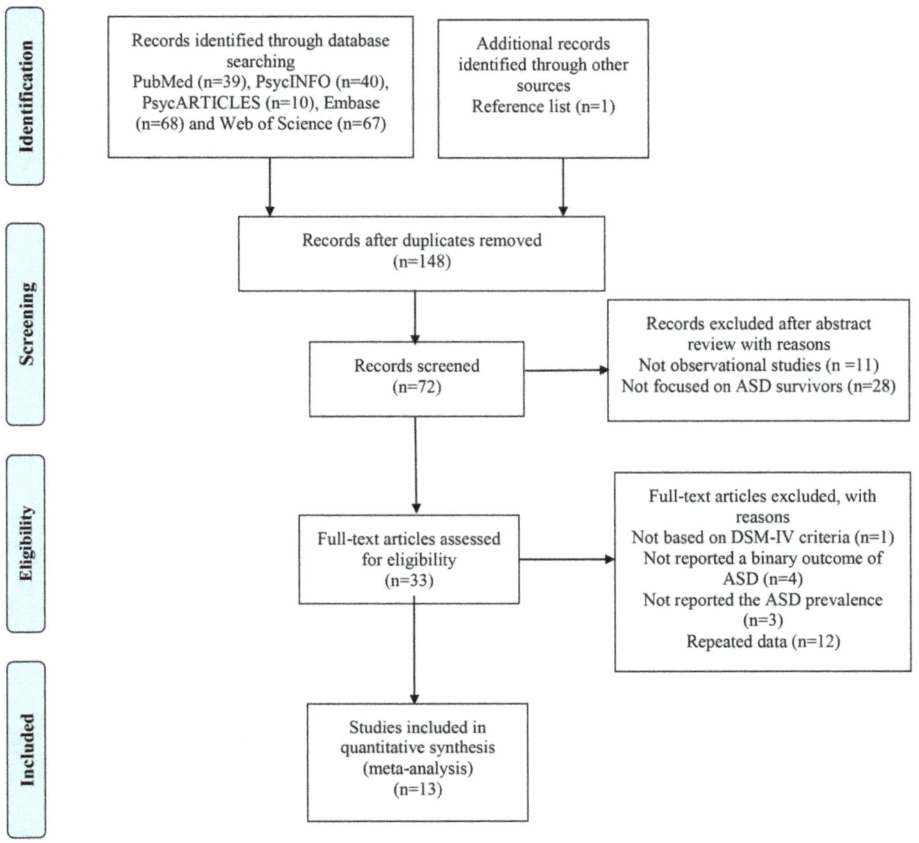

Fig. 1 PRISMA flow chart of study identification process

2 had a sample size of > 300 and all used established instruments to identify ASD. According to the Loney criteria, 1 scored 7 points, 9 scored 5 points and 3 scored 4 points.

Pooled prevalence of ASD among RTA survivors

The prevalence of ASD reported among the eligible studies varied from 3.0 to 41.1%, with the highest found among adult RTA survivors in Turkey and lowest found among child or adolescent RTA survivors in Switzerland [14, 17]. The overall heterogeneity was high across studies (I^2=96.8%, $P < 0.001$), and the pooled prevalence of ASD among RTA survivors was 15.81% (95% CI: 8.27–25.14%) by a random effects model (Fig. 2).

Subgroup analyses

The results of subgroup analyses are presented in Table 3. The pooled prevalence of ASD among RTA survivors in USA, UK, and Australia was 11.16% (95% CI: 0.00–48.57%), 14.24% (95% CI: 7.34–22.88%) and 12.11% (95% CI: 8.73–15.95%), respectively. The pooled prevalence of ASD among RTA survivors identified by self-report questionnaire and structured interview was 17.82% (95% CI: 4.05–38.11%) and 15.26% (95% CI: 7.03–25.81%), respectively. The pooled prevalence of ASD among child or adolescent RTA survivors and adult RTA survivors was 9.03% (95% CI: 2.90–17.89%) and 21.51% (95% CI: 11.82–33.08%), respectively. Additionally, the pooled prevalence of ASD among male and female RTA survivors was 7.43% (95% CI: 4.90–10.42%) and 17.89% (95% CI: 12.50–23.96%), respectively. Furthermore, the pooled prevalence of ASD among RTA survivors with and without TBI was 17.09% (95% CI: 11.30–23.75%) and 13.27% (95% CI: 3.69–27.13%), respectively. Also, the results of subgroup analyses indicated that the prevalence of ASD among RTA survivors differed significantly with regard to the country of study, instrument used to identify ASD, age and gender ($P < 0.05$).

Meta-regression analyses

The results of meta-regression analyses are presented in Table 4. The proportion of hospitalized participants, the proportion of male participants, and instrument used to identify ASD were not significant moderators for heterogeneity ($P > 0.05$). Mean age of participants and quality assessment score were significant moderators for heterogeneity ($P < 0.05$). Specifically, mean age of participants accounted for 32.40% of the heterogeneity and quality assessment score accounted for 36.80% of the heterogeneity across studies.

Table 1 Characteristics of the eligible studies

First author	Year of publication	Country of study	Recruitment site	Proportion of hospitalized participants, %	Proportion of male participants, %	Mean age (SD), years	Instrument used to identify ASD		Trauma- assessment interval	Number of survivors with ASD	Sample size
							Self-report questionnaire	Structured interview			
Bryant [46]	1998	Australia	Hospital-based	100.0	69.6	29.45 (12.62)	–	ASDI	2–28 days	11	79
Bryant [8]	2003	Australia	Hospital-based	100.0	63.7	Male: 29.95 (11.49) Female: 33.36 (13.28)	–	ASDI	Within 1 month	23	171
Fuglsang [52]	2004	Denmark	Hospital-based	6.7	45.6	33.99 (11.3)	ASDS	–	7–31 days	25	90
Jones [47]	2005	UK	Hospital-based	100.0	39.7	36.75 (12.77)	–	ASDI	Within 14 days	27	131
Hamanaka [53]	2006	Japan	Hospital-based	100.0	77.0	32.8 (14.5)	–	ASDI	Within 1 month	9	100
Yasan [14]	2009	Turkey	Hospital-based	100.0	70.5	33.93 (19.78)	–	SCID	4 days	39	95
van den Heuvel [54]	2016	South Africa	Hospital-based	NR	56.9	32.3 (10.6)	ASDS	–	10 days	47	115
Winston [55]	2002	USA	Hospital-based	100.0	72.0	10.4 (3.3)	CASQ	–	3–30 days	27	95
Bryant [56]	2004	UK	Hospital-based	21.0	55.0	12.27 (2.86)	Questions based on DSM-IV	–	2 weeks	13	86
Winston [13]	2005	USA	Population-based	NR	45.8	6.9	Questions based on DSM-IV	–	Within 30 days	24	1483
Salmon [15]	2007	Australia	Hospital-based	100.0	65.8	9.92 (2.55)	CASQ	–	6–28 days	6	76
Meiser-Stedman [16]	2007	UK	Hospital-based	100.0	68.1	11.88 (2.6)	Questionnaire based on DSM-IV	Interview based on DSM-IV	2–4 weeks	33	367
Haag [17]	2015	Switzerland	Hospital-based	61.4	58.4	11.55 (2.70)	–	IBS-A-KJ	10 days	3	101

SD standard deviation, *ASDI* Acute Stress Disorder Interview, *ASDS* Acute Stress Disorder Scale, *SCID* Structured Clinical Interview for DSM Disorders, *CASQ* Child Acute Stress Questionnaire, *IBS-A-KJ* Interview zur Akuten Belastungsstorung bei Kindern und Jugendlichen, *NR* not reported

Table 2 Methodological quality assessment of the eligible studies

Study	Random sample or whole population	Unbiased sampling frame	Adequate sample size (> 300 subjects)	Standard measures	Outcomes measured by unbiased assessors	Adequate response rate (> 70%) and refusers described	Confidence intervals and subgroups analysis	Study subjects described	Total score
Bryant et al. [46]	0	0	0	1	1	1	1	1	5
Bryant et al. [8]	0	0	0	1	1	1	1	1	5
Fuglsang et al. [52]	0	0	0	1	0	1	1	1	4
Jones et al. [47]	0	0	0	1	1	1	1	1	5
Hamanaka et al. [53]	0	0	0	1	1	1	1	1	5
Yasan et al. [14]	0	0	0	1	1	1	1	1	5
van den Heuvel et al. [54]	0	0	0	1	0	1	1	1	4
Winston et al. [55]	0	0	0	1	1	1	1	1	5
Bryant et al. [56]	0	0	0	1	0	1	1	1	4
Winston et al. [13]	1	1	1	1	0	1	1	1	7
Salmon et al. [15]	0	0	0	1	1	1	1	1	5
Meiser-Stedman et al. [16]	0	0	1	1	1	0	1	1	5
Haag et al. [17]	0	0	0	1	1	1	1	1	5

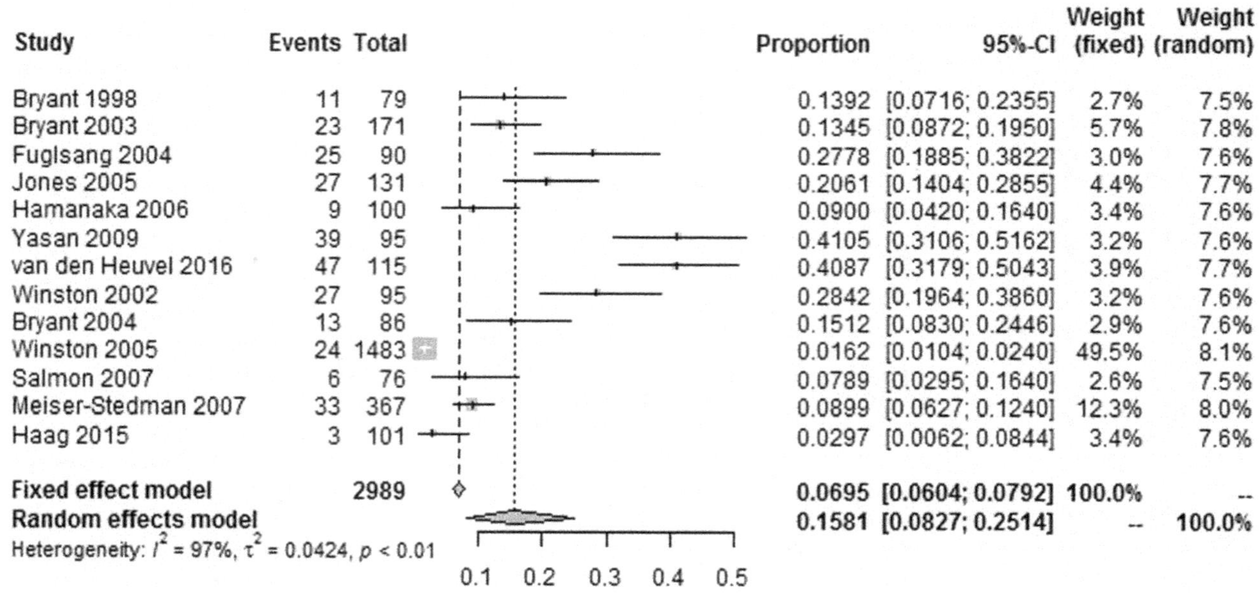

Fig. 2 Forest plot of the eligible studies

Sensitivity analysis and publication bias

After one-by-one removals of 13 studies, the pooled prevalence of ASD among RTA survivors varied from 14.09% (95% CI: 7.27–22.61%) to 17.66% (95% CI: 11.28–25.08%), and the I^2 statistic varied from 91.7 to 97.1%. Specifically, after removing one study which used both the self-report questionnaire and structured interview to identify ASD, the pooled prevalence of ASD was 16.50% (7.77–27.58%) and the I^2 statistic was 96.8%. Additionally, after excluding one population-based study, the pooled prevalence of ASD was 14.90% (7.44–24.28%), and the I^2 statistic was 97.1%. Moreover, after removing three studies

Table 3 Subgroup analyses of the pooled prevalence of ASD among RTA survivors

Subgroup		Number of studies	Number of survivors with ASD	Total sample	Pooled prevalence (95% CI) (%)	Test of difference within each subgroup	
						Chi-square value	*P* value
Country of study						79.111	< 0.001*
	USA	2	51	1578	11.16 (0.00–48.57)		
	UK	3	73	584	14.24 (7.34–22.88)		
	Australia	3	40	326	12.11 (8.73–15.95)		
Instrument used to identify ASD						49.038	< 0.001*
	Self-report questionnaire	6	112	677	17.82 (4.05–38.11)		
	Structured interview	6	142	1945	15.26 (7.03–25.81)		
Age						170.088	< 0.001*
	Child or adolescent	6	106	2208	9.03 (2.90–17.89)		
	Adult	5	111	495	21.51 (11.82–33.08)		
Gender						13.667	< 0.001*
	Male	2	27	361	7.43 (4.90–10.42)		
	Female	2	32	177	17.89 (12.50–23.96)		
TBI						0.779	0.377
	Yes	2	25	145	17.09 (11.30–23.75)		
	No	2	19	141	13.27 (3.69–27.13)		

*$P < 0.05$

Table 4 Meta-regression analyses of the effects of potential moderators

	Number of studies	Coefficient	Standard error	*Z* value	*P* value	tau^2
Proportion of hospitalized participants, %	11	−0.030	0.139	−0.217	0.828	0.021
Proportion of male participants, %	13	0.101	0.464	0.217	0.828	0.033
Mean age of participants, years	13	0.009	0.004	2.467	0.014*	0.020
Instrument used to identify ASD	13	−0.046	0.103	−0.455	0.649	0.032
Quality assessment score	13	−0.142	0.054	−2.661	0.008*	0.019

*$P < 0.05$

with quality assessment score of 4, the pooled prevalence decreased to 12.85% (95% CI: 5.94–21.79%), and the I^2 statistic was 96.4%.

Publication bias was not observed in this meta-analysis, with *P* value for the Begg's rank test being 0.760 (z = 0.306). A Begg's funnel plot is presented in Fig. 3.

Discussion

This meta-analysis synthesized the evidence on the prevalence of ASD among RTA survivors. Thirteen eligible studies conducted in 8 countries were included. A total of 2989 RTA survivors were assessed, of which 287 were identified with ASD. Results showed that the pooled prevalence of ASD among RTA survivors was 15.81% (95% CI: 8.27–25.14%). To the best of our knowledge, this study provides the first quantitative estimate of the pooled prevalence of ASD among RTA survivors.

The pooled prevalence of ASD among RTA survivors (15.81, 95% CI: 8.27–25.14%) found in this study was lower than the prevalence of ASD found among earthquake survivors (28.4%), victims of major burn injuries (23.6%), and victims of physical assault (24%) [31–33]. However, it was much higher than the prevalence of ASD among myocardial infarction patients (3.6%) and victims of typhoon (7.2%) [34, 35]. Given the rapid increase in the occurrence of RTA worldwide and the high pooled prevalence of ASD among RTA survivors found in this study, health care providers should pay more attention to the assessment of early trauma responses among RTA survivors and implement early psychological interventions accordingly.

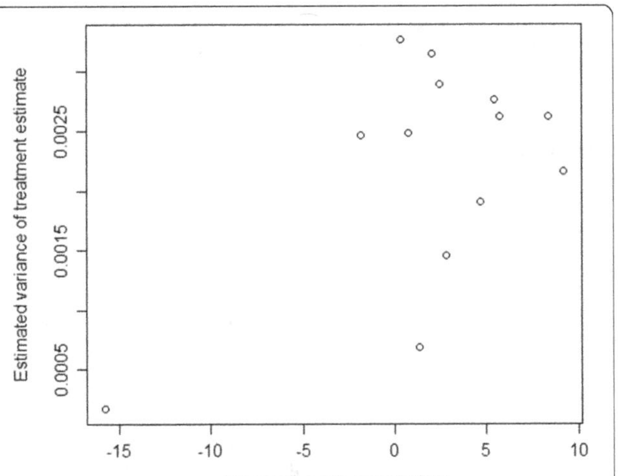

Fig. 3 Begg's funnel plot of the eligible studies

A significant difference in the pooled prevalence of ASD among RTA survivors across countries was observed by subgroup analyses, which could be mainly associated with cultural difference across countries. For example, it has been well-established that the profile of ASD symptoms varies greatly across cultures, especially with regard to the symptom cluster of dissociation [36]. Furthermore, the disparity of genetic background across ethnicities may have played a role in the different pooled prevalence observed across countries [37].

In terms of the instruments used to identify ASD, structured interview is the "gold standard" to diagnose ASD, while some self-report questionnaires with high specificity and sensitivity, such as the ASDS, have been widely used when structured interview was not feasible [38]. Numerous studies have shown that compared with structured interview, self-report questionnaires tend to overestimate the prevalence of some psychiatric disorders [39, 40]. For example, Swartzman et al. synthesized the results of 11 studies and found that the pooled prevalence of PTSD among cancer patients assessed using structured interview was 4.0% (95% CI:2.6–6.2%), while that assessed using self-report questionnaire was 12.8% (95% CI: 10.8–15.0%) [40]. Consistently, this study found that the pooled prevalence of ASD among RTA survivors identified by self-report questionnaires (17.82, 95% CI: 4.05–38.11%) was significantly higher than that identified by structured interviews (15.26, 95% CI: 7.03–25.81%), which indicated that caution should be applied when using self-report questionnaires to identify ASD among RTA survivors.

Subgroup analyses also found that the pooled prevalence of ASD was significantly higher among female RTA survivors. Gender difference in the pooled prevalence of ASD could be attributed to the gender difference in the coping strategy and interpretation of the trauma. Specifically, compared with men, women interpret trauma more stressfully and are more likely to take negative coping strategies when exposed to a trauma [41]. Additionally, women could report their post-traumatic response more easily than men [42].

The prevalence of ASD among child and adolescent RTA survivors was estimated to be low in many studies [13, 17], and our study found that the pooled prevalence of ASD was significantly higher among adult RTA survivors than child or adolescent RTA survivors. Also, meta-regression analyses indicated that the mean age of the participants was a significant source of heterogeneity. The profile of ASD symptoms is different between adults and children or adolescents. In particular, the occurrence of the dissociative symptom on the DSM-IV criteria was quite low among children and adolescents. For example, Meiser-Stedman et al. found that the symptom cluster that prevented a full ASD diagnosis among child and adolescent was overwhelmingly (73.5%) the dissociative criterion [16].

Numerous studies have consistently shown that moderate to severe TBI could lead to negative alterations in cognition, and individuals who sustained TBI exhibit more severe post-traumatic stress symptoms [43–45]. However, though this study found that the pooled prevalence of ASD was higher among those with TBI than those without TBI, the difference was not significant, which could be explained by the fact that the severity of TBI among RTA survivors who were able to participate in studies conducted at an early period after trauma was mostly mild [46, 47]. Additionally, it's worth noting here that only 2 eligible studies reported relevant data when estimating the pooled prevalence of ASD in relation to TBI. Therefore, more studies are needed to clarify the association between TBI and ASD among RTA survivors.

The result of sensitivity analyses indicated that the quality of study may affect the stability of the pooled results. After excluding 3 studies with relatively low quality, the pooled prevalence decreased greatly from 15.81% (95% CI: 8.27–25.14%) to 12.85% (95% CI: 5.94–21.79%). Also, meta-regression analyses showed that quality assessment score was a significant moderator for heterogeneity. Generally, studies with low quality are more likely to apply biased sampling frame with small sample size, and thus tend to overestimate the effect size [48, 49]. Therefore, more studies with unbiased sampling frame and large sample size are warranted to obtain a more reliable estimate.

This study has several limitations. First, this meta-analysis included exclusively studies which identified ASD using the instruments according to the DSM-IV criteria, which may preclude generalizing the findings of this study to studies identifying ASD according to the DSM-V criteria. Second, though evidence has shown that history of prior trauma, history of prior psychiatric disorders, and perceived social support level may be related to post-traumatic stress symptoms [14, 50, 51], subgroup analyses according to these factors were unable to be conducted since few studies reported relevant information. Additionally, subgroup analyses were carried out without adjustment for potential confounders.

Conclusions

The pooled prevalence of ASD among RTA survivors is 15.81% (95% CI: 8.27–25.14%) and varies significantly with regard to the country of study, instrument used to identify ASD, gender and age. Mean age of participants and quality assessment score were significant moderators for heterogeneity. The high pooled prevalence of ASD among RTA survivors underscores the importance of regular assessment of early trauma responses among RTA survivors, and the implementation of effective psychological interventions is recommended.

Abbreviations

ASD: Acute stress disorder; ASDI: Acute stress disorder interview; ASDS: Acute stress disorder scale; CASQ: Child acute stress questionnaire; CI: Confidence interval; DSM: Diagnostic and statistical manual of mental disorders; IBS-A-KJ: Interview zur Akuten Belastungsstorung bei Kindern und Jugendlichen; NR: Not reported; PRISMA: Preferred reporting items for systematic reviews and meta-analyses; PTSD: Post-traumatic stress disorder; RTA: Road traffic accidents; SCID: Structured clinical interview for DSM disorders; SD: Standard deviation; TBI: Traumatic brain injury; WHO: World health organization

Acknowledgments

The authors are grateful to all authors of the eligible articles.

Funding

This study was supported in part, by the Canadian Institutes of Health Research (FDN-148438), the Specialized Research Fund for the Doctoral Program of Higher Education (20130162110054), the Natural Science Foundation of Hunan Province, China (2016JJ2153), the Fundamental Research Funds for the postgraduates of Central South University (2015zzts282), and the Applied Basic Research Project of Shanxi Province (2016011092).

Authors' contributions

AL and SWW contributed to the study design. WD, ACK and JD contributed to the eligibility assessment and data extraction. Statistical analyses and data interpretation were performed by WD, ACK, JD, ZL and JY. WD, AL and SWW drafted the manuscript. All authors confirmed approval for the submission of the manuscript.

Competing interests

The authors declare that they have no competing interests.

Author details

[1]Department of Epidemiology and Health Statistics, Xiangya School of Public Health, Central South University, Changsha, Hunan, China. [2]OMNI Research Group, Department of Obstetrics and Gynecology, Faculty of Medicine, University of Ottawa, Ottawa, ON, Canada. [3]Ottawa Hospital Research Institute, Clinical Epidemiology Program, Ottawa, ON, Canada. [4]School of Epidemiology, Public Health, and Preventive Medicine, Faculty of Medicine, University of Ottawa, Ottawa, ON, Canada. [5]Department of Mathematics, Mzuzu University, Mzuzu, Malawi. [6]Immunization Programme Department, Hunan Provincial Center for Disease Control and Prevention, Changsha, Hunan, China. [7]Department of Preventive Medicine, Changzhi Medical College, Changzhi, Shanxi, China.

References

1. Ladeira RM, Malta DC, OLN M, MMS M, AMF S, Vasconcelos CH, et al. Road traffic accidents: Global Burden of Disease study, Brazil and federated units, 1990 and 2015. Rev Bras Epidemiol. 2017;20(Suppl 01):157–70. https://doi.org/10.1590/1980-5497201700050013.
2. Wilson JL, Gruffydd-Jones TJ, Murray JK. Risk factors for road traffic accidents in cats up to age 12 months that were registered between 2010 and 2013 with the UK pet cat cohort ('Bristol Cats'). Vet Rec. 2017;180(8):195. https://doi.org/10.1136/vr.103859.
3. Yang CS, Chen SC, Yang YC, Huang LC, Guo HR, Yang HY. Epidemiology and patterns of facial fractures due to road traffic accidents in Taiwan: a 15-year retrospective study. Traffic Inj Prev. 2017;18(7):724–9. https://doi.org/10.1080/15389588.2017.1309650.
4. Harvey AG, Bryant RA. The relationship between acute stress disorder and posttraumatic stress disorder: a prospective evaluation of motor vehicle accident survivors. J Consult Clin Psychol. 1998;66(3):507–12. https://doi.org/10.1037/0022-006X.66.3.507.
5. Bryant RA, Harvey AG. The influence of traumatic brain injury on acute stress disorder and post-traumatic stress disorder following motor vehicle accidents. Brain Inj. 1999;13(1):15–22. https://doi.org/10.1080/026990599121836.
6. Harvey AG, Bryant RA. The relationship between acute stress disorder and posttraumatic stress disorder: a 2-year prospective evaluation. J Consult Clin Psychol. 1999;67(6):985–8. https://doi.org/10.1037/0022-006X.67.6.985.
7. American Psychiatric Association. Diagnostic and statistical manual of mental disorders. 4th edition (DSM-IV) ed. Washington: American psychiatric press; 1994.
8. Bryant RA, Harvey AG. Gender differences in the relationship between acute stress disorder and posttraumatic stress disorder following motor vehicle accidents. Aust N Z J Psychiatry. 2003;37(2):226–9. https://doi.org/10.1046/j.1440-1614.2003.01130.x.
9. Bryant RA, Friedman MJ, Spiegel D, Ursano R, Strain J. A review of acute stress disorder in DSM-5. Depress anxiety. 2011;28(9):802–17. https://doi.org/10.1002/da.20737.
10. Koopman C, Classen C, Cardena E, Spiegel D. When disaster strikes, acute stress disorder may follow. J Trauma Stress. 1995;8(1):29–46.
11. American Psychiatric Association. Diagnostic and statistical manual of mental disorders, 5th edition (DSM-V). Washington: American psychiatric press; 2013.
12. Norris FH. Epidemiology of trauma: frequency and impact of different potentially traumatic events on different demographic groups. J Consult Clin Psychol. 1992;60(3):409–18.
13. Winston FK, Baxt C, Kassam-Adams NL, Elliott MR, Kallan MJ. Acute traumatic stress symptoms in child occupants and their parent drivers after crash involvement. Arch Pediatr Adolesc Med. 2005;159(11):1074–9. https://doi.org/10.1001/archpedi.159.11.1074.
14. Yasan A, Guzel A, Tamam Y, Ozkan M. Predictive factors for acute stress disorder and posttraumatic stress disorder after motor vehicle accidents. Psychopathology. 2009;42(4):236–41. https://doi.org/10.1159/000218521.
15. Salmon K, Sinclair E, Bryant RA. The role of maladaptive appraisals in child acute stress reactions. Br J Clin Psychol. 2007;46(2):203–10. https://doi.org/10.1348/014466506X160704.
16. Meiser-Stedman R, Dalgleish T, Smith P, Yule W, Bryant B, Ehlers A, et al. Dissociative symptoms and the acute stress disorder diagnosis in children and adolescents: a replication of the Harvey and Bryant (1999) study. J Trauma Stress. 2007;20(3):359–64. https://doi.org/10.1002/jts.20211.
17. Haag AC, Zehnder D, Landolt MA. Guilt is associated with acute stress symptoms in children after road traffic accidents. Eur J Psychotraumatol. 2015;6:29074. https://doi.org/10.3402/ejpt.v6.29074.
18. Alisic E, Jongmans MJ, van Wesel F, Kleber RJ. Building child trauma theory from longitudinal studies: a meta-analysis. Clin Psychol Rev. 2011;31(5):736–47. https://doi.org/10.1016/j.cpr.2011.03.001.
19. Pailler ME, Kassam-Adams N, Datner EM, Fein JA. Depression, acute stress and behavioral risk factors in violently injured adolescents. Gen Hosp Psychiatry. 2007;29(4):357–63. https://doi.org/10.1016/j.genhosppsych.2007.04.003.
20. Brewin CR, Andrews B, Rose S, Kirk M. Acute stress disorder and posttraumatic stress disorder in victims of violent crime. Am J Psychiatry. 1999;156(3):360–6. https://doi.org/10.1176/ajp.156.3.360.
21. Siqveland J, Hussain A, Lindstrom JC, Ruud T, Hauff E. Prevalence of posttraumatic stress disorder in persons with chronic pain: a Meta-analysis. Front Psychiatry. 2017;8:164. https://doi.org/10.3389/fpsyt.2017.00164.
22. Williamson V, Stevelink SAM, Greenberg K, Greenberg N. Prevalence of mental health disorders in elderly U.S. military veterans: a Meta-analysis and systematic review. Am J Geriatr Psychiatry. 2018;26(5):534–45. https://doi.org/10.1016/j.jagp.2017.11.001.
23. Dai W, Chen L, Lai Z, Li Y, Wang J, Liu A. The incidence of post-traumatic stress disorder among survivors after earthquakes:a systematic review and meta-analysis. BMC psychiatry. 2016;16:188. https://doi.org/10.1186/s12888-016-0891-9.
24. Spottswood M, Davydow DS, Huang H. The prevalence of posttraumatic stress disorder in primary care: a systematic review. Harv Rev Psychiatry. 2017;25(4):159–69. https://doi.org/10.1097/hrp.0000000000000136.
25. Griffiths J, Fortune G, Barber V, Young JD. The prevalence of post traumatic stress disorder in survivors of ICU treatment: a systematic review. Intensive Care Med. 2007;33(9):1506–18. https://doi.org/10.1007/s00134-007-0730-z.
26. Loney PL, Chambers LW, Bennett KJ, Roberts JG, Stratford PW. Critical appraisal of the health research literature: prevalence or incidence of a health problem. Chronic Dis Can. 1998;19(4):170–6.
27. Bassuk EL, Richard MK, Tsertsvadze A. The prevalence of mental illness in homeless children: a systematic review and meta-analysis. J Am Acad Child Adolesc Psychiatry. 2015;54(2):86–96.e2. https://doi.org/10.1016/j.jaac.2014.11.008.
28. Ades AE, Lu G, Higgins JP. The interpretation of random-effects meta-analysis in decision models. Med Decis Mak. 2005;25(6):646–54. https://doi.org/10.1177/0272989x05282643.
29. Li X, Wang J, Zhou J, Huang P, Li J. The association between post-traumatic stress disorder and shorter telomere length: a systematic review and meta-analysis. J Affect Disord. 2017;218:322–6. https://doi.org/10.1016/j.jad.2017.03.048.
30. Zhang L, Fu T, Yin R, Zhang Q, Shen B. Prevalence of depression and anxiety in systemic lupus erythematosus: a systematic review and meta-analysis. BMC Psychiatry. 2017;17(1):70. https://doi.org/10.1186/s12888-017-1234-1.
31. Zhou P, Zhang Y, Wei C, Liu Z, Hannak W. Acute stress disorder as a predictor of posttraumatic stress: a longitudinal study of Chinese children exposed to the Lushan earthquake. Psych J. 2016;5(3):206–14. https://doi.org/10.1002/pchj.136.
32. McKibben JB, Bresnick MG, Wiechman Askay SA, Fauerbach JA. Acute stress disorder and posttraumatic stress disorder: a prospective study of prevalence, course, and predictors in a sample with major burn injuries. J Burn Care Res. 2008;29(1):22–35. https://doi.org/10.1097/BCR.0b013e31815f59c4.
33. Elklit A, Brink O. Acute stress disorder in physical assault victims visiting a Danish emergency ward. Violence Vict. 2003;18(4):461–72.
34. Roberge MA, Dupuis G, Marchand A. Acute stress disorder after myocardial infarction: prevalence and associated factors. Psychosom Med. 2008;70(9):1028–34. https://doi.org/10.1097/PSY.0b013e318189a920.
35. Staab JP, Grieger TA, Fullerton CS, Ursano RJ. Acute stress disorder, subsequent posttraumatic stress disorder and depression after a series of typhoons. Anxiety. 1996;2(5):219–25.
36. Yahav R, Cohen M. Symptoms of acute stress in Jewish and Arab Israeli citizens during the second Lebanon war. Soc Psychiatry Psychiatr Epidemiol. 2007;42(10):830–6. https://doi.org/10.1007/s00127-007-0237-5.
37. Melroy-Greif WE, Wilhelmsen KC, Yehuda R, Ehlers CL. Genome-wide association study of post-traumatic stress disorder in two high-risk populations. Twin Res Hum Genet. 2017;20(3):197–207. https://doi.org/10.1017/thg.2017.12.
38. Bryant RA, Moulds ML, Guthrie RM. Acute stress disorder scale: a self-report measure of acute stress disorder. Psychol Assess. 2000;12(1):61–8.
39. Einsle F, Kraft D, Kollner V. Post-traumatic stress disorder (PTSD) in cardiology and oncology–which diagnostic tools should be used? J Psychosom Res. 2012;72(6):434–8. https://doi.org/10.1016/j.jpsychores.2012.02.008.
40. Swartzman S, Booth JN, Munro A, Sani F. Posttraumatic stress disorder after cancer diagnosis in adults: a meta-analysis. Depress Anxiety. 2017;34(4):327–39. https://doi.org/10.1002/da.22542.
41. Muldoon OT. Perceptions of stressful life events in northern Irish school children: a longitudinal study. J Child Psychol Psychiatry. 2003;44(2):193–201.
42. Ehlers A, Mayou RA, Bryant B. Psychological predictors of chronic posttraumatic stress disorder after motor vehicle accidents. J Abnorm Psychol. 1998;107(3):508–19.
43. Tousignant B, Jackson PL, Massicotte E, Beauchamp MH, Achim AM, Vera-Estay E, et al. Impact of traumatic brain injury on social cognition in adolescents and contribution of other higher order cognitive functions. Neuropsychol Rehabil. 2018;28(3):429–47. https://doi.org/10.1080/09602011.2016.1158114.
44. Yurgil KA, Barkauskas DA, Vasterling JJ, Nievergelt CM, Larson GE, Schork NJ, et al. Association between traumatic brain injury and risk of posttraumatic stress disorder in active-duty marines. JAMA Psychiatry. 2014;71(2):149–57. https://doi.org/10.1001/jamapsychiatry.2013.3080.
45. Vasterling JJ, Aslan M, Lee LO, Proctor SP, Ko J, Jacob S, et al. Longitudinal associations among posttraumatic stress disorder

symptoms, traumatic brain injury, and neurocognitive functioning in Army soldiers deployed to the Iraq war. J Int Neuropsychol Soc. 2018; 24(4):311–23. https://doi.org/10.1017/s1355617717001059.

46. Bryant RA, Harvey AG. Relationship between acute stress disorder and posttraumatic stress disorder following mild traumatic brain injury. Am J Psychiatry. 1998;155(5):625–9. https://doi.org/10.1176/ajp.155.5.625.
47. Jones C, Harvey AG, Brewin CR. Traumatic brain injury, dissociation, and posttraumatic stress disorder in road traffic accident survivors. J Trauma Stress. 2005;18(3):181–91. https://doi.org/10.1002/jts.20031.
48. Moher D, Pham B, Jones A, Cook DJ, Jadad AR, Moher M, et al. Does quality of reports of randomised trials affect estimates of intervention efficacy reported in meta-analyses? Lancet. 1998;352(9128):609–13. https://doi.org/10.1016/s0140-6736(98)01085-x.
49. Kjaergard LL, Villumsen J, Gluud C. Reported methodologic quality and discrepancies between large and small randomized trials in meta-analyses. Ann Intern Med. 2001;135(11):982–9.
50. Kessler RC, Aguilar-Gaxiola S, Alonso J, Benjet C, Bromet EJ, Cardoso G, et al. Trauma and PTSD in the WHO world mental health surveys. Eur J Psychotraumatol. 2017;8(sup5):1353383. https://doi.org/10.1080/20008198.2017.1353383.
51. Fernandez CA, Vicente B, Marshall BD, Koenen KC, Arheart KL, Kohn R, et al. Longitudinal course of disaster-related PTSD among a prospective sample of adult Chilean natural disaster survivors. Int J Epidemiol. 2017;46(2):440–52. https://doi.org/10.1093/ije/dyw094.
52. Fuglsang AK, Moergeli H, Schnyder U. Does acute stress disorder predict post-traumatic stress disorder in traffic accident victims? Analysis of a self-report inventory. Nord J Psychiatry. 2004;58(3):223–9. https://doi.org/10.1080/08039480410006278.
53. Hamanaka S, Asukai N, Kamijo Y, Hatta K, Kishimoto J, Miyaoka H. Acute stress disorder and posttraumatic stress disorder symptoms among patients severely injured in motor vehicle accidents in Japan. Gen Hosp Psychiatry. 2006;28(3):234–41. https://doi.org/10.1016/j.genhosppsych.2006.02.007.
54. van den Heuvel L, Suliman S, Malan-Muller S, Hemmings S, Seedat S. Brain-derived neurotrophic factor Val66met polymorphism and plasma levels in road traffic accident survivors. Anxiety Stress Coping. 2016;29(6):616–29. https://doi.org/10.1080/10615806.2016.1163545.
55. Winston FK, Kassam-Adams N, Vivarelli-O'Neill C, Ford J, Newman E, Baxt C, et al. Acute stress disorder symptoms in children and their parents after pediatric traffic injury. Pediatrics. 2002;109(6):e90.
56. Bryant B, Mayou R, Wiggs L, Ehlers A, Stores G. Psychological consequences of road traffic accidents for children and their mothers. Psychol Med. 2004; 34(2):335–46. https://doi.org/10.1017/s0033291703001053.

4

Does presence of metabolic syndrome impact anxiety and depressive disorder screening results in middle aged and elderly individuals?

Jurate Butnoriene[1*], Vesta Steibliene[2], Ausra Saudargiene[3,4] and Adomas Bunevicius[4]

Abstract

Background: Depressive and anxiety disorders are common in primary care setting but often remain undiagnosed. Metabolic syndrome (MetS) is also prevalent in the general population and can impair recognition of common mental disorders due to significant co-morbidity and overlap with psychiatric symptoms included in self-reported depression/anxiety screening tools. We investigated if MetS has an impact on the accuracy of current major depressive disorder (MDD) and generalized anxiety disorder (GAD) screening results using the Hospital Anxiety and Depression scale (HADS).

Methods: A total of 1115 (562 men; mean age 62.0 ± 9.6 years) individuals of 45+ years of age were randomly selected from the general population and evaluated for current MetS; depressive and anxiety symptoms (HADS); and current MDD and GAD (Mini International Neuropsychiatric Interview [MINI]).

Results: The MetS was diagnosed in 34.4% of the study participants. Current MDD and GAD were more common in individuals with MetS relative to individuals without MetS (25.3% vs 14.2%, respectively, $p < 0.001$; and 30.2% vs 20.9%, respectively, $p < 0.001$). The ROC analyses demonstrated that optimal thresholds of the HADS-Depression subscale for current MDE were ≥9 in individuals with MetS (sensitivity = 87%, specificity = 73% and PPV = 52%) and ≥8 in individuals without MetS (sensitivity = 81%, specificity = 78% and PPV = 38%). At threshold of ≥9 the HADS-Anxiety subscale demonstrated optimal psychometric properties for current GAD screening in individuals with MetS (sensitivity = 91%, specificity = 85% and PPV = 72%) and without MetS (sensitivity = 84%, specificity = 83% and PPV = 56%).

Conclusions: The HADS is a reliable screening tool for current MDE and GAD in middle aged and elderly population with and without MetS. Optimal thresholds of the HADS-Depression subscale for current MDD is ≥9 for individuals with MetS and ≥8 - without MetS. Optimal threshold of the HADS-Anxiety subscale is ≥9 for current GAD in individuals with and without MetS. The presence of MetS should be considered when interpreting depression screening results.

Keywords: Depressive disorder, General anxiety disorder, Hospital anxiety and depression scale, Metabolic syndrome, Mini international neuropsychiatric interview, Screening

* Correspondence: jurate.butnoriene@fc.lsmuni.lt
[1]Institute of Endocrinology, Lithuanian University of Health Sciences, Eiveniu str. 2, LT-50161 Kaunas, Lithuania
Full list of author information is available at the end of the article

Background

Anxiety disorders are the most common psychiatric disorders in primary care patients [1–4]. Patients suffering from anxiety disorders are more likely to seek treatment from primary care provider than from mental health specialist [5]. However, only up to one third of anxiety cases are recognized by primary care providers [3, 6, 7] and only a small proportion of patients receive treatment for anxiety disorders [4, 8, 9]. Generalized anxiety disorder (GAD) is characterized by persistent anxiety and worry, and is the most common anxiety disorder with reported prevalence rates ranging between 2.8% and 8.5% [6, 10]. Untreated GAD causes extreme distress, severe functional impairment [11, 12] significant economic costs [10], and is independently associated with elevated suicide risk [13, 14]. Implementation of effective screening strategies for detection of GAD in primary care setting could increase availability of treatment interventions and consequently contribute towards improved patient outcomes [15–18].

Major depressive disorder (MDD) affects from 5% to 14% of primary care patients [3, 19–21], but only less than 65% of depressed patients are diagnosed with depressive disorders [3, 22, 23] and less than 50% of depressed patients receive antidepressant treatment [23, 24]. Previous clinical practice guidelines did not recommend depression screening in primary care [25–27] due to lack of evidence of benefit of such intervention [28] and concerns for high false positive rate [29]. However, the US Preventive Services Task Force (USPSTF) has recently concluded that depression screening in primary care setting improves identification of depressed patients and treatment availability [30].

Metabolic Syndrome (MetS) encompasses a cluster of cardiovascular disease and type 2 diabetes risk factors [31]. The prevalence of MetS is steadily growing wordwide [32, 33]. Significant co-morbidity and bi-directional association of MetS with depressive and anxiety disorders is well-documented [34–39]. An accumulating body of evidence suggests that biological mechanisms underlying the MetS and MDD can overlap. For example, chronic stress, hyperactivity of hypothalamic-pituitary-adrenal (HPA) axis, noradrenergic dysregulation, inflammatory cytokines and endothelial dysfunction were implicated in both MDD and MetS [40]. Furthermore, behavioral changes attributed to MDD, such as smoking, physical inactivity and sleep disturbances, can also contribute towards development of MetS. On the other hand, metabolic disturbance in MetS patients may contribute to impaired brain functioning and development of GAD, MDD and other affective disorders [41, 42].

These observations indicate the importance of timely identification and adequate management of MDE and GAD among patients with established MetS [31, 36]. However, the MetS is highly co-morbid with other somatic conditions and complaints, which are common in middle aged and elderly population [43]. Symptoms of co-morbid cardiovascular disease, diabetes and obesity (such as fatigue and sleep impairment) can overlap with symptoms included in depression/anxiety self-rating scales leading to impaired recognition of mental disorders and high false positive screening rates due to inclusion of patients reporting symptoms caused by MetS rather than mental disorder. Indeed, previous studies indicated stronger association of MetS with depression evaluated using self-rating scales than structured clinical diagnostic interviews [31, 44]. Therefore, different thresholds of depression/anxiety screening may be needed for patients with co-morbid MetS. The Hospital Anxiety and Depression Scale (HADS) is widely used for screening of depressive and anxiety disorders in medically ill patients [45, 46]. There are no universally accepted thresholds of the HADS as studies documented different optimal thresholds across different somatic disorders [47]. To our knowledge, there are no studies evaluating psychometric properties of the HADS for depressive and anxiety disorder screening purposes as a function of current MetS diagnosis. Therefore, the aim of our study was to investigate if presence of MetS diagnosis has an impact on the accuracy of current MDE and GAD screening using the HADS. We hypothised that due to overlap of MetS-related symptoms with depression, optimal depression (but not anxiety) screening threshold value would be greater in patients with MetS versus patients without MetS.

Methods

Patient recruitment in this cross-sectional observational cohort study took place from February 2003 until January 2004 at the Primary Health Care Centre (PHCC). Men and women of 45 years old and older were randomly selected from the database of inhabitants registered at the PHCC by using the probability systematic method. Invitation letters were sent to 1624 selected individuals via regular mail. One-thousand one-hundred and twenty (response rate 69%) subjects attended the study visit. Women who did not respond to the study invitation letter were older when compared to women that were studied ($p < 0.05$). Other socio-demographic characteristics were similar between responders and non-responders. However, five individuals were excluded from the analyses because they were not evaluated for the MetS or refused from psychiatric assessment leaving the final sample of 1115 subjects (562 men and 553 women).

All study participants completed a battery of questionnaires that included assessment of socio-demographic characteristics (education, residence, marital status and employment history), and depressive and anxiety symptoms severity (HADS) [46]. Past medical histories and current medication use were evaluated by reviewing medical records. All study participants were evaluated by a trained interviewer for current MDE and GAD using the Mini International Neuropsychiatric Interview or MINI [48].

The study protocol and informed consent procedure were approved by the Regional Bioethics Committee at the Lithuanian University of Health Sciences, Kaunas, Lithuania (2003–01-21 No. 6B/2003). The investigation was carried out in accordance with the Declaration of Helsinki. Each participant gave written informed consent prior to all study procedures.

Psychiatric evaluation

The HADS [46] is a self-rating questionnaire comprised of two 7-item subscales of anxiety (HADS-A) and depression (HADS-D) that are designed to evaluate respective symptom severity during the preceding 2 weeks. Each HADS item is rated on a 4-point Likert-type scale with total scores on each subscale ranging from 0 to 21, and with higher scores corresponding to greater respective symptom severity [47].

Diagnoses of current MDE and GAD were established using the MINI interview, version 5.0.0 [48]. The MINI interview is a semi-structured diagnostic psychiatric interview designed for evaluation for current psychiatric disorders according to the *Diagnostic and Statistical Manual of Mental Disorders 4th edition, Text revision* (DSM-IV-TR) [49]. The MINI has modular structure pertaining to specific psychiatric diagnoses. For the purpose of the present study we used the MINI modules pertaining to current MDE (module A) and current GAD (module O). The Lithuanian translation of the MINI interview is widely used for research purposes in hospitalized patients [50] and in primary patients [1].

Assessment of the metabolic syndrome

Participants were asked to fast for at least 12 h prior to the study visit and to collect the first morning urine sample into a special container. During the study visit, fasting blood samples were drawn from an antecubital vein, were centrifuged and stored frozen at −70 °C for measurements of fasting plasma lipid panel and at −20 ° C for evaluation of fasting plasma insulin concentration. Serum samples were enzymatically assayed for total cholesterol, high-density lipoprotein (HDL), and triglyceride (TG) concentrations. Low-density lipoprotein (LDL) serum concentration was determined using the Friedwald equation. Fasting glucose (oxidase-phenol aminophenazone method) and insulin (Immunoradiometric method; BioSource INS-IRMA; Belgium) concentrations were also assessed and oral glucose tolerance test [51] was performed in all participants with an exception of diabetic patients. Insulin resistance index was calculated using the Homeostasis Model Assessment ($HOMA_{IR}$) [52]. Urine albumin concentration was determined using immunological semi-quantitative method (Roche Diagnostic; UK). Anthropometric characteristics were measured using standard procedures and included height (in cm), weight (in kg), and waist and hip circumference (in cm). Waist-to-hip ratio (WHR) and body mass index (BMI) were subsequently calculated using standard methods [53, 54]. Blood pressure (BP) was measured using a random-zero mercury sphygmomanometer after the subject sat still for about 5 min.

The diagnosis of the current MetS was established according to the World Health Organization (WHO) criteria that covers impaired insulin resistance or elevated fasting glucose or impaired glucose tolerance or type 2 diabetes mellitus; and any two of the following criteria: (1) arterial hypertension (blood pressure ≥ 140/ 90 mmHg); (2) current use of antihypertensive medication; (3) elevated TG concentration (≥ 1.7 mmol/l); (4) reduced HDL cholesterol concentration (< 0.9 mmol/l for men or <1.0 mmol/l for women); (5) obesity (BMI > 30 kg/ m^2, or WHR > 0.9 for men or >0.85 for women); or (6) microalbuminuria [40, 55].

Statistical analyses

First, we compared socio-demographic characteristics, adverse health behaviors, past medical histories, current medication use, and prevalence of the MINI diagnoses of mental disorders in subjects with MetS versus subjects without MetS by applying the independent sample t-test for continuous factors and Pearson's chi-squared test for categorical factors.

Next, we sought to identify optimal thresholds of the HADS-D and HADS-A subscales to predict the MINI diagnoses of current MDE and current GAD, respectively, in subjects diagnosed with MetS and in subjects without MetS. We computed sensitivity, specificity, positive predictive value (PPV), negative predictive value (NPV), accuracy and area under the receiver operating characteristic (ROC) curve (AUC), with 95% confidence intervals (CIs). The estimate of the area under the ROC curve was computed nonparametrically. The optimal HADS-D and HADS-A thresholds correctly identifying individuals with MDE and GAD, respectively, were determined as the threshold values that gave the closest to the ideal point on the ROC curve, i.e. that made the resulting binary prediction as close to the perfect predictor as possible [56]. A perfect predictor is represented by a point in the upper left corner in the plot and has 100% sensitivity and 100% specificity. The distance between this optimal point and the ROC curve is estimated using the Euclidean distance. The minimal Euclidean distance indicates the point on the ROC curve with the optimal threshold value.

The SPSS 20.0 for Windows (IBM Corporation, Chicago, IL, USA) and Matlab 7.11 were used for data analysis.

Results

As presented in Table 1, 34% of the study subjects were diagnosed with current MetS. Subjects with MetS were older (63.7 ± 9.2 years vs 61.1 ± 9.7, respectively; $p <$ 0.0001) and were more likely to live in the city (36.5% vs 26.3%, respectively; $p < 0.0001$), be retired or disabled (70.3% vs 59.5%, respectively; $p = 0.002$), be physically non-active (60.9% vs 48.0%, respectively; $p < 0.0001$) and do not consume alcohol (14.1% vs 9.7, respectively; $p =$ 0.024) when compared to subjects without MetS. Significantly greater prevalence of past medical histories of myocardial infarction (8.6%), stroke (6.8%), cardiovascular disorder (71.6%), type 2 diabetes mellitus (11.7%) and other endocrine disorders (26.8%) was reported in subjects with MetS when compared to patients without MetS. Current medication use was also more common in subjects with MetS.

Prevalence rates of current MDE and GAD were significantly higher among subjects with MetS in comparison to subjects without MetS (25.3% vs. 14.2%, respectively; $p < 0.001$; and 30.2% vs 20.9%, respectively; $p < 0.0001$).

The ROC analyses showed that AUCs of the HADS-D for current MDE in subjects with MetS and without MetS were at levels of 0.83 (95% CI: 0.79–0.87) and 0.86 (95% CI: 0.82–0.89), respectively. Psychometric properties of the HADS-D at different thresholds for current MDE in individuals with and without MetS are presented in Table 2. Optimal thresholds of the HADS-D for current MDE were ≥9 in subjects with MetS (sensitivity = 87%, specificity = 73% and PPV = 52%) and ≥8 in subjects without MetS (sensitivity = 81%, specificity = 78% and PPV = 38%). In the total sample, the HADS-D at threshold of ≥8 demonstrated optimal psychometric properties for current MDE screening (sensitivity = 87%, specificity = 74% and PPV = 42%) (Fig. 1).

AUCs of the HADS-A for current GAD were 0.95 (95% CI: 0.92–0.97) in subjects with MetS and 0.91 (95% CI: 0.89–0.94) in subjects without MetS. Psychometric properties of the HADS-A at different thresholds as a function of presence of the MetS for screening of current GAD are presented in Table 3. We found that at threshold of ≥9 the HADS-A demonstrated optimal psychometric properties for current GAD in subjects with MetS (sensitivity = 91%, specificity = 85% and PPV = 72%) and without MetS (sensitivity = 84%, specificity = 83% and PPV = 56%) (Fig. 2).

Discussion

We found that the HADS is a reliable screening tool for current MDE and GAD irrespectively of the presence of the MetS. Optimal thresholds of the HADS-D for current MDE were ≥9 for subjects with MetS and ≥8 for subjects without MetS. Optimal threshold of the HADS-A for current GAD was ≥9 in subjects with and without MetS. At optimal thresholds the HADS-D and HADS-A demonstrated adequate sensitivity, specificity and PPV for current MDE and GAD, respectively, in subjects with and without MetS.

Optimal thresholds of the HADS-D for current MDE screening was higher in participants with MetS, relative to participants without MetS. These findings suggest that somatic symptoms attributed to conditions co-morbid with MetS can overlap with depressive symptoms and consequentially inflate the total HADS-D score. For example, central obesity is among the cardinal MetS features that can cause symptoms similar to depressive disorders, such as general tiredness, fatigue and reduced physical activity. Consequentially patients with MetS can rate the HADS-D item "feeling of slowed down" higher due to obesity rather than depression. From social perspective, obese patients can have lower self-esteem resulting in decreased enjoyment in the social activities [57] and therefore rate higher the HADS-D items "the ability still enjoy the things, were used to enjoy" and "the loss of interest in personal appearance". Similar findings were reported in a systematic review and meta-analysis by Pan et al., [31], showing that self-reported depression instruments among subjects with MetS allow inclusion of patients who do not meet the DSM diagnostic criteria for current MDD resulting in increased false-positive rate. Our findings suggest that higher optimal HADS-D threshold (≥9) for current MDE screening purposes should be used in subjects with MetS, as this approach would reduce the likelihood of false positive screening results by excluding individuals with MetS-related symptoms mimicking clinical depressive symptoms. Optimization of false-positive depression screening results by using greater threshold could potentially reduce delivery of unnecessary treatment interventions and reduce burden on available healthcare resources.

In our cohort, patients diagnosed with MetS were slightly older, had more somatic co-morbidities and used more prescription medication relative to non-MetS patients, suggesting that greater somatic symptom burden among individuals with MetS that can mimic depressive symptoms and impact depression screening. Indeed, optimal HADS-D threshold of ≥9 for current MDD screening were previously reported in other somatic patient populations. For example, optimal HADS-D threshold of ≥9 (sensitivity 0.846 and specificity 0.903) was found in

Table 1 Baseline Characteristics in Subjects with MetS and without MetS

	With MetS $n = 384$ (34.4%)	Without MetS $n = 731$ (65.6%)	*P*-value*
Age (years)	63.7 ± 9.2	61.1 ± 9.7	**0.0001**
Gender			0.05
Women	206 (53.6%)	347 (47.5%)	
Men	178 (46.4%)	384 (52.5%)	
Residence			**0.0001**
Rural	244 (63.5%)	539 (73.7%)	
Urban	140 (36.5%)	192 (26.3%)	
Education			0.219
High school or lower	193 (50.3%)	341 (46.6%)	
Graduated from high school	150 (39.1%)	324 (44.3%)	
University degree	41 (10.7%)	66 (9.0%)	
Marital status			0.152
Currently married	260 (67.7%)	531 (72.6%)	
Never married	20 (5.2%)	40 (5.5%)	
Divorced or widower	104 (27.1%)	160 (21.9%)	
Employment status			**0.002**
Currently employed	71 (18.5%)	188 (25.7%)	
Currently unemployed	43 (11.2%)	108 (14.8%)	
Retired/disabled	270 (70.3%)	435 (59.5%)	
Current smoking			0.329
Non-smokers	266 (69.3%)	478 (65.4%)	
Smokes 1–9 cigarettes/day	19 (4.9%)	54 (7.4%)	
Smokes 10–19 cigarettes/day	38 (9.9%)	69 (9.4%)	
Smokes ≥20 cigarettes/day	61 (15.9%)	130 (17.8%)	
Alcohol consumption			**0.024**
Non-consumers	54 (14.1%)	71 (9.7%)	
Several times/year	210 (54.7%)	384 (52.5%)	
Monthly or more	120 (31.2%)	276 (37.8%)	
Physical activity [a]			**0.0001**
Several times/month or more	75 (19.5%)	124 (17.0%)	
Several times/year	75 (19.5%)	256 (35.0%)	
Non-active	234 (60.9%)	351 (48.0%)	
Past medical histories			
Myocardial infarction	33 (8.6%)	29 (4.0%)	**0.001**
Stroke	26 (6.8%)	28 (3.8%)	**0.030**
Cardiovascular disorders	275 (71.6%)	388 (53.1%)	**0.0001**
Respiratory disorders	138 (35.9%)	232 (31.7%)	0.157
Gastrointestinal disorders	131 (34.1%)	241 (33.0%)	0.70
Musculoskeletal disorders	204 (53.1%)	387 (52.9%)	0.953
Neurological disorders	86 (22.4%)	175 (23.9%)	0.563
Genitourinary tract disorders	110 (28.6%)	187 (25.6%)	0.271
Type 2 diabetes mellitus	45 (11.7%)	8 (1.1%)	**0.0001**
Other endocrine disorders	103 (26.8%)	118 (16.1%)	**0.0001**

Table 1 Baseline Characteristics in Subjects with MetS and without MetS *(Continued)*

	With MetS *n* = 384 (34.4%)	Without MetS *n* = 731 (65.6%)	*P*-value*
Other diseases	135 (35.2%)	231 (31.6%)	0.230
Current medication use			
ACE inhibitors	144 (37.5%)	97 (13.3%)	**0.0001**
Beta-blockers	41 (10.7%)	29 (4.0%)	**0.0001**
Calcium channel blockers	43 (11.2%)	26 (3.6%)	**0.0001**
Other medication	98 (25.5%)	107 (14.6%)	**0.0001**
Current MINI mental disorders			
Generalized Anxiety Disorder	116 (30.2%)	153 (20.9%)	**0.001**
Major Depressive Episode	97 (25.3%)	104 (14.2%)	**0.0001**

Values are expressed as no. of subjects (%) or mean ± SD
ACE angiotensin-converting-enzyme inhibitor, *MINI* Mini International Neuropsychiatric Interview, *SD* standard deviation
[a]At least 30 min of physical exercise per day
* *p* value were calculated using independent sample t-test or Pearson's chi-squared test
In **bold** *p* values <0.05

the general medical ward patients [58]; and ≥10 (sensitivity 0.77 and specificity 0.82) in patients with chronic fatigue syndrome [59] and general medical out-patients with unexplained somatic symptoms (sensitivity 0.56 and specificity 0.92) [60]. Also, optimal threshold of the HADS-D at ≥11 was reported in patients with advanced breast cancer (sensitivity 0.75 and specificity 0.75) [61], Hodgkin's lymphoma and non-Hodgkin lymphoma (0.84 sensitivity and 0.66 specificity) [62]; and in mixed sample of breast cancer, head and neck cancers, and lymphoma outpatients (0.43 sensitivity and 0.96 specificity) [63]. These findings suggest that MDD screening results using the HADS-D should be interpreted with caution in the context of patients' functional status and other somatic co-morbidities, including the MetS.

We found that histories of cardiovascular disorder (CVD) and type 2 diabetes were more common in subjects with MetS relative to subjects without MetS.

Table 2 Receiver-operating Characteristics for Current Major Depressive Episode using Different Thresholds of the Depression Subscale of the Hospital Anxiety and Depression Scale (HADS-D)

Thresholds	*n* (%)	Sensitivity, % (95% CI)	Specificity, % (95% CI)	PPV, % (95% CI)	NPV, % (95% CI)	Accuracy, % (95% CI)	AUC (95% CI)
All study participants, *n* = 1115							
≥ 6	610 (55)	94 (89–96)	54 (51–57)	31 (27–35)	97 (96–99)	61 (58–64)	0.86 (0.83–0.88)
≥ 7	499 (45)	90 (84–93)	65 (62–68)	36 (32–40)	97 (95–98)	70 (67–72)	
≥ 8	**414 (37)**	**87 (81–91)**	**74 (71–77)**	**42 (38–47)**	**96 (95–98)**	**76 (74–79)**	
≥ 9	336 (30)	77 (71–83)	80 (77–83)	46 (41–52)	94 (92–96)	80 (77–82)	
≥ 10	263 (24)	64 (57–71)	85 (83–88)	49 (43–55)	92 (89–93)	81 (79–84)	
With Metabolic syndrome only (WHO definition), *n* = 384							
≥ 6	252 (66)	97 (91–100)	45 (39–51)	37 (31–44)	98 (93–100)	58 (53–63)	0.83 (0.79–0.87)
≥ 7	215 (56)	94 (86–98)	57 (51–63)	42 (36–49)	96 (92–99)	66 (61–71)	
≥ 8	194 (51)	94 (86–98)	64 (58–70)	47 (40–54)	97 (93–99)	72 (67–76)	
≥ 9	**161 (42)**	**87 (78–93)**	**73 (68–78)**	**52 (44–60)**	**94 (90–97)**	**77 (72–81)**	
≥ 10	128 (33)	69 (59–78)	79 (73–83)	52 (43–61)	88 (84–92)	88 (84–92)	
Without Metabolic syndrome only (WHO definition), *n* = 731							
≥ 6	358 (49)	90 (83–95)	58 (54–62)	26 (22–31)	97 (95–99)	63 (59–66)	0.86 (0.82–0.89)
≥ 7	284 (39)	86 (77–92)	69 (65–72)	31 (26–37)	97 (94–98)	71 (68–75)	
≥ 8	**220 (30)**	**81 (72–88)**	**78 (75–81)**	**38 (32–45)**	**96 (94–98)**	**79 (75–82)**	
≥ 9	175 (24)	68 (58–77)	83 (80–86)	41 (33–48)	94 (92–96)	81 (78–84)	
≥ 10	135 (18)	60 (50–69)	88 (86–91)	46 (37–55)	93 (91–95)	84 (81–87)	

PPV positive predictive value, *NPV* negative predictive value, *AUC* area under the receiver operating curve, *CI* confidence interval
Optimal thresholds in **bold**

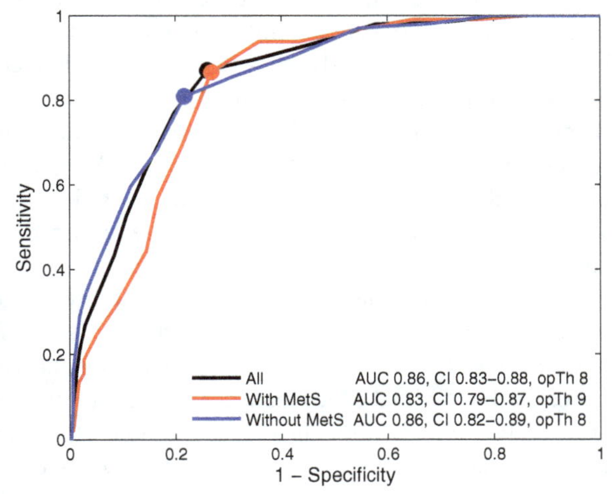

Fig. 1 The areas under the ROC curves and the optimal thresholds of the HADS-D for current MDE in all study participants, subjects with MetS and subjects without MetS

However, previous studies in patients with established CVD reported lower optimal HADS-D thresholds for screening of depressive disorders relative to our study. Optimal HADS-D thresholds was ≥4 (sensitivity 0.864, a specificity 0.788) in out-patients with chronic heart failure [64]; ≥5 (sensitivity 0.77%, specificity 0.69 and PPD 0.23%) in CVD patients attending cardiac rehabilitation [65]; and ≥8 in stable coronary heart disease (CHD) patients [66]. These findings suggest that in MetS population, non-CVD related symptoms other comorbid non-CVD disorders can account for inflation self-reported depressive symptom severity. In patients with diabetes, glucose metabolism impairment can also account for greater self-reported depressive symptom severity because it is known that greater self-perceived depression among patients with MetS is associated with larger waist circumference among women and with elevated plasma glucose concentration among men [67]. Studies examining potential impact of co-morbid diabetes on depression screening results should be attempted.

In the present cohort, patients with MetS were more likely to be retired/ disabled, live in urban area, report less physical activity and greater alcohol consumption. These socioeconomic, environmental and behavioral markers were also linked to depressive disorders [68] indicating that common mental disorders and MetS can share environmental risk factors. Better understanding of common features underlying common mental disorders and MetS could potentially help to identify vulnerable populations, and to develop more accurate recognition strategies and effective interventions leading to reduced global burden of the two disorders.

In our study, the optimal HADS-D cutoff score of the current MDE was at level of ≥8 in subjects without MetS

Table 3 Receiver-operating Characteristics for Generalized Anxiety Disorder using Different Thresholds of the Anxiety Subscale of the Hospital Anxiety and Depression Scale (HADS-A)

Thresholds	*n* (%)	Sensitivity, % (95% CI)	Specificity, % (95% CI)	PPV, % (95% CI)	NPV, % (95% CI)	Accuracy, % (95% CI)	AUC (95% CI)
All study participants, *n* = 1115							
≥ 6	661 (59)	98 (95–99)	53 (50–56)	40 (36–44)	99 (97–100)	64 (61–67)	0.93 (0.91–0.94)
≥ 7	554 (50)	96 (92–98)	65 (62–68)	46 (42–51)	98 (96–99)	72 (70–75)	
≥ 8	456 (41)	94 (90–96)	76 (73–79)	55 (51–60)	97 (96–98)	80 (78–82)	
≥ 9	**373 (33)**	**87 (82–90)**	**84 (81–86)**	**63 (57–67)**	**95 (93–97)**	**84 (82–86)**	
≥ 10	301 (27)	79 (73–83)	90 (87–91)	70 (65–76)	93 (91–95)	87 (85–89)	
With Metabolic syndrome only (WHO definition), *n* = 384							
≥ 6	242 (63)	98 (93–100)	52 (46–58)	47 (41–54)	99 (95–100)	66 (61–71)	0.95 (0.92–0.97)
≥ 7	205 (53)	97 (92–100)	66 (60–71)	55 (48–62)	98 (95–100)	75 (71–79)	
≥ 8	171 (45)	95 (89–98)	77 (72–82)	64 (57–71)	97 (94–99)	83 (78–86)	
≥ 9	**146 (38)**	**91 (83–95)**	**85 (80–89)**	**72 (64–79)**	**95 (92–98)**	**86 (83–90)**	
≥ 10	119 (31)	84 (75–90)	92 (88–95)	82 (73–88)	93 (89–96)	89 (86–92)	
Without Metabolic syndrome only (WHO definition), *n* = 731							
≥ 6	419 (57)	98 (94–100)	53 (49–58)	36 (31–41)	99 (97–100)	63 (59–66)	0.91 (0.89–0.94)
≥ 7	349 (48)	94 (89–97)	65 (60–68)	41 (36–47)	98 (95–99)	71 (67–74)	
≥ 8	285 (39)	93 (87–96)	75 (72–79)	50 (44–56)	98 (95–99)	79 (76–82)	
≥ 9	**227 (31)**	**84 (77–89)**	**83 (80–86)**	**56 (50–63)**	**95 (93–97)**	**83 (80–86)**	
≥ 10	182 (25)	75 (67–82)	88 (85–91)	63 (56–70)	93 (91–95)	86 (83–88)	

PPV positive predictive value, *NPV* negative predictive value, *AUC* area under the receiver operating curve, *CI* confidence interval
Optimal thresholds in **bold**

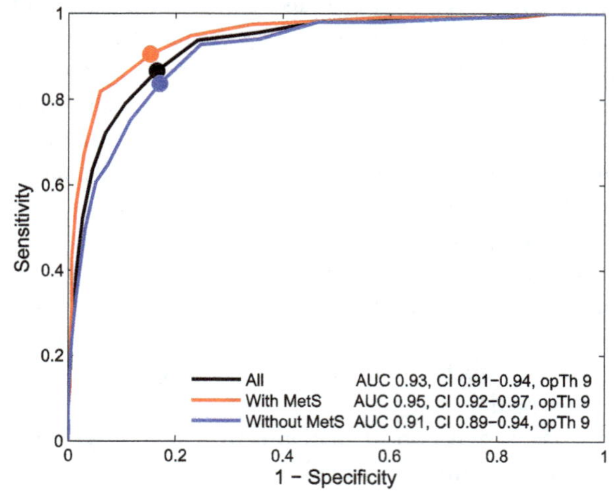

Fig. 2 The areas under the ROC curves and the optimal thresholds of the HADS-A for current MDE in all study participants, subjects with MetS and subjects without MetS

and in the total sample of the study participants. Lower optimal HADS-D thresholds of ≥6 (sensitivity 0.66; specificity 0.97) and ≥7 (sensitivity 0.8; specificity 0.69) for current MDD screening were previously reported by other studies in primary care patients [58]. These findings can be explained that we considered only middle aged and elderly patients as opposed to consecutive primary care patients included in the latter two studies. Elderly patients are expected to have more co–morbidities that can interfere with depression screening. Our findings suggest that HADS-D cutoff score of ≥8 should be used for current MDE screening purposes in middle aged and elderly patients.

We found that the optimal threshold (≥9) of the HADS-A was the same for screening for current GAD in subjects with and without MetS. These findings suggest that GAD symptoms do not overlap with symptoms of MetS and MetS related co–morbidities. The same optimal threshold of the HADS-A at a level of ≥9 for current GAD [45, 69] was reported by other groups in primary care populations. Screening for current GAD should be considered in patients with MetS, because GAD and MetS can increase cardiovascular mortality risk in women independently from each other [70]. Unrecognized and untreated GAD can significantly impair quality of life and level of functioning, and impose burden to societies [71].

Both HADS subscales had high sensitivity for MDD and GAD screening; however, positive predictive values were low. These findings indicate high-false positive rate of current MDE and GAD screening using the HADS. Therefore, all patients screened positive using the HADS scale should be referred for psychiatric consultation prior to initiation of treatment interventions. Further studies investigating optimal mental disorders screening algorithms in primary care setting are encouraged.

Limitations of our study should be acknowledged. Inclusion of patients from predominantly rural area can put our results at risk for selection bias and limit generalizability to urban population. Also, only middle aged and elderly patients were invited in the study, therefore our results cannot be generalized to younger patients.

There is a debate in literature about the validity of the MetS definition criteria [72, 73]. We used the MetS definition proposed by the WHO that considers insulin resistance as the cardinal MetS feature and it is among the most widely studied MetS diagnostic criteria. However, studies examining potential impact of the MetS diagnosed using other commonly used sets of diagnostic criteria for mental disorder screening can be attempted. We evaluated psychometric properties of one scale (the HADS) that is commonly used for screening purposes in clinical setting. Psychometric properties of other commonly used depression screening scales, such as the Patient Health Questionnaire, remain to be investigated in patients with MetS. On the other hand, strengths of our study include large and representative sample of middle aged and elderly general population, use of validated diagnostic psychiatric interview and the use of well-established WHO criteria for diagnosis of current MetS.

Conclusions

In conclusion, the HADS has adequate psychometric properties for current MDE and GAD screening purposes in middle aged and elderly patients with and without MetS. For current MDD screening, the HADS-D threshold of ≥9 should be used in patients with MetS and ≥8 in patients without MetS with acceptable sensitivity (≥87%) and specificity (≥73%). For current GAD screening the HADS-A threshold of ≥9 has adequate psychometric (sensitivity ≥87% and specificity ≥84%) in patients with and without MetS. Further studies investigating optimal mental disorder screening strategies in primary care settings are encouraged.

Abbreviations

ACE: Angiotensin-converting-enzyme inhibitor; AUC: Area under the receiver operating curve; BMI: Body mass index; BP: Blood pressure; CHD: Coronary heart disease; CI: Confidence interval; CVD: Cardiovascular disorders; DSM-IV-TR: Diagnostic and statistical manual of mental disorders 4th edition, text revision; GAD: Generalized anxiety disorders; HADS: Hospital anxiety and depression scale; HADS-A: Hospital anxiety and depression scale - anxiety subscale; HADS-D: Hospital anxiety and depression scale - depression subscale; HDL: High-density lipoprotein; $HOMA_{IR}$: Homeostasis model assessment; LDL: Low-density lipoprotein; MDD: Major depressive disorder; MDE: Major depressive episode; MetS: Metabolic syndrome; MINI: Mini International neuropsychiatric interview; NPV: Negative predictive value; PHCC: Primary health care centre; PPV: Positive predictive value; ROC: The receiver operating characteristic; SD: Standard deviation; TG: Triglyceride; USPSTF: US preventive services task force; WHO: World health organization; WHR: Waist-to-hip ratio

Acknowledgements
The authors wish to thank all patients for participation in the study.

Funding
Not applicable / No funding was received.

Authors' contributions
JB: Conception and design, Statistical Analysis, Interpretation of the data, Drafting manuscript, Critical revision of the manuscript. VS: Interpretation of the data, Drafting the manuscript, Critical revision of the manuscript. AS: Statistical Analysis, Interpretation of the data, Critical revision of the manuscript. AB: Conception and design, Interpretation of data, Critical revision of the manuscript. All authors have contributed to and have approved the final manuscript.

Consent for publication
Not Applicable.

Competing interests
The authors declare that they have no competing interests.

Author details
[1]Institute of Endocrinology, Lithuanian University of Health Sciences, Eiveniu str. 2, LT-50161 Kaunas, Lithuania. [2]Psychiatry Clinic, Lithuanian University of Health Sciences, Kaunas, Lithuania. [3]Lithuanian University of Health Sciences, Kaunas, Lithuania. [4]Neuroscience Institute, Lithuanian University of Health Sciences, Kaunas, Lithuania.

References

1. Bunevicius R, Liaugaudaite V, Peceliuniene J, Raskauskiene N, Bunevicius A, Mickuviene N. Factors affecting the presence of depression, anxiety disorders, and suicidal ideation in patients attending primary health care service in Lithuania. Scand J Prim Health Care. 2014;32(1):24–9. https://doi.org/10.3109/02813432.2013.873604.
2. Kessler RC, McGonagle KA, Zhao S, Nelson CB, Hughes M, Eshleman S, et al. Lifetime and 12-month prevalence of DSM-III-R psychiatric disorders in the United States. Results from the National Comorbidity Survey. Arch Gen Psychiatry. 1994;51(1):8–19.
3. Wittchen HU, Kessler RC, Beesdo K, Krause P, Hofler M, Hoyer J. Generalized anxiety and depression in primary care: prevalence, recognition, and management. The Journal of clinical psychiatry. 2002;63(Suppl 8):24–34.
4. Kroenke K, Spitzer RL, Williams JB, Monahan PO, Lowe B. Anxiety disorders in primary care: prevalence, impairment, comorbidity, and detection. Ann Intern Med. 2007;146(5):317–25.
5. Combs H, Markman J. Anxiety disorders in primary care. The Medical clinics of North America. 2014;98(5):1007–23. https://doi.org/10.1016/j.mcna.2014.06.003.
6. Roy-Byrne PP, Wagner A. Primary care perspectives on generalized anxiety disorder. J Clin Psychiatry. 2004;65(Suppl 13):20–6.
7. Kessler RC, Keller MB, Wittchen HU. The epidemiology of generalized anxiety disorder. The Psychiatric clinics of North America. 2001;24(1):19–39.
8. Stein MB, Sherbourne CD, Craske MG, Means-Christensen A, Bystritsky A, Katon W, et al. Quality of care for primary care patients with anxiety disorders. Am J Psychiatry. 2004;161(12):2230–7. https://doi.org/10.1176/appi.ajp.161.12.2230.
9. Munk-Jorgensen P, Allgulander C, Dahl AA, Foldager L, Holm M, Rasmussen I, et al. Prevalence of generalized anxiety disorder in general practice in Denmark, Finland, Norway, and Sweden. Psychiatr Serv. 2006;57(12):1738–44. https://doi.org/10.1176/appi.ps.57.12.1738.
10. Stein MB. Public health perspectives on generalized anxiety disorder. The Journal of clinical psychiatry. 2004;65(Suppl 13):3–7.
11. Rickels K, Rynn MA. What is generalized anxiety disorder? J Clin Psychiatry. 2001;62(Suppl 11):4–12. discussion 3-4
12. Andrews G, Hobbs MJ, Borkovec TD, Beesdo K, Craske MG, Heimberg RG, et al. Generalized worry disorder: a review of DSM-IV generalized anxiety disorder and options for DSM-V. Depress Anxiety. 2010;27(2):134–47. https://doi.org/10.1002/da.20658.
13. Hawgood J, De Leo D. Anxiety disorders and suicidal behaviour: an update. Current opinion in psychiatry. 2008;21(1):51–64. https://doi.org/10.1097/YCO.0b013e3282f2309d.
14. Cougle JR, Keough ME, Riccardi CJ, Sachs-Ericsson N. Anxiety disorders and suicidality in the National Comorbidity Survey-Replication. J Psychiatr Res. 2009;43(9):825–9. https://doi.org/10.1016/j.jpsychires.2008.12.004.
15. Culpepper L. Generalized anxiety disorder in primary care: emerging issues in management and treatment. J Clin Psychiatry. 2002;63(Suppl 8):35–42.
16. Roberge P, Normand-Lauziere F, Raymond I, Luc M, Tanguay-Bernard MM, Duhoux A, et al. Generalized anxiety disorder in primary care: mental health services use and treatment adequacy. BMC Fam Pract. 2015;16(1):146. https://doi.org/10.1186/s12875-015-0358-y.
17. Katon W, Roy-Byrne P. Anxiety disorders: efficient screening is the first step in improving outcomes. Ann Intern Med. 2007;146(5):390–2.
18. Garcia-Campayo J, del Hoyo YL, Valero MS, Yus MC, Esteban EA, Guedea MP, et al. Primary prevention of anxiety disorders in primary care: a systematic review. Prev Med. 2015;76(Suppl):S12–5. https://doi.org/10.1016/j.ypmed.2014.10.015.
19. Screening for depression in adults. U.S. preventive services task force recommendation statement. Ann Intern Med. 2009;151(11):784–92. https://doi.org/10.7326/0003-4819-151-11-200912010-00006.
20. Kessler RC, Berglund P, Demler O, Jin R, Merikangas KR, Walters EE. Lifetime prevalence and age-of-onset distributions of DSM-IV disorders in the National Comorbidity Survey Replication. Arch Gen Psychiatry. 2005;62(6):593–602. https://doi.org/10.1001/archpsyc.62.6.593.
21. Qin X, Wang W, Jin Q, Ai L, Li Y, Dong G, et al. Prevalence and rates of recognition of depressive disorders in internal medicine outpatient departments of 23 general hospitals in Shenyang, China. J Affect Disord. 2008;110(1–2):46–54. https://doi.org/10.1016/j.jad.2007.12.237.
22. Sartorius N, Ustun TB, Costa e Silva JA, Goldberg D, Lecrubier Y, Ormel J, et al. An international study of psychological problems in primary care. Preliminary report from the World Health Organization collaborative project on 'Psychological problems in general health Care'. Arch Gen Psychiatry. 1993;50(10):819–24.
23. Lecrubier Y. Widespread underrecognition and undertreatment of anxiety and mood disorders: results from 3 European studies. The Journal of clinical psychiatry. 2007;68(Suppl 2):36–41.
24. Simon GE, VonKorff M. Recognition, management, and outcomes of depression in primary care. Arch Fam Med. 1995;4(2):99–105.
25. Guide to Clinical Preventive Services. 2 ed. Baltimore: Williams & Wilkins; 1996.
26. Depression: The Treatment and Management of Depression in Adults (Updated Edition). National Institute for Health and Clinical Excellence: Guidance. Leicester (UK)2010.
27. Thombs BD, Ziegelstein RC. Does depression screening improve depression outcomes in primary care? BMJ. 2014;348:g1253. https://doi.org/10.1136/bmj.g1253.
28. Allaby M. Revised report. Screening for depression: a report for the UK National Screening Committee. 2010;
29. Joffres M, Jaramillo A, Dickinson J, Lewin G, Pottie K, Shaw E, et al. Recommendations on screening for depression in adults. CMAJ : Canadian Medical Association journal = journal de l'Association medicale canadienne. 2013;185(9):775–82. https://doi.org/10.1503/cmaj.130403.
30. Siu AL, Bibbins-Domingo K, Grossman DC, Baumann LC, Davidson KW, Ebell M, et al. Screening for depression in adults: US preventive services task force recommendation statement. JAMA. 2016;315(4):380–7. https://doi.org/10.1001/jama.2015.18392.
31. Pan A, Keum N, Okereke OI, Sun Q, Kivimaki M, Rubin RR, et al. Bidirectional association between depression and metabolic syndrome: a systematic review and meta-analysis of epidemiological studies. Diabetes Care. 2012;35(5):1171–80. https://doi.org/10.2337/dc11-2055.
32. Procopiou M, Philippe J. The metabolic syndrome and type 2 diabetes: epidemiological figures and country specificities. Cerebrovasc Dis. 2005;20(Suppl 1):2–8. https://doi.org/10.1159/000088231.
33. van Vliet-Ostaptchouk JV, Nuotio ML, Slagter SN, Doiron D, Fischer K, Foco L, et al. The prevalence of metabolic syndrome and metabolically healthy obesity in Europe: a collaborative analysis of ten large cohort studies. BMC Endocr Disord. 2014;14:9. https://doi.org/10.1186/1472-6823-14-9.
34. Dunbar JA, Reddy P, Davis-Lameloise N, Philpot B, Laatikainen T, Kilkkinen A, et al. Depression: an important comorbidity with metabolic

syndrome in a general population. Diabetes Care. 2008;31(12):2368–73. https://doi.org/10.2337/dc08-0175.

35. Heiskanen TH, Niskanen LK, Hintikka JJ, Koivumaa-Honkanen HT, Honkalampi KM, Haatainen KM, et al. Metabolic syndrome and depression: a cross-sectional analysis. The Journal of clinical psychiatry. 2006;67(9):1422–7.
36. Skilton MR, Moulin P, Terra JL, Bonnet F. Associations between anxiety, depression, and the metabolic syndrome. Biol Psychiatry. 2007;62(11):1251–7. https://doi.org/10.1016/j.biopsych.2007.01.012.
37. Carroll D, Phillips AC, Thomas GN, Gale CR, Deary I, Batty GD. Generalized anxiety disorder is associated with metabolic syndrome in the Vietnam experience study. Biol Psychiatry. 2009;66(1):91–3. https://doi.org/10.1016/j.biopsych.2009.02.020.
38. Butnoriene J, Bunevicius A, Norkus A, Bunevicius R. Depression but not anxiety is associated with metabolic syndrome in primary care based community sample. Psychoneuroendocrinology. 2014;40:269–76. https://doi.org/10.1016/j.psyneuen.2013.11.002.
39. Tziallas D, Kostapanos MS, Skapinakis P, Milionis HJ, Athanasiou T, SE M, et al. The association between type D personality and the metabolic syndrome: a cross-sectional study in a university-based outpatient lipid clinic. BMC research notes. 2011;4:105. https://doi.org/10.1186/1756-0500-4-105.
40. Kaur J. A comprehensive review on metabolic syndrome. Cardiol Res Pract. 2014;2014:943162. https://doi.org/10.1155/2014/943162.
41. Martinac M, Pehar D, Karlovic D, Babic D, Marcinko D, Jakovljevic M. Metabolic syndrome, activity of the hypothalamic-pituitary-adrenal axis and inflammatory mediators in depressive disorder. Acta clinica Croatica. 2014; 53(1):55–71.
42. Remus JL, Stewart LT, Camp RM, Novak CM, Johnson JD. Interaction of metabolic stress with chronic mild stress in altering brain cytokines and sucrose preference. Behav Neurosci. 2015;129(3):321–30. https://doi.org/10.1037/bne0000056.
43. Miettola J, Niskanen LK, Viinamaki H, Kumpusalo E. Metabolic syndrome is associated with self-perceived depression. Scand J Prim Health Care. 2008; 26(4):203–10. https://doi.org/10.1080/02813430802117624.
44. Kessler RC. The categorical versus dimensional assessment controversy in the sociology of mental illness. J Health Soc Behav. 2002;43(2):171–88.
45. Bunevicius A, Peceliuniene J, Mickuviene N, Valius L, Bunevicius R. Screening for depression and anxiety disorders in primary care patients. Depression and anxiety. 2007;24(7):455–60. https://doi.org/10.1002/da.20274.
46. Zigmond AS, Snaith RP. The hospital anxiety and depression scale. Acta Psychiatr Scand. 1983;67(6):361–70.
47. Bjelland I, Dahl AA, Haug TT, Neckelmann D. The validity of the hospital anxiety and depression scale. An updated literature review. J Psychosom Res. 2002;52(2):69–77.
48. Sheehan DV, Lecrubier Y, Sheehan KH, Amorim P, Janavs J, Weiller E, et al. The Mini-international neuropsychiatric interview (M.I.N.I.): the development and validation of a structured diagnostic psychiatric interview for DSM-IV and ICD-10. The Journal of clinical psychiatry. 1998;59(Suppl 20):22–33. quiz 4-57
49. DSM-IV-TR. Diagnostic and statistical manual of mental disorders. Fourth ed. text revision ed. Washington: American Psychiatric Association; 2000.
50. Bunevicius A, Staniute M, Brozaitiene J, Pop VJ, Neverauskas J, Bunevicius R. Screening for anxiety disorders in patients with coronary artery disease. Health Qual Life Outcomes. 2013;11:37. https://doi.org/10.1186/1477-7525-11-37.
51. Genuth S, Alberti KG, Bennett P, Buse J, Defronzo R, Kahn R, et al. Follow-up report on the diagnosis of diabetes mellitus. Diabetes Care. 2003;26(11):3160–7.
52. Katsuki A, Sumida Y, Gabazza EC, Murashima S, Furuta M, Araki-Sasaki R, et al. Homeostasis model assessment is a reliable indicator of insulin resistance during follow-up of patients with type 2 diabetes. Diabetes Care. 2001;24(2):362–5.
53. International Standards for Anthropometric Assessment. International Society for the Advancement of Kinanthropometry (ISAK); 2001.
54. Clinical Guidelines on the Identification, Evaluation, and Treatment of Overweight and Obesity in Adults–The Evidence Report. National Institutes of Health. Obes Res. 1998;6(Suppl 2):51S–209S.
55. Alberti KG, Zimmet PZ. Definition, diagnosis and classification of diabetes mellitus and its complications. Part 1: diagnosis and classification of diabetes mellitus provisional report of a WHO consultation. Diabetic medicine : a journal of the British Diabetic Association. 1998;15(7):539–53. https://doi.org/10.1002/(SICI)1096-9136(199807)15:7<539::AID-DIA668>3.0.CO;2-S.
56. Gonen M. Selecting an optimal threshold. Analyzing receiver operating characteristic curves with SAS. Cary: SAS Institute Inc; 2007. p. 25–6.
57. Strauss RS. Childhood obesity and self-esteem. Pediatrics. 2000;105(1):e15.
58. Botega NJ, Bio MR, Zomignani MA, Garcia CJ, Pereira WA. Mood disorders among inpatients in ambulatory and validation of the anxiety and depression scale HAD. Rev Saude Publica. 1995;29(5):355–63.
59. Morriss RK, Wearden AJ. Screening instruments for psychiatric morbidity in chronic fatigue syndrome. J R Soc Med. 1998;91(7):365–8.
60. Spinhoven P, Ormel J, Sloekers PP, Kempen GI, Speckens AE, Van Hemert AM. A validation study of the hospital anxiety and depression scale (HADS) in different groups of Dutch subjects. Psychol Med. 1997;27(2):263–70.
61. Hopwood P, Howell A, Maguire P. Screening for psychiatric morbidity in patients with advanced breast cancer: validation of two self-report questionnaires. Br J Cancer. 1991;64(2):353–6.
62. Razavi D, Delvaux N, Bredart A, Paesmans M, Debusscher L, Bron D, et al. Screening for psychiatric disorders in a lymphoma out-patient population. Eur J Cancer. 1992;28A(11):1869–72.
63. Berard RM, Boermeester F, Viljoen G. Depressive disorders in an out-patient oncology setting: prevalence, assessment, and management. Psychooncology. 1998;7(2):112–20.
64. Haworth JE, Moniz-Cook E, Clark AL, Wang M, Cleland JG. An evaluation of two self-report screening measures for mood in an out-patient chronic heart failure population. International journal of geriatric psychiatry. 2007; 22(11):1147–53. https://doi.org/10.1002/gps.1807.
65. Bunevicius A, Staniute M, Brozaitiene J, Bunevicius R. Diagnostic accuracy of self-rating scales for screening of depression in coronary artery disease patients. J Psychosom Res. 2012;72(1):22–5. https://doi.org/10.1016/j.jpsychores.2011.10.006.
66. Martin CR, Thompson DR, Barth J. Factor structure of the hospital anxiety and depression scale in coronary heart disease patients in three countries. J Eval Clin Pract. 2008;14(2):281–7. https://doi.org/10.1111/j.1365-2753.2007.00850.x.
67. Miettola J, Niskanen LK, Viinamäki H, Kumpusalo E. Metabolic syndrome is associated with self-perceived depression. Scand J Prim Health Care. 2008; 26(4):2013–0. https://doi.org/10.1080/02813430802117624.
68. Freeman A, Tyrovolas S, Koyanagi A, Chatterji S, Leonardi M, Ayuso-Mateos JL, et al. The role of socio-economic status in depression: results from the COURAGE (aging survey in Europe). BMC Public Health. 2016;16(1):1098. https://doi.org/10.1186/s12889-016-3638-0.
69. el-Rufaie OE, Absood GH. Retesting the validity of the Arabic version of the hospital anxiety and depression (HAD) scale in primary health care. Soc Psychiatry Psychiatr Epidemiol. 1995;30(1):26–31.
70. Butnoriene J, Bunevicius A, Saudargiene A, Nemeroff CB, Norkus A, Ciceniene V, et al. Metabolic syndrome, major depression, generalized anxiety disorder, and ten-year all-cause and cardiovascular mortality in middle aged and elderly patients. Int J Cardiol. 2015;190:360–6. https://doi.org/10.1016/j.ijcard.2015.04.122.
71. Lecrubier Y. The burden of depression and anxiety in general medicine. J Clin Psychiatry. 2001;62(Suppl 8 (4-9)):discussion 10–1.
72. Kassi E, Pervanidou P, Kaltsas G, Chrousos G. Metabolic syndrome: definitions and controversies. BMC Med. 2011;9:48. https://doi.org/10.1186/1741-7015-9-48.
73. Alberti KG, Eckel RH, Grundy SM, Zimmet PZ, Cleeman JI, Donato KA, et al. Harmonizing the metabolic syndrome: a joint interim statement of the international diabetes federation task force on epidemiology and prevention; National Heart, Lung, and Blood Institute; American Heart Association; world heart federation; international atherosclerosis society; and International Association for the Study of obesity. Circulation. 2009;120(16): 1640–5. https://doi.org/10.1161/CIRCULATIONAHA.109.192644.

5

The implementation and adherence to evidence-based protocols for psychotherapy for depression: the perspective of therapists in Dutch specialized mental healthcare

Sanne J. E. Bruijniks[1*], Gerdien Franx[2] and Marcus J. H. Huibers[1,3]

Abstract

Background: Although psychotherapy is an effective treatment for depression, a large number of patients still do not receive care according to the protocols that are used in clinical trials. Instead, patients often receive a modified version of the original intervention. It is not clear how and when treatment protocols are used or modified in the Dutch specialized mental health care and whether these changes lead to suboptimal adherence to treatment protocols.

Methods: In the context of an ongoing multicenter trial that investigates whether twice-weekly sessions of protocolized interpersonal psychotherapy (IPT) and cognitive behavioral therapy (CBT) for depression lead to better treatment outcomes compared to once-weekly sessions, two focus groups using semi-structured interviews were organized. Aims were to increase insight in the adherence to and modifications of CBT and IPT protocols in the Dutch specialized mental health care for depression. Participants were fifteen therapists from seven mental health locations part of five mental health organizations. Verbatim transcripts were coded and analyzed using qualitative software.

Results: Three themes emerged: modification as the common practice, professional and patient factors influencing the adherence to protocols and organizational boundaries and flexibility. Treatment modification appeared to happen on a frequent basis, even in the context of a trial. Definitions of treatment modifications were multiple and varied from using intuition to flexible use of the same protocol. Therapist training and supervision, the years of work experience and individual characteristics of the therapist and the patient were mentioned to influence the adherence to protocols. Modifications of the therapists depended very much on the culture within the mental health locations, who differed in terms of the flexibility offered to therapists to choose and modify treatment protocols.

Conclusions: Not all treatment modifications were in line with existing evidence or guidelines. Regular supervision, team meetings and a shared vision were identified as crucial factors to increase adherence to treatment protocols, whereas additional organizational factors, among which a change of mindset, may facilitate adequate implementation.

Keywords: Cognitive-behavioral therapy, Interpersonal psychotherapy, Psychotherapy, Implementation, Protocol adherence, Specialized mental healthcare, Depression

* Correspondence: s.j.e.bruijniks@vu.nl
[1]Department of Clinical Psychology, VU Amsterdam, Van der Boechorststraat 1, 1081, BT, Amsterdam, the Netherlands
Full list of author information is available at the end of the article

Background

Adequate implementation of protocolized, evidence-based psychotherapy such as cognitive behavioral therapy (CBT) and interpersonal psychotherapy (IPT) has been associated with better treatment outcomes [1, 2]. Unfortunately, a large number of patients still receives inadequate or suboptimal psychological treatment [3–9]. Although CBT and IPT are the most investigated psychotherapies for depression [10, 11] and among the first-choice treatments for different levels of severity and subtypes of depression [12], therapists have been observed to drift from treatment protocols and modify them in different ways. For example, therapists may drift from treatment protocols by focusing on an immediate stressor, rushing into third-wave therapies before offering the first-choice of treatment or by leaving elements out [7, 13]. Also, it was shown that therapists may modify treatment protocols on the basis of their own, or patient preferences, even when these are inconsistent with evidence-based treatment guidelines [9, 14].

Not all modifications of treatment protocols might lead to suboptimal treatment or worse treatment outcomes. A systematic review on the use of various preventive, promoting or treatment interventions in mental health care pointed to twelve different ways in which a protocol can be modified and defined treatment fidelity as the adherence to the intervention components, competence with which the intervention is delivered and the differentiation from other treatments. In addition, the authors distinguish between fidelity-consistent modifications that do not alter core elements of treatment enough to reduce adherence to a protocol and do not reduce ability to differentiate between treatments, and fidelity-inconsistent modifications, such as modifications that reduce or preclude the delivery of core elements or decrease ability to differentiate between treatments [15, 16]. Removing treatment elements, losing structure, drifting from protocol or using inconsistent treatment strategies were framed as fidelity-inconsistent, and changing the length of the intervention or adding consistent modules were hypothesized as fidelity-consistent. The study of Levitz and colleagues provides a good example of modifications that seem to be in line with the protocol. In this study, flexible use of the CBT protocol for posttraumatic stress disorder (PTSD) was defined as skipping protocol sessions if the therapist did not deem the material appropriate for the patient, repeating certain protocol sessions if the material was particularly relevant to the given patient, ending therapy with a patient before completing all 16 sessions or having non- protocol sessions in order to discuss a current life stressor that required significant session time. Although patients in the flexible protocol group received on average three more sessions, of which one non-protocol session, using the protocol in a flexible way led to the same results as strict adherence to the protocol in this randomized controlled trial (RCT) [17]. Also, other studies found no evidence that small modifications such as refining the protocol or using protocols in a flexible way may lead to diminished effects of treatment outcomes and have even related treatment flexibility to more engagement in CBT for children with anxiety disorders [18, 19].

Information about how treatment protocols are used and modified in Dutch clinical practice is limited. Yet serious concerns about the quality of CBT in the Netherlands have been raised: it was suggested that limited educational programs, the tendency to attend to new interventions that are popular, but less evidence-based and limitations within the organization, such as insufficient supervision or high workload, may hinder adequate implementation of CBT [20]. Also, one of the possible reasons for why a recent observational study showed that supportive therapy was the most registered treatment among patients with a major depressive disorder in the Netherlands [21], is that therapists combined elements of CBT with elements from other therapies and therefore registered the treatment as supportive therapy [21].

In the Netherlands, a RCT is currently conducted [22] into the effectiveness of a higher session frequency of protocolized CBT and IPT for depression in specialized mental health care. CBT for depression is based on the manual by Beck [23], whereas IPT is based on the manual by Klerman [24]. The goal of the trial is to investigate whether twice-weekly sessions will lead to better treatment outcomes compared to once-weekly sessions. This trial was considered to be a good context to generate more in-depth knowledge of adherence to and modifications of protocols for IPT and CBT for depression by therapists from different mental health locations and areas in the Netherlands.

The aim of the present qualitative study was to learn about the perspective of therapists of providing CBT or IPT treatment according to protocols in daily practice. Insight in how treatment protocols are used or modified by clinicians might help to design strategies to improve the implementation and delivery of CBT and IPT in specialized mental health care the Netherlands.

Method

Study design

The study used a qualitative approach by conducting two focus groups with therapists from specialized mental health organizations that participated in a randomized trial in the Netherlands, called the FreqMech study [22]. In the FreqMech study, 200 patients were randomized into: a) 16 twice-weekly CBT sessions followed by 4 sessions during the last 8 weeks, b) 16 twice-weekly IPT sessions followed by 4 sessions during the last 8 weeks, c) 16 once-weekly CBT sessions followed by 4 sessions during the last 8 weeks, d) 16 once-weekly IPT sessions followed by 4 sessions during the last 8 weeks. All patients receive 12 to 20 sessions, 45 min in length of protocolized IPT [24] or CBT [23], depending on the individual progress of the patient. Both treatments are time-limited and target the present symptoms. However, the treatments have a different focus: key elements of the CBT protocol are behavioral activation and challenging dysfunctional beliefs (i.e. negative beliefs about the self, other or the world), whereas the IPT protocol focuses on the interpersonal context of the depressive symptoms. The focus groups were conducted in parallel with the data collection of the trial, which provided a good context to study the perspective of professionals on the adherence to treatment protocols.

Data collection and participants

A representative selection of therapists from nine locations of six mental health organizations that had been, or were currently involved in the FreqMech study, were invited by a formal letter from the research group to participate in a two-hour focus group session. Selection criteria of the therapists are given in Table 1.

For each mental health location, initially 3–5 therapists with different professions and different levels of experience, were invited. In case of no response, additional therapists in the same mental health location were invited. This selection procedure resulted in a total of forty-six therapists that were invited, out of a total of 70 therapists that had been involved in the Freqmech trial until May 2017. The invitations resulted in two focus groups with six and nine participants respectively from seven different mental health locations in five different mental health care organizations. We were not able to recruit therapists from two of the nine mental health locations participating in the FreqMech study, due to a lack of time expressed by the therapists to participate in the focus groups. Therapists represented different professions, different levels of experience, different types of organizations (academic versus non-academic) and worked in different areas of the Netherlands. The sample seemed a representative selection of the therapists in the FreqMech study, were the largest profession groups were: licensed mental health psychologists (30.88%), psychologists MSc (25%), psychologists MSc in training for licensed mental health psychologists (13.23%) or psychotherapists (7.35%). Characteristics of the participants in the present and the FreqMech study (i.e. until May 2017) can be found in Table 2.

Table 1 Therapist selection criteria

• Mental health center
• Professional background
• Years of work experience
• Years of work experience with CBT and/or IPT

The focus groups were held at the Vrije Universiteit Amsterdam and were facilitated by a moderator (GF) and assistant moderator (SB). We used a semi-structured interview guide for both focus groups, developed by the researchers. All researchers were involved and played a different role in the development of the semi-structured interview guide. MH was involved as a professor in Clinical Psychology and a psychotherapist working in one of the mental health care organizations, GF was involved as an expert on implementation of protocols and was not involved in the data collection of the FreqMech study, and SB was involved as a researcher (PhD student) who conducted the data collection for the FreqMech study. The interview guide consisted of questions related to: (1) adherence to treatment protocols, (2) which type of modifications are applied in daily practice, (3) which patient and therapist characteristics influence the modification of the protocols chosen by the therapists and, (4) in what way the organizational context influenced the way therapists adhere to protocols. Each focus group discussion started with an introduction in which the moderators and the participants presented themselves and in which the moderators the purpose of the study was explained. The rationale of the study that was told to the therapists was that we encountered an increasing use of terms such as 'personalizing treatments' during the data collection of the FreqMech study and that this led to the research questions we identified in our interview guide. During the second focus group, in order to gain more in-depth information and prevent a repetition of responses, the moderator and assistant moderator briefly summarized the content of the first focus group and asked the group to verify, add to and elaborate on the issues raised during the first group.

Data analyses

Focus groups were videotaped and transcribed verbatim by an independent research assistant. Participants were given anonymous identification codes (i.e. participant 1–16). Data analyses followed golden standard methodology for analyzing qualitative data: quotes were labeled in the raw data and categorized in subsequent codes and concepts to come at a final model [25, 26]. Content analysis was conducted by two researchers (SB and GF) that independently examined the data. Open coding was used by SB and GF to independently examine the data for relevant quotes and group them together in codes. Subsequently, similar codes were grouped together into more general concepts by SB. Next, the codes and concepts were discussed between the two independent researchers (SB and GF) and themes were created and discussed. Last, interpretation of results and resulting themes were discussed with a third researcher, MH.

Table 2 Demographics, professions and years of clinical experience of the participants

	Focus group 1 (*n* = 6)	Focus group 2 (*n* = 9)	FreqMech therapist sample (*n* = 70)
Demographics			
Female (%)	83.4%	100%	81.4%
Age (years + range)	36.80 (26.61–55.25)	40.63 (27.91–58.49)	39.02 (25–60)
Profession (n)[a]			
Clinical Nurse Specialist	1 (16.66%)	0	4 (5.71%)
Clinical Psychologist	0	0	2 (2.85%)
Licensed mental health psychologist (GZ-psycholoog) in training for clinical psychologist	1 (16.66%)	1 (11.11%)	3 (4.28%)
Licensed mental health psychologist (GZ-psycholoog) & psychotherapist	0	0	3 (4.28%)
Licensed mental health psychologist (GZ-psycholoog)	2 (33.33%)	2 (22.22%)	22 (30.88%)
Psychologist MSc in training for licensed mental health psychologist	1 (16.66%)	4 (44.44%)	9 (13.23%)
Psychologist MSc	1 (16.66%)	0	18 (25%)
Psychotherapist	0	1 (11.11%)	5 (7.35%)
Psychotherapist in training	0	0	2 (2.85%)
Psychiatrist	0	1 (11.11%)	2 (2.85%)
Clinical experience (in years)			
General (median + range)	7.75 (10; 2–14)	11.22 (8; 5–28)	10.02 (7; 1–29)
CBT (median + range)	5.83 (4; 2–12)	7.11 (6; 0–28)	7.20 (5; 1–26)
IPT (median + range)	1.75 (1; 0–3)	3.66 (1; 0–22)	3.25 (.5; 0–25)

[a]Professions according to the Dutch educational system; psychologist MSc refers to psychological training on master level, a clinical nurse specialist is a nurse with three additional years of postgraduate training in mental health care and licensed to provide CBT and IPT treatment; licensed mental health psychologists, psychotherapists, and clinical psychologists received two, three and six additional years of postgraduate training, respectively. For FreqMech sample, years of therapist experience at the start of participating on the FreqMech study was noted. In addition, some data was missing on the age and years of experience variables, available data per variable was: age (*n* = 60), years of experience (*n* = 58), CBT experience (*n* = 54), IPT experience (*n* = 37)

Coding was done using qualitative software Atlas.ti to facilitate the labeling of quotes and the subsequent categorizing of these quotes into codes and concepts.

Results

Three themes emerged from our focus groups: modification as the common practice, professional and patient factors influencing the decisions to adhere to or to modify protocols and organizational boundaries and flexibility as important contextual factors. Examples of concepts, codes and quotes related to the three themes can be found in Table 3.

Theme 1: Modification as the common practice

Although CBT and IPT protocols were known and used as a guidance by all participants, the therapists pictured a situation within their organizations where modification of protocols seemed to be common practice and happened in a range of different ways. On one extreme end of the range, participants mentioned that they thought treatment protocols are being ignored by some of their colleagues, who act on what they personally think is best for the patient. In contrast, on the other end of the range, participants mentioned the very strict adherence to a protocol. Between these two contrasts, participants mentioned four additional ways in which treatment protocols can be modified. For example, treatment protocols can be modified by combining different treatment protocols directly from the start to create an individualized treatment protocol adjusted to the patient. Examples are the combination of CBT protocols for different disorders, a combination of the CBT protocol with the protocol for eye movement desensitization reprocessing (EMDR) or combining the CBT protocol with protocols focused on sleep problems. It was mentioned that this method may lead to loss of focus. Another way to use treatment protocols was by starting with one protocol and switching to another protocol without finishing the protocol that was started first. In addition, it was mentioned that ingredients can be added or removed from treatment protocols. Examples mentioned were: CBT without behavioral activation, to add assertiveness training or running therapy to the CBT protocol or to spend one session on another intervention. Last, therapists mentioned flexible adherence to a protocol without losing

Table 3 Examples of concepts, codes and codes for each theme

Concept(s)	Code (s)	*Quote*
Theme 1 Modification as the common practice		
Definition of personalizing treatments / Personalizing treatments	Intuition / How to personalize treatments: methods	*'I think some therapists feel that they need to work according to their own insight and standards. And although this pattern seems less than a while ago, some therapists may still need a certain amount of freedom to do so' … 'for example: eclectic work, a bit of schema therapy, talking about modi, making a sociogram and talking about the past week'* (participant 15).
Definition of personalizing treatments / Knowledge about colleagues	Combine treatments from the start / Differences in conducting treatments	*'I think that there are colleagues that forget the protocol and combine different techniques to form a protocol. The danger of this strategy is that this may lead to never ending treatments'* (participant 5).
Personalizing treatments	Do you personalize treatments?	*'In patients with comorbid personality problems I will start with CBT, and if that does not work continue with schema therapy, and if there are topics I can use EMDR, I will also start EMDR, but not before discussing it with our team'* (participant 9).
Definition of personalizing treatments / Personalizing treatments	Flexible use within the protocol / Personalizing within CBT	*'There is CBT, and then you personalize: what does this person need first from the protocol?... If somebody already has an active lifestyle, I will spend less time on behavioral activation compared to someone who has no activities'* (participant 6).
How are protocols being used? / Role of the organization	Opinions / Differences between organizations	*'Both ways are not great, doing a lot of different interventions may lead to less focus, but it can be also very difficult to force people into a protocol'* (participant 4).
Knowledge about colleagues	Little knowledge	*'I would like to see that every therapist uses the protocol, but I doubt whether this is the case in day-to-day practice'* (participant 10).
How are protocols being used?	Opinions	*'That is why I like online or blended treatment, it helps you and the patient to really work through the protocol* (participant 2) … *while also leaving some space for topics that are not directly related to the protocol during the offline sessions'* (participant 14).
Theme 2 Professional and patient factors influencing the adherence to protocols		
How are protocols being used?	Therapist discipline	*'A therapist needs discipline to adhere to protocol, because there will always be the temptation to get stuck in a nice and friendly conversation about things that are not related to the primary goal of treatment'* (participant 11).
Solutions for better use of protocols	Experience and knowledge	*'I believe it might be the way of thinking we need to change … If you change your mindset to 'this intervention is helpful, or more effective', you will make yourself, or aim to, organize the circumstances that are necessary to adapt the intervention'* (participant 15).
Moderators of personalizing treatment protocols / Personalizing treatments	Patient factors / When to personalize?	*'Some patients need more space, sometimes when I try to closely adhere to the protocol the patient will tell me his motivation is decreasing. In those cases, I had to stop strict adherence to the protocol'* (participant 12).
Reasons to modify protocols	Patient factors	*'For example, patients that experience crisis all the time, or when you just haven't been able to use the protocol yet'* (participant 4).
Theme 3 Organizational boundaries and flexibility		
What is needed to adhere to treatment protocols?	Reports and evaluation of treatments and clear treatment structure	*'Regular patient evaluations in the team help to structure the treatment for the therapist and the patient, while my colleagues help to focus on the treatment protocol and notice possible distractions from the treatment protocol'* (participant 15).
Role of the organization	A lot of freedom	*'The advantage is that it is easier to do something you think is important, and sometimes that is very useful, at other times it will dilute your approach'* (participant 4).
Solutions for better use of protocols	Role of the manager and team	*'It is important that the manager is motivated and has a clear rationale for what and why we are doing what we do'* (participant 9).
What is missing but necessary for adhering to protocols?	Having the same professional vision	*'What I sometimes miss, is coming together and feeling supported by other colleagues. Having the same vision. This makes our job more difficult'* (participant 4)

Some quotes were incorporated into multiple codes and concepts the main lines of the protocol. Thus, mainly using one protocol while also making small adjustments, for example by giving more attention to some parts of the protocol.

Participants were ambivalent about these modifications. On the one hand, modifications were considered as unhelpful and not in line with the scientific evidence, which was considered the norm, whereas on the other hand strictly following protocols might interfere with the treatment process too. In addition, participants mentioned differences in modifications for different forms of psychotherapy: compared to IPT, CBT was experienced as a more structured treatment and therefore easier to adhere to.

Theme 2: Professional and patient factors influencing the decision to adhere to or modify protocols

Participants described both professional- and patient-related factors that influenced the modification of treatment protocols. Factors related to the professional were: the type of training and supervision received, the years of work experience and some characteristics of the therapist as a person. Therapists trained in multiple therapeutic techniques will be more likely to try out different treatment techniques in the same treatment and modify treatment protocols quicker compared to therapists that were trained in a single treatment technique.

It was suggested that supervisors in the Netherlands follow and teach different approaches in terms of protocol adherence: whereas some supervisors seem to strictly adhere to protocols and use ratings scales to investigate which therapist skills were (not) used during the sessions, other supervisors seem less strict in protocol adherence. Not all supervisions use audio or video tapes to evaluate therapy sessions, which was suggested to increase adherence to protocols. Also, years of work experience seems to play a role in protocol adherence, with young psychologists having a stronger inclination to adhere to a protocol than more experienced therapists who might feel more flexibility to use and choose from different protocols. The use of e-health (i.e. structured online environments in which different sessions address different elements of the treatment protocol) was suggested to help to keep up with the protocol in case of distractions to topics that are not directly related to the treatment protocol but, according to the therapists, need to be addressed in the session (such as substantial life events or crisis).

A few personal characteristics of the therapists and patients were also considered relevant. For example, factors related to the patient were: being in a crisis, low cognitive abilities, the presence of suicidal behavior or suicidal intrusions, not accepting the protocol, low motivation for treatment, or the presence of comorbid problems (i.e. PTSD, personality disorders). There was some disagreement among the therapists about when to modify the adherence to the protocols, for example in the case of a higher session frequency. While some therapists who thought that two weekly sessions were unhelpful for patients with high levels of avoidance, other therapists believed that in case of avoidance, the first weekly session may help to tackle avoidance so that in the second session, after only a few days, one could entirely focus on the actual therapy content. In the same way, while some therapists mentioned that a higher session frequency may deepen therapy and enhance activation in severe depression, other therapists mentioned that this might just be too much for patients that are severely depressed. Beside these patient factors, therapists mentioned that it can be hard to accept that some patients do not improve, and that this may lead to longer treatments than is necessary or helpful for the patient. Also, being disciplined was considered important to prevent unnecessary distractions from the protocol, whereas therapists agreed that a change of mindset of the therapist is essential for successful implementation and adherence to treatment protocols.

Theme 3: Organizational boundaries and flexibility

Participants indicated that a number of organizational factors strongly influence the way they adhere to or modify treatment protocols. These factors included: the attitude of the manager towards protocolised care, reorganizations, planning capacity and workspace, a coherent team vision on protocol implementation, or a main focus on production targets. Overall, limited planning capacity and workspace, a main focus on production targets and changes in the organization were mentioned to hinder the adherence to and implementation of treatment protocols. Combining these factors, three types of organizational cultures in terms of protocol implementation, appeared from the discussions with the therapists.

In the first type of mental health care location, therapists were confronted with standardized mental health care programs with hardly any options to change or adapt the treatment during the course of the treatment process. This helps to adhere to the protocol and to focus on one specific disorder, but may also be a disadvantage in the case the protocol does not fit the patient. For example, if during the first sessions it appears that the patient treated for depression is also suffering from comorbid post-traumatic stress disorder (PTSD), it would not be possible to apply PTSD techniques. The patient would first have to switch to another therapeutic team and overcome a waiting list period or finish the depression treatment before he or she can receive a treatment focused on PTSD.

In the second type of mental health care location, described in a very positive way by some of the therapists, there was some flexibility, but also a coherent shared vision and room for discussion within the team about which treatment protocol to use, and in what cases the therapist will have to deviate from this protocol. One of the locations that recently successfully switched from individualizing treatments to adherence to protocols as a standard, ingredients that were described for successful implementation were: an active, enthusiastic manager, enough supervision, team meetings and the possibility to try the new procedures before definitely implementing them.

In the third type of mental health care location, therapists experienced a lot of flexibility and limited social control by the team. In these organizations, therapists seemed less bothered by the organizational barriers, organize their own agenda and seemed able to decide independently of their manager whether or not to apply a new protocol, such as a higher session frequency. However, this amount of flexibility was also linked to the risk of less focused treatment.

Discussion

In the context of a randomized trial, we investigated the perspective of fifteen therapists on the adherence to CBT and IPT protocols in specialized mental health care in the Netherlands. Modification and deviation from protocols by therapists was viewed as common practice within the organizations involved in the study. We identified a range of ways in which treatment protocols were modified and different professional and patient factors that influenced the decisions of therapists to divert from the protocol. In addition, adherence to protocols was strongly related to the organizational context, especially to the flexibility offered to therapists to choose and modify treatment protocols. The organizations involved in the study varied from a very inflexible culture to a very flexible culture in terms of adherence to protocols.

Modifications from treatment protocols described by the interviewed therapists were partly in line with current research evidence or clinical guidelines. For example, acting on what you personally think might be best or combining protocols from the start of treatment is not supported by any research or guidelines [12, 27]. On the other hand, therapists also mentioned to adapt treatment protocols by making modifications that seem to be fidelity consistent. This method seems an excellent example of how to modify treatment protocols without losing focus or guidelines [17] and is in line with a recent study that showed that flexibility of the use of treatment techniques was related to better treatment outcomes [28]. Other modifications mentioned, such as switching to another protocol, or adding or removing elements from the intervention were less straightforwardly linked to research outcomes and guidelines and might even be seen as fidelity-inconsistent [16]. Beside treatment modifications, therapists' suggestions concerning patient characteristics that influence their decisions to adhere to protocol were consistent with the literature. For example, research and guidelines show that trauma should be treated before the depression [29], and that in the case of complex depression (i.e. comorbid problems, previous inadequate response), treatment for a comorbid personality disorder should be considered as one of the first choices [27]. In addition, studies have come up with adaptions to treatment protocols to deal with suicidal problems [30, 31] or to target problems with memory during CBT [32].

Therapists pointed to multiple factors that can help to decide when to modify protocols and how to decrease the undesirable lack of adherence to protocols. Suggestions were in line with studies showing that training, supervision or the years of work experience of the therapist are related to better delivery of treatment [20, 33–36], feedback, observation and consultation improve the adoption and retention of innovations [34] and that regular meetings with colleagues may increase the use of research findings [37, 38]. Besides, therapists mentioned that social pressure, for example by use of consistent patient evaluations or observational measures such as video-tapes of sessions, might be an important factor that would help to increase adherence to protocol. This is in line with other studies that suggested that the use of observational techniques, such as video material, is essential for the adequate reflection and feedback [39]. Nevertheless, a recent pilot study indicated that compared to social rewards (i.e. defined as being publicly recognized for adherent CBT delivery), financial rewards (i.e. $100 if a session that was selected and watched in the context of the study met criterion for adherent CBT delivery) may even lead to better increase of adherence to treatment protocols [40].

The present study has several strengths and limitations. A strength of the present study was that it was the first to investigate the adherence to and modifications of CBT and IPT protocols and its relation with professional, patient and organizational factors in the Dutch specialized mental health care for depression from a therapist viewpoint. The focus group method enabled the discussion of protocol fidelity issues in depth with clinicians. Also, a large variation of therapists and organizations participated and by presenting issues that came up in the first focus group to the participants in the second group, the current study was able to confirm the themes and enrich the data. The study led to clear recommendations for therapists and organizations to improve the adherence to treatment protocols in Dutch specialized mental health care. A limitation of the study was a lack of representation from all organizations participating in the original trial. Also, focus groups generate data on what clinician's say they do, but this might not reflect actual behavior in daily practice.

Another limitation was that the majority of the clinicians involved in the focus group were still in training. Although there is yet little literature on the relation between therapist experience and protocol adherence, it is possible that less experienced therapists have different views on protocols adherence in clinical practice compared to more experienced therapists. Finally, the selection of therapists may have led to selection bias as it might be possible that the therapists who volunteered to participate in the focus groups might be more amenable to protocol-based treatments.

These findings lead to several recommendations for therapists and organizations. First, protocol use and adherence in clinical practice can be increased by distinguishing between types of modification and relating these changes to clinical guidelines. Second, use of observational material, such as video or audio tapes of treatment sessions, may improve treatment evaluations. Third, in regard to the organization, time and space for supervision and regular team meetings should be created. Regular team meetings may not only help to increase adherence to protocol (i.e. for example by enabling discussion of patient characteristics that make it difficult to adhere to protocol, decreasing unnecessary distractions due to other interventions or helping to prevent the continuation of never-ending treatments), but also create room for discussion about what factors should lead to a modification of the protocol and increase a shared treatment vision. As therapists indicated that more social control will lead to better treatments, organizations should implement regular patient evaluations and monitor not only the quality of treatment, but also that of supervision. Managers may play an important role in increasing a positive environment that enables discussion about the adherence to treatment protocols and could play a role in monitoring what modifications are in line with the scientific literature and the team vision. In addition, piloting of a new intervention before definite implementation (for example: testing the intervention by a small group of employees) may help to increase support of the intervention and adherence to its protocol. Recommendations for clinical practice are summarized in Table 4.

Table 4 Recommendations for clinical practice to increase adherence and a shared vision on treatment protocols

Recommendations for clinical practice
Therapists
• Distinguish between ways of modifying treatment protocols and relate these modifications to clinical guidelines
• Use observational material (i.e. video/audio) during supervision
• Discuss treatment modifications with colleagues
• Plan regular patient evaluations
Mental health centers
• Create time and space for supervision of treatments and monitor it's quality
• Organize regular team meetings for discussions about protocol modifications
• Recognize and define the role of the manager in relation to protocol implementation
• Pilot protocols for new interventions or methods

The present study led to multiple hypotheses about what common protocol deviations are and what drives them that should be addressed in future studies to help therapists make informed choice about how and when to modify treatment protocols and enhance evidence-based practice. First, further research into the adherence to protocols for specific patient characteristics, such as comorbid disorders, cognitive abilities, patient motivation for treatment or suicidality, is needed. Studies should not only investigate the effects of additional interventions or techniques, but also specify how these specific patient characteristics can be treated within the protocol and, when therapists should modify or switch to another protocol. The study of Beidas and colleagues [41] provides a good example of how to provide a manual that discusses the implementation of a flexible manualized treatment protocol without losing fidelity. Their study presents an elaborate discussion (including video material) of how their specific treatment protocol can be used in a flexible way for different challenges that might be encountered when using the protocol, such as social skill deficits or depressive symptoms, and may serve as an example for future studies on flexible adherence to treatment protocols for depression. In addition, it is possible that protocol modifications will be less needed if we can find out what treatment or protocol works for whom. Recent studies already showed that treatment outcomes can be improved by using patient characteristics to predict from which one of two treatments the individual patient benefits most [42, 43] and future studies should investigate how these predictions can be applied in a clinical setting. Second, future studies should focus on the effects of flexible adherence to CBT and IPT protocols on treatment outcomes and should investigate whether different forms of protocol use will lead to different treatment outcomes. Third, the role of team influence and supervision (i.e. the frequency, structure, and methods of supervision) in the adherence to treatment protocols, quality of treatment and subsequent treatment outcome should be investigated [36, 44]. Following a recent study, future studies should investigate whether and how standardized assessments can be used improve training and supervision in the adherence to treatment protocols [45].

Conclusions

According to therapists, treatment protocols for CBT and IPT in Dutch specialized mental healthcare are modified in multiple ways and not all of these modifications are in line with existing research evidence or guidelines. Differences between therapists in how treatment protocols are used and modified are related to professional and patient characteristics and to the flexibility offered by the organizational context. Regular supervision, team meetings and a shared vision were identified as potentially crucial factors to increase adherence to treatment protocols, while additional organizational factors, among which a change in mindset, may facilitate adequate implementation. Gaps in current research evidence should be addressed to help therapists make an informed choice about how and when to modify treatment protocols and enhance evidence-based practice.

Abbreviations

CBT: Cognitive behavioral therapy; EMDR: Eye movement desensitization reprocessing; IPT: Interpersonal therapy; PTSD: Posttraumatic stress disorder; RCT: Randomized controlled trial

Acknowledgements

The authors would like to thank the therapists for participating in the focus groups.

Funding

This study is funded by ZonMw (project number 837002401). ZonMw did not have a role in the design of the study, data collection, data-analysis, interpretation of the data and in writing the manuscript.

Authors' contributions

SB, GF and MH contributed to the design. SB and GF conducted the data collection and analysis. SB wrote the manuscript. All authors read, contributed and approved the final manuscript.

Competing interests

The authors declare that they have no competing interests.

Author details

[1]Department of Clinical Psychology, VU Amsterdam, Van der Boechorststraat 1, 1081, BT, Amsterdam, the Netherlands. [2]113 Zelfmoordpreventie, Amsterdam, the Netherlands. [3]Department of Psychology, University of Pennsylvania, Philadelphia, USA.

References

1. Hollon SD. The efficacy and acceptability of psychological interventions for depression: where we are now and where we are going. Epidemiol Psychiatr Sci. 2016;25(4):295–300. Available from: http://www.journals.cambridge.org/abstract_S2045796015000748
2. DeRubeis RJ, Hollon SD, Amsterdam M, Shelton M, Paula R, Young P, Ronald M, Salomon M, et al. Cognitive therapy vs medications in the treatment of moderate to severe depression. Arch Gen Psychiatry. 2005;62(4):409–16.
3. Simon GE, Von Korff M, Rutter CM, Peterson DA. Treatment process and outcomes for managed care patients receiving new antidepressant prescriptions from psychiatrists and primary care physicians. Arch Gen Psychiatry. 2001;58(4):395. Available from: http://archpsyc.jamanetwork.com/article.aspx?doi=10.1001/archpsyc.58.4.395
4. Kessler RC, Demler O, Frank RG, Olfson M, Pincus HA, Walters EE, et al. Prevalence and treatment of mental disorders, 1990 to 2003. N Engl J Med. 2005;352(24):2515–23. Available from: http://content.nejm.org/cgi/content/abstract/352/24/2515
5. Kazdin AE. Addressing the treatment gap: A key challenge for extending evidence-based psychosocial interventions. Behav Res Ther. 2017;88:7–18. Available from: http://www.sciencedirect.com/science/article/pii/S0005796716300997
6. Institute of Medicine. Improving the Quality of Health Care for Mental and Substance-Use Conditions. Health Care. 2006;12:629–34. Available from: https://www.ncbi.nlm.nih.gov/books/NBK19830/
7. Stobie B, Taylor T, Quigley A, Ewing S, Salkovskis PM. "Contents May Vary": A Pilot Study of Treatment Histories of OCD Patients. Behav Cogn Psychother. 2007;35(3):273. Available from: http://www.journals.cambridge.org/abstract_S135246580700358X
8. Haddock G, Eisner E, Boone C, Davies G, Coogan C, Barrowclough C. An investigation of the implementation of NICE-recommended CBT interventions for people with schizophrenia. J Ment Heal. 2014;23(4):162–5. Available from: http://www.tandfonline.com/doi/full/10.3109/09638237.2013.869571
9. Shafran R, Clark DM, Fairburn CG, Arntz A, Barlow DH, Ehlers A, et al. Mind the gap: improving the dissemination of CBT. Behav Res Ther. 2009;47(11):902–9.
10. Cuijpers P, Berking M, Andersson G, Quigley L, Kleiboer A, Dobson KS. A meta-analysis of cognitive-behavioural therapy for adult depression, alone and in comparison with other treatments. Can J Psychiatr. 2013;58(7):376–85.
11. LGHM L, Galindo-Garre F, Arntz A, Peeters F, Hollon SD, DeRubeis RJ, et al. Exploring mechanisms of change in cognitive therapy and interpersonal psychotherapy for adult depression. Behav Res Ther. 2017;94:81–92. Available from: http://www.sciencedirect.com/science/article/pii/S0005796717300980
12. Trimbos Instituut. GGZ Richtlijnen. 2013. Available from: https://www.ggzrichtlijnen.nl/depressie
13. Waller G. Evidence-based treatment and therapist drift. Behav Res Ther. 2009;47(2):119–27.
14. Perlis RH. Abandoning personalization to get to precision in the pharmacotherapy of depression. World Psychiatry. 2016;15(3):228–35.
15. Stirman SW, Miller CJ, Toder K, Calloway A. Development of a framework and coding system for modifications and adaptations of evidence-based interventions. Implement Sci. 2013;8(1):65. Available from: http://implementationscience.biomedcentral.com/articles/10.1186/1748-5908-8-65
16. Wiltsey Stirman S, A Gutner C, Crits-Christoph P, Edmunds J, Evans AC, Beidas RS. Relationships between clinician-level attributes and fidelity-consistent and fidelity-inconsistent modifications to an evidence-based psychotherapy. Implement Sci. 2015;10(1):115. Available from: http://www.implementationscience.com/content/10/1/115
17. Levitt JT, Malta LS, Martin A, Davis L, Cloitre M. The flexible application of a manualized treatment for PTSD symptoms and functional impairment related to the 9/11 world trade center attack. Behav Res Ther. 2007;45(7):1419–33.
18. Chu BC, Kendall PC. Therapist responsiveness to child engagement: flexibility within manual-based CBT for anxious youth. J Clin Psychol. 2009;65(7):736–54.
19. Merrill KA, Tolbert VE, Wade WA. Effectiveness of cognitive therapy for depression in a community mental health center: a benchmarking study. J Consult Clin Psychol. 2003;71(2):404–9.
20. Huibers MJH, Bockting CL, Van Oppen P, Cuijpers P. De kwaliteit van cognitieve therapie in Nederland. Gedragstherapie. 2010;(43):115–18.
21. Boerema AM, Cuijpers P, Beekman ATF, Hellenthal A, Voorrips L, van Straten A. Is duration of psychological treatment for depression related to return into treatment? Soc Psychiatry Psychiatr Epidemiol. 2016;51(11):1495–507.
22. Bruijniks SJE, Bosmans J, Peeters FPML, Hollon SD, van Oppen P, van den Boogaard M, et al. Frequency and change mechanisms of psychotherapy among depressed patients: study protocol for a multicenter randomized trial comparing twice-weekly versus once-weekly sessions of CBT and IPT. BMC Psychiatry. 2015;15(1)
23. Beck AT, Rush AJ, Shaw BF, Emery G. Cognitive therapy of depression. New York: Guilford; 1979. p. 425.
24. Klerman GL, Weissman MM, Rounsaville B, Chevron E. Interpersonal therapy of depression (IPT). New York: Basic Books; 1984.
25. Miles MB, Huberman MA, Saldaña J. Qualitative data analysis. A Methods Sourcebook Zeitschrift für Pers. 2014;28(4):485–7.

26. Bradley EH, Curry LA, Devers KJ. Qualitative data analysis for health services research: developing taxonomy, themes, and theory. Health Serv Res. 2007;42(4):1758–72.
27. National Institute for Health and Care Excellence. NICE, concept guidelines. 2017. Available from: https://www.nice.org.uk/guidance/indevelopment/gid-cgwave0725
28. Owen J, Hilsenroth MJ. Treatment adherence: the importance of therapist flexibility in relation to therapy outcomes. J Couns Psychol. 2014;61(2):280–8. Available from: http://doi.apa.org/getdoi.cfm?doi=10.1037/a0035753
29. Green BL, Krupnick JL, Chung J, Siddique J, Kruase ED, Revicki D, et al. Impact of PTSD comorbidity on one-year outcomes in a depression trial. J Clin Psychol. 2006;62(7):815–35.
30. Van Bentum JS, Sijbrandij M, Huibers MJH, Huisman A, Arntz A, Holmes EA, et al. Treatment of intrusive suicidal imagery using eye movements. Int J Environ Res Public Health. 2017;14(7):1–14.
31. Stanley. Cognitive-Behavioral Therapy for Suicide Prevention (CBT-SP): Treatment Model, Feasibility, and Acceptability. J Am Acad Child Adolesc Psychiatry. 2009;48(10):1005–13. Available from: http://www.sciencedirect.com/science/article/pii/S0890856709601659
32. Dong L, Lee JY, Harvey AG. Memory support strategies and bundles: a pathway to improving cognitive therapy for depression? J Consult Clin Psychol. 2017;85(3):187–99.
33. Driessen E, Hollon SD. NIH Public Access. Psychiatr Clin North Am. 2010;33(3):1–18.
34. Herschell A, Kolko DJ, Baumann BL, Davis AC. The role of therapist training in the implementation of psychosocial treatments: a review and critique with recommendations. Clin Psychol Rev. 2010;30(4):448–66.
35. Lambert MJ, Hawkins EJ. Using information about patient progress in supervision : are outcomes enhanced? Aust Psychol. 2001;36(2):131–8.
36. Watkins CE. Does psychotherapy supervision contribute to patient outcomes? Considering thirty years of research. Clin Superv. 2011;30(2):235–56. Available from: http://www.tandfonline.com/doi/abs/10.1080/07325223.2011.619417
37. Humphris D, Littlejohns P, Victor C, O'Halloran P, Peacock J. Implementing evidence-based practice: factors that influence the use of research evidence by occupational therapists. Br J Occup Ther. 2000;63(11):516–22. Available from: http://bjo.sagepub.com/lookup/doi/10.1177/030802260006301102
38. Fadden G, Heelis R. The Meriden Family Programme: lessons learned over 10 years. J Ment Health. 2011;20(1):79–88. Available from: http://www.ncbi.nlm.nih.gov/pubmed/20812854
39. Gonsalvez CJ, Brockman R, Hill HRM. Video feedback in CBT supervision: review and illustration of two specific techniques. Cogn Behav Ther. 2016; 9(2016):e24. Available from: http://www.journals.cambridge.org/abstract_S1754470X1500029X
40. Beidas RS, Becker-Haimes EM, Adams DR, Skriner L, Stewart RE, Wolk CB, et al. Feasibility and acceptability of two incentive-based implementation strategies for mental health therapists implementing cognitive-behavioral therapy: a pilot study to inform a randomized controlled trial. Implement Sci. 2017;12(1):148. Available from: https://implementationscience.biomedcentral.com/articles/10.1186/s13012-017-0684-7
41. Beidas RS, Benjamin CL, Puleo CM, Edmunds JM, Kendall PC. Flexible applications of the coping cat program for anxious youth. Cogn Behav Pract 2010;17(2):142–153. Available from: https://doi.org/10.1016/j.cbpra.2009.11.002
42. Huibers MJH, Cohen ZD, Lemmens LHJM, Arntz A, Peeters FPML, Cuijpers P, et al. Predicting optimal outcomes in cognitive therapy or interpersonal psychotherapy for depressed individuals using the personalized advantage index approach. PLoS One 2015;10(11):1–16. Available from: https://doi.org/10.1371/journal.pone.0140771
43. Lutz W, Zimmermann D, Müller VNLS, Deisenhofer A-K, Rubel JA. Randomized controlled trial to evaluate the effects of personalized prediction and adaptation tools on treatment outcome in outpatient psychotherapy: study protocol. BMC Psychiatry. 2017;17(1):306. Available from: https://www.ncbi.nlm.nih.gov/pubmed/28836954
44. Alfonsson S, Spännargård Å, Parling T, Andersson G, Lundgren T. The effects of clinical supervision on supervisees and patients in cognitive-behavioral therapy: a study protocol for a systematic review. Syst Rev. 2017;6(1):94. Available from: https://www.ncbi.nlm.nih.gov/pubmed/28490376
45. Schmidt ID, Strunk DR, Derubeis RJ, Conklin LR, Braun JD. Revisiting how we assess therapist competence in cognitive therapy. Cognit Ther Res. 2018;0(0):0. Available from: https://doi.org/10.1007/s10608-018-9908-7

6

Prevalence of anxiety and depression symptoms and their associated factors in mild COPD patients from community settings, Shanghai, China

Tian Xiao[1†], Hua Qiu[2†], Yue Chen[3], Xianfeng Zhou[2], Kang Wu[2], Xiaonan Ruan[2], Na Wang[1*] and Chaowei Fu[1*]

Abstract

Background: Chronic obstructive pulmonary disease (COPD) is a serious disease frequently accompanied by anxiety and depression. Few studies have focused on anxiety and depression for mild COPD patients in China. This study aimed to assess the prevalence and associated factors for anxiety and depression among patients with mild COPD in urban communities.

Methods: A cross-sectional survey of 275 mild COPD patients was conducted in 6 communities randomly sampled from Pudong New Area of Shanghai, China, in 2016. Data on socioeconomic factors and health conditions were acquired through a face-to-face interview as well as a physical examination. The Hospital Anxiety and Depression Scale (HAD) and EQ-5D visual analogue ($EQ\text{-}5D_{vas}$) were applied to evaluate their mental health and quality of life, respectively. Logistic regression model was used to estimate adjusted odds ratios (aORs) and their 95% confidential intervals (CI) for risk factors associated with anxiety or depression.

Results: Among 275 subjects, 8.1% had anxiety and 13.4% had depression. Logistic regression analysis indicated that female patients were more likely to suffer from anxiety than male patients (aOR = 6.41, 95% CI:1.73-23.80). Poor health status ($EQ\text{-}5D_{vas}$ score < 70) was significantly associated with increased risks of anxiety (aOR = 5.99, 95% CI: 2.13-16.82) and depression (aOR = 2.67, 95% CI: 1.29-5.52).

Conclusions: There were increased risks of anxiety and depression in mild COPD patients living in urban communities. Female sex and poor health status were significantly correlated to anxiety or depression. More interventions should be developed to reduce the risks of anxiety and depression at the early stage of COPD.

Keywords: Depression, Anxiety, Quality of life, COPD, Mild

Background

Chronic obstructive pulmonary disease (COPD) was the fifth leading cause of mortality globally in 2011, and was expected to be the third leading cause by 2030 [1]. In 2010, the total cost of COPD was 50 billion US dollars and the average cost per patient was over 4000 US dollars in the US, while they were respectively 36.9 billion and 2259 US dollars in China [2–6].

Patients of COPD are at a considerable risk of suffering from symptoms of depression and anxiety [7]. The prevalence of anxiety symptoms varied from 30 to 90%, and that of depressive symptoms ranged from 13 to 70% among COPD patients (mostly inpatients) [8–13]. Previous studies indicated that anxiety and depressive symptoms in COPD patients were correlated with various factors including age, gender,

* Correspondence: fcw@fudan.edu.cn; na.wang@fudan.edu.cn
†Equal contributors
[1]Department of Epidemiology, School of Public Health; Key Laboratory of Public Health Safety; Pudong Institute of Prevention Medicine, Fudan University, Shanghai 200032, China
Full list of author information is available at the end of the article

severity of COPD, general health status, smoking, physical endurance and social performance [14–18]. These studies were mainly conducted among inpatients who had severe COPD, and few of them focused on the prevalences of depression and anxiety and their influencing factors among mild COPD patients in community settings [8–19]. The aim of this study was to estimate the prevalences of anxiety and depression among mild COPD patients living in urban Chinese communities and their associated factors.

Methods

Study site and population

A cross-sectional study was carried out in Pudong New Area of Shanghai, China, from June to August in 2016. A register system including data of diagnosed COPD patients from all secondary and tertiary hospitals was created in 2014. Six out of 46 communities were selected randomly to recruit patient with mild COPD. At the enrollment, spirometry function test was implemented on each patient to verify their COPD severity. Inclusion criteria were as follows: 1) a person was previously diagnosed as mild COPD according to the Global Initiative for Chronic Obstructive Lung Disease (GOLD) (forced expiratory volume in one second of percent predicted (FEV1% predicted) ≥80%, the ratio of FEV1 to forced vital capacity (FVC) < 0.7) [20]; 2) a person provided informed consent and medical records were available; and 3) a person was a local resident aged 40 to 70 years and was capable of participating in the study by themselves. Patients with serious or unstable disease(s) (such as cardiovascular, neurological and musculoskeletal diseases) or inpatients were excluded. Patients with cognitive impairment and mobility limitation were excluded as well. Among 300 patients who participated in the study, 275 (91.7%) met all the criteria and were included in this analysis.

Data collection and quality control

All information was collected by using a structured questionnaire and a physical examination. Demographic information included age, alcohol drinking history (Yes/No), smoking history (Yes/No), years of education (< 9 years/≥9 years), monthly household income (< 3000 RMB/≥3000 RMB), and regular exercise (Yes/No). Clinical information collected included disease duration, regular use of COPD medications in the past 12 months (Yes/No), exacerbation in the past 12 months (Yes/No) and comorbid conditions (hypertension, diabetes, kidney disease, stroke, cardiovascular diseases or others).

All field investigators received specific trainings in questionnaire interviewing, data recording and specific medical testing (scale assessment and spirometry function test) before the study was conducted. Questionnaire data were double-checked for its accuracy and completeness.

Measurements of anxiety and depression symptoms as outcome variables

The Hospital Anxiety and Depression Score (HAD) is a concise and commonly used questionnaire to assess the existence of depression and anxiety symptoms for COPD patients [21–25] (Additional file 1). The HAD is a self-administered questionnaire with two subscales (HAD-A for anxiety symptom and HAD-D for depression symptom) and each subscale contains seven items. Each item score ranges from 0 to 3, and the total score for each subscale ranges from 0 to 21 (0 manifests rare symptom, and 3 indicates apparent symptom) [21, 22]. Studies showed that HADs with ≥8 points as cut-off points for anxiety and depression symptoms performed great sensitivity and specificity in Chinese patients [19, 26]. Participants with a HAD score greater than 8 points were more likely to suffer from anxiety or depression, and a higher score implies more advanced severity of clinically anxious or depressed symptom [15, 18, 21, 27].

In the current study, we defined a patient with "anxiety" or "depression" as having a HAD-A or HAD-D score of 8 points or higher.

Spirometry function test, physical examination and health status assessment

Spirometry function test was performed at enrollment to acquire FEV1 and FVC values as well as FEV1% predicted to determine COPD severity or stage according to the guideline for COPD [20]. Each patient inhaled 20 ml salbutamol before pulmonary function testing was conducted and then complied with steps required for a spirometry function test. Final pulmonary function testing values were the average values of two satisfactory tests. Height and weight were measured to calculate body mass index (BMI, weight (kg)/height^2 (m^2)). In addition, health status was assessed with EQ-5D visual analogue (EQ-5D$_{vas}$), which was considered to be a reliable and efficient tool for previous COPD studies [28–30]. Two previous studies used the visual analogue as a measure of quality of life in the association with depressive and anxious symptoms [31, 32]. For the EQ-5D$_{vas}$ test, each patient drew a horizontal line on a scale to represent their health status, ranging from 0 (worst imaginable health status) at the bottom to 100 (best imaginable health status) at the top.

Statistical analysis

Data analysis was performed by using SAS 9.2 for Windows (SAS Institute, Inc., Cary, NC). Pearson Chi square test or Fisher exact test was used for comparisons of categorical variables. Student t-test or Wilcoxon test was applied for two-group comparisons of continuous variables with or without a normal distribution. Logistic regression analysis was used to estimate crude odds ratios (cORs) and adjusted OR (aOR) as well as their 95% confidential intervals (CI) for risk factors associated with anxiety or depression. The p value of <0.05 was considered statistically significant.

Results

Basic characteristics of subjects

Among 275 patients, 134 (48.7%) were male. The average age and BMI were 61.5 ± 6.0 years and 25.1 ± 4.0 (Kg/m^2), respectively. Nearly 40% of participants had a history of smoking, with a higher proportion of ever smoking in male patients than in female patients. Women had a longer average duration of COPD (13.2 years) and were more likely to have a comorbid condition (59.6%), compared to men. There were no significant differences in EQ-5D$_{vas}$ scores, regular use of COPD medications, as well as exacerbation in the past 12 months between male and female patients (Table 1).

Prevalences of anxiety and depression

The overall prevalences of anxiety and depression were 7.6 and 13.1%, respectively. Figure 1 shows the prevalences according to sex, smoking history and health status. An increased risk of anxiety was observed in female patients (12.8%, $P<0.001$), smokers (11.3%, $P=0.008$) and those with poor health status (EQ-5D$_{vas}$ score < 70) (15.6%, $P=0.0003$). Patients with poor health status (EQ-5D$_{vas}$ score < 70) (20.8%) were more likely to suffer from depression than those with better health status (8.9%) ($P=0.005$) (Fig. 2).

Factors associated with anxiety and depression

After adjustment for covariates, female patients were more likely to suffer from anxiety (aOR = 6.41, 95% CI: 1.73-23.80), and patients with poor health status (EQ-5D$_{vas}$ score < 70) had a higher risk of anxiety (aOR = 5.99, 95% CI: 2.13-16.82) (Table 2). Similarly, poor health status was significantly associated with an increased risk of depression (aOR = 2.67, 95% CI: 1. 29-5.52) after important covariates were taken into account (Table 3).

Discussion

In this cross-sectional study, the prevalence was 7.6% for anxiety and 13.1% for depression (13.1%) among mild COPD patients living in urban community. The prevalences for COPD patients were higher as compared with those for general populations [19, 33–35].

Table 1 Basic information among male and female patients with mild COPD

Characteristics	Total	Male	Female	*P* value
Number [*n*(%)]	275	134(48.7)	141(51.3)	.
Age, years [mean(SD)]	61.5(6.0)	62.1(5.4)	60.9(6.5)	0.113
BMI (kg/m2) [mean(SD)]	25.1(4.0)	24.7(3.9)	25.5(4.2)	0.074
Ever alcohol drinking [*n*(%)]	54(19.6)	49(36.6)	5(3.5)	**< 0.0001**
Ever smoking [*n*(%)]	115(41.8)	113(84.3)	2(1.4)	**< 0.0001**
Regular exercise [*n*(%)]	98(35.6)	48(35.8)	50(35.5)	0.95
Years of education [*n*(%)]				
< 9	229(83.3)	109(81.3)	120(85.1)	0.403
≥ 9	46(16.7)	25(18.7)	21(14.9)	
Monthly household income per capita/Yuan [*n*(%)]				
< 3000/per month	141(51.3)	57(42.5)	84(59.6)	**0.005**
≥ 3000/per month	134(48.7)	77(57.5)	57(40.4)	
Duration of COPD, year [mean(SD)]	11.3(14.1)	9.4(13.9)	13.2(14.1)	**0.004**
EQ-5Dvas score [mean(IQR)]	70.6(14.3)	70.1(14.6)	71.0(14.1)	0.322
Regular COPD medication use, in recent 12 months [*n*(%)]	97(35.3)	48(35.8)	49(34.8)	0.853
Exacerbation, in recent 12 months [*n*(%)]	77(28.0)	35(26.1)	42(29.8)	0.498
Comorbidity [*n*(%)]	145(52.7)	61(45.5)	84(59.6)	**0.020**

Abbreviations: BMI body mass index
For comparison, χ^2 test used for binary variables, and Student's t test or Wilcoxon non-parametric test employed for continuous variables; the bold *P* values indicated the statistical significance

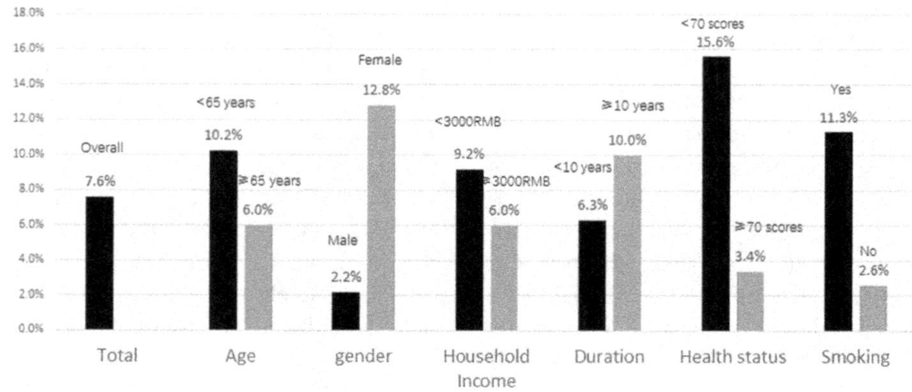

Fig. 1 Prevalence of anxiety symptoms among patients of mild COPD

Among the general adult population in China, the prevalences of anxiety and depression were 5.3 and 7.2%, respectively, when assessed by the HADs scale, and were 5.6 and 6.1% when assessed by the Diagnostic and Statistical Manual of Mental Disorders fourth edition (DSM-IV) scale [19, 29]. Another Chinese cohort study of 0.5 million adults found that the prevalence of depressive symptoms was as low as 2.4%, which was similar to the finding from a meta-analysis of 21 studies covering 11 provinces [30, 33]. The prevalence of anxiety varied from 10 to 100%, while that of depression varied from 7 to 79% depending on the stage of COPD [34]. Most previous studies, which recruited COPD patients with moderate to extremely severe stages from hospitals, found inconsistent relationships between severity of COPD and mental health [19, 35–38]. Different instruments measuring anxiety and depression symptoms were used in different studies, which is one reason for study discrepancies [39, 40]. In this study, only mild COPD patients from community settings were included. Our prevalence estimates were lower than those using the same scale of HAD (9.6 to 49% for anxiety and 22.8 to 52% for depression) [11, 38] except for one that included patients with mild COPD only [19].

For COPD patients, women were more likely to suffer from anxiety, and poor health status assessed by using EQ-5D was associated with increased risks of both anxiety and depression. A systematic review of 10 studies showed that women were significantly more likely to suffer from anxiety than men (56% vs 35%, $P = 0.04$), and similar sex disparity also existed in other studies [36, 40, 41]. One possibility would be that female patients with COPD had a lower income level, a longer duration and more comorbid conditions, compared to male patients. However, sex difference remained significant after taking these factors into consideration. Similar finding for the relationships between health status and anxiety/depression were observed in other studies [14, 42, 43]. In one hand, those who have positive symptoms of anxiety or depression in general tend to report worse health status. In another hand, those with worse health status worry more about their conditions, which could worsen their anxiety or depression symptoms. A cross-sectional study provided no information on the direction of the associations. Therefore, cohort study

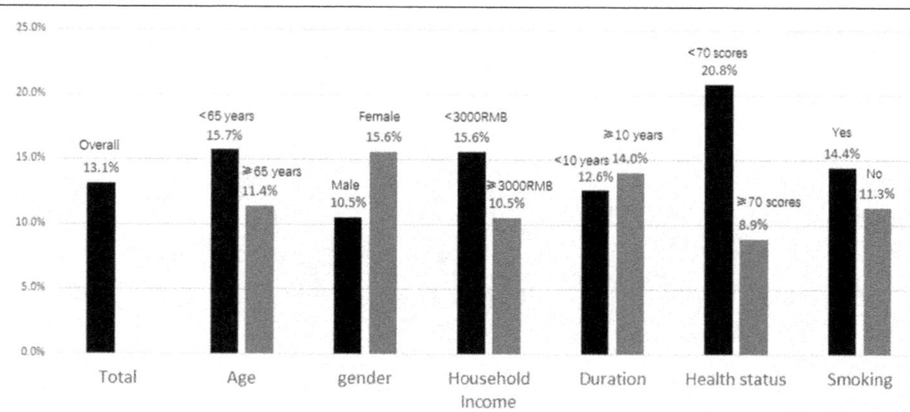

Fig. 2 Prevalence of depression symptoms among patients of mild COPD

Table 2 Possible factors associated with anxiety symptoms among mild COPD patients

Characteristics	cOR(95%CI)[a]	aOR(95%CI)[b]
Gender		
Male	1.00	1.00
Female	**6.39(1.84~ 22.23)**	**6.41(1.73~ 23.79)**
Age, years		
< 65	1.00	1.00
≥ 65	0.56(0.23~ 1.37)	0.58(0.21~ 1.55)
Household income per capita/Yuan		
< 3000/per month	1.00	1.00
≥ 3000/per month	0.86(0.63~ 1.16)	1.04(0.74~ 1.46)
Duration, years		
< 10	1.00	1.00
≥ 10	1.66(0.68~ 4.05)	1.21(0.45~ 3.19)
EQ-5Dvas score		
≥ 70	1.00	1.00
< 70	**5.34(1.20~ 14.27)**	**5.99(2.13~ 16.82)**
Comorbidities		
No	1.00	1.00
Yes	0.98(0.40~ 2.40)	0.90(0.33~ 2.43)

Abbreviations: cOR crude odds ratio, *aOR* adjusted odds ratio
[a] Data represents univariate association as determined by logistic regression model
[b] Variable included in the multivariate logistic regression model: gender, age, monthly household per capita, disease duration, EQ-5Dvas score and comorbidity; the bold OR (95% CI) indicated the statistical relationship

Table 3 Possible factors associated with depression symptoms among COPD patients

Characteristics	cOR(95%CI)[a]	aOR(95%CI)[b]
Gender		
Male	1.00	1.00
Female	1.58(0.77~ 3.24)	1.48(0.69~ 3.19)
Age, years		
< 65	1.00	1.00
≥ 65	0.69(0.34~ 1.39)	0.68(0.32~ 1.41)
Household income per capita/Yuan		
< 3000/per month	1.00	1.00
≥ 3000/per month	0.86(0.68~ 1.09)	0.91(0.71~ 1.17)
Duration, year		
< 10	1.00	1.00
≥ 10	1.13(0.55~ 2.33)	0.95(0.44~ 2.02)
EQ-5Dvas score		
≥ 70	1.00	1.00
< 70	**2.68(1.32~ 5.46)**	**2.67(1.29~ 5.52)**
Comorbidities		
No	1.00	1.00
Yes	0.88(0.44~ 1.78)	0.89(0.43~ 1.86)

Abbreviations: cOR crude odds ratio, *aOR* adjusted odds ratio
[a] Data represents univariate association as determined by logistic regression model
[b] Variable included in the multivariate logistic regression model: gender, age, monthly household per capita, disease duration, EQ-5Dvas score and comorbidity; the bold OR (95% CI) indicated the statistical relationship

design is required to further explore the nature of these associations.

There are strengths and limitations in this study. This study was conducted in urban communities and all invited subjects participated in the study. All subjects included in the study were confirmed to be at the mild stage of COPD based on a free post-bronchodilator pulmonary function test. However, a cross-sectional study design provided no evidence for causal associations between risk factors and presence of psychological symptoms. Since severe COPD cases were not included in this study and we could not assess the overall occurrences of anxiety and depression for COPD. In addition, the exclusion of any inpatients might result in an underestimation of the prevalences of anxiety and depression in mild COPD patients.

Conclusions

In conclusion, anxiety and depression were common in patients with mild COPD living in urban communities and mental health care services should be provided to these patients. Female sex and poor health status were significantly correlated to anxiety and depression symptoms. More interventions should be developed to reduce the risks of anxiety and/or depression at the early stage of COPD in community settings.

Abbreviations

CI: Confidence interval; DSM-IV: Diagnostic and statistical manual fourth edition; HAD: The Hospital Anxiety and Depression Score; IQR: Interquartile range; OR: Odds ratio; SD: Standard deviation

Acknowledgements

All authors would like to give their thanks for the health professionals in community health centers and the individuals who participated in this study.

Funding

This work was founded by the Health Science Foundation of Shanghai (201540415), Shanghai 3-Year Public Health Action Plan (GWTD2015S04) and Shanghai Leading Academic Discipline Project of Public Health (15GWZK80101). The sponsors have no role in the study design, survey process, data analysis and manuscript preparation.

Authors' contributions

CY, RX, QH, WN, and FC contributed in study protocol and creation of questionnaire. XT, QH, ZX, WK, and RX investigated and acquired information. XT, QH, CY, WN, and FC analyzed and interpreted the data and drafted and revised different sections of the manuscript. FC and WN are accountable for all aspects of the work in ensuring that questions related to the accuracy of any part of the manuscript are appropriate investigated and resolved. All authors read and approved the final manuscript.

Authors' information

Not applicable

Consent for publication

Not applicable.

Competing interests

The authors declare that they have no competing interests.

Author details

[1]Department of Epidemiology, School of Public Health; Key Laboratory of Public Health Safety; Pudong Institute of Prevention Medicine, Fudan University, Shanghai 200032, China. [2]Department of Chronic Disease, Pudong New Area Center for Disease Control and Prevention, Shanghai 200136, China. [3]School of Epidemiology and Public Health, Faculty of Medicine, University of Ottawa, Ottawa, ON K1G 5Z3, Canada.

References

1. World Health Organization (WHO): Burden of COPD. Available from: http://www.who.int/respiratory/copd/burden/en. Accessed 22 Mar 2018.
2. Soriano JB, Rodriguez-Roisin R. Chronic obstructive pulmonary disease overview: epidemiology, risk factors, and clinical presentation. Proc Am Thorac Soc. 2011;8(4):363–7.
3. Buist AS, McBurnie MA, Vollmer WM, Gillespie S, Burney P, Mannino DM, Menezes AM, Sullivan SD, Lee TA, Weiss KB, et al. International variation in the prevalence of COPD (the BOLD study): a population-based prevalence study. Lancet. 2007;370(9589):741–50.
4. Wu M, Zhao Q, Chen Y, Fu C, Xu B. Quality of life and its association with direct medical costs for COPD in urban China. Health Qual Life Outcomes. 2015;13:57.
5. Guarascio AJ, Ray SM, Finch CK, Self TH. The clinical and economic burden of chronic obstructive pulmonary disease in the USA. Clinicoecon Outcomes Res. 2013;5:235–45.
6. Chen X, Wang N, Chen Y, Xiao T, Fu C, Xu B. Costs of chronic obstructive pulmonary disease in urban areas of China: a cross-sectional study in four cities. Int J Chron Obstruct Pulmon Dis. 2016;11:2625–32.
7. Wagena EJ, van Amelsvoort LG, Kant I, Wouters EF. Chronic bronchitis, cigarette smoking, and the subsequent onset of depression and anxiety: results from a prospective population-based cohort study. Psychosom Med. 2005;67(4):656–60.
8. Bentsen SB, Miaskowski C, Rustoen T. Demographic and clinical characteristics associated with quality of life in patients with chronic obstructive pulmonary disease. Qual Life Res. 2014;23(3):991–8.
9. Di Marco F, Verga M, Reggente M, Maria CF, Santus P, Blasi F, Allegra L, Centanni S. Anxiety and depression in COPD patients: the roles of gender and disease severity. Respir Med. 2006;100(10):1767–74.
10. Eckerblad J, Todt K, Jakobsson P, Unosson M, Skargren E, Kentsson M, Theander K. Symptom burden in stable COPD patients with moderate or severe airflow limitation. Heart Lung. 2014;43(4):351–7.
11. Kunik ME, Roundy K, Veazey C, Souchek J, Richardson P, Wray NP, Stanley MA. Surprisingly high prevalence of anxiety and depression in chronic breathing disorders. Chest. 2005;127(4):1205–11.
12. Reinke LF, Slatore CG, Udris EM, Moss BR, Johnson EA, Au DH. The association of depression and preferences for life-sustaining treatments in veterans with chronic obstructive pulmonary disease. J Pain Symptom Manag. 2011;41(2):402–11.
13. Walke LM, Byers AL, Tinetti ME, Dubin JA, McCorkle R, Fried TR. Range and severity of symptoms over time among older adults with chronic obstructive pulmonary disease and heart failure. Arch Intern Med. 2007; 167(22):2503–8.
14. Cleland JA, Lee AJ, Hall S. Associations of depression and anxiety with gender, age, health-related quality of life and symptoms in primary care COPD patients. Fam Pract. 2007;24(3):217–23.
15. Gudmundsson G, Gislason T, Janson C, Lindberg E, Suppli UC, Brondum E, Nieminen MM, Aine T, Hallin R, Bakke P. Depression, anxiety and health status after hospitalisation for COPD: a multicentre study in the Nordic countries. Respir Med. 2006;100(1):87–93.
16. Dowson C, Laing R, Barraclough R, Town I, Mulder R, Norris K, Drennan C. The use of the hospital anxiety and depression scale (HADS) in patients with chronic obstructive pulmonary disease: a pilot study. N Z Med J. 2001; 114(1141):447–9.
17. Lewis KE, Annandale JA, Sykes RN, Hurlin C, Owen C, Harrison NK. Prevalence of anxiety and depression in patients with severe COPD: similar high levels with and without LTOT. COPD. 2007;4(4):305–12.
18. Ng TP, Niti M, Tan WC, Cao Z, Ong KC, Eng P. Depressive symptoms and chronic obstructive pulmonary disease: effect on mortality, hospital readmission, symptom burden, functional status, and quality of life. Arch Intern Med. 2007;167(1):60–7.
19. Lou P, Zhu Y, Chen P, Zhang P, Yu J, Zhang N, Chen N, Zhang L, Wu H, Zhao J. Prevalence and correlations with depression, anxiety, and other features in outpatients with chronic obstructive pulmonary disease in China: a cross-sectional case control study. BMC Pulm Med. 2012;12:53.
20. Global Initiative for Chronic Obstructive Lung Disease. Global strategy for the diagnosis, management, and prevention of chronic obstructive pulmonary disease. 2017. Available from: http://goldcopd.org/global-strategy-diagnosis-management-prevention-copd-2016. Accessed 22 Mar 2018.
21. Zigmond AS, Snaith RP. The hospital anxiety and depression scale. Acta Psychiatr Scand. 1983;67(6):361–70.
22. Bjelland I, Dahl AA, Haug TT, Neckelmann D. The validity of the hospital anxiety and depression scale. An updated literature review. J Psychosom Res. 2002;52(2):69–77.
23. McKenzie DK, Frith PA, Burdon JG, Town GI. The COPDX plan: Australian and New Zealand guidelines for the management of chronic obstructive pulmonary disease 2003. Med J Aust. 2003;178(Suppl):S7–S39.
24. Coventry PA, Bower P, Keyworth C, Kenning C, Knopp J, Garrett C, Hind D, Malpass A, Dickens C. The effect of complex interventions on depression and anxiety in chronic obstructive pulmonary disease: systematic review and meta-analysis. PLoS One. 2013;8(4):e60532.
25. Maurer J, Rebbapragada V, Borson S, Goldstein R, Kunik ME, Yohannes AM, Hanania NA. Anxiety and depression in COPD: current understanding, unanswered questions, and research needs. Chest. 2008;134(4 Suppl):43S–56S.
26. Zhang Q, Liao J, Liao X, Wu X, Wan M, Wang C, Ma Q. Disease knowledge level is a noteworthy risk factor of anxiety and depression in patients with chronic obstructive pulmonary disease: a cross-sectional study. BMC Pulm Med. 2014;14:92.
27. Janssen DJ, Spruit MA, Leue C, Gijsen C, Hameleers H, Schols JM, Wouters EF. Symptoms of anxiety and depression in COPD patients entering pulmonary rehabilitation. Chron Respir Dis. 2010;7(3):147–57.
28. Wacker ME, Jorres RA, Karch A, Wilke S, Heinrich J, Karrasch S, Koch A, Schulz H, Watz H, Leidl R, et al. Assessing health-related quality of life in COPD: comparing generic and disease-specific instruments with focus on comorbidities. BMC PULM MED. 2016;16(1):70.
29. Phillips MR, Zhang J, Shi Q, Song Z, Ding Z, Pang S, Li X, Zhang Y, Wang Z. Prevalence, treatment, and associated disability of mental disorders in four provinces in China during 2001-05: an epidemiological survey. Lancet. 2009; 373(9680):2041–53.
30. Chen Y, Bennett D, Clarke R, Guo Y, Yu C, Bian Z, Ma L, Huang Y, Sun Q, Zhang N, et al. Patterns and correlates of major depression in Chinese adults: a cross-sectional study of 0.5 million men and women. Psychol Med. 2017;47(5):958–70.
31. Racic M, Todorovic R, Ivkovic N, Masic S, Joksimovic B, Kulic M. Self-perceived stress in relation to anxiety, depression and health-related quality of life among health professions students: a cross-sectional study from Bosnia and Herzegovina. Zdr Varst. 2017;56(4):251–9.
32. El FA, Bentata Y, Ada N, Oneib B. Depression and anxiety disorders in chronic hemodialysis patients and their quality of life: a cross-sectional study about 106 cases in the northeast of Morocco. Saudi J Kidney Dis Transpl. 2017;28(2):341–8.
33. Guo X, Meng Z, Huang G, Fan J, Zhou W, Ling W, Jiang J, Long J, Su L.

Meta-analysis of the prevalence of anxiety disorders in mainland China from 2000 to 2015. Sci Rep. 2016;6:28033.
34. Andenaes R. Psychological characteristics of patients with chronic obstructive pulmonary disease: a review. J Psychosom Res. 2005;59(6):427–8.
35. Balcells E, Gea J, Ferrer J, Serra I, Orozco-Levi M, de Batlle J, Rodriguez E, Benet M, Donaire-Gonzalez D, Anto JM, et al. Factors affecting the relationship between psychological status and quality of life in COPD patients. Health Qual Life Outcomes. 2010;8:108.
36. Kim KU, Park HK, Jung HY, Ahn JJ, Moon E, Kim YS, Lee MK, Lee H. Association of depression with disease severity in patients with chronic obstructive pulmonary disease. Lung. 2014;192(2):243–9.
37. Iguchi A, Senjyu H, Hayashi Y, Kanada R, Iwai S, Honda S, Kitagawa C, Ozawa H, Rikitomi N. Relationship between depression in patients with COPD and the percent of predicted FEV(1), BODE index, and health-related quality of life. Respir Care. 2013;58(2):334–9.
38. Eisner MD, Blanc PD, Yelin EH, Katz PP, Sanchez G, Iribarren C, Omachi TA. Influence of anxiety on health outcomes in COPD. Thorax. 2010;65(3):229–34.
39. Matte DL, Pizzichini MM, Hoepers AT, Diaz AP, Karloh M, Dias M, Pizzichini E. Prevalence of depression in COPD: a systematic review and meta-analysis of controlled studies. Respir Med. 2016;117:154–61.
40. Willgoss TG, Yohannes AM. Anxiety disorders in patients with COPD: a systematic review. Respir Care. 2013;58(5):858–66.
41. Laurin C, Lavoie KL, Bacon SL, Dupuis G, Lacoste G, Cartier A, Labrecque M. Sex differences in the prevalence of psychiatric disorders and psychological distress in patients with COPD. Chest. 2007;132(1):148–55.
42. Chavannes NH, Huibers MJ, Schermer TR, Hendriks A, van Weel C, Wouters EF, van Schayck CP. Associations of depressive symptoms with gender, body mass index and dyspnea in primary care COPD patients. Fam Pract. 2005;22(6):604–7.
43. Miravitlles M, Molina J, Quintano JA, Campuzano A, Perez J, Roncero C. Factors associated with depression and severe depression in patients with COPD. Respir Med. 2014;108(11):1615–25.

7

Anxiety in women - a Swedish national three-generational cohort study

Gunilla Sydsjö[1*], Sara Agnafors[2], Marie Bladh[1] and Ann Josefsson[1]

Abstract

Background: Findings from animal and human studies indicate that anxiety and stress have a negative influence on the child and mother. The aim of this study was to explore the risk for having an anxiety diagnosis and the impact of the diagnosis in a three generational perspective.

Methods: The information was retrieved from Swedish population-based registries. All women who gave birth between 1973 and 1977 (n 169,782), their daughters (n 244,152), and subsequently also the offspring of the daughters (n 381,953) were followed until 2013.

Results: We found that 4% of the mothers and 6% of the grandmothers had been diagnosed with anxiety. Women who had mothers with an anxiety disorder were more than twice as likely to have an anxiety disorder themselves compared to all other women (OR = 2.20, 95% CI = 2.04–2.30). In the third generation, the children born to mothers with an anxiety disorder, the odds ratio of being diagnosed with anxiety was more than twice as high than for the rest of the population (OR = 2.54, 95% CI = 2.01–3.20). If both the mother and the grandmother had had an anxiety disorder the odds ratio for the child having a diagnosis of anxiety was three times higher (OR = 3.11, 95% CI = 2.04–4.75). Anxiety diagnosis in the two previous generations also increased the likelihood of the child having either more than two inpatient visits or more than 10 outpatient visits (OR = 2.64, 95% CI = 2.40–2.91 and OR = 2.21, 95% CI = 2.01–2.43, respectively).

Conclusions: The intergenerational effect on anxiety is high. In order to minimize the risk for further transmission of anxiety disorders, increased awareness and generous use of effective treatment regimes might be of importance.

Keywords: Anxiety, Multi-generation, Women, Offspring

Background

Anxiety related diagnoses are prevalent among women in reproductive age groups [1]. In the clinical setting these conditions may be difficult to detect and therefore may be difficult to diagnose. Consequently, women suffering from these conditions are often undertreated or not treated at all. This may lead to a lower quality of life for these women, may have negative effects on family relations, and also have adverse effects on the children's mental health and wellbeing. Anxiety may also have an impact on the woman's behavior leading to, for example, problems such as increased drug abuse or becoming prone to accidents, which have a deleterious effect on the woman [2]. It has also been suggested that some individuals with anxiety disorders are genetically predisposed to develop drug addiction [3]. Comorbidity with other mental disorders is common, and the prevalence of individuals with both general anxiety disorders (GAD) and depression is high. In a recent Swedish prevalence study with 3000 participants it was found that among men and women with clinically significant depression or anxiety, nearly 50% had comorbid disorders. The point prevalence of major depression was 5.2, and 8.8% had GAD [4]. Women's lifetime prevalence of being diagnosed with an anxiety disorder is around 30% [1]. For women of reproductive age, pregnancy and childbirth are sometimes triggers for worsening an already manifested anxiety disorder or for deterioration of an existing anxiety disorder. Thus, pregnant women with mental health problems are common in the antenatal care setting [5, 6]. Anxiety symptoms in pregnant women who

* Correspondence: Gunilla.Sydsjo@liu.se; gunilla.sydsjo@regionostergotland.se
[1]Department of Obstetrics and Gynaecology and Department of Clinical and Experimental Medicine, Linköping University, SE-581 85 Linköping, Sweden
Full list of author information is available at the end of the article

may or may not have been given an anxiety diagnosis present themselves in a number of different ways. For example, some of these women might have a severe fear of childbirth, be anxious about the child's health, anxious about the future, about their relationship with their partner, and even about their new role as a parent [7, 8]. For pregnant women in a population-based community sample, the prevalence of anxiety symptoms was found to be almost 16% in early pregnancy [9]. The study found that women under 25 years of age were at an increased risk for anxiety symptoms during early pregnancy and also revealed that women who were more psychosocially disadvantaged were more often nicotine users before pregnancy. A psychiatric history of depression increased the risk of anxiety symptoms, as did a prior history of anxiety disorders. Women who showed symptoms of anxiety expressed a greater fear of childbirth than those who showed no such symptoms. The adverse effect of anxiety on the fetus and the pregnant woman is not fully understood. In a review, Alder and colleagues examined 35 studies published between 1990 and 2005 and found that enhanced levels of anxiety symptoms during pregnancy contributed independently of other biomedical risk factors to adverse obstetric, fetal, and neonatal outcomes [10].

Findings from animal studies have shown a link between antenatal stress, measured as the occurrence of major life events, and impact on behavior and emotional adjustment as well as cognitive impairment of the offspring both in childhood but also later in adulthood [11]. The interpretation of these findings is that changes in the function of the hypothalamic – pituitary - adrenal (HPA) axis account for these relationships [12].

In a review by Monk et al., evidence for the impact of human maternal distress on fetal and infant outcomes through epigenetic mechanisms was outlined. Prenatal exposure to maternal anxiety and depression can have lasting effects on infant development with consequences for risk of psychopathology [13]. The recurrence rate and chronicity of anxiety conditions are high. In addition, many women with anxiety are not clinically recognized which means that many children are exposed to maternal anxiety not just temporarily but during a substantial part of their childhood.

Hence, the findings from both animal and human studies indicate that anxiety have a negative influence on both child and mother. In a long-term perspective these findings provide a solid foundation on which to form hypotheses concerning how anxiety may shape risks for coming generations. To our knowledge there are no studies based on a national population investigating whether there is an impact beyond the two generations i.e. mother and child.

The aim of the present study was therefore to investigate the intergenerational transmission of anxiety in a national population comprising three generations. More specifically, the primary aim was to investigate the risk for being diagnosed with anxiety given that previous generation(s) of mothers had been diagnosed with anxiety. Additional aim was to examine the use of specialized health care among third generation children, if either or both previous generation of mothers had been diagnosed with anxiety.

Methods

Data collection

The information on all the participants in this study was retrieved from Swedish population-based registries. All Swedish residents are given unique personal identification numbers that allow us to individually link the information about each person from different registers.

Background variables such as educational level, marital status, and parity were registered in the Swedish Medical Birth Register (MBR) at the time of admission to antenatal care. From the other registers we collected information on parents' country of birth, the women's marital status, highest attained educational level as well as anxiety diagnosis and use of specialized health care. More specifically, data were collected from the following registers:

- The Swedish Medical Birth Register (MBR): Medical information on all births since 1973 and onwards has been stored in the MBR which is held by the Swedish National Board of Health and Welfare [14].
- The Total Population Register (TPR): The TPR is held by Statistics Sweden and was established in 1968 [15, 16]. The register contains information on variables such as births, deaths, migrations, and marital status.
- The Causes of Death Register: The Causes of Death Register, which is held by the Swedish National Board of Health and Welfare, contains information on the cause of death and was established in 1961 [17, 18].
- The Education Register and the Population and Housing Census: Since 1985, Statistics Sweden has continuously collected information on the educational level of the population in the Education Register [19–21].
- The National Patient Register (NPR): The NPR was originally established in 1964, with its main focus being on psychiatric diagnoses. From 1987 all inpatient visits are included and in 2001 outpatient visits were added to the register.

These registers have all been evaluated [14, 22–26]; The Inpatient Register was most recently evaluated by Ludvigsson et al. in 2011, who concluded that the register is of good quality with a high validation rate [22].

Similarly, The Education Register, The Medical Birth Register, The Total Population Register and The Cause of Death Register have been evaluated and deemed to be of a high quality.

Study population

For the purpose of this study we selected all women who gave birth between 1973 and 1977 ($n = 169{,}782$, all of these women were born between 1924 and 1963), their daughters ($n = 244{,}152$ who were born between 1973 and 1977), and subsequently also the offspring of the daughters ($n = 381{,}953$ who were born between 1987 and 2012); all three groups were followed until the 31 December, 2012. At time of data collection no further data were available by the registers holder for a longer follow-up, since data have to be validated before being released to researchers. The data collection included identifying if the two first generations of women had become mothers, and their socio-demographic characteristics, whether the individuals in the study (all generations) had been diagnosed with an anxiety diagnosis during the entire follow-up time, as well as how many times they had used specialized hospital care, either as an outpatient or inpatient resulting in an anxiety diagnosis.

Diagnoses

To study these women and third-generation children, we used The National Patient Register (NPR), which contains all psychiatric inpatient care diagnoses and from 2001 all outpatient-diagnoses in a hospital setting.

The anxiety diagnoses are based on the Swedish version of *The International Classification of Diseases* (ICD) from the World Health Organization [27]. Between 1969 and 1986 ICD version 8 was in use. In 1987 a new version of ICD was released and was in use until 1997 when the health care system changed the ICD-version used from ICD-9 to ICD-10. During this year ICD-9 and ICD-10 were used interchangeably. Anxiety diagnoses in ICD-8 were identified as codes 300–301, 305–308, ICD-9 codes were identified as codes 290–319 and in ICD-10 codes F40-F42 (24), this includes diagnoses such as phobic anxiety, panic disorders, generalized anxiety disorder, and obsessive compulsive disorders. Therefore we searched for both ICD-9 and 10 codes in 1997 and only ICD-10 in 1998 to 2004. ICD-8 and ICD-9 codes were translated to ICD-10 using a conversion table [27].

Definitions

Anxiety disorders in all three generations were divided into two categories according to ICD-10 (24), diagnosis present and diagnosis not present. Socio-demographic variables on the grandmothers included parity (previous children/no previous children), highest attained level of education (Elementary, High school and Graduate/Post-graduate), region of origin (Nordic/Non-Nordic), marital status (Married, Unmarried and Divorced/widowed), age when giving birth (< 20 years, 20–26 years, 27–33 years and > 33 years). The same set of socio-demographic factors was collected for the mothers, except for origin since all mothers were born in Sweden.

In addition to anxiety diagnosis according to ICD-10, patient data regarding the total number of outpatient and inpatient visits were collected for the third-generation children, and arbitrarily cut off incidences of 0–1 visits/≥ 2 visits for inpatient data and 0–10 visits/≥11 visits for out-patient data were chosen. These served as proxies for overall morbidity among the third-generation children.

Statistical analysis

To examine the risk for anxiety disorder in the studied generation of women and their children we analyzed the data by using Pearson's chi-square to analyze bivariate differences. Data were also analyzed by unadjusted as well as adjusted logistic regression in order to estimate the odds ratio of being diagnosed with anxiety, each generation modeled separately. The dependent variable was the presence of anxiety diagnoses and the independent variables were educational level, marital status, and parity. For the third-generation children the same set of independent variables were used to estimate the odds ratios for having a larger amount of inpatient or outpatient visits to the hospital, or being diagnosed with anxiety. These models also included an additional independent variable; a three level indicator on the presence of anxiety in the two previous generations (only 1st generation woman diagnosed with anxiety, only 2nd generation woman diagnosed with anxiety, or both generations diagnosed with anxiety).

All analyses were performed using SPSS, version 22.0 (IBM SPSS Inc., Armonk, NY).

Results

The study population is shown in Table 1. Approximately 4% of the second-generation mothers and 6% of the first-generation mothers had, at some point, been diagnosed with anxiety. Out of 381,953 children a total of 65,838 of the children (i.e. the third-generation) had had more than 10 outpatient visits for at some kind of medical or psychiatric disorder (median = 5, range = 1–261) and 53,649 had had two or more inpatient visits for some kind of disorder (median = 10, range = 2–504) as presented in Table 1.

The background characteristics of the first- and second-generation mothers are shown in Table 2.

We found that second-generation women diagnosed with anxiety were more likely to have had mothers with

Table 1 The study population encompassing two generations of women and their offspring

	Study population n (%)
Total no. of children (third generation)	381,953
No. of children with anxiety diagnosis	749 (0.2)
No. of children with ≥10 outpatient visits	65,838 (17.2)
No. of children with ≥2 inpatient visits	53,649 (14.0)
Total no of mothers (second generation)	244,153
No of mothers with anxiety diagnosis	10,285 (4.2)
Total no. of grandmothers (first generation)	169,782
No of grandmothers with anxiety diagnosis	10,301 (6.1)

a lower level of education, with higher rates of divorce or widowhood, and higher rates of having been diagnosed with anxiety than the mothers of second-generation women who had not been diagnosed with anxiety.

Moreover, second-generation women diagnosed with anxiety were less likely to have given birth during the study period, and those who had given birth to at least one child, had reproduced at a younger age than women who had not been diagnosed with anxiety. Limiting the study population to second-generation women who had had at least one child it was found that second-generation mothers diagnosed with anxiety were more likely to have had mothers with a lower level of education, more often had mothers who had been divorced or become a widow, and who had had their child at a younger age, Table 3. They themselves also had a lower level of education, were more often divorced or widowed, and had had children at a younger age compared to mothers not diagnosed with anxiety. Furthermore, second-generation mothers diagnosed with anxiety were also more prone to have children who had been diagnosed with anxiety and children who more frequently received specialized medical care; both as inpatients and outpatients.

The unadjusted odds ratio of having been diagnosed with anxiety was more than twice as high among second-generation mothers who themselves had mothers who at some point had been diagnosed with anxiety (OR = 2.58, 95% CI = 2.43–2.74), Table 4. Among the 3rd generation children, the lowest increased odds ratios were seen for those for whom only the first-generation mothers had been diagnosed with anxiety (OR = 2.14 95% CI 1.68–2.73), Table 4, while children where both 1st and 2nd generation women had been diagnosed with anxiety exhibited the highest odds ratio for being diagnosed with anxiety (OR = 7.74, 95% CI = 5.18–11.59).

Among the third generation children, the odds ratios of being diagnosed with anxiety, having more than two inpatient visits and/or having more than 10 outpatient visits were highest among those children for whom both the first- and second-generation mothers had been diagnosed with anxiety (OR = 2.64, 95% CI = 2.40–2.91 and OR = 2.21, 95% CI = 2.01–2.43, respectively) compared to children where none of the previous generations had an anxiety diagnosis, Table 4. Stratifying by gender revealed that the increased likelihood of having an anxiety diagnosis, having more than two inpatient visits and/or more than 10 inpatient visits were approximately the same among both boys and girls whose mothers and grandmothers had been diagnosed with anxiety, in comparison to boys and girls where none of the previous generations had had an anxiety diagnosis, Table 4.

After adjusting for socio-demographic factors (educational level, marital status and parity) the odds ratios decreased. However, having a mother and/or a grandmother diagnosed with anxiety still remained an important factor in determining whether the child had a relatively higher number of visits for specialized medical care and an anxiety diagnosis, Table 5. If both mother and grandmother were diagnosed with anxiety the odds ratio was almost twice as high for in- and outpatient care (OR = 1.94, 95% CI = 1.75–2.14 and OR = 1.74, 95% CI = 1.58–1.92, respectively) while having been diagnosed with anxiety the odds ratio was threefold (OR = 3.11, 95% CI = 2.04–4.75) compared to children where none of the previous generations had been diagnosed with anxiety, Table 5. Moreover, in the gender stratified analysis, both boys and girls where the two previous generations had been diagnosed with anxiety, had an increased likelihood of being diagnosed with anxiety, having two or more inpatient visits and/or 10 or more outpatient visits compared to children where none of the previous generations had been diagnosed with anxiety. This increased likelihood was approximately of the same magnitude among both boys and girls, Table 5. To further elucidate the impact of previous generation's anxiety diagnosis, the 3rd generation was divided into two strata, 0–12 year olds, and 13 or older. This analysis validates the increased risk for an anxiety diagnosis among the third generation children if any or both of the previous generations have been diagnosed with anxiety, Table 6. This was especially evident among girls, where the ORs, were higher and with a narrower confidence interval, indicating a more reliable estimate. Also, among both boys and girls, there were increased risks for having been diagnosed with anxiety in the younger groups (0–12 years of age), but the estimates did not always reach statistical significance or had very wide confidence intervals. This was probably due to the limited number of children having received specialized hospital care due to anxiety.

Discussion

In this nationwide population-based study we have been able to shed light on the intergenerational transmission

Table 2 Socio-demographic characteristics of the study participants – limited to study persons born between 1973 and 1977, indifferent on future child

	Anxiety	Anxiety		*p*-value[a]
		No	Yes	
		n (%)	n (%)	
First-generation mothers				
Educational level	Elementary	50,015 (22.1)	2539 (25.2)	< 0.001
	High school	110,512 (48.9)	4937 (49.1)	
	Graduate/post-graduate	65,699 (29.0)	2589 (25.7	
Civil status	Married	190,869 (84.2)	7830 (78.6)	< 0.001
	Unmarried[b]	17,493 (7.7)	990 (9.9)	
	Divorced/widowed	18,261 (8.1)	1144 (11.5)	
Parity	No previous children	102,328 (43.8)	4444(43.2)	0.275
	Previous children	131,540 (56.2)	5841 (56.8)	
Age when giving birth	< 20	16,099 (6.9)	1018 (9.9)	< 0.001
	20–26	111,212 (47.6)	4792 (46.6)	
	27–33	88,450 (37.8)	3626 (35.3)	
	> 33	18,107 (7.7)	849 (8.3)	
Origin	Nordic	9905 (4.2)	408 (4.0)	0.185
	Non-Nordic	223,963 (95.8)	9877 (96.0)	
Second-generation women				
Educational level	Elementary	9954 (4.4)	1513 (15.0)	< 0.001
	High school	89,281 (39.2)	4466 (44.2)	
	Graduate/post-graduate	128,453 (56.4)	4129 (40.8)	
Civil status	Married	123,020 (52.6)	4596 (44.7)	< 0.001
	Unmarried[a]	107,549 (46.0)	5387 (52.4)	
	Divorced/widowed	3298 (1.4)	302 (2.9)	
Parity	No previous children	94,215 (54.9)	3891 (56.8)	0.003
	Previous children	77,348 (45.1)	2964 (43.2)	
Age when giving birth	< 20	3220 (1.9)	422 (6.2)	< 0.001
	20–26	37,956 (22.1)	2119 (30.9)	
	27–33	95,051 (55.4)	3093 (45.1)	
	> 33	35,336 (20.6)	1221 (17.8)	
Childbirth	No	48,825 (20.9)	2893 (28.1)	< 0.001
	Yes	185,043 (79.1)	7392 (71.9)	
First-generation mother diagnosed with anxiety	Yes	13,480 (5.8)	8884 (86.4)	< 0.001
	No	220,388 (94.2)	1401 (13.6)	
First-generation mother, no. of visits to hospital due to anxiety	0–3 visits	104,551 (44.7)	3162 (30.7)	< 0.001
	4- visits	129,317 (55.3)	7123 (69.3)	< 0.001
Second-generation women, no. of visits to hospital due to anxiety	0–3 visits	133,878 (57.2)	652 (6.3)	
	4- visits	99,990 (42.8)	9633 (93.7)	

[a]Chi2-test
[b]The category Unmarried includes women cohabiting with the child's father though they are not legally married and women who are considered single (i.e. not married or cohabiting with the child's father)

Table 3 Socio-demographic characteristics of the study participants, limited to women born between 1973 and 1977 who had become mothers

	Anxiety	Anxiety		p-value
		No	Yes	
		n (%)	n (%)	
First-generation mothers				
Educational level	Elementary	87,638 (22.6)	4197 (26.7)	< 0.001
	High school	191,237 (49.3)	7869 (50.0)	
	Graduate/post-graduate	108,767 (28.1)	3661 (23.3)	
Civil status	Married	322,053 (84.8)	12,314 (79.0)	< 0.001
	Unmarried[a]	27,341 (7.2)	1458 (9.4)	
	Divorced/widowed	30,443 (8.0)	1811 (11.6)	
Parity	No previous children	107,573 (43.5)	7009 (43.6)	0.720
	Previous children	221,502 (56.5)	9049 (56.4)	
Age when giving birth	< 20	30,254 (7.7)	2020 (12.6)	< 0.001
	20–26	191,791 (48.9)	7857 (48.9)	
	27–33	142,058 (36.2)	5013 (31.2)	
	> 33	27,972 (7.1)	1168 (7.3)	
Origin	Nordic	379,255 (96.7)	15,459 (96.3)	0.001
	Non-Nordic	12,820 (3.3)	599 (3.7)	
Second-generation mothers				
Educational level	Elementary	17,193 (4.4)	2452 (15.3)	< 0.001
	High school	156,213 (39.9)	7297 (45.5)	
	Graduate/post-graduate	218,399 (55.7)	6297 (39.2)	
Civil status	Married	254,795 (65.0)	9559 (59.5)	< 0.001
	Unmarried[a]	129,781 (33.1)	5766 (35.9)	
	Divorced/widowed	7498 (1.9)	733 (4.6)	
Parity	No previous children	174,958 (47.7)	6979 (46.4)	0.002
	Previous children	191,962 (52.3)	8054(53.6)	
Age when giving birth	< 20	8067 (2.2)	1003 (6.7)	< 0.001
	20–26	86,576 (23.6)	4862 (32.3)	
	27–33	203,016 (55.3)	6706 (44.6)	
	> 33	69,261 (18.9)	2461 (16.4)	
Second-generation mother diagnosed with anxiety	Yes	23,073 (5.9)	2172 (13.5)	< 0.001
	No	369,002 (94.1)	13,886 (86.5)	
First-generation mother, no. of visits to hospital due to anxiety	0–3 visits	169,608 (43.3)	4721 (29.4)	< 0.001
	4- visits	222,467 (56.7)	11,337 (70.6)	
Second-generation mother, no. of visits to hospital due to anxiety	0–3 visits	171,508 (43.7)	346 (2.2)	< 0.001
	4- visits	220,567 (56.3)	15,712 (97.8)	
Children (3rd generation)				
Gender	Boy	188,199 (51.3)	7753 (51.6)	0.498
Outpatient visits	Girl	178,721 (48.7)	7280 (48.2)	
	0–10	305,181 (83.2)	10,934 (72.7)	< 0.001
	≥11	61,739 (16.8)	4099 (27.3)	

Table 3 Socio-demographic characteristics of the study participants, limited to women born between 1973 and 1977 who had become mothers *(Continued)*

	Anxiety	Anxiety		*p*-value
		No	Yes	
		n (%)	n (%)	
Inpatient visits	0–1	316,924 (86.4)	11,380 (75.7)	< 0.001
	≥2	49,996 (13.6)	3653 (24.3)	
Anxiety diagnosis (child)	Yes	391,447 (99.8)	15,397 (99.2)	< 0.001
	No	628 (0.2)	121 (0.8)	

[a]The category Unmarried includes women cohabiting with the child's father though they are not legally married and women who are considered single (i.e. not married or cohabiting with the child's father)

of anxiety in three generations. It was found that the transmission of anxiety from one generation to the next is very high. More specifically, we found that women (2nd generation) who had mothers (1st generation) with an anxiety disorder were more than twice as likely to have an anxiety disorder themselves in comparison to all other women. Moreover, in the third generation, among children born to mothers with an anxiety disorder, the unadjusted odds ratio of being diagnosed with anxiety was more than four times higher compared to children (3rd generation) where none of the previous generations had been diagnosed with anxiety disorders. If both the mother and the grandmother had had an anxiety disorder the unadjusted odds ratio for the child having a diagnosis of anxiety close to eight times higher. Adjusting confounding factors such as marital status, educational level and parity, the odds ratios decreased but still remained elevated at three, and two and a half times higher, respectively, compared to children where none of the previous generations had an anxiety diagnosis. An explanation for this might be that the specialist care is more prone to investigate a child's problem

Table 4 Unadjusted odds ratios (OR) and corresponding 95% confidence intervals (CI) on the intergenerational effect of anxiety disorder in three generations[a,b,c]

	Total	Boys	Girls
	OR (95% CI)	OR (95% CI)	OR (95% CI)
OR Second-generation mother diagnosed with anxiety			
First-generation mother diagnosed with anxiety	2.58 (2.43–2.74)	2.61 (2.36–2.88)	2.56 (2.31–2.84)
First-generation mother not diagnosed with anxiety	Reference	Reference	Reference
OR child (3rd generation) has inpatient care[d]			
First- and second-generation mother diagnosed with anxiety	2.64 (2.40–2.91)	2.36 (2.06–2.69)	3.02 (2.63–3.47)
Only second-generation mother diagnosed with anxiety	1.98 (1.90–2.07)	1.92 (1.81–2.03)	2.08 (1.95–2.12)
Only first-generation mother diagnosed with anxiety	1.30 (1.25–1.35)	1.25 (1.19–1.32)	1.36 (1.29–1.44)
None diagnosed with anxiety	Reference	Reference	Reference
OR child (3rd generation) has outpatient care[e]			
First- and second-generation mother diagnosed with anxiety	2.21 (2.01–2.43)	2.28 (2.01–2.59)	2.14 (1.86–2.46)
Only second-generation mother diagnosed with anxiety	1.83 (1.76–1.90)	1.79 (1.70–1.89)	1.87 (1.77–1.99)
Only first-generation mother diagnosed with anxiety	1.23 (1.19–1.27)	1.22 (1.16–1.28)	1.24 (1.81–1.31)
None diagnosed with anxiety	Reference	Reference	Reference
OR child (3rd generation) diagnosed with anxiety			
First- and second-generation mother diagnosed with anxiety	7.74 (5.18–11.59)	6.73 (3.15–14.35)	8.40 (5.21–13.53)
Only second-generation mother diagnosed with anxiety	4.63 (3.72–5.75)	4.40 (2.97–6.52)	4.92 (3.78–6.40)
Only first-generation mother diagnosed with anxiety	2.14 (1.68–2.73)	2.36 (1.57–3.57)	2.06 (1.52–2.80)
None diagnosed with anxiety	Reference	Reference	Reference

[a]All second-generation mothers are born between 1973 and 1977
[b]All children (third-generation) are born between 1987 and 2012
[c]All first-generation mothers are born between 1924 and 1963
[d]Inpatient care categorized into 0–1 visits and ≥ 2 visits
[e]Outpatient care categorized into 0–10 visits and ≥ 11 visits

Table 5 Adjusted odds ratios (OR) and corresponding 95% confidence intervals (CI) on the intergenerational effect of anxiety disorder in three generations[a,b,c]

	Total OR (95% CI)	Boys OR (95% CI)	Girls OR (95% CI)
OR second generation mother diagnoses with anxiety			
First-generation mother diagnosed with anxiety	2.20 (2.04–2.38)	2.20 (1.98–2.44)	2.22 (1.99–2.47)
First-generation mother not diagnosed with a anxiety	Reference	Reference	Reference
OR child (3rd generation) has inpatient care[d]			
First- and second-generation mother diagnosed with anxiety	1.94 (1.75–2.14)	1.76 (1.53–2.02)	2.17 (1.88–2.52)
Only second-generation mother diagnosed with anxiety	1.66 (1.59–1.74)	1.63 (1.53–1.73)	1.72 (1.60–1.83)
Only first-generation mother diagnosed with anxiety	1.14 (1.10–1.19)	1.11 (1.05–1.07)	1.19 (1.12–1.26)
None diagnosed with anxiety	Reference	Reference	Reference
OR child (3rd generation) has outpatient care[e]			
First- and second-generation mother diagnosed with anxiety	1.74 (1.58–1.92)	1.84 (1.61–2.10)	1.63 (1.41–1.89)
Only second-generation mother diagnosed with anxiety	1.62 (1.55–1.69)	1.62 (1.52–1.71)	1.63 (1.53–1.74)
Only first-generation mother diagnosed with anxiety	1.11 (1.07–1.15)	1.12 (1.06–1.18)	1.11 (1.05–1.17)
None diagnosed with anxiety	Reference	Reference	Reference
OR child (3rd generation) diagnosed with anxiety			
First- and second-generation mother diagnosed with anxiety	3.11 (2.04–4.75)	2.97 (1.37–6.45)	3.14 (1.88–5.22)
Only second-generation mother diagnosed with anxiety	2.54 (2.01–3.20)	2.38 (1.57–3.62)	2.63 (1.99–3.49)
Only first-generation mother diagnosed with anxiety	1.46 (1.14–1.88)	1.57 (1.02–2.42)	1.42 (1.04–1.93)
None diagnosed with anxiety	Reference	Reference	Reference

[a]All second-generation mothers are born between 1973 and 1977
[b]All children (third-generation) are born between 1987 and 2012
[c]All first-generation mothers are born between 1924 and 1963
[d]Inpatient care categorized into 0–1 visits and ≥ 2 visits
[e]Outpatient care categorized into 0–10 visits and ≥ 11 visits

and to be more precise in collecting medical history in order to diagnose appropriately. Another possible explanation might be that the parents who seek help for anxiety related disorders are able to present a child's problem or help the child to present his or her problems in an accurate way since they themselves have knowledge of anxiety disorders and how anxiety has affected them. Lastly, the child might also be able to present his or hers problems more systematically when seeking help.

The children in the third generation of mothers with anxiety also had a higher consumption of relatively advanced medical care such as inpatient, and outpatient specialist care. With the exception of anxiety disorders, the children's exact medical diagnoses and interventions are outside the scope of this study and were therefore

Table 6 Unadjusted odds ratios (OR) and corresponding 95% confidence intervals (CI) on the intergenerational effect of anxiety in three generations, stratified by age and gender of the child (3rd generation) [a,b,c]

	Total		Boys		Girls	
	0–12 years	13- years	0–12 years	13- years	0–12 years	13- years
OR child (3rd generation) diagnosed with anxiety						
First- and second-generation diagnosed with anxiety	6.41(2.03–20.23)	3.74 (2.42–5.77)	3.83 (0.53–27.23)	9.07 (2.35–40.14)	3.58 (1.57–8.19)	3.96 (2.36–6.62)
Second-generation mother diagnosed with anxiety	2.13 (0.99–4.58)	3.14 (2.49–3.96)	1.06 (0.26–4.35)	3.54 (1.40–8.95)	3.48 (2.28–5.30)	3.06 (2.32–4.05)
Only first-generation mother diagnosed with anxiety	2.07 (1.14–3.77)	1.51 (1.16–1.98)	2.73 (1.35–5.52)	1.20 (0.37–3.87)	1.55 (0.93–2.58)	1.51 (1.10–2.07)
None diagnosed with anxiety	Reference	Reference	Reference	Reference	Reference	Reference

[a]All second-generation mothers are born between 1973 and 1977
[b]All children (third-generation) are born between 1987 and 2012
[c]All first-generation mothers are born between 1924 and 1963

not investigated. However, a study of the full medical record might be expected to show a higher level of somatic ill-health that in turn might be a signal of additional problems within the family, the personality of the child, and even childhood experiences outside the family [28].

The transmission of anxiety from parents to offspring is well known, but the underlying processes are poorly understood [29–32]. Most studies have evaluated the risks from a two-generation perspective and there is no evidence that allows us to determine the relative importance of genetic factors and environmental factors, respectively, on the transmission of anxiety disorders for the 3rd generation. In this study we only have information on anxiety disorders in the maternal probands [13, 29–32]. Little is known about the effect of paternal anxiety disorders on children's psychopathology but in a study by Cooper et al. 2006 it was evident that there is a strong familiality of anxiety disorders in general but the impact of maternal anxiety was more evident [30]. In a Swedish twin study, the authors argue that environmental transmission from parents is stronger than genetic factors because the children learn an anxious behavior from their parents through modeling [33]. Different paths of environmental transmission are plausible. For example, maternal anxiety has been shown to be associated with reduced tolerance to negative emotions in children [34]. Anxious mothers were also shown to have lower expectations of their children's performance compared to non-anxious mothers [34]. Another study found anxiety in children to be associated with overinvolved and critical parenting [35]. Whether these parenting behaviors are influenced by anxiety in the offspring, or whether the rearing environment increases the risk of the development of anxiety in children is not fully understood. While parenting styles were not investigated in this study, family structure and socioeconomic factors such as education was found to impact the risk for anxiety. These findings underline the multifactorial etiology of anxiety conditions, and the importance to address the psychosocial environment. Moreover, there are studies suggesting that different genetic factors impact the development of anxiety disorders during childhood, adolescence and early adulthood respectively [36], indicating genetic innovation and attenuation or possibly epigenetic mechanisms. Kendler et al. (2008) found support for a developmentally dynamic hypothesis of genetic effects on anxiety and depression, which could explain the low level of homotypic continuity of anxiety disorders from childhood to adulthood [36]. In a recent study by Weissman and colleagues [37], it was found that offspring to depressed parents had a risk for major depression and that the period of peak for first onset was between ages 15–25. Onsets before adolescence were uncommon; there was also an increase in morbidity and mortality indicating a greater vulnerability in general [37].

In a prevalence study on mental health, the results showed that among individuals with depression or anxiety, around one third did not receive treatment. Comorbidity was associated with higher symptom severity and lower health-related quality of life and that these mental disorders form a unit and thus depression and anxiety can be seen together as a rule rather than an exception. [4] Overall, comorbidity is of great importance to acknowledge and to investigate. Mainly in order to understand the effect of comorbidity, but also to better screen the patient and design individual treatment and care for the patients. A high recurrence rate of anxiety conditions has also been found [38].

Reproductive events and particularly childbirth are risk factors for acquiring mental disorders for women. In a register study from Denmark it was concluded that primiparous women had an increased risk of incident-related hospital admission to a psychiatric hospital for a mental disorder through the first 3 months after childbirth but among fathers there was no increase of severe mental disorders that required their admission to a hospital [39].

Animal as well as human studies have shown associations between antenatal stress and or anxiety development and behavioral/emotional disturbance in the child. Yet, the strength of this link was unclear since these studies did not examine the covariance of antenatal risks and did not distinguish between ante- and postnatal stress. The large Avon Longitudinal Study of Parents and Children (ALSPAC) cohort showed a strong relationship between maternal anxiety in late pregnancy and behavioral/emotional problems in their children at age four [40].

Animal studies have shown that offspring of mothers who have suffered antenatal stress are over-reactive to stressors and hypersecrete cortisol compared with controls. Both the behavioral and physiological disturbances last into adulthood in rodents and for several years, suggesting that the HPA axis can be 'programmed' during the fetal period [12].

In most prevalence studies there are, generally, significant gender differences with mental health disorders being more common in women than in men. The effect on the families and generations might therefore be of significance as our results show. Since mental health problems seem to have an impact on subsequent generations it is of the utmost importance to detect and treat anxiety.

A limitation of this study is that only diagnoses set at hospitals or specialist clinics such as psychiatric outpatient clinics are used. Therefore one can suspect that the true percentage of individuals with an anxiety disorder is higher as a number of individuals may have been diagnosed and treated by their general practitioners. Thus, only including diagnoses from a hospital or specialist clinic setting implies that only the most severe forms of anxiety are included. This may cause an overestimation of the intergenerational transmission. Also, misclassification problems caused by unrecorded cases and/or incorrect registration of diagnostic codes are known limitations in register studies. If so, the incorrect registration is random and not systematic. Moreover, the children (third-generation) in the present study were born between 1987 and 2012. While anxiety disorders develop relatively early in life with a mean onset age of 11 years [1], the results are strengthened by the presence of an intergenerational effect already evident at an early age. Another limitation is the lack of information of the timing of anxiety in relation to childbirth. Anxiety symptoms during pregnancy have been shown to increase the risk for adverse obstetric, fetal, and neonatal outcomes [10], while maternal anxiety during early childhood might impact the children through negative or over-controlling parenting behaviors [35]. Moreover, recurrent or chronic anxiety episodes would have a greater impact on both the woman and her children, compared to a single anxiety episode.

Conclusion

Second-generation mothers diagnosed with anxiety had children who had been diagnosed with anxiety and children who more frequently received medical care; both as inpatients and outpatients. Anxiety disorders have a three-generational effect. Since intergenerational effect on anxiety is high and in order to minimize the risk for further transmission of anxiety disorders, increased awareness and generous use of effective treatment regimes might be important.

Acknowledgements
Professor Lawrence Lundgren for language corrections.

Authors' contributions
All the authors fulfill the authorship criteria. GS and AJ have been responsible for the idea and the design of the study. GS, SA, MB and AJ have been responsible of the writing and the critical discussion of the manuscript. MB has done the statistical analysis together with GS and AJ. All authors have approved the final version of the manuscript.

Authors' information
Gunilla Sydsjö is professor in psychosocial obstetrics and gynecology with main research focus on mental health issues for women and children, Sara Agnafors is MD, PhD presently working and doing research in the area of child and adolescent psychiatry, Marie Bladh is PhD and a statistician, with primary interest in medical epidemiology, Ann Josefsson is professor and MD in obstetrics and gynecology, with main research focus in women's mental health issues.

Competing interests
The material contained in the manuscript has not been published or submitted elsewhere for publication. The authors declare that they have no competing interests.

Author details
[1]Department of Obstetrics and Gynaecology and Department of Clinical and Experimental Medicine, Linköping University, SE-581 85 Linköping, Sweden. [2]Department of Child and Adolescent Psychiatry and Department of Clinical and Experimental Medicine, Linköping University, Linköping, Sweden.

References
1. Kessler RC, Berglund P, Demler O, Jin R, Merikangas KR, Walters EE. Lifetime prevalence and age-of-onset distributions of DSM-IV disorders in the National Comorbidity Survey Replication. Arch Gen Psychiatry. 2005;62:593–602.
2. Brady K, Tolliver B, Verdiun M. Alcohol use and anxiety: diagnostic and management issues. Am J Psychiatry. 2007;164:217–21.
3. Pandey SC, Zhang H, Roy A, Xu T. Deficits in amygdaloid cAMP-responsive element-binding protein signaling play a role in genetic predisposition to anxiety and alcoholism. J Clin Invest. 2005;115:2762–73.
4. Johansson R, Carlbring P, Heedman Å, Paxling B, Andersson G. Depression, anxiety and their comorbidity in the Swedish general population: point prevalence and the effect on health-related quality of life. Peer J. 2013;1:e98. https://doi.org/10.7717/peerj.98.
5. Andersson L, Sundström-Poromaa I, Bixo M, Wulff M, Bondestam K, Åström M. Point prevalence of psychiatric disorders during the second trimester of pregnancy: a population-baser study. Am J Obstet Gynecol. 2003;189:148–54.
6. Josefsson A, Berg G, Nordin C, Sydsjö G. Prevalence of depressive symptoms in late pregnancy and postpartum. Acta Obstet Gynecol Scand. 2001;80:251–5.
7. Feinberg ME, Jones DE, Roettger ME, Hostetler ML, Sakuma KL, Paul IM, Ehrenthal DB. Preventive effects on birth outcomes: buffering impact of maternal stress, depression and anxiety. Matern Child Health J. 2016;20:55–65.
8. Storksen HT, Eberhard-Grahn M, Garthus-Niegel S, Eskild A. Fear of childbirth: the relation to anxiety and depression. Acta Obstet Gynecol Scand. 2012;91:237–42.
9. Rubertsson C, Hellström J, Cross M, Sydsjö G. Anxiety in early pregnancy: prevalence and contributing factors. Arch Womens Ment Health. 2014;17: 221–8.
10. Alder J, Fink N, Bitzer J, Hösli I, Holzgreve W. Depression and anxiety during pregnancy: a risk factor for obstetric, fetal and neonatal outcome? A critical review of the literature. J Matern Fetal Neonatal Med. 2007;20:189–209.
11. Weinstock M. Alterations induced by gestational stress in brain morphology and behaviour of the offspring. Prog Neurobiol. 2001;65:427–51.
12. Schneider ML, Moore CF, Roberts AD, Dejesus O. Prenatal stress alters early neurobehaviour, stress reactivity and learning in non-human primates: a brief review. Stress. 2001;4:183–93.
13. Monk C, Spicer J, Champagne FA. Linking prenatal maternal adversity to developmental outcomes in infants: the role of epigenetic pathways. Dev Psychopatol. 2012;24:1361–76.
14. Centre for Epidemiology, National Board of Health and Welfare. The Swedish Medical Birth Register; A summary of content and quality National Board of Health and Welfare. Stockholm, Sweden. 2003. (http://www.socialstyrelsen.se/Lists/Artikelkatalog/Attachments/10655/2003-112-3_20031123.pdf). Accessed 24 May 2018.
15. Population and welfare department, Statistics Sweden. The total population register. The population as at 31 December 2011. Statistics Sweden, Örebro, Sweden. 2012. (http://ec.europa.eu/eurostat/cache/metadata/Annexes/demo_gind_esms_se_an1.docx).
16. Statistics Sweden. Registret över totalbefolkningen (RTB) (https://www.scb.se/vara-tjanster/bestalla-mikrodata/vilka-mikrodata-finns/individregister/registret-overtotalbefolkningen-rtb/. Accessed 24 May 2018.
17. Centre for Epidemiology, National Board of Health and Welfare. Dödsorsaksstatistik Historik, produktionsmetoder och tillförlitlighet. Komplement till rapporten Dödsorsaker 2008. Stockholm, Sweden: National Board of Health and Welfare; 2008. http://www.socialstyrelsen.se/Lists/Artikelkatalog/Attachments/18019/2010-4-33.pdf. Accessed 24 May 2018.
18. Centre for Epidemiology, National Board of Health and Welfare. Dödsorsaksregistret (http://www.socialstyrelsen.se/register/dodsorsaksregistret). Accessed 24 May 2018.

19. Statistics Sweden. Educational attainment of the population 2002. (publication no. UF0506). Örebro: Statistics Sweden; 2003. (https://www.scb.se/statistik/UF/UF0506/2003M00/UF37SM0301.pdf). Accessed 24 May 2018.
20. Statistics Sweden. Population and housing census 1970 (SOS). Part 12. Stockholm, Sweden: National Central Bureau of Statistics.
21. Statistics Sweden. The Swedish register of education. Örebro: Statistics Sweden; 2004. (http://www.scb.se/statistik/UF/UF0506/Produktbeskrivning_short_English_UF0506_20040101r.doc). Accessed 24 May 2018.
22. Ludvigsson JF, Andersson E, Ekbom A, Feychting M, Kim JL, Reuterwall C, Heurgren M, Otterbladh Olausson P. External review and validation of the Swedish national inpatient register. BMC Public Health. 2011;11:450.
23. Cnattingius S, Ericson A, Gunnarskog J, Källén B. A quality study of a medical birth registry. Scand J Soc Med. 1990;18:143–8.
24. Statistics Sweden. Evalvering av utbildningsregistret. Örebro, Sweden: Author. 2006. Retrieved from https://www.scb.se/statistik/_publikationer/be9999_2006a01_br_be96st0604.pdf. Accessed 24 May 2018.
25. National Board of Health and Welfare, Centre for Epidemiol- ogy. *Kodningskvalitet i patientregistret, slutenvård 2008*. Stockholm, Sweden: 2010. Author. Retrieved from http://www.socialstyrelsen.se/Lists/Artikelkatalog/Attachments/18082/2010-6-27.pdf. Accessed 24 May 2018.
26. D'Amico M, Agozzino E, Biagino A, Simonetti A, Marinelli P. Ill-defined and multiple causes on death certificates: a study of misclassification in mortality statistics. Eur J Epidemiol. 1999;15:141–8.
27. Internationell statistisk klassifikation av sjukdomar och relaterade hälsoproblem – Systematisk förteckning – Svensk version 2018. http://www.socialstyrelsen.se/Lists/Artikelkatalog/Attachments/20928/2018-4-12.pdf. http://www.socialstyrelsen.se/Lists/Artikelkatalog/Attachments/20929/2018-4-13.pdf. http://www.socialstyrelsen.se/Lists/Artikelkatalog/Attachments/20930/2018-4-14.pdf.
28. Jenkins JM, McGowan P, Knafo-Noam A. Parent-offspring transaction: mechanisms and the value of within family designs. Horm Behav. 2016;77:53–61.
29. Biederman J, Faraone SV, Hirshfeld-Becker DR, Friedman D, Robin JA, Rosenbaum JF. Patterns of psychopatology and dysfunction in high-risk children of parents with panic disorder and major depression. Am J Psychiatry. 2001;158:49–57.
30. Cooper PJ, Fearn V, Willetts L, Seabrook H, Parkinson N. Affective disorders in a clinical sample of children with anxiety disorders. J Affect Disord. 2006; 93:205–12.
31. Micco JA, Henin A, Mick E, Kim S, Hopkins CA, Biederman J, Hirshfeld-Becker DR. Anxiety and depressive disorders in offspring at high risk for anxiety: a meta-analysis. J Anxiety Disord. 2009;23:1158–64.
32. Hirshfeld-Becker DR, Micco JA, Henin A, Petty C, Faraone SV, Mazursky H, Bruett L, Rosenbaum JF, Biederman J. Psychopatology in adolescent offspring of parents with panic disorder, major depression, or both: a 10-year follow-up. Am J Psychiatry. 2012;169:1175–84.
33. Eley TC, McAdams TA, Rijsdik FV, Lichtenstein P, Narusyte J, Reiss D, Spotts EL, Ganiban JM, Neiderhiser JM. The intergenerational transmission of anxiety: a children-of-twins study. Am J Psychiatry. 2015;172:630–7.
34. Creswell C, Apetroaia A, Murray L, Cooper P. Cognitive, affective, and behavioral characteristics of mothers with anxiety disorders in the context of child anxiety disorder. J Abnorm Psychol. 2013;122(1):26–38.
35. Gar NS, Hudson JL. An examination of the interactions between mothers and children with anxiety disorders. Behav Res Ther. 2008; 46(12):1266–74.
36. Kendler KS, Gardner CO, Lichtenstein P. A developmental twin study of symptoms of anxiety and depression: evidence for genetic innovation and attenuation. Psychol Med. 2008;38(11):1567–75.
37. Weissman MM, Wickramaratne P, Gameroff MJ, Warner V, Pilowsky D, Kohad RG, Verdeli H, Skipper J, Talati A. Offspring of depressed parents: 30 years later. Am J Psychiatry. 2016;173:1024–32.
38. Scholten WD, Batelaan NM, van Balkom AJ, Wjh Penninx B, Smit JH, van Oppen P. Recurrence of anxiety disorders and its predictors. J Affect Disord. 2013;147(1–3):180–5.
39. Munk-Olsen T, Laursen TM, Pedersen CB, Mors O, Mortensen PB. New parents and mental disorders: a population-based register study. JAMA. 2006;296(21):2582–9.
40. O'Connor TG, Heron J, Glover V. Alspac study Team.Antenatal anxiety predicts child behavioral/emotional problems independently of postnatal depression. J Am Acad Child Adolesc Psychiatry. 2002;41(12):1470–7.

8

Prevalence of depression or depressive symptoms among people living with HIV/AIDS in China

Tingting Wang[1], Hanlin Fu[1], Atipatsa Chiwanda Kaminga[1,2], Zhanzhan Li[3], Guiping Guo[4], Lizhang Chen[1*] and Qiongxuan Li[1*]

Abstract

Background: The number of people living with HIV/AIDS (PLHA) in China continues to increase. Depression, a common mental disorder in this population, may confer a higher likelihood of worse health outcomes. An estimate of the prevalence of this disorder among PLHA is required to guide public health policy, but the published results vary widely and lack accuracy in China. The goal of this study was to estimate the pooled prevalence of depression or depressive symptoms among PLHA in China.

Methods: A systematic literature search of several databases was conducted from inception to June 2017, focusing on studies reporting on depression or depressive symptoms among PLHA in China. The risk of bias of individual studies was assessed using a modified version of the Newcastle-Ottawa scale. The overall prevalence estimates were pooled using random-effects meta-analysis. Differences according to study-level characteristics were examined using stratified meta-analysis and meta-regression.

Results: Seventy-four observational studies including a total of 20,635 PLHA were included. The pooled prevalence of depression or depressive symptoms was 50.8% (95% CI: 46.0–55.5%) among general PLHA, 43.9% (95% CI: 36.2–51.9%) among HIV-positive men who have sex with men, 85.6% (95% CI: 64.1–95.2%) among HIV-positive former blood/plasma donors, and 51.6% (95% CI: 31.9–70.8%) among other HIV-positive populations. Significant heterogeneity was detected across studies regarding these prevalence estimates. Heterogeneity in the prevalence of depression among the general population of PLHA was partially explained by the geographic location and baseline survey year.

Conclusions: Because of the significant heterogeneity detected across studies regarding these prevalence estimates of depression or depressive symptoms, the results must be interpreted with caution. Our findings suggest that the estimates of depression or depressive symptoms among PLHA in China are considerable, which highlights the need to integrate screening and providing treatment for mental disorders in the treatment package offered to PLHA, which would ultimately lead to better health outcomes in PLHA.

Keywords: Prevalence, Depression, Depressive symptoms, HIV/AIDS, Systematic review, Meta-analysis

* Correspondence: liche4005@126.com; xuanlqx@126.com
[1]Department of Epidemiology and Health Statistics, Xiangya School of Public Health, Central South University, Changsha, Hunan Province, China
Full list of author information is available at the end of the article

Background

Human immunodeficiency virus (HIV) infection remains a significant social issue worldwide. Estimates reported by the World Health Organization (WHO) suggested that 36.7 million people were living with HIV infection and acquired immune deficiency syndrome (AIDS) at the end of 2015, with 2.1 million new infections and 1.1 million deaths due to HIV-related causes. Most people living with HIV/AIDS (PLHA) are in low-income and middle-income countries [1]. As a middle-income country, the number of PLHA continues to increase in China, although the nationwide epidemic situation of HIV/AIDS remains at a low rate. According to the Chinese Center for Disease Control and Prevention, there were 0.50 million people infected with HIV at the end of 2014 in China [2], and in June 2017, this number increased to 0.66 million, 41.7% of whom were AIDS patients [3]. From 2014 to 2016, more than 10,000 people were infected with HIV every year [2–4].

Since the introduction of highly active antiretroviral therapy (ART) in the late 1990s, a large percentage of individuals with HIV-infection have been able to avoid death and live longer in a healthy condition. Nevertheless, due to social stigma, sexual dysfunction, long-term physical discomfort and illness, side effects of antiretroviral therapy, and neurobiological changes [5, 6], PLHA are at a higher risk of mental disorders, particularly depression. Evidence suggests that, depression occurs more commonly in HIV-positive individuals, with a prevalence that is two to four times higher compared with comparable HIV-negative individuals or the general population [7–9]. Individuals with HIV infection and depression perform more poorly on clinical outcomes [10]. In fact, evidence suggests that depression may reduce antiretroviral therapy adherence and quality of life, weaken the physical function and therapeutic effect [11, 12], and confer a higher rate of medical comorbidities [13, 14]. Moreover, in several studies, depression has been found to be associated with higher HIV viral loads and lower CD4 counts, even after controlling for the effects of adherence, which predict a worsening disease progression and mortality [11, 15–20]. Even depressive symptoms, which do not necessarily meet the entire diagnostic criteria for a depressive disorder, have been identified as a significant factor associated with worse health outcomes among people with HIV infection, including impaired immunological response and mortality [21–27]. Therefore, screening for depression or depressive symptoms is an overriding concern in identifying significant risk factors for health outcomes among those who are living with HIV/AIDS.

Given the importance of the association between HIV infection and depression, scholars have been committed to the epidemiological study of depression in China. While revealing a high occurrence of depression or depressive symptoms among PLHA, the results of existing studies have been fragmentary and inconsistent. For example, the prevalence among PLHA in Changsha City was 18.3% [28], whereas among PLHA in Wuhan City, it was 40.4% [29], among PLHA in Shanghai City, it was 60.3% [29], and among PLHA in Kunming City, it was 81.5% [30]. This knowledge gap is an obstacle to policy and practice. For example, the success of a screening program is sensitive to base prevalence. As the inconsistencies are outstanding in the current literature, it would be useful to analyze the data provided in the scientific literature using integrated approaches to establish the extent of depression or depressive symptoms among PLHA and clarify the reasons for the differences.

Therefore, in the present study, the objective was to conduct a systematic review and meta-analysis of studies to determine the prevalence of depression or depressive symptoms among PLHA in China and to explore the possible causes of the inconsistencies in the current estimates.

Methods

Search strategy

Two reviewers independently searched the EMBASE, Web of Science, PubMed, Wanfang, China Biology Medicine disc, China National Knowledge Infrastructure, and Weipu databases from inception to June 2017 for articles in English and Chinese, with no restriction on the year of the study.. The following search terms were used: human immunodeficiency virus, acquired immune deficiency syndrome, HIV, AIDS, depression, depressive disorder, depressive symptom, mental disorder, mental health, mood disorder, affective disorder, psychological health, and psychiatric. Search strategy details are shown in Additional file 1. In addition, the reviewers manually searched the reference lists of identified articles to identify any relevant studies missed in the initial search.

Study selection

At the stage of titles and abstracts screening, we purposely broadened the inclusion criteria to obtain any relevant study. First, studies were considered for inclusion if they were published in Chinese or English and reported on depression or depressive symptoms among PLHA. Then, the full texts of all selected studies were reviewed. Articles were included if they 1) were cross-sectional or cohort in design, 2) reported PLHA in China as a primary study population, 3) used a standard instrument to assess for depression or depressive symptoms, and 4) provided information about prevalence estimate of depression or depressive symptoms among PLHA. Conversely, articles were excluded if they 1) were review papers, conference abstracts, case reports, experimental studies, qualitative studies or case-control studies, 2) had incomplete or unclear data, or 3) were duplicate publications. Studies using only the data obtained from the National Health Insurance Research Database (NHIRD) were also excluded because of the possibility of underestimation. When there was more than one study involving the same population of PLHA, only the most recent published or comprehensive one was included. In addition, if the same data were published in both Chinese and English, then the articles published in Chinese were excluded.

Data extraction

Two reviewers independently extracted and evaluated the data for each included article using a self-designed data abstraction form. Disagreements were resolved through discussion or consultation with a third reviewer when consensus could not be achieved. The following data were extracted: the first author, year of publication, duration of data collection, geographic location, study design, sample source, subjects, sample size, average age of participants (mean or median), number and percentage of male participants, screening or diagnostic method, outcome definition (screening instrument cutoff or diagnostic criteria) and reported prevalence estimates of depression or depressive symptoms among PLHA. If a study reported more than one estimate assessed by different measurement tool, the one detected by the more valid measurement tool (i.e., the tool with higher specificity and sensitivity) was extracted. When there were multiple estimates over time in the same sample of a study, the first one was chosen.

Assessment of risk of bias

The risk of bias in the included studies was assessed using a modified version of the Newcastle-Ottawa scale (NOS) which was referred to the version used in the meta-analysis conducted by Rotenstein et al. to estimate the prevalence of depression or depressive symptoms in medical students [31]. The tool contained five items, which determine the risk of bias, including sample representativeness, sample size, response rate, ascertainment of depression, and quality of descriptive statistics reporting (for details, see Additional file 2). The five criteria were assessed as either "1 point" or "0 point". The higher the score, the lower the risk of bias in an individual study. According to Rotenstein et al. [31], a study was rated as having a high risk of bias if less than 3 points were given, and a low risk of bias if 3 or more points were given.

Statistical analysis

All analyses were performed using R version 3.4.1 (R Foundation for Statistical Computing), 'meta' package (version 4.8–4). In the presence of between-study heterogeneity, the pooled prevalence estimates and corresponding 95% confidence intervals (CIs) were calculated using random-effects meta-analyses. Data from studies based on HIV-positive sub-populations with specific characteristics (i.e., men who have sex with men [MSM], pregnant women, tuberculosis [TB] patients, injected drug users [IDUs] and former blood/plasma donors [FBPD]) were analyzed separately when at least six studies were available. As fewer than six studies reported data on HIV-positive pregnant women, HIV-TB co-infected individuals and HIV-positive IDUs, studies on those sub-populations were combined as "other HIV-positive population" to estimate the pooled prevalence. Cochran Q test and the I^2 statistic were used to assess the between-study heterogeneity. The Cochran Q test was used to evaluate whether the variation across studies was compatible with chance, and $p < 0.1$ was considered to indicate significant heterogeneity. The I^2 statistic was a quantitative indicator used to evaluate the percentage of total variance in prevalence estimates due to statistical heterogeneity rather than chance, or sampling error ($I^2 >$ 75% indicates high heterogeneity, 51–75% indicates substantial heterogeneity, 26–50% indicates moderate heterogeneity, and ≤ 25% indicates low heterogeneity).

Results from included studies were grouped according to pre-specified study-level characteristics, and then they were compared using subgroup meta-analysis (for screening instrument cut-off or diagnostic criteria, geographic location, sample source and total NOS score) or random-effects meta-regression (for baseline survey year, sample size, age and sex). The difference between subgroups was examined using the Cochran Q test ($p < 0.05$ indicated statistically significant differences). To determine the influence of individual studies on the pooled prevalence estimates, sensitivity analyses were performed by serially repeating the meta-analysis after the exclusion of each included study. If the point estimate of the new pooled prevalence is outside of the 95% confidence interval of the original pooled prevalence, it can be determined that the study which has been excluded to get the new prevalence has an significant effect on the original pooled prevalence. Publication bias was evaluated using Egger's line regression test ($p < 0.05$ indicated statistically significant differences). Preferred Reporting Items for Systematic Reviews and Meta-analysis guidelines were strictly adhered to wherever appropriate [32].

Results

Identification and characteristics of studies

In total, 54,005 unique citations were identified after an initial search, 53,771 of which were excluded after removing duplicate papers and screening titles and abstracts (Fig. 1). Then, the full text of 234 articles were reviewed, 74 of

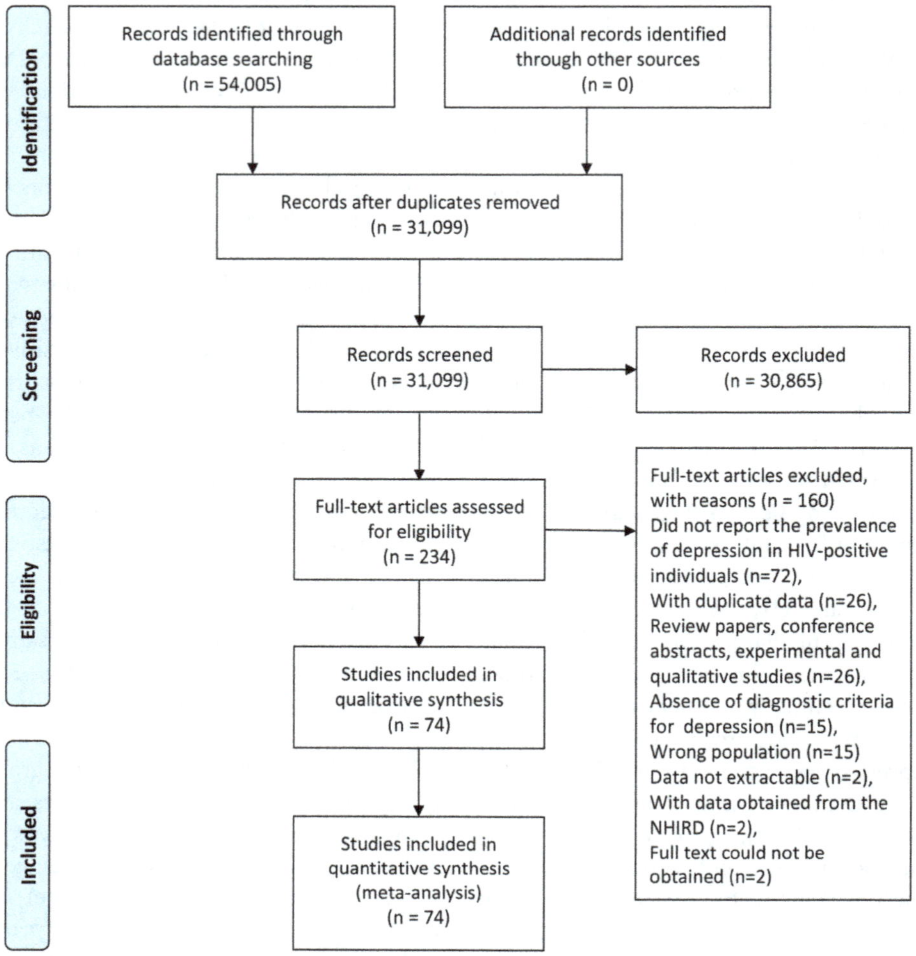

Fig. 1 Flow diagram of included/excluded studies

which [9, 28–30, 33–102] were considered to be eligible and included in the systematic review and meta-analysis.

In the 74 studies, there were a total of 20,635 PLHA. The median number of participants in those studies was 185 (range: 28 to 4103). Sixty-seven studies were conducted in one of the seven areas (twenty-one in East China, seventeen in Central China, ten in South China, nine in Southwest China, six in North China, three in Northeast China and one in Northwest China), six studies were conducted in two or more areas and one study did not report the study site. The papers were published between 2004 and 2017, and more than 70% (54/74 studies) were published between 2011 and 2017. Seventy-one cross-sectional studies ($n = 20{,}154$) and three longitudinal studies ($n = 481$) reported on the prevalence of depression or depressive symptoms, and twenty-three of the seventy-three observational studies focused on specific sub-populations (ten on MSM, seven on FBPD, two on pregnant women, two on HIV-TB co-infected individuals, and two on IDUs). More details are shown in an additional table file (see Additional file 3).

Study quality

Modified NOS score components for all 74 individual studies are shown in Additional file 4 and Additional file 5. Fifty-seven studies (77.0%) had an overall rating of low risk, while the rest were rated as high. One-fifth of the studies scored 1 point on each of these five items. The overall sample representativeness was fair, as more than half of the studies (41, 55.4%) sampled PLHA from HIV-infected individuals databases of the provincial or municipal Center for Disease Control and Prevention or from multiple study sites. Forty-one studies reported responses of at least 70%, and of these more than 90% sampled 100 or more PLHA.

Depression or depressive symptoms among the general PLHA

Estimate of overall prevalence of depression or depressive symptoms among the general population of PLHA

The prevalence estimates of depression or depressive symptoms among the general PLHA reported by 50 included studies ranged from 18.3 to 86.9%. Meta-analytic pooling of these prevalence estimates yielded a crude summary prevalence of 50.8% (8023/14,824 individuals, 95% CI: 46.0–55.5%), with significant between-study heterogeneity present ($I^2 = 96.4\%$, $p < 0.001$) (Fig. 2). No evidence of publication bias was detected using the Egger's test ($t = -1.549$, $p = 0.128$). Sensitivity analysis showed that none of the studies had a significant influence on the pooled prevalence estimate (see Additional file 6).

To further characterize the range of prevalence estimates of depression or depressive symptoms, a stratified analysis was conducted, based on the screening instruments and cut-off scores used in these methodologically diverse studies (Table 1). Summary prevalence estimates of depression or depressive symptoms ranged from 18.3% (95% CI: 13.0–24.8%) for Psychological "Computerized Tomography" 4.0 Vision (PCT V4.0) to 75.0% (95% CI: 55.1–89.3%) for the Beck Depression Inventory (BDI), with a cut-off score of 10 or greater. The median summary prevalence estimate was 48.2% (95% CI: 43.2–53.1%) for the 20-item Center for Epidemiological Studies Depression Scale (CES-D-20), with a cut-off score of 17 or greater.

Subgroup analysis and meta-regression

Statistically significant differences in prevalence estimates were identified among studies conducted in different areas ($Q = 41.3$, $p < 0.001$). When stratified by the sample source, the pooled prevalence estimates among the PLHA from the 20 community-based samples (55.3, 95% CI: 47.0–63.4%) was comparable to the PLHA from the 30 studies reporting on hospital-based samples (47.6, 95% CI: 41.7–53.6%) ($Q = 2.2$, $p = 0.141$). Similarly, there were no significant differences in the prevalence estimates of depression or depressive symptom between studies with total NOS score < 3 points and studies with total ≥ 3 points ($Q = 2.5$, $p = 0.117$). Data are shown in Table 2.

The results of the random-effects meta-regression showed that the prevalence estimates of depression or depressive symptoms significantly varied with the baseline survey year (slope = – 8.3% per 1-year increase [95% CI: -14.2% to – 2.4%]; $Q = 7.5$, $p = 0.006$). but did not significantly vary with the sample size (slope = 1.5% per 100-individual increase [95% CI: -2.1 to 5.0%]; $Q = 0.7$, $p = 0.418$), mean or median age (slope = 3.9% per 1-year increase [95% CI: -0.1 to 8.8%]; $Q = 2.5$, $p = 0.115$), sex (slope = – 0.7% per percentage increase in male individuals [95% CI: -2.0 to 0.7%]; $Q = 1.0$, $p = 0.323$) or antiretroviral therapy (ART) (slope = – 0.1% per percentage increase in individuals with ART [95% CI: -0.9 to 0.6%]; $Q = 0.1$, $p = 0.740$).

Heterogeneity within the depression survey instruments

To identify potential sources of heterogeneity independent of assessment method, stratified meta-analysis and univariate meta-regression analysis were conducted within subgroups of studies using the same instruments when at least five studies were available. An additional file shows this process in more detail (see Additional file 7). No significant differences were observed between community-based and hospital-based studies, as well as studies with total NOS score < 3 points and ≥ 3 points, within any instruments. Heterogeneity was partially accounted for by geographic location, as studies conducted in North China yielded lower depression or depressive symptoms prevalence estimates than studies conducted in Central China (24.0% [95% CI: 14.2–37.7%] vs 62.9% [95% CI: 59.0–66.7%]), as well as studies conducted in Central China (24.0% [95% CI: 14.2–37.7%] vs 70.0% [95% CI: 63.0–76.2%]) among five studies using the CES-D-20 with a cutoff score of 16 or greater (see Additional file 7 Table S1).

The baseline survey year significantly contributed to the observed notable heterogeneity among the studies using the Zung Self-Rating Depression Scale (Zung SDS), with a cut-off score of 50 or greater, and the 90-item Symptom Checklist (SCL-90), with a cut-off score of 2 or greater. Similarly, age also accounted for between-study heterogeneity within two instruments, Zung SDS score ≥ 50 and CES-D-20 score ≥ 16. Sample size also significantly contributed to the observed notable heterogeneity within three instruments (Zung SDS score ≥ 50, SCL-90 score ≥ 2 and CES-D-20 score ≥ 16), although the results were inconsistent (i.e., two analyses suggested that the prevalence estimate of depression was increasing with sample size, while a third one suggested that it was decreasing). Sex and ART did not significantly contribute to the between-study heterogeneity within any of the four instruments (see Additional file 7 Table S2).

Depression or depressive symptoms in specific PLHA

The overall pooled prevalence of depression or depressive symptoms was 43.9% (1171/2785 individuals, 95% CI: 36.2–51.9%) among HIV-positive MSM, 85.6% (941/1233 individuals, 95% CI: 64.1–95.2%) among HIV-positive FBPD, and 51.6% (457/1122 individuals, 95% CI: 31.9–70.8%) among other HIV-positive populations. Significant heterogeneity was detected across studies in the prevalence estimates of depression or depressive symptoms in these specific sub-populations (I^2 range: 93.9–97.8%; all $p < 0.05$) (Fig. 3).

Discussion

In the present systematic review and meta-analysis, we quantified the proportion of depression or depressive symptoms among PLHA using data from seventy-four studies involving 20,635 individuals in seven areas of China. On average, the pooled prevalence estimates were 50.8% for depression or depressive symptoms among the

Study	No.Depressed	Total No.	Prevalence	95% CI	Weight
BDI Score ≥ 10					
Jin H/2006	21	28	0.750	[0.551; 0.893]	1.5%
BDI Score ≥ 16					
Bo P/2012	65	145	0.448	[0.366; 0.533]	2.0%
BDI-II Score ≥ 11					
Yen CF/2004	28	41	0.683	[0.519; 0.819]	1.7%
BDI-II Score ≥ 14					
Rong H/2017	159	394	0.404	[0.355; 0.454]	2.1%
Hou WL/2014	44	108	0.407	[0.314; 0.506]	2.0%
Su XY/2013	186	258	0.721	[0.662; 0.775]	2.1%
Yeh ML/2012	68	160	0.425	[0.347; 0.506]	2.0%
CES-D-10 Score ≥ 10					
Liu HJ/2014	80	148	0.541	[0.457; 0.623]	2.0%
Rao D/2012	59	120	0.492	[0.399; 0.584]	2.0%
CES-D-20 Score ≥ 16					
Li XH/2015	75	114	0.658	[0.563; 0.744]	2.0%
Dwyer R/2014	12	50	0.240	[0.131; 0.382]	1.7%
Sun W/2014	564	772	0.731	[0.698; 0.762]	2.1%
Wang HH/2014	309	496	0.623	[0.579; 0.666]	2.1%
Liu L/2013	212	320	0.662	[0.608; 0.714]	2.1%
CES-D-20 Score ≥ 17					
Guo ZH/2015	197	409	0.482	[0.432; 0.531]	2.1%
CES-D-20 Score ≥ 20					
Sun YP/2016	150	406	0.369	[0.322; 0.418]	2.1%
HADS-D Score ≥ 8					
Huang XJ/2017	2370	3873	0.612	[0.596; 0.627]	2.2%
Li YL/2016	41	118	0.347	[0.262; 0.441]	2.0%
Peng L/2014	385	443	0.869	[0.834; 0.899]	2.1%
Zhou G/2014	133	356	0.374	[0.323; 0.426]	2.1%
HAMD-24 Score ≥ 8					
Chen FQ/2014	38	142	0.268	[0.197; 0.348]	2.0%
PCT V4.0					
Jiang Y/2016	33	180	0.183	[0.130; 0.248]	2.0%
PHQ-9 Score ≥ 5					
Zhao L/2017	334	410	0.815	[0.774; 0.851]	2.1%
Liu Y/2014	159	262	0.607	[0.545; 0.666]	2.1%
Yang GL/2014	101	190	0.532	[0.458; 0.604]	2.1%
PHQ-9 Score ≥ 10					
Qiu YY/2014	149	370	0.403	[0.352; 0.455]	2.1%
SCID-I					
Huang TL/2006	22	60	0.367	[0.246; 0.501]	1.9%
SCL-90 Score ≥ 2					
Li C/2016	93	150	0.620	[0.537; 0.698]	2.0%
Zhang CH/2016	45	103	0.437	[0.339; 0.538]	2.0%
Zhang X/2016	14	57	0.246	[0.141; 0.378]	1.8%
Zhou J/2016	46	110	0.418	[0.325; 0.516]	2.0%
Zhou ZH/2014	30	41	0.732	[0.571; 0.858]	1.7%
Jin C/2010	152	214	0.710	[0.645; 0.770]	2.1%
Chen G/2008	152	192	0.792	[0.727; 0.847]	2.0%
Zung SDS Score ≥ 50					
Hu J/2017	92	360	0.256	[0.211; 0.304]	2.1%
Sun YH/2012	13	36	0.361	[0.208; 0.538]	2.1%
Lu L/2010	94	144	0.653	[0.569; 0.730]	2.0%
Wang HY/2017	194	498	0.390	[0.346; 0.434]	1.7%
Yang YJ/2013	69	144	0.479	[0.395; 0.564]	2.1%
Dong WY/2011	185	400	0.462	[0.413; 0.513]	2.1%
Liu TZ/2010	186	624	0.298	[0.262; 0.336]	2.0%
Li BG/2008	60	95	0.632	[0.526; 0.728]	2.0%
Zhu XY/2008	67	105	0.638	[0.539; 0.730]	2.0%
Liao Q/2004	25	71	0.352	[0.242; 0.475]	1.9%
Zung SDS Score ≥ 53					
Mo XY/2017	169	321	0.526	[0.470; 0.582]	2.1%
Li L/2016	34	166	0.205	[0.146; 0.274]	2.0%
Sun HM/2015	126	298	0.423	[0.366; 0.481]	2.1%
Shi K/2014	72	120	0.600	[0.507; 0.688]	2.0%
Yao HJ/2014	82	136	0.603	[0.516; 0.686]	2.0%
Li J/2008	29	66	0.439	[0.317; 0.567]	1.9%
Random effects model		**14824**	**0.508**	**[0.460; 0.555]**	**100.0%**

Heterogeneity: $I^2 = 96.4\%$, $\tau^2 = 0.438$, $p < 0.001$

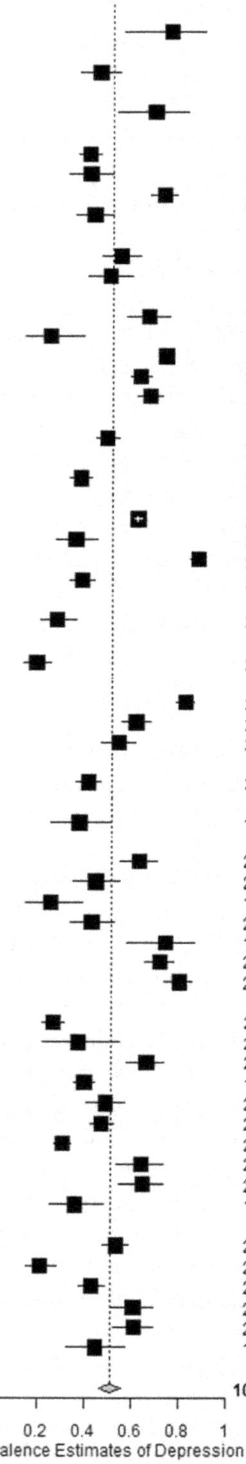

Fig. 2 Forest plot of the prevalence of depression or depressive symptoms among the general people living with HIV/AIDS in China. The vertical dotted line indicates the overall effect size of all studies combined. The studies are ordered alphabetically by screening instrument and cutoff score, and then sorted by decreasing publication year within each instrument. BDI, Beck Depression Inventory; CES-D-10, 10-item Center for Epidemiological Studies Depression Scale; CES-D-20, 20-item Center for Epidemiological Studies Depression Scale; HADS-D, Hospital Anxiety and Depression Scale; HAMD-24, 24-item Hamilton Depression Rating Scale; PCT V4.0, Psychological 'Computerized Tomography' 4.0 Vision; PHQ-9, 9-item Patient Health Questionnaire; SCID-I, Structured Clinical Interview for the fourth edition of the Diagnostic and Statistical Manual for Mental Disorders Axis I Disorders; SCL-90, 90-item Symptom Check List; Zung-SDS, Zung Self-Rating Depression Scale

Table 1 Meta-analyses of the prevalence of depression or depressive symptoms among the general PLHA in China stratified by instrument and cutoff score

Screening instrument and cutoff score	No. of Studies	No. Depressed	Total No.	Prevalence, % (95% CI)	I^2 (%)	*P* value for heterogeneity
Beck Depression Inventory Score ≥ 10	1	21	28	75.0 (55.1, 89.3)	–	–
Beck Depression Inventory Score ≥ 16	1	65	145	44.8 (36.6, 53.3)	–	–
Beck Depression Inventory II Score ≥ 11	1	28	41	68.3 (51.9, 81.9)	–	–
Beck Depression Inventory II Score ≥ 14	4	457	920	49.3 (33.2, 65.5)	95.6	< 0.001
10-item Center for Epidemiologic Studies Depression Scale Score ≥ 10	2	139	268	51.9 (45.9, 57.8)	0	0.426
20-item Center for Epidemiologic Studies Depression Scale Score ≥ 16	5	1172	1752	60.9 (51.2, 69.8)	91.9	< 0.001
20-item Center for Epidemiologic Studies Depression Scale Score ≥ 17	1	197	409	48.2 (43.2, 53.1)	–	–
20-item Center for Epidemiologic Studies Depression Scale Score ≥ 20	1	150	406	36.9 (32.2, 41.8)	–	–
Hospital Anxiety and Depression Scale Score ≥ 8	4	2929	4790	57.6 (36.7, 76.0)	98.6	< 0.001
24-item Hamilton Depression Rating Scale Score ≥ 8	1	38	142	26.8 (20.1, 34.6)	–	–
Psychological "Computerized Tomography"4.0 Vision	1	33	180	18.3 (13.0, 24.8)	–	–
9-item Patient Health Questionnaire Score ≥ 5	3	594	862	66.4 (46.9, 81.6)	96.5	< 0.001
Patient Health Questionnaire-9 Score ≥ 10	1	149	370	40.3 (35.2, 45.5)	–	–
Structured Clinical Interview for the fourth edition of the Diagnostic and Statistical Manual for Mental Disorders Axis I Disorders	1	22	60	36.7 (24.6, 50.1)	–	–
90-item Symptom Check List Score ≥ 2	7	532	867	57.4 (42.9, 70.7)	93.4	< 0.001
Zung Self-Rating Depression Scale Score ≥ 50	10	985	2477	44.8 (36.3, 53.6)	93.8	< 0.001
Zung Self-Rating Depression Scale Score ≥ 53	6	512	1107	46.0 (35.0, 57.5)	92.4	< 0.001

PLHA people living with HIV/AIDS

general PLHA. We also quantified these proportion among specific PLHA. As significant heterogeneity was detected across studies for all these prevalence estimates, the results must be interpreted with caution. To the best of our knowledge, this study represents the first time that the epidemic of depression among PLHA in China was exhaustively reviewed. As depression among PLHA is a public health issue, the risk of burden on human resources and the health care systems is considerable. The study could help to estimate the public health burden of depression among PLHA in China and to guide policy, as well as advocacy efforts. Furthermore, the study represents the first step in developing effective interventions to prevent and treat associated sequelae.

Evidence suggested that the prevalence of depression among the general population in China ranged between 1.2 and 6.9% [103, 104], significantly lower than the prevalence rate reported in our study, which further confirmed that depression was an outcome conforming to logic among PLHA [105]. However, due to the common symptoms associated with HIV illness, such as pain, fatigue, insomnia, anorexia and cognitive impairment, it is difficult to diagnose depression among PLHA [106–110]. Based on a nationally representative sample, it is demonstrated that depression among PLHA is under-diagnosed in clinical practice in the United States [111]. Although there is no study on this issue in China, we can speculate that depression in the Chinese people with HIV/AIDS is also under-diagnosed in clinical practice because more than three-quarters of non-psychiatric clinicians in China lack adequate knowledge of depression [112], which has proven to contribute to the difficulty in identifying individuals with depression [113]. Moreover, a strong stigma against PLHA lead them to defer seeking health care services or to disclose their own HIV status to the health care workers [114], which is an additional obstacle to early detection and treatment of depression among PLHA. In fact, the serious shortness and uneven distribution of mental health resources are obstacles to directing adequate attention toward those health issues [115, 116]. To improve the current situation, the National Heath and Family Planning Commission of the People's Republic of China issued the *Nation Mental Health Program (2015–2020)* [116] in 2015, in which a series of specific goals aimed at ultimately promoting public mental health have been proposed, including

Table 2 Meta-analyses of the prevalence of depression or depressive symptoms among PLHA in China stratified by study-level characteristics

Characteristics	No. of Studies	No. Depressed	Total No.	Prevalence, % (95% CI)	I^2 (%)	*P* value for heterogeneity	Test for subgroup differences	
							Q (df)	*P* value
Geographic location							41.3 (7)	< 0.001
Central China	13	1836	3927	48.8 (40.3, 57.5)	96.3	< 0.001		
Cross-region	4	2649	4279	65.7 (58.3, 72.4)	78.8	0.003		
East China	14	927	2165	47.4 (38.5, 56.5)	93.3	< 0.001		
North China	4	126	345	33.5 (22.9, 46.0)	79.9	0.002		
Northeast	3	869	1242	67.8 (60.9, 74.0)	80.1	0.007		
Northwest	1	45	103	43.7 (33.9, 53.8)	–	–		
South China	7	1019	1831	52.0 (37.2, 66.5)	97.1	< 0.001		
Southwest	4	552	932	55.7 (29.1, 79.4)	98.1	< 0.001		
Sample source							2.2 (1)	0.141
Community-based	20	2773	4840	55.3 (47.0, 63.4)	96.5	< 0.001		
Hospital-based	30	5250	9984	47.6 (41.7, 53.6)	96.3	< 0.001		
Total score							2.5 (1)	0.117
< 3 points	12	504	1167	43.8 (34.4, 53.8)	90.2	< 0.001		
≥ 3 points	38	7519	13,657	52.9 (47.5, 58.2)	96.9	< 0.001		

PLHA people living with HIV/AIDS

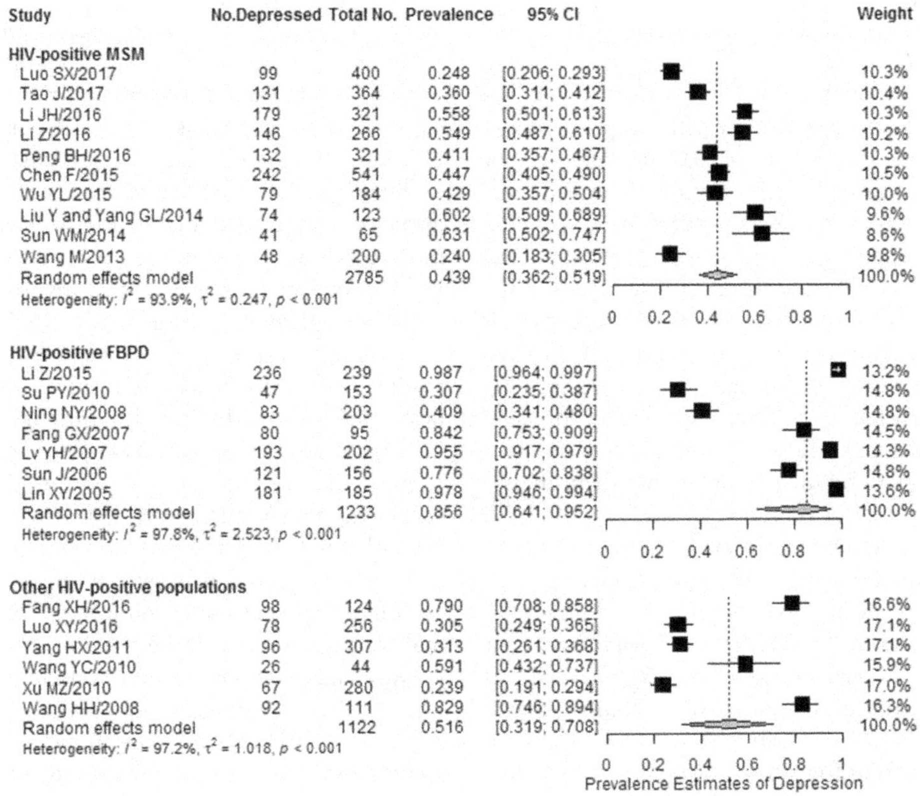

Fig. 3 Forest plot of the prevalence of depression or depressive symptoms among the subgroups of people living with HIV/AIDS in China. The vertical dotted lines indicate the overall effect sizes of all studies combined within each sub-population who were living with HIV/AIDS in China. MSM, men who have sex with men; FBPD, former blood/plasma donors

general improvement of the public cognition of depression and other common mental disorders and the public awareness of forwardly seeking medical advice, as well as obvious improvement in ability of medical workers to identify depression.

In our study, depression was found to be associated with the baseline survey time, on the decrease over time, even among some studies using common instruments. Economic development in the past decades may be a possible reason for this decrease in depression prevalence, which has greatly increased the investment of mental health as well as the availability of mental health services [115]. The growing awareness of AIDS-related knowledge among the public [117, 118] helps to reduce discrimination against PLHA and, hence, may be conductive to decreasing the prevalence of depression.

Even today, no consensus has been reached on the impact of ART on depression among PLHA in China. Several studies [54, 61, 68, 72, 78, 119, 120] have reported a higher prevalence of depression or depressive symptoms among PLHA who have undergone ART when compared with those who have not, and only two studies have reported a statistical significance [119, 120]. Nevertheless, some other studies [53, 58, 73, 121] have found the prevalence to be lower in patients who had received ART than in those who had not, while only one study has reported statistical significance for this opposite result [121]. Due to the lack of data available on depression prevalence estimates among the people using and not using ART, stratified meta-analyses could not be conducted in these two sub-populations. Instead, random-effects meta-regression analysis was used to explore the relationship between ART and depression or depressive symptoms prevalence. As a result, there was no significant association between them.

Given the higher reported prevalence estimates of depression among females in the general population, females were considered to be more vulnerable than males to the onset of depression [122], a finding supported by evidence from studies conducted in PLHA populations. In a observational cross-sectional study conducted in central India recruiting a large sample of 1181 PLHA, Deshmukh et al. have found that a greater percentage of females was screened positive for depressive symptoms when compared with males (59.9% vs 43.7%, $p <$ 0.001) [123]. In another cross-sectional study conducted in Nigeria, a significantly higher prevalence of major depressive disorders was reported among females than among males [124]. However, in a current study targeted on newly diagnosed HIV-patients, being female was found to be protective against depression but without significance (OR = 0.48, $p = 0.078$) [125]. In our study, no significant association between the prevalence estimates of depression or depressive symptoms and gender was determined. In addition, in the general population, age has also been proven to be associated with variations in the prevalence estimates of depression, with younger participants having higher prevalence of current and lifetime depression than participants older than 50 or 55 years [126]. However, the association between age and depression among PLHA remained unclear. The results showed that a younger age was significant associated with the higher prevalence of depression screened by CES-D-20 [127], as well as diagnoses by psychiatrists, according to DSM-IV-TR [128], even after adjusting for confounding factors. However, the study conducted in HIV-infected adults undergoing anti-retroviral treatment demonstrated that participants older than 50 years old had a two times higher risk of depression when compared with participants with between 18 and 30 years old [129]. In addition, the result from the study which used the Depression, Anxiety, Stress subscales, and full Scale (DASS-21) for depression screening showed that no significant effect of age on the rate of depression was found among PHLA [123]. In this meta-analysis, although no significant association was found between age and the pooled prevalence of depression, age was demonstrated to be linked with a higher risk of depression in studies with Zung SDS scores ≥50 or CES-D-20 scores ≥16 as the criteria for screening positive, which might support the positive association between age and depression among PLHA to some extent. However, as there were few studies using those two screening instrument cut-offs as screening criteria, the results must be interpreted with caution. Further studies are needed to clarify the associations between gender/age and the risk of depression among PLHA, which will help to identify individuals in high-risk.

When interpreting the results of this study, note that the data synthesized in this meta-analysis were nearly entirely extract from studies using self-report inventories of depressive symptoms as the survey instruments, which had a wide range of sensitivity and specificity for diagnosing major depressive disorder (Additional file 4). Instruments such as the Psychological "Computerized Tomography" 4.0 Vision (PCT V4.0) have high specificity and sensitivity for diagnosing depression, whereas others instruments, such as the SCL-90, have low specificity and should be regarded as screening tools. Furthermore, evidences suggest that screening tools tend to over-estimate prevalence relative to diagnostic tools, which may lead to an over-estimation of true rates in the meta-analysis with all the included studies relying on screening instruments. Despite the limitations in self-report inventories of depressive symptoms, these inventories are still essential for assessing depression in HIV-positive individuals because they are easier and more cost-effective for use in busy specialty medical clinics and epidemiological surveys than formal diagnostic interviews [130, 131], particularly in epidemiological surveys. Because of the high prevalence in China, it is nearly impossible to assess depression through formal interviews between psychiatrists and HIV-positive individuals in epidemiological studies. As an alternative, self-report inventories are the best choice. Nevertheless, for primary care physicians, it is better to remember that the diagnosis of depression should not be based solely on the results of the screening questionnaire [132]. In this meta-analysis, to control the diversity in these inventories, stratified analyses were conducted based on survey instrument and cut-off scores that identified a range of prevalence estimates not presented in the previous review [133].

This study has important limitations. As with other meta-analyses, significant heterogeneity was found in the prevalence estimates in our study, which was incompletely explained by the stratified meta-analyses and meta-regressions analyses. We hypothesize that other variables might affect the heterogeneity, such as poor income adequacy, unemployment, homeless, lower CD4 counts, higher viral loads, the severity of depressive symptoms, duration of HIV/AIDS, poor self-efficacy and lack of social support. However, we were unable to obtain adequate information about these variables. For example, less than 1/3 of the studies reported the average or median counts of CD4 cells among HIV infected populations, and fewer than 10 studies provided employment-specific prevalence estimates of depression. In addition, although an extensive document retrieve was performed in multiple databases, the existence of non-indexed studies in those databases might have led to some relevant studies being ignored. Moreover, although an attempt was made to minimize the possible bias in the process of document retrieving with specific searches in major English-Chinese databases (including master and doctoral theses), there may still be some unidentified papers. Fortunately, as the results of Egger's test results showed, there was no publication bias found in all results because we obtained a certain percentage of data from unpublished papers (fourteen theses [38, 56, 57, 66, 70, 71, 75, 82, 87, 89, 91, 94, 96, 99]).

Conclusions

Our findings suggest that the estimates of depression or depressive symptoms among PLHA in China are considerable. Given that the progression of depression are associated with a higher short-term suicide risk and a higher long-term risk of cardiovascular disease and cancer [134, 135], the findings in this study highlight the need for screening and treatment for mental disorders to be integrated in the treatment package offered to PLHA, which will ultimately lead to better health outcomes for PLHA [136].

Additional files

Additional file 1: "Search strategy used in the current systematic review and meta-analysis".

Additional file 2: "Modified Newcastle-Ottawa risk of bias scoring guide".

Additional file 3: "Selected characteristics of the 74 studies on the prevalence of depression or depressive symptoms among people living with HIV/AIDS in China".

Additional file 4: "Modified Newcastle-Ottawa risk of bias score for the 74 studies included in this systematic review and meta-analysis".

Additional file 5: "Sensitivities and specificities of commonly used instruments for diagnosing depression".

Additional file 6: "Sensitivity analysis of the prevalence of depression or depressive symptoms among people living with HIV/AIDS in China".

Additional file 7: "Within-instrument heterogeneity analyses of studies reporting on the prevalence of depression or depressive symptoms among people living with HIV/AIDS in China: stratified meta-analyses and meta-regression analyses".

Abbreviations

AIDS: acquired immune deficiency syndrome; ART: antiretroviral therapy; BDI: Beck Depression Inventory; CDC: Center for Disease Control and Prevention; CES-D-20: 20-item Center for Epidemiological Studies Depression Scale; CIs: confidence intervals; FBPD: former blood/plasma donors; HIV: human immunodeficiency virus; IDUs: injected drug users; MSM: men who have sex with men; NHIRD: National Health Insurance Research Database; NOS: Newcastle-Ottawa scale; PCT V4.0: Psychological "Computerized Tomography" 4.0 Vision; PLHA: people living with HIV/AIDS; SCL-90: 90-item Symptom Checklist; TB: tuberculosis; Zung SDS: Zung Self-Rating Depression Scale

Acknowledgments

We thank all our colleagues working in Department of Epidemiology and Health Statistics, Xiangya School of public health of Central South University, Dr. Li working in Department of Oncology, Xiangya Hospital of Central South University and Dr. Guo working in Department of Medical Psychology, the Second Xiangya Hospital of Central South University.

Authors' contributions

TTW, HLF and LZC designed this study and contributed substantially to the design of the search strategy. TTW and ACK searched and selected the literatures and extracted data. ZZL and GPG performed the analysis and interpreted the data. TTW and QXL wrote the manuscript. HLF and QXL critically reviewed the manuscript. TTW, HLF and ACK participated in the data extraction and critically revised it. LZC and QXL proofread the final version. All authors read and approved the final manuscript.

Competing interests

The authors declare that they have no competing interests.

Author details

[1]Department of Epidemiology and Health Statistics, Xiangya School of Public Health, Central South University, Changsha, Hunan Province, China. [2]Department of Mathematics, Mzuzu University, Mzuzu 2, Malawi. [3]Department of Oncology, Xiangya Hospital, Central South University, Changsha, Hunan Province, China. [4]Department of Medical Psychology, The Second Xiangya Hospital of Central South University, Changsha, Hunan Province, China.

References

1. World Health Organization. 10 facts on HIV/AIDS. 2017. http://www.who.int/features/factfiles/hiv/en/. Accessed 16 Sept 2017
2. Chinese Center for Disease Control and Prevention. Update on the AIDS/STD epidemic in China and main response in control and prevention in December, 2014. Chinese Journal of AIDS & STD. 2015;21:87.
3. Chinese Center for Disease Control and Prevention. Update on the AIDS/STD epidemic in China in the second quarter of 2017. Chinese Journal of AIDS & STD. 2017;23:677.
4. Chinese Center for Disease Control and Prevention. Update on the AIDS/STD epidemic in China and main response in control and prevention in December, 2015. Chinese Journal of AIDS & STD. 2016;22:69.
5. Phillips KD, Sowell RL, Rojas M, Tavakoli A, Fulk LJ, Hand GA. Physiological and psychological correlates of fatigue in HIV disease. Biol Res Nurs. 2004;6:59–74.
6. Schuster R, Bornovalova M, Hunt E. The influence of depression on the progression of HIV: direct and indirect effects. Behav Modif. 2012;36:123–45.
7. Ciesla JA, Roberts J. Meta-analysis of the relationship between HIV infection and risk for depressive disorders. Am J Psychiatry. 2001;158:725–30.
8. Bing EG, Burnam MA, Longshore D, Fleishman JA, Sherbourne CD, London AS, et al. Psychiatric disorders and drug use among human immunodeficiency virus-infected adults in the United States. Arch Gen Psychiatry. 2001;58:721–8.
9. Chen F, Li F, Chen L, Li Y, Li Y, Guo Z, et al. Analysis of depression and anxiety in HIV / AIDS patients. Journal of dermatology and. Venereology. 2014;36:110–2.
10. Mayston R, Kinyanda E, Chishinga N, Prince M, Patel V. Mental disorder and the outcome of HIV/AIDS in low-income and middle-income countries: a systematic review. AIDS. 2012;26:S117–35.
11. Carrico AW, Bangsberg DR, Weiser SD, Chartier M, Dilworth SE, Riley ED. Psychiatric correlates of HAART utilization and viral load among HIV-positive impoverished persons. AIDS. 2011;25:1113–8.
12. Sumari-de Boer IM, Sprangers MA, Prins JM, Nieuwkerk PT. HIV stigma and depressive symptoms are related to adherence and virological response to antiretroviral treatment among immigrant and indigenous HIV infected patients. AIDS Behav. 2012;16:1681–9.
13. Sabin CA, Ryom L, De Wit S, Mocroft A, Phillips AN, Worm SW, et al. Associations between immune depression and cardiovascular events in HIV infection. AIDS. 2013;27:2735–48.
14. Katon W, Schulberg H. Epidemiology of depression in primary care. Gen Hosp Psychiatry. 1992;14:237–47.
15. Bouhnik AD, Préau M, Vincent E, Carrieri MP, Gallais H, Lepeu G, et al. Depression and clinical progression in HIV-infected drug users treated with highly active antiretroviral therapy. Antivir Ther. 2005;10:53–61.
16. Ammassari A, Antinori A, Aloisi MS, Trotta MP, Murri R, Bartoli L, et al. Depressive symptoms, neurocognitive impairment, and adherence to highly active antiretroviral therapy among HIV-infected persons. Psychosomatics. 2004;45:394–402.
17. Kleeberger CA, Buechner J, Palella F, Detels R, Riddler S, Godfrey R, et al. Changes in adherence to highly active antiretroviral therapy medications in the multicenter AIDS cohort study. AIDS. 2004;18:683–8.
18. Alciati A, Gallo L, Monforte AD, Brambilla F, Mellado C. Major depression-related immunological changes and combination antiretroviral therapy in HIV-seropositive patients. Hum Psychopharmacol. 2007;22:33–40.
19. Leserman J. HIV disease progression: depression, stress, and possible mechanisms. Biol Psychiatry. 2003;54:295–306.
20. Leserman J. Role of depression, stress, and trauma in HIV disease progression. Psychosom Med. 2008;70:539–45.

21. Burack JH, Barrett DC, Stall RD, Chesney MA, Ekstrand ML, Coates TJ. Depressive symptoms and CD4 lymphocyte decline among HIV-infected men. JAMA. 1993;270:2568–73.
22. Leserman J, Petitto JM, Perkins DO, Folds JD, Golden RN, Evans DL. Severe stress, depressive symptoms, and changes in lymphocyte subsets in human immunodeficiency virus-infected men. A 2-year follow-up study. Arch Gen Psychiatry. 1997;54:279–85.
23. Vedhara K, Nott KH, Bradbeer CS, Davidson EA, Ong EL, Snow MH, et al. Greater emotional distress is associated with accelerated CD4+ cell decline in HIV infection. J Psychosom Res. 1997;42:379–90.
24. Ironson G, O'Cleirigh C, Fletcher MA, Laurenceau JP, Balbin E, Klimas N, et al. Psychosocial factors predict CD4 and viral load change in men and women with human immunodeficiency virus in the era of highly active antiretroviral treatment. Psychosom Med. 2005;67:1013–21.
25. Patterson TL, Shaw WS, Semple SJ, Cherner M, McCutchan JA, Atkinson JH, et al. Relationship of psychosocial factors to HIV disease progression. Ann Behav Med. 1996;18:30–9.
26. Page-Shafer K, Delorenze GN, Satariano WA, Winkelstein W Jr. Comorbidity and survival in HIV-infected men in the San Francisco Men's health survey. Ann Epidemiol 1996;6:420–430.
27. Ickovics JR, Hamburger ME, Vlahov D, Schoenbaum EE, Schuman P, Boland RJ, et al. Mortality, CD4 cell count decline, and depressive symptoms among HIV-seropositive women: longitudinal analysis from the HIV epidemiology research study. JAMA. 2001;285:1466–74.
28. Jiang Y, Wang M, Wei X, He J, Guo T, Huang G, et al. Prevalence of depression and related factors in 180 HIV/AIDS patients receiving highly active antiretroviral therapy. Zhonghua Liu Xing Bing Xue Za Zhi. 2016;37:638–42.
29. Rong H, Nianhua X, Jun X, Lianguo R, Si W, Sheng W, et al. Prevalence of and risk factors for depressive symptoms among people living with HIV/AIDS receiving antiretroviral treatment in Wuhan, China: a short report. AIDS Care. 2017;29:1–5.
30. Yao H, Zhu X, Wang H, Gu K. Analysis of mental health status among people with HIV/AIDS in shanghai. Chinese Primary Health Care. 2014;28:48–9.
31. Zhao L, Cai L, Cui W, Wang G, Zhao G, Prevalence HJ. Influencing factors of depression and anxiety among people living with HIV/AIDS in Yunnan province. Chin J Public Health. 2017;0:1–4.
32. Rotenstein LS, Ramos MA, Torre M, Segal JB, Peluso MJ, Guille C, et al. Prevalence of depression, depressive symptoms, and suicidal ideation among medical students: a systematic review and Meta-analysis. JAMA. 2016;316:2214–36.
33. Moher D, Liberati A, Tetzlaff J, Altman D, PRISMA Group. Preferred reporting items for systematic reviews and meta-analyses: the PRISMA statement. Open Med 2009;3:e123–e130.
34. Tao J, Vermund S, Lu H, Ruan Y, Shepherd B, Kipp A, et al. Impact of depression and anxiety on initiation of antiretroviral therapy among men who have sex with men with newly diagnosed HIV infections in China. AIDS Patient Care STDs. 2017;31:96–104.
35. Hu J, Zhou X, Qu F, Xu T, Wang S, Yi Y, et al. Depression of HIV/AIDS outpatients and its influence factors. Journal of Nursing. 2017;24:5–8.
36. Huang X, Li H, Meyers K, Xia W, Meng Z, Li C, et al. Burden of sleep disturbances and associated risk factors: a cross-sectional survey among HIV-infected persons on antiretroviral therapy across China. Sci Rep. 2017;7:3657.
37. Luo S, Zhou H, Zhou C, Li Y. The psychological health status and sexual behavior in the HIV-infected men who have sex with men. Journal of Preventive Medicine Information. 2017;33:450–3.
38. Mo X. Investgate the psychological distress status and evaluate the effect of individualized psychological intervention in HIV/AIDS. Guangxi medical university (Nanning); 2017. MA thesis.
39. Wang H, Wang M, Jiang F, Liu Z, Wang H, Li J. Socio-psychological factors relevant to suicidal ideation among patients with AIDS in Changsha. Zhong Nan Da Xue Xue Bao Yi Xue Ban. 2017;42:687–94.
40. Yu N. The effects of beliefs about AIDS-related death on quality of life in Chinese married couples with both husband and wife infected with HIV: examining congruence using the actor-partner interdependence model. Health Qual Life Outcomes. 2017;15:127.
41. Zhou J, Cheng H, Xu F, Zhang X, Zhu J, Wang P. The psychological and social support status of people living with HIV/AIDS in Wuxi. Chinese Journal of Disease Control & Prevention. 2016;20:1265–9.
42. Fang X, Ma D, Zou Z, Kan X, Tang L. Social support and mental health among patients with TB/HIV double infection in Anhui Province. Chinese Rural Health Service Administration. 2016;36:228–31.
43. Li C, Chen Y, Xing J, Zhang Q, Xiong B, Zhao Z, et al. Investigation of psychological health of people living with HIV/AIDS in Dalian. Studies of Trace Elements and Health. 2016;33:65–6.
44. Li J, Mo PKH, Kahler CW, Lau JTF, Du M, Dai Y, et al. Prevalence and associated factors of depressive and anxiety symptoms among HIV-infected men who have sex with men in China. AIDS Care. 2016;28:465–70.
45. Li L, Lyu C, Zhang X, Dong L, Fu J. Survey on quality of life among AIDS patients who received ART. Jinan city Preventive Medicine Tribune. 2016;22:847–8.
46. Li Y, Song X, Zhao X, Li T. The level of anxiety and depression in HIV/AIDS patients receiving highly active antiretroviral therapy. J Nurs Adm. 2016;16:241–3.
47. Li Z, Hsieh E, Morano JP, Sheng Y. Exploring HIV-related stigma among HIV-infected men who have sex with men in Beijing, China: a correlation study. AIDS Care. 2016;28:1394–401.
48. Luo X, Jimu M, Yang Q, Shama X. Analysis of depressive status of AIDS patients co-infected with tuberculosis in Liangshan Yi autonomous prefecture. Chinese Journal of AIDS & STD. 2016;22:825–7.
49. Peng B, Luo D, Liu Y, Niu L, Wang M, Chen X, et al. HIV/AIDS stress, emotional problems and social support among newly HIV-infected men who have sex with men. China Journal of Modern Medicine. 2016;26:131–6.
50. Zhang H, Zeng C, Cai W, Guo Z, Zhu Y, Sun Y, et al. Suicidal status and related factors between male and female people living with HIV/AIDS. Chinese Journal of AIDS & STD. 2016;22:601–4.
51. Zhang X, Tan W, Zhang Z, Wu D, Xu H, Sun Y. A follow-up survey on mental health of people with HIV/AIDS in the early stage of antiviral therapy. Journal of Preventive Medicine of Chinese People's Liberation Army. 2016;34:835–7.
52. Zhao C, Zhou Z. Psychological status of HIV/AIDS patients and their relatives in Shufu county of Xinjiang. Chinese Journal of AIDS & STD. 2016;22:717–20.
53. Chen F, Ding F, Lin X, Wang X, He H, Huang W, et al. Prevalence rates of depression and anxiety in HIV-infected men who have sex with men. Chin Ment Health J. 2015;29:251–7.
54. Guo Z, Cai W, Zhou Q, Zhu Y, Guo Y. Gender differences in factors associated with depression among people living with HIV/AIDS in Guangzhou. South China. J Prev Med. 2015;41:501–6.
55. Li X, Li L, Wang H, Fennie KP, Chen J, Williams AB. Mediation analysis of health-related quality of life among people living with HIV infection in China. Nurs Health Sci. 2015;17:250–6.
56. Li Z. Investigation on the status of perceived discrimination in HIV / AIDS patients and its influencing factors. Peking union medical college (Beijing); 2015. MA thesis.
57. Sun HM. Adherence to antiretroviral therapy, anxiety and depression of AIDS patients in Anhui, China. Anhui Medical University (Hefei); 2015. MA thesis.
58. Wu Y, Yang H, Wang J, Yao H, Zhao X, Chen J, et al. Prevalence of suicidal ideation and associated factors among HIV-positive MSM in Anhui, China. Int J STD AIDS. 2015;26:496–503.
59. Wang H, Zhang C, Ruan Y, Li X, Fennie K, Williams A. Depressive symptoms and social support among people living with HIV in Hunan, China. J Assoc Nurses AIDS Care. 2014;25:568–76.
60. Qiu Y, Luo D, Cheng R, Xiao Y, Chen X, Huang Z, et al. Emotional problems and related factors in patients with HIV/AIDS. Zhong Nan Da Xue Xue Bao Yi Xue Ban. 2014;39:835–41.
61. Dwyer R, Wenhui L, Cysique L, Brew BJ, Lal L, Bain P, et al. Symptoms of depression and rates of neurocognitive impairment in HIV positive patients in Beijing, China. J Affect Disord. 2014;162:89–95.
62. Hou WL, Chen CE, Liu HY, Lai YY, Lee HC, Lee NY, et al. Mediating effects of social support on depression and quality of life among patients with HIV infection in Taiwan. AIDS Care. 2014;26:996–1003.
63. Liu H, He X, Levy JA, Xu Y, Zang C, Lin X. Psychological impacts among older and younger people living with HIV/AIDS in Nanning, China. J Aging Res. 2014;2014:576592.
64. Liu Y. Impact of perceived stigma of HIV/AIDS patients on mental health and unsafe sexual behavior. China Journal of Modern Medicine. 2014;24:76–80.
65. Liu Y, Yang G, Gong H, Yan J. Association of perceived stigma, psychological status and sexual behavior in the HIV-infected persons among men who have sex with men. Chinese Journal of Modern Medicine. 2014;24:51–5.
66. Peng M. Research on current situation of medical discrimination against person living with HIV/AIDS (PLWHA) in Guangdong province. Jinan University (Guangzhou); 2014. MA thesis.
67. Shi K, He Y, Zou Y. Personal and family's factors influencing the self-discrimination of AIDS patients. Chinese Journal of Disease Control & Prevention. 2014;18:1206–8.

68. Sun W, Wu M, Qu P, Lu C, Wang L. Psychological well-being of people living with HIV/AIDS under the new epidemic characteristics in China and the risk factors: a population-based study. Int J Infect Dis. 2014;28:e147–52.
69. Sun W, Lu L, Yuan Y, Xu D, Chen X, Zou Q, et al. The anxiety and depression of male homosexual with HIV/AIDS in Nanchang City: current situation and related factors. Chinese Journal of Disease Control & Prevention. 2014;18:1143–6.
70. Yang G. Retention in care and its related factors of people living with HIV/AIDS in Changsha. Central South University (Changsha); 2014. MA thesis.
71. Zhou G. A survey on psychological states and coping styles in HIV/AIDS during the antiretroviral therapy in three hospitals in Yunnan Province. Kunming Medical University (Kunming); 2014. MA thesis.
72. Zhou Z, Gao Y. Mental health of AIDS/HIV positive clients. China Journal of Health Psychology. 2014;22:22–4.
73. Liu L, Pang R, Sun W, Wu M, Qu P, Lu C, et al. Functional social support, psychological capital, and depressive and anxiety symptoms among people living with HIV/AIDS employed full-time. BMC Psychiatry. 2013;13:324.
74. Su X, Lau JTF, Mak WWS, Choi KC, Chen L, Song J, et al. Prevalence and associated factors of depression among people living with HIV in two cities in China. J Affect Disord. 2013;149:108–15.
75. Wang M. Health status and health service utilization in a sample of HIV-positive men who have sex with men in shanghai. Anhui Medical University (Hefei); 2013. MA thesis.
76. Yang Y, Qin X, Zhang H, Huang G, Li G, Li Y. The study on depression and influencing factors among people living with HIV/AIDS. Journal of Tropical Medicine. 2013;13:1381–4.
77. Bo P. The evaluation of degree of depression and quality of life of HIV/AIDS patients. Chinese and Foreign Medical Research. 2012;10:61–2.
78. Rao D, Chen WT, Pearson CR, Simoni JM, Fredriksen-Goldsen K, Nelson K, et al. Social support mediates the relationship between HIV stigma and depression/quality of life among people living with HIV in Beijing, China. Int J STD AIDS. 2012;23:481–4.
79. Yeh ML, Hsu ST, Ko WC, Ko NY. Depressive symptoms in people living with HIV: related factors. Hu li za zhi. 2012;59:40–50.
80. Dong W, Geng W, Huang J, Qin Y, Ou R, Qin Y. Multi-variate logistic regression analysis of influencing factors of the depression in the HIV-infected out-patients. Chinese journal of new Clinical Medicine. 2011;04:429–33.
81. Sun Y, Fan A, Yan X. Survey on psychology status and related factors among population with HIV/ AIDS. Chinese journal of public. Health Management. 2011;27:314–6.
82. Yang HX. Research on the stress and its correlates of HIV-infected pregnant women. Kunming Medical University (Kunming); 2011. MA thesis.
83. Liu T, Fu J, Kang D, Qian Y, Lyu C, Zhang X. Investigation on living condition among HIV-infected patients in Shandong Province. Preventive Medicine Tribune. 2010;16:228–30.
84. Lu L, He C, Yang Y. Analysis and persuasion of depression during AIDS patients in rural areas. China Modern Doctor. 2010;48:85–6.
85. Su P, Tao F, Hao J, Huang K, Zhu P. Mental health and risk behavior of married adult HIV/AIDS subjects derived from paid blood donation in the rural of Anhui Province. Journal of Hygiene Research. 2010;39:739–42.
86. Wang Y, Li AA. Study on depression, anxiety and related factors in pregnant women infected with human immunodeficiency virus. Chinese Journal of Family Planning. 2010;18:340–3.
87. Xu MZ. Attempted suicide and mental disorders among HIV-positive drug users in Guangdong. Guangdong pharmaceutical university (Guangzhou); 2010. MA thesis.
88. Jin C, Zhao G, Zhang F, Feng L. Wu N. The psychological status of HIV-positive people and their psychosocial experiences in eastern China. HIV MED. 2009;11:253–9.
89. Chen G. Study of the mental health and the influencing factors with rural area PLWHA in a county of Henan. Third Military Medical University (Chongqing); 2008. MA thesis.
90. Li B, Zhu Y, Mo J, Zhang J. Psychological evaluation of anxiety and depression response for 95 cases of HIV positive people. Journal of Kunming Medical University. 2008;29:20–4.
91. Li J. Study on PLWHA demand for psychological care evaluation and intervention in rural area. Anhui Medical University (Hefei); 2008. MA thesis.
92. Ning N, Shi C, Yu X, Chen Y, Wu Z, Jin H, et al. Depression and quality of life investigation among HIV/AIDS subjects infected by plasma donation. Chin Ment Health J. 2008;22:501–4.
93. Wang H, Zhou J, Huang L. Adherence to highly active antiretroviral treatment and related factors in drug users with HIV/AIDS. Chinese journal of behavioral medicine and brain. Science. 2008;17:881–3.
94. Zhu XY. Research and evaluation on the psychology and quality of life among HIV/AIDS cases and correlated people. Shandong Academy of Medical Sciences (Jinan); 2008. MA thesis.
95. Fang G, Jiang Q, Dong Y. Analysis and study of psychological state among paid blood donors infected with HIV in rural areas. Chinese Journal of Disease Control & Prevention. 2007;11:127–9.
96. Lyu YH. A cross-sectional study on the mental health among people living with HIV/AIDS. Peking union medical college (Beijing); 2007. MA thesis.
97. Huang T, Leu H, Liu J. Lymphocyte subsets and viral load in male AIDS patients with major depression: naturalistic study. Psychiatry Clin Neurosci. 2006;60:687–92.
98. Jin H, Hampton Atkinson J, Yu X, Heaton RK, Shi C, Marcotte TP, et al. Depression and suicidality in HIV/AIDS in China. J Affect Disord. 2006;94:269–75.
99. Sun J. Study examines the living situation of people living with HIV/AIDS in Suizhou City of Hubei Province. Huazhong University of Science and Technology (Wuhan); 2006. MA thesis.
100. Lin X, Wu H, Zhang T, Fu Y, Wang J. Analysis of depression and anxiety among paid blood donors infected with HIV in rural areas. Chinese Journal of AIDS & STD. 2005;11:178–81.
101. Liao J, Ma Y, Xiong J, Kuang W, Shi Q, Xiao Y. Investigation of depressive status of patients with HIV/AIDS and their family members. Chinese. J Dermatol. 2004;37:8–9.
102. Yen CF, Tsai JJ, Lu PL, Chen YH, Chen TC, Chen PP, et al. Quality of life and its correlates in HIV/AIDS male outpatients receiving highly active antiretroviral therapy in Taiwan. Psychiatry Clin Neurosci. 2004;58:501–6.
103. Luo H, Li Y. Study on the status quo of the domestic depression disorder prevalence and its distribution characteristics. Foreign Medical Sciences (Section of Medgeography). 2012;33:254–5.
104. Lu J, Ruan Y, Huang Y, Yao J, Dang W, Gao C. Major depression in Kunming: prevalence, correlates and co-morbidity in a south-western city of China. J Affect Disord. 2008;111:221–6.
105. Bernard C, Dabis F, Prevalence d RN. Factors associated with depression in people living with HIV in sub-Saharan Africa: a systematic review and meta-analysis. PLoS One. 2017;12:e181960.
106. Benton TD. Depression and HIV/AIDS. Curr Psychiatry Rep. 2008;10:280–5.
107. Kalichman SC, Rompa D, Cage M. Distinguishing between overlapping somatic symptoms of depression and HIV disease in people living with HIV-AIDS. J Nerv Ment Dis. 2000;188:662–70.
108. Gibbie T, Mijch A, Ellen S, Hoy J, Hutchison C, Wright E, et al. Depression and neurocognitive performance in individuals with HIV/AIDS: 2-year follow-up. HIV Med. 2006;7:112–21.
109. Castellon SA, Hardy DJ, Hinkin CH, Satz P, Stenquist PK, van Gorp WG, et al. Components of depression in HIV-1 infection: their differential relationship to neurocognitive performance. J Clin Exp Neuropsychol. 2006;28:420–37.
110. Grant I. Neurocognitive disturbances in HIV. Int Rev Psychiatry. 2008;20:33–47.
111. Asch SM, Kilbourne AM, Gifford AL, Burnam MA, Turner B, Shapiro MF, et al. Underdiagnosis of depression in HIV: who are we missing. J Gen Intern Med. 2003;18:450–60.
112. Liang H, Fei L, Zhang Y, Xue D, Wei L, Cui Y, et al. A preliminary investigation on the knowledge of depression in non-psychiatric clinic staff in three cities in developing countries. Chinese Journal of Nervous and Mental Diseases. 2007;33:48–50.
113. Akena D, Stein DJ, Joska J. Does screening HIV-positive individuals in Uganda for major depressive disorder improve case detection rates and antidepressant prescription? AIDS Behav. 2013;17:2802–7.
114. Zhang X, Miège P, Zhang Y. Decentralization of the provision of health services to people living with HIV/AIDS in rural China: the case of three counties. Health Res Policy Syst. 2011;9:9.
115. Jiang Z. Research progress on the status quo and needs of mental health resources in China. Journal of Youjiang Medical University for Nationalities. 2016;38:442–3.
116. National Heath and Family Planning Commission of the People's Republic of China. National mental health program (2015 - 2020). 2015. http://www.gov.cn/zhengce/content/2015-06/18/content_9860.htm. Accessed 16 Sept 2017
117. Du W, Guo L, Wei N, Tao M, Tian X, An J, et al. An analysis of AIDS related knowledge among Chinese citizens and its influencing factors. Chinese Journal of AIDS & STD. 2011;17:332–5.
118. Zhang X, Su X, Song W, Wang C, Wang L, Zhang L, et al. Telephone survey on awareness of HIV/AIDS and related policy among residents in 19 provinces of China. Chinese Journal of AIDS & STD. 2013;19:683–93.

119. Liu Q, Yang JJ, Guo Y. Investigation on depression and social support among people living with HIV/AIDS. Medical Journal of Wuhan University. 2011;32:273–6.
120. Li L. A study on living status of people living with HIV/AIDS in high HIV prevalence districts. Peking union medical college (Beijing); 2007. MA thesis.
121. Wang H, Zhou J, Huang L, Li X. Adherence to highly active antiretroviral therapy and quality of life in patients with acquired immunodeficiency syndrome. Chinese Journal of Nursing. 2008;43:776–9.
122. Richards D. Prevalence and clinical course of depression: a review. Clin Psychol Rev. 2011;31:1117–25.
123. Deshmukh NN, Borkar AM, Deshmukh JS. Depression and its associated factors among people living with HIV/AIDS: can it affect their quality of life? J Family Med Prim Care. 2017;6:549–53.
124. Egbe CO, Dakum PS, Ekong E, Kohrt BA, Minto JG, Ticao CJ. Depression, suicidality, and alcohol use disorder among people living with HIV/AIDS in Nigeria. BMC Public Health. 2017;17:542.
125. L'Akoa RM, Noubiap JJ, Fang Y, Ntone FE, Kuaban C. Prevalence and correlates of depressive symptoms in HIV-positive patients: a cross-sectional study among newly diagnosed patients in Yaoundé, Cameroon. BMC Psychiatry. 2013;13:228.
126. Kessler RC, Berglund P, O D, Merikangas KR, Rush AJ, Walters EE, et al. The epidemiology of major depressive disorder: results from the National Comorbidity Survey Replication (NCS-R). JAMA 2003;289:3095–3105.
127. Seth P, Kidder D, Pals S, Parent J, Mbatia R, Chesang K, et al. Psychosocial functioning and depressive symptoms among HIV-positive persons receiving care and treatment in Kenya, Namibia, and Tanzania. Prev Sci. 2014;15:318–28.
128. Akena D, Musisi S, Joska J, Stein DJ. The association between aids related stigma and major depressive disorder among HIV-positive individuals in Uganda. PLoS One. 2012;7:e48671.
129. Kaharuza FM, Bunnell R, Moss S, Purcell DW, Bikaako-Kajura W, Wamai N, et al. Depression and CD4 cell count among persons with HIV infection in Uganda. AIDS Behav. 2006;10:S105–11.
130. Vilagut G, Forero CG, Barbaglia G, Alonso J. Screening for depression in the general population with the Center for Epidemiologic Studies Depression (CES-D): a systematic review with Meta-analysis. PLoS One. 2016;11:e155431.
131. Wang YP, Gorenstein C. Assessment of depression in medical patients: a systematic review of the utility of the Beck depression inventory-II. Clinics (Sao Paulo). 2013;68:1274–87.
132. Kerr LK, Kerr LD Jr. Screening tools for depression in primary care: the effects of culture, gender, and somatic symptoms on the detection of depression. West J Med 2001;175:349–352.
133. Niu L, Luo D, Liu Y, Silenzio VM, Xiao S. The mental health of people living with HIV in China, 1998-2014: a systematic review. PLoS One. 2016;11:e153489.
134. Clarke DM, Depression CK. Anxiety and their relationship with chronic diseases: a review of the epidemiology. risk and treatment evidence Med J Aust. 2009;190:S54–60.
135. Glassman AH, Shapiro PA. Depression and The course of coronary artery disease. Am J Psychiatry. 1998;155:4–11.
136. Gaynes BN, O'Donnell J, Nelson E, Heine A, Zinski A, Edwards M, et al. Psychiatric comorbidity in depressed HIV-infected individuals: common and clinically consequential. Gen Hosp Psychiatry. 2015;37:277–82.

9

Knowledge, attitudes and practices regarding depression among primary health care providers in Fako division, Cameroon

Isabelle Dibu Mulango[1*], Julius Atashili[2], Bradley N. Gaynes[3] and Tsi Njim[4,5]

Abstract

Background: Mental health and mental illness are often overlooked in the management of patients in our health services. Depression is a common mental disorder worldwide. Recognising and managing mental illnesses such as depression by primary health care providers (PHCPs) is crucial. This study describes the knowledge, attitudes and practices (KAP) of PHCPs regarding depression in Fako Division.

Methods: A cross-sectional study was conducted among PHCPs (general practitioners, nurses, pharmacy attendants and social workers) in public-owned health facilities in the four health districts in Fako Division. Participants were selected by a consecutive convenience sampling. A structured questionnaire including the Depression Attitude Questionnaire (DAQ) was used to collect information about their socio-demographic characteristics, professional qualifications and KAP about depression.

Results: The survey had a response rate of 56.7%. Most of the 226 participants (92.9%) were aware that depression needs medical intervention. Only 1.8% knew a standard tool used to diagnose depression. Two-thirds agreed that majority of the cases of depression encountered originate from recent misfortune. About 66% felt uncomfortable working with depressed patients. Also, 45.1% of PHCPs did not know if psychotropic drugs were available at pharmacies within their health area. Very few (15.2%) reported to have prescribed psychotropic drugs. Less than half (49.1%) of the participants had prior formal training in mental health.

Conclusion: PHCPs in Fako Division tend to have limited knowledge and poor attitudes regarding depression. Practices towards diagnosis and management of depression tend to be inadequate. There is an urgent need to train PHCPs in mental health in general and depression diagnosis and management in particular.

Keywords: Primary health care providers, Depression, Knowledge, Attitudes, Practices, Fako, Cameroon

Background

Health is defined by the World Health Organization (WHO) as "a state of complete physical, mental and social well-being and not merely the absence of disease or infirmity" [1]. Mental health is an inherent component of health.

However, screening and treatment for depression and other mental health diseases in general are limited in sub-Saharan Africa. Research concerning routine screening of depression indicates benefits were greater among the general adult population, pregnant and postpartum women than in older adults, nonetheless accurate screening of all populations and provision of treatment were recommended [2]. Few studies have been done on the prevalence of mental disorders and associated factors [3–5]. In Cameroon, neuropsychiatric disorders are estimated to contribute to 6.1% of the global burden of disease. There are no official data on the prevalence of depression in the general population [6]. Furthermore, health care providers' attitudes towards mental disorders have not been adequately assessed even

* Correspondence: mulangoi@yahoo.com
[1]District Hospital Kumba, Kumba, South West Region, Cameroon
Full list of author information is available at the end of the article

though adequate knowledge on mental health by primary health care providers (PHCPs) is vital for the provision and integration of mental health services [7]. This is important as PHCPs are usually the first to encounter patients.

In Zambia, a recent study showed that among PHCPs, there was great stigma and discrimination towards mental illness [8]. Another study in Tanzania showed that the number of depressed persons is reported to have increased. The authors concluded on the need for PHCPs to undergo more training to ameliorate the management of depression [9].

While mortality is still mostly the result of infectious diseases and malnutrition, the morbidity associated to mental illnesses receives minimal attention from most governments. As a result, mental health services are poorly developed [3, 10]. It is projected that depression will cause the highest burden of disease by 2020 [11]. Mental illnesses-associated morbidity thereby requires that public policy makers and PHCPs change their attitudes towards mental and neurological disorders [3, 12].

In Cameroon, to the best of our knowledge, the knowledge, attitudes and practices (KAP) among PHCPs towards depression has not been assessed. We conducted this study to describe the KAP regarding depression among PHCPs to address these information gaps. As the range of mental disorders is vast, depression was used as representative of mental disorders. Information on current perceptions, diagnosis and management for depression, and mental health services may have an impact on the overall management of depression in a way best to suite our context and potentially improve mental health care in Cameroon.

Methods

Study design and setting

Fako Division is one of the six divisions of the South West Region of Cameroon. Fako Division has a population of about 534,854 people and an area of 2093km^2 [13]. Fako Division has four health districts namely: Buea, Limbe, Tiko and Muyuka health districts [14]. There are 37 functional public-owned health facilities out of 89 health facilities within the four health districts. These health facilities include health centers and hospitals which represent the peripheral and intermediate levels of the Cameroon health system classification. Data on the exact number of health personnel in these health facilities is unavailable. There are two mental health nurses within Fako Division, one mental health nurse in each of the regional hospitals in Buea and Limbe.

We conducted an observational cross-sectional study of all PHCPs within public-owned health facilities in the four health districts in Fako Division who consented voluntarily to participate. PHCPs were selected by a consecutive convenience sampling.

Participants and sampling

The study population was made of PHCPs (all general practitioners, social workers, pharmacy attendants and nurses). This study population was deliberately chosen because they are expected to provide primary health care which includes early detection of mental illness. Eligible participants were PHCPs aged ≥21 years who provided informed written consent. PHCPs less than 21 years of age were excluded from the study.

Participants were enrolled at their work station between July and December 2013. Every eligible participant available was approached by the principal investigator. Participation was voluntary and participants who gave their consent were given questionnaires to fill and return within one week. Questionnaires were anonymous. The questionnaire was pilot tested prior to the survey proper. A total of 400 PHCPs agreed to participate in this study and 226 returned completely filled questionnaires.

Data collection, variables and measurements

The study was carried out using a structured questionnaire (Additional file 1) which was self-administered. The questionnaire was divided into four main sections. Section one which collected information on the key socio-demographic variables of the PHCPs (age, gender, marital status, profession, and duration of practice). Section two had 15 questions to assess the knowledge of PHCPs about depression. Section four had twelve items on the practice about depression and prior training in mental health. Knowledge and practice questions were selected from questions found in other studies [8, 15–18] and the questions were modified or rephrased for better understanding.

Section three used the DAQ to assess the attitudes of the PHCPs to depression. The DAQ was originally devised for use in the United Kingdom and it has been used successfully by various health professionals in other developed countries [19–21] as well as in African settings [9, 22]. The initial DAQ was a self-reported measure comprising of 20 items spanning 100 mm on a visual analogue scale ranging from "strongly agree" to "disagree" [23]. Sections two, three and four had questions were in 'Agree/yes', 'Disagree/no' or 'Neutral/I don't know' format. This format was used in among PHCPs in Tanzania and GPs in Nigeria [9, 22].

Data management and statistical analysis

Data from the questionnaires were entered into an Epi-Info version 7.0 database and analyzed using Epi-Info Version 7.0, Simple Interactive Statistical Analysis (SISA) and Microsoft Excel. Participants' characteristics were described using absolute and relative frequencies of various responses for categorical variables and means and standard deviations were used for continuous variables such as age. The socio-demographic variables of PHCPs such as past training (on mental health and illness during their degree/certificate training) were compared to randomly selected KAP statements (amitriptyline is a psychotropic drug; depression reflects a characteristic response that is not amendable to change; you have prescribed a psychotropic drug to a patient with a depressive disorder). The association were assessed using Chi-square tests or Fisher's exact tests as appropriate. Statistical significance was set at $p < 0.05$.

Ethical approval

This research was approved by the Faculty of Health Sciences Institutional Reviews Board and the South West Regional Delegation of Public Health of Cameroon. Informed written consent was obtained from all participants. Participation was voluntary, and participants could withdraw at any time from the study.

The manuscript was written following the STROBE guidelines for reporting observational studies [24].

Results

Of the 400 questionnaires distributed, 226 were returned (response rate = 56.7%). The characteristics of the 226 PHCPs who participated in the study are summarised in Table 1. Most (73.9%) of the participants were females. Almost half (41.6%) belonged to the age group 30–39 years. The mean age of study participants was 33.3 ± 7.6 years. PHCPs had an average duration of practice of 6.4 ± 6.4 years. A majority (61.1%) of them had worked for more than five years.

Table 1 Distribution of the study population according to socio-demographic variables

Variable	Category	Frequency	Proportion (%)
Gender	Male	59	16.1
	Female	167	73.6
Marital status	Single	196	52.7
	Married	96	42.5
	Widow	96	3.1
	Divorced	7	1.8
Age (years)	21–29	83	36.7
	30–39	94	41.6
	40–49	39	17.2
	50–59	10	4.5
Duration of practice (years)	≤ 1	47	20.8
	2–5	91	40.3
	6–9	34	15.0
	10–14	31	13.7
	15–19	8	3.5
	20–24	8	3.5
	25–29	5	2.2
	≥30	2	1.0
Profession	Nurses	184	81.4
	GPs	25	11.1
	Social Workers	7	3.1
	Pharmacy attendants	10	4.4

A vast majority (81.4%, $n = 184$) of the respondents were nurses with 11.1% ($n = 25$) being general practitioners (GPs), 3.1% ($n = 7$) social workers and pharmacy attendants (4.4%, $n = 10$). Nurses include: state registered nurses and nurse assistants.

Knowledge towards etiology of depression

Table 2 details the KAP towards depression. Majority (85.4%) disagreed that depression is caused by witchcraft, charms or evil spirits. 92.9% reported that depression can lead to suicide or suicide attempts.

Knowledge about the treatment and classification of depression

Majority (85.8%) accepted that depression can be treated with pharmacological methods and psychotherapy. Only 28.3% agreed that fluoxetine is an anti-depressant drug.

Attitudes towards the prevalence and origin of depression

Attitudes towards depression for each item are listed in Table 3. More than a third (45.1%) reported to have seen an increase in the number of depressed patients presenting with depressive symptoms during the last five years. More than 60% agreed that the majority of depressed cases they see originated from recent misfortune and perceived that depressed patients are more likely to have experienced deprivation in early life than other people. However, few (31.9%) felt that patients with depression are discriminated by and avoided by the general public.

Attitudes about the diagnosis and prognosis of depression

Less than half (42.5%) of the respondents disagreed that it is difficult to differentiate unhappiness from a clinical depressive disorder that needs treatment. More than half (61.5%) perceived that antidepressants usually produce a satisfactory result in treatment of depressed patients.

Attitudes regarding treatment of depression

Nearly two thirds (67.3%) believed that most depressive disorders improve without medication. A vast majority (82.7%) endorsed the statement that PHCPs could be a useful person to support depressed patients. More than 60% of PHCPs agreed that if depressed patients need antidepressants or psychotherapy they are better off with psychiatrists.

Table 2 Responses to knowledge items of 226 PHCPs who responded to a survey on the Knowledge, Attitudes and Practices regarding depression in Fako Division, Cameroon

No.	Statement	Agree n (%)	Disagree n (%)	Don't know[a] n (%)	Total n (%)
1	Have you ever heard about depression?	226 (100)	0 (0)	0(0)	226 (100)
2	Do you consider depression as a health problem?	210 (92.9)	11 (5)	5 (2.1)	226 (100)
3	Depression affects people of a particular age group.	60 (26.5)	152 (67.3)	14 (6.2)	226 (100)
4	Depression is caused by witchcraft, charms or evil spirits.	14 (6.2)	193 (84.4)	19 (8.4)	226 (100)
5	Patients with depression can break down at any time.	203 (89.8)	12 (5.3)	11 (4.9)	226 (100)
6	Patients with depression are dangerous to themselves and others.	167 (73.9)	48 (21.2)	11 (4.9)	226 (100)
7	Depression can lead to suicide and suicide attempts.	210 (92.9)	12 (5.3)	1 (1.9)	226 (100)
8	Depression can be treated with pharmacological methods and psychotherapy.	194 (85.9)	18 (8.0)	14 (6.1)	226 (100)
9	Depression is best managed by traditional doctors/healers.	5 (2.2)	206 (91.2)	15 (6.6)	226 (100)
10	Depression responds better to traditional remedies than orthodox treatment most of the time.	8 (3.5)	181 (80.1)	37 (16.4)	226 (100)
11	Amitriptyline is an anti-depressant drug.	91 (40.3)	15 (6.6)	120 (53.1)	226 (100)
12	Methotrexate is an anti-depressant drug.	35 (15.5)	58 (25.7)	133 (58.9)	226 (100)
13	Fluoxetine is an anti-depressant drug.	64 (28.3)	23 (10.2)	139 (61.5)	226 (100)
14	Carbamazepine is an anti-depressant drug.	91 (40.3)	23 (10.2)	112 (49.5)	226 (100)
15	Do you know of a tool used to classify depressed patients? If response is yes, please specify the tool.	4 (1.8)	222 (98.2)	NA	226 (100)

[a]or Neutral; NA: Not applicable

Working with depressed patients

Only 26.5% of PHCPs felt comfortable dealing with depressed patients and a majority (74.3%) agreed that working with depressed patients is "heavy going", tedious or difficult. However, nearly two thirds endorsed the statement that it is rewarding to spend time looking after depressed patients.

Practices towards recognition and management of depression

Very few (12%) of PHCPs were routinely screening patients for depression, while 16.4% never screened patients for depression. More than a third (43.8%) of the participants agreed that time constraints is a limiting factor to managing depressed patients.

Majority (78.4%) reported that they would send patients with depression for counseling or medical management, while 21.6% of the sample would send depressed patients home, for prayers or to traditional healers.

Training in mental health and illness

Less than half (49.1%) of the sample had prior training in mental health during their undergraduate studies: 84% of GPs and 46.7% of all nurses (Fig. 1). This training covered depression, anxiety disorders, schizophrenia and epilepsy (Fig. 2). However, only 1.8% knew of a standard tool used in the classification of depression such as the Diagnostic Statistical Manual Fourth Edition (DSM-IV), Neurobehavioral functioning inventory Yale tool (NFI), Hospital anxiety and depression scale (HAD).

All the PHCPs with prior undergraduate training agreed that the training on mental health and disorders was less as compared to the time spent on training in infectious diseases and chronic illnesses. Only 0.9% ($n = 2$) of the respondents went for further training on mental health after undergraduate studies. One general practitioner had a 6 months training on mental health and one mental health nurse had 1-year training on mental health.

Availability and prescription of psychotropic drugs

Few (6.6%) agreed that psychotropic drugs were always available at pharmacies within their health area. Furthermore, 15.1% agreed to have prescribed psychotropic drugs such as amitriptyline, fluoxetine, haloperidol and risperidone. GPs prescribed psychotropic drugs more than any other category of health professionals.

Associations of selected KAP items with some socio-demographic variables

PHCPs who had prior training during their undergraduate training were significantly more likely to know that amitriptyline is a psychotropic drug (OR = 0.34, 95% CI [0.19–0.6], $p = 0.001$). In addition, these PHCPs were more likely to agree that depression reflects a characteristic

Table 3 Participants' responses to Depression Attitude Questionnaire

No.	Statement	Agree n (%)	Disagree n (%)	Don't know[a] n (%)	Total n (%)
1	During the last 5 years I have seen an increase in the number of patients presenting with depressive symptoms	102 (45.1)	93 (41.2)	31 (13.7)	226 (100)
2	The majority of depression cases I see originated from recent misfortune	146 (64.6)	51 (22.6)	29 (12.8)	226 (100)
3	Biochemical abnormality is at the basis of more severe depression	80 (35.4)	66 (29.2)	80 (35.4)	226 (100)
4	It is possible to distinguish two groups of depression, one psychological in origin and the other caused by biochemical mechanisms.	139 (61.5)	40 (17.7)	47 (20.8)	226 (100)
5	Depressed patients are more likely to have experienced deprivation in early life than other people.	134 (59.6)	59 (26.2)	32 (14.2)	226 (100)
6	Becoming depressed is a way that people with poor stamina deal with life difficulties	116 (51.6)	73 (32.4)	36 (16.0)	226 (100)
7	Becoming depressed is a natural part of becoming old	60 (26.6)	155 (68.6)	11 (4.8)	226 (100)
8	Are patients with depression discriminated by the general public and avoided?	72 (31.9)	128 (56.6)	26 (11.5)	26 (11.5)
9	Difficult to differentiate unhappiness or a clinical depressive disorder that needs treatment	90 (39.8)	96 (42.5)	40 (17.7)	226 (100)
10	Depression reflects a characteristic response which is not amendable to change	35 (15.5)	149 (65.9)	23 (10)	226 (100)
11	Antidepressants usually produce a satisfactory result in the treatment of depressed patients in general practice	139 (61.5)	44 (19.5)	43 (19.0)	226 (100)
12	Most depressive disorders improve without medication	152 (67.3)	50 (22.6)	24 (10.6)	226 (100)
13	The primary health care worker could be a useful person to support depressed patients	197 (87.2)	17 (7.5)	12 (5.3)	226 (100)
14	There is little to be offered those depressed patients who do not respond to what primary health care workers do	64 (28.4)	122 (54.2	39 (17.3)	226 (100)
15	If depressed patients need antidepressants, they are better off with psychiatrists than with primary health care workers	162 (71.7)	30 (13.3)	34 (15.0)	226 (100)
16	Psychotherapy for depressed patients should be left to a specialist	154 (64.4)	58 (25.8)	13 (5.7)	226 (100)
17	If psychotherapy were freely available, this would be more beneficial than antidepressants for most depressed patients	162 (71.7)	30 (13.3)	34 (15.0)	226 (100)
18	I feel comfortable dealing with depressed patients	60 (26.6)	149 (65.9)	17 (7.5)	226 (100)
19	Working with depressed patients is heavy going, tedious or difficult	168 (74.3)	45 (19.9)	13 (5.8)	226 (100)
20	It is rewarding to spend time looking after depressed patients	148 (65.5)	49 (21.7)	29 (12.8)	226 (100)

[a]= or Neutral

response that is amendable to change (OR = 2.0, 95%CI [0.95–4.23], p-value = 0.03). Also, these PHCPs were significantly more likely to prescribe psychotropic drugs (OR = 3.45, 95% CI [1.52–7.81], p = 0.003).

Discussion

Participants' knowledge on depression was generally low in our study. Attitudes regarding depression reported negative responses and PHCPs had limited training on

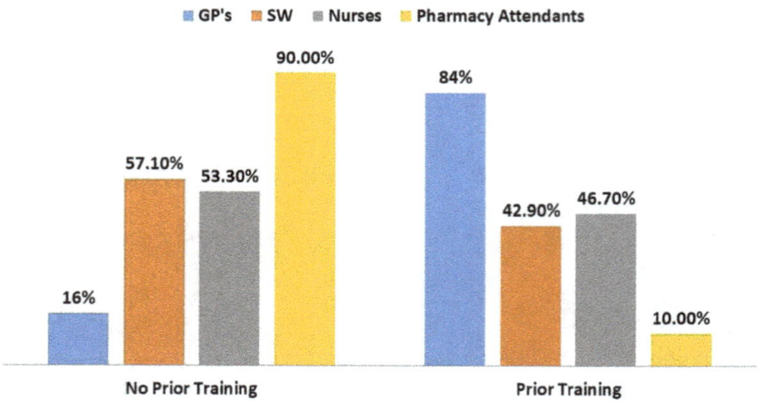

Fig. 1 PHCPs training on Mental Health and Illnesses during undergraduate studies in Fako Division, Cameroon

mental disorders. Depression is a significant public health problem worldwide [11]. PHCPs play a major role in the diagnosis and management of depression.

In this study, PHCPs have good knowledge on the causation of depression in general. There were some misconceptions on depression, as a vast majority agreed that depressed patients can breakdown at any time [15].

Regarding the knowledge on management of depression, the large majority knew the effectiveness of pharmacological methods and psychotherapy. However, few PHCPs were knowledgeable about a standard tool used in the screening of depression. Recent evidence suggest PHCPs should use a standardized screening tool for depression to reduce underdiagnosis and to determine the diagnosis of depression with DSM-V criteria to avoid overuse and unneeded detrimental effects of pharmacotherapy [2]. The underdiagnosis of depression has been associated with increased morbidity in other studies [9, 16, 22]. Our data are in contrast with those of Seehusen et al. in the United States where a higher proportion (30.6%) of family physicians used a validated screening tool for postpartum depression [25]. Moreover, the use of validated tools has proven to be important in screening for depression [21, 26, 27]. Furthermore, only few of the respondents knew that amitriptyline, an anti-depressant is a psychotropic drug and similar results were observed in Nigeria [28].

Less than half of the respondents reported an increase in the number of depressed patients, and this has been observed in prior studies among non-psychiatric doctors in Japan and health workers in Tanzania [9, 29]. Although the prevalence of depression in the general population of Cameroon is not known [6], PHCPs recognize the burden of depression in primary health care. More data from future studies are needed to assess if the rate of depression is increasing in the general population. Recently, few studies have been carried out on the prevalence of depression in specific populations

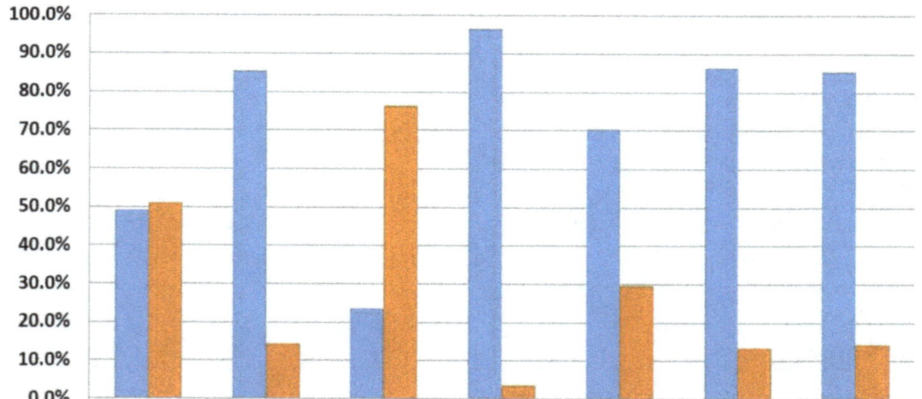

	Learning disorders	Anxiety disorders	Tics	Depression	Suicide	Schizophrenia	Epilepsy
Yes	49.10%	85.60%	23.60%	96.40%	70.30%	86.50%	85.60%
No	50.90%	14.40%	76.40%	3.60%	29.70%	13.50%	14.40%

Fig. 2 Distribution of prior mental health training and mental disorders covered by PHCPs in Fako Division, Cameroon

such as HIV/AIDS patients. A study conducted by Gaynes et al. in Bamenda, Cameroon among HIV-infected patients ($n = 11$) revealed a low prevalence of last month major depression (3%) among that specific sample [4]. Another study by L'akoa et al. in Yaounde, Cameroon revealed that the prevalence of depression (63%) among newly diagnosed HIV patients ($n = 100$) was higher [5]. Although both studies used the same cut-off score of ≥10 as a positive screen of depression with PHQ-9, the vast difference in the prevalence of major depression among HIV-infected patients in the above studies may be due to differences in sample size.

PHCPs had misconceptions on the risk factors and cause of depression. Most of the respondents believed that depression is caused by misfortune. Similar findings have been reported elsewhere [20, 30]. Discriminatory attitudes and stigma towards depression has been shown to limit depressed patients to seek help [7, 31]. The stigma associated with this condition could also explain the unwillingness of about half of the target population to participate in the study. A recent study in Canada and Cameroon revealed that persons from Cameroon had more stigmatizing attitudes towards mentally ill patients when compared to persons from Canada [17]. Variations in PHCPs and patients' views on depression may strongly be influenced by social and cultural factors [15].

In our study, majority of PHCPs felt uncomfortable working with depressed patients. This is consistent with prior studies [22, 26]. One in three PHCPs reported to have difficulty differentiating unhappiness from a clinical depressive state that needs treatment. Our results are similar with a study among GPs in Brazil [32] but in contrast to GPs in France [20]. This can be accounted for by the fact that physicians in developed world have more training on mental illness.

Majority of the respondents preferred depressed patients to be managed by specialists. Similar findings were seen in other studies [9, 15, 29, 33]. PHCPs have limited skills to offer adequate management options hence prefer the management of depression by mental health professionals.

Regarding practices, only few PHCPs agreed to always screen patients for depression. PHCPs identified time constraints, limited skills and training as limitations in the diagnosis and management of depression as earlier documented [11, 15]. The workforce in the mental health sector in Cameroon is severely limited and cannot meet the needs to care for mentally ill patients [6]. In the United Kingdom, a study done by Haddad et al. reported that if nurses in general practice were provided adequate training in mental health, they could provide better mental health services [23], supporting the findings of other studies [27, 28, 34, 35].

The two main mental health treatment centers in the Cameroon: Jamot Hospital Yaounde and Laquintinie Hospital Douala are found in the Center and Littoral Regions respectively [14]. Hence referral from primary care to specialized mental health services is inadequate [15, 36].

About a third of the PHCPs agreed that psychotropic drugs were available at pharmacies within their health area. Studies by Olugbile et al. report that only a fifth of GPs had psychotropic drugs available in their drug stocks [18]. This can be linked to the fact that psychotropic drugs are limited in primary health care.

The study had the following limitations. This study used a non-random sampling method and was done among PHCPs working in public-owned health facilities in the four health districts in Fako Division in the South West Region of Cameroon, these results may not be a representation of the rest of the country. The DAQ was first used in United Kingdom. Although it has been widely used with GPs and health workers success in African settings, the scale may not have been transferable to a different country or culture. We did not evaluate the validation (general test score characteristics, internal reliability, factor structure) of the DAQ nor it's psychometric properties. In addition, there have been questions on the psychometric inadequacy of the DAQ in relation to its differing subscales and modest internal consistency [37]. However, using the DAQ provided us with the opportunity to compare findings in studies in African settings and elsewhere which implemented the same tool. Thus, there may be a need to carry out a larger survey among PHCPs in Cameroon using a revised version of the DAQ [30] assessing psychometric properties and accounting for some of its psychometric inadequacies.

The survey's low response rate can be accounted by participants unwillingness to participate due to the stigma associated with depression. Also, there was a problem of recall bias as majority of those who had training in mental health could not correctly estimate the duration of training or type of mental illness studied. These limitations should be considered when interpreting the results.

Notwithstanding these limitations, this paper does present new data on the KAP among primary health care providers regarding depression.

Implications

Educational intervention programs in areas of mental health to improve the knowledge, attitudes and practices of PHCPs towards depression is paramount. If this is implemented, PHCPs will be more confident in dealing with depressed cases. Previous studies have shown that continued medical education is linked to better diagnosis and management of depressed patients.

Conclusions

PHCPs have insufficient KAP about the management of depression. There was paucity in depression management options. PHCPs generally had negative views regarding depression. PHCPs felt uncomfortable and perceived difficulty when working with depressed patients. This study revealed that in practice, PHCPs do not or rarely screen or assess patients for depression, which is a very common mental disorder encountered within primary health care. PHCPs had limited training in mental health. We recommend that, the government through the Ministry of Public Health should draft and implement a national mental health policy. In addition, the resources allocated to mental health should be increased and the creation of more mental health services. We also recommend the provision of schools and training programs in the area of mental health, to increase the number of mental health professionals. Furthermore, the creation of awareness education programmes on mental illnesses.

Additional file

Additional file 1: Mental Health Questionnaire. Title of data: Questions used during the study "Knowledge, Attitudes and Practices regarding Depression among Primary Health Care Providers in Fako Division, Cameroon". Description of data: The study was carried out using a 52 items structured questionnaire which was self-administered from July 2013 to December 2013. The questionnaire was divided into four main sections. Section one which collected information on the key socio-demographic variables of the PHCPs. Section two had 15 items to assess the knowledge of PHCPs about depression. Section four had 12 items on the practice about depression and prior training in mental health. The knowledge and practice items were selected from questions found in other studies [8, 15–18] and the questions were modified or rephrased for better understanding. Section three used the DAQ to assess the attitudes of the PHCPs to depression. The DAQ was originally devised for use in the United Kingdom and it has been used successfully by various health professionals in other developed countries [19–21] as well as in African settings [9, 22].

Abbreviations

AIDS: Acquired immune deficiency syndrome; DAQ: Depression attitude questionnaire; DSM-IV: Diagnostic Statistical Manual Fourth Edition (DSM-IV)DSM-VDiagnostic Statistical Manual Fourth Edition (DSM-V); GP: General practitioner; HAD: Hospital anxiety and depression scale (HAD); HIV: Human immuno-deficiency virus; KAP: Knowledge, attitudes and practices; NFI: Neurobehavioral functioning inventory; PHCP: Primary health care providers; SISA: Simple Interactive Statistical Analysis; WHO: World Health Organization

Acknowledgements

The study team wishes to thank the PHCPs who took their time to participate in this study. Thank you to BNG for supporting this work. Moreover, thank you to Mrs. Joan Mulango-Namoango and Dr. Kahwah-Sumbele.

Funding

This study received support from grant R34 MH084673 of the National Institute of Mental Health, National Institutes of Health, Bethesda, MD, USA to Professor Bradley N. Gaynes of the University of North Carolina at Chapel Hill, USA. The funders had no role in study design, data collection and analysis, decision to publish, or preparation of the manuscript.

Authors' contributions

Conception of study: JA, BNG, IDM. Data collection: IDM. Data analysis: IDM, JA. Writing of first draft: IDM, JA, BNG, TN. Manuscript revisions: IDM, JA, BNG, TN. All authors read and approved the final manuscript.

Consent for publication

Not applicable.

Competing interests

The authors declare they have no competing interests.

Author details

[1]District Hospital Kumba, Kumba, South West Region, Cameroon. [2]Medicine Programme, Faculty of Health Sciences, University of Buea, Buea, Cameroon. [3]Department of Psychiatry, University of North Carolina School of Medicine, Chapel Hill, North Carolina, USA. [4]Health and Human Development Research Group, Douala, Littoral Region, Cameroon. [5]Nuffield Department of Health, Centre for Global Health and Tropical Medicine, University of Oxford, Oxfordshire, UK.

References

1. WHO. Health for all, World Health Organization. Geneva: WHO Publication; 1948.
2. O'Connor E, Rossom RC, Henninger M, Groom HC, Burda BU, Henderson JT, Bigler KD, Whitlock EP. Screening for depression in adults: an updated systematic evidence review for the U.S. preventive services task force. 2016..
3. Okasha A. Mental health in Africa: the role of the WPA. World Psychiatry. 2002;1(1):32–5.
4. Gaynes BN, Pence BW, Atashili J, O'Donnell J, Kats D, Ndumbe PM. Prevalence and predictors of major depression in HIV-infected patients on antiretroviral therapy in Bamenda, a semi-urban center in Cameroon. PLoS One. 2012;7(7):e41699.
5. L'akoa R, Noubiap JJN, Fang Y, Ntone F, Kuaban C. Prevalence and correlates of depressive symptoms in HIV-positive patients: a cross-sectional study among newly diagnosed patients in Yaoundé, Cameroon. BMC Psychiatry. 2013;13(1):228.
6. WHO. Mental health atlas. In: Department of mental health and substance abuse, vol. 2011. Geneva: World Health Organization Publication; 2011. p. 7.
7. Mansouri N, Gharaee B, Shariat SV, Bolhari J, Nooraie RY, Rahimi-Movaghar A, Alirezaie N. The change in attitude and knowledge of health care personnel and general population following trainings provided during integration of mental health in primary health Care in Iran: a systematic review. Int J Ment Health Syst. 2009;3(1):15.
8. Kapungwe A, Cooper S, Mayeya J, Mwanza J, Mwape L, Sikwese A, Lund C. And the mental health and poverty research Programme and consortium. Attitudes of primary health care providers towards people with mental illness: evidence from two districts in Zambia. Afr J Psychiatry. 2011;14(4):290–7.
9. Mbatia J, Shah A, Jenkins R. Knowledge, attitudes and practice pertaining to depression among primary health care workers in Tanzania. Int J Ment Health Syst. 2009;3(1):5.
10. Pence BW, Gaynes BN, Atashili J, O'Donnell JK, Tayong G, Kats D, Whetten R, Whetten K, Njamnshi AK, Ndumbe PM. Validity of an interviewer-administered patient health questionnaire-9 to screen for depression in HIV-infected patients in Cameroon. J Affect Disord. 2012; 143(1–3):208–13.
11. Chen S, Conwell Y, Xu B, Chiu H, Tu X, Ma Y. Depression care management for late-life depression in China primary care: protocol for a randomized controlled trial. Trials. 2011;12(1):121.
12. Baingana F, Thomas R Comblain C. HIV/AIDS and mental health. 2005.
13. Statoids. Annuaire Statistique du Cameroun 2006. Obtained from Institut National de la Statitique du Cameroun. 2009. http://www.statoids.com/ycm.html. Accessed 10 Mar 2018.
14. SWRDPH Demographic data, health districts and public health census for the south west region. 2010.
15. Ndetei DM, Khasakhala LI, Mutiso V, Mbwayo AW. Knowledge, attitude and practice (KAP) of mental illness among staff in general medical facilities in Kenya: practice and policy implications. Afr J Psychiatry. 2011;14(3):225–35.
16. Mahmood-Abadi H, Kayhani M, Rabi M, Mohammadi M. A survey of knowledge and attitudes of non-psychiatrists (medical specialists) treating depression. Thrita. 2012;1:30–3.
17. St. Louis K, Roberts P. Public attitudes toward mental illness in Africa and North America. Afr J Psychiatry. 2013;16:123–33.

18. Olugbile O, Zachariah M, Coker O, Kuyin O, Isichei B. Provision of mental health services in Nigeria. Int Psychiatry. 2008;5(2):32–4.
19. Kerr M, Blizard R, Mann A. General practitioners and psychiatrists: comparison of attitudes to depression using the depression attitude questionnaire. Br J Gen Pract. 1995;45(391):89–92.
20. Norton J, Pommie C, Cogneau J, Haddad M, Ritchie K, Mann A. Beliefs and attitudes of French family practitioners toward depression: the impact of training in mental health. Int J Psychiatry Med. 2011;41(2):107–22.
21. van Rijswijk E, van Hout H, van de Lisdonk E, Zitman F, van Weel C. Barriers in recognizing, diagnosing and managing depressive and anxiety disorders as experienced by family physicians; a focus group study. BMC Fam Pract. 2009; 10(1):52.
22. James B, Jenkins R, Lawani A, Omoaregba J. Depression in primary care: knowledge, attitudes and practice of general practitioners in Benin City, Nigeria. South Afr Fam Pract. 2012;54(1):55–60.
23. Haddad M, Walters P, Tylee A. District nursing and depression: a psychometric evaluation of depression attitude questionnaire findings. Int Journal of Nursing Study. 2007;44(3):447–56.
24. Vandenbroucke JP, von Elm E, Altman DG, Gotzsche PC, Cynthia MD, Pocock SJ, Poole C, Schlessman JJ, Egger M. Strengthening the reporting of observational studies in epidemiology (STROBE): explanation and elaboration. PLoS Med. 2007;4(10):1628–54.
25. Seehusen DA, Baldwin L-M, Runkle GP, Clark G. Are family physicians appropriately screening for postpartum depression? J Am Board Fam Med. 2005;18(2):104–12.
26. Smolders M, Laurent M, Verhaak P, Prins M, Marwijk H, Prenninx B, Wensing M, Grol R. Which physician and practices characteristics are associated with adherence to evidence-based guidelines for depressive and anxiety disorders? Med Care. 2010;48(3):240–8.
27. Thapa P, Rawal N, Bista Y. A study of depression and anxiety in cancer patients. Nepal Med Coll J. 2010;12(3):171–5.
28. Odejide AO, Morakinyo JJ, Oshiname FO, Ajuwon AJ, Kola L. Integrating mental health into primary health care in Nigeria: management of depression in a local government (district) area as a paradigm. Seishin Shinkeigaku Zasshi. 2002;104(10):802–9.
29. Ohtsuki T, Kodaka M, Sakai R, Ishikura F, Watanabe Y, Mann A, Haddad M, Yamada M, Inagki M. Attitudes toward depression among Japanese non-psychiatric medical doctors: a cross-sectional study. BMC Res Notes. 2012;5(1):441.
30. Haddad M, Waqas A, Qayyum W, Shams M, Malik S. The attitudes and beliefs of Pakistani medical practitioners about depression: a cross-sectional study in Lahore using the revised depression attitude questionnaire (R-DAQ). BMC Psychiatry. 2016;16:349.
31. Centers for Disease Control and Prevention, Substance Abuse and Mental Health Services Administration, National Association of County Behavioral Health & Developmental Disability Directors, National Institute of Mental Health, The Carter Center Mental Health Program. Attitudes Toward Mental Illness: Results from the Behavioral Risk Factor Surveillance System. Atlanta; Centers for Disease Control and Prevention; 2012.
32. Botega N, Silveira G. General practitioners' attitudes towards depression: a study in primary care setting in Brazil. Int J Soc Psychiatry. 1996;42(3):230–7.
33. Saeed M, McCall L. General practitioners knowledge and attitude towards anxiety and depression in Abu Dhabi. Middle East J Fam Med. 2006;4(1):1–5.
34. Dowrick C, Gask L, Dixon C, Usherwood T. Do general practitioners' attitudes towards depression predict their clinical behavior? Psychol Med. 2000;30(2):413–9.
35. Furegato ARF, Ferreira da Silva Candido MC, Lobo da Costa M Jr. Comparing knowledge and opinions on depression among nurses in the health services. Rev Salud Pública. 2009;11(2):200–11.
36. Mwape L, Sikwese A, Kapungwe A, Mwanza J, Flisher A, Lund C, Cooper J. Integrating mental health into primary health care in Zambia: a care provider's perspective. Int J Ment Health Syst. 2010;4(1):21.
37. Haddad M, Menchetti M, Walters P, Norton J, Tylee A, Mann A. Clinicians' attitudes to depression in Europe: a pooled analysis of depression attitude questionnaire findings. Fam Pract. 2012;29(2):121–30.

10

Major anxiety disorders in Iran: prevalence, sociodemographic correlates and service utilization

Ahmad Hajebi[1,2], Seyed Abbas Motevalian[1,3*], Afarin Rahimi-Movaghar[4], Vandad Sharifi[5,6], Masoumeh Amin-Esmaeili[4], Reza Radgoodarzi[4] and Mitra Hefazi[4]

Abstract

Background: It has been shown in the past two decades that anxiety disorders are the most common mental disorders in general population across the world. This study sought to assess the prevalence of major anxiety disorders, their sociodemographic correlates and mental health service utilization as part of the Iranian Mental Health Survey (IranMHS).

Methods: A national household face-to-face survey was carried out on a representative sample of Iranian adults from January to June 2011 using Composite International Diagnostic Interview (CIDI 2.1). A total of 7886 subjects between 15 and 64 years who can understand Persian language were included. The 12-month prevalence of anxiety disorders according to Diagnostic and Statistical Manual of Mental Disorders, Fourth Edition (DSM-IV), their socio-demographic correlates, health service use and days out of role were measured in this study.

Results: The 12-month prevalence of anxiety disorders (not including specific phobias) was 15.6%. The prevalence was 12.0% in males and 19.4% in females. The three most prevalent anxiety disorders were generalized anxiety disorder (5.2%), obsessive-compulsive disorder (5.1%) and social phobia (3.2%), respectively. Factors found to be significantly associated with anxiety disorders were: female gender (OR = 1.16, 95% CI: 1.09–1.23), middle (OR = 1.23, 95%CI: 1.01–1.50) or low (OR = 1.66, 95%CI: 1.31–2.10) socioeconomic status, unemployment (OR = 1.98, 95%CI: 1.49–2.62), and urban residence (OR = 1.31, 95%CI: 1.10–1.57). Comorbidity with non-anxiety disorders significantly increased service utilization. In all subgroups, service utilization was higher among females while the number of days out of role was higher among males.

Conclusions: Anxiety disorders are common conditions with a higher prevalence among the female gender, unemployed individuals, and people with low socioeconomic conditions living in urban areas. Comorbidity of anxiety disorders with other psychological disorders aggravates the disability and significantly increases the number of days out of role.

Keywords: Anxiety disorders, Generalized anxiety disorder, Obsessive-compulsive disorder, PTSD, Social phobia, Mental health services

* Correspondence: motevalian.a@iums.ac.ir
[1]Research Center for Addiction and Risky Behavior (ReCARB), Iran University of Medical Sciences, Tehran, Iran
[3]Department of Epidemiology, School of Public Health, Iran University of Medical Sciences, Crossroads of Hemmat and Chamran Highways, Tehran, Iran
Full list of author information is available at the end of the article

Background

Anxiety disorders are a group of psychological conditions characterized by an intense sense of anxiety and fear. Patients are mainly anxious about the future and their fear is a reaction to the current events. Several types of anxiety disorders exist, each with specific characteristics. However, they all share the signs and symptoms of anxiety. Anxiety disorders are often accompanied by other psychological conditions particularly major depressive disorder [1].

Epidemiologic studies conducted in the past two decades worldwide have shown that anxiety disorders are the most common mental disorders in general population [2–4]. The 12-month prevalence of anxiety disorders in different regions ranged from 6.4% in European nations [2] to 14.4 and 18.1% in Australia [3] and United States [4], respectively. Most of the anxiety disorders are more prevalent among women [5] and in developed compared to developing countries [6].

Epidemiologic studies have revealed that a significant percentage of Iranians are afflicted with mental disorders and psychological conditions. Study of the burden of diseases in Iran indicated that mental disorders ranked second after unintentional injuries in terms of burden of disease in Iran, comprising 16% of the overall burden of diseases [7]. In another study, the lifelong prevalence of psychological disorders was 10.8% in Iran, and anxiety disorders with a prevalence of 8.4% were reported to be the most common condition [8].

The Iranian Mental Health Survey (IranMHS) was carried out to estimate the prevalence, severity, service utilization pattern and costs of mental disorders. It has been the first study to assess the prevalence of psychological disorders in the national scale using the 12-month version of the Composite International Diagnostic Interview (CIDI 2.1) [9]. The current study aimed to assess the 12-month prevalence and severity of different types of anxiety disorders and their sociodemographic correlates in Iran.

Methods

Sample and study setting

The IranMHS was a national household survey with face-to-face interview carried out on a representative sample of Iranian adults aged 15–64 years. The exclusion criteria were: a) not understanding Persian language (4.8% of eligible individuals), b) not to be able to respond because of any severe illness (0.7%), c) not accessible at household during the study period (3.7%). The detailed methodology of the study has already been published [10]. A three-stage random sampling scheme was applied. In the first stage, 1525 blocks were chosen proportional to size of the population of each province based on the most recent national census. In the second stage, six households in each block were chosen by systematic random sampling and in the third stage, one member of each household was selected using the Kish grid tables. The study was carried out from January to June 2011 with a sample size of 7886 individuals. Among the 9150 households identified by interviewers; 506 (5.5%), 230 (2.5%), 329 (3.6%) and 98 (1.1%) did not participate in the study; respectively because of household refusal, household unavailability after at least 3 in-person contact, individual refusal and individual unavailability after 3 in-person contacts. Besides this, 17 (0.2%) respondents were found ineligible during interview and 84 (0.9%) questionnaires were eliminated because of their low quality. So, finally 7886 individuals out of 9150 households successfully participated in the study and the response rate was 86.2%.

Variables and instruments

To assess the prevalence of anxiety disorders, Composite International Diagnostic Interview (CIDI2.1) was applied. This tool is a comprehensive, standard interview designed by the World Health Organization (WHO) to assess the 12-month prevalence of psychological disorders according to Diagnostic and Statistical Manual of Mental Disorders, Fourth Edition (DSM-IV). The anxiety disorders studied in IranMHS included: panic disorders (with and without agoraphobia), agoraphobia without panic disorder, Obsessive-Compulsive Disorder (OCD), social phobia, Generalized Anxiety Disorder (GAD) and Post-Traumatic Stress Disorder (PTSD). Sheehan Disability Scale (SDS) was used to assess the disability associated with psychiatric disorders [11]. Persian version of SDS, similar to its English version, has adequate validity and reliability [12]. We developed a service use questionnaire and evaluated its psychometric properties in the preliminary phase of the Iran-MHS as described elsewhere [10]. Socioeconomic status of participants was assessed using a household asset questionnaire. Principal component analysis was performed to estimate a socioeconomic score for each of the participants.

Interviewer training, quality control, ethics and informed consent

Interviewers were 232 professionals with a university degree in psychology. Training consisted of a 56-h workshop of instruction and practice sessions that took place in 7 consecutive days in Tehran. Each Interviewer also took part in at least 2 pilot interviews with real subjects before the main phase of the study; and received appropriate feedback from experienced interviewers. In each province, a local executive manager and a supervisor (a member of research team) were assigned to ensure the quality of the procedures. The feasibility and acceptability of the interviews and the study limitations were assessed in a pilot study in selected urban and rural areas of Tehran and Khoozestan province. All interviews were conducted face-to-face at subjects' place of residence. We made our best efforts to make sure that all interviews were conducted in privacy. All completed questionnaires were reviewed and edited by the local executive manager. A third of all questionnaires were double-checked by a supervisor. Errors or inconsistencies were returned to the interviewers for resolution. This involved re-interview with the participants in some cases.

Sampling weights and statistical analysis

Sampling weights were calculated so that each respondent can be inflated to represent other individuals in Iran. The consolidated weights (w) were the joint product of inverse probability of unit selection into the sample (w1), non-response weights (w2) and post-stratification weights (w3): w = w1*w2*w3.

To calculate the post-stratification weights (w3), the proportion of subjects in each stratum in National Census 2006 was divided by the proportion of the same group in the sample. Based on 5-year age groups, sex and urban\-rural place of residence in each of 31 country provinces, 1240 post-stratification weights were generated.

The sample sociodemographic structure was slightly different with national census data in terms of over-presentation of women, rural residents, homemakers and married individuals. However, after applying weighting procedures and doing complex sample analysis; the weighted proportions of different sociodemographic groups in the sample were found very similar to the census structure. The details are available in study protocol paper [10].

All statistical analyses including point prevalence estimates and their confidence interval were carried out using complex sample analysis procedures for taking into account the multi-stage sampling method and sampling weights. Data were analyzed using STATA/SE 10.0 software. Logistic regression (taking into account the complex sample structure) was applied to assess the association between independent variables and the study outcomes.

Results

The overall prevalence of anxiety disorders in the past 12 months in the national MHS was found to be 15.6%. This rate was 12% in males and 19.4% in females. Higher prevalence of anxiety disorders in females compared to males was found for all types of anxiety disorders (Table 1). The three most common anxiety disorders in the study population were generalized anxiety disorder (5.2%), obsessive-compulsive disorder (5.1%) and social phobia (3.2%).

The sex-specific interval estimates for 12-month prevalence of any anxiety disorder by demographic factors including: age groups, marital status, education, occupation, place of residence and socioeconomic status are described in Table 2. The findings shows that the higher prevalence of anxiety disorders in women is more prominent in younger age groups and it almost disappears in the oldest age group. Similarly, the gender difference of anxiety disorders is observed in both currently married and never married groups but the prevalence is almost equal between men and women in previously married participants. Another interesting finding is the decreasing trend of anxiety disorders by increasing educational level in male participants. Among female subjects, prevalence of anxiety disorders is highest in the middle education groups.

The association of sociodemographic variables with any anxiety disorder and the four most common diagnoses (namely: GAD, OCD, social phobia and PTSD) were assessed by applying five separate multivariate logistic regression analyses whose results are summarized in Table 3. The findings showed that female sex (Adjusted Odds Ratio = 1.16), unemployment (AOR = 1.98), urban living (AOR = 1.31) and moderate (AOR = 1.23) or low (AOR = 1.49) socioeconomic status were significantly associated with higher prevalence of any anxiety disorders. Being married (AOR = 1.51), unemployment (AOR = 2.15), urban living (AOR = 1.77) and low socioeconomic status (AOR = 1.54) were significantly associated with GAD. Young age, female sex (AOR = 1.17), unemployment (AOR = 2.45) and urban living (AOR = 1.37) were significantly associated with OCD. Female sex (AOR = 1.19), retirement (AOR = 3.79) and moderate (AOR = 1.76) and low (AOR = 2.85) socioeconomic status were significantly associated with social phobia. The only variable showing a significant association with PTSD was being divorced or widowed (AOR = 2.68).

Table 1 Twelve-month prevalence of anxiety disorders in IranMHS ($n = 7886$)

Type of disorder	n	Total % (95%CI)	Female % (95%CI)	Male % (95%CI)
Any anxiety disorder		15.6 (14.5–16.6)	19.4 (17.9–20.9)	12.0 (10.6–13.4)
Panic disorder with/ without agoraphobia	178	1.9 (1.6–2.3)	2.5 (2.0–3.0)	1.4 (0.9–1.8)
Agoraphobia without panic	118	1.5 (1.1–1.8)	2.0 (1.5–2.5)	0.9 (0.5–1.4)
Social phobia	274	3.2 (2.7–3.6)	4.1 (3.4–4.8)	2.3 (1.7–2.9)
Generalized anxiety disorder	427	5.2 (4.6–5.8)	5.9 (5.2–6.7)	4.5 (3.7–5.4)
Obsessive-compulsive disorder	408	5.1 (4.5–5.7)	6.8 (5.9–7.6)	3.4 (2.7–4.1)
Post-traumatic stress disorder	169	2.1 (1.7–2.4)	2.4 (1.9–3.0)	1.7 (1.2–2.3)

Table 2 Twelve-month prevalence of any anxiety disorders by socio-demographic characteristics

Variables	*n*	Any anxiety disorder			
		Female (*n* = 4499)		Male(*n* = 3387)	
		%	95% CI	%	95% CI
Age groups					
15–19	998	20.1	16.0–24.2	11.0	7.7–14.4
20–29	2549	19.7	17.4–22.0	11.6	9.3–13.9
30–39	2200	19.2	16.7–21.8	12.8	10.3–15.2
40–49	1188	19.2	15.5–22.8	12.8	9.4–16.3
50–59	704	19.6	14.7–24.6	11.6	6.7–16.4
60–64	247	13.8	7.6–20.0	13.5	4.0–23.1
Marital status					
Never married	2025	18.9	15.9–21.8	11.9	9.7–14.2
Married	5527	19.5	17.8–21.2	11.8	10.2–13.5
Previously Married	332	20.3	14.6–25.9	18.3	5.2–31.3
Education					
Illiterate	646	17.7	13.6–21.9	19.3	9.9–28.7
Primary	1917	22.3	19.2–25.3	12.2	9.3–15
Secondary	1280	24.1	20.1–28.2	12.9	9.9–15.9
High school	2823	18.1	15.7–20.5	11.9	9.6–14.1
University	1208	16	12.8–19.1	10.5	7.5–13.4
Occupation					
Employed	2803	17.9	14–21.8	10.9	9.4–12.5
Student	937	16.3	12.5–20.2	9.2	6.1–12.4
Retired	166	16.3	6.7–25.9	11.5	4.9–18.1
Housekeeper	3241	19.6	17.8–21.3	NA	
Unemployed	737	29.4	22.5–36.3	20.5	15.9–25.2
Place of Residence					
Urban	4380	19.1	17.2–21.0	12.5	10.7–14.2
Rural	3506	20.1	17.8–22.4	10.8	8.8–12.8
Socio-economic status					
Low	2152	23.3	20.4–26.2	16.1	12.9–19.3
Moderate	3191	19.5	17.3–21.8	12	9.8–14.2
High	2330	16.5	14.1–19.0	9.6	7.6–11.6

In Table 4; health service utilization, days out of role and severity of functional impairment are compared between four groups: [1] no disorder at all, [2] subjects with anxiety disorders only, [3] subjects with non-anxiety disorders only, and [4] subjects suffering from both anxiety and non-anxiety disorders. Comparison of service utilization showed that group 4 had the highest rate of utilization of services followed by groups 3 and 2. In other words, subjects with anxiety disorders alone had used health services less frequently than the other two groups of patients. Another important finding was that in all four groups, females had used services more frequently than males. However, this difference in some of the groups did not reach statistical significance. Both number of days out of role and severity of impairment were highest in group 4 followed by groups 3 and 2. None of these two were had statistically significant difference between men and women.

The prevalence of major depressive disorder (single or recurrent episode) among individuals who had any anxiety disorders was 42.9% (CI95%: 39.4–46.5%) while this prevalence proportion was 6.8% (CI95%: 6.0–7.6%) among those who did not have any anxiety disorders.

Discussion

This study was the first to determine the prevalence of psychiatric disorders in the national level in Iran using a diagnostic tool like CIDI. Application of this tool allows for the comparison of results of this study with those conducted in other countries. In our study, the prevalence of anxiety disorders (15.6%) was higher than that of other psychiatric disorders. In the World Mental Health Survey, in all countries except for Ukraine, the prevalence of anxiety disorders was higher than that of other psychiatric disorders [13]. It is also noteworthy that the prevalence of anxiety disorders in all countries participating in the World Mental Health Survey except for the United States (18.2%) was lower than the rate in Iran [13]. Although some other diagnostic tools have been used in previous studies conducted in Iran, they reported higher prevalence of anxiety compared to other conditions, similar to the current investigation [8, 14, 15].

The current study results also showed that among anxiety disorders, the highest prevalence belonged to generalized anxiety disorder (5.2%) and obsessive-compulsive disorder (5.1%) while the lowest prevalence belonged to panic disorder with agoraphobia (0.5%). The results of our study regarding the prevalence of anxiety disorders are different from those of Mohammadi et al., [8]. In their study, the prevalence of phobia disorders (2.1%) was the highest followed by obsessive-compulsive disorder (1.8%) and panic disorder (1.5%). In a national survey in Australia [3], the most common anxiety disorder was PTSD (6.4%). In a study in Northern Ireland [16], the most common anxiety disorders were specific phobia (7.2%) and PTSD (5.1%), followed by social phobia (4.0%). In the United States [4], the highest prevalent anxiety disorders were specific phobia (8.7%), social phobia (6.8%), PTSD (3.5%) and GAD (3.1%), respectively. A study in Greece, showed that the prevalence (past seven days) of GAD, panic disorder and OCD were 4.1, 1.9 and 1.7%, respectively [17].

In the current study, assessment of the prevalence of anxiety disorders in the past 12 months prior to the interview showed that these disorders were more prevalent among women. This predilection for female gender was true for all types of anxiety disorders. Previous

Table 3 Socio-demographic correlates of anxiety disorders, findings of multiple logistic regression analysis

Variables	Any anxiety disorder	GAD	OCD	Social Phobia	PTSD
	Adjusted OR (95% CI)	Adjusted OR (95% CI)	Adjusted OR (95% CI)	Adjusted OR (95% CI)	Adjusted OR (95% CI)
Age groups					
15–19	1.0	1.0	1.0	1.0	1.0
20–29	0.88(0.66–1.20)	1.41(0.81–2.47)	1.17(1.06–1.30)[a]	1.20(0.70–2.06)	0.77(0.36–1.67)
30–39	0.89(0.64–1.24)	1.43(0.77–2.64)	0.86(0.55–1.35)	1.73(0.92–3.28)	0.70(0.32–1.55)
40–49	0.88(0.61–1.27)	1.47(0.76–2.86)	0.77(0.46–1.28)	1.09(0.53–2.26)	1.02(0.44–2.34)
50–59	0.85(0.55–1.31)	1.98(0.98–3.99)	0.52(0.29–0.94)	0.48(0.18–1.27)	1.15(0.43–3.08)
60–64	0.71(0.36–1.36)	2.16(0.79–5.93)	0.12(0.03–0.57)	0.29(0.07–1.23)	0.25(0.05–1.33)
Gender					
Male	1.0	1.0	1.0	1.0	1.0
Female	1.16(1.09–1.23)[a]	1.06(0.97–1.16)	1.17(1.06–1.30)[a]	1.19(1.08–1.32)[a]	1.11(0.95–1.28)
Marital status					
Never married	1.0	1.0	1.0	1.0	1.0
Married	1.08(0.85–1.36)	1.51(1.06–2.16)[a]	0.97(0.68–1.39)	0.58(0.38–0.89)	1.66(0.92–3.01)
Previously Married	1.09(0.71–1.67)	1.31(0.69–2.53)	1.01(0.51–2.00)	0.87(0.41–1.85)	2.68(1.02–7.04)[a]
Education					
Illiterate	1.0	1.0	1.0	1.0	1.0
Primary	1.09(0.78–1.53)	1.56(0.94–2.59)	0.84(0.48–1.46)	0.74(0.39–1.40)	1.41(0.64–3.10)
Secondary	1.19(0.83–1.71)	1.14(0.65–1.98)	0.87(0.50–1.52)	1.33(0.66–2.67)	1.34(0.57–3.17)
High school	1.01(0.71–1.44)	1.35(0.77–2.34)	0.63(0.36–1.12)	0.95(0.48–1.87)	1.16(0.50–2.69)
University	0.96(0.63–1.46)	1.59(0.82–3.10)	0.53(0.27–1.03)	1.17(0.52–2.63)	0.54(0.15–1.97)
Occupation					
Employed	1.0	1.0	1.0	1.0	1.0
Student	0.94(0.66–1.34)	0.82(0.45–1.51)	1.20(0.67–2.15)	1.22(0.66–2.26)	0.78(0.28–2.19)
Retired	1.16(0.64–2.11)	0.80(0.33–1.92)	1.54(.54–4.43)	3.79(1.19–12.1)[a]	0.27(0.03–2.28)
Housekeeper	1.07(0.82–1.40)	1.08(0.71–1.64)	1.29(0.80–2.07)	1.04(0.63–1.73)	0.81(0.42–1.58)
Unemployed	1.98(1.49–2.62)[a]	2.15(1.43–3.22)[a]	2.45(1.62–3.71)[a]	1.39(0.81–2.37)	1.44(0.71–2.89)
Place of Residence					
Rural	1.0	1.0	1.0	1.0	1.0
Urban	1.31(1.10–1.57)[a]	1.77(1.34–2.35)[a]	1.37(1.05–1.78)[a]	1.08(0.77–1.53)	0.96(0.66–1.41)
Socio-economic status					
High	1.0	1.0	1.0	1.0	1.0
Moderate	1.23(1.01–1.50)[a]	1.19(0.88–1.61)	1.13(0.81–1.57)	1.76(1.12–2.75)[a]	1.02(0.61–1.70)
Low	1.66(1.31–2.10)[a]	1.54(1.08–2.18)[a]	1.15(0.79–1.66)	2.85(1.71–4.74)[a]	1.37(0.82–1.41)

[a]highlights the statistically significant Odds Ratios

studies (both in Iran and other countries) yielded the same results as well [3, 4, 8]. The reasons behind the higher prevalence of anxiety disorders in females have yet to be clearly understood. Some previous studies have discussed the possible role of genetics in combination with environmental factors [18]. Others suggest the possible role of female sex hormones and related cycles in this regard [19, 20]. Imaging studies have shown that the anterior cingulate cortex in females with high fear response and harm avoidance is larger and more active than that in males with similar characteristics [21]. Although these findings have not been evaluated for all types of anxiety disorders, preliminary results show the higher susceptibility of women to anxiety disorders compared to men.

The results of the current study showed that the prevalence of anxiety disorders in females during the study period was higher in adolescents and young adults

Table 4 Comparison of health service use and days out of role by anxiety and co-morbidity disorders

Variable		*n*	Health service use % (95% CI)	Days out of roles Mean (95% CI)	Severe impairment[a] % (95% CI)
No disorder	Male	2575	5.85 (4.70–7.00)	2.52 (1.93–3.11)	3.07 (2.19–3.96)
	Female	3033	12.85 (11.43–14.28)	2.36 (1.93–2.79)	3.50 (2.79–4.27)
Any anxiety disorder without comorbidity	Male	182	21.06 (14.54–27.58)	12.35 (7.44–17.27)	13.41 (7.48–19.35)
	Female	422	26.75 (21.86–31.64)	10.48 (6.07–14.90)	13.01 (8.65–17.37)
Any mental disorder not including anxiety disorders	Male	253	26.46 (20.21–32.71)	24.40 (16.83–31.97)	16.33 (10.96–21.70)
	Female	302	38.43 (31.54–45.32)	10.99 (8.16–13.81)	23.16 (17.70–28.61)
Any anxiety disorder comorbid with other mental disorders	Male	205	34.97 (27.19–42.75)	31.99 (23.57–40.42)	33.54 (25.92–41.16)
	Female	400	54.42 (48.52–60.31)	26.91 (21.60–32.16)	33.35 (27.82–38.87)

[a]At least two items of Sheehan with 70% or more disability

compared to other age groups. However, in males, this rate was reported to be higher among the middle-aged. Since the current study had a cross-sectional design, the obtained results can only indicate the higher prevalence of anxiety disorders in women at younger ages compared to men during the study period. Therefore, longitudinal studies are required to further scrutinize this topic.

This study revealed that aside from the significant role of female sex in prevalence of anxiety disorders, some other demographic factors could significantly affect the prevalence of these conditions. Low socioeconomic status, illiteracy, low level of education, unemployment and urban living are among the most important factors found in the current study. Evidence shows that people with lower socioeconomic status have poorer health indices [22]. Low level of education, low income, unhealthy lifestyle and occupational conditions and stress are among the socioeconomic factors often associated with poor health [23]. Evidence shows that illiteracy and low level of education marginalize people [24], decrease the access and utilization of available mental health services and interfere with some valuable goals in a community such as health promotion and access to social support and health care services [25, 26]. Low level of education is also correlated with poverty, unemployment and incarceration [26]. However, some studies have reported that if other factors such as social support are controlled, low level of education cannot serve as an independent risk factor for mental health problems [27]. Unemployment increases the risk of development and progression of psychiatric disorders and strong evidence is available in this regard for depression and anxiety disorders [28, 29]. Understanding of the fact that unemployment is a risk factor for occurrence of mental disorders plays a critical role in clinical and socioeconomic interventions. Although, this association might be the consequence of reverse causality. It means that unemployment might be the outcome of a psychiatric disorder, for example, Mojtabi et al. showed that having a mental illness can be accompanied by an increase in the chance of unemployment in the future [30]. Evidence shows that urban living has some advantages and disadvantages [31] and has been proposed as a risk factor for mental health disturbances [32, 33]. Air pollution, traffic noise, deprived districts, crime and poor social communication can adversely affect mental health [34]. Studies using magnetic resonance imaging have revealed increased activity of amygdala in urban residents when processing social stresses due to urban environment. Also, changed activity of perigenual anterior cingulate cortex has been found in subjects raised in urban areas. This region of the brain regulates the activity of amygdala, negative emotions and stresses [35]. However, it is difficult to recognize what specific characteristic of urban living/environment causes psychiatric disorders [36].

The current study revealed that presence of comorbidity in patients with anxiety disorders increased the percentage of service utilization, number of days out of role due to disorder and the percentage of individuals that developed severe disability. These results are in accord with the findings of studies showing that presence of a comorbidity in patients with anxiety disorders increased the severity of psychopathology, caused dysfunction and disability [37] and decreased the quality of life [38]. Presence of comorbidity can also affect the outcome of treatment of anxiety disorders [39] and is associated with an increase in signs and symptoms of anxiety disorders even after treatment [40]. The results of our study showed that both males and females with anxiety disorders used services more than subjects with no disorder, which is in accord with the findings of NCS-R study [41].

In our study, number of days out of role was higher in men compared to women, which is in contrast to the findings of a study conducted in the United States on the data provided by the collaborative psychiatric epidemiology studies (CPES) [5]. They showed that anxiety disorders in women were associated with higher number of days out of role. Possible reasons may be comorbidity of anxiety disorders with other conditions in women, higher social acceptance of sickness absence of women or a combination of both. One possible, yet important, reason of low number of days out of role in women in the national MHS in Iran is the attitude of a significant number of Iranian women towards being a housewife. A considerable percentage of women in our study were housewives. In most Iranian subcultures, being a housewife is not considered an occupation and therefore, it is not reported as one. Not being able to perform household tasks due to psychiatric disorders is not normally noticed and therefore, it is not reported by the subjects; this results in underestimation of data in this regard.

Limitations

The major limitation of this study is not including specific phobias. In most population-based studies, specific phobias are found to be the most common type of anxiety disorders. So, the prevalence of any anxiety disorders we presented in this study is underestimated. In contrast to the World Mental Health Survey which had been administered in two steps [2], IranMHS was implemented in a single step. So the questionnaire was too long, and after exhaustive consultations, the study team decided to not include specific phobias in this study because of their less impact on the burden of psychiatric disorders [7].

Also, in this study it was not possible to translate CIDI to local languages; thus, those who were not able to understand Persian were excluded. This group of individuals comprised 4.8% of the target population and we have no information about the prevalence of anxiety disorders in this group. Thus, this may be considered as another limitation of this study. Considering the cross-sectional design of our study, we were not able to determine the precedence order of the factors such as socioeconomic status or unemployment and occurrence of anxiety disorders to analyze the role of influential factors. This is an inherent limitation of causal inference in all cross-sectional studies.

Conclusion

The national MHS showed that anxiety disorders in Iran, similar to most countries participating in the World Mental Health Survey [2], were the most common type of psychiatric disorders. The prevalence of anxiety disorders (of all types) in females was 1.5 times the rate in males. These disorders were more commonly reported in adolescent and young-adult females and middle-aged males. Moreover, these disorders were more prevalent among the widowed, divorced, illiterate and unemployed female urban residents and male rural residents. Approximately, 50% of patients suffering from an anxiety disorder had at least one other psychiatric comorbidity. Based on the results, special attention must be paid to anxiety disorders because these conditions along with comorbidity significantly increase the severity of disability, number of days out of role and percentage of health service utilization. Increasing the quantitative capacity and promoting the quality of health care services provided, especially in the primary health care system, can enhance early detection and prompt treatment of these conditions and consequently decrease their prevalence and risk of chronicity.

Acknowledgments

We wish to thank Dr. Ronald C. Kessler and Dr. Ramin Mojtabai for their invaluable contributions to our study. We also acknowledge supports received from Dr. Hassan Emami Razavi, Dr. Ali Reza Mesdaghinia, Dr. Akbar Fotoohi, Dr. Masood Younesian, Dr. Mohammad Bagher Saberi Zafarghandi, Dr. Abbas Ali Nasehi, Dr. Mohammad Reza Mohammadi and Dr. Minoo Mohraz and contributions of Dr. Samaneh Kariman, Maryam Gholamrezaei, Leila Moazami Goodarzi, Farideh Kolahi Heshmat, Dr. Reza Mahdavi, Dr. Siamak Molavi and Fahima Farrahi in conducting the study. We also wish to thank provincial executive managers and interviewers, as well as all the participants in the study.

Funding

The Iranian Mental Health Survey (IranMHS) was supported by supported by the Ministry of Health through the contract number 132–1491 of Tehran University of Medical Sciences and the contract number 89-D-432-143 of Mental Health Research Network. The funding source had no role in the study design, the collection, analysis and interpretation of data, the writing of the report, or in the decision to submit the article for publication.

Authors' contributions

All authors were involved in study conceptualization, design, training of the interviewers, quality control and interpretation of the results. ARM was the principal investigator of IranMHS. Statistical analyses were performed by SAM. All authors had full access to all of the data in the study. Preparation of the manuscript was performed by AH and SAM. All authors have read and approved the final manuscript.

Consent for publication

Not applicable.

Competing interests

The authors declare that they have no competing interests.

Author details

[1]Research Center for Addiction and Risky Behavior (ReCARB), Iran University of Medical Sciences, Tehran, Iran. [2]Department of Psychiatry, School of Medicine, Iran University of Medical Sciences, Tehran, Iran. [3]Department of Epidemiology, School of Public Health, Iran University of Medical Sciences, Crossroads of Hemmat and Chamran Highways, Tehran, Iran. [4]Iranian National Center for Addiction Studies (INCAS), Tehran University of Medical Sciences, Tehran, Iran. [5]Psychiatry and Psychology Research Center, Tehran University of Medical Sciences, Tehran, Iran. [6]Department of Psychiatry, School of Medicine, Tehran University of Medical Sciences, Tehran, Iran.

References

1. Aina Y, Susman JL. Understanding comorbidity with depression and anxiety disorders. J Am Osteopath Assoc. 2006;106(5 Suppl 2):S9–14. [PubMed]
2. Alonso J, Lepine JP. Overview of key data from the European study of the epidemiology of mental disorders (ESEMeD). J Clin Psychiatry. 2007; 68(Suppl. 2):3–9. [PubMed]

3. Slade T, Johnston A, Teesson M, Whiteford H, Burgess P, Pirkis J, Saw S. The Mental Health of Australians 2. Report on the 2007 National Survey of mental health and wellbeing. Canberra: Department of Health and Ageing; 2009.
4. Kessler RC, Chiu WT, Demler O, Merikangas KR, Walters EE. Prevalence, severity, and comorbidity of 12-month DSM-IV disorders in the National Comorbidity Survey Replication. Arch Gen Psychiatry. 2005;62(6):617–27.
5. McLean CP, Asnaani A, Litz BT, Hofmann SG. Gender differences in anxiety disorders: prevalence, course of illness, comorbidity and burden of illness. J Psychiatr Res. 2011;45(8):1027–35.
6. Kessler RC, Aguilar-Gaxiola S, Alonso J, Chatterji S, Lee S, Ormel J, Ustün TB, Wang PS. The global burden of mental disorders: an update from the WHO world mental health (WMH) surveys. Epidemiol Psichiatr Soc. 2009;18(1):23–33.
7. Naghavi M, Abolhassani F, Pourmalek F, Lakeh M, Jafari N, Vaseghi S, Mahdavi Hezaveh N, Kazemeini H. The burden of disease and injury in Iran 2003. Popul Health Metr. 2009;7:9.
8. Mohammadi MR, Davidian H, Noorbala AA, Malekafzali H, Naghavi HR, Pouretemad HR, et al. An epidemiological survey of psychiatric disorders in Iran. Clin Pract Epidemiol Ment Health. 2005;1:16.
9. Sharifi V, Amin-Esmaeili M, Hajebi A, Motevalian A, Radgoodarzi R, Hefazi M, Rahimi-Movaghar A. Twelve-month prevalence and correlates of psychiatric disorders in Iran: the Iranian mental health survey, 2011. Arch Iran Med. 2015;18(2):76–84. [PubMed]
10. Rahimi-Movaghar A, Amin-Esmaeili M, Sharifi V, Hajebi A, Radgoodarzi R, Hefazi M, Motevalian A. Iranian mental health survey: design and field procedures. Iran J Psychiatry. 2014;9:96–109. [PubMed]
11. Sheehan DV, Harnett-Sheehan K, Raj BA. The measurement of disability. Int Clin Psychopharmacol. 1996;11 Suppl 3:89–95.
12. Amin-Esmaeili M, Motevalian SA, Rahimi-Movaghar A, Hajebi A, Hefazi M, Rad Goodarzi R, Sharifi V. Sheehan disability scale: translation and psychometric assessment of the Persian version. Iran J psych. 2014;9(3):125–32.
13. The WHO World Mental Health Survey Consortium. Prevalence, severity, and unmet need for treatment of mental disorders in the World Health Organization world mental health surveys. JAMA. 2004;291(21):2581–90.
14. Noorbala AA, Yazdi SAB, Yasamy MT, Mohammad K. Mental health survey of the adult population in Iran. Br J Psychiatry. 2004;184:70–3.
15. Noorbala AA, Bagheri Yazdi SA, Hafezi M. Trends in change of mental health status in the population of Tehran between 1998 and 2007. Arch Iran Med. 2012;15(4):201–4. [PubMed]
16. Bunting B, Murphy S, O'Neill S, Ferry F. Prevalence and treatment of 12-month DSM-IV disorders in the Northern Ireland study of health and stress. Soc Psychiatry Psychiatr Epidemiol. 2013;48(1):81–93.
17. Skapinakis P, Bellos S, Koupidis S, Grammatikopoulos I, Theodorakis PN, Mavreas V. Prevalence and sociodemographic associations of common mental disorders in a nationally representative sample of the general population of Greece. BMC Psychiatry. 2013;13:163.
18. Kendler KS, Walters EE, Neale MC, Kessler RC, Heath AC, Eaves LJ. The structure of the genetic and environmental risk factors for six major psychiatric disorders in women. Phobia, generalized anxiety disorder, panic disorder, bulimia, major depression, and alcoholism. Arch Gen Psychiatry. 1995;52(5):374–83.
19. Shear MK. Anxiety disorders in women: gender-related modulation of neurobiology and behavior. Semin Reprod Endocrinol. 1997;15(1):69–76.
20. Redmond G. Mood disorders in the female patient. Int J Fertil Womens Med. 1997;42(2):67–72. [PubMed]
21. Butler T, Pan H, Epstein J, Protopopescu X, Tuescher O, Goldstein M, et al. Fear-related activity in subgenual anterior cingulate differs between men and women. Neuroreport. 2005;16(11):1233–6.
22. Marmot M. The status syndrome: how social standing affects our health and longevity. New York: Owl Books; 2004.
23. World Health Organization. Closing the gap: policy into practice on social determinants of health: discussion paper. Rio de Janeiro: WHO; 2011.
24. Luke A. Critical literacy: foundational notes. Theory Pract. 2012;51(1):4–11.
25. Lincoln A, Espejo D, Johnson P, Paasche-Orlow M, Speckman JL, Webber TL, White RF. Limited literacy and psychiatric disorders among users of an urban safety-net hospital's mental health outpatient clinic. J Nerv Ment Dis. 2008;196(9):687–93.
26. Vijayalakshmi P. Ramachandra, Reddemma K, math SB. Perceived human rights violation in persons with mental illness: role of education. Int J Soc Psychiatry. 2013;59(4):351–64.
27. Lincoln A, Paasche-Orlow MK, Cheng DM, Lloyd-Travaglini C, Caruso C, Saitz R, Samet JH. Impact of health literacy on depressive symptoms and mental health-related: quality of life among adults with addiction. J Gen Intern Med. 2006;21(8):818–22.
28. Zhang S, Bhavsar V. Unemployment as a risk factor for mental illness: combining social and psychiatric literature. Adv Appl Sociol. 2013;3(2):131–6.
29. Paul KI, Moser K. Unemployment impairs mental health: meta-analysis. J Vocat Behav. 2009;74:264–82.
30. Mojtabai R, Stuart EA, Hwang I, Susukida R, Eaton WW, Sampson N, Kessler RC. Long-term effects of mental disorders on employment in the National Comorbidity Survey ten-year Follow-up. Soc Psychiatry Psychiatr Epidemiol. 2015;50(11):1657–68.
31. Eckert S, Kohler S. Urbanization and health in developing countries: a systematic review. World Health Popul. 2014;15:7–20.
32. Heinz A, Deserno L, Reininghaus U. Urbanicity, Social Adversity and Psychosis. World Psychiatry. 2013;12:187–97.
33. Vassos E, Pedersen CB, Murray RM, Collier DA, Lewis CM. Meta-analysis of the association of urbanicity with schizophrenia. Schizophr Bull. 2012;38(6):1118–23.
34. Vlahov D, Galea S. Urbanization, urbanicity, and health. J Urban Health. 2002;79(Suppl 1):S1–S12.
35. Lederbogen F, Kirsch P, Haddad L, Streit F, Tost H, Schuch P, Wüst S, Pruessner JC, Rietschel M, Deuschle M, Meyer-Lindenberg A. City living and urban upbringing affect neural social stress processing in humans. Nature. 2011;474(7352):498–501.
36. Mair C, Diez Roux AV, Galea S. Are neighbourhood characteristics associated with depressive symptoms? A review of evidence. J Epidemiol Community Health. 2008;62(11):940–6. 8 p following 946
37. Coryell W, Endicott J, Andreasen NC, Keller MB, Clayton PJ, Hirschfeld RM, Scheftner WA, Winokur G. Depression and panic attacks: the significance of overlap as reflected in follow-up and family study data. Am J Psychiatry. 1988;145(3):293–300.
38. Lochner C, Mogotsi M, du Toit PL, Kaminer D, Niehaus DJ, Stein DJ. Quality of life in anxiety disorders: a comparison of obsessive-compulsive disorder, social anxiety disorder, and panic disorder. Psychopathology. 2003;36(5):255–62.
39. Tsao JC, Mystkowski JL, Zucker BG, Craske MG. Impact of cognitive-behavioral therapy for panic disorder on comorbidity: a controlled investigation. Behav Res Ther. 2005;43(7):959–70.
40. Ledley DR, Huppert JD, Foa EB, Davidson JR, Keefe FJ, Potts NL. Impact of depressive symptoms on the treatment of generalized social anxiety disorder. Depress Anxiety. 2005;22(4):161–7.
41. Wang PS, Lane M, Olfson M, Pincus HA, Wells KB, Kessler RC. Twelve-month use of mental health services in the United States: results from the National Comorbidity Survey Replication. Arch Gen Psychiatry. 2005;62(6):629–40.

11

Validation of the Edinburgh Postnatal Depression Scale against both DSM-5 and ICD-10 diagnostic criteria for depression

Johanne Smith-Nielsen[1*], Stephen Matthey[2], Theis Lange[3] and Mette Skovgaard Væver[1]

Abstract

Background: The Edinburgh Postnatal Depression Scale (EPDS) is widely used in many countries to screen women for depression in the perinatal period. However, across studies the psychometric properties and cutoff scores of the EPDS have varied considerably; potentially due to different depression criteria and diagnostic systems being used. Therefore, we validated the Danish EPDS against a depression diagnosis according to both DSM-5 and ICD-10. Furthermore, we examined whether the Danish EPDS is multidimensional, as it has previously been suggested.

Methods: Women ($N = 324$) were recruited after routine screenings with the EPDS between 2 and 10 months postpartum (T1). At a subsequent home visit (T2), the EPDS and the Structured Clinical Interview for DSM-5 were administered. Diagnostic interviews were audio recorded to enable subsequent coding for ICD-10 diagnoses and inter-rater reliability analysis. A two-phase stratified sampling strategy with three sampling categories (EPDS-score at T1) was used. Using the distribution of 4931 T1 EPDS-scores from the same population from which we sampled the participants, we used sampling weighing to reweight the sample. The calculation of weights was based upon the mother's sampling category at T1 (i.e. the probability of being sampled) and the weights were applied when assessing the receiver operation characteristics (ROCs) of the EPDS. Sensitivity, specificity, positive predictive value, negative predictive value and area under the ROC curve were computed from the reweighted data for all relevant cutoff values. CIs were computed by embedding the calculations in a weighted logistic regression. Exploratory factor analysis was done using oblique rotation. Parallel analysis was used to assess the number of factors.

Results: A score of 11 or more was found to be the optimal cutoff for depression according to both DSM-5 and ICD-10 criteria. Factor analysis suggested that the Danish EPDS consists of three factors, including an 'anxiety factor'.

Conclusions: The Danish EPDS has reasonable sensitivity and specificity at a cutoff score of 11 or more. There are no notable differences with respect to using ICD-10 or DSM-5 criteria for depression in terms of optimal cutoff. The variation in cutoff scores is likely to be due to cultural variations in the expression of depressive symptoms.

Keywords: Depression, Postnatal, Two-phase design, Screening, Exploratory factor analysis, Perinatal anxiety

Background

The Edinburgh Postnatal depression Scale (EPDS) [1] has been established as a useful screening instrument for detection of women at risk for depression in the perinatal period [2, 3]. In addition, it has been identified as the most frequently validated instrument to screen for perinatal depression [4], and in 2014 the EPDS had been validated against a diagnosis of depression in at least 37 languages [5]. Although recently, a discussion has begun to emerge regarding several shortcomings in the scale, including the multitude of different validated cutoff scores required for women (and men) from different cultures and during the ante- and postnatal periods, as well as the exclusion of certain types of psychological distress often occurring in the perinatal period (e.g. perinatal anxiety) [6], the current use of the EPDS in Denmark warrants understanding its properties further.

* Correspondence: johanne.smith-nielsen@psy.ku.dk
[1]Centre for Early Intervention and Family Studies, Department of Psychology, University of Copenhagen, Oester Farimagsgade 2A, DK-1353 Copenhagen, Denmark
Full list of author information is available at the end of the article

For almost two decades, a translation of the EPDS [7] has been in used for screening purposes in primary care in Denmark by public health visitors, and this translation was also used in a large-scale study to assess risk factors and point prevalence of postnatal depression in Danish women [7]. Nevertheless, the Danish EPDS has not been validated in a Danish population, and no official guidelines exist regarding cutoff scores for further monitoring of symptoms or referral to other services. This has resulted in various cutoff scores being used across the public health visiting districts where the scale is most frequently used. Moreover, the scale has only rarely been used in general practice or as part of perinatal psychiatric services where it is required that a screening instrument must go through a formal validation before implemented in practice.

The most commonly used cutoff score in postnatal women is 13 or more [8]. However, across studies, and in particular across languages, the optimal cutoff scores of the EPDS have varied considerably [5]. For example, the optimal cutoff for a diagnosis of depression in postnatal woman was found to be 7 or more in a Lithuanian population [9], 9 or more in a Sinhala population [10], 11 or more in a French population [11], and 12 or more in a Swedish population [12]. These differences in identified cutoff scores may be due to cultural variation in the expression of depressive symptoms in the perinatal period [13, 14], and consequently, researchers stress that the EPDS should be validated in a particular population before implementation in screening programs [15].

Another reason for the differing identified cutoff scores may be that across studies different diagnostic criteria and different diagnostic systems have been used [16]. Some, (e.g. [17]) have used criteria for depression according to their current version of the Diagnostic and Statistical Manual for Mental disorders (DSM–III–R; IV–TR; 5) [18, 19]. Others, (e.g. [10]) have used the International Classification of Diseases 10th revision (ICD-10) [20]. The original and some subsequent early validation studies [1, 21] used the Research Diagnostic Criteria (RDC) [22]. Differences between the diagnostic systems, with respect to diagnoses of depression, are marked. Whereas DSM-IV allows for a diagnosis of minor depression, this diagnosis does not exist in DSM-III, DSM-5, or ICD-10. Some studies have reported the optimal cutoff score for detecting just DSM major depression [12], while others have reported the optimal cutoff score for minor *and* major depression, sometimes referred to as 'combined depression' [23, 24]. Yet other studies have reported separate cutoffs, i.e. for minor or major as well as for just major depression [25]. Yet another difference between the ICD and DSM is that ICD-10 requires a minimum of two out of three core symptoms (depressed mood, anhedonia, and energy loss) for a diagnosis of depression, whereas DSM (III, IV, and 5) only requires the presence of one of two core symptoms (depressed mood and anhedonia). Moreover, none of the ICD-10 diagnoses of mild, moderate, or severe depression correspond to DSM-IV minor or DSM-III/IV/5 major depression in terms of symptom requirements (ICD-10 mild: 2 core symptoms + 2 or 3 associated symptoms; ICD-10 moderate: 2 core symptoms + 4 or 5 associated symptoms; ICD-10 severe: 3 core symptoms + 5–7 associated symptoms. DSM-IV minor: at least 1 core symptom + 2–4 symptoms; DSM-III/ IV/ 5 major: at least 1 core symptom + 5–9 symptoms). Similar discrepancies occur in the RDC diagnostic system in which a diagnosis of major depression requires at least one core symptom and at least five associated symptoms [22]. It is not, known whether ICD-11 which, if endorsed by member states, is planned to come into use in 2022, will be any different in these respects from ICD-10. Finally, some diagnoses have been made determining if criteria are met using in-depth diagnostic interviews, such as the Structured Clinical Interview for DSM-IV axis I disorders [26] which allows for probing and further exploration of answers, i.e. to determine if a symptom is in fact present, while others have used interviews that do not allow such probing, e.g., the Mini-International Neuropsychiatric Interview [27].

All of these issues could account for some of the differences in optimal cutoff scores reported across EPDS studies, notwithstanding the language or cultural differences [16]. As yet, however, no study has investigated whether using different diagnostic systems influence receiver operating characteristics of the EPDS. Therefore, we validate the EPDS against both ICD-10 and DSM-5. Whilst the DSM is most frequently used in EPDS validation studies, and in research more generally [28], the ICD is the official coding system in most of the countries where the EPDS is being used for screening purposes. Indeed, the ICD-10 has been identified as the most frequently used in clinical practice across countries [29], and hence, from a clinical perspective, it is relevant to include ICD criteria in a validation of the EPDS.

Apart from the EPDS's utility in screening for depression, several investigators [30, 31] have commented on its properties for screening for perinatal anxiety given that this mood disorder is also prevalent, often co-occurs with depression, and has significant impacts not only on the mother's well-being but also on her offspring [32, 33]. Although the EPDS was intended to be unidimensional, using exploratory factor analysis (EFA), many studies have suggested that the scale contains two factors, a depressive factor and an anxiety factor (e.g. [11, 34, 35]). Other studies have suggested that a three-factor structure with depression, anxiety, and anhedonia (e.g. [36, 37]), or depression, anxiety, and self-harm/suicide (e.g. [38, 39]) fits the data better. There is also variation as to which items load on the anxiety scale. While the anxiety factor most frequently include items 3 (guilt),4 (anxiety),and 5 (panic attacks) [40], some studies have found other item combinations to comprise the anxiety factor, e.g. Italian version: items 4, 5 & 6 [41]; Iranian version: items 3,4,5 and 8 [42]. More recently, a researchers have questioned the utility of continously conducting EFA as opposed to data and theory-driven confirmatory factor analyses (CFAs), (e.g. [40, 43]) and related to this, the optimal length of the EPDS has been questioned [44]. However, as there is currently no genereally agreed upon factor structure that could serve as the basis for a CFA, in the present study, we decided to assesss the factor structure of the EPDS using EFA.

Aims of the study

To address these issues, the aims of the present study were to a) validate the Danish version of the EPDS against a diagnosis of depression in a sample of new mothers by assessing the sensitivity, specificity, and predictive values of different cutoff scores; b) investigate whether these receiver operating characteristics (ROCs) of the scale differ depending upon whether the DSM-5 or the ICD-10 is used, and (3) using an exploratory factor analytic approach, examine the factor structure of the Danish EPDS.

As ICD-10 mild depression in some contexts is considered to be subthreshold [45], for comparison, we conducted ROC analyses with and without including ICD-10 mild depression as 'depressed'. In the determination of the optimal cutoff, for first-phase screening purposes, we intended to select a value that provides good sensitivity (the true-positive rate) and high specificity (the true-negative rate) without lowering the positive predictive value (PPV: proportion of subjects with positive test results who are correctly diagnosed) so much that it would overwhelm clinical services. Based on the view that a missed case of depression in the postnatal period can have significant negative consequences, we aimed at a sensitivity of 80% or more, a specificity of 90% or more, and a positive predictive value of 50% or more.

Methods

Study setting and procedure

As part of the general social security and health care system in Denmark, all families in are offered health visits by public health visitors (specialized nurses) in their home during the first year postpartum. This study was conducted in collaboration with the health visitors from the municipality of Copenhagen and was part of a larger project, the Copenhagen Infant Mental Health Project (CIMHP), which also includes a treatment trial (Clinical trials identifier: NCT02497677) [46]. Enrollment of participants started July 2015 and data collection for the present study terminated June 2017.

During the project period, all mothers in Copenhagen received home visits at 2 and 8 months postpartum by public health visitors. First-time mothers received an additional visit at 4 months postpartum. The EPDS was routinely administered at the two month visit, however, in addition, some women were also administered the EPDS at 4 or 8 months based upon the clinical judgement of the health visitor. This score is the Time 1 (T1) EPDS score. To ensure that sufficient numbers of women who met criteria for depression were recruited, an oversampling strategy was used, similar to that used in other studies [17, 21, 47]. Therefore, all mothers scoring 10 or more at T1 were invited to participate in CIMHP. Additionally, a subgroup of health visitors, equally distributed across districts, invited (from April 2016 – February 2017) not only mothers scoring 10 or more, but also those who scored 0–9 at the routine two month visit to the project. The sampling strategy is described in further detail below.

After screening with the EPDS, the health visitor informed the mother about the research project, and if interested, contact information was given to the research team. Interested mothers were offered a home visit by a clinical psychologist from CIMHP (Time 2: T2). During this visit, written informed consent was obtained, the EPDS was again administered, and a diagnostic interview was conducted. For logistic and practical reasons, the time-period from T1 to T2 could vary from a few days to several weeks. Therefore, to obtain the most precise ROC estimates, the EPDS score obtained at the T2 was validated in the current study.

Sampling strategy and weighting

Mothers were eligible for participation in the current study if they were at least 18 years old, if they had an infant between 8 weeks and 10 months, and if they could read and speak Danish. We used a two-phase stratified sampling design [48] also used in other validation studies e.g. [17, 49]. A data extraction from the health visitors' digital filing system (14 February 2016) including the latest 4931 EPDS-screenings (i.e. T1 scores) from mothers with infants under one year in Copenhagen showed that 69% of all screened mothers scored in the range 0–5, and 21% scored in the range 6–9, and 10% scored 10 or more. Thus, the vast majority were expected to score less than 6. In order to enrich the sample in the range where the cutoff was expected to be found, and to ensure roughly equal representation of these groups, we included all mothers scoring 10 or above (probable cases) at T1, and a larger proportion of those in the range 6–9 (possible cases) than of those scoring in range 0–5 (probable non-cases). The aim was to include at least 35 mothers from each of the two lower groups. To obtain these goals after October 2016 we only invited mothers who scored 6–9 or 10 or more at T1. The 4931 scores effectively gave us the population wide distribution and we could therefore use sampling weighing to reweight the sample corresponding to if we had done a random sample from the full population. The calculation of weights was based upon the mother's sampling category at T1 (i.e. the probability of being sampled), and the weights were subsequently applied to the ROC analyses of T2 EPDS scores. Because all mothers scoring 10 or above were included, this group had the weight 1. The 0–5 and 6–9 groups got the sampling weights 28.8 and 16.9, respectively. By construction, after applying these weights, the distribution of T1 scores in our weighted sample matched the one observed in the full population, and as no other systematic effects of the sampling procedure exists, the weighted analysis can therefore be thought of as a simple random sample from the full population, but with substantial higher statistical power compared to a true random sample from the full population. This mimics well known techniques from survey literature (see [50]).

Measures

The Edinburgh Postnatal Depression Scale [1] is a 10-item self-report questionnaire (range 0–30) designed to screen for possible depression in new mothers, and was completed by the mothers at T1 and T2. While the original published version of the Danish translation [7] had some formatting differences to the English version (i.e. inclusion of response scores; altering the item wording, and exclusion of the introduction), these were amended so that the Danish version used in the study was identical to the English version, having gone through the usual translation and back-translation methodology and complied with the principles for translation of the EPDS described in the EPDS manual [5]. The Danish EPDS is provided as Additional files 1 and 2.

The Structured Clinical Interview for the DSM-5 (SCID-5) [51] was used at T2 to establish a diagnosis of major depression according to DSM-5 as well as to assess history of depression. The interviewers were trained to explore the mothers' answers to the standardized questions to be able to differentiate between normal and depressive reactions in the postnatal period (such as sleep problems and changes in appetite) because it has been found that depression might be otherwise over diagnosed in new mothers [52]. The interviews were conducted by trained SCID-5 interviewers who received ongoing supervision, and the interviews were audiotaped to allow for inter-rater reliability analyses to be conducted. The SCID-5 scorings and audio recordings of the interviews were also used to diagnose mothers according to ICD-10 diagnostic criteria for depression (mild, moderate, and severe depression). The interviewers did not score the T2 EPDS filled in by the mother prior to the interview. However, it was not possible to blind the interviewers entirely to the T1 or T2 EPDS scores (e.g., sometimes, the mother mentioned her T1 score prior to or during the interview). Therefore, to prevent interviewer-biases and ensure interrater reliability, a randomly selected subset ($n = 70$, 22%) of the audio recorded interviews were rated by a certified SCID-5 interviewer. This rater had no previous knowledge about the mothers and was blind to EPDS score and the diagnoses made by the interviewers. Interrater agreement for DSM-5 diagnostic status (no depression vs. major) was 90.2%, $\kappa = .89$ ($p = .000$); for ICD-10 diagnostic status (no depression vs. mild or more) interrater agreement was 94.6%, $\kappa = .94$ ($p = .000$), and for ICD-10 diagnostic status, four-way, interrater agreement was 94.6% (no depression); 81.8% (Mild), 78,6%; (Moderate), and 80% (Severe), $\kappa = .76$, ($p = .000$) which are all considered to represent excellent levels of interrater reliability [53].

Statistical methods

Sensitivity, specificity, positive predictive value (PPV), negative predictive value (NPV) and area under the ROC curve (AUC) were computed directly from the reweighted data and the calculations were done for all relevant cutoff values. Confidence intervals were computed by embedding the calculations in a weighted logistic regression as implemented in R version 3.3.1. Confidence intervals corrected for weights were then obtained. Exploratory factor analysis (EFA) was done in R using the Psych Package [54]. To allow for factors' inter-correlation, as would be expected of the underlying assumed dimensions of depression, anhedonia, and anxiety [55] we employed oblique rotation (promax). We used parallel analysis, i.e. using scree plots comparing actual loadings with random data with the same properties as the real data, to assess the appropriate number of factors. Continuous variables were summarized using means and standard deviations while categorical variables were summarized using raw counts and percentages.

Results

A total of 350 mothers agreed to be contacted by the research team after T1 screening. Of these, 23 declined to participate when contacted, 2 did not consent to participate after having received a home visit from the research team, and one mother was not able to fill in the EPDS in Danish, and was therefore excluded, resulting in a final sample size of 324 women for whom we had T2 EPDS scores and a diagnostic interview. For four of these mothers, the T1 EPDS score was not available, and therefore data from these mothers were only included in unweighted analyses and not in the weighted analyses for which $n = 320$.

The distribution of mothers across the three sampling categories at T1 were as following: EPDS range 0–5: n = 56 (17.5%), EPDS range 6–9: n = 29 (9.1%), and EPDS range 10–30: n = 235 (73.4%). Thus, the desired size of 35 mothers from the each of the two lowest sampling groups (at T1) was achieved for the lowest group and almost for the middle group. The distribution of raw EPDS scores at T2 is presented in Fig. 1. The unusual distribution is due to the sampling mechanism. The reweighted distribution, reflecting the distribution in the population, i.e. based on the distribution of the latest 4931 EPDS screenings in Copenhagen, is presented in Fig. 2.

Sample characteristics and distribution across diagnostic categories are presented in Table 1. As shown in Table 1, the majority (83%) of the mothers had an infant between 8 and 20 weeks at T2 when the diagnostic interview was conducted. Non-weighted EPDS means for the diagnostic categories were: DSM-5 Major: $M = 15.0$ ($SD = 4.5$), not depressed: 7.0 ($SD = 4.5$); ICD-10 mild: $M = 12.5$ ($SD = 4.0$), ICD-10 moderate: $M = 14.9$ ($SD = 4.2$), ICD-10 severe: 18.4 ($SD = 3.8$), not depressed: $M = 7.1$ ($SD = 4.9$).

Table 2 shows the overlap between the two diagnostic systems. As shown, 10 mothers had a discrepant diagnostic status: four of the 118 mothers fulfilling criteria for DSM-5 major depression, did not fulfill criteria for any ICD-10 diagnosis. Inspecting the data further showed that these mothers only had one core symptom (but five symptoms in total), and hence, they did not get a ICD-10 diagnosis. Of the 38 mothers fulfilling criteria for ICD-10 mild depression, six did not fulfill criteria for DSM major depression. These mothers all had four symptoms (two core and two associated symptoms), thereby lacking one symptom to fulfill criteria for DSM-5 major depression but had the lowest possible number of symptoms to fulfill criteria for ICD-10 mild depression.

Cronbach's alpha, a measure of a scale's reliability, was 0.822 in the raw data, and in the weighted data it was 0.835, indicating good internal consistency [56].

Receiver operating characteristics

Tables 3 presents estimates of sensitivity, specificity, PPV, NPV, and AUC for DSM Major depression, ICD-10 mild depression or more, and ICD-10 moderate+severe depression for different EPDS cutoff-scores and based on the reweighted data. For all three diagnostic categories of depression, the AUC values were close to 1 (ranging from 0.957–0.960) indicating that the Danish EPDS has a high discriminative power (i.e. how well the test separates the group being tested into those with and without the condition).

For DSM-5 major depression as well as ICD-10 mild depression or more, a cutoff score of 11 or more is suggested by the data, both yielding a sensitivity close to 80%, a specificity above 90%, and a PPV close to 50%. For ICD-10 moderate and severe depression, a cutoff score of 12 or more was suggested with a sensitivity of 77%, specificity of 96% and a PPV of 49.5%.

As shown in Table 3, the ROC values between DSM-5 major and ICD-10 (any) are very similar. This is because

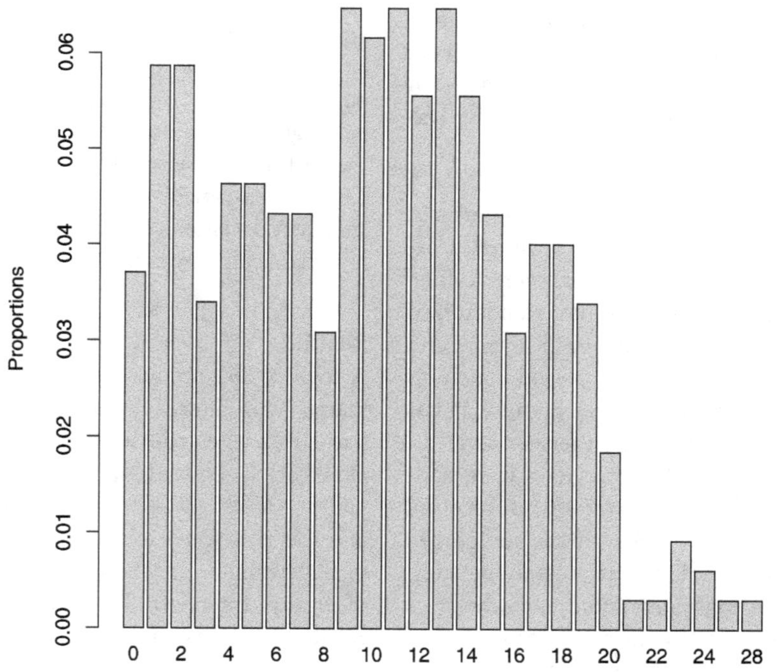

Fig. 1 EPDS scores (T2 raw counts)

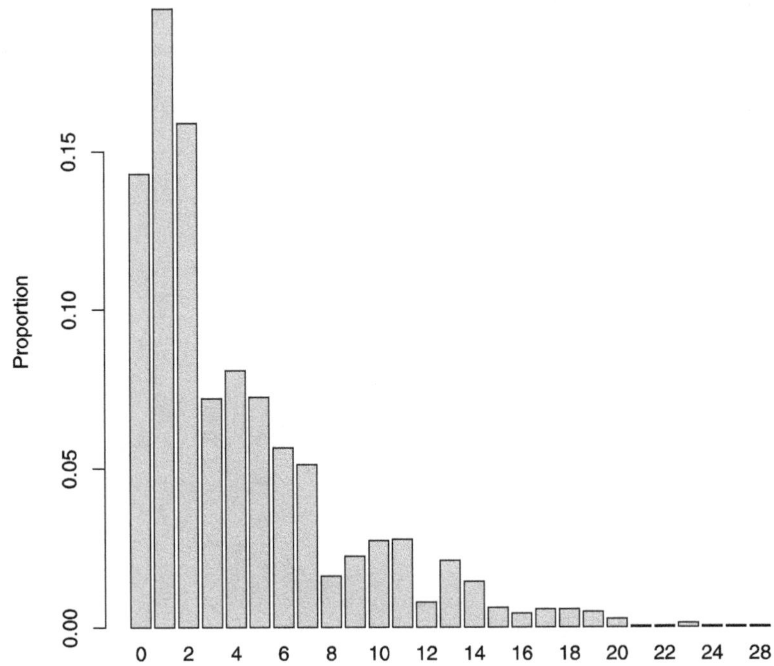

Fig. 2 EPDS scores (T2 weighted)

only 10 women had a discrepant diagnostic status. However, the ROC values for ICD-10 moderate+severe are in some cases more different than DSM-5 because using this classification as 'depressed', and the ICD-10 mild as 'not depressed', resulted in 38 having a discrepant diagnostic status.

Factor analysis

Using parallel analysis [54] we found that either two or three factors would be appropriate. To ensure a good fit we employ three factors, and the associated factor loadings are presented in Table 4. For clarity, only loadings of 0.3 and above are reported.

As shown in Table 4, items 6 and 7 cross loaded on factor 1 and factor 2. Likewise, the factor loadings of item 6 and 7 did not discriminate adequately to be included in either factor 1 or factor 2, and these were therefore omitted from both factors. Following, the result indicated that the Danish EPDS consists of three factors: Factor 1 (depression): items 1,2,8, and 9; Factor 2 (anxiety): items 3,4, and 5; and Factor 3 (self-harm/suicide): item 10. As shown, Factor 1 and Factor 2 are vastly more important than Factor 3 in terms of explained variance. It is noted that the third factor included essentially only loads on Item 10 (self-harm and suicidal ideas) and that this item did not load on the two other factors. For these reasons Factor 3 did not truly meet the criteria for being a factor as it is essentially just a rescaled version of item 10. We did, however, include it in this EFA, because it is important to realize that this item works in a different dimensionality from the rest.

Discussion

In the EPDS literature, there is a wide variation as to what criteria have been used when the receiver operating characteristics of the scale have been assessed (i.e., the 'gold standard' has been defined by different diagnoses within and between different diagnostic systems). As previously suggested [16], we suspected that the variation in optimal cutoff scores reported across studies might at least partly be explained by this. Therefore, we validated the Danish EPDS against both DSM-5 and ICD-10 diagnostic criteria for depression.

In this Danish postnatal sample, for DSM-5 major as well as for ICD-10 mild, moderate or severe depression, a cutoff score of 11 or more was suggested by the data as the best cutoff. With sensitivities of 79.2 and 78.2%, specificities of 94.4%, and PPVs of 49% respectively, this value reflected the best trade-off in terms of the EPDS's ability to detect the majority of cases of depression without an undue sacrifice of PPV.

Interestingly, four mothers met criteria for DSM-5 major depression but not ICD-10 mild depression (Table 2). This was due to the ICD-10 requirement of having at least two core symptoms out of three (as opposed to one of two in DSM-5), suggesting that there is an unfortunate inconsistency between the two diagnostic systems.

Because ICD-10 mild depression (which requires at least four versus five depressive symptoms in DSM-5

Table 1 Sample characteristics and distribution of diagnostic categories

Variable	N = 324	
Maternal age, mean (*SD*)	32.7	(4.6)
Range	22–45	
Infant age[a] in weeks, mean (*SD*)	16.2	(8.2)
Infant age 8–14 weeks, *n* (%)	211	(65.1)
Infant age 15–20 weeks, *n* (%)	58	(17.9)
Infant age 21–30 weeks, *n* (%)	30	(9.3)
Infant age 31–49 weeks, *n* (%)	25	(7.7)
Infant gender, boys, *n* (%)	174	(53.7)
Maternal country of origin		
Danish, *n* (%)	271	(83.6)
Immigrant, *n* (%)	32	(9.9)
Descendants of immigrants, *n* (%)	9	(2.8)
Missing, *n* (%)	12	(3.7)
Mother single parent or not		
Married or living with partner, *n* (%)	293	(90.4)
Single, *n* (%)	14	(4.3)
Other, *n* (%)	6	(1.9)
Missing, *n* (%)	11	(3.4)
Primiparous *n* (%)	192	(63.6)
Maternal ISCED level of education		
Level 1–3 (lower secondary or less), *n* (%)	29	(9.0)
Level 4 and 5 (post secondary + short-cycle tertiary), *n* (%)	37	(11.4)
Level 6 (bachelor or equivalent), *n* (%)	113	(34.9)
Level 7 and 8 (master + doctor or equivalent), *n* (%)	134	(41.4)
Other or missing, *n* (%)	11	(3.4)
Mothers endorsing item 10 above zero, *n* (%)	26	(8.0)
Depression history status[b]		
No current or past depression, *n* (%)	132	(40.7)
Not currently depressed but a history of depression, *n* (%)	75	(23.1)
Currently depressed with a history of depression, *n* (%)	62	(19.1)
First episode of depression, *n* (%)	55	(17.0)
DSM-5 Major depression[c]		
Depressed, *n* (%)	118	(36.4)
Not depressed, *n* (%)	206	(63.6)
ICD-10 any (mild, moderate, or severe depression)[c]		
Depressed *n* (%)	120	(37.0)
Not depressed, *n* (%)	204	(63.0)
ICD-10 moderate or severe depression[c]		
Depressed *n* (%)	82	(25.3)
Not depressed, *n* (%)	242	(74.7)

Note. ISCED = International Standard Classification of Education (UNESCO). ICD-10 = International Classification of mental and behavioural disorders 10th edition (WHO, 1992); DSM-5 = Diagnostic and Statistical Manual of Mental Disorders, 5th edition (American Psychiatric Association, 2013)
[a]Infant age at the day for diagnostic interview and EPDS screening (T2)
[b]History of depression status was established according to DSM-5 criteria
[c]Due to the oversampling strategy, these are not prevalence estimates. See text

Table 2 Cross tabulation of distributions of ICD-10 and DSM-5 diagnoses

	DSM-5 diagnostic status		
ICD-10 diagnostic status	No depression	Major depression	Total
No depression	200	4	204
Mild depression	6	32	38
Moderate depression	0	60	60
Severe depression	0	22	22
Total	206	118	324

Note. ICD-10 = International Classification of mental and behavioural disorders 10th edition (WHO, 1992); DSM-5 = Diagnostic and Statistical Manual of Mental Disorders, 5th edition (American Psychiatric Association, 2013)

major depression) in clinical practice sometimes is considered "subthreshold", for comparison, we also conducted analyses not including ICD-10 mild depression as 'depressed'. In this case, and using our a priori defined 'criteria' for selecting cutoff scores, the optimal cutoff was 12 or more (sensitivity: 77.0%, specificity: 96%, PPV: 49.5%). However, given that the symptom threshold for ICD-10 moderate and severe depression is higher than for DSM-5 major depression (at least six symptoms in ICD-10 moderate versus at least five symptoms in DSM-5 Major), a missed case of moderate or severe depression is highly undesirable, and increasing sensitivity at the cost of PPV seems reasonable in this context. Hence, for the use in first-phase screening of Danish postnatal mothers, for ICD-10 moderate and severe

Table 3 Sensitivity, specificity, PPV, NPV, and AUC for DSM-5 major depression, ICD-10 mild, moderate, and severe depression, and ICD-10 moderate and severe depression

EPDS cutoff[a]	Sensitivity	95% CI	Specificity	95% CI	PPV	95% CI	NPV	95% CI	AUC
DSM-5 major									
6 +[b]	98.0		77.0		22.4		99.8		0.960
7+	96.6		83.0		27.9		99.7		
8+	84.6		87.7		31.9		98.8		
9+	83.9		89.4		35.0		98.8		
10+	81.2		91.6		39.7		98.6		
11+	**79.2**	[60.3, 98.1]	**94.4**	[90.5, 98.3]	**49.0**	[29.4, 68.7]	**98.5**	[96.9, 1.0]	
12+	72.5		96.9		61.4		98.1		
13+	66.5		97.3		62.7		97.7		
ICD-10, any									
6+	98.0		77.1		22.8		99.8		0.959
7+	96.7		83.1		28.2		99.7		
8+	84.1		87.8		32.1		98.8		
9+	83.5		89.4		35.3		98.7		
10+	80.2		91.6		39.7		98.5		
11+	**78.2**	[59.6, 96.7]	**94.4**	[90.5, 98.3]	**49.0**	[29.4, 68.7]	**98.4**	[96.8, 1.0]	
12+	72.2		96.9		62.0		98.1		
13+	65.6		97.3		62.7		97.6		
ICD-10 moderate+severe									
6+	98.2		75.8		17.1		99.9		0.957
7+	97.3		81.7		21.3		99.8		
8+	82.3		86.4		23.5		99.0		
9+	82.3		88.1		26.0		99.0		
10+	82.3		90.5		30.5		99.0		
11+	82.3		93.4		38.6		99.0		
12+	**77.0**	[52.8, 1.0]	**96.0**	[93.4, 98.7]	**49.5**	[29.9, 69.1]	**98.8**	[97.2, 1.0]	
13+	72.6		96.6		51.9		98.6		

Note. PPV = positive predictive value; NPV = Negative predictive value; AUC = the area under the ROC curve; ICD-10 = International classification of mental and behavioural disorders 10th edition (WHO, 1992); DSM-5 = Diagnostic and Statistical Manual of Mental Disorders, 5th edition (American Psychiatric Association, 2013) CI = confidence Interval. Values in bold represent the most adequate combination of sensitivity, specificity, and PPV. For the sake of clarity 95% CIs provided only for the optimal cutoff-scores. 95% CIs for all values are reported in Table 3b which is provided by request to the first author. [a]A value score exactly equal to the cutoff is understood as being depressed. [b]'+' signifies 'or more'

Table 4 Factor loadings in an EFA of the Danish EPDS

	Factor 1	Factor 2	Factor 3
% of variance	0.257	0.198	0.082
Item			
1 (anhedonia)	**0.888**		
2 (anhedonia)	**0.773**		
3 (guilt)		**0.605**	
4 (anxiety)		**0.805**	
5 (Panic attacks)		**0.748**	
6 (overwhelmed)	0.381	0.445	
7 (sleep problems)	0.357	0.309	
8 (sadness)	**0.701**		
9 (tearfulness)	**0.640**		
10 (self-harm and suicidal ideas)			**0.875**

Note. EFA: Exploratory Factor Analysis; only loadings of 0.300 or more are reported
Values in bold represent factor loadings included in either factor 1, 2, or 3

depression, we recommend using a cutoff of 11 or more (sensitivity of 82.3%, specificity of 93.4%, and a PPV of 38.6%).

In sum, our results suggest that there are no notable differences with respect to using ICD-10 or DSM-5 criteria for depression in terms of optimal cutoff on the EPDS. Indeed, the ROC values are almost identical given that there were only 10 cases that showed discrepant caseness status. Thus, the optimum postpartum Danish cutoff (11 or more) differs from the English-speaking cutoff (13 or more for DSM major depression) as well as from a number of the cutoff scores found for other translations of the scales (e.g. [9, 10, 12, 14]). As also proposed previously [15], our results may suggest that the variation in cutoff scores across studies reflect differences in the expression of psychological distress across cultures, though, to our knowledge, no perinatal study have tested this assumption. More generally, our study stresses the importance of validating self-report instruments, originally validated in another culture (and another language), before use in a specific culture because cultural differences may impact results.

In the vast majority of EPDS validation studies, a diagnosis of depression has been used as the criterion or 'gold standard' against which the scale has been validated. This was also the case in our study where we used a thorough diagnostic interview. It should, however, be realized that some would argue that using such a criterion will miss many women who have significant levels of worry or low mood, yet do not meet diagnostic criteria for a mood disorder (e.g. [57–59]). Diagnostic status, therefore, may not be the most suitable criterion against which to validate mood screening instruments, but currently, this is the accepted methodology in the perinatal mental health field.

Another reason for the various cutoffs reported across studies could also be that, within the EPDS literature, there exist no agreed upon standards for what are acceptable levels of sensitivity, specificity, PPV and NPV. For screening purposes, high sensitivity is often desirable to ensure the detection of the majority of cases in the screened population. This was the case in the present study where we aimed at a sensitivity of 80% or more, a specificity of 90% or more, and a positive predictive value of 50% or more. However, high sensitivity is not always the first priority. For example, in a recent study, where a cutoff of 19 or more was selected, high specificity was prioritized and a sensitivity of 30% was considered acceptable for screening purposes in order to use the available resources in the most effective way and not overwhelm clinical services with many inappropriate referrals [60]. More generally, when using validated cutoff scores, the context in which the EPDS score is used is of crucial importance. For some research purposes, using an EPDS score as a measure of depression without further assessment (which is sometimes the case in epidemiological studies, e.g. [61]) it could be argued that the PPV should have a higher priority than sensitivity. This would ensure that those screening positive are very likely to meet diagnostic criteria for depression (if the PPV is, for example, 80% or 90%). In the current sample, if using a cutoff of 11 or more as a measure of depression, only approximately 5 out of every 10 screen positive mothers would, in fact, be depressed, which in turn would overestimate the prevalence of clinical depression in the population by a factor of two.

Using an exploratory factor analytic approach, our results indicate that the Danish EPDS is multidimensional as previously suggested. The first 'depression factor' included item 1 (anhedonia), item 2 (anhedonia), item 8 (sadness), and item 9 (tearfulness); the second 'anxiety factor' included item 3 (guilt), item 4 (anxiety), item 5 (panic attacks). As such, this result is in line with previous studies that have found an 'anxiety factor' of the EPDS to include items 3,4,5 [34, 35, 37, 38, 52, 62]. The anxiety subscale is sometimes referred to as the EPDS-3A or the EDS-3A in pregnancy [34, 63], and there is some evidence suggesting that it can be used to screen for perinatal anxiety [34, 52, 64]. However, more research is warranted to establish a separate cutoff score if this subscale should be used in clinical practice to screen for perinatal anxiety. Consistent with three previous studies [38, 39, 64], a third 'self-harm/suicide factor' (only including item 10) also emerged. However, in terms of proportion of explained variance, the two first factors were far more important than the third factor which accounted for less than 10% of the variance and fit statistics (parallel analysis) do not firmly establish whether the correct number of factors is two or three.

A limitation of the current study is that only women from urban Copenhagen area were included. This may limit generalizability to the whole population. Another limitation is that we did not have access to the number of mothers initially screened at T1 but who did not agree to be referred to the project, and thus we cannot report on the number of approached mothers who declined to participate. Neither are we able to report whether these mothers differ from our sample in terms of sociodemographic characteristics or EPDS scores. However, of the 350 mothers who were referred to the project, only 25 (7%) declined to participate. Yet, as these mothers did not give consent to participate, all of these mothers' data were deleted, and therefore we were not able to report EPDS scores or sociodemographic characteristics on these mothers either. This problem, however, is very common within the EPDS literature, and to our knowledge, only two previous studies [25, 65] have reported on the number of approached women who declined to participate.

As we assessed depression according to the current diagnostic standards, we used the DSM-5 and ICD-10 diagnostic systems. Because the notion of minor depression (requiring two but less than five depressive symptoms) does not exist in DSM-5, this meant that the diagnostic interviews were not coded for DSM-IV minor depression. It could be argued that this would be relevant in terms of comparing our results with previous studies that have included women meeting criteria for minor depression as cases of depression and have reported cutoff scores for 'combined depression'; and as such, this can be considered as a limitation of our study. Finally, when interpreting our findings the timeframe for T2 assessments should be considered. One of our inclusion criteria was that the mother had an infant between 2 and 10 months and although the majority (83%) of the T2 assessments were conducted between 8 and 20 weeks postpartum, T2 assessments were conducted with a quite wide timeframe (Table 1). Recently, a paper by Martin and Redshaw reported that mothers, who did not differ on other background variables, scored significantly different on the EPDS at three and six months postpartum [43]. However, based on the current data, it is not possible to address the question of whether an EPDS-score obtained for example at two months postpartum is more or less likely to reflect an underlying depression than at a later time point in the postpartum period.

Strengths of the study include the use of oversampling to ensure that a high number of depressed women were included, the sampling weighting method yielding good statistical power, and conducting interrater-reliability check of the clinicians who conducted the diagnostic interviews.

Conclusions

The Danish EPDS is a valid and reliable screening instrument to detect possible depression in new mothers in a Danish postnatal population. The best cutoff score for the EPDS to screen for depression according to both DSM-5 and ICD-10 in Danish women is 11 or more. It should be noted, however, that the antenatal cutoff could be different, and possible, different for each trimester [15], and consequently, the scale should be validated in a antenatal sample before it is used to screen for depression in pregnancy. Moreover, the Danish EPDS is multi-dimensional, and, additional to measuring depressive symptoms and self-harm/suicidal ideas, it also contains a subscale measuring symptoms of anxiety. Thus, the appropriate validated cutoff score for this subscale would also need to be calculated for both the ante- and postnatal periods before being used to screen for perinatal anxiety.

Abbreviations

AUC: Area under the ROC curve; AUC: Area under the ROC curve; CIMHP: Copenhagen Infant Mental Health Project; DSM-III-R: Diagnostic and Statistical Manual for Mental disorders, third edition, revised; DSM-5: Diagnostic and Statistical Manual for Mental disorders, fifth edition; DSM-IV-TR: Diagnostic and Statistical Manual for Mental disorders, fourth edition, revised; EFA: Exploratory factor analysis; EPDS: The Edinburgh Postnatal depression Scale; ICD-10: International Classification of Diseases 10th revision; NPV: Negative predictive value; PPV: Positive predictive value; ROCs: Receiver operating characteristics; SCID-5: The Structured Clinical Interview for the DSM-5; T1: Time 1; T2: Time 2

Acknowledgements

The authors wish to thank the health visitors and The Children and Youth Administration (Børne- Ungdoms Forvaltningen) in the City of Copenhagen for a fruitful collaboration. Special thanks go to the health visitors who agreed to recruit control mothers.

The authors wish to declare that the first and last authors' institution have paid BMC Psychiatry a substantial 'processing fee'. This is in accordance with the Journal's requirement for all manuscripts, stating that this then allows for the manuscripts to be available on 'Open Access'.

Funding

The project was funded by a grant from the charitable foundation Tryg Foundation (Grant ID no 107616). The Tryg Foundation had no role in the design of the study, data collection, analyses, interpretation of data, or in writing the manuscript.

Authors' contributions

JSN was overall responsible for the study design and writing of the manuscript, managed data collection, and interpreted the results. SM contributed to data analysis, interpreted the data, and contributed in writing the manuscript. TL contributed to the study design, performed the statistical analyses, and contributed in writing the manuscript. MSV received the original grant financing the project, contributed to the study design, supervised the project, and reviewed and contributed to drafting the manuscript. All authors read and approved the final manuscript.

Consent for publication
Not applicable.

Competing interests
The authors declare that they have no competing interests.

Author details
[1]Centre for Early Intervention and Family Studies, Department of Psychology, University of Copenhagen, Oester Farimagsgade 2A, DK-1353 Copenhagen, Denmark. [2]South West Sydney Local Health District, Liverpool Hospital, University of Sydney, Sydney, Australia. [3]Department of Public Health, Section of Biostatistics, University of Copenhagen, Copenhagen, Denmark.

References
1. Cox JL, Holden JM, Sagovsky R. Detection of postnatal depression. Development of the 10-item Edinburgh postnatal depression scale. Br J Psychiatry. 1987;150(6):782–6.
2. Chaudron LH, Szilagyi PG, Kitzman HJ, Wadkins HI, Conwell Y. Detection of postpartum depressive symptoms by screening at well-child visits. Pediatrics. 2004;113(3):551–8.
3. Sheeder J, Kabir K, Stafford B. Screening for postpartum depression at well-child visits: is once enough during the first 6 months of life? Pediatrics. 2009;123(6):e982–8.
4. Hewitt CE, Gilbody SM, Mann R, Brealey S. Instruments to identify post-natal depression: which methods have been the most extensively validated, in what setting and in which language? Int J Psychiatry Clin Pract. 2010;14(1):72–6.
5. Cox J, Holden J, Henshaw C: Perinatal mental health: the Edinburgh postnatal depression scale (EPDS) manual (2nd edn): RCPsych publications; 2014.
6. Matthey S, Agostini F. Using the Edinburgh postnatal depression scale for women and men-some cautionary thoughts. Archives of Women's Mental Health. 2017;20(2):345–54.
7. Nielsen D, Videbech P, Hedegaard M, Dalby J, Secher N. Postpartum depression: identification of women at risk. BJOG Int J Obstet Gynaecol. 2000;107(10):1210–7.
8. Mann R, Evans J. Screening tools and methods of identifying perinatal depression. Identifying Perinatal Depression and Anxiety: Evidence-based Practice in Screening, Psychosocial Assessment and Management. 2015;76.
9. Bunevičius A, Kusminskas L, Bunevičius R. Validation of the Lithuanian version of the Edinburgh postnatal depression scale. Medicina. 2009; 45(7):544–8.
10. Rowel D, Jayawardena P, Fernando N: Validation of the Sinhala translation of Edinburgh Postnatal Depression Scale. 2008.
11. Guedeney N, Fermanian J. Validation study of the French version of the Edinburgh postnatal depression scale (EPDS): new results about use and psychometric properties. European psychiatry. 1998;13(2):83–9.
12. Wickberg B, Hwang C. The Edinburgh postnatal depression scale: validation on a Swedish community sample. Acta Psychiatr Scand. 1996;94(3):181–4.
13. Oates MR, Cox JL, Neema S, Asten P, Glangeaud-Freudenthal N, Figueiredo B, Gorman LL, Hacking S, Hirst E, Kammerer MH. Postnatal depression across countries and cultures: a qualitative study. Br J Psychiatry. 2004;184(46):s10–6.
14. Barnett B, Matthey S, Gyaneshwar R. Screening for postnatal depression in women of non-English speaking background. Archives of women's Mental Health. 1999;2(2):67–74.
15. Kozinszky Z, Dudas RB. Validation studies of the Edinburgh postnatal depression scale for the antenatal period. J Affect Disord. 2015;176:95–105.
16. Gibson J, McKenzie-McHarg K, Shakespeare J, Price J, Gray R. A systematic review of studies validating the Edinburgh postnatal depression scale in antepartum and postpartum women. Acta Psychiatr Scand. 2009;119(5):350–64.
17. Garcia-Esteve Ls AC, Ojuel J, Navarro P. Validation of the Edinburgh postnatal depression scale (EPDS) in Spanish mothers. J Affect Disord. 2003;75(1):71–6.
18. Diagnostic and statistical manual of mental disorders fifth edition (DSM-5®): American Psychiatric Association; 2013.
19. Diagnostic and statistical manual of mental disorders fourth edition DSM-IV-TR. Washington. DC: American Psychiatric Association; 2000.
20. The ICD-10 classification of mental and behavioural disorders. clinical descriptions and diagnostic guidelines, vol. 1. Geneva: World Health Organization; 1992.
21. Cox JL, Chapman G, Murray D, Jones P. Validation of the Edinburgh postnatal depression scale (EPDS) in non-postnatal women. J Affect Disord. 1996;39(3):185–9.
22. Spitzer R, Endicott J, Robins E. Research diagnostic criteria: instrument no. 58. New York: New York State Psychiatric Institute; 1975.
23. Alvarado-Esquivel C, Sifuentes-Alvarez A, Salas-Martinez C, Martínez-García S. Validation of the Edinburgh postpartum depression scale in a population of puerperal women in Mexico. Clin Pract Epidemiol Ment Health. 2006;2(1):33.
24. Aydin N, Inandi T, Yigit A, Hodoglugil NNS. Validation of the Turkish version of the Edinburgh postnatal depression scale among women within their first postpartum year. Soc Psychiatry Psychiatr Epidemiol. 2004;39(6):483–6.
25. Töreki A, Andó B, Keresztúri A, Sikovanyecz J, Dudas RB, Janka Z, Kozinszky Z, Pál A. The Edinburgh postnatal depression scale: translation and antepartum validation for a Hungarian sample. Midwifery. 2013;29(4):308–15.
26. First MB. User's guide for the structured clinical interview for DSM-IV axis I disorders SCID-I: clinician version. Washington DC: American Psychiatric Press; 1997.
27. Sheehan D, Janavs J, Baker R, Harnett-Sheehan K, Knapp E, Sheehan M, Lecrubier Y, Weiller E, Hergueta T, Amorim P. MINI-Mini international neuropsychiatric interview-english version 5.0. 0-DSM-IV. J Clin Psychiatry. 1998;59:34–57.
28. Jenkins R, Goldberg D, Kiima D, Mayeya J, Mayeya P, Mbatia J, Mussa M, Njenga F, Okonji M, Paton J. Classification in primary care: experience with current diagnostic systems. Psychopathology. 2002;35(2–3):127–31.
29. Mezzich JE. International surveys on the use of ICD-10 and related diagnostic systems. Psychopathology. 2002;35(2–3):72–5.
30. Bowen A, Bowen R, Maslany G, Muhajarine N. Anxiety in a socially high-risk sample of pregnant women in Canada. Can J Psychiatry. 2008;53(7):435–40.
31. Matthey S, Fisher J, Rowe H. Using the Edinburgh postnatal depression scale to screen for anxiety disorders: conceptual and methodological considerations. J Affect Disord. 2013;146(2):224–30.
32. Heron J, O'Connor TG, Evans J, Golding J, Glover V, Team AS. The course of anxiety and depression through pregnancy and the postpartum in a community sample. J Affect Disord. 2004;80(1):65–73.
33. Kingston D, Tough S, Whitfield H. Prenatal and postpartum maternal psychological distress and infant development: a systematic review. Child Psychiatry Hum Dev. 2012;43(5):683–714.
34. Matthey S. Using the Edinburgh postnatal depression scale to screen for anxiety disorders. Depression and anxiety. 2008;25(11):926–31.
35. Pop VJ, Komproe IH, Van Son MJ. Characteristics of the Edinburgh post natal depression scale in the Netherlands. J Affect Disord. 1992;26(2):105–10.
36. King PAL. Replicability of structural models of the Edinburgh postnatal depression scale (EPDS) in a community sample of postpartum African American women with low socioeconomic status. Archives of women's mental health. 2012;15(2):77–86.
37. Kubota C, Okada T, Aleksic B, Nakamura Y, Kunimoto S, Morikawa M, Shiino T, Tamaji A, Ohoka H, Banno N. Factor structure of the Japanese version of the Edinburgh postnatal depression scale in the postpartum period. PLoS One. 2014;9(8):e103941.
38. Jomeen J, Martin CR. Replicability and stability of the multidimensional model of the Edinburgh postnatal depression scale in late pregnancy. J Psychiatr Ment Health Nurs. 2007;14(3):319–24.
39. Small R, Lumley J, Yelland J, Brown S. The performance of the Edinburgh postnatal depression scale in English speaking and non-English speaking populations in Australia. Soc Psychiatry Psychiatr Epidemiol. 2007;42(1):70–8.
40. Kozinszky Z, Töreki A, Hompoth EA, Dudas RB, Németh G. A more rational, theory-driven approach to analysing the factor structure of the Edinburgh postnatal depression scale. Psychiatry Res. 2017;250:234–43.
41. Petrozzi A, Gagliardi L. Anxious and depressive components of Edinburgh postnatal depression scale in maternal postpartum psychological problems1. J Perinat Med. 2013;41(4):343–8.
42. Montazeri A, Torkan B, Omidvari S. The Edinburgh postnatal depression scale (EPDS): translation and validation study of the Iranian version. BMC psychiatry. 2007;7(1):11.
43. Martin CR, Redshaw M. Establishing a coherent and replicable measurement model of the Edinburgh postnatal depression scale. Psychiatry Res. 2018; 264:182–91.
44. Gollan JK, Wisniewski SR, Luther JF, Eng HF, Dills JL, Sit D, Ciolino JD, Wisner KL. Generating an efficient version of the Edinburgh postnatal depression scale in an urban obstetrical population. J Affect Disord. 2017;208:615–20.

45. Depression in adults: recognition and management. Clinical guideline [CG90]. [https://www.nice.org.uk/guidance/cg90].
46. Væver MS, Smith-Nielsen J, Lange T. Copenhagen infant mental health project: study protocol for a randomized controlled trial comparing circle of security–parenting and care as usual as interventions targeting infant mental health risks. BMC psychology. 2016;4(1):57.
47. Edmondson OJ, Psychogiou L, Vlachos H, Netsi E, Ramchandani PG. Depression in fathers in the postnatal period: assessment of the Edinburgh postnatal depression scale as a screening measure. J Affect Disord. 2010; 125(1):365–8.
48. Dunn G, Pickles A, Tansella M, Vázquez-Barquero JL. Two-phase epidemiological surveys in psychiatric research. Br J Psychiatry. 1999.
49. Lasa L, Ayuso-Mateos J, Vazquez-Barquero J, Dıez-Manrique F, Dowrick C. The use of the Beck depression inventory to screen for depression in the general population: a preliminary analysis. J Affect Disord. 2000;57(1):261–5.
50. Cochran WG. Sampling techniques. In., 3rd edn. New York: Wiley & Sons; 1977.
51. First M, Williams J, Karg R, Spitzer R. Structured clinical interview for DSM-5—research version (SCID-5 for DSM-5, research version; SCID-5-RV). Arlington, VA: American Psychiatric Association; 2015.
52. Matthey S, Ross-Hamid C. The validity of DSM symptoms for depression and anxiety disorders during pregnancy. J Affect Disord. 2011;133(3):546–52.
53. Fleiss JL, Levin B, Paik MC. Statistical methods for rates and proportions: John Wiley & Sons; 2013.
54. Revelle WR. Psych: procedures for personality and. Psychol Res. 2017.
55. Watson D. Rethinking the mood and anxiety disorders: a quantitative hierarchical model for DSM-V. J Abnorm Psychol. 2005;114(4):522.
56. Tavakol M, Dennick R. Making sense of Cronbach's alpha. Int J Med Educ. 2011;2:53.
57. Tyrer P. A comparison of DSM and ICD classifications of mental disorder. Adv Psychiatr Treat. 2014;20(4):280–5.
58. Green JM. Postnatal depression or perinatal dysphoria? Findings from a longitudinal community-based study using the Edinburgh postnatal depression scale. Journal of Reproductive and Infant Psychology. 1998; 16(2–3):143–55.
59. Goodman JH, Tyer-Viola L. Detection, treatment, and referral of perinatal depression and anxiety by obstetrical providers. J Women's Health. 2010; 19(3):477–90.
60. van der Westhuizen C, Brittain K, Koen N, Maré K, Zar HJ, Stein DJ. Sensitivity and specificity of the SRQ-20 and the EPDS in diagnosing major depression ante-and postnatally in a south African birth cohort study. Int J Ment Heal Addict. 2017:1–12.
61. Tharner A, Luijk MP, Van IJzendoorn MH, Bakermans-Kranenburg MJ, Jaddoe VW, Hofman A, Verhulst FC, Tiemeier H. Maternal lifetime history of depression and depressive symptoms in the prenatal and early postnatal period do not predict infant–mother attachment quality in a large, population-based Dutch cohort study. Attach Hum Dev. 2012;14(1):63–81.
62. Brouwers EPM, van Baar AL, Pop VJM. Does the Edinburgh postnatal depression scale measure anxiety? J Psychosom Res. 2001;51(5):659–63.
63. Ayers S, Coates R, Matthey S. Identifying perinatal anxiety. Identifying Perinatal Depression and Anxiety: Evidence-Based Practice in Screening, Psychosocial Assessment, and Management. 2015:93–107.
64. Ross LE, Evans SG, Sellers E, Romach M. Measurement issues in postpartum depression part 1: anxiety as a feature of postpartum depression. Archives of Women's Mental Health. 2003;6(1):51–7.
65. Rubertsson C, Börjesson K, Berglund A, Josefsson A, Sydsjö G. The Swedish validation of Edinburgh postnatal depression scale (EPDS) during pregnancy. Nordic journal of psychiatry. 2011;65(6):414–8.

12

Impact of seasons on stroke-related depression, mediated by vitamin D status

Yingying Gu[1], Xiaoqian Luan[2], Wenwei Ren[2], Lin Zhu[3] and Jincai He[2*]

Abstract

Background: This study aimed to describe the seasonal variation of depression prevalence among stroke patients at 1 month and to explore whether vitamin D plays a role in the association between seasons and post-stroke depression (PSD).

Methods: Data were collected from 402 acute stroke patients. Seasons were stratified by summertime (June to November) and wintertime (December to May) based on vitamin D status. The impact of seasons on PSD was assessed via binary logistic regression, with summertime considered the referent category. The mediating effect was used to evaluate whether vitamin D plays a role in the association between seasons and PSD.

Results: The prevalence of PSD was significantly higher in the wintertime group than in the summertime group ($P = 0.003$). The serum vitamin D level was lower in wintertime than in summertime ($P < 0.001$). Lower vitamin D levels were associated with higher HAMD scores ($P < 0.001$). In the multivariate analysis, patients in the wintertime group had a higher prevalence of PSD compared with those in the summertime group across all binary logistic regression models after adjusting for potential confounders. When serum vitamin D was added to the above model, there was no association between seasons and PSD ($P = 0.056$). Vitamin D was independently associated with PSD (OR 0.95, 95% CI 0.935–0.966, $P < 0.001$).

Conclusion: There was a clear seasonal variation in depression prevalence among stroke patients. Vitamin D status plays a critical mediating role in the relationship between season and post-stroke depression.

Keywords: Season, Depression, Stroke, Vitamin D, Biomarker

Introduction

In China, with a large population of 1.4 billion people, the stroke mortality rate is almost 1.6 million each year, and stroke has become the primary cause of death and adult disability [1]. In addition, China annual new stroke cases is approximately 2.5 million and stroke survivors is almost 7.5 million [2]. Among the complications of stroke, post-stroke depression (PSD) has high clinical relevance. Recently, a meta-analysis of 43 researches that included approximately 2 million stroke survivors suggested that 29% of patients developed depression within the first 5 years following the stroke [3]. PSD aggravated stroke-related adverse events in the form of higher mortality, greater functional disability, raised the risk of recurrent stroke, and lower the quality of life [4], and in the end, with worse rehabilitation outcomes. Although psychological, social and biological factors in the mechanism of depression have been explored [5], the potential pathophysiology of PSD is still uncertain and several diverse mechanisms may be relevant to the development of PSD.

Vitamin D is an essential neurosteroid hormone in human body that may be related to the development of depression. Several studies have been performed in humans demonstrated that vitamin D receptors and vitamin D-activating enzymes existed intracerebral structures such as the hippocampus, the prefrontal cortex, and the amygdala [6, 7]. In addition, vitamin D plays an important role in many brain processes including brain development, regulation of neurotrophic factors, neuroplasticity, neuroprotection, and neuroimmunomodulation [8], which suggesting that vitamin D might be related to the development of depression. Increasing evidence suggests that, low serum levels of 1,25-dihydroxyvitamin D had an association with the

* Correspondence: hjc@wmu.edu.cn
[2]Department of Neurology, the First Affiliated Hospital of Wenzhou Medical University, Wenzhou 325000, Zhejiang Province, China
Full list of author information is available at the end of the article

increased risk of depression in non-stroke patients [9–12]. Compared with placebo, several studies demonstrated that vitamin D supplementation improved depressive symptom in clinical patients [13, 14]. Nevertheless, in other intervention studies, no significant effect of vitamin D supplementation, compared with placebo, was found on changes in depressive symptom scores [15, 16]. Meanwhile, several studies examining the relationship between vitamin D and depression have been performed in stroke patients, and the results from these studies confirmed an inverse relationship between serum vitamin D levels and PSD [17–19].

Increasing evidence suggests that, there was a seasonal variation in depression. One study demonstrated that depressive symptoms during autumn and winter were more common than during the summer among senior high school students in Swedish [20]. Similarly, a study with 11054 general population suggested that seasonality is associated with depression [21]. In addition, another study suggested that the prevalence of postpartum depression (PD) in winter time was higher than other seasons in Taiwan [22]. Depressive symptoms are common during wintertime when vitamin D levels may be reduced due to inadequate ultraviolet B radiation leading to decreased vitamin D synthesis in the skin [23, 24]. Since serum vitamin D levels were usually higher in summertime than wintertime, if reduced vitamin D levels were a reason of PSD, then depression was supposed to be more common in wintertime when compared to summertime in stroke survivors. This study aimed to describe the seasonal variation of depression prevalence among stroke patients at 1 month post stroke and explore whether serum vitamin D levels plays an important role in the association between seasons and PSD.

Methods

Study design

This was an observational study. The study was performed from October 2013 to May 2015 and was made up of acute stroke patients aged 18-80 years at Department of Neurology, the First Affiliated Hospital of Wenzhou Medical University, Zhejiang, China (27°-28° degrees latitude). All patients had been hospitalized within 7 days of stroke first symptom, and a clinical diagnosis of acute stroke was confirmed by computerized tomography (CT) reports or magnetic resonance imaging (MRI). Patients with their serum vitamin D levels measured were included. The exclusion criteria were the following: (1) patients with a malignant tumor, a pre-stroke diagnosis dementia or a severe cognitive impairment, visual or auditory impairment or aphasia making them unable to participate in the clinical psychological tests, (2) patients with a history of mental disorders (especially depression, anxiety and other psychiatric disorders), (3) patients with another significant neurology diseases (e.g., Parkinson's disease), (4) patients suffered from osteoporosis or had used vitamin D and/or calcium supplementation previously.

This study was approved by the Medical Ethics Committee of the First Affiliated Hospital of Wenzhou Medical University and was performed in line with the principles of the Declaration of Helsinki. We have obtained written informed consent from participants or their closest relatives.

Data collection and measures

At admission, the health examination included demographic data (age and gender) and the records of weight, height, and blood pressure, and the characteristic data such as years of education, history of conventional vascular risk factors, family history of mental disorders, and smoking and drinking history. BMI was calculated based on the information of height and weight.

At 1 month after the stroke, a psychological evaluation was performed by a trained psychiatrist/neurologist who was unaware of the patients' other information. The 17-item Hamilton Rating Scale for Depression (HAMD) was used to assess the presence of depressive symptoms at the same time [25]. The diagnosis of depression was in line with the Diagnostic and Statistical Manual of Mental Disorders, fourth edition (DSM-IV) criteria on the basis of the depressive symptoms (HAMD score > 7). The severity of stroke was evaluated at admission with the National Institutes of Health Stroke Scale (NIHSS) by trained neurologists [26].

A fasting blood sample was drawn for analyses of serum vitamin D levels within 24 h of admission. The measurement of serum vitamin D levels was carried out using a competitive protein-binding assay at the First Affiliated Hospital of Wenzhou Medical University's laboratory. The intraassay coefficient of variation was 7%–10%. The season of the blood sampling was grouped as spring (March to May), summer (June to August), autumn (September to November) and winter (December to February). Vitamin D serum levels were higher during autumn 55.88 (37.28-68.61) nmol/L and summer 64.29 (47.39-81.00) nmol/L and were lower during spring 41.87 (28.34-58.39) nmol/L and winter 47.29 (33.94-60.31) nmol/L. According to the Osteoporosis Committee of China Gerontological Society for vitamin D and bone health in adult Chinese, the definition (25(OH) D < 30 nmol/L indicating deficiency, 30 to 49.9 nmol/L indicating insufficiency, and ≥50 nmol/L indicating sufficiency) [27], the extended seasons were categorized as summertime (June to November) and wintertime (December to May) based on vitamin D status [28].

Statistical analysis

Analyses were conducted to describe and to compare demographic and clinical characteristics at baseline between patients with and without depression. In addition, all analyses were conducted between seasons stratified by summertime and wintertime. The Kolmogorov-Smirnov test was used for a normal distribution. Serum vitamin D levels were not normal distribution. Non-normal distributed variables were expressed as medians (quartiles) and analyzed with the Mann-Whitney test. Normal distributed variables were presented as the mean ± standard deviation (SD) and analyzed with Student's t-test. Categorical variables were expressed as percentages and numbers and analyzed with the chi-squared test. The correlation between vitamin D and depression was examined by Spearman correlation coefficients. The impact of seasons on PSD was performed via binary logistic regression, with summertime considered the referent category. The mediating effect was used to evaluate whether vitamin D played a role in the association between seasons and PSD. The variables associated with PSD and seasons at baseline with P values < 0.1 were taken into account as potential confounders. Age, BMI, gender were also selected. Analyses were adjusted for gender and age in Model 1. Analyses were further adjusted for BMI, history of diabetes mellitus, history of hyperlipidemia, history of stroke, history of coronary heart disease, alcohol consumption, and active smoking status in Model 2. In Model 3, analyses were additionally adjusted with stroke subtypes, and the NIHSS score at admission was taken into account. Model 4 included model 3 and added vitamin D. The results were presented as adjusted odds ratios (OR) along with the corresponding 95% confidence intervals (CI). All the analyses were conducted in SPSS 20.0 (IBM, SPSS, and Chicago, IL). For all analyses, a P-value < 0.05 based on a two-sided test was considered statistically significant.

Results

Baseline characteristics of study samples

The study enrolled 551 acute stroke patients at admission. This analysis was limited to stroke survivors who were followed up at 1 month. There were 149 such patients excluded from the study: 143 patients had missing data and 6 patients passed away. Thus, the final sample comprised 402 acute stroke patients. When compared to the 149 patients excluded from the study, there were no statistically significant differences in gender, age, BMI and NIHSS scores.

In the study sample, the mean age of the stroke patients was 62.41± 10.24 years. 270 (67.2%) of the included patients were male and 132 (32.8%) were female. The median serum vitamin D level was 49.52 (32.71-64.14) nmol/L with no significant difference between women and men (50.16 (32.70-63.86) nmol/L vs 46.98 (31.63-66.01) nmol/L, P = 0.67). The median HAND score was 4 (2-8).

Vitamin D

As shown in Table 1, patients in the wintertime group showed lower serum vitamin D levels than those in the summertime group (46.98 (30.90-57.88) nmol/L vs 52.44 (46.04-68.11) nmol/L, P < 0.001). Serum vitamin D levels were statistically significant higher in the non-PSD patients than in the PSD patients (51.06(36.44-63.95) nmol/L vs 43.80(30.40-55.88) nmol/L, P = 0.011). A higher HAMD score was significantly associated with lower serum vitamin D levels (r = -0.406, P < 0.001) Fig. 1.

Season and post-stroke depression

Table 1 summarized the characteristics of the study population according to stratification of season and for patients with or without depression. Compared to the patients without depression, characteristics associated with depression in the univariate analyses were active alcohol consumption, hemorrhagic stroke, higher initial stroke severity and lower vitamin D levels. There were no statistically significant differences in demographic data. In our study, 26.6% of acute stroke patients (107 patients) were diagnosed as PSD. The prevalent rate of PSD was significantly higher in the wintertime group than in the summertime group (31.3% vs 17.5%, P =0.003) (Table 2). In addition, patients in the wintertime group had higher HAMD scores than those in the summertime group (5 (2-9) vs 3 (2-6.5), P < 0.0001). There were no statistically significant differences in other demographic characteristics and clinical data with regard to stratification of the seasons (Table 1).

Table 3 showed the results of binary logistic regression analysis for the association between PSD and stratification of the seasons. The prevalent rate of PSD was significantly higher in the wintertime group compared with those in the summertime group in an unadjusted model (OR: 2.14; 95% CI: 1.28-3.58, P = 0.003). Furthermore, patients in the wintertime group had a higher prevalent rate of PSD compared with those in the summertime group across all binary logistic regression models after adjusted potential confounders. In Model 1, after adjustment for age and gender, and summertime taken as the reference, wintertime was independently related to the prevalence of PSD (OR:2.17; 95% CI:1.29-3.63). After full adjustment numerous underlying confounding factors, the relationship between season and PSD was further strengthened with an OR (95% CI) of 2.37(1.29-4.34). While when serum vitamin D was added in above described model 3, there was no association between seasons and PSD (P = 0.056), and vitamin D was independently related to PSD (OR 0.95, 95% CI 0.935-0.966, P < 0.001).

Table 1 Characteristics of the study population ($n = 402$) according to stratification of season and post-stroke depression

	Stratification of season			Post-stroke depression		
	Wintertime ($n = 265$)	Summertime ($n = 137$)	*P*-value	Non-PSD ($n = 295$)	PSD ($n = 107$)	*P*-value
Demographic characteristics						
Age (years), mean ± SD	62.47 ± 10.22	62.29 ± 10.31	0.871	62.85 ± 10.29	61.18 ± 10.04	0.149
Female, n (percent)	86 (32.5)	46 (33.6)	0.82	94 (31.9)	38 (35.5)	0.491
BMI (kgm^{-2}), mean ± SD	24.00 ± 3.28	23.97 ± 3.29	0.899	23.84 ± 3.18	24.42 ± 2.94	0.1
Education (years), median (IQR)	5 (0–7)	4.5 (1–7)	0.889	4.5 (0–7)	5 (0–7)	0.862
Vascular risk factors (%)						
Hypertension	192 (72.7)	101 (73.7)	0.831	211 (71.8)	82 (76.6)	0.331
Diabetes mellitus	55 (20.9)	46 (33.6)	0.006	76 (25.9)	25 (23.4)	0.6
Hyperlipidemia	18 (6.9)	6 (4.4)	0.316	14 (4.8)	10 (9.4)	0.086
Coronary heart disease	19 (7.3)	4 (2.9)	0.076	20 (6.9)	3 (2.9)	0.136
History of stroke	23 (8.8)	20 (14.6)	0.075	32 (10.9)	11 (10.4)	0.877
Active smokers	82 (31.5)	37 (27.6)	0.421	93 (32.2)	26 (24.8)	0.156
Alcohol consumption	94 (37.3)	46 (35.9)	0.794	111 (39.8)	29 (28.7)	0.048
Systolic blood pressure (mmHg), mean ± SD	153.68 ± 21.38	158.45 ± 24.54	0.055	154.78 ± 22.91	156.76 ± 21.72	0.439
Diastolic blood pressure (mmHg), mean ± SD	82.96 ± 13.16	85.34 ± 13.03	0.085	83.40 ± 13.34	84.79 ± 12.63	0.149
Stroke subtype			0.629			0.001
Hemorrhagic stroke	47 (17.7)	27 (19.7)		43 (14.6)	31 (29.0)	
Ischemia stroke	218 (82.3)	110 (80.3)		252 (85.4)	76 (71.0)	
NIHSS score	3 (1–4)	3 (1–4)	0.909	2 (1–4)	3 (2–6)	< 0.001
Vitamin D (nmol/L), median (IQR)	46.98 (30.90–57.88)	52.44 (46.04–68.11)	< 0.001	51.06 (36.44–63.95)	43.80 (30.40–55.88)	0.011
HAMD at 1 month, median (IQR)	5 (2–9)	3 (2–6.5)	0.005	3 (1–5)	10 (9–13)	< 0.001

Values are shown as number (percentage) or as medians (IQR) and means (±SD)
PSD post-stroke depression, *SD* standard deviation, *IQR* interquartile range, *BMI* body mass index, *NIHSS* National Institutes of Health Stroke Scale, *HAMD* Hamilton Rating Scale for Depression

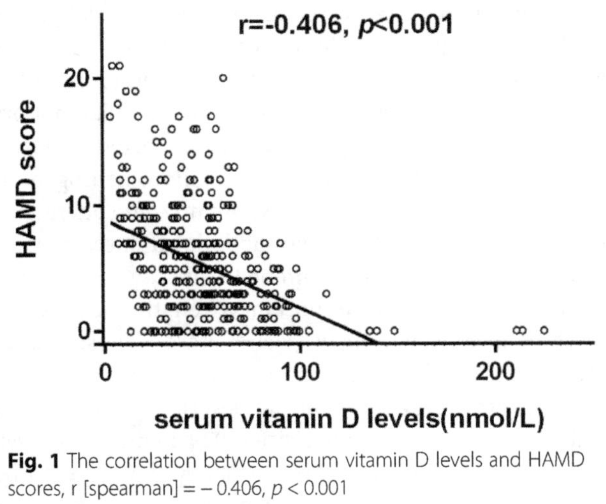

Fig. 1 The correlation between serum vitamin D levels and HAMD scores, r [spearman] = − 0.406, $p < 0.001$

Discussion

To the best of my knowledge, this is the first study investigating the impact of seasons on stroke-related depression. The present study suggested that there was a higher prevalent rate of PSD in the wintertime, when serum vitamin D levels were expected to be lower. Full adjustment for all the potential confounders related to seasons and PSD at admission had minimal effect on the results. In addition, lower serum vitamin D levels were associated with a higher HAMD score. Our results suggest that seasons were associated with the prevalence of PSD and that the association was mediated by vitamin D

Table 2 Prevalent of post-stroke depression by season

	Summertime ($n = 137$)	Wintertime ($n = 265$)	*P*-value
All stroke patients ($n = 402$)			0.003
Stroke with depression ($n = 107$)	24 (17.5)	83 (31.3)	
Stroke without depression ($n = 295$)	113 (82.5)	182 (68.7)	

Table 3 Odds ratio (95% confidence interval) for 1-month post-stroke depression by season

	Post-stroke depression	
	OR (95% CI)	*P*-value
Unadjusted Model	2.14 (1.28–3.58)	0.003
Model 1	2.15 (1.28–3.60)	0.003
Model 2	2.23 (1.28–3.88)	0.005
Model 3	2.60 (1.43–4.72)	0.002
Model 4	1.87 (0.98–3.56)	0.064

Take summertime as the referent category. Model 1 included age and gender. Model 2 included model 1 and added BMI, history of hyperlipidemia, history of Diabetes mellitus, history of Coronary heart disease, history of stroke, smoke, alcohol consumption. Model 3 included model 2 and added admission NIHSS score, and stroke subtype. Model 4 included model 3 and added vitamin D
OR odds ratios, *CI* confidence intervals

status. Low vitamin D levels induced by seasonal variation play a vital role in the presence of PSD.

In this study, we found that 26.6% patients (107 patients) were diagnosed as PSD at 1 month post stroke, and the prevalent rate of PSD was significantly higher in the wintertime group compared to those in the summertime group, which was in line with previous researches. A few studies have demonstrated seasonal mood changes to be related to various mental diseases. For example, a recent study consisting of 202 individuals suggested that the highest prevalence depressive symptoms in bipolar I disorder was observed around the winter solstice and the lowest frequency in the summer [29]. In another study, a group of 2107 women with PD were analyzed, and the results demonstrated that the prevalent rate of PD for winter deliveries was higher than other seasons in Taiwan [22]. In addition, Cobb et al found that there exists statistically significant peak in depressive symptoms from the winter solstice to the spring equinox in unipolar major depressive disorder [30]. Moreover, a recent study found that the highest proportion of major depressive episodes occurred in winter and the lowest proportions occurred in summer; seasonal variation was clearly evident [31]. Regarding the abovementioned studies, depressive symptoms are more common during wintertime than summertime, our findings are consistent with previous results.

In addition, we demonstrated that patients in the summertime group were more possibly to have higher serum vitamin D levels than those in the wintertime group, similar to previously reported results [32–34], because of enhanced sun/UVB irradiation dose which was an efficient way to acquire adequate vitamin D levels [35]. Sun exposure and estimated UV radiation significantly predicted serum vitamin D levels, and result in higher serum vitamin D levels during summer months. Moreover, serum vitamin D levels were significantly higher in non-PSD patients compared with in PSD patients, and a higher HAMD score was significantly related to lower vitamin D levels, which was in line with the results of previous researches. Previous studies have founded a strong association between depression and vitamin D in non-stroke patients [10, 11, 36–38], whereas others show no association [39, 40]. However, there have been few studies conducted in stroke patients. One study found that vitamin D deficiency was associated with depression symptoms in stroke patients [17], and others found a relationship between increased depression prevalent rate and lower serum vitamin D levels in stroke patients [18, 19].

A number of plausible pathogenesis underlying the relationship between low vitamin D level and PSD could be speculated about. As a unique neurosteroid hormone that has acrossed the blood–brain barrier, vitamin D plays an important role in many brain processes such as brain development, neuroplasticity, and regulation of neurotrophic factors [8], which may contribute to the pathophysiology of depression. Second, another probable pathogenesis between depression and low vitamin D levels is by regulating neurotransmitters such as norepinephrine, dopamine, and serotonin, which involved in the pathogenesis of depression, which are target neurotransmitters for antidepressants treatment [41]. The impact of vitamin D on neurotransmission may contribute to depression [42–44]. Moreover, vitamin D affects inflammatory pathways (promoting anti-inflammatory pathways by VDR-mediated gene transcription and down-regulating autoimmune pathways producing proinflammatory cytokines) [45, 46] that in turn to play a role in neuroprotection. In acute stroke, clinical studies and experimental have found that the ischemic brain tissue reacts to ischemic injury with a prolonged and acute inflammatory process, characterized by production of proinflammatory mediators, rapid activation of resident cells, and infiltration of all kinds of inflammatory cells [47]. A number of studies confirmed proof for the vital role of inflammation in the pathophysiologic mechanisms of depression by neurotransmitter systems, regulating neuroplasticity [48], and HPA axis activation [49]. In acute stroke survivors, lower vitamin D may contribute to PSD due to modulating the relationship between depression and inflammatory responses. Overall, the pathophysiology between lower vitamin D and PSD includes inflammation, neurogenesis in response to ischemia and low vitamin D, and alterations in serotonergic, noradrenergic, and dopaminergic pathways that lead to changes in amine levels.

Our study has some important strengths, this is the first study investigating the impact of seasons on stroke-related depression. Furthermore, our study included a measure of actual serum vitamin D levels, a diagnoses of depression, and a large sample size (402 patients). However, there are several limitations of this study that need to be addressed. First, participants with depression or other severe aphasia and severe cognitive impairment were excluded, which are likely to be underrepresented in the present study sample. Second, serum vitamin D levels was only tested at admission; therefore, our study have no data about how vitamin D was changed during the follow up. Third, we failed to acquire information on weather or temperature, physical functioning and participation in sports activities for the amount of time spent outdoors and during sunlight exposure, which may have a significant impact on vitamin D levels. In addition, information on whether patients with thyroid diseases were not recorded. Furthermore, only one point (1 month) was for the evaluation of PSD and a longer time point (e.g., 3 month or 6 month) would strengthen the manuscript. Finally, this study was conducted in a purely Chinese ethnic background and patients aged from18 to 80 years.

Conclusion

In summary, we found that PSD is more common in wintertime when serum vitamin D levels are expected to be lower compared with those in summertime, and a higher HAMD score were related to lower serum vitamin D levels; these data support the suggestion that the association is mediated by vitamin D status. Our results suggest that seasons are associated with the prevalence of PSD and the association is mediated by vitamin D status. Future studies should be performed in stroke patients followed through numerous seasons, meanwhile to explore the role of other confounders that influence by season, include daylight length, temperature, and physical activity.

Abbreviations

BMI: Body mass index; CI: Confidence intervals; CT: Computerized tomography; DSM-IV: The Diagnostic and Statistical Manual of Mental Disorders, fourth edition; HAMD: Hamilton Rating Scale for Depression; MRI: Magnetic resonance imaging; NIHSS: National Institutes of Health Stroke Scale; OR: Odds ratios; PSD: Post-stroke depression; SD: Standard deviation

Acknowledgements

We express our gratitude to all the patients and the staff who participated in our study, and thereby made this work possible.

Funding

This study was supported by the National Key Technology Research and Development Program of the Ministry of Science and Technology of China (grant number: 2015BAI13B01) and Wenzhou Municipal Sci-Tech Bureau Program (Y20160002).

Authors' contributions

YG and JH conceived of the study, conception and design, supervised the statistical analyses, and prepared manuscript, and wrote the protocol and the paper. XL, WR and LZ were responsible for interpretation of the data, drafting the manuscript, critical revision of the manuscript. All authors have contributed to and have approved the final manuscript.

Consent for publication

Not applicable

Competing interests

The authors declare that they have no competing interests.

Author details

[1]Department of Psychiatry, the First Affiliated Hospital of Wenzhou Medical University, Wenzhou 325000, Zhejiang Province, China. [2]Department of Neurology, the First Affiliated Hospital of Wenzhou Medical University, Wenzhou 325000, Zhejiang Province, China. [3]Department of Pediatrics, the First Affiliated Hospital of Wenzhou Medical University, Wenzhou 325000, Zhejiang Province, China.

References

1. Liu L, Wang D, Wong KS, Wang Y. Stroke and stroke care in China: huge burden, significant workload, and a national priority. Stroke. 2011;42(12): 3651–4.
2. Johnston SC, Mendis S, Mathers CD. Global variation in stroke burden and mortality: estimates from monitoring, surveillance, and modelling. Lancet Neurol. 2009;8(4):345–54.
3. Ayerbe L, Ayis S, Wolfe CD, Rudd AG. Natural history, predictors and outcomes of depression after stroke: systematic review and meta-analysis. Br J Psychiatry. 2013;202(1):14–21.
4. Ayerbe L, Ayis S, Crichton S, Wolfe CD, Rudd AG. The long-term outcomes of depression up to 10 years after stroke; the South London Stroke Register. J Neurol Neurosurg Psychiatry. 2014;85(5):514–21.
5. Krishnan V, Nestler EJ. Linking molecules to mood: new insight into the biology of depression. Am J Psychiatry. 2010;167(11):1305–20.
6. Zehnder D, Bland R, Williams MC, McNinch RW, Howie AJ, Stewart PM, Hewison M. Extrarenal expression of 25-hydroxyvitamin d (3)-1 alpha-hydroxylase. J Clin Endocrinol Metab. 2001;86(2):888–94.
7. Eyles DW, Smith S, Kinobe R, Hewison M, McGrath JJ. Distribution of the vitamin D receptor and 1 alpha-hydroxylase in human brain. J Chem Neuroanat. 2005;29(1):21–30.
8. Fernandes de Abreu DA, Eyles D, Feron F, Vitamin D. a neuro-immunomodulator: implications for neurodegenerative and autoimmune diseases. Psychoneuroendocrinology. 2009;34(Suppl):1S265–77.
9. Johansson P, Alehagen U, van der Wal MH, Svensson E, Jaarsma T. Vitamin D levels and depressive symptoms in patients with chronic heart failure. Int J Cardiol. 2016;207:185–9.
10. Milaneschi Y, Hoogendijk W, Lips P, Heijboer AC, Schoevers R, van Hemert AM, Beekman AT, Smit JH, Penninx BW. The association between low vitamin D and depressive disorders. Mol Psychiatry. 2014;19(4):444–51.
11. Anglin RE, Samaan Z, Walter SD, McDonald SD. Vitamin D deficiency and depression in adults: systematic review and meta-analysis. Br J Psychiatry. 2013;202:100–7.
12. Brouwer-Brolsma EM, Dhonukshe-Rutten RA, van Wijngaarden JP, van der Zwaluw NL, Sohl E, In't Veld PH, van Dijk SC, Swart KM, Enneman AW, Ham AC, et al. Low vitamin D status is associated with more depressive symptoms in Dutch older adults. Eur J Nutr. 2016;55(4):1525–34.
13. Sepehrmanesh Z, Kolahdooz F, Abedi F, Mazroii N, Assarian A, Asemi Z, Esmaillzadeh A. Vitamin D Supplementation Affects the Beck Depression Inventory, Insulin Resistance, and Biomarkers of Oxidative Stress in Patients with Major Depressive Disorder: A Randomized, Controlled Clinical Trial. J Nutr. 2016;146(2):243–8.
14. Stokes CS, Grunhage F, Baus C, Volmer DA, Wagenpfeil S, Riemenschneider M, Lammert F. Vitamin D supplementation reduces depressive symptoms in patients with chronic liver disease. Clin Nutr. 2016;35(4):950–7.
15. Bertone-Johnson ER, Powers SI, Spangler L, Larson J, Michael YL, Millen AE, Bueche MN, Salmoirago-Blotcher E, Wassertheil-Smoller S, Brunner RL, et al. Vitamin D supplementation and depression in the women's health initiative calcium and vitamin D trial. Am J Epidemiol. 2012;176(1):1–13.
16. Kjaergaard M, Waterloo K, Wang CE, Almas B, Figenschau Y, Hutchinson MS, Svartberg J, Jorde R. Effect of vitamin D supplement on depression scores in people with low levels of serum 25-hydroxyvitamin D: nested case-control study and randomised clinical trial. Br J Psychiatry. 2012;201(5):360–8.

17. Kim SH, Seok H, Kim DS. Relationship Between Serum Vitamin D Levels and Symptoms of Depression in Stroke Patients. Ann Rehabil Med. 2016;40(1): 120–5.
18. Yue W, Xiang L, Zhang YJ, Ji Y, Li X. Association of serum 25-hydroxyvitamin D with symptoms of depression after 6 months in stroke patients. Neurochem Res. 2014;39(11):2218–24.
19. Han B, Lyu Y, Sun H, Wei Y, He J. Low serum levels of vitamin D are associated with post-stroke depression. Eur J Neurol. 2015;22(9):1269–74.
20. Rastad C, Ulfberg J, Sjoden PO. High prevalence of self-reported depressive mood during the winter season among Swedish senior high school students. J Am Acad Child Adolesc Psychiatry. 2006;45(2):231–8.
21. Oyane NM, Bjelland I, Pallesen S, Holsten F, Bjorvatn B. Seasonality is associated with anxiety and depression: the Hordaland health study. J Affect Disord. 2008;105(1–3):147–55.
22. Yang SN, Shen LJ, Ping T, Wang YC, Chien CW. The delivery mode and seasonal variation are associated with the development of postpartum depression. J Affect Disord. 2011;132(1–2):158–64.
23. Engelsen O, Brustad M, Aksnes L, Lund E. Daily duration of vitamin D synthesis in human skin with relation to latitude, total ozone, altitude, ground cover, aerosols and cloud thickness. Photochem Photobiol. 2005; 81(6):1287–90.
24. Tsiaras WG, Weinstock MA. Factors influencing vitamin D status. Acta Derm Venereol. 2011;91(2):115–24.
25. Hamilton M. A rating scale for depression. J Neurol Neurosurg Psychiatry. 1960;23:56–62.
26. Brott T, Adams HPJ, Olinger CP, Marler JR, Barsan WG, Biller J, Spilker J, Holleran R, Eberle R, Hertzberg V, et al. Measurements of acute cerebral infarction: a clinical examination scale. Stroke. 1989;20(7):864–70.
27. Liao XP, Zhang ZL, Zhang HH, Zhu HM, Zhou JL, Huang QR, Wang ZX, Wang L, Liu ZH. Application Guideline for Vitamin D and Bone Health in Adult Chinese (2014 Standard Edition). In: Chin J Osteopor; 2014. p. 1011–30.
28. Meyer HE, Robsahm TE, Bjorge T, Brustad M, Blomhoff R. Vitamin D, season, and risk of prostate cancer: a nested case-control study within Norwegian health studies. Am J Clin Nutr. 2013;97(1):147–54.
29. Akhter A, Fiedorowicz JG, Zhang T, Potash JB, Cavanaugh J, Solomon DA, Coryell WH. Seasonal variation of manic and depressive symptoms in bipolar disorder. Bipolar Disord. 2013;15(4):377–84.
30. Cobb BS, Coryell WH, Cavanaugh J, Keller M, Solomon DA, Endicott J, Potash JB, Fiedorowicz JG. Seasonal variation of depressive symptoms in unipolar major depressive disorder. Compr Psychiatry. 2014;55(8):1891–9.
31. Patten SB, Williams JV, Lavorato DH, Bulloch AG, Fiest KM, Wang JL, Sajobi TT. Seasonal variation in major depressive episode prevalence in Canada. Epidemiol Psychiatr Sci. 2017;26:20161–8.
32. Park KY, Chung PW, Kim YB, Moon HS, Suh BC, Won YS, Kim JM, Youn YC, Kwon OS. Serum Vitamin D Status as a Predictor of Prognosis in Patients with Acute Ischemic Stroke. Cerebrovasc Dis. 2015;40(1–2):73–80.
33. Perna L, Felix JF, Breitling LP, Haug U, Raum E, Burwinkel B, Schottker B, Brenner H. Genetic variations in the vitamin D binding protein and season-specific levels of vitamin D among older adults. Epidemiology. 2013;24(1):104–9.
34. Klenk J, Rapp K, Denkinger MD, Nagel G, Nikolaus T, Peter R, Koenig W, Bohm BO, Rothenbacher D. Seasonality of vitamin D status in older people in Southern Germany: implications for assessment. Age Ageing. 2013;42(3): 404–8.
35. Howe WR, Dellavalle R. Vitamin D deficiency. N Engl J Med. 2007;357(19): 1981 author reply 1981-1982.
36. Lee DM, Tajar A, O'Neill TW, O'Connor DB, Bartfai G, Boonen S, Bouillon R, Casanueva FF, Finn JD, Forti G, et al. Lower vitamin D levels are associated with depression among community-dwelling European men. J Psychopharmacol. 2011;25(10):1320–8.
37. Milaneschi Y, Shardell M, Corsi AM, Vazzana R, Bandinelli S, Guralnik JM, Ferrucci L. Serum 25-hydroxyvitamin D and depressive symptoms in older women and men. J Clin Endocrinol Metab. 2010;95(7):3225–33.
38. Polak MA, Houghton LA, Reeder AI, Harper MJ, Conner TS. Serum 25-hydroxyvitamin D concentrations and depressive symptoms among young adult men and women. Nutrients. 2014;6(11):4720–30.
39. Chan R, Chan D, Woo J, Ohlsson C, Mellstrom D, Kwok T, Leung P. Association between serum 25-hydroxyvitamin D and psychological health in older Chinese men in a cohort study. J Affect Disord. 2011;130(1–2):251–9.
40. Pan A, Lu L, Franco OH, Yu Z, Li H, Lin X. Association between depressive symptoms and 25-hydroxyvitamin D in middle-aged and elderly Chinese. J Affect Disord. 2009;118(1–3):240–3.
41. Tekes K, Gyenge M, Folyovich A, Csaba G. Influence of neonatal vitamin A or vitamin D treatment on the concentration of biogenic amines and their metabolites in the adult rat brain. Horm Metab Res. 2009;41(4):277–80.
42. Brown J, Bianco JI, McGrath JJ, Eyles DW. 1,25-dihydroxyvitamin D3 induces nerve growth factor, promotes neurite outgrowth and inhibits mitosis in embryonic rat hippocampal neurons. Neurosci Lett. 2003;343(2):139–43.
43. Cass WA, Smith MP, Peters LE. Calcitriol protects against the dopamine- and serotonin-depleting effects of neurotoxic doses of methamphetamine. Ann N Y Acad Sci. 2006;1074:261–71.
44. Patrick RP, Ames BN. Vitamin D and the omega-3 fatty acids control serotonin synthesis and action, part 2: relevance for ADHD, bipolar disorder, schizophrenia, and impulsive behavior. FASEB J. 2015;29(6):2207–22.
45. Howren MB, Lamkin DM, Suls J. Associations of depression with C-reactive protein, IL-1, and IL-6: a meta-analysis. Psychosom Med. 2009;71(2):171–86.
46. Shang YX, Ding WQ, Qiu HY, Zhu FP, Yan SZ, Wang XL. Association of depression with inflammation in hospitalized patients of myocardial infarction. Pak J Med Sci. 2014;30(4):692–7.
47. Jin R, Yang G, Li G. Inflammatory mechanisms in ischemic stroke: role of inflammatory cells. J Leukoc Biol. 2010;87(5):779–89.
48. Fuchs E, Czeh B, Kole MH, Michaelis T, Lucassen PJ. Alterations of neuroplasticity in depression: the hippocampus and beyond. Eur Neuropsychopharmacol. 2004;14(Suppl):5S481–90.
49. Himmerich H, Binder EB, Kunzel HE, Schuld A, Lucae S, Uhr M, Pollmacher T, Holsboer F, Ising M. Successful antidepressant therapy restores the disturbed interplay between TNF-alpha system and HPA axis. Biol Psychiatry. 2006;60(8):882–8.

13

Prevalence and determinants of antepartum depressive and anxiety symptoms in expectant mothers and fathers: results from a perinatal psychiatric morbidity cohort study in the east and west coasts of Malaysia

Hashima E. Nasreen[1*], Jamalludin Ab Rahman[1†], Razman Mohd Rus[1†], Mira Kartiwi[2†], Rosnah Sutan[3†] and Maigun Edhborg[4†]

Abstract

Background: Research on antepartum psychiatric morbidities investigating depressive and anxiety symptoms in expectant mothers and fathers is lacking in low- and middle-income countries. This study aimed to estimate the prevalence of antepartum depressive, anxiety and co-occurring significant symptoms and explore the associated factors in a cross-section of Malaysian expectant mothers and fathers.

Methods: We used cross-sectional data from a prospective cohort study of 911 expectant mothers and 587 expectant fathers during their third trimester of pregnancy, from health clinics of two states in the east and west coasts of Malaysia. The validated Malay version of Edinburgh Postnatal Depression Scale and the anxiety sub-scale of Depression, Anxiety and Stress Scale were used to measure the depressive and anxiety symptoms. Multiple logistic regression analyses identified the determinants of antepartum depressive and anxiety symptoms (ADS and AAS).

Results: Prevalence of ADS was 12.2% in expectant mothers and 8.4% in expectant fathers, while AAS was 28.8% in expectant mothers and 13.3% in expectant fathers, and co-occurring significant symptoms was 8.0% in expectant mothers and 4.0% in expectant fathers. Expectant mothers and fathers having perceived social/family support were less likely to suffer from ADS. Intimate partner violence, poor relationship with husbands, depression in earlier pregnancy and husband's depression in current pregnancy in expectant mothers, and living in rented house, sex preference for the unborn child, stressful life events and wife's depression in current pregnancy in expectant fathers were associated with a greater likelihood of ADS. The determinants for AAS were living in rented house and with parents/in-laws, poor relationship with husbands, restrictions during pregnancy and stressful life events for expectant mothers, and stressful life events and being unsupportive towards wives in household chores for expectant fathers.

(Continued on next page)

* Correspondence: drnasreen@iium.edu.my
†Jamalludin Ab Rahman, Razman Mohd Rus, Mira Kartiwi, Rosnah Sutan and Maigun Edhborg contributed equally to this work.
[1]Faculty of Medicine, International Islamic University Malaysia, Jalan Sultan Ahmad Shah, 25200 Kuantan, Pahang, Malaysia
Full list of author information is available at the end of the article

(Continued from previous page)

Conclusion: Both ADS and AAS are prevalent in expectant mothers and fathers, and largely an undetected problem in Malaysia. Administration of couple-based screening and referral program during antenatal check-up should be universal practices to identify and treat the psychiatric morbidities.

Keywords: Antepartum, Depressive symptoms, Anxiety symptoms, Associated factors, Expectant mothers and fathers, Malaysia

Background

High maternal perinatal depressive and anxiety symptoms are traditionally evident [1]. It is widely believed that only mothers are affected by depression during pregnancy and postpartum period. Therefore, most research are focused on mothers. However, contemporary research findings, mostly from high-income countries, suggest that fathers are also affected by depression during ante and postpartum period [2]. Recent research findings in high-income countries show that anxiety is more prevalent than depression among mothers during their perinatal period [1, 3]. Moreover, anxiety and depressive symptoms are more prevalent during pregnancy than postpartum period both in mothers [1, 4] and fathers [1, 5]. Meta-analysis indicates the mean weighted prevalence for maternal antepartum depressive symptoms (ADS) is 12% in high income countries [6] and about 20% in Asia [7]. The meta-estimation of paternal ADS was 8% with significant heterogeneity observed among prevalence rates ranging from 2 to 19% [2, 4]. Emerging literature reported that 18–25% of expectant mothers [1, 3] and 8–20% of expectant fathers showed antepartum anxiety symptoms (AAS) [1]. Comorbid depressive and anxiety symptoms in mothers are common during pregnancy [1, 8], however, very few data are available about expectant fathers [1].

The prevalence of ADS and AAS tends to be higher in low- and middle-income countries (LMIC) than in high-income countries [9, 10]. Although the World Health Organization (WHO) ranks depression as the leading cause of disease burden for women of childbearing age (15–44 years) [11], often both ADS and AAS go unrecognized and untreated in LMIC [12]. However, ADS has impact on infants, such as low birth weight [13], premature delivery [14], poor nutrition [15], difficult temperament, impaired cognitive development and conduct disorder during childhood [16], and more direct impact on mothers, such as impaired mother-infant relationship [17], poor partner relationship [12], alcohol and substance use [18], the postpartum depression itself and suicidal ideation [19]. Evidences from high-income countries indicate that maternal AAS has similar effects on children's emotional, behavioral and physical development as do maternal depression [20]. Paternal ADS is negatively associated with intimate relationship satisfaction [2], parenting practices [21], and emotional and behavioral outcome of children [22].

Risks for maternal ADS differ between high-income countries and LMIC [8, 12]. Studies from Asian countries reported that risk factors for maternal ADS included socioeconomic disadvantage, unintended pregnancy, intimate partner violence (IPV), lack of social and family support, life stress, insufficient emotional and practical support, having hostile in-laws, sex preference for the unborn child, and history of mental illness [12, 23, 24]. A systematic review of 97 papers indicated that the risk factors for maternal AAS are analogous to the risk factors of maternal ADS [25]. However, the risk factors for paternal ADS are poorly understood. Based on the systematic review by Wee et al. [2], the most common correlate for paternal ADS were having a partner with elevated depressive symptoms and poor relationship satisfaction. Similar evidence is lacking in LMIC.

Research in Asia including Malaysia mostly reported on maternal postpartum depression, a few on maternal ADS [10, 26] and AAS [10, 23]. Data on expectant fathers are not available. ADS and AAS have not yet been investigated together and simultaneously for expectant mothers and fathers in Malaysia. This study aimed to estimate the prevalence and to identify the determinants of ADS and AAS in expectant mothers and fathers. The study also compared the prevalence of ADS, AAS and co-occurring significant symptoms between expectant mothers and fathers in the east and west coasts of Malaysia.

Methods

Study design and setting

Data for this cross-sectional study were originated from the baseline phase (third trimester of pregnancy) of a larger prospective cohort study of parents and their infants, which aimed to assess the impact of parental perinatal depressive and anxiety symptoms on infants' growth and development. The prospective cohort study recruited expectant mothers and fathers during the third trimester of pregnancy, and followed up mothers, fathers and infants at birth, 2–3 and 6–8 months postpartum on parents' depressive and anxiety symptoms and infants' growth and development. The study was conducted in health clinics in Pahang and Selangor states in the east and west coasts of the peninsular Malaysia, respectively. The population in Pahang is largely rural, religious and poor, where the economic mainstay is agriculture and mining contributing 4.2% to country's gross domestic product (GDP). The majority of women in Pahang are involved in unpaid domestic work including child care. On the contrary, Selangor is one of the most developed and populous state which is predominantly urban and contemporary. The major sources economy in Selangor are manufacturing and services sectors that contributed 22.6% to GDP (27). Pregnant women in Malaysia get free antenatal and postnatal care from government health clinics and hospitals, and majority of the births occur at hospitals. Whatever they plan to give birth in a government or private hospital, they can register and attend periodic check-ups at the nearest government health clinics.

Sample

Considering a prevalence of maternal depression of 21–22% [26, 27], ratio between exposed and unexposed is 1:5, prevalence of child outcomes on underweight and wasting 12% and stunting 16% [28], a significance level of 5% and a power of 80%, the estimated sample size for the larger prospective cohort study was 586 women (98 from exposed and 488 from unexposed). Taking into account a non-response rate of 30% and attrition rate 20%, the calculated sample size at baseline was 900 expectant mothers and fathers. To attain the required sample, 10 health clinics (four from west coast and six from east coast) were selected, where the highest number of attendance for antenatal check-up was observed.

Expectant mothers and fathers who attended the health clinics for their routine antenatal care at the third trimester of pregnancy, in other words when the length of pregnancy is 7 months and onward, were invited to participate in this study. Exclusion criteria for the original cohort study included non-Malaysian, illiterate, multiple pregnancy (as it may affect the child outcome) and intrauterine death. The trained clinic nurses explained the aims and procedures of the study, and respondent's right to refuse to participate or to terminate the interview at any point. Of the 911 couples approached, 904 expectant mothers (454 from east coast and 450 from west coast) and 587 expectant fathers (440 from east coast and 147 from west coast) signed the informed consent and agreed to take part indicating participation rate of 99 and 64% in expectant mothers and fathers, respectively.

Data collection

Data for the prospective cohort study were collected during March 2016 to August 2017. Data at baseline (third trimester of pregnancy) include information on socioeconomic condition, reproductive health, perceived social support, intimate partner violence (IPV), stressful life event, previous/family history of depression, and depressive and anxiety symptoms. Data from expectant mothers were collected through self-reported structured questionnaire at the health clinics. Information from expectant fathers was collected in the same manner in a separate room, if they accompanied their wives in the clinics. Questionnaires and informed consent forms were given to expectant mothers whose husbands did not accompany them to clinics. The expectant fathers who agreed to participate signed the informed consent and filled out questionnaires, and sent them back to the respected health clinics by their wives during subsequent visits. The clinic nurses and research assistants received training on the questionnaire and data collection procedures, and scrutinized the filled in questionnaires for any missing data. The questionnaire was pretested with pregnant women in a clinic other than the study sites, and was revised based on feedback received in the field test.

Assessment of explanatory variables

Age of the respondents was calculated in years. Socioeconomic status was indicated by respondent's educational level (primary, secondary or tertiary), income earner (yes or no), occupation (government employee, non-government employee, self-employed or unemployed/homemaker), monthly household income and living condition (own house, rental house or living with parents/in-laws). Based on the monthly household income, the household was ranked as high (>RM 5599), middle (RM 2300–RM 5599) or low income (<RM 2300) [29]. The obstetric indicators encompassed parity (primi or multipara), number of children, whether the current pregnancy was planned or unplanned, and preferences for gender on unborn child. Facing restriction during pregnancy was assessed if the expectant mothers were confronting any involuntary dietary restriction or movement restriction or both during pregnancy.

IPV was indicated by a lifetime experience of physical violence ever by the husband, forced sex ever, and physical violence during pregnancy. Physical violence included being slapped, shoved, punched, kicked or dragged on the ground by the partner [30]. The total score of physical violence was ranging from 0 to 4, and categorized as no act of physical violence (0) and acts of physical violence (1–4). Respondent's perceived relationship with spouse was measured as categorical and dichotomized as good (included very good and good) and poor (included not so good and bad). Expectant fathers' support towards their wives in household chores was considered as a proxy indicator of good spousal relationship.

Perceived social support was assessed by the validated Malay version of Multidimensional Scale of Perceived Social Support (MSPSS) [31]. MSPSS included 12 items, scored on a 7-point scale from 1 (very strongly disagree) to 7 (very strongly agree). The scale was categorized as low support (mean score 1–2.9), moderate support (mean score 3–5) and high support (mean score 5.1–7). MSPSS comprised of three subscales, including family support (4 items), friends' support (4 items) and significant other support (4 items), a higher score indicating more support [32]. The scale demonstrated good internal consistency in the present study with the Cronbach's alpha between 0.87 and 0.94 on the three subscales.

Stressful life event was assessed by six questions, scored 1 (yes) or 0 (no): 1) any life-threatening illness, 2) any life-threatening accident, 3) loss of family members/ friends that affects daily living activities, 4) any event/ torture/abuse that emotionally putting down, 5) severe financial difficulty, 6) any other situation that extremely frightening or horrifying in which they felt extremely helpless. A scale was composed ranging from 0 to 6, and dichotomized as 0 indicating experiencing no stressful life events and 1–6 experiencing stressful life events.

Measurement of depressive symptoms

The Edinburgh Postnatal Depression Scale (EPDS) was used to detect depressive symptoms among parents during pregnancy [33]. The EPDS is a 10-item self-administered questionnaire, where each item is rated on a 4-point scale (0–3), with total score ranging from 0 to 30. The scale rates the intensity of depressive symptoms in the last 7 days where higher score indicates more depressive symptoms. The items assessed dysphoric mood (five items), anxiety (two items), guilt (one item), ability to cope with everyday life (one item), and suicidal thought (one item). The reliability and validity of the Malay version of the EPDS was verified, whereby a score of 11.5 represented the optimum cut-off point for 72.7% sensitivity, 95% specificity and 80% positive predictive value [34]. Therefore, expectant mothers with an EPDS score ≥ 12 was categorized as having depressive symptoms and ≥ 16 as severe depressive symptoms in this study. The EPDS was also validated for use among expectant fathers, and the recommended cut-off point is ≥10 for them [35]. The scale presented good reliability in the study with Cronbach's alpha of 0.75.

Measurement of anxiety symptoms

General anxiety was assessed using the validated Malay version of the anxiety sub-scale of Depression, Anxiety and Stress Scale (DASS 21) [36]. It was used to screen and measure the level of anxiety over the previous week. DASS 21 comprised of 21 questions, which are subdivided into three domains with seven questions in each, to represent domains of depression, anxiety and stress. The choice of response ranged from 0 ('did not apply at all') to 3 ('applied very much' or 'most of the time'). In this research we used only the anxiety scale items of 2, 4, 7, 9, 15, 19 and 20. As we used the short version of DASS (21 v 42 items), score on the DASS 21 anxiety was multiplied by 2 to calculate final score of anxiety symptoms [37]. The cut-off point used in the study was ≥8 to estimate the prevalence and ≥ 15 to estimate severe anxiety symptoms [37]. The DASS 21 anxiety scale showed a good reliability in this study with Cronbach's alpha of 0.74.

Co-occurring significant symptoms were assessed if the expectant mothers scored ≥12 on EPDS and ≥ 8 on DASS 21 anxiety scale, and expectant fathers scored ≥10 on EPDS and ≥ 8 on DASS 21 anxiety scale.

Analysis

Descriptive analyses were performed for background characteristics of the respondents and prevalence of ADS and AAS. Point prevalence of ADS and AAS during third trimester of pregnancy was calculated by dividing the number of cases by the total number of non-missing outcome data at that time. An independent t-test was used to compare means of age, family support, friends' support and significant other support of MSPSS between expectant mothers and fathers. Bivariate analyses (χ^2 test, Fisher's exact test and Pearson's point bi-serial correlation coefficient) were conducted between each independent variable and the outcome variables ADS and AAS independently to identify the possible contributory factors. The independent variables with $p < 0.05$ were considered as possible contributory factors and included in the multiple logistic regression enter models. The outcome variables i.e. ADS and AAS were measured as both numerical and dichotomous. However, as there were well-known and recommended cut-off points on both variables, we used the outcome variables as dichotomous in multiple logistic regression. Subsequently a final model was emerged using only the significant variables ascertained in multiple regression models. We reported an odds ratio (OR) at 95% confidence level to indicate the likelihood of reporting depressive and anxiety symptoms. Any violation of assumption was observed by examining the interaction between explanatory variables in the models.

Results

Sample profile

The final sample included 904 expectant mothers (50.2% from west coast and 49.8% from east coast) with a mean age of 29 years and 583 expectant fathers (24.5% from west coast and 75.5% from east coast) with a mean age of 32 years in the third trimester of pregnancy after excluding four men because of missing outcome data. Expectant mothers were more educated than fathers in east coast, while no difference was observed in west coast. Half of the expectant mothers in east coast and one-third in west coast were homemakers. More expectant fathers were employed in private or public sector in west coast than in east coast. Nearly all the participants (> 90%) were Muslim and the majority were Malay

(Table 1). Approximately 53% of the participants were from middle income level with median monthly household income of RM 3300 and 26% from low income level with significantly higher proportion fitted in east coast (36.5%) than in west coast (16.2%). Three quarters of the respondents were living in nuclear family with husband and children, amongst 60% lived in rented houses (data not shown).

No significant differences were observed between the expectant mothers whose spouse agreed or disagreed to participate in the study in terms of age, race, religion and parity. However, a higher percentage of expectant mothers whose spouse did not agree to participate were from west cost ($\chi^2 = 555.53$; $p < 0.001$), richer ($\chi^2 = 39.789$; $p < 0.001$), more likely to be income earner ($\chi^2 = 13.993$; $p < 0.001$) or empolyed ($\chi^2 = 28.891$; $p < 0.001$), and had a tertiary level of education ($\chi^2 = 26.067$; $p = 0.001$).

Obstetric profile

Almost 36% of the respondents were primiparas with higher proportion fitted in west coast ($\chi^2 = 6.778$; $p = 0.009$). The mean number of children was two. Six percent of the parents experienced the death of 1–2 children, including stillbirth; and 18% of the mothers experienced abortion. Three out of every 10 expectant mothers faced cultural restrictions related to food and/or movement during pregnancy with higher proportion ($p = 0.001$) in west coast (36%) than in east coast (25.8%) (data not shown). Half of the respondents stated that the current pregnanacy was planned. More expectant fathers than expectant mothers expressed a desire to have son in both settings (Table 1).

Social support, intimate partner violence and stressful life event

Expectant mothers received higher perceived social support than expectant fathers, with a mean score of 23.0 (SD 3.5) for expectant mothers and 21.9 (SD 3.7) for expectant fathers on MSPSS-family support, and 20.5 (SD 4.0) for expectant mothers and 19.6 (SD 3.9) for expectant fathers on MSPSS-friend's support (data not shown). However, no significant difference between expectant mothers and fathers was noted in perceived social support after stratification by sites. More than 90% of the expectant fathers support their wives in household chores. Three percent of the expectant mothers in both west and east coasts reported of being the victim of at least a single act of IPV ever, including 1.4% ($n = 13$) reporting physical abuse during the current pregnancy (Table 1). About 2 % of the expectant mothers experienced of being forced to have sex with their spouse (data not shown). One-fifth of the expectant mothers and one-tenth of the expectant fathers reported that their relationship with their spouses was poor, with significantly higher proportion fitted in west coast. Conversely, more expectant fathers than expectant mothers experienced single or multiple stressful life events in their life. Overall, expectant mothers were more likely to report depression in earlier pregnancy and history of previous depressive symptoms than expectant fathers (Table 1).

Prevalence of antepartum depressive and anxiety symptoms

Of the 904 expectant mothers assessed during their third trimester of pregnancy, 110 had EPDS scores ≥12 and 206 had DASS 21 anxiety scores ≥8 indicating an ADS point prevalence of 12.2% (CI_{95} 10.7–13.7%) and AAS point prevalence of 28.8% (CI_{95} 25.8–31.8%). Similarly, the point prevalence of ADS was 8.4% (CI_{95} 6.1–10.7%) and AAS was 13.3% (CI_{95} 10.5–16.1%) in expectant fathers. The expectant mothers had higher rate of ADS ($\chi^2 = 5.26$, $p = .022$) and AAS ($\chi^2 = 48.64$, $p < 0.001$) than expectant fathers. Similarly the expectant mothers had twice as high the prevalence of co-occuring significant symptoms than expectant fathers ($\chi^2 = 49.06$, $p.0 < 001$) (Fig. 1). The point prevalence of AAS was found to be higher in west coast than in east coast in both expectant mothers (34.0% vs. 23.6%, $p = .001$) and fathers (18.4% vs. 11.6%, $p = .037$). However, no differences were noted between two sites in the prevalence of ADS (13.0% in west cost vs. 11.0% in east coast, $p = .445$ in expectant mothers, and 9.8% in west coast vs. 8.0% in east coast, $p = .492$ in expectant fathers) and co-occurring significant symptoms (8.2% in west cost vs. 7.8% in east coast, $p = .829$ in expectant mothers, and 3.5% in west coast vs. 4.1% in east coast, $p = .773$ in expectant fathers) in expectant mothers and fathers (data not shown).

Twenty-eight expectant mothers (3.1%) and seven expectant fathers (1.2%) ($p = .019$) scored ≥16 on EPDS, and 39 (4.3%) expectant mothers and nine expectant fathers (1.5%) ($p = .009$) scored ≥15 on DASS anxiety. Seven depressed expectant mothers and one depressed expectant father thought of harmimg themselves quite often (data not shown).

Determinants of antepartum depressive and anxiety symptoms

After adjusting with possible associated factors, the multiple logistic regression models showed both protective and risk factors for ADS among the expectant mothers and fathers. The protective factors included high perceived social support for expectant mothers and higher family support for expectant fathers (Tables 2 and 3). Maternal depressive symptoms were independently and positively associated with IPV ever, poor relationship with husband, depression in earlier pregnancy, and husband's depression in current pregnancy (Table 2). On the contrary, the risk of paternal depression increased with living condition (if living in a rented house), son

Table 1 Background profile of the respondents at third trimester of pregnancy (in percent unless otherwise specified)

	East Coast			West coast				
	Mothers N^a=450	Fathers N^a=440	*p* value	N[a]	Mothers N = 454	N[a]	Fathers N = 143	*p* value
Socioeconomic profile								
Age, mean (SD)	29.3(5.0)	32.3(6.1)	< 0.001	448	28.9(4.1)	134	30.1(5.1)	0.005
Race				453		138		
Malay	94.7	82.7	< 0.001		91.8		89.9	0.469
Chinese/Indian/aboriginal	5.3	17.3			8.2		10.1	
Religion				453		138		
Islam	94.9	94.8	0.943		92.5		94.9	0.325
Hindu/Buddhist/Christian	5.1	5.2			7.5		5.1	
Education				449		132		
Primary	4.0	4.1	0.012		0.4		2.3	0.136
Secondary	52.0	61.6			31.6		31.1	
Tertiary	44.0	34.3			67.9		66.7	
Occupation				454		134		
Government employee	24.0	26.1	< 0.001		19.6		20.9	< 0.001
Non-government employee	19.8	41.8			37.0		57.5	
Self employed	5.6	31.8			9.0		21.6	
Home maker/unemployed	50.7	0.2			34.4		0.0	
Obstetric information								
Parity				454				
Primipara	31.8	–			40.1		–	
Multipara	68.2				59.9			
Planned current pregnancy	49.1	53.9	0.156	449	45.0	129	45.0	0.996
Sex preference				449		131		
Boy	14.4	27.0	< 0.001		19.4		28.2	< 0.001
Girl	16.7	12.3			17.8		4.6	
No preference	68.9	60.7			62.8		67.2	
Social support				453		143		
Low	1.3	0.9	0.083		0.9		0.0	0.090
Moderate	35.1	42.3			23.4		31.5	
High	63.6	56.8			75.7		68.5	
Family support, mean (SD)	22.5(3.5)	21.8(3.7)	0.004		23.4(3.5)		22.4(3.9)	0.003
Friends support, mean (SD)	20.2(4.1)	19.7(3.9)	0.079		20.9(3.9)		19.5(4.1)	< 0.001
Significant other support, mean (SD)	22.9(4.5)	22.6(4.5)	0.412		23.6(4.2)		24.2(4.5)	0.151
Intimate partner violence								
Poor relations with spouse	15.6	14.1	0.213	452	22.1	132	4.5	0.012
Physical abuse ever	2.7	–		452	2.7		–	
Physical abuse during current pregnancy	1.3	–		453	1.5		–	
Experienced stressful life event	13.6	20.2	0.008	452	18.1	142	35.2	< 0.001
Previous history of mental illness				448		126		
Previous depressive symptoms	3.6	2.0	0.173		12.7		7.1	0.083
Depressive symptoms in earlier pregnancy	6.7	2.7	0.006		12.3		8.0	0.182

[a]Data available for analysis

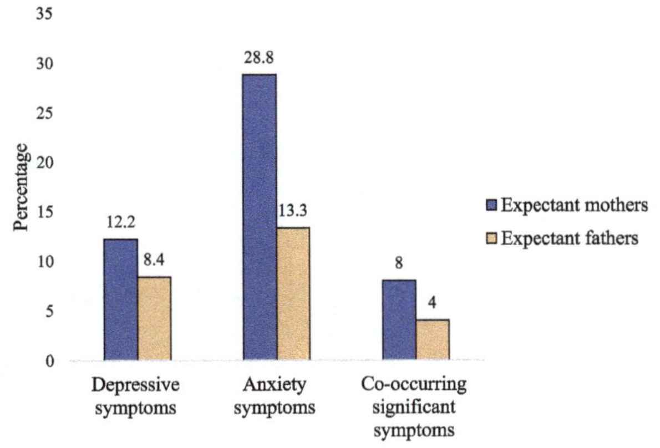

Fig. 1 Prevalence of parental antepartum depressive and anxiety symptoms

preference, stressful life event, and depression during wife's earlier pregnancy (Table 3). No significant interaction between explanatory variables was found. The Hosmer and Lemeshow tests ($p = .281$ for expectant mothers' model and $p = .748$ for expectant fathers' model) indicated that the models fit the data well. Site was not included in multiple logistic regression as it was not associated with ADS in bi-variate analysis in both expactant mothers and fathers.

The adjusted logistic regression models also identifed the determinants for AAS. The risk of AAS increased for expectant mothers with living condition (living with parents/in-laws), high family support, poor relationship with husband, restriction during preganacy, and stressful life event (Table 4). The risk of AAS for expectant fathers decreased if he supported his wife in household chores, and increased with stressful life event (Table 5). There was no association between AAS and the variation of study sites. No interaction effect of explanatory variables was observed.

Discussion

The current study is the first study that we are aware of to examine the depressive, anxiety and co-occurring significant symptoms both in expectant mothers and fathers in Malaysia. The result shows that ADS is prevalent in almost one in every eight expectant mothers and one in every 12 expectant fathers in the east and west coasts of Malaysia. Our prevalence of ADS in expectant mothers (12.2%) is in line with the previous report from a systematic review (12%) [6] and from Sabah (13.8%) in Borneo island in Malaysia [26]. However, the prevalence reported in the study is lower than the prevalence from Penang (20%) [38], but higher than the report from Ipoh (8.6%) in the northern part of Malaysia [39]. The heterogeneity observed in the prevalence rates may be potentially related to different assessment methods, multiple cut-off scores, different assessment times, or differences between populations [40].

The prevalence of ADS in expectant fathers (8.4%) in the current study is lower compared to expectant mothers' rate and identical with the meta-estimate of 8.4% reported in an updated meta-analysis of paternal depression in pregnancy [4]. A prevalence of ADS of 8% in expectant fathers seems rather high, nonetheless Cameron et al. [4] suggested that the prevalence of expectant father's depressive symptoms during their partners' pregnancy are nearly twice as high as the rate of depressive symptoms in the general male population. Thus, it indicates that transition to parenthood in men are at high risk of developing depression like women. Moreover, 3.1% of expectant mothers and 1.2% of expectant fathers had an episode of severe depression. These expectant mothers and fathers should be closely monitored and supported after birth, since not only the presence of ADS increases the risk of depressive symptoms after birth, also the severity of ADS matters [41].

This study reported that AAS occurred in just over 1 in 4 expectant mothers and 1 in 10 expectant fathers indicating that AAS is more common than ADS both in expectant mothers and fathers during the third trimester of pregnancy as expected from literature review [1]. A recent meta-analysis conducted in 34 countries (including Malaysia) reported a mean weighted prevalence of AAS of 24.6% in expectant mothers during the third trimester, and this prevalence is higher in LMIC than in high-income countries [42]. The current study confirms the meta-analysis results as the prevalence of AAS was high in Malaysia, and in line with the prevalence in Bangladeshi expectant mothers (29.4%) during their third trimester of pregnancy [23].

The prevalence of co-occurring significant symptoms in expectant mothers was double (8%) than that for expectant fathers (4%). Consistent with Austin et al. [43], we found that two-thirds of the expectant mothers with ADS also experienced anxiety symptoms. Our prevalence is compatible with a meta-estimate of comorbid symptoms of 9.5% in expectant mothers across all trimesters from 30 different countries [44], and 10% in expectant mothers and 3% in expectant fathers during third trimester of pregnancy from Portugal [1]. However, we found a higher rate compared with 4% in expectant mothers from Vietnam [45].

Systematic reviews assessed stressful life event and lack of social support as important risk factors for ADS and AAS [2, 8, 25]. The positive association of stressful life events was pronounced in our study on the outcome of ADS in expectant mothers and fathers, and AAS in expectant mothers not expectant fathers. Pregnancy is a well-recognized time of stress because of potential changes and challenges, and the occurrence of one or more stressful events can lead to an increase in the probability that mothers and fathers experience psychiatric

Table 2 Logistic regression model examining associated factors of expectant mothers' depressive symptoms

Associated factors	Full model		Final model	
	Adjusted OR	$CI_{95\%}$	Adjusted OR	$CI_{95\%}$
Socioeconomic status				
Income earner				
No	1			
Yes	1.08	0.51–2.26	–	
Economic status				
High income	1			
Middle income	1.07	0.44–2.59	–	
Low income	1.55	0.53–4.49	–	
Social support				
Low support	1		1	
Moderate support	0.12	0.02–0.65	0.16	0.03–0.73
High support	0.09	0.02–0.50	0.13	0.03–0.59
Intimate partner violence				
Experienced physical violence ever				
No	1		1	
Yes	10.93	2.79–42.83	12.13	3.48–42.23
Relationship with husband				
Good	1		1	
Poor	3.50	1.78–6.87	3.92	2.05–7.53
Pregnancy related indicators				
Planned current pregnancy				
No	1			
Yes	0.65	0.35–1.21	–	
Husband's sex preference				
No	1			
Yes	1.18	0.62–2.23	–	
Restriction during pregnancy				
No	1			
Yes	1.73	0.90–3.35	–	
Stressful life event				
No	1			
Yes	1.86	0.89–3.88	–	
History of mental illness				
Previous history of depression				
No	1			
Yes	0.96	0.31–2.98	–	
Depression in earlier pregnancy				
No	1		1	
Yes	5.48	2.35–12.79	6.78	3.21–14.34
Husband's depression in current pregnancy				
No	1		1	
Yes	2.68	1.16–6.17	3.95	1.79–8.70

Table 3 Logistic regression showing factors associated with expectant fathers' depressive symptoms

Associated factors	Full model		Final model	
	Adjusted OR	$CI_{95\%}$	Adjusted OR	$CI_{95\%}$
Socioeconomic status				
Living condition				
Own house	1		1	
Rented house	2.67	1.11–6.45	2.53	1.08–5.92
Living with parents/others	0.70	0.20–2.48	0.77	0.23–2.59
Social support				
Family support	0.82	0.72–0.94	0.83	0.76–0.90
Friends support	1.03	0.91–1.16	–	
Significant other support	1.04	0.95–1.13	–	
Partner relationship				
Relationship with wife				
Good	1			
Poor	1.91	0.72–5.06	–	
Help wife in household chores				
No	1			
Yes	0.51	0.17–1.57	–	
Pregnancy related indicator				
Son preference				
No	1		1	
Yes	2.35	1.13–4.86	2.32	1.15–4.67
Stressful life event				
No	1		1	
Yes	2.62	1.25–5.47	2.92	1.45–5.85
History of mental illness				
Depression in wife's earlier pregnancy				
No	1		1	
Yes	21.26	6.34–71.32	19.69	6.66–58.23
Wife's depression in current pregnancy				
No	1			
Yes	2.40	0.96–5.97	–	

morbidities [25]. However, the study highlighted the importance of perceived social/family support in protecting expectant mothers and fathers from ADS and adds to the prior studies from Malaysia during ante [38] and postpartum period [29]. Several studies indicate social/family support during pregnancy and childbirth may be of special significance in the context of traditional Asian society, including in Malaysia [29, 46]. Adequate support may act as a buffer against the harmful effect of other stressors and difficulties experienced in the transition to parenthood, protecting parental mental health [25]. Surprisingly, this study shows that expectant mothers living in extended families together with parents or in-laws with high family support were more likely to experience AAS, compared to expectant mothers cohabiting with their partners in their own houses. Similar association with depressive symptoms was reported from Italy [47] and Malaysia [29]. Azidah et al. [29] clarified that mothers who had good social support involved in traditional practices related to birth, were more likely to show depressive symptoms compared to mothers who did not follow traditional practices [29]. These findings contradicted the view that traditional practices with family support related to birth is protective against depressive symptoms [46]. Rashid and Mohd [38] explained that in a contemporary society mothers might feel pressure to carry out traditional activities in which they no longer believed in.

Despite a low prevalence of IPV ever (2.6%) and physical abuse during the current pregnancy (1.3%), IPV was

Table 4 Logistic regression model showing determinants of expectant mothers' anxiety symptoms

Associated factors	Full model		Final model	
	Adjusted OR	$CI_{95\%}$	Adjusted OR	$CI_{95\%}$
Socioeconomic status				
Site				
East coast	1			
West coast	1.22	0.87–1.71	–	
Education				
Primary	1			
Secondary	2.42	0.53–11.08	–	
Tertiary	3.53	0.76–16.37	–	
Income earner				
No	1		1	
Yes	0.60	0.42–0.84	0.73	0.53–1.00
Living condition				
Own house	1		1	
Rented house	1.29	0.87–1.91	1.47	1.01–2.13
Living with parents/in-laws	1.82	1.15–2.88	2.18	1.41–3.37
Social support				
Family support	1.05	1.01–1.13	1.07	1.03–1.13
Intimate partner violence				
Physical violence during pregnancy				
No	1			
Yes	3.87	0.94–15.90	–	
Relationship with husband				
Good	1		1	
Poor	1.49	0.98–2.27	1.74	1.17–2.57
Pregnancy related indicators				
Parity				
Multi	1			
Primi	1.08	0.66–1.70	–	
Number of children	0.88	0.74–1.06	–	
Husband's sex preference				
No	1			
Yes	1.09	0.78–1.53	–	
Restriction during pregnancy				
No	1		1	
Yes	2.22	1.59–3.11	2.30	1.63–3.13
Stressful life event				
No	1		1	
Yes	1.77	1.16–2.68	1.84	1.23–2.75

found to be one of the strongest predictors of ADS in the current study. There are robust evidences of the adverse impact of IPV on women's mental health [9], and on depression in particular during the perinatal period [48], when a mother is more dependent. IPV during pregnancy has serious consequences for both the mother and her unborn baby, such as miscarriage, risk of low birth-weight, pre-term labor, and fetal death [48]. Consistent with other research [2, 49], this study shows that poor relationship with husband is another strong predictor of

Table 5 Logistic regression examining determinants of expectant fathers' anxiety symptoms

Associated factors	Full model		Final model	
	Adjusted OR	$CI_{95\%}$	Adjusted OR	$CI_{95\%}$
Demographic indicator				
Site				
East coast	1			
West coast	1.38	0.79–2.43	–	
Social support				
Friends support	0.94	0.88–1.00	–	
Spousal relations				
Help wife in household chores				
No	1		1	
Yes	0.37	0.17–0.83	0.40	0.18–0.87
Pregnancy related indicator				
Number of children	0.88	0.72–1.07	–	
Stressful life event				
No	1		1	
Yes	2.62	1.56–4.39	2.82	1.70–4.70

ADS in expectant mothers. Although 19% of the study expectant mothers acknowledged poor relationship with their husbands, its impact on women's mental health is clearly noticeable in their increased likelihood of reporting depressive symptoms. Risk is also increased among the expectant fathers with the expected sex of the unborn child. The gender preference in favour of a boy has been deeply ingrained in some Asian societies [12], possibly more in expectant fathers than in expectant mothers. Although the participants were not aware about the sex of the unborn child, surprisingly more than one-quarter of expectant fathers in both sites preferred for a boy child. Gender preference and the manifestations of sex preferential behavior are expected to be intrinsically influenced by family, community, and sociocultural norms and expectations, and should not be considered solely the result of parental desires [12].

Previous depression at any time during lifetime and depression during previous pregnancies have been recognised as potential predictors for ADS [2, 8, 25]. In our study, we found only depression in earlier pregnancy both among expectant mothers and fathers, husband's depression in current pregnancy in expectant mothers, but not previous depression in life predicted ADS at third trimester of pregnancy. The association between ADS in expectant mothers and having a depressed husband has been confirmed by Nath et al. [40], which indicates that the family may be more vulnerable if men, who often is the breadwinner in the family becomes ill. There are growing evidences that depression either in expectant mothers or in expectant fathers, increases the likelihood for both to develop ADS [2, 5].

Studies that have examined the association between socioeconomic status and depressive and anxiety symptoms have reported contradictory results [2, 5, 8, 9]. Contrasting findings reported by Wee et al. [2] and Paulson and Bazemore [5] that no association between ADS/AAS and socioeconomic factors was observed either in expectant mothers or in expectant fathers in the current study. However, consistent with a systematic review by Biaggi et al. [25], our study indicates that expectant mothers are protected against AAS if they are income earner, and expectant fathers are more likely to experience ADS if they live in rented houses. Nath et al. [40] explained that the economy may not be directly associated with ADS/AAS, but it may moderate the relationship between other risk factors and ADS/AAS in expectant mothers and fathers. Contrary to prior research [50], this study did not find any association between ADS/AAS and deviances associated with urbanization. This may be because the sampling was not implemented with independent sample to compare between two study sites.

Several methodological limitations should be considered when interpreting the findings. EPDS is known to have a high rate of false positive as the detection of depression can be impeded by respondent's culture, gender, and/or predominance of somatic symptoms. However, the positive predictive value at the recommended cut-off point was 80% in the validation study in Malaysia [34], indicating that 80% of the cases might be correctly diagnosed. The DASS anxiety scale has been administered in isolation, which may affect the psychometrics of the scale. Instruments used to measure IPV and stressful life event were not validated. However, translation and back translation of the items of those instruments were done by two bilingual social science researchers. Previous depressive symptoms were identified subjectively by asking question if the respondents were encountered similar depressive symptoms ever in lifetime and in earlier pregnancies, may introduce bias through over-estimation. In the case of reporting physical violence, expectant mothers may not have reported the actual scenario due to its sensitive nature. Several other important variables were not controlled for, such as physical illness, gynaecological morbidities, previous infertility, complications during pregnancy, other mental disorders and smoking. Because of self-reported nature of the interviews, the study recruited only the literate participants that may create a selection bias against those with low education or who have literacy difficulties. Moreover, for highly urban areas, such as Selangor state, there is a greater concern about nonresponse bias, since response rates are lower among expectant fathers; they are not only harder to contact but also less likely to cooperate even after contact. As the study was carried out in purposively selected health clinics in two states of east and west coasts of Malaysia, the findings cannot be generalised.

Conclusion

Our study confirms that ADS, AAS and co-occurring significant symptoms during the third trimester of pregnancy are common in both expectant mothers and fathers, and that stressful life events, IPV, poor relationship with husband, lack of perceived social/family support, depression in earlier pregnancy, and sex preference for unborn child (expectant fathers only) are independent factors associated with ADS and AAS. The main implication of the results is to integrate a couple-focused screening intervention into the antenatal care services to prevent ADS, AAS and co-occurring significant symptoms. Because of the high costs associated with clinical interviews, research suggested to use screening instruments to identify psychiatric morbidities in LMIC. All pregnant women and their accompanying husbands attending the health clinics for antenatal check-up should be screened for ADS and AAS by the clinic nurses using the locally validated EPDS and DASS-Anxiety. The more structured clinical interview can be followed only for those who screen positive, both expectant mothers and fathers. Moreover, the policies aimed at referring couples with depressive and anxiety symptoms to the nearest health care facilities where psychological treatment is available may help couples in receiving appropriate support.

Abbreviations

AAS: Antepartum anxiety symptoms; ADS: Antepartum depressive symptoms; DASS: Depression, anxiety and stress scale; EPDS: Edinburgh postnatal depressive scale; IPV: Intimate partner violence; LMIC: Low- and middle-income countries; MSPSS: Multidimensional scale of perceived social support

Acknowledgments

The authors thank all clinic nurses and staff involved in helping the data collection. The authors also express gratitude to the women and men who participated in the study for generously giving their time and energy and providing personal details to the interviews. We would like to thank the Director General of Health, Malaysia for his permission to publish this article.

Funding

The study was supported by grants from the Ministry of Higher Education, Malaysia under the Fundamental Research Grant Scheme (FRGS15–238-0479).

Authors' contributions

All authors (HEN, JAR, RMR, MK, RS, ME) participated in the planning and conception of the research questions and the study design. HEN was the principal investigator of the study and primarily conceptualized the research. RMR, RS and MK were responsible for retrieving the data, and HEN and JAR were responsible for analyzing the data. HEN and ME participated in interpreting the data and drafted the article. All authors critically revised the manuscript for important intellectual content. All authors read and approved the manuscript.

Authors' information

Hashima E Nasreen, MBBS, MPH, PhD, Assistant Professor of Epidemiology; Department of Community Medicine, Faculty of Medicine, International Islamic University Malaysia, Kuantan Campus, Pahang, Malaysia.
Jamalludin Ab Rahman, MBBS, MPH, Professor of Biostatistics, Department of Community Medicine, Faculty of Medicine, International Islamic University Malaysia, Kuantan Campus, Pahang, Malaysia.
Razman Mohd Rus, MBBS, Masters in Community Medicine (Occupational Health), Associate Professor, Department of Community Medicine, Faculty of Medicine, International Islamic University Malaysia, Kuantan Campus, Pahang, Malaysia.
Mira Kartiwi, PhD, Associate Professor, Department of Information Systems, Faculty of Information and Communication Technology, International Islamic University Malaysia, Kuala Lumpur, Malaysia.
Rosnah Sutan, MBBS, PhD, Associate Professor, Public Health Specialist (Family Health Group), Community Health Department, Universiti Kebangsaan Malaysia Medical Centre, Kuala Lumpur, Malaysia.
Maigun Edhborg, PhD, Senior Lecturer, Department of Neurobiology, Care Science and Society, Division of Nursing, Karolinska Institutet, Stockholm, Sweden.

Consent for publication

Not applicable.

Competing interests

The authors declare that they have no competing interests.

Author details

[1]Faculty of Medicine, International Islamic University Malaysia, Jalan Sultan Ahmad Shah, 25200 Kuantan, Pahang, Malaysia. [2]Faculty of Information and Communication Technology, International Islamic University Malaysia, Jalan Gombak, 53100 Kuala Lumpur, Malaysia. [3]Community Health Department, Universiti Kebangsaan Malaysia, Bandar Tun Razak Cheras, 56000 Kuala Lumpur, Malaysia. [4]Department of Neurobiology, Care Sciences and Society, Karolinska Institute, SE-141 83 Huddinge, Stockholm, Sweden.

References

1. Figueiredo B, Conde A. Anxiety and depression in women and men from early pregnanacy to 3-months postpartum. Arch Womens Ment Health. 2011;14:247–55.
2. Wee KY, Skouteris H, Pier C, Richardson B, Milgrom J. Correlates of ante- and postnatal depression in fathers: a systematic review. J Affect Disord. 2011; 130:358–77.

3. Lee AM, Lam SK, Sze Mun Lau SM, Chong CS, Chui HW, Fong DY. Prevalence, course, and risk factors for antenatal anxiety and depression. Obstet Gynecol. 2007;110:1102–12.
4. Cameron EE, Sedov ID, Tomfohr-Madsen LM. Prevalence of paternal depression in pregnancy and the postpartum: an updated meta-analysis. J Affect Disord. 2016;206:189–203.
5. Paulson JF, Bazemore SD. Prenatal and postnatal depression in fathers and its association with maternal depression: a metal analysis. JAMA. 2010;303:1961–9.
6. Bennett HA, Einarson A, Taddio A, Koren G, Einarson TR. Prevalence of depression during pregnancy: systematic review. Obstet Gynecol. 2004;103:698–709.
7. Roomruangwong C, Epperson CN. Perinatal depression in Asian women: prevalence, associated factors and cultural aspects. Asian Biomed. 2011;5:179–93.
8. Lancaster CA, Gold KJ, Flynn HA, Yoo H, Marcus SM, Davis MM. Risk factors for depressive symptoms during pregnancy: a systematic review. Am J Obstet Gynecol. 2010;202:5–14.
9. Fisher J, Cabral de Mello M, Patel V, Rahman A, Tran T, Holton S, et al. Prevalence and determinants of common perinatal mental disorders in women in low- and lower-middle-income countries: a systematic review. Bull World Health Organ. 2012;90:139–49G.
10. Karmaliani R, Asad N, Bann C, Moss N, Mcclure EM, Pasha O, et al. Prevalence of anxiety, depression and associated factors among pregnant women of Hyderabad, Pakistan. Int J Soc Psychiatry. 2009;55:414–24.
11. Bergman K, Sarkar P, Glover V, O'Connor TG. Maternal prenatal cortisol and infant cognitive development: moderation by infant-mother attachment. Biol Psychiatry. 2010;67:1026–32.
12. Klainin P, Arthur DG. Postpartum depression in Asian cultures: a literature review. Int J Nurs Stud. 2009;46:1355–73.
13. Nasreen HE, Kabir ZN, Forsell Y, Edhborg M. Low birth weight in offspring of women with depressive and anxiety symptoms during pregnancy: results from a population based study in Bangladesh. BMC Public Health. 2010;10:515.
14. Lui C, Cnattingius S, Bergström M, Östberg V, Hjern A. Prenatal parental depression and preterm birth: a national cohort study. BJOG. 2016;123:1973–82.
15. Rahman A, Iqbal Z, Bunn J, Lovel H, Hurrington R. Impact of maternal depression on infant nutritional status and illness: a cohort study. Arch Gen Psychiatry. 2004;61:946–52.
16. Glover V. Maternal depression, anxiety and stress during pregnancy and child outcome: what needs to be done. Best Pract Res Clin Obstet Gynaecol. 2014;28:25–35.
17. Tronick E, Reck C. Infants of depressed mothers. Harv Rev Psychiatry. 2009; 17:147–56.
18. Harrison PA, Sidebottom AC. Alcohol and drug use before and during pregnancy: an examination of use patterns and predictors of cessation. Matern Child Health J. 2009;13:386–94.
19. Freitas GV, Cais CF, Stefanello S, Botega NJ. Psychological conditions and suicidal behavior in pregnant teenagers: a case-control study in Brazil. Eur Child Adolesc Psychiatry. 2008;17:336–42.
20. Glasheen C, Richardson GA, Fabio A. A systematic review of the effects of postnatal maternal anxiety on children. Arch Womens Ment Health. 2010;13:61–74.
21. Wilson S, Durbin CE. Effects of paternal depression on father's parenting behaviors: a meta-analytic review. Clin Psychol Rev. 2010;30:167–80.
22. Ramchandani PG, O'Connor TG, Evans J, Heron J, Murray L, Stein A. The effect of pre- and postnatal depression in fathers: a natural experiment comparing the effects of exposure to depression on offspring. J Child Psychol Psychiatry. 2008;49:1069–78.
23. Nasreen HE, Kabir ZN, Forsell Y, Edhborg M. Prevalence and associated factors of depressive and anxiety symptoms during pregnancy: a population based study in rural Bangladesh. BMC Womens Health. 2011;11:22.
24. Shidhaye R, Patel V. Association of socioeconomic, gender, and health factors with common mental disorders in women: a population-based study of 5703 married rural women in India. Int J Epidemiol. 2010;39:1510–21.
25. Biaggi A, Conroy S, Pawlby S, Pariante CM. Identifying the women at risk of antenatal anxiety and depression: a systematic review. J Affect Disord. 2016; 191:62–77.
26. Yusuff ASM, Tang L, Binns CW, Lee AH. Prevalence of antenatal depressive symptoms among women in Sabah, Malaysia. J Matern Fetal Neonatal Med. 2016;29:1170–4.
27. Azidah AK, Shaiful BI, Rusli N, Jamil MY. Postnatal depression and socio-cultural practices among postnatal mothers in Kota Bahru, Kelantan, Malaysia. Med J Malaysia. 2006;61:76–83.
28. UNICEF for every child: Malaysia. UNICEF. 2013. http://www.unicef.org/infobycountry/malaysia_statistics.html. Accessed 12 May 2015.
29. Government of Malaysia. Tenth Malaysia Plan 2011–2015. Putrajaya: The Economic Planning Unit, Prime Minister's Department; 2010.
30. Garcia-Moreno C, Jansen HAFM, Ellsberg M, Heise L, Watts CH. Prevalence of intimate partner violence: findings from the WHO multi-country study on women's health and domestic violence. Lancet. 2006;368:1260–9.
31. Ng CG, Nurasikin MS, Loh HS, Anne Yee HA, Zainal NZ. Factorial validation of the Malay version of multidimensional scale of perceived social support among a group of psychiatric patients. Malaysian J Psychiatry. 2012;21:2.
32. Zimet GD, Dahlem NW, Zimet SG, Farley GK. The multidimesional scale of perceived social support. J Pers Assess. 1988;52:30–41.
33. Cox JL, Holden JM, Sagovsky R. Detection of postnatal depression: development of the 10-item Edinburgh postnatal depression scale. Br J Psychiatry. 1987;150:782–6.
34. Azidah AK, Nordin R, Ismail SB, Yaacob MJ, Mustapha WMRW. Validation of the Malay version of Edinburgh postnatal depression scale. Asia Pac J Fam Med. 2004;3:9–18.
35. Matthey S, Barnett B, Kavanagh DJ, Howie P. Validation of the Edinburgh postnatal depression scale for men, and comparison of item endorsement with their partners. J Affect Disord. 2001;64:175–84.
36. Ramli M, Mohd AF, Zaini Z. Translation, validation and psychometric properties of Bahasa Malaysia version of the depression, anxiety and stress scale (DASS). Asian J Psychiatry. 2007;8:82–9.
37. Lovibond SH, Lovibond PF. Manual for the depression, anxiety and stress scales. 2nd ed. Sydney: Psychology Foundation; 1995.
38. Rashid A, Mohd R. Poor social support as a risk factor for antenatal depressive symptoms among women attending public antennal clinics in Penang, Malaysia. BMC Reprod Health. 2017;14:144.
39. Fadzil A, Balakrishnan K, Razali R, Sidi H, Malapan T, Japaraj RP, et al. Risk factors for depression and anxiety among pregnant women in hospital Tuanku, Bainum, Ipoh Malaysia. Asia Pac Psychiatry. 2013;5(Supp 1):7–13.
40. Nath S, Psychogiou L, Kuyken W, Ford T, Ryan E, Russel G. The prevalence of depressive symptoms among fathers and associated risk factors during the first seven years of their child's life: findings from the millennium cohort study. BMC Public Health. 2016;16:509–22.
41. Underwood L, Waldie KE, D'Souza S, Peterson E, Morton SMB. A longitudinal study of pre-pregnancy and pregnancy risk factors associated with antenatal and postnatal symptoms of depression: Evidence from growing up in New Zealand. Matern Child Health J. 2017;21:915–31.
42. Dennis C-L, Falah-Hassani K, Shiri R. Prevalence of antenatal and postnatal anxiety: systematic review and meta-analysis. Br J Psychiatry. 2017;210:315–23.
43. Austin MP, Hadzi-Pavlovic D, Priest SR, Reilly N, Wilhelm K, Saint K, et al. Depressive and anxiety disorders in the postpartum period: how prevalent are they and can we improve their detection? Arch Womens Ment Health. 2010;13:395–401.
44. Falah-Hassani K, Shiri R, Dennis CL. The prevalence of antenatal and postnatal co-morbid anxiety and depression: a meta-analysis. Psychol Med. 2017;47:2041–53.
45. Fisher J, Tran T, La BT, Kriitmaa K, Rosenthal D, Tran T. Common perinatal mental disorders in northern Viet Nam: community prevalence and health care use. Bull World Health Organ. 2010;88:737–45.
46. Lee DTS, Chan SSM, Sahota DS, Yip ASK, Tsui M, Chung TKA. A prevalence study of antenatal depression among Chinese women. J Affect Disord. 2004;82:93–9.
47. Balestrieri M, Isola M, Bisoffi G, Calo S, Conforti A, Driul L, et al. Determinants of antepartum depression: a multicenter study. Soc Psychiatry Psychiatr Epidemiol. 2012;47:1959–65.
48. Beydoun HA, Beydoun MA, Kaufman JS, Lo B, Zonderman AB. Intimate partner violence against adult women and its associations with major depressive disorders, depressive symptoms and postpartum depression: a systematic review and meta-analysis. Soc Sci Med. 2012;75:959–75.

14

Evaluating patterns and predictors of symptom change during a three-week intensive outpatient treatment for veterans with PTSD

Alyson K. Zalta[1,2*], Philip Held[1], Dale L. Smith[3], Brian J. Klassen[1], Ashton M. Lofgreen[1], Patricia S. Normand[1], Michael B. Brennan[1], Thad S. Rydberg[1], Randy A. Boley[1], Mark H. Pollack[1] and Niranjan S. Karnik[1]

Abstract

Background: Intensive delivery of evidence-based treatment for posttraumatic stress disorder (PTSD) is becoming increasingly popular for overcoming barriers to treatment for veterans. Understanding how and for whom these intensive treatments work is critical for optimizing their dissemination. The goals of the current study were to evaluate patterns of PTSD and depression symptom change over the course of a 3-week cohort-based intensive outpatient program (IOP) for veterans with PTSD, examine changes in posttraumatic cognitions as a predictor of treatment response, and determine whether patterns of treatment outcome or predictors of treatment outcome differed by sex and cohort type (combat versus military sexual trauma [MST]).

Method: One-hundred ninety-one veterans (19 cohorts: 12 combat-PTSD cohorts, 7 MST-PTSD cohorts) completed a 3-week intensive outpatient program for PTSD comprised of daily group and individual Cognitive Processing Therapy (CPT), mindfulness, yoga, and psychoeducation. Measures of PTSD symptoms, depression symptoms, and posttraumatic cognitions were collected before the intervention, after the intervention, and approximately every other day during the intervention.

Results: Pre-post analyses for completers ($N = 176$; 92.1% of sample) revealed large reductions in PTSD ($d = 1.12$ for past month symptoms and $d = 1.40$ for past week symptoms) and depression symptoms ($d = 1.04$ for past 2 weeks). Combat cohorts saw a greater reduction in PTSD symptoms over time relative to MST cohorts. Reduction in posttraumatic cognitions over time significantly predicted decreases in PTSD and depression symptom scores, which remained robust to adjustment for autocorrelation.

Conclusion: Intensive treatment programs are a promising approach for delivering evidence-based interventions to produce rapid treatment response and high rates of retention. Reductions in posttraumatic cognitions appear to be an important predictor of response to intensive treatment. Further research is needed to explore differences in intensive treatment response for veterans with combat exposure versus MST.

Keywords: Veteran, Military, Posttraumatic stress disorder, Combat, Military sexual trauma, Intensive treatment, Cognitive processing therapy, Mindfulness

* Correspondence: azalta@uci.edu
[1]Rush University Medical Center, Chicago, IL 60612, USA
[2]University of California, Irvine, Irvine, CA 92697, USA
Full list of author information is available at the end of the article

Background

According to a recent meta-analysis, approximately 23% of veterans returning from Operation Enduring Freedom and Operation Iraqi Freedom develop posttraumatic stress disorder (PTSD) [1]. Although evidence-based psychotherapies for PTSD such as Cognitive Processing Therapy (CPT) [2, 3] and Prolonged Exposure [4] exist, many veterans do not receive these treatments or fail to receive a sufficient dose of treatment [5]. Research shows that nearly 40% of veterans terminate evidence-based PTSD treatment prior to receiving therapeutic benefit [6]. Several barriers may contribute to low utilization of evidence-based PTSD treatment among veterans including avoidance [7] and poor accessibility of treatment [8, 9].

It is clear that there is a need for greater provision of evidence-based PTSD treatment that is able to address these barriers to its effective utilization. An increasingly popular approach is to deliver these therapies intensively (i.e., daily treatment with patients often living at or near the treatment site during the treatment period) to reduce the susceptibility to external distractions and practical barriers to engaging in treatment, and provide less opportunity for avoidance. Intensive treatments also allow for the integration of multiple treatment modalities, including case management and integrative modalities, which may support treatment adherence and provide more comprehensive care as compared to traditional outpatient therapy. For example, research has shown that the addition of case management services can reduce dropout from cognitive behavioral therapy in vulnerable populations [10].

Residential treatment programs for PTSD typically offer daily treatment over the course of 6–12 weeks with evidence-based treatment (e.g., CPT) delivered twice per week [11–15]. In addition to evidence-based treatment, these programs offer other therapeutic interventions including medication management, psychoeducation, and wellness interventions. Evidence suggests that the delivery of CPT in residential treatment is effective in reducing PTSD and depression symptoms in veterans with different types of trauma (e.g., combat, MST) and comorbidities (e.g., traumatic brain injury, substance abuse) [11–15]. However, the length of time required to complete these programs is often a significant practical barrier for veterans due to concerns about being away from family and work for such a significant period of time.

Several recent studies have shown that more intensive outpatient programs that offer daily evidence-based treatment delivered over the course of 3 weeks are also effective for active duty service members and veterans with PTSD [16, 17]. Lande and colleagues [16] evaluated a three-week intensive outpatient program (IOP) for 39 active duty service members with combat-related PTSD that incorporated daily group and individual cognitive behavioral therapy, coping skill education, medication management, art therapy, and biofeedback. Participation in the IOP resulted in significant reductions in PTSD and depressive symptoms with medium effect sizes [16]. Beidel and colleagues [17] evaluated a 3-week IOP treatment for post 9/11 veterans ($N = 112$) that incorporated daily individual exposure therapy and daily group therapy focusing on behavioral activation, social skills, and anger management. The study revealed large reductions in PTSD symptoms, depression symptoms, guilt, and anger from pre- to posttreatment and these gains were maintained at 6-month follow-up. Moreover, in this study, treatment dropout was much lower than what is typically seen in traditional outpatient treatment.

These findings suggest that IOPs are a promising avenue for delivering evidence-based treatment to veterans and service members with PTSD. However, existing studies have only evaluated key outcomes before and after treatment and have not evaluated the patterns of symptom change of symptom change over the course of treatment. Understanding how veterans improve over the course of intensive treatment is important for establishing the proper dose of treatment, a key question for balancing the feasibility and effectiveness of these programs. Specifically, examining treatment change during the intervention will allow us to determine whether patients plateau and whether shorter interventions would be worthwhile. Moreover, evaluating predictors of treatment response to determine who is most likely to benefit and how they benefit is critical for optimizing the dissemination of intensive treatments.

With women having an increasingly larger presence in the military, it is important to evaluate whether intensive PTSD treatment programs work equally well for men and women and for different trauma types (i.e., combat and military sexual trauma [MST]). One large Veteran's Administration (VA) study combining data across seven different PTSD intensive treatment programs showed that sex and a history of military sexual assault did not predict treatment outcome [18]. However, this study was limited by the fact that they combined data across very different types of treatment programs and overall the treatment effect sizes were small, suggesting that these programs were not as effective as the intensive outpatient programs [16, 17]. Another VA study examining a 7-week residential PTSD treatment showed that women had a greater decrease in clinician-rated and self-reported PTSD symptoms than men over the course of treatment, but having MST as the index trauma did not predict treatment response [12]. To our knowledge, no studies to date have examined sex and MST as a predictor of treatment response to more condensed intensive outpatient treatment programs.

With respect to how individuals benefit from treatment, current evidence suggests that changes in posttraumatic cognitions may be an important mechanism of cognitive-behavioral treatments for PTSD [19], including Cognitive Processing Therapy [20]. Schumm and colleagues [21] reported that changes in posttraumatic cognitions preceded changes in PTSD symptoms for veterans receiving CPT in a 7-week residential treatment program. However, this study relied on only 3 time points of measurement (pre, mid, post) and no studies have evaluated whether changes in posttraumatic cognitions predict treatment response in more intensive treatment models.

The current study sought to address these important gaps in the literature using effectiveness data from an all-day three-week, cohort-based IOP for service members and veterans with PTSD. The IOP included two treatment tracks (combat-based PTSD and MST-based PTSD), both of which included co-ed cohorts. The goals of the current study were to 1) evaluate patterns of PTSD and depression symptom change over the course of the IOP, 2) examine sex and cohort type (combat vs. MST) as predictors of treatment response, 3) examine changes in posttraumatic cognitions as a predictor of treatment response, and 4) examine whether the relationship between changes in posttraumatic cognitions and treatment response differed by sex or cohort type (combat vs. MST).

Method

Intervention

Service members and veterans in this sample participated in a three-week, co-ed, cohort-based IOP designed to treat PTSD secondary to military trauma. The program is housed within a non-VA, mental health clinic that provides services to individuals who served in the U.S. military and their family members free-of-charge. The program runs from 8:00 am to 5:00 pm from Monday through Friday over the course of 3 weeks (15 days of treatment delivered over 19 days). Following the clinical intake evaluation, eligible IOP participants were assigned to one of two IOP tracks (combat or MST) based on their identified index trauma; the treatment tracks ran non-concurrently (for a description of patient flow into the program see Held et al.: Feasibility and acceptability of a three-week intensive outpatient treatment program for service members and veterans with PTSD, in submission). The combat track was designed to meet the needs of veterans experiencing PTSD secondary to combat or warzone stressors. The MST track was offered to veterans with PTSD who experienced military sexual trauma and reported a sexual trauma as their index trauma. Interventions offered in both tracks were largely the same, although some minor modifications were made to address issues specific to each population (e.g., topic-specific psychoeducation sessions for MST). Cohort sizes for both tracks of the program ranged from 5 to 14 participants ($M = 10.05$, $SD = 2.27$), and most cohorts were co-ed. Clinicians were mindful in informing patients about the co-ed groups prior to treatment initiation and worked to ensure that at least 2 individuals of the same sex were in each MST cohort.

The primary IOP intervention components included daily trauma-focused treatment comprised of individual and group CPT [2, 3], as well as daily group integrative health treatment comprised of a mindfulness program that was based on Mindfulness-Based Stress Reduction [22] and yoga. Over the course of the 3 weeks, IOP participants received 15 sessions of individual CPT, 13 sessions of group CPT, 13 sessions of group mindfulness, and 12 sessions of yoga. IOP participants were also assigned daily CPT homework and mindfulness practice. These interventions were modified slightly depending on cohort type (combat vs. MST). For example, the MST track emphasized the esteem and interpersonal difficulties often characteristic of relational trauma.

In addition to these primary intervention components, several secondary intervention components were offered during the three-week IOP program. IOP participants attended experiential and didactic sessions on healthy living that focused on nutrition and physical activity. They also participated in art therapy and groups with a chaplain that focused on making meaning from military service. Psychoeducation sessions focused on common challenges in service members with PTSD such as sleep, pain, relationships, and cognitive health. IOP participants had the option to do up to 6 sessions of acupuncture, meet with a psychiatrist or nurse practitioner for medication management, and meet with a VA Liaison for case management services to assist with continuity of care upon discharge. They were also offered referrals for neuropsychological assessment in cases of suspected traumatic brain injury. Case management services were provided to address legal, financial, or other psychosocial needs. IOP participants attended planned weekend social outings in the city both for enjoyment and as opportunities to practice newly acquired skills (e.g., sports events, city tours). Psychoeducation sessions were offered to family members during the third week of the program in-person or via telehealth. Finally, outreach coordinators worked with participants routinely to ensure that veterans were connected to appropriate aftercare resources (e.g., psychotherapy, pharmacotherapy, vocational services, meditation groups, yoga classes).

Cognitive processing therapy

Cognitive Processing Therapy (CPT) is an evidence-based, cognitive-behavioral treatment for PTSD secondary to a range of traumatic experiences, including military trauma and sexual assault [23–25]. The group and individual CPT protocols were structured to accommodate the 3-week format of the IOP (see Appendix A). The content of the individual CPT aligned closely with the CPT protocol [2, 3]. CPT groups were used mainly to practice CPT skills, such as stuck point identification and cognitive restructuring using Socratic dialogue. The initial Impact Statement assignment was modified to facilitate the early identification of assimilated "stuck points." All participants were encouraged to share their Impact Statement in the groups and group-based Socratic dialogue often led to uncovering specific details about the various index traumas, which appeared to foster group cohesion. Individual and group CPT sessions were conducted by licensed psychologists, psychology postdoctoral fellows, licensed clinical social workers, and licensed professional counselors. All clinicians were trained in CPT by a national subject matter expert. Clinicians were required to participate in official CPT consultation calls following the training and were either rostered on the CPTforPTSD.com website when seeing patients as part of the IOP or working toward becoming rostered. In addition, all clinicians who saw patients as part of the IOP received weekly on-site CPT-consultation from a licensed psychologist with extensive CPT training and experience. Communication between individual and group providers was facilitated through weekly CPT consultation in which the veterans' stuck points were identified and prioritized for treatment, as well as twice-weekly conference calls among all the IOP providers.

Mindfulness based resiliency training

Our intervention, Mindfulness Based Resiliency Training (MBRT) was based on Mindfulness-Based Stress Reduction (MBSR) [22]. Mindfulness, non-judgmental attention on present moment experience, was taught as a way to help participants learn cognitive objectivity, decrease reactivity, and increase affect tolerance. Sessions were delivered by trained MBSR teachers. Content of the MBSR curriculum was maintained but the program was adapted to accommodate the 3-week format of the IOP. Specifically, the 13 sessions were delivered in 75–90 min and one of the sessions in week 2 was a mini retreat of practice without didactics. The yoga (mindful movement) content of MBSR was taught as a separate hour to have sufficient time for the MBRT curriculum and to allow family members who accompanied participants in the last week to participate. The order of the MBSR curriculum content was modified to better align with the CPT curriculum and two sessions of mindful self-compassion [26] were added as a way of helping participants who had experienced moral injury. One session also included an introduction to the mindfulness smartphone apps, Mindfulness Coach [27] and Headspace [28]. The daily home practice sessions, consisting of approximately 15 min of formal and informal mindfulness meditations, were shorter than the standard MBSR home practice.

Participants

Local and non-local service members and veterans were referred to the program through a variety of sources, including mental health providers/programs, program outreach coordinators, non-profit veteran and social service organizations, other veterans, as well as self-referral. Potential participants completed a comprehensive psychosocial and diagnostic assessment and a series of online screening measures. To be eligible for the IOP, veterans had to report a history of military trauma (e.g., combat or exposure to warzone, military sexual trauma) and to have met the diagnostic criteria for PTSD, which was verified by the Clinician Administered PTSD Scale for DSM-5 - past month version (CAPS-5) [29]. Service members and veterans were ineligible for the program and referred for a higher of level of care if they were experiencing clinical issues that would interfere with their ability to engage in the IOP. Exclusion criteria included active suicidality or homicidality, current engagement in non-suicidal self-harm, active mania or psychosis, active eating disorders, and/or active substance use that would interfere with ability to participate or pose risk of physiological withdrawal. Individuals were also excluded if current medical, legal, or other psychosocial issues would interfere with their ability to fully engage in treatment (for rates and reasons for exclusion see Held et al.: Feasibility and acceptability of a three-week intensive outpatient treatment program for service members and veterans with PTSD, in submission).

The sample for the present study consisted of 191 veterans and service members (94% discharged/retired; 6% on active duty, reserves, or National Guard; henceforth collectively referred to as "veterans") who completed a 3-week IOP between April 2016 and December 2017. This sample represents 19 cohorts including 12 cohorts of the combat track ($n = 122$; 88.5% male) and 7 cohorts of the MST track ($n = 69$; 18.8% male). On average, veterans were 41.4 years old ($SD = 9.4$, range = 25–69). The majority served in the military after the September 11th terrorist attacks (89.0%), had been deployed (81.5%), and were not local (i.e., greater than 60-mile line-of-sight distance from the mental health clinic; $n = 170$, 89.0%). Other demographic and military characteristics are reported in Table 1.

Assessment procedures

As part of the IOP, veterans completed baseline, post-treatment, and daily assessments. Prior to enrolling into the IOP, veterans participated in two 60–90 min clinical intake evaluations with a licensed psychologist, psychology postdoctoral fellow, social worker, or licensed professional counselor. During the intake evaluations, veterans completed a semi-structured psychosocial interview, were assessed for PTSD using the CAPS-5, and were asked to complete a battery of self-report assessments. On average, intake self-report questionnaires were completed

Table 1 Demographic and Military Characteristics

Variable	*n* (%)
Male	121 (63.4)
Ethnicity	
Not Hispanic or Latino	154 (80.6)
Hispanic or Latino	36 (18.9)
Refused	1 (0.5)
Race	
White or Caucasian	130 (68.1)
Black or African American	34 (17.8)
Asian	1 (0.5)
American Indian or Alaskan Native	5 (2.6)
Native Hawaiian or Pacific Islander	3 (1.6)
Other	18 (9.4)
Marital Status	
Single	38 (19.9)
Married/domestic partner	90 (47.1)
Divorced/separated	60 (31.4)
Widowed	3 (1.6)
Last or Current Military Pay Grade	
E1-E3	23 (12.0)
E4-E9	156 (81.7)
Officer/Warrant Officer	12 (6.3)
Branch	
Army/Army Reserve/Army National Guard	124 (64.9)
Air Force/Air Force Reserve/Air National Guard	18 (9.4)
Marine	26 (13.6)
Navy	21 (11.0)
Coast Guard	2 (1.1)
Military Service Status	
Discharged / Retired / Medically Retired	180 (94.2)
Active Duty / Reserves / Inactive Ready Reserve / National Guard	11 (5.8)

Note. $N = 191$

8.25 days ($SD = 5.15$) before they started the IOP program. Veterans were asked to complete additional self-report assessments during the IOP and upon completion of the IOP. All self-report assessments were conducted via Qualtrics [30], a secure online survey tool. This study was approved by the Institutional Review Board at Rush University Medical Center. A waiver of consent was obtained because all assessments were collected as part of routine care procedures.

Measures

Demographics

At intake, veterans provided demographic information, such as age, sex, ethnicity, and education level, as well as military characteristics, such as service branch, last or current military pay grade, service era, and discharge status.

Posttraumatic stress disorder

The primary outcome measure for the study was the PTSD Checklist for DSM-5 (PCL-5) [31], a 20-item self-report measure of the DSM-5 symptoms of PTSD. When completing the measure, veterans were directed to rate symptoms in relation to their index trauma. As part of their intake and post-treatment assessments, veterans were asked to rate their PTSD symptoms experienced during the past month. On 9 days during the IOP (every other day with additional assessments to capture the beginning and end of treatment), veterans were asked to report PTSD symptoms experienced during the past week. The past week version of the PCL-5 was used for the daily measures and endpoint scores because it was hypothesized to be more sensitive to any changes that would occur during treatment given that the treatment was shorter than a one-month period. The PCL-5 has been validated and shown to have good internal consistency in samples of veterans and treatment-seeking service members [31–33]. Internal reliability for the past month PCL-5 at intake was .88. Internal reliability of the past week PCL-5 on day 2 of the program was .88.

Depression

Depression symptoms were assessed as a secondary outcome measure using the Patient Health Questionnaire – 9 (PHQ-9) [34]. The PHQ-9 is a 9-item self-report measure of DSM-IV criteria for a Major Depressive Episode. The measure asks patients to report on symptoms occurring in the past 2 weeks. The PHQ-9 was assessed during at intake, post-treatment, and on 7 days during the IOP. The measure has been validated and shown to be a have good reliability and internal consistency with a variety of samples, including veterans [35, 36]. Internal reliability for the PHQ-9 at intake was .80.

Posttraumatic cognitions

Posttraumatic cognitions were assessed with the Posttraumatic Cognitions Inventory (PTCI) [37]. The PTCI is a 33-item self-report scale that measures trauma-related thoughts and beliefs including negative cognitions about the self, self-blame, and negative cognitions about others and the world. Items are scored from 1 (*totally disagree*) to 7 (*totally agree*). A total score was calculated as the sum of all items with higher scores indicating stronger endorsement of posttraumatic cognitions. The PTCI has demonstrated strong reliability and validity [37] including in military populations with PTSD [38]. Internal reliability for the PTCI at intake was .95.

Analytic approach for trajectory analysis

Mixed-effects regression models were conducted to examine the trajectory of treatment response over the course of the IOP program due to their less restrictive assumptions regarding the variance-covariance structure, their utility in accommodating some missing measurements across timepoints, and their ability to model individual change over time [39]. Likelihood ratio tests were used for significance testing in mixed effects model comparisons. Some sporadic missing data existed for responses across time points used in longitudinal analyses during the program, though 87.31% of participants utilized in this analysis completed measurements for PTSD symptoms, and 91.04% participants completed depression assessments measurements, during the final two program measurements. Additionally, missingness was not associated with outcome measures at any timepoint or any measured variable. All analyses were conducted in Stata 14 (Statacorp) [40] and Supermix 1.1 (Scientific Software International) [41]. Figures were created in Sigmaplot 13 (Systat Software) [42].

Initial examinations of the correlation structure of PTSD symptom severity (PCL-5) and depression (PHQ-9) scores over time suggested that measurements closer in time were indeed more highly correlated, and that correlations within the same time lags were moderately consistent. This suggested that first-order autoregressive or unstructured covariance pattern models were likely appropriate for errors, which were used for PTSD symptoms and depression scores, respectively, based on Akiake Information Criterion (AIC) analysis. Likelihood ratio tests and AIC values indicated that random intercepts models were a significantly better fit than linear models for both PTSD symptoms and depression ($ps < .001$), and random intercepts and trends models were a significantly better fit compared to random intercepts-alone models ($ps < .001$). A random quadratic trend component also significantly improved fit for PTSD symptom score ($p < .001$) and thus was retained for all mixed effects regression models predicting PCL-5 score that did not include time-varying covariates.[1] To test the hypothesized prognostic factors (sex and cohort type), we examined the main effects of these variables in the model as well as their interactions with time to determine whether treatment response differed over time based on these variables.[2]

We further examined PTCI scores across the treatment program as a lagged time-varying covariate to assess the relationships between changes in cognitions over the course of the program and PTSD and depression symptoms. PTCI measurements taken on days 2, 4, 9, 11, and 16 served as predictors of both PCL-5 and PHQ-9 outcomes on days 3, 5, 10, 12, and 17 while including time, sex, and cohort type in the models. This also included examining the interaction of the PTCI with time, decomposing within-subject and between-subjects PTCI effects, as well as adjusting for autocorrelation by including the most recent PTSD or depression prior outcome measurements as predictors. Of note, intra-class correlations (ICCs) were greater than .60 for both outcomes, suggesting that a high proportion of unexplained variance existed at the subject level.

Results

Treatment engagement

On average, participants completed 13.69 days (*SD* = 1.92) of the 15 days of the program. Of the 191 participants, 176 (92.1%) completed the program. There were no differences in treatment completion by sex (χ^2 (1) = 1.94, $p = .163$) or cohort type (χ^2 (1) = 0.06, $p = .815$). Of the 15 participants who did not complete the program, four voluntarily withdrew from the program seemingly due to avoidance, one withdrew due to a family emergency, one withdrew due to perceived lack of improvement, seven were removed due to verbal and physical aggression, one was removed for a medical problem, and one was removed due to failure to attend treatment sessions.

Pre-post treatment comparison

Paired *t*-tests were conducted to examine changes in symptoms from pre-treatment to post-treatment for treatment completers (see Table 2). Analyses were conducted for the entire sample and by cohort type. Results indicated significant and large reductions in PCL-5 scores (past month $d = 1.12$, past week $d = 1.40$), PHQ-9 scores ($d = 1.04$), and PTCI scores ($d = 0.75$) from pre- to post-treatment. For veterans in the MST cohort, effect sizes were medium to large ($d = 0.62$ to 0.88) whereas effect sizes for veterans in the combat cohorts were large to very large ($d = 0.85$ to 1.81). At post-treatment, 53.4% of veterans no longer met criteria for probable PTSD based on a past-week PCL-5 score ≤ 33 [32]. Rates of remission were significantly different based on cohort type with 62.9% of veterans treated in combat cohorts and 35.7% of veterans treated in MST cohorts no longer meeting criteria for probable PTSD at post-treatment ($\chi^2(1) = 10.81$, $p = .001$).

Trajectory of treatment response

All participants (completers and non-completers) were included in mixed-effects regression analyses. Examination of time trends in the mixed-effects regression models indicated that significant reductions occurred in both PCL-5 past week and PHQ-9 scores during the course of the treatment program (*ps* < .001; see Table 3). Figures 1 and 2 illustrate the general reduction in PCL-5 and PHQ-9 scores over time, respectively. The significant linear time estimates for PHQ-9 predict a 0.28 point reduction per day in depression score during the treatment program. The quadratic time trend for PCL-5 predicts an accelerating reduction over time for PTSD symptoms from .17 point in the second day to 3.78 point daily reductions at mid-program. These effects remained significant after adjusting for main effects of sex and cohort type. Neither of these covariates were significant predictors of average PCL-5 or PHQ-9 scores.

Interactions between time and both sex and cohort type were also examined. A significant cohort type by time interaction was found for PTSD symptoms ($p = .04$) but not for depression ($p = .38$), suggesting differences in PTSD outcome time trends based on cohort type (i.e., combat vs. MST; see Fig. 3). Time by sex interactions were not significant.

Changes in posttraumatic cognitions as a predictor of changes in PTSD and depression symptoms

Posttraumatic cognitions were examined as a lagged time-varying covariate to assess the relationship between changes in cognitions and changes in PTSD and depression symptoms. PTCI scores were obtained the day prior to PCL-5 and PHQ-9 score assessment, resulting in a one-day lag. In both models, PTCI scores were a significant predictor of subsequent PCL-5 and PHQ-9 scores. Lagged PTCI score remained a significant predictor of both PTSD and depression symptoms following adjustment for autocorrelation using time-lagged PCL-5 or PHQ-9 score (*ps* < .001; see Table 4). Estimates suggest that a 10-point reduction in PTCI score is associated with a PCL-5 decrease of 2.2 and a PHQ-9 decrease of 0.8 (see Table 4).

Within-subjects and between-subjects effects of PTCI were then disaggregated to examine whether they contributed equally to PTSD and depression outcomes [43]. Separation of these effects resulted in greater model fit for both PCL-5 and PHQ-9 (*ps* < .001), suggesting invariance in the contribution of these effects. Further examination revealed that although both within and between-subjects effects of PTCI were significant predictors of PCL-5 and PHQ-9 scores over time (*ps* < .001), within-subjects reductions in PTCI resulted in greater decreases for both PCL-5 and PHQ-9 relative to cross-sectional between-subjects changes.

Inclusion of PTCI did not alter the significance pattern of sex, cohort type, or the sex by time interaction. However the cohort by time interaction was no longer

Table 2 Paired *T*-tests of Pre- and Post-Treatment Scores for Treatment Completers

Variable	Total Sample				Combat Cohorts				MST Cohorts			
	n	Pre-tx *M (SD)*	Post-tx *M (SD)*	*d*	*n*	Pre-tx *M (SD)*	Post-tx *M (SD)*	*d*	*n*	Pre-tx *M (SD)*	Post-tx *M (SD)*	*d*
PCL-5 month	176	57.13 (11.34)	39.78 (18.04)	1.12***	112	57.23 (10.69)	36.94 (17.23)	1.40***	64	56.94 (12.49)	44.77 (18.49)	0.74***
PCL-5 week	157	55.89 (11.67)	33.32 (18.48)	1.40***	104	55.39 (11.25)	29.60 (16.35)	1.81***	53	56.85 (12.51)	40.62 (20.30)	0.88***
PHQ-9	176	17.79 (4.88)	12.05 (5.99)	1.04***	112	17.71 (4.59)	11.03 (5.55)	1.31***	64	17.92 (5.39)	13.83 (6.34)	0.69***
PTCI	176	146.77 (36.05)	115.41 (46.47)	0.75***	112	142.65 (33.25)	109.81 (43.13)	0.85***	64	153.97 (39.74)	125.20 (50.66)	0.62***

Note. Pre-tx = Pre-treatment; Post-tx = Post-treatment. PCL-5 month = PTSD Checklist for DSM-5 scores evaluated for the past month. PCL-5 week = PTSD Checklist for DSM-5 scores evaluated for the past week. PHQ-9 = Patient Health Questionnaire – 9. PTCI = Posttraumatic Cognitions Inventory
***$p < .001$

Table 3 Fixed Effects Parameter Estimates for Models of PTSD and Depression Scores

Variable	PCL-5	PHQ-9
	b (SE)	*b (SE)*
Time	0.03 (0.30)	−0.28 (0.08)*
Time^2	− 0.05 (0.01)*	
Sex (male = 0)	0.08 (2.38)	0.83 (1.05)
Cohort Type (MST = 0)	−0.03 (2.39)	−0.32 (1.06)
Sex x Time	0.02 (0.20)	−0.04 (0.08)
Cohort Type x Time	−0.42 (0.20)*	− 0.12 (0.08)

Note. $N = 191$. PCL-5 = PTSD Checklist for DSM-5 scores evaluated for the past week. PHQ-9 = Patient Health Questionnaire – 9. Parameter estimates reflect final outcome model estimates, which included all terms. Significance pattern of time trends were the same when covariates were excluded, though parameter estimates differed slightly. The quadratic time component was not significant in models of PHQ-9, and was thus excluded from final models
$^*p < .05$

significant when adjusting for the PTCI. Two-way interactions of sex/cohort and PTCI and three-way interactions of sex/cohort, PTCI, and time were not significant for any outcome. This suggests that the relationship between changes in PTCI and symptom changes were equivalent for men and women and for the different cohort types. The relationships between time-varying PTCI and both PCL-5 and PHQ-9 were also robust to adjustment for autocorrelation (see Table 4).

Discussion

We evaluated patterns and predictors of symptom change over the course of a 3-week co-ed cohort-based IOP for veterans with PTSD. Consistent with previous research on intensive outpatient programs [17], our intervention resulted in large and clinically meaningful changes in PTSD and depression symptoms. Our effect size for past week PTSD symptoms ($d = 1.40$) was on par with effect sizes established in efficacy trials of psychotherapy for PTSD ($d = 1.43$) [44], suggesting that intensive treatment programs may lead to comparable levels of symptom change as traditional outpatient treatment over a much shorter timeframe (3 weeks compared to 10–12 weeks for typical outpatient treatment). Moreover, adherence and retention in our program was notably high; 92% of patients completed the program and on average, patients completed more than 13 days of the 15-day program. High rates of retention have also been reported for other IOP programs. Beidel and colleagues [17] reported that 89.3% of veterans completed their IOP intervention with only 1.8% of veterans dropping

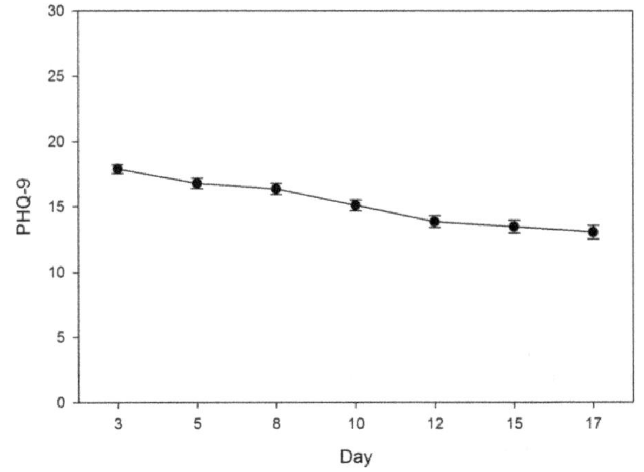

Fig. 2 Depression scores across time during treatment. Note: Error bars represent standard errors. Day represents the day the assessment was taken over the course of the 19 days that participants were in the program (15 treatment days plus 4 weekend days)

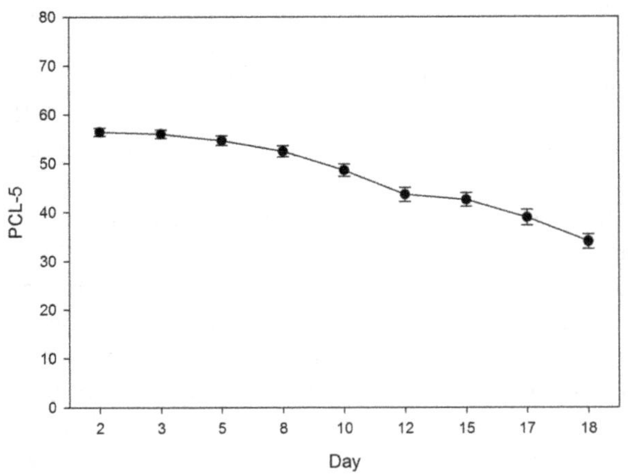

Fig. 1 PTSD symptom scores across time during treatment. Note: Error bars represent standard errors. Day represents the day the assessment was taken over the course of the 19 days that participants were in the program (15 treatment days plus 4 weekend days)

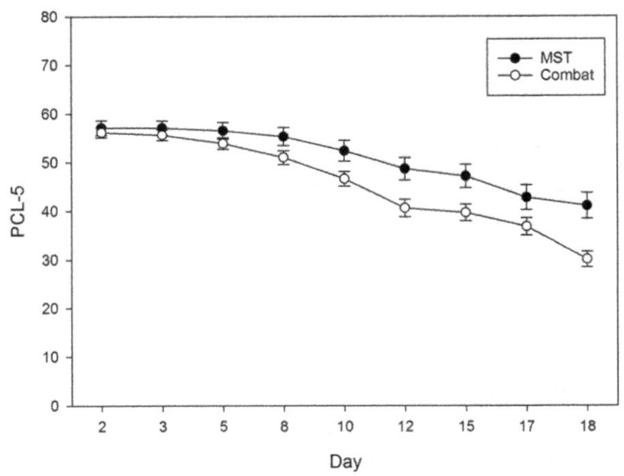

Fig. 3 PTSD symptom scores across time by cohort type. Note: Error bars represent standard errors. Day represents the day the assessment was taken over the course of the 19 days that participants were in the program (15 treatment days plus 4 weekend days)

Table 4 Parameter Estimates for PTCI as a Lagged Predictor of PTSD and Depression Scores

Lagged PTCI model variable	PCL-5	PHQ-9
	b(SE)	*b(SE)*
PTCI as time-varying covariate	0.22 (0.01)*	0.08 (0.01)*
PTCI disaggregated Within-Subjects	0.32 (0.02)*	0.10 (0.01)*
PTCI disaggregated Between-Subjects	0.21 (0.02)*	0.05 (0.01)*
PTCI adjusting for autocorrelation	0.19 (0.02)*	0.05 (0.01)*
Autocorrelation	0.46 (0.04)*	0.46 (0.04)*

Notes. $N = 188$. Parameter estimates reflect final outcome model estimates, which included time (as previously characterized), sex, and cohort type
*$p < .05$

out of treatment and 8.9% of veterans administratively discharged. A recent review describing four IOP programs across the United States, including the current program, reported that across the sites, 95% of veterans completed IOP treatment [45]. The results from these IOP programs compare favorably to previous research showing that nearly 40% of veterans drop out of traditional outpatient PTSD treatment programs [6]. Collectively, these findings suggest that the IOP format can lead to rapid treatment response and help to ensure that patients receive an adequate dose of treatment. However, it is important to note that all of these IOP programs have been administered outside of the VA system, which may also impact treatment adherence and response for a variety of reasons (e.g., differences in patient population, patient expectancy, etc.). Further research is needed to compare IOP and traditional outpatient treatment modalities in a randomized trial to evaluate how treatment delivery format affects adherence and treatment outcome. Moreover, research evaluating the implementation of similar IOP programs within the VA system would help to determine whether this model is equally effective within VA settings.

PTSD symptoms and depression symptoms demonstrated different patterns of change over the course of treatment. Depression symptoms demonstrated a linear decline over the course of treatment whereas PTSD symptoms revealed a quadratic pattern with little symptom change over the first week and an acceleration in symptom reduction over the 2nd and 3rd weeks of the program. Galovski and colleagues [46] evaluated different patterns of symptom reduction over the course of a modified CPT in which the end of treatment was determined by the patient's individual trajectory. They identified 3 different trajectories of PTSD symptom change, however the trajectory in which patients exhibited high initial symptoms and accelerating change (i.e., patients with the same negative quadratic pattern we observed) was the least common (7.2% of the sample). For depression symptoms, the consistent responders (i.e. patients with the same linear reduction we observed) were one of the more common groups (47.8% of the sample). This may suggest that initial PTSD symptom change may be slower in terms of number of sessions using an intensive approach. This could be due to the time it takes to build trust with providers or the time it takes for patients to consolidate the information they learn and translate that into meaningful changes. Anecdotal evidence suggests that over the first weekend, patients were able to digest the intensive work that was conducted over the first week. Thus, having brief rest periods may be beneficial for the consolidation of gains over the course of intensive treatment. By contrast, depression symptoms may be more liable to change early in intensive treatment given the level of behavioral activation as part of a full-day program. It is also possible that the initiation of an intensive program increases patients' sense of hope in recovery. Notably, there was no plateau in either PTSD or depressive symptoms at the end of the treatment program. It is possible that a longer treatment program could lead to further symptom reduction, though potentially at the cost of feasibility for patients.

Consistent with previous research in outpatient and residential samples [20, 21], changes in posttraumatic cognitions predicted subsequent changes in PTSD and depression symptoms in our IOP program. Given that CPT directly targets maladaptive cognitions, these results suggest that CPT is an important active ingredient in our integrative IOP treatment, though we are unable to disentangle the effects of the various treatment components that may have impacted cognitions (e.g., mindfulness practice). Regardless of what is driving changes in cognitions, our findings clearly indicate that reductions in posttraumatic cognitions can occur rapidly using an intensive treatment approach and that these changes are meaningfully associated with treatment outcomes. We have shown in the same sample of participants that pre-treatment posttraumatic cognitions predict post-treatment suicidal ideation even when accounting for pre-treatment suicidal ideation, PTSD symptoms, and depression symptoms [47]. Thus, posttraumatic cognitions may be important indicators of treatment response in terms of both symptoms and overall functioning. Future research is needed to evaluate whether posttraumatic cognitions at post-treatment predict long-term functional outcomes and risk for relapse.

Unexpectedly, the combat cohorts revealed a greater reduction in PTSD symptoms over time relative to MST cohorts reflecting an approximate 10-point difference in PTSD symptoms between combat and MST cohorts at treatment endpoint. These findings are inconsistent with previous research showing that MST status did not predict treatment response across several VA intensive PTSD treatment programs [12, 18]. There are several potential explanations that could help to account for these discrepancies. All of the treatments offered at the VA were delivered over longer time period. One possibility is that individuals with MST may not respond as well to treatment over a shortened timeframe. Individuals with MST may have higher rates of interpersonal trauma in childhood [48, 49], which could contribute to more entrenched posttraumatic cognitions that are more difficult to change for individuals with MST compared to those with combat trauma [50]. Notably, the cohort by time interaction was no longer significant after adding posttraumatic cognitions to the model. This may suggest that differences in posttraumatic cognitions across the cohorts drove differences in treatment response; however, it is also possible that this variable became non-significant due to issues of statistical power. Another possibility is that differences in group dynamics affected the cohorts differently. Anecdotally, clinicians reported a larger number of interpersonal issues that arose over the course of group treatment in MST cohorts relative to combat cohorts, which delayed treatment progress. Specifically, interpersonal conflicts among group members in MST cohorts sometimes interfered with the delivery of the CPT group content. It is possible that a greater focus on distress tolerance and interpersonal effectiveness skills early in the IOP program may be beneficial for individuals with MST. Despite the differences across the MST and combat cohorts, it is important to recognize that individuals in the MST cohorts revealed large and clinically meaningful symptom reductions, suggesting that an intensive treatment approach is promising for producing large and rapid symptom reductions for individuals with MST.

Consistent with what has been demonstrated in other intensive PTSD programs [16, 17] as well as traditional outpatient treatment [44], many patients were still symptomatic and did not reach remission at treatment endpoint. These findings may be indicative of several things. First, it is possible that these results are affected by our measurement approach in conjunction with an intensive delivery format. PTSD symptoms are typically assessed over the past month; at treatment endpoint, this would include the time period before the veteran even started treatment. We attempted to correct for this by assessing past week PTSD symptoms and the effect sizes for past week symptoms were notably higher. However, even a past week assessment would mean that veterans would have to account for symptoms occurring before one-third of the treatment was delivered. It is possible that veterans will continue to experience symptom reduction following the IOP treatment without further intervention as they apply newly acquired skills in their home environment and become more confident in their treatment gains. Our findings may also suggest that for many patients, IOP programs can help to stimulate initial symptom reduction, but further outpatient treatment may be needed to achieve remission. Finally, it is also possible that these findings suggest that there may be ways of optimizing our treatment approach to improve outcomes even further, particularly for veterans with MST as their index trauma. For example, booster sessions using telehealth may be indicated.

Our treatment approach is unique in conducting co-ed treatment cohorts; the vast majority of research on intensive treatment for veterans has been done exclusively on single sex groups [11–14]. Although the cohorts were imbalanced with a higher proportion of women in the MST cohorts and a higher proportion of men in the combat cohorts, our findings indicate that male and female veterans benefitted similarly from the IOP. Given the small sample of men with MST, we did not have sufficient power to evaluate whether interactions between sex and MST status predicted treatment response. However, our findings provide preliminary evidence that co-ed cohorts based on trauma type are tolerable and effective for veterans with PTSD.

Several limitations should be taken into consideration when interpreting our results. Because all measures were conducted as part of routine clinical practice, we relied on the use of self-report measures (PCL-5, PHQ-9) as our primary treatment outcomes, rather than gold-standard clinician administered measures such as the CAPS-5. As is typical in effectiveness research, we also did not have a control group in this study. Therefore, we cannot evaluate the degree to which changes over time were due to non-specific treatment components (e.g., therapeutic alliance) versus specific treatment components (e.g., the use of cognitive restructuring techniques). Although all IOP clinicians were CPT trained and received on-site consultation during the IOP, we did not conduct formal treatment fidelity ratings; therefore, we cannot empirically establish the degree to which the CPT protocol was followed. Moreover, our treatment approach was multifaceted with the integration of trauma-focused treatment, wellness, psychoeducation, and case management. We are unable to determine which of these treatment components are necessary for treatment outcomes.

Conclusions

This study is the first to evaluate patterns and predictors of symptom change over the course of an intensive outpatient PTSD treatment for veterans. This study suggests that IOPs show great promise in delivering full doses of evidence-based treatment and producing rapid and clinically meaningful symptom reduction for different types of veterans including men and women as well as combat and MST trauma survivors. Moreover, our findings suggest that reductions in posttraumatic cognitions may be a key treatment target in CPT-based intensive programs. Given that large amount of subject-level variance observed, more research is needed to determine which factors impact treatment outcomes in this intensive treatment approach to help improve treatment selection and effectiveness.

Appendix A

Table 5 CPT Session Outlines

Day	Group CPT Session Content	Individual CPT Session Content	Homework
Pre-IOP	N/A	• Call client • Introductions • Program overview • Cognitive Processing Therapy ○ 15 daily sessions ○ Trauma-focused ○ Can initially be challenging but we have found it to help with symptom reductions • Questions? • Motivation for treatment • Barriers • Needed support • Check-in about reactions to call	• Call therapist if questions come up
Week 1 Monday	N/A	• Set agenda, make introductions and explain check-in process • PTSD symptoms ○ Intrusions ○ Avoidance ○ Negative alterations in cognitions and mood ○ Hyperarousal • Trauma recovery and Fight-Flight-Freeze response • Cognitive theory • Role of emotions in trauma recovery • Brief review of most traumatic event • Therapy rationale – stuck points • Anticipating avoidance and increasing compliance • Overview of treatment – structured • Discuss group readiness • Check-in about reactions to session	• Write Impact Statement
Week 1 Tuesday	• Agenda, introductions, and check-ins • Group rules • Provide treatment rationale ○ Cognitive theory ○ Types of emotions ○ Biological basis of PTSD • Not everyone responds to trauma the same • Importance of support among group members • First Impact Statement • Reminder: Impact Statement assignment and problem solve completion • Check-in about reactions to session	• Brief check-in • Complete practice assignment review and set agenda • Patient to read Impact Statement • Discuss meaning of Impact Statement • Describe stuck points more fully • Identify stuck points & generate Stuck Point Log • Examine connections among events, thoughts, and feelings • Introduce ABC Worksheets • Check-in about reactions to session	• Complete 3 ABC Worksheets focused on assimilated stuck points
Week 1 Wednesday	• Agenda and check-ins • Share Impact Statements • Introduce connections between events, thoughts, and feelings • Reminder: ABC Worksheet assignment and problem solve completion • Check-in about reactions to session	• Brief check-in • Complete practice assignment review and set agenda • Review ABC Worksheets, further differentiating between thoughts and feelings • Use Socratic questioning on ABC worksheets related to the index event to help patient identify alternative hypotheses • Continue to add to Stuck Point Log • Check-in about reactions to session	• Complete 3 ABC Worksheets focused on assimilated stuck points • Write first Trauma Account
Week 1 Thursday	• Agenda and check-ins • Continue to share Impact Statements • Discuss ABC Worksheets • Introduce Socratic questioning in group, practice challenging assimilated stuck points ○ Up to two patients share • Reminder: ABC Worksheet assignment, Trauma Account assignment, and problem solve completion • Check-in about reactions to session	• Brief check-in • Complete practice assignment review and set agenda • Patient to read full Trauma Account aloud with affective expression • Identification of stuck points • Use Socratic questioning to challenge assimilated stuck points • Explain difference between responsibility and blame • Continue to add to Stuck Point Log • Check-in about reactions to session	• Complete 3 ABC Worksheets focused on assimilated stuck points • Write second Trauma Account
Week 1 Friday	• Agenda and check-ins • Share thoughts and feelings about writing	• Brief check-in • Complete practice assignment review and set agenda	• Complete 3 Challenging Questions Worksheet

Table 5 CPT Session Outlines *(Continued)*

Day	Group CPT Session Content	Individual CPT Session Content	Homework
	Trauma Account • Practice challenging assimilated stuck points ○ Up to two patients share • Reminder: ABC Worksheet assignment, Trauma Account assignment, and problem solve completion • Check-in about reactions to session	• Patient to read full Trauma Account aloud with affective expression; help identify differences between first and second account • Introduce Challenging Questions Worksheet • Use Socratic questioning to challenge assimilated stuck points • Check-in about reactions to session	
Week 2 Monday	• Agenda and check-ins • Discuss re-writing Trauma Account • Assess for and normalize strong emotions at this phase of therapy • Practice challenging assimilated stuck points ○ Up to two patients share • Reminder: Challenging Questions Worksheet assignment and problem solve completion • Check-in about reactions to session	• Brief check-in • Complete practice assignment review and set agenda • Review Challenging Questions Worksheet ○ Focus on assimilated stuck points • Continue cognitive therapy for stuck points • Introduce Patterns of Problematic Thinking Worksheet • Check-in about reactions to session	• Complete 1 Patterns of Problematic Thinking Worksheet
Week 2 Tuesday	• Agenda and check-ins • Practice challenging assimilated stuck points ○ Up to two patients share • Reminder: Patterns of Problematic Thinking Worksheet assignment and problem solve completion • Check-in about reactions to session	• Brief check-in • Complete practice assignment review and set agenda • Review Patterns of Problematic Thinking Worksheet ○ Complete challenging Questions if patient is still struggling with content • Continue cognitive therapy for stuck points • Introduce Challenging Beliefs Worksheets • Introduce first of five problem areas: Safety • Check-in about reactions to session	• Complete 3 Challenging Beliefs Worksheets • Review Safety Module
Week 2 Wednesday	• Agenda and check-ins • Practice challenging assimilated stuck points ○ Up to two patients share • Reminder: Challenging Beliefs Worksheet assignment and problem solve completion • Check-in about reactions to session	• Brief check-in • Complete practice assignment review and set agenda • Review Challenging Beliefs Worksheet ○ Address remaining assimilated stuck points or Safety stuck points • Help patient confront problematic cognitions and generate alternative beliefs using the Challenging Beliefs Worksheet • Assign Challenging Beliefs Worksheets • Introduce second of five problem areas: Trust • Check-in about reactions to session	• Complete 3 Challenging Beliefs Worksheets • Review Trust Module
Week 2 Thursday	• Agenda and check-ins • Practice challenging assimilated stuck points ○ Up to two patients share • Reminder: Challenging Beliefs Worksheet assignment and problem solve completion • Check-in about reactions to session	• Brief check-in • Complete practice assignment review and set agenda • Review Challenging Beliefs Worksheet ○ Address remaining assimilated stuck points or Trust stuck points • Help patient confront problematic cognitions and generate alternative beliefs using the Challenging Beliefs Worksheet • Assign Challenging Beliefs Worksheets • Introduce third of five problem areas: Power/Control • Check-in about reactions to session	• Complete 3 Challenging Beliefs Worksheets • Review Power / Control Module
Week 2 Friday	• Agenda and check-ins • Practice challenging assimilated/over-accommodated stuck points ○ Up to two patients share • Reminder: Challenging Beliefs Worksheet assignment and problem solve completion • Check-in about reactions to session	• Brief check-in • Complete practice assignment review and set agenda • Review Challenging Beliefs Worksheet ○ Address remaining assimilated stuck points or Power/Control stuck points • Help patient confront problematic cognitions and generate alternative beliefs using the Challenging Beliefs Worksheet • Assign Challenging Beliefs Worksheets • Introduce fourth of five problem areas: Esteem • Check-in about reactions to session	• Complete 3 Challenging Beliefs Worksheets • Review Esteem Module
Week 3 Monday	• Agenda and check-ins • Practice challenging assimilated/over-accommodated stuck points ○ Up to two patients share	• Brief check-in • Complete practice assignment review and set agenda • Review Challenging Beliefs Worksheet ○ Address remaining assimilated stuck points or	• Complete 3 Challenging Beliefs Worksheets • Review Intimacy Module

Table 5 CPT Session Outlines *(Continued)*

Day	Group CPT Session Content	Individual CPT Session Content	Homework
	○ Focus on trauma themes • Reminder: Challenging Beliefs Worksheet assignment and problem solve completion • Check-in about reactions to session	Esteem stuck points • Help patient confront problematic cognitions and generate alternative beliefs using the Challenging Beliefs Worksheet • Assign Challenging Beliefs Worksheets • Introduce fifth of five problem areas: Intimacy • Initiate contact with community provider in patient's area • Check-in about reactions to session	
Week 3 Tuesday	• Agenda and check-ins • Practice challenging assimilated/over-accommodated stuck points ○ Up to two patients share ○ Focus on trauma themes • Reminder: Challenging Beliefs Worksheet assignment and problem solve completion • Check-in about reactions to session	• Complete practice assignment review and set agenda • Review Challenging Beliefs Worksheet ○ Address remaining stuck points • Help patient confront problematic cognitions and generate alternative beliefs using the Challenging Beliefs Worksheet • Assign Challenging Beliefs Worksheets • Continue to establish contact with community provider in patient's area • Check-in about reactions to session	• Complete 3 Challenging Beliefs Worksheets
Week 3 Wednesday	• Agenda and check-ins • Practice challenging assimilated/over-accommodated stuck points ○ Up to two patients share ○ Focus on trauma themes • Reminder: Challenging Beliefs Worksheet assignment and problem solve completion • Check-in about reactions to session	• Complete practice assignment review and set agenda • Review Challenging Beliefs Worksheet ○ Address remaining stuck points • Help patient confront problematic cognitions and generate alternative beliefs using the Challenging Beliefs Worksheet • Assign Final Impact Statement • Continue to establish contact with community provider in patient's area • Check-in about reactions to session	• Final Impact Statement
Week 3 Thursday	• Agenda and check-ins • Discuss Final Impact Statement • Involve patients in reviewing the course of treatment and patient's progress • Help identify goals for the future and delineate strategies for meeting them • Check-in about reactions to session/program	• Complete practice assignment review and set agenda • Review Challenging Beliefs Worksheet ○ Address remaining stuck points • Help patient confront problematic cognitions and generate alternative beliefs using the Challenging Beliefs Worksheet • Patient to read Final Impact Statement • Involve patient in reviewing the course of treatment and patient's progress • Help identify goals for the future and delineate strategies for meeting them • Continue to establish contact with community provider in patient's area • Check-in about reactions to session	N/A
Week 3 Friday	N/A - Graduation	• Review course of treatment and patient progress • Go over discharge plan • Assess patient goals for the future • Continue to establish contact with community provider in patient's area • Review referrals and plan for aftercare	N/A - Graduation

Endnotes

[1]Quadratic time effects were non-significant for both PCL and PHQ outcomes when including lagged time-varying PTCI as a covariate, and were thus excluded from model estimates.

[2]To examine clustering by cohort, three-level mixed models were also examined. However, because trends and significance patterns for time and covariates of interest were nearly identical, and due to our interest in including cohort type (MST and combat), only two-level models were reported here.

Acknowledgements

We would like to thank the participating veterans and their families. We also wish to acknowledge Walter Faig for preparing the dataset for analysis as well as the Road Home Program administrators, research assistants, and clinicians for their contributions to this work.

Funding

We thank the Wounded Warrior Project for their support of the Road Home Program and the resulting research. AKZ's effort is partially supported by a career development award from the National Institute of Mental Health (K23 MH103394). NSK's effort is partially supported by the National Center for Advancing Translational Science of the National Institutes of Health (UL1 TR002389). The content is solely the responsibility of the authors and does not necessarily represent the official views of the National Institutes of Health or Wounded Warrior Project.

Authors' contributions
AKZ was involved in the development of the treatment program, acquisition of the data, data analysis, interpretation of the data, and drafting the manuscript. PH was involved in the development of the treatment program, treatment delivery, acquisition of the data, data analysis, interpretation of the data, and drafting of the manuscript. DLS was involved in data analysis, and drafting the manuscript. BJK, AML, PSN, MBB, TSR, and NSK were involved in the development of the treatment program, treatment delivery, interpretation of the data, and drafting the manuscript. RAB was involved in the acquisition of the data, data analysis, and drafting the manuscript. MHP was involved in establishing the treatment clinic, interpretation of the data, and editing the manuscript. All authors read and approved the final manuscript.

Consent for publication
Not applicable.

Competing interests
AKZ receives grant support from the National Institute of Mental Health and the Brain & Behavior Research Foundation. PH receives grant support from the Boeing Company and the American Psychological Association. MHP receives research funding from National Institutes of Health and Janssen Pharmaceuticals; he provides consultation to Aptinyx, Clintara, and Palo Alto Health Sciences; he has equity in Argus, Doyen Medical, Mensante Corporation, Mindsite, and Targia Pharmaceuticals; he receives royalties from SIGH-A, SAFER interviews. NSK receives grant support from Welcome Back Veterans, an initiative of the McCormick Foundation and Major League Baseball; the Bob Woodruff Foundation; the Substance Use & Mental Health Services Administration; the National Institute on Drug Abuse; and the National Center for Advancing Translational Science of the National Institutes of Health. All other authors declare that they have no competing interests.

Author details
[1]Rush University Medical Center, Chicago, IL 60612, USA. [2]University of California, Irvine, Irvine, CA 92697, USA. [3]Olivet Nazarene University, Bourbonnais, IL 60914, USA.

References

1. Fulton JJ, Calhoun PS, Wagner HR, Schry AR, Hair LP, Feeling N, et al. The prevalence of posttraumatic stress disorder in operation enduring freedom/ operation Iraqi freedom (OEF/OIF) veterans: A meta-analysis. J Anxiety Disord. 2015;31:98–107.
2. Resick PA, Monson CM, Chard KM. Cognitive processing therapy: veteran/ military version: therapist and patient materials manual. Washington: Department of Veterans Affairs; 2014.
3. Resick PA, Monson CM, Chard KM. Cognitive processing therapy for PTSD: a comprehensive manual. New York: Guilford Press; 2016.
4. Foa EB, Hembree EA, Rothbaum BO. Prolonged exposure therapy for PTSD: emotional processing of traumatic experiences: therapist guide. New York: Oxford University Press; 2007.
5. Hoge CW, Grossman SH, Auchterlonie JL, Riviere LA, Milliken CS, Wilk JE. PTSD treatment for soldiers after combat deployment: low utilization of mental health care and reasons for dropout. Psychiatr Serv. 2014;65:997–1004.
6. Kehle-Forbes SM, Meis LA, Spoont MR, Polusny MA. Treatment initiation and dropout from prolonged exposure and cognitive processing therapy in a VA outpatient clinic. Psychol Trauma. 2016;8:107–14.
7. Hundt NE, Mott JM, Miles SR, Arney J, Cully JA, Stanley MA. Veterans' perspectives on initiating evidence-based psychotherapy for posttraumatic stress disorder. Psychol Trauma. 2015;7:539–46.
8. Kehle SM, Greer N, Rutks I, Wilt T. Interventions to improve veterans' access to care: a systematic review of the literature. J Gen Intern Med. 2011;26:689.
9. Seal KH, Maguen S, Cohen B, Gima KS, Metzler TJ, Ren L, et al. VA mental health services utilization in Iraq and Afghanistan veterans in the first year of receiving new mental health diagnoses. J Trauma Stress. 2010;23:5–16.
10. Miranda J, Azocar F, Organista KC, Dwyer E, Areane P. Treatment of depression among impoverished primary care patients from ethnic minority groups. Psychiatr Serv. 2003;54:219–25.
11. Chard KM, Schumm JA, McIlvain SM, Bailey GW, Parkinson RB. Exploring the efficacy of a residential treatment program incorporating cognitive processing therapy-cognitive for veterans with PTSD and traumatic brain injury. J Trauma Stress. 2011;24:347–51.
12. Voelkel E, Pukay-Martin ND, Walter KH, Chard KM. Effectiveness of cognitive processing therapy for male and female US veterans with and without military sexual trauma. J Trauma Stress. 2015;28:174–82.
13. Zappert LN, Westrup D. Cognitive processing therapy for posttraumatic stress disorder in a residential treatment setting. Psychotherapy (Chic). 2008;45:361–76.
14. Alvarez J, McLean C, Harris AHS, Rosen CS, Ruzek JI, Kimerling R. The comparative effectiveness of cognitive processing therapy for male veterans treated in a VHA posttraumatic stress disorder residential rehabilitation program. J Consult Clin Psychol. 2011;79:590–9.
15. McDowell J, Rodriguez J. Does substance abuse affect outcomes for trauma-focused treatment of combat-related PTSD? Addict Res Theory. 2013;21:357–64.
16. Lande RG, Banks Williams L, Francis JL, Gragnani C, Morin ML. Characteristics and effectiveness of an intensive military outpatient treatment program for PTSD. J Aggress Maltreat Trauma. 2011;20:530–8.
17. Beidel DC, Frueh BC, Neer SM, Lejuez CW. The efficacy of trauma management therapy: a controlled pilot investigation of a three-week intensive outpatient program for combat-related PTSD. J Anxiety Disord. 2017;50:23–32.
18. Tiet QQ, Leyva YE, Blau K, Turchik JA, Rosen CS. Military sexual assault, gender, and PTSD treatment outcomes of US veterans. J Trauma Stress. 2015;28:92–101.
19. Zalta AK. Psychological mechanisms of effective cognitive–behavioral treatments for PTSD. Curr Psychiatry Rep. 2015;17:23.
20. Scher CD, Suvak MK, Resick PA. Trauma cognitions are related to symptoms up to 10 years after cognitive behavioral treatment for posttraumatic stress disorder. Psychol Trauma. 2017;9:750–7.
21. Schumm JA, Dickstein BD, Walter KH, Owens GP, Chard KM. Changes in posttraumatic cognitions predict changes in posttraumatic stress disorder symptoms during cognitive processing therapy. J Consult Clin Psychol. 2015;83:1161–6.
22. Kabat-Zinn J, University of Massachusetts Medical Center/Worcester. Stress reduction clinic. Full catastrophe living: using the wisdom of your body and mind to face stress, pain, and illness: the program of the stress reduction clinic at the University of Massachusetts Medical Center. New York: Dell; 1990.
23. Monson CM, Schnurr PP, Resick PA, Friedman MJ, Young-Xu Y, Stevens SP. Cognitive processing therapy for veterans with military-related posttraumatic stress disorder. J Consult Clin Psychol. 2006;74:898–907.
24. Resick PA, Williams LF, Suvak MK, Monson CM, Gradus JL. Long-term outcomes of cognitive–behavioral treatments for posttraumatic stress disorder among female rape survivors. J Consult Clin Psychol. 2012;80:201–10.
25. Resick PA, Nishith P, Weaver TL, Astin MC, Feuer CA. A comparison of cognitive-processing therapy with prolonged exposure and a waiting condition for the treatment of chronic posttraumatic stress disorder in female rape victims. J Consult Clin Psychol. 2002;70(4):867–79.
26. Neff KD. The role of self-compassion in development: a healthier way to relate to oneself. Hum Dev. 2009;52:211–4.
27. US Department of Veterans Affairs. Mindfulness Coach [App]; http://www.ptsd.va.gov/public/materials/apps/mobileapp_mindfulness_coach.asp.
28. Headspace Inc. Headspace [App]; https://www.headspace.com/headspace-meditation-app.
29. Weathers FW, Blake DD, Schnurr PP, Kaloupek DG, Marx BP, Keane TM. The clinician-administered PTSD scale for DSM-5 (CAPS-5). 2013. Interview available from the National Center for PTSD at http://www.ptsd.va.gov.
30. Qualtrics. Provo, UT. 2017. http://www.qualtrics.com
31. Weathers FW, Litz BT, Keane TM, Palmieri P, Marx B, Schnurr P. The PTSD checklist for DSM-5 (PCL-5). 2013. Scale available from the National Center for PTSD at www.ptsd.va.gov.
32. Bovin MJ, Marx BP, Weathers FW, Gallagher MW, Rodriguez P, Schnurr PP, et al. Psychometric properties of the PTSD checklist for diagnostic and

statistical manual of mental disorders–fifth edition (PCL-5) in veterans. Psychol Assess. 2016;28:1379–91.
33. Wortmann JH, Jordan AH, Weathers FW, Resick PA, Dondanville KA, Hall-Clark B, et al. Psychometric analysis of the PTSD Checklist-5 (PCL-5) among treatment-seeking military service members. Psychol Assess. 2016;28:1392–403.
34. Kroenke K, Spitzer RL, Williams JBW. The PHQ-9: validity of a brief depression severity measure. J Gen Intern Med. 2001;16:606–13.
35. Corson K, Gerrity MS, Dobscha SK. Screening for depression and suicidality in a VA primary care setting: 2 items are better than 1 item. Am J Manag Care. 2004;10:839–45.
36. Louzon SA, Bossarte R, McCarthy JF, Katz IR. Does suicidal ideation as measured by the PHQ-9 predict suicide among VA patients? Psychiatr Serv. 2016;67:517–22.
37. Foa EB, Ehlers A, Clark DM, Tolin DF, Orsillo SM. The posttraumatic cognitions inventory (PTCI): development and validation. Psychol Assess. 1999;11:303–14.
38. Sexton MB, Davis MT, Bennett DC, Morris DH, Rauch SA. A psychometric evaluation of the posttraumatic cognitions inventory with veterans seeking treatment following military trauma exposure. J Affect Disord. 2018;226:232–8.
39. Hedeker D, Gibbons RD. Longitudinal data analysis. Hoboken: John Wiley & Sons; 2006.
40. Stata Corp. Stata Statistical Software: Release 14; 2015. College Station, TX: StataCorp LP.
41. Hedeker D, Gibbons R, Du Toit M, Cheng Y. SuperMix 1.1. 2007.
42. Systat Software Inc. Sigmaplot 13; 2014. San Jose, CA.
43. Rabe-Hesketh S, Skrondal A. Multilevel and longitudinal modeling using Stata. 2nd ed. College Station: Stata Press; 2015.
44. Bradley R, Greene J, Russ E, Dutra L, Westen D. A multidimensional meta-analysis of psychotherapy for PTSD. Am J Psychiatry. 2005;162:214–27.
45. Harvey MM, Rauch SAM, Zalta AK, Sornborger J, Pollack MH, Bothbaum BO, Laifer LM, Simon NM. Intensive treatment models to address posttraumatic stress among post-9/11 warriors: the warrior care network. Focus. 2017;15:378–83.
46. Galovski TE, Harik JM, Blain LM, Farmer C, Turner D, Houle T. Identifying patterns and predictors of PTSD and depressive symptom change during cognitive processing therapy. Cogn Ther Res. 2016;40:617–26.
47. Horwitz AG, Held P, Klassen BJ, Karnik NS, Pollack MH, Zalta AK. Posttraumatic cognitions and suicidal ideation among veterans receiving PTSD treatment. Cogn Ther Res. 2018; https://doi.org/10.1007/s10608-018-9925-6 online advance publication.
48. Merrill LL, Newell CE, Thomsen CJ, Gold SR, Milner JS, Koss MP, Rosswork SG. Childhood abuse and sexual revictimization in a female navy recruit sample. J Trauma Stress. 1999;12(2):211–25.
49. Schry AR, Beckham JC, Workgroup TV, Calhoun PS. Sexual revictimization among Iraq and Afghanistan war era veterans. Psychiatry Res. 2016;240:406–11.
50. Sexton MB, Davis MT, Bennett DC, Morris DH, Rauch SA. A psychometric evaluation of the posttraumatic cognitions inventory with ceterans seeking treatment following military trauma exposure. J Affect Disord. 2018;226:232–8.

15

Time trends in depression prevalence and health-related correlates: results from population-based surveys in Germany 1997–1999 vs. 2009–2012

Julia Bretschneider[1*], Silke Janitza[1], Frank Jacobi[2], Julia Thom[1], Ulfert Hapke[1], Tobias Kurth[3] and Ulrike E. Maske[1]

Abstract

Background: Although an "epidemic" of depression is frequently claimed, empirical evidence is inconsistent, depending on country, study design and depression assessment. Little is known about changes in depression over time in Germany, although health insurance companies report frequency increases. Here we examined time trends in depression prevalence, severity and health-related correlates in the general population.

Methods: Data were obtained from the mental health module of the "German Health Interview and Examination Survey for Adults" (2009–2012, $n = 3265$) and the mental health supplement of the "German National Health Interview and Examination Survey 1998" (1997–1999, $n = 4176$), excluding respondents older than 65. 12-month major depressive disorder (MDD), severity and symptoms were assessed based on the WHO Composite International Diagnostic Interview. Health-related quality of life (SF-36), self-reported sick days or days with limitations in normal daily life activities were examined, too. Calculations were carried out population-weighted. Additional age-standardized analyses were conducted to account for demographic changes.

Results: Overall, MDD 12-month prevalence remained stable at 7.4%. Women showed a shifted age distribution with increased prevalence at younger ages, and increasing MDD severity. Time trends in health-related correlates occurred both in participants with and without MDD. Mental health disability increased over time, particularly among men with MDD, reflected by the mental component score of the SF-36 and days with activity limitation due to mental health problems. Demographic changes had a marginal impact on the time trends.

Conclusions: In contrast to the ongoing international debate regarding increased depression rates in western countries, we found no increase in overall MDD prevalence in Germany over a long period. In conclusion, increased depression frequencies in national health insurance data and growing health care costs associated with depression are not attributable to overall prevalence changes at a population level. However, shifted age distribution and increased severity among women may reflect a rising depression risk within this specific subgroup, and changes in health-related correlates indicate a growing mental health care need for depression, particularly among men.

Keywords: Major depressive disorder, Depression, Prevalence, Time trends, Health-related quality of life, Disease burden, General population, Germany, Epidemiology, Cross-sectional studies

* Correspondence: BretschneiderJ@rki.de
[1]Unit 26 Mental Health, Department of Epidemiology and Health Monitoring, Robert Koch-Institute, Berlin, Germany
Full list of author information is available at the end of the article

Background

An "epidemic" of depression as a disease of modernity has been frequently claimed [1–3]. Given the high prevalence and enormous personal and economic disease burden, this discourse highlights a global core health challenge of the 21st century [4–6].

According to the World Health Organization (WHO), over 300 million people were estimated to be affected by depression globally in 2015, an increase of 18.4% since 2005 [7]. However, changes were mainly attributable to the overall growth of the global population and its changing age structure [7, 8]. Likewise, a meta-analysis of 116 epidemiological studies revealed no change in the prevalence of major depressive disorder (MDD) between 1990 and 2010 using age-adjusted estimates, challenging the notion of an epidemic [3]. However, the empirical evidence is inconsistent, depending on country, study design, disorder definition and assessment of depression, and several previous studies also indicate a slight increase of depressive symptoms over time [9–12]. The evaluation of time trends based on direct comparisons of population-based data is difficult, and different depression measures lead to varying results [1]. Even if assessed with a fully-structured clinical diagnostic interview based on diagnostic criteria of the Diagnostic and Statistical Manual of Mental Disorders (DSM), the "gold standard" for estimating depression prevalence [13, 14], prevalence estimates are affected by minor changes in the diagnostic criteria and revisions of clinical interviews or diagnostic algorithms used in mental health survey replications [15]. Thus, there is little agreement about whether depression prevalence is increasing over time or not. However, there is no evidence for a reduction in prevalence [16, 17].

In Germany, little is currently known about changes in depression prevalence over time. However, health insurance companies have reported an increasing depression frequency [18], and health care costs attributable to depression have increased considerably [19]. Besides the possibility of increasing depression prevalence in the general population, time trends in health insurance data could also reflect a rising need for mental health care (e.g., due to increasing functional disability). Therefore, the current study sought to examine changes over a period of 13 years for MDD prevalence, severity, symptoms, and health-related correlates for the general population in Germany.

Methods

Study design and population

Mental disorders, including MDD, were assessed in the mental health module of the first wave of the "German Health Interview and Examination Survey for Adults" (DEGS1-MH, data collection 2009–2012, age range 18–79 years) and the mental health supplement of its predecessor, the "German National Health Interview and Examination Survey 1998" (GHS-MHS, data collection 1997–1999, age range 18–65 years). Both surveys were part of the German health monitoring system at the Robert Koch-Institute. They provide representative nationwide data about the health of the non-institutionalized adult population in Germany. Design and methods are described in detail elsewhere [20–24]. In brief, the core surveys GHS and DEGS1 were conducted using two-stage clustered random sampling (step 1: random selection of study locations from all municipal communities; step 2: random selection of participants from population-registries in each selected study location). The net samples of GHS ($n = 7124$, response rate: 61%) and DEGS1 ($n = 7115$, including 3959 participants who participated in both surveys, response rates: 64% among former GHS participants and 42% for newly sampled individuals) enable representative cross-sectional and trend analyses [25]. The mental health assessment was completed by $n = 4181$ participants in GHS (conditional response rate: 87.6%, see [23]) and $n = 4483$ participants in DEGS1 (conditional response rate: 88.2%, see [24]). Excluding participants with missing data regarding 12-month MDD from both surveys and participants older than 65 from DEGS1-MH, the final study sample was $n = 4176$ for GHS-MHS and $n = 3265$ for DEGS1-MH.

Assessment of depression

Major depressive disorder (MDD) during the last 12 months was assessed by trained interviewers based on the WHO Composite International Diagnostic Interview (CIDI). The CIDI is a standardized fully-structured computer-assisted clinical face-to-face interview. It is widely used internationally in the assessment of mental disorders according to the diagnostic criteria of the DSM [13, 26, 27]. A modified German version of the CIDI, the Munich Composite International Diagnostic Interview, was used in the GHS-MHS (DIA-X/M-CIDI; [28]) and modified for DEGS1-MH (DEGS-CIDI; [24]) to assess mental disorders, according to the diagnostic criteria of the DSM-IV and DSM-IV-TR, respectively [29]. MDD requires the persistence of at least five of nine depression symptoms on nearly every day for 2 weeks or longer, of which at least one is depressed mood or decreased interest/pleasure (DSM criterion A). Furthermore, clinically significant distress and impairment associated with these symptoms are necessary (DSM criterion C). MDD exclusion criteria include lifetime manic/hypomanic episodes and depressive symptoms solely attributable to the direct physiological effects of a substance, a general medical condition or attributable to grief. The questions related to depression assessment were similar in the versions of the CIDI in both the

GHS-MHS and DEGS1-MH. However, skip rules, and diagnostic algorithms for deduction of 12-month MDD diagnosis differed slightly. Therefore, trend analyses were based on a specific unified diagnostic algorithm. In brief, the algorithm for 12-month MDD was limited to information about the last 12 months without considering lifetime information on symptoms and disorders, and the operationalization of exclusion criteria was harmonized between DEGS1-MH and GHS-MHS. This modified algorithm enables the estimation of prevalence changes over time but also leads to slightly different estimates compared with previously published MDD prevalence data for Germany [30–32]. For participants with 12-month MDD, depression severity was categorized based on the number of depression symptoms into "mild" (5 symptoms), "moderate" (6–7 symptoms) and "severe" (8–9 symptoms) (see [33]).

Other measures

In the core surveys (GHS and DEGS1), socio-demographic variables were assessed, including sex, marital status (married and living with partner, married and not living with partner, single, divorced, widowed), socio-economic status (SES; classified in low, middle and high based on information on education, occupational, status and net household income, see [34]) and community size [categorized in rural (< 5000 inhabitants), small town (5000 to < 20,000), mid-sized town (20,000 to < 100,000) and large town, see [25]. Age was assessed in years at the time of mental health assessment (GHS-MHS and DEGS1-MH) and categorized into age groups (18–34, 35–49 and 50–65).

Self-rated health and health-related quality of life (past 4 weeks) were assessed with a self-administered questionnaire using the German version of the Short Form 36 (SF-36) version 1 in the GHS [35, 36] and version 2 in the DEGS1 [37, 38]. The first question in the SF-36 (identical in both versions) measuring self-rated health was dichotomized into poor/fair vs. good/very good/excellent (see [39]). The SF-36 distinguishes eight domains for health-related quality of life: physical functioning, role physical, bodily pain, general health, vitality, social functioning, role emotional and mental health. A physical component score (PCS) and a mental component score (MCS) are constructed as total scales. "Norm-based scoring" enabled comparability between SF-36 versions (see [37]). Thus, SF-36 scales of both versions were standardized to the 1998 American normative random sample then transformed to an average value of 50 and a standard deviation of 10. Higher values indicate better health-related quality of life.

The number of days with limitations in normal daily life activities due to mental or physical health problems (past 4 weeks) were assessed in the same way in both survey mental health modules [23, 24]: participants were asked on how many days during the past 4 weeks they were totally limited in daily life activities due to mental and physical health problems. In this study, answers were dichotomized into "no" vs. "any" days with limitation. The number of sick days (past 12 months) was assessed in an identical way in both survey mental health modules using a self-administered questionnaire [21, 40] and dichotomized into "no" vs. "any" sick days for this study.

Statistical analysis

All statistical analyses were performed using survey-specific weighting factors adjusting the study samples to the demographic-geographic distribution of the population in Germany, as on 12/31/1997 (for GHS-MHS) and 12/31/2010 (for DEGS-MH). Adjustment took sex, age, educational status, federal state, and nationality into account, as well as the probability of re-participation in the mental health module subsequent to the core survey [23–25]. Statistical analyses were performed using Stata 14.1 and survey design procedures accounting for clustering and weighting. Statistical significance was based on a two-sided significance level of 0.05. Analyses were not adjusted for multiple testing. Prevalence, frequencies, means and 95% confidence intervals (95%-CI) for all measures were reported for each sex for participants aged 18–65 years in the GHS-MHS and DEGS1-MH. In addition, estimates from age-standardized analyses were reported where appropriate. Note that the provided age-standardized values cannot be interpreted as valid cross-sectional population estimates themselves, but reflect changes over time that are unaffected by demographic changes in the underlying population. To calculate age-standardized prevalence estimates, participants from the GHS-MHS were weighted to the demographic-geographic population structure underlying the DEGS1-MH (as on 12/31/2010).

Distribution of depression severity and prevalence of depression symptoms were reported for cases with 12-month MDD. The Rao-Scott chi-square test was used to test time trends. Age-adjusted results are described for depression severity based on multinomial logistic regression model with depression severity as dependent variable including time point (GHS-MHS vs. DEGS1-MH) and age as independent variables (reference: 1997–1999). Health-related correlates are reported for participants with and without 12-month MDD to enable evaluation of time trends for MDD cases compared with the remaining population. The number of sick days was examined if participants reported any sick days. Effect estimates for time trends were calculated based on linear, logistic and negative binomial regression models, including MDD, time point (GHS-MHS vs. DEGS1-MH) and the interaction between MDD and time point as independent variables (reference: 1997–1999).

Results of additional age-adjusted regression models are supplementary and described only if divergent from unadjusted results.

Results

Demographic features of GHS-MHS and DEGS1-MH are shown in Table 1. Overall, the sample characteristics showed little change in the underlying population between 1997–1999 and 2009–2012 regarding the included variables, except for age distribution (shift towards older age) and marital status (being married and living with a partner became less frequent, while the proportion of singles increased).

12-month prevalence of MDD

Overall 12-month MDD prevalence was stable over time (GHS-MHS: 7.4%, 95%-CI: 6.5–8.5 vs. DEGS1-MH: 7.4%, 95%-CI: 6.1–8.8; $p = 0.93$ when testing for differences), as well as age-standardized prevalence (GHS-MHS: 7.4%, 95%-CI: 6.4–8.6 vs. DEGS1-MH: 7.4%, 95%-CI: 6.1–8.8; $p = 0.96$). Although prevalence estimates slightly increased in women and decreased in men, these changes were not statistically significant (see Fig. 1). This was also the case with age-standardization (women: GHS-MHS: 9.6%, 95%-CI: 8.0–11.5 vs. DEGS1-MH: 10.5%, 95%-CI: 8.6–12.8; $p = 0.53$; men: GHS-MHS: 5.2%, 95%-CI: 4.1–6.5 vs. DEGS1-MH: 4.2%, 95%-CI: 3.3–5.4; $p = 0.22$). There were no significant sex differences regarding prevalence trends (logistic model with MDD as dependent variable, $p = 0.30$ for testing the interaction between sex and time point, resp. 0.13 with age-standardization). Prevalence among women was significantly higher than among men at both time points.

There were significant age-specific time trends for women (see Table 2): 12-month prevalence of MDD increased in women aged 18 to 34 years ($p = 0.005$) from 8.8% (95%-CI: 6.6–11.6) to 15.6% (95%-CI: 11.3–21.0) and decreased in the oldest age group ($p = 0.002$) from 9.8% (95%-CI: 7.3–13.0) to 5.0% (95%-CI: 3.5–7.1). In contrast, for women aged 35 to 49 years the prevalence remained constant, at approximately 11%. For men, prevalence estimates did not significantly differ within age groups. There were also no significant changes over time depending on socioeconomic status for men and women.

Table 1 Sample characteristics of GHS-MHS (1997–1999)[1] and DEGS1-MH (2009–2012)[2]

	Men		Women	
	GHS-MHS ($n = 1911$)	DEGS1-MH ($n = 1522$)	GHS-MHS ($n = 2265$)	DEGS1-MH ($n = 1743$)
Age group (years), % (95%-CI)				
18–34	36.4 (33.5–39.5)	30.0 (26.9–33.2)	35.4 (33.0–37.9)	31.3 (28.8–34.0)
35–49	34.0 (31.4–36.7)	36.0 (33.1–39.0)	33.3 (31.0–35.8)	36.1 (33.4–39.0)
50–65	29.6 (27.0–32.3)	34.0 (31.3–36.9)	31.3 (29.3–33.4)	32.5 (30.0–35.2)
Socioeconomic status[3], % (95%-CI)				
Low	17.0 (14.7–19.6)	18.2 (15.4–21.3)	17.6 (15.4–20.1)	16.9 (14.5–19.6)
Medium	61.4 (58.8–63.9)	58.3 (54.9–61.6)	62.9 (60.4–65.4)	63.1 (59.5–66.6)
High	21.7 (19.1–24.5)	23.5 (20.8–26.5)	19.4 (17.2–21.9)	20.0 (17.6–22.6)
Community size[4], % (95%-CI)				
Rural (< 5000 inhabitants)	20.8 (14.0–29.8)	15.9 (10.6–23.2)	18.9 (12.6–27.4)	14.5 (9.4–21.5)
Small town (5000 to < 20,000)	21.9 (14.7–31.5)	23.8 (17.4–31.7)	19.9 (13.3–28.5)	24.0 (17.6–31.8)
Mid-sized town (20,000 to < 100,000)	26.7 (19.1–36.0)	29.2 (22.1–37.6)	28.7 (20.7–38.3)	29.8 (22.7–37.9)
Large town (≥ 100,000)	30.6 (22.5–40.1)	31.0 (23.8–39.3)	32.6 (24.1–42.4)	31.8 (24.5–40.1)
Marital status, % (95%-CI)				
Married and living with partner	63.3 (60.2–66.2)	57.9 (54.4–61.2)	65.3 (62.2–68.3)	59.2 (55.8–62.4)
Married and not living with partner	1.9 (1.2–3.0)	1.7 (1.0–3.0)	2.9 (2.1–3.9)	2.5 (1.6–3.7)
Single (never been married)	28.9 (26.3–31.7)	34.3 (31.2–37.6)	20.7 (18.5–23.0)	28.1 (25.3–31.0)
Divorced	4.9 (3.9–6.3)	5.2 (3.9–6.9)	6.7 (5.4–8.3)	6.9 (5.6–8.6)
Widowed	1.0 (0.6–1.6)	0.9 (0.4–1.9)	4.4 (3.4–5.7)	3.4 (2.5–4.7)

[1]German National Health Interview and Examination Survey 1998, mental health supplement (GHS-MHS, 1997–1999): weighted for population structure as of 12/31/1997; age range: 18–65; $n = 4176$ with full mood disorders section within the Composite International Diagnostic Interview (CIDI)

[2]German Health Interview and Examination Survey for Adults, mental health module (DEGS1-MH, 2009–2012): weighted for population structure as of 12/31/2010; age range: 18–65; $n = 3265$ with full mood disorders section within the Composite International Diagnostic Interview (CIDI)

[3]Based on information regarding education, occupational status and net household income

[4]GHS-MHS: community size as of 12/31/1996; DEGS1-MH: community size as of 12/31/2006

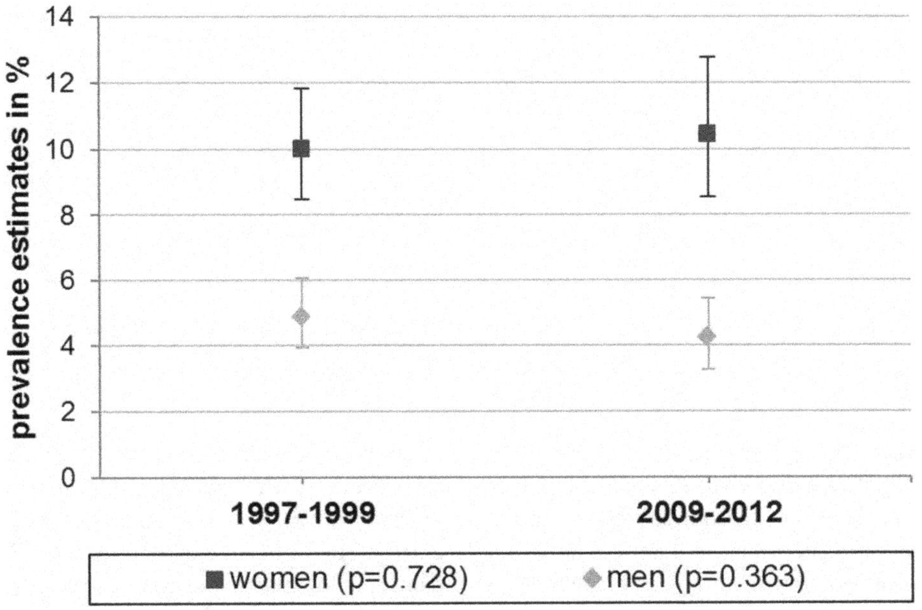

Fig. 1 12-month prevalence of MDD 1997–1999 (GHS-MHS: German National Health Interview and Examination Survey 1998, mental health supplement, weighted for population structure as of 12/31/1997) vs. 2009–2012 (DEGS1-MH: German Health Interview and Examination Survey for Adults, mental health module, weighted for population structure as of 12/31/2010). Age range: 18–65; *p*-values: Rao-Scott chi-square test for testing differences between 1997–1999 and 2009–2012

Further analyses revealed similar significant differences and comparable prevalence estimates within age groups, and, with regard to socioeconomic status, when controlling for sociodemographic variables (logistic models adjusting for socioeconomic status, or age, as well as community size and marital status; results not shown).

Distribution of depression severity and depression symptoms in cases with 12-month MDD

Overall, for men and women with 12-month MDD, moderate severity was most frequent (> 40% at both time points). There was a slight decrease in mild depression over time, while severe depression increased (see Table 3). However, these changes were statistically significant only

Table 2 12-month prevalence of MDD 1997–1999[1] vs. 2009–2012[2] by age group and socioeconomic status

	Men			Women		
	1997–1999 (*n* = 1911)	2009–2012 (*n* = 1522)	*p*-value[3]	1997–1999 (*n* = 2265)	2009–2012 (*n* = 1743)	*p*-value[3]
Total, % (95%-CI)	4.9 (3.9–6.1)	4.2 (3.3–5.4)	0.363	10.0 (8.5–11.8)	10.5 (8.6–12.8)	0.728
Age group (years), % (95%-CI)						
18–34	4.4 (3.0–6.5)	4.0 (2.4–6.7)	0.761	**8.8 (6.6–11.6)**	**15.6 (11.3–21.0)**	**0.005**
35–49	5.4 (3.9–7.5)	4.0 (2.4–6.7)	0.333	11.5 (9.2–14.3)	11.0 (8.1–14.7)	0.787
50–65	4.9 (3.4–6.9)	4.6 (3.1–6.8)	0.812	**9.8 (7.3–13.0)**	**5.0 (3.5–7.1)**	**0.002**
SES, % (95%-CI)						
Low	5.6 (2.9–10.5)	5.1 (2.7–9.5)	0.864	11.7 (8.4–16.0)	17.0 (11.1–25.2)	0.128
Middle	5.3 (4.1–6.9)	4.4 (3.1–6.2)	0.331	10.1 (8.2–12.3)	9.3 (7.1–12.1)	0.610
High	3.3 (2.2–5.0)	3.1 (1.7–5.7)	0.874	8.6 (6.4–11.5)	8.6 (5.6–12.7)	0.981

[1]German National Health Interview and Examination Survey 1998, mental health supplement (GHS-MHS, 1997–1999): weighted for population structure as of 12/31/1997; age range: 18–65

[2]German Health Interview and Examination Survey for Adults, mental health module (DEGS1-MH, 2009–2012): weighted for population structure as of 12/31/2010; age range: 18–65

[3]*p*-value based on Rao-Scott chi-square test. Bold type indicates significant differences between 1997–1999 and 2009–2012 (local significance level α = 0.05)

Table 3 Depression severity in cases with 12-month MDD 1997–1999[1] vs. 2009–2012[2]

	Men			Women		
	1997–1999 (*n* = 110)	2009–2012 (*n* = 71)	*p*-value[3]	1997–1999 (*n* = 238)	2009–2012 (*n* = 159)	*p*-value[3]
Depression severity, % (95%-CI)						
Mild (5/9 symptoms)	31.7 (22.3–42.9)	27.1 (16.2–41.7)	0.574	**24.1 (18.3–30.9)**	**13.8 (8.0–22.7)**	**0.045**
Moderate (6 + 7/9 symptoms)	45.0 (35.2–55.1)	43.0 (31.0–55.9)	0.803	41.5 (34.2–49.2)	47.2 (37.0–57.7)	0.329
Severe (8 + 9/9 symptoms)	23.3 (15.8–33.1)	29.9 (19.0–43.7)	0.373	34.5 (27.2–42.6)	39.0 (28.2–51.1)	0.466

[1]German National Health Interview and Examination Survey 1998, mental health supplement (GHS-MHS, 1997–1999): weighted for population structure as of 12/31/1997; age range: 18–65

[2]German Health Interview and Examination Survey for Adults, mental health module (DEGS1-MH, 2009–2012): weighted for population structure as of 12/31/2010; age range: 18–65

[3]*p*-value based on Rao-Scott chi-square test. Bold type indicates significant differences between 1997–1999 and 2009–2012 (local significance level α = 0.05)

for women with mild depression, decreasing from 24.1% to 13.8% ($p = 0.045$). Comparable results were obtained when controlling for age in a multinomial logistic model (results not shown). Furthermore, differences observed were not attributable to changes only within specific age groups (results not shown).

Prevalence of the nine depression symptoms in cases with 12-month MDD was heterogeneous (see Additional file 1). Over time, there was a significant increase in the frequency of reporting a feeling of guilt/worthlessness in men ($p = 0.035$) and women ($p = 0.019$). In addition, women reported significant weight/appetite change more frequently in 2009–2012 ($p < 0.001$) and diminished interest/pleasure less frequently ($p = 0.018$).

Health-related correlates

Overall, men and women with 12-month MDD exhibited worse outcomes for all health-related correlates than participants without MDD at both time points (see Table 4). Participants with 12-month MDD reported fair/poor self-rated health significantly more often, had significantly lower health-related quality of life in all SF-36 sub-scales, and reported days with activity limitation due to mental health problems and sick days more frequently than participants without MDD.

The proportion of women with 12-month MDD reporting fair/poor self-rated health significantly decreased over time from 40.4% to 21.3% (odds ratio [OR] = 0.4, $p = 0.001$, see Table 5). This decrease was significantly more pronounced among women with 12-month MDD ($p = 0.043$) compared with the trend in women without MDD (OR = 0.7). However, the trends converged when effect estimates were adjusted for age (OR = 0.5 vs. OR = 0.7, $p = 0.39$, see Additional file 2). For men with MDD, there was no significant change in self-rated health over time (OR = 1.0) and no significant divergence ($p = 0.37$) from the trend in men without MDD (OR = 0.7).

Health-related quality of life (past 4 weeks) changed over time: women with 12-month MDD showed a significant improvement for the physical component by an average of 3.8 points and a small but non-significant deterioration in the mental component (by −1.2 points), when comparing participants between 1997–1999 and 2009–2012. These trends did not significantly differ from female participants without MDD ($p = 0.11$ and $p = 0.87$, respectively). For men with 12-month MDD, there was no significant change over time in the physical component (by −0.8 points), but also no significant divergence ($p = 0.25$) from the improvement observed in men without MDD. In contrast, aggravation of the mental component over time in men with MDD (by −5.2 points) was significantly more pronounced ($p = 0.033$) compared with men without MDD (see Fig. 2). The outlined effect estimates for the total scales were comparable when adjusted for age, except for minor differences (see Additional file 2). The results for the total scales reflect changes regarding the SF-36 sub-scales. Women with 12-month MDD showed significant improvement in bodily pain over time (by 6.1 points). For all sub-scales, time trends did not significantly differ between women with and without MDD. In contrast, men showed a slight aggravation over time on all SF-36 subscales, reaching significance for social role functioning (by −4.4 points) and emotional role functioning (by −8.3 points). These time trends among men with MDD differed significantly from men without MDD in emotional role functioning ($p = 0.006$) and bodily pain ($p = 0.030$).

The risk of experiencing any days with activity limitation (past 4 weeks) due to mental health problems was significantly higher in 2009–2010 compared with 1997–1999 for men and women, whether MDD was present or not (with ORs ranging from 2.3 to 6.5). However, there was a trend towards a more pronounced increase in women with MDD compared with women without MDD ($p = 0.056$). In contrast, the risk of experiencing days with activity limitation due to physical health problems did not significantly change over time. The proportion of days with limitations due to physical health problems was already significantly higher in 1997–1999 compared with

Table 4 Health-related correlates in participants with and without 12-month MDD in 1997–1999[1] and 2009–2012[2]

	Men				Women			
	With MDD		Without MDD		With MDD		Without MDD	
	1997–1999 ($n = 110$)	2009–2012 ($n = 71$)	1997–1999 ($n = 1801$)	2009–2012 ($n = 1451$)	1997–1999 ($n = 238$)	2009–2012 ($n = 159$)	1997–1999 ($n = 2027$)	2009–2012 ($n = 1584$)
Fair/poor self-rated health, % (95%-CI)	36.8 (26.7–48.3)	37.1 (24.6–51.6)	**13.9 (12.0–16.1)**	**10.1 (8.3–12.3)**	**40.4 (32.7–48.5)**	**21.3 (13.9–31.2)**	**14.6 (12.7–16.6)**	**10.9 (9.2–13.0)**
Health-related quality of life (4 weeks)[3], mean (95%-CI)								
Physical functioning	50.3 (48.4–52.1)	48.8 (46.0–51.6)	**52.9 (52.5–53.3)**	**53.6 (53.2–54.0)**	47.8 (46.3–49.3)	49.3 (46.9–51.7)	**51.6 (51.1–52.0)**	**52.5 (52.1–52.9)**
Physical role functioning	47.4 (44.8–50.0)	43.1 (39.6–46.6)	52.8 (52.3–53.2)	52.2 (51.7–52.7)	46.5 (44.7–48.2)	46.6 (44.4–48.9)	**51.6 (51.2–52.1)**	**50.7 (50.2–51.2)**
Bodily pain	45.1 (42.6–47.5)	43.4 (40.0–46.7)	**51.1 (50.4–51.7)**	**54.1 (53.4–54.8)**	**41.8 (39.8–43.8)**	**47.9 (45.3–50.6)**	**48.0 (47.4–48.6)**	**51.3 (50.6–52.0)**
General health	42.8 (41.0–44.6)	42.2 (39.3–45.1)	**49.0 (48.5–49.4)**	**50.6 (50.0–51.2)**	43.2 (41.4–44.9)	45.4 (43.3–47.5)	**49.1 (48.6–49.7)**	**50.5 (50.1–51.0)**
Vitality	45.3 (43.2–47.4)	43.1 (39.8–46.3)	52.9 (52.4–53.3)	53.1 (52.6–53.6)	43.0 (41.7–44.3)	43.7 (41.2–46.2)	50.8 (50.3–51.3)	51.2 (50.7–51.8)
Social role functioning	**44.0 (41.7–46.3)**	**39.6 (36.0–43.2)**	52.6 (52.2–53.0)	52.4 (51.9–52.9)	41.4 (39.4–43.4)	41.6 (39.2–44.1)	51.1 (50.6–51.6)	50.9 (50.4–51.5)
Emotional role functioning	**44.6 (41.5–47.7)**	**36.3 (32.4–40.1)**	**52.9 (52.5–53.2)**	**51.6 (51.1–52.1)**	43.1 (40.9–45.3)	40.4 (37.3–43.5)	**52.0 (51.6–52.5)**	**49.4 (48.7–50.0)**
Mental health	39.0 (36.9–41.1)	37.0 (34.1–39.8)	50.2 (49.8–50.7)	50.8 (50.2–51.3)	36.8 (35.0–38.6)	38.7 (36.7–40.8)	**47.6 (47.1–48.2)**	**48.6 (48.0–49.2)**
Physical component score	49.2 (47.1–51.2)	48.4 (45.3–51.5)	**51.8 (51.3–52.3)**	**53.4 (52.8–53.9)**	**47.6 (45.9–49.4)**	**51.4 (49.2–53.6)**	**50.6 (50.1–51.1)**	**52.3 (51.9–52.8)**
Mental component score	**40.5 (38.0–42.9)**	**35.3 (32.0–38.5)**	**51.6 (51.2–52.0)**	**50.9 (50.4–51.5)**	38.5 (36.5–40.4)	37.2 (34.5–40.0)	**49.8 (49.3–50.4)**	**48.9 (48.3–49.5)**
Any days with activity limitation (4 weeks), % (95%-CI)								
due to mental health problems	**9.1 (4.9–16.5)**	**25.9 (14.8–41.3)**	**0.4 (0.2–0.7)**	**1.7 (1.0–3.0)**	**5.9 (3.1–10.8)**	**29.0 (19.3–41.0)**	**1.6 (1.0–2.6)**	**3.7 (2.6–5.2)**
due to physical health problems	21.0 (13.4–31.2)	26.7 (16.3–40.5)	14.0 (11.8–16.4)	12.7 (10.6–15.2)	20.0 (14.6–26.7)	26.5 (17.8–37.6)	14.6 (12.8–16.7)	13.6 (11.5–16.0)
Any sick days (12 month), % (95%-CI)	69.3 (57.6–79.0)	74.5 (59.6–85.2)	**49.9 (47.0–52.8)**	**59.5 (56.0–62.9)**	68.1 (60.4–74.9)	76.5 (65.6–84.7)	**55.4 (52.5–58.1)**	**63.8 (60.7–66.8)**
No. of sick days if any[4], mean (95%CI)	62.8 (38.0–87.6)	62.4 (24.9–100.0)	25.0 (20.5–29.5)	19.7 (16.3–23.0)	39.6 (27.4–51.8)	26.2 (16.6–35.9)	19.6 (17.4–21.7)	19.1 (15.1–23.1)

Bold type indicates significant differences between 1997–1999 and 2009–2012 (local significance level $\alpha = 0.05$; see Table 5)

[1]German National Health Interview and Examination Survey 1998, mental health supplement (GHS-MHS, 1997–1999): weighted for population structure as of 12/31/1997; age range: 18–65

[2]German Health Interview and Examination Survey for Adults, mental health module (DEGS1-MH, 2009–2012): weighted for population structure as of 12/31/2010; age range: 18–65

[3]SF-36: Norm-based scoring

[4]In GHS-MHS $n = 77$ men and $n = 166$ women with MDD and $n = 895$ men and $n = 1110$ women without MDD reported any sick days in the last 12 months; in DEGS1-MH $n = 49$ men and $n = 117$ women with MDD and $n = 828$ men and $n = 961$ women without MDD reported any sick days in the last 12 months

Table 5 Effect estimates for time trends in health-related correlates: 1997–1999[1] (reference) vs. 2009–2012[2]

		Men					Women				
		With MDD		Without MDD			With MDD		Without MDD		
		Effect estimate (95%-CI)	p_{trend}	Effect estimate (95%-CI)	p_{trend}	$p_{MDD \times trend}$	Effect estimate (95%CI)	p_{trend}	Effect estimate (95%-CI)	p_{trend}	$p_{MDD \times trend}$
Fair/poor self-rated health	OR	1.0 (0.5–2.1)	0.972	0.7 (0.5–0.9)	**0.006**	0.370	0.4 (0.2–0.7)	**0.001**	0.7 (0.6–0.9)	**0.007**	**0.043**
Health-related quality of life (4 weeks)											
Physical functioning	β	−1.5 (− 4.8–1.9)	0.391	0.7 (0.1–1.3)	**0.021**	0.214	1.5 (−1.1–4.1)	0.252	0.9 (0.4–1.5)	**0.001**	0.668
Physical role functioning	β	−4.3 (− 8.8–0.2)	0.061	−0.6 (−1.3–0.1)	0.098	0.116	0.2 (− 2.7–3.0)	0.897	−1.0 (− 1.6–−0.3)	**0.005**	0.433
Bodily pain	β	−1.7 (− 5.8–2.4)	0.413	3.0 (2.1–4.0)	**< 0.001**	**0.030**	6.1 (3.0–9.2)	**< 0.001**	3.3 (2.5–4.1)	**< 0.001**	0.077
General health	β	−0.6 (−4.1–2.9)	0.727	1.6 (0.9–2.3)	**< 0.001**	0.230	2.2 (−0.4–4.9)	0.097	1.4 (0.7–2.1)	**< 0.001**	0.534
Vitality	β	− 2.2 (− 6.4–1.9)	0.281	0.2 (−0.4–0.9)	0.448	0.237	0.7 (− 2.1–3.5)	0.612	0.4 (−0.2–1.1)	0.180	0.851
Social role functioning	β	−4.4 (− 8.9–0.0)	**0.048**	−0.2 (−0.8–0.4)	0.529	0.063	0.2 (−2.7–3.2)	0.870	−0.2 (− 0.9–0.6)	0.654	0.790
Emotional role functioning	β	−8.3 (−13.3–−3.3)	**0.001**	−1.3 (−1.9–−0.7)	**< 0.001**	**0.006**	−2.7 (− 6.7–1.2)	0.177	−2.6 (−3.4–−1.9)	**< 0.001**	0.966
Mental health	β	−2.0 (− 5.7–1.6)	0.273	0.5 (−0.1–1.2)	0.118	0.171	2.0 (−0.6–4.5)	0.131	1.0 (0.2–1.7)	**0.012**	0.482
Physical component score	β	−0.8 (−4.5–3.0)	0.694	1.6 (0.8–2.3)	**< 0.001**	0.248	3.8 (1.2–6.3)	**0.004**	1.8 (1.1–2.4)	**< 0.001**	0.113
Mental component score	β	−5.2 (−9.4–−1.1)	**0.014**	−0.7 (−1.3–0.0)	**0.040**	**0.033**	−1.2 (−4.6–2.2)	0.477	−0.9 (−1.8–−0.1)	**0.023**	0.874
Any days with activity limitation (4 weeks)											
due to mental health problems	OR	3.5 (1.4–9.0)	**0.010**	4.9 (2.0–11.7)	**< 0.001**	0.607	6.5 (2.8–15.4)	**< 0.001**	2.3 (1.3–4.2)	**0.007**	0.056
due to physical health problems	OR	1.4 (0.6–3.3)	0.482	0.9 (0.7–1.2)	0.403	0.363	1.5 (0.8–2.7)	0.251	0.9 (0.7–1.2)	0.494	0.196
Any sick days (12 month)	OR	1.3 (0.5–3.1)	0.569	1.5 (1.2–1.8)	**< 0.001**	0.787	1.5 (0.8–2.9)	0.198	1.4 (1.2–1.7)	**< 0.001**	0.846
No. of sick days if any	IRR	1.0 (0.5–2.1)	0.988	0.8 (0.6–1.0)	0.058	0.542	0.7 (0.4–1.1)	0.089	1.0 (0.8–1.2)	0.848	0.150

Models include MDD, time point and the interaction between MDD and time point (see Additional file 2 for age adjusted effect estimates). OR: Odds ratio from logistic regression (reference: 1997–1999); β: β coefficient from linear model; IRR: incidence rate ratio from negative binomial regression (reference: 1997–1999); p_{trend}: p-value for testing a trend (test for OR/IRR = 1 or β = 0); $p_{MDD \times trend}$: p-value for testing differences in effect estimates of participants with MDD and without MDD (interaction). Bold type indicates significant results (local significance level α = 0.05)

[1]German National Health Interview and Examination Survey 1998, mental health supplement (GHS-MHS, 1997–1999): weighted for population structure as of 12/31/1997; age range: 18–65

[2]German Health Interview and Examination Survey for Adults, mental health module (DEGS1-MH, 2009–2012): weighted for population structure as of 12/31/2010; age range: 18–65

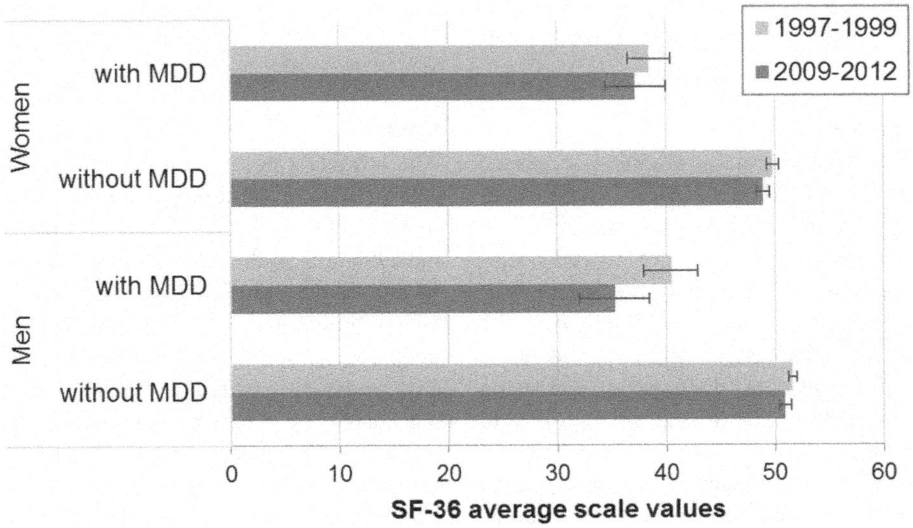

Fig. 2 Health-related quality of life in 1997–1999 (GHS-MHS: German National Health Interview and Examination Survey 1998, mental health supplement, weighted for population structure as of 12/31/1997. Age range: 18–65) vs. 2009–2012 (DEGS1-MH: German Health Interview and Examination Survey for Adults, mental health module, weighted for population structure as of 12/31/2010. Age range: 18–65): Mental Component Score (based on SF-36 and norm-based scoring)

limitation days due to mental health problems. In 2009–2010, at least 25% of cases with 12-month MDD reported some days involving limitations due to each type of problem.

The risk of having any sick days (past 12 months) slightly rose over time (with ORs ranging from 1.3–1.5), but these changes were significant only for participants without MDD. In 2009–2010, approximately 75% of cases with 12-month MDD reported sick days. For women with 12-month MDD reporting any sick days, there was a trend towards a decreased number of sick days over time, from an average of 39.6 days to 26.2 days (incidence rate ratio 0.7, $p = 0.089$), but no change for women without MDD. For men with depression, there was no change over time in the number of sick days, but also no significant divergence ($p = 0.54$) from the decline in men without MDD (incidence ratio 0.8, $p = 0.058$, and incidence ratio 0.7, $p = 0.005$ when adjusted for age, see Additional file 2).

Discussion

Prevalence stability

Based on nationally representative samples of the general adult population, this study revealed no increase in overall 12-month MDD prevalence in Germany over a long period, irrespective of whether the data were standardized for demographic changes. Thus, the increased depression frequencies in health insurance data and increasing costs do not appear to reflect an "epidemic of depression" on a population level. Overall, the current results are in line with the initially presented meta-analysis and findings of the Global Burden of Disease Study, indicating no substantial change in MDD prevalence between 1990 and 2010, or 2005 and 2015, when adjusting for demographic changes [3, 7, 8]. However, women exhibited an MDD prevalence that was twice as high in the youngest age-group and a decrease in mild depression, corresponding to previous findings of increasing depression prevalence or chronicity in (younger) women [41–43].

Overall prevalence stability has previously been discussed as a potential outcome of improved prevention, mental health care and treatment benefits over time, possibly masking rising depression incidence or severity of illness [17, 44]. Meanwhile, exposure to risk factors for mental disorders in the population may have increased (e.g., higher levels of stress due to growing social inequality, isolation, urbanization and modernization in general; [2, 3]). International findings of increased lifetime depression prevalence and chronicity in younger cohorts appear to support this hypothesis [43, 45, 46]. However, societal changes could also result in reductions of depression risks (e.g., improved education). Furthermore, a general decrease in psychological distress or psychosocial stressors [47, 48], stable or even decreasing depression incidence [41, 43, 44], unchanged episode duration [44], and stable severity [49] have also been reported. A recent review concluded that there is no support for the first hypothesis of increasing exposure to risk factors in industrialized countries [17]. Likewise, potential changes in sociodemographic correlates were negligible for prevalence estimates in the current study, even within population subgroups (e.g., age groups). However, understanding the extent to which changes among women reflect growing exposure to risk factors over time within this specific subgroup requires further investigation.

Rising mental health care need?

Changes in health-related correlates revealed increased disability over time in the MCS of SF-36, particularly among men with MDD, and an increased risk of experiencing days with activity limitation due to mental health problems. Thus, the current study provides some evidence of an increased need for mental health care for depression over time, particularly among men. Likewise, national health insurance data documents increasing work day loss attributable to depression (e.g. [50]), and treatment-seeking rates for major depression have been reported to be increasing internationally [51]. However, only relatively small changes were observed in the current study, and only slight improvement in non-help-seeking was reported for participants with mental disorders between 1997–1999 and 2009–2012 (62% vs. 57%) in Germany [52]. Thus, increasing depression frequency in health insurance data and growing costs cannot be explained solely by an increased need for mental health care in depression.

However, changes in health-related correlates also occurred in participants without MDD, while the perception of general health improved (see [37]). Likewise, international findings also indicate increasing mental health disability [53] and worsening of perceived mental health status [47, 48]. Thus, declining mental wellbeing may indicate an increasing need for mental health care in general (e.g., due to rising psychosocial demands over time). Another potential explanation is related to time trends in the process of reporting depressive symptoms themselves. The findings of several previous studies indicate that increased mental health literacy in the general population over time [54, 55] is associated with increased (public) awareness, recognition of psychological symptoms, and willingness to disclose [9, 11, 48, 56], as well as elevated help-seeking behavior [57, 58]. Thus, increased mental health literacy may have led to a more negative evaluation of stressors and perceived mental health over time, associated with rising subjective health care needs. International findings have indicated such a decrease in perceived mental health, while levels of distress were unchanged [47, 48, 53]. Having poor or fair mental health literacy has even been reported to be protective against MDD [9]. Furthermore, several results indicate age- and sex-dependent symptom expression [59–61], and mental health literacy [9]. Thus, even findings of increasing lifetime prevalence in younger cohorts or rising depression prevalence among younger women may be specifically associated with increased reporting of symptoms. However, only minor changes in health-related correlates were observed overall, and little evidence of rising mental health literacy is available in view of the enormous increases in national health insurance data (see [17]).

Limitations

The following potential limitations should be considered interpreting the findings of the current study. Underestimation of MDD prevalence at both time points may have been caused by "recall bias", selective non-response of less healthy participants and exclusion of institutionalized individuals in both surveys [21, 22, 24]. Thus, people with severe depression may have been particularly underrepresented. In addition, participants' "reporting bias" and varying diagnostic accuracy between population subgroups may have led to prevalence underestimation in older participants and male participants [62, 63]. Moreover, the inclusion of some longitudinal data could lead to an underestimation of MDD prevalence in 2009–2012, due to a potentially higher rate of re-participation among healthier participants. Moreover, in the statistical analysis the two survey populations were considered to be independent, neglecting potential correlations related to re-participation of some participants in the DEGS1-MH. The particularly small number of men with MDD in the surveys resulted in low statistical power for detecting time trends within this subgroup. A further potential limitation could be related to the time lags between the core surveys and mental health supplements, which may have led to an underestimation of associations between 12-month MDD and health-related correlates. However, associations may also have been overestimated due to a construct overlap of depressive symptoms (e.g., energy loss) with outcome measures such as SF-36 and self-reported disability.

Conclusions

The current study provides valid, up-to-date information about time trends in depression prevalence, severity and symptoms in the general population in Germany over a long period with a high-quality diagnostic level. To date, national cross-sectional data has been lacking comparability over time due to divergent measures or diagnostic algorithms. Moreover, this is the first study comparing DSM-IV-based major depression prevalence over time while also considering health-related correlates. Furthermore, the current study also provides an evaluation of time trends in view of demographic changes in the underlying population. Thus, the current findings contribute significantly to the ongoing national and international debate regarding the potential increase of depression in western countries.

In contrast to the frequently claimed "epidemic" of depression, we found stable overall prevalence in Germany between 1997–1999 and 2009–2012. Demographic changes had a marginal impact on the examined time trends within the considered age range. In conclusion, increased depression frequencies in national health insurance data and associated growing health care costs are not attributable to overall prevalence changes at a population level.

However, shifted age distribution and increased severity among women may reflect a rising depression risk within this specific subgroup. Furthermore, we found some evidence for an increased need for mental health care for depression over time, particularly among men. However, changes in mental wellbeing also occurred in the general population, which may have also contributed to an increase in depression diagnoses in the health care system. Thus, the observed time trends suggest the need for further investigations of potentially rising psychosocial demands in the general population, and specifically increasing depression risks among women, considering age- and sex-specific developments in mental health literacy.

Finally, divergent time trends in primary and secondary data indicate the need for a critical review of mental health care in Germany, rising questions about the effects of simultaneously expanded services and provision of treatment (e.g. [64]). Jorm AF, Patten SB, Brugha TS and Mojtabai R [17] already highlighted the impact of a "treatment gap", "quality gap" and "prevention gap" for the lack of improvement in population prevalence. In Germany, only 34.6% of participants with 12-month MDD reported any service use due to mental health problems in 2009–2012 [65]. Locally varying access to mental health care has previously been identified as an important determinant of help-seeking behavior [66, 67]. In addition, increasing acceptance of mental health care services [55] and rising public knowledge appear to not have resulted in improved social acceptance of people with mental illness over time [54]. Furthermore, targeting of treatment seems to be questionable: concordance of self-reported clinician diagnosed depression and DSM-IV-based MDD diagnosis is remarkably low [33, 62]. False positive depression diagnoses were particularly high in primary care [68], also indicating "over-representation" of depression within the German health care system, concurrent with the persisting treatment gap. Moreover, national health insurance data provides evidence for lacking quality of treatment [69–73]. These findings suggest that public health initiatives in Germany should continue to reduce access barriers to mental health care services, and focus on improving targeting and quality of treatment for depression. Furthermore, primary and secondary data seem to fundamentally lack comparability with regard to their respective depression indicators. Thus, the current findings emphasize the potential benefits of linking secondary data regarding health care utilization and service provision with standardized measures of depression based on primary data.

Abbreviations

CIDI: Composite International Diagnostic Interview; DEGS1: German Health Interview and Examination Survey for Adults; DEGS1-MH: Mental health module of DEGS1; DSM-IV: Diagnostic and Statistical Manual of Mental Disorders, 4th edition; DSM-IV-TR: Diagnostic and Statistical Manual of Mental Disorders, 4th edition, Text Revision; GHS: German National Health Interview and Examination Survey 1998; GHS-MHS: Mental health supplement of GHS; MCS: Mental component score; MDD: Major depressive disorder; PCS: Physical component score; SES: Socio-economic status; SF-36: Short Form 36

Acknowledgements

We thank Benjamin Knight, MSc., from Edanz Group (www.edanzediting.com) for editing a draft of this manuscript.

Funding

This work was supported by the German Ministry of Health (funding No. ZMV1−2516-FSB-703). GHS was supported by the German Federal Ministry of Research, Education and Science (BMBF, grant 01EH970/8) and conducted by the Robert Koch-Institute, Berlin. Reported data on mental disorders were assessed in GHS-MHS, conducted by the Max-Planck-Institute of Psychiatry, Munich. DEGS1 and DEGS1-MH were funded primarily by the German Ministry of Health (Bundesministerium für Gesundheit, BMG, grant numbers for DEGS1-MH: 1368–1124 and 1501–54401). Supplementary funding for DEGS1-MH was provided by the Technische Universität Dresden, and by the Foundation for Mental Health (Stiftung Seelische Gesundheit) inaugurated by the German Association for Psychiatry, Psychotherapy and Psychosomatics (Deutsche Gesellschaft für Psychiatrie und Psychotherapie, Psychosomatik und Nervenheilkunde, DGPPN).

Authors' contributions

JB and UEM devised the main conceptual ideas. JB, SJ and UEM designed the study and prepared and analyzed the data. TK contributed by mentoring the analysis. JB interpreted the results and wrote the manuscript. UEM, FJ, JT, UH and TK contributed to the interpretation of results and critically revised the article. All authors read and approved the final manuscript.

Consent for publication

Not applicable.

Competing interests

In the past 3 years, TK has received honoraria for providing methodological advice to Lilly, for a presentation on neuroepidemiology from Novartis, from providing a presentation about clinical research methods from Daiichi-Sankyo, and for providing editorial services from the BMJ. TK has provided methodological advice to CoLucid and Amgen, for which the Charité – Universitätsmedizin Berlin has received unrestricted funds. The remaining authors declare that they have no competing interests.

Author details

[1]Unit 26 Mental Health, Department of Epidemiology and Health Monitoring, Robert Koch-Institute, Berlin, Germany. [2]Psychologische Hochschule Berlin, Berlin, Germany. [3]Institute of Public Health, Charité – Universitätsmedizin Berlin, Berlin, Germany.

References

1. Busfield J. Challenging claims that mental illness has been increasing and mental well-being declining. Soc Sci Med. 2012;75:581–8.
2. Hidaka BH. Depression as a disease of modernity: explanations for increasing prevalence. J Affect Disord. 2012;140:205–14.

3. Baxter AJ, Scott KM, Ferrari AJ, Norman RE, Vos T, Whiteford HA. Challenging the myth of an "epidemic" of common mental disorders: trends in the global prevalence of anxiety and depression between 1990 and 2010. Depress Anxiety. 2014;31:506–16.
4. Hewlett E, Moran V. Making mental health count. The social and economic costs of neglecting mental health care. Paris: OECD Publishing; 2014.
5. Demyttenaere K, Bruffaerts R, Posada-Villa J, Gasquet I, Kovess V, Lepine JP, Angermeyer MC, Bernert S, de Girolamo G, Morosini P, et al. Prevalence, severity, and unmet need for treatment of mental disorders in the World Health Organization world mental health surveys. Jama. 2004;291:2581–90.
6. Wittchen HU, Jacobi F, Rehm J, Gustavsson A, Svensson M, Jonsson B, Olesen J, Allgulander C, Alonso J, Faravelli C, et al. The size and burden of mental disorders and other disorders of the brain in Europe 2010. Eur Neuropsychopharmacol. 2011;21:655–79.
7. Vos T, Allen C, Arora M, Barber RM, Bhutta ZA, Brown A, Carter A, Casey DC, Charlson FJ, Chen AZ, et al. Global, regional, and national incidence, prevalence, and years lived with disability for 310 diseases and injuries, 1990–2015: a systematic analysis for the global burden of disease study 2015. Lancet. 2016;388:1545–602.
8. Ferrari AJ, Charlson FJ, Norman RE, Patten SB, Freedman G, Murray CJ, Vos T, Whiteford HA. Burden of depressive disorders by country, sex, age, and year: findings from the global burden of disease study 2010. PLoS Med. 2013;10: e1001547.
9. Goldney RD, Eckert KA, Hawthorne G, Taylor AW. Changes in the prevalence of major depression in an Australian community sample between 1998 and 2008. Aust N Z J Psychiatry. 2010;44:901–10.
10. Kovess-Masfety V, Briffault X, Sapinho D. Prevalence, risk factors, and use of health care in depression: a survey in a large region of France between 1991 and 2005. Can J Psychiatr. 2009;54:701–9.
11. Andersen I, Thielen K, Bech P, Nygaard E, Diderichsen F. Increasing prevalence of depression from 2000 to 2006. Scand J Public Health. 2011;39:857–63.
12. Spiers N, Brugha TS, Bebbington P, McManus S, Jenkins R, Meltzer H. Age and birth cohort differences in depression in repeated cross-sectional surveys in England: the National Psychiatric Morbidity Surveys, 1993 to 2007. Psychol Med. 2012;42:2047–55.
13. Wittchen HU, Lachner G, Wunderlich U, Pfister H. Test-retest reliability of the computerized DSM-IV version of the Munich-composite international diagnostic interview (M-CIDI). Soc Psychiatry Psychiatr Epidemiol. 1998;33:568–78.
14. Haro JM, Arbabzadeh-Bouchez S, Brugha TS, de Girolamo G, Guyer ME, Jin R, Lepine JP, Mazzi F, Reneses B, Vilagut G, et al. Concordance of the composite international diagnostic interview version 3.0 (CIDI 3.0) with standardized clinical assessments in the WHO world mental health surveys. Int J Methods Psychiatr Res. 2006;15:167–80.
15. Karlsson L, Marttunen M, Karlsson H, Kaprio J, Hillevi A. Minor change in the diagnostic threshold leads into major alteration in the prevalence estimate of depression. J Affect Disord. 2010;122:96–101.
16. Richter D, Berger K. Are mental disorders increasing? Update of a systematic review on repeated cross-sectional studies. Psychiatr Prax. 2013;40:176–82.
17. Jorm AF, Patten SB, Brugha TS, Mojtabai R. Has increased provision of treatment reduced the prevalence of common mental disorders? Review of the evidence from four countries. World Psychiatry. 2017;16:90–9.
18. Gerste B, Roick C. Prävalenz und Inzidenz sowie Versorgung depressiver Erkrankungen in Deutschland - Eine Analyse auf Basis der in Routinedaten dokumentierten Depressionsdiagnosen. In: Klauber J, Günster C, Gerste B, Robra B-P, Schmacke N, editors. *Versorgungs-Report 2013/2014*. Stuttgart: Schattauer; 2014. p. 21–54.
19. Statistisches Bundesamt (Destatis): Gesundheit: Krankheitskosten 2015. 2017.
20. Bellach BM, Knopf H, Thefeld W. The German Health Survey. 1997/98. Gesundheitswesen. 1998;60(Suppl 2):S59–68.
21. Scheidt-Nave C, Kamtsiuris P, Gößwald A, Hölling H, Lange M, Busch MA, Dahm S, Dölle R, Ellert U, Fuchs J, et al. German health interview and examination survey for adults (DEGS) - design, objectives and implementation of the first data collection wave. BMC Public Health. 2012;12:730.
22. Gosswald A, Lange M, Kamtsiuris P, Kurth BM. DEGS: German Health Interview and Examination Survey for Adults. A nationwide cross-sectional and longitudinal study within the framework of health monitoring conducted by the Robert Koch Institute. Bundesgesundheitsbl. 2012;55:775–80.
23. Jacobi F, Wittchen HU, Holting C, Sommer S, Lieb R, Hofler M, Pfister H. Estimating the prevalence of mental and somatic disorders in the community: aims and methods of the German National Health Interview and examination survey. Int J Methods Psychiatr Res. 2002;11:1–18.
24. Jacobi F, Mack S, Gerschler A, Scholl L, Hofler M, Siegert J, Burkner A, Preiss S, Spitzer K, Busch M, et al. The design and methods of the mental health module in the German health interview and examination survey for adults (DEGS1-MH). Int J Meth Psychiatr Res. 2013;22:83–99.
25. Kamtsiuris P, Lange M, Hoffmann R, Schaffrath Rosario A, Dahm S, Kuhnert R, Kurth BM. The first wave of the German health interview and examination survey for adults (DEGS1): sample design, response, weighting and representativeness. Bundesgesundheitsbl. 2013;56:620–30.
26. Kessler RC, Ustun TB. The World Mental Health (WMH) survey initiative version of the World Health Organization (WHO) composite international diagnostic interview (CIDI). Int J Methods Psychiatr Res. 2004;13:93–121.
27. Wittchen H-U. Reliability and validity studies of the WHO-composite international diagnostic interview (CIDI): a critical review. J Psychiatr Res. 1994;28:57–84.
28. Wittchen H-U, Pfister H. DIA-X-Interviews: Manual für Screening-Verfahren und Interview. Frankfurt: Swets und Zeitlinger; 1997.
29. American Psychiatric Association. Diagnostic and statistical manual of mental disorders, fourth edition, text revision (DSM-IV-TR). Washington, DC: American Psychiatric Association; 2000.
30. Jacobi F, Höfler M, Siegert J, Mack S, Gerschler A, Scholl L, Busch MA, Hapke U, Maske U, Seiffert I, et al. Twelve-month prevalence, comorbidity and correlates of mental disorders in Germany: the mental health module of the German health interview and examination survey for adults (DEGS1-MH). Int J Methods Psychiatr Res. 2014;23:304–19.
31. Jacobi F, Höfler M, Strehle J, Mack S, Gerschler A, Scholl L, Busch MA, Hapke U, Maske U, Seiffert I, et al. Twelve-months prevalence of mental disorders in the German health interview and examination survey for adults - mental health module (DEGS1-MH): a methodological addendum and correction. Int J Methods Psychiatr Res. 2015;24:305–13.
32. Jacobi F, Wittchen HU, Holting C, Hofler M, Pfister H, Muller N, Lieb R. Prevalence, co-morbidity and correlates of mental disorders in the general population: results from the German health interview and examination survey (GHS). Psychol Med. 2004;34:597–611.
33. Maske UE, Hapke U, Riedel-Heller SG, Busch MA, Kessler RC. Respondents' report of a clinician-diagnosed depression in health surveys: comparison with DSM-IV mental disorders in the general adult population in Germany. BMC Psychiatry. 2017;17:39.
34. Lampert T, Kroll LE, von der Lippe E, Muters S, Stolzenberg H. Measurement of socioeconomic status in the German health interview and examination survey for adults (DEGS1). Bundesgesundheitsbl. 2013;56:814–21.
35. Bullinger M, Kirchberger I. SF-36 Fragebogen zum Gesundheitszustand. Göttingen: Hogrefe; 1998.
36. Ware JE Jr, Sherbourne CD. The MOS 36-item short-form health survey (SF-36). I. Conceptual framework and item selection. Med Care. 1992;30:473–83.
37. Ellert U, Kurth BM. Health related quality of life in adults in Germany: results of the German health interview and examination survey for adults (DEGS1). Bundesgesundheitsbl. 2013;56:643–9.
38. Ware JE Jr. SF-36 health survey update. Spine. 2000;25:3130–9.
39. Maske U, Buttery A, Beesdo-Baum K, Riedel-Heller S, Hapke U, Busch M. Prevalence and correlates of DSM-IV-TR major depressive disorder, self-reported diagnosed depression and current depressive symptoms among adults in Germany. J Affect Disord. 2016;190:167–77.
40. Jacobi F, Klose M, Wittchen H-U. Mental disorders in the community: healthcare utilization and disability days. Bundesgesundheitsbl. 2004;47: 736–44.
41. Eaton WW, Kalaydjian A, Scharfstein DO, Mezuk B, Ding Y. Prevalence and incidence of depressive disorder: the Baltimore ECA follow-up, 1981-2004. Acta Psychiatr Scand. 2007;116:182–8.
42. Compton WM, Conway KP, Stinson FS, Grant BF. Changes in the prevalence of major depression and comorbid substance use disorders in the United States between 1991-1992 and 2001-2002. Am J Psychiatry. 2006;163: 2141–7.
43. Murphy JM, Laird NM, Monson RR, Sobol AM, Leighton AH. Incidence of depression in the Stirling County study: historical and comparative perspectives. Psychol Med. 2000;30:505–14.
44. Patten SB, Williams JV, Lavorato DH, Bulloch AG, Wiens K, Wang J. Why is major depression prevalence not changing? J Affect Disord. 2016;190:93–7.
45. WHO International Consortium in Psychiatric Epidemiology. Cross-national comparisons of the prevalences and correlates of mental disorders. Bull World Health Organ. 2000;78:413–26.

46. Kessler RC, Angermeyer M, Anthony JC, De Graaf R, Demyttenaere K, Gasquet I, De Girolamo G, Gluzman S, Gureje O, Haro JM, et al. Lifetime prevalence and age-of-onset distributions of mental disorders in the World Health Organization's world mental health survey initiative. World Psychiatry. 2007;6:168–76.
47. Patten SB, Williams JV, Lavorato DH, Fiest KM, Bulloch AG, Wang J. Changing perceptions of mental health in Canada. Can J Psychiatr. 2014;59: 591–6.
48. Jorm AF, Reavley NJ. Changes in psychological distress in Australian adults between 1995 and 2011. Aust N Z J Psychiatry. 2012;46:352–6.
49. Kessler RC, Berglund P, Demler O, Jin R, Merikangas KR, Walters EE. Lifetime prevalence and age-of-onset distributions of dsm-iv disorders in the national comorbidity survey replication. Arch Gen Psychiatry. 2005;62: 593–602.
50. Bundespsychotherapeutenkammer. BPtK-Studie zur Arbeits-und Erwerbsunfähigkeit: Psychische Erkrankungen und gesundheitsbedingte Frühverrentung. Berlin: BPtK - Bundespsychotherapeutenkammer; 2013.
51. Bristow K, Patten S. Treatment-seeking rates and associated mediating factors among individuals with depression. Can J Psychiatr. 2002;47:660–5.
52. Brandstetter S, Dodoo-Schittko F, Speerforck S, Apfelbacher C, Grabe H-J, Jacobi F, Hapke U, Schomerus G, Baumeister S. Trends in non-help-seeking for mental disorders in Germany between 1997-1999 and 2009-2012: a repeated cross-sectional study. Soc Psychiatry Psychiatr Epidemiol. 2017: 1005–13.
53. Mojtabai R. National trends in mental health disability, 1997-2009. Am J Public Health. 2011;101:2156–63.
54. Schomerus G, Schwahn C, Holzinger A, Corrigan PW, Grabe HJ, Carta MG, Angermeyer MC. Evolution of public attitudes about mental illness: a systematic review and meta-analysis. Acta Psychiatr Scand. 2012;125:440–52.
55. Angermeyer MC, van der Auwera S, Carta MG, Schomerus G. Public attitudes towards psychiatry and psychiatric treatment at the beginning of the 21st century: a systematic review and meta-analysis of population surveys. World Psychiatry. 2017;16:50–61.
56. Mojtabai R, Jorm AF. Trends in psychological distress, depressive episodes and mental health treatment-seeking in the United States: 2001-2012. J Affect Disord. 2015;174:556–61.
57. Mojtabai R. Americans' attitudes toward mental health treatment seeking: 1990-2003. Psychiatr Serv. 2007;58:642–51.
58. Corrigan P. How stigma interferes with mental health care. Am Psychol. 2004;59:614–25.
59. Hybels CF, Landerman LR, Blazer DG. Age differences in symptom expression in patients with major depression. Int J Geriatr Psychiatry. 2012; 27:601–11.
60. Wuthrich VM, Johnco CJ, Wetherell JL. Differences in anxiety and depression symptoms: comparison between older and younger clinical samples. Int Psychogeriatr. 2015;27:1523–32.
61. Wang K, Lu H, Cheung EF, Neumann DL, Shum DH, Chan RC. "Female preponderance" of depression in non-clinical populations: a meta-analytic study. Front Psychol. 2016;7:1398.
62. Bramesfeld A, Grobe T, Schwartz F. Who is diagnosed as suffering from depression in the German statutory health care system? An analysis of health insurance data. Eur J Epidemiol. 2007;22:397–403.
63. Karger A. Gender differences in depression. Bundesgesundheitsbl. 2014;57: 1092–8.
64. Kowitz S, Zielasek J, Gaebel W. Mental healthcare in Germany-current situation and perspectives. Dtsch Med Wochenschr. 2014;139:1249–52.
65. Mack S, Jacobi F, Gerschler A, Strehle J, Höfler M, Busch MA, Maske UE, Hapke U, Seiffert I, Gaebel W, et al. Self-reported utilization of mental health services in the adult German population - evidence for unmet needs? Results of the DEGS1-mental health module (DEGS1-MH). Int J Methods Psychiatr Res. 2014;23:289–303.
66. Rommel A, Bretschneider J, Kroll LE, Prütz F, Thom J. The utilization of psychiatric and psychotherapeutic services in Germany – individual determinants and regional differences. J Health Monitor. 2017;2.
67. Jacobi F, Becker M, Bretschneider J, Müllender S, Thom J, Hapke U, Maier W. Provision of outpatient specialist care for mental disorders : minor regional differences in treatment needs, major regional differences in availability. Nervenarzt. 2016;87:1211–21.
68. Höfler M, Wittchen H-U. Why do primary care doctors diagnose depression when diagnostic criteria are not met? Int J Methods Psychiatr Res. 2000;9: 110–20.
69. Melchior H, Schulz H, Härter M. Faktencheck Gesundheit - Regionale Unterschiede in der Diagnostik und Behandlung von Depressionen. Gütersloh: Bertelsmann Stiftung; 2014.
70. Bramesfeld A, Grobe T, Schwartz F. Who is treated, and how, for depression? Soc Psychiatry Psychiatr Epidemiol. 2007;42:740–6.
71. Gaebel W, Kowitz S, Zielasek J. The DGPPN research project on mental healthcare utilization in Germany: inpatient and outpatient treatment of persons with depression by different disciplines. Eur Arch Psychiatry Clin Neurosci. 2012;262(Suppl 2):S51–5.
72. Trautmann S, Beesdo-Baum K. The treatment of depression in primary care. Dtsch Arztebl Int. 2017;114:721–8.
73. Sundmacher L, Fischbach D, Schuettig W, Naumann C, Augustin U, Faisst C. Which hospitalisations are ambulatory care-sensitive, to what degree, and how could the rates be reduced? Results of a group consensus study in Germany. Health Policy. 2015;119:1415–23.

16

Depression and its psychosocial risk factors in pregnant Kenyan adolescents

Judith Osok[1], Pius Kigamwa[2], Ann Vander Stoep[3], Keng-Yen Huang[4] and Manasi Kumar[5,6*]

Abstract

Background: Adolescent pregnancies within urban resource-deprived settlements predispose young girls to adverse mental health and psychosocial adversities, notably depression. Depression in sub-Saharan Africa is a leading contributor to years lived with disability (YLD). The study's objective was to determine the prevalence of depression and related psychosocial risks among pregnant adolescents reporting at a maternal and child health clinic in Nairobi, Kenya.

Methods: A convenient sample of 176 pregnant adolescents attending antenatal clinic in Kangemi primary healthcare health facility participated in the study. We used PHQ-9 to assess prevalence of depression. Hierarchical multivariate linear regression was performed to determine the independent predictors of depression from the psychosocial factors that were significantly associated with depression at the univariate analyses.

Results: Of the 176 pregnant adolescents between ages 15-18 years sampled in the study, 32.9% ($n = 58$) tested positive for a depression diagnosis using PHQ-9 using a cut-off score of 15+. However on multivariate linear regression, after various iterations, when individual predictors using standardized beta scores were examined, having experienced a stressful life event ($B = 3.27$, $P = 0.001$, $\beta = 0.25$) explained the most variance in the care giver burden, followed by absence of social support for pregnant adolescents ($B = -2.76$, $P = 0.008$, $\beta = -0.19$), being diagnosed with HIV/AIDS ($B = 3.81$, $P = 0.004$, $\beta = 0.17$) and being young ($B = 2.46$, $P = 0.038$, $\beta = 0.14$).

Conclusion: Depression is common among pregnant adolescents in urban resource-deprived areas of Kenya and is correlated with well-documented risk factors such as being of a younger age and being HIV positive. Interventions aimed at reducing or preventing depression in this population should target these groups and provide support to those experiencing greatest stress.

Keywords: Adolescent pregnancies, Prevalence of depression, Psychosocial risk factors

Background

Adolescents are defined as people aged between 10 and 19 years according to the World Health Organization (WHO) [1]. Kenya is a country with an overwhelming population of children and youth, with more than half the estimated population of 36 million under the age of 18 years [2]. Two thirds of young people, worldwide are growing up in countries like Kenya where preventable and treatable health problems like HIV/AIDS, early pregnancy, unsafe sex and depression are common and where injury and violence remain a daily threat to their health, wellbeing and prospects in life [3–6]. In the African continent the rate of urbanization soared from 15% in 1960 to 40% in 2010 and is projected to reach 60% in 2050 [7]. Rapid urbanization has meant that economic growth and opportunities are centered in bigger cities and these pockets also fuel huge inequalities such as high unemployment and low incomes;

* Correspondence: manni_3in@hotmail.com
[5]Department of Psychiatry, College of Health Sciences, University of Nairobi, Nairobi 00100 (47074), Kenya
[6]Research Department of Clinical Health and Educational Psychology, University College London, London WC1E 7BT, UK
Full list of author information is available at the end of the article

inadequate housing together with tenure insecurity; and limited access to services such as health, education, safe water and sanitation, with limited physical and environmental infrastructure [8]. With the growth of urban informal settlements, populated with an emerging class of citizens known as 'urban poor'; a large number of whom are children and young people with poor access to health, education or even basic sanitation and resources in an additional challenge in several African counties including Kenya [9]. Poor family planning, sexual and reproductive health education and services and absence of robust maternity services are common problems in these informal settlements [10]. Adolescent pregnancy is then unintended and unplanned, fueled by socioeconomic and cultural factors and their prevalence aggravated by poor dissemination of sexual and reproductive health knowledge and access to adolescent friendly health services. In the urban resource-deprived settlements it predisposes young girls to adverse mental health outcomes and enormous psychosocial stresses including stigma and discrimination [3].

Being an adolescent: Risk factor for both perinatal health and depression

Pregnancy is ordinarily a natural developmental process however evidence shows that a significant portion of adolescent fertility is unintended–either unwanted or mistimed–across countries in SSA [9]. Adolescent pregnancy is associated with poor health outcomes, including maternal deaths and injuries and adverse infant outcomes [11]. Eleven percent of all births occur in women between 15 and 19 years [12] with lower-and-middle income countries (LMICs) accounting for 95% of births before 18 years. Almost 10% of girls in LMICs become mothers by the age of 16, with the highest prevalence rates of early pregnancies seen in Sub-Saharan Africa (SSA) and in South Central and Southeast Asian regions [13] In Kenya, 26% of adolescents become mothers between 15 to 19 years of age [14] About 41% of these pregnancies are unintended, 26% are mistimed and 15% are unwanted [9]. These unintended and early pregnancies also make adolescents prone to STIs and HIV, adolescents experiencing an unwanted pregnancy are more likely to resort to abortions, which are often illegal and done by unskilled attendants leading to several pregnancy and birth-related complications [15]. Adolescent pregnancy predisposes young girls to adverse mental health [3] with depression and anxiety being the most common mental health disorders [16, 17]. Worldwide prevalence of depression during pregnancy is estimated to be between 11 and 18% [4, 18]. A higher prevalence is reported in women in LMICs with point prevalence of 15.6% during pregnancy and 19.8% postpartum [19, 20]. Major depressive disorder (MDD) accounts for approximately 40% of YLDs yet mental health services in Sub-Saharan Africa are mostly restricted to tertiary psychiatric facilities [21–23]. Recent studies have shown that the prevalence of depression across sub-Saharan Africa to be high with antenatal depression reported to be 27 and 33% respectively in Ghana and Côte d'Ivoire [24]. In Ethiopia, the prevalence of antenatal depression was 24.94% [25] and 39.5% in Tanzania [26]. In Kenya, a longitudinal study of women attending maternal and child health clinics in two major public hospitals in Nairobi (using Kiswahili version of EPDS with a cut off of 13 or more) found a prevalence of 18% for antepartum depression [27]. Given this context, and how rampant adolescent pregnancies are in LMICs like Kenya, the clear implementation gap has been to provide timely integrated sexual and reproductive health, maternity and mental health services in these informal settlements. For this implementation gap to be addressed we need robust epidemiological studies that look at depression prevalence, its severity and the associated risk factors that aggravate mental illness in this vulnerable group.

Depression and mental health problems in pregnant adolescents

In Kenya and other SSA countries, adolescent pregnancy is widely prevalent public health problem which poses a significant mental health burden. Despite this only a few studies on adolescent mental health needs during perinatal context can be found. Women living in LMICs are exposed to multiple risk factors for depression as their adverse life circumstances commonly include poverty and lack of family structure, low level of education, high rates of HIV/AIDS diagnosis, stigma and lack of social support [28–31]. There is a huge evidence now which suggests that the risk of depression is heightened when there is a previous adolescent pregnancy, low partner age, and adolescents whose mothers themselves had early unintended pregnancies [32, 33]. Furthermore, there is evidence of an association between a mood disorder and concomitant alcohol and substance use in adolescents in SSA which presents additional pregnancy and birth related risks [34]. One study reported that 43.7% of adolescents attending public secondary schools sample in Nairobi had clinically significant depression scores; nearly the same proportion were detected with moderate to severe anxiety along with depression symptoms [35]. Our study aims to determine the prevalence of depression in pregnant adolescents living in a resource-poor urban settlement of Nairobi County and an associated objective is to identify related psychosocial risk factors accompanying depression in this vulnerable population.

Method

Study design, population and setting

We carried out a cross-sectional study assessing depression and associated psychosocial risk factors in pregnant adolescents attending a Maternal Child Health clinic at a Nairobi community health care center located within the informal settlement. The facility is operated through the County Council of Nairobi giving free maternity services and caters for low-and-middle income wage earners from nearby informal settlements. It receives between 12 and 15 pregnant women every day and operates every weekday. We recruited 176 participants between ages 15-18 years using a prevalence rate of 13% from a study [36]; using Cochran sample size estimation (1977) for a cross-sectional study keeping alpha at $p < 0.05$.

Study procedures

This study was approved by Kenyatta National Hospital and University of Nairobi Ethics Review Committee (approval no. P499/07/2015). We collected data between November, 2015 to January, 2016. The study's purpose was explained to the participants and their caregivers. A written informed consent was signed based on willingness to participate in the study and for future uses of data, such as publication, preservation and long-term use of research data. About 6.8% ($n = 12$) of pregnant adolescents we approached during data collection declined to participate in the study and despite our assurance of anonymity and confidentiality, it was mostly due to a strong feeling of stigma associated with their pregnancy. We suspect that their partners or caregivers prohibited them from participation. Adolescent pregnancy has a significant social stigma associated with it in the community context where we were working.

Once data was collected, confidentiality was assured by other means such as by de-identifying the data by use of serial numbers and the paper data was kept in sealed boxes in the Department of Psychiatry office. The study was conducted in a small cubicle within the ANC clinic in the health facility. Participants completed the researcher-designed demographic and psychosocial risk factors questionnaire and PHQ-9 Kiswahili version. There was no incentive given for participation. The lead author, who carried out this study as part of her post-graduate research, is a trained clinical psychologist with wide experience in working with adolescents and young children in the informal settlements of Kenya.

The study team discussed the data collection, referral mechanisms and use of the tools with the lead researcher who collected all the data herself. The participants recording high scores with a cut off of 15+ on the PHQ-9 were referred to one of two places: (a) Psychiatric clinic operated on Wednesdays within the facility or (b) provided alternative of the Youth/Reproductive Health Centre at Kenyatta National Hospital where they could be seen free of charge. Within this inquiry, we had a nested small qualitative study exploring participants' interpersonal, practical and cultural challenges and barriers to accessing depression and general mental health care. The substantive findings of this qualitative inquiry are under process [37].

Measures

Research designed questionnaire

We inquired from our participants about their living conditions, access to food, care and education, whether they lived with parents, relatives or partners, income source/s, parental and partner social support and education, alcohol/substance abuse, experience of sexual/domestic violence, and STI/HIV status. These are social risk factors known to be associated with adolescent pregnancy and are also commonly found in adolescents with depression.

Perinatal depression screening tool

We used Kiswahili translated version of Edinburgh Postnatal Depression Screen (EPDS) [38]. EPDS has demonstrated acceptable clinical utility as a screening scale in Kenya and SSA. Our study team at the University of Nairobi has been using it to assess perinatal depression including carrying out a formal Kiswahili translation of EPDS and cross-cultural emic-etic issues in translation [39] and it was this version of the tool that was administered orally to the participants. The lead researcher first gave the socio-demographic tool followed by EPDS. A cut off of 13+ confirmed presence of peri-partum depression. A cut-off of 13 is recommended for probable major depression and a cut-off of 10 is recommended for probable minor depression [40]. We used this instrument as a primary screener and to enhance comparability with other studies carried out in Kenya.

Depression diagnosis and severity assessment

We used PHQ-9 as our main outcome variable (> 15+) and also to identify severity [41], the higher scores are an indication of greater severity depression.

Due to the peripartum nature of depression in adolescents, we used EPDS as a screener to identify likelihood of depression. We reported scores on PHQ- 9 for those who tested positive in EPDS primarily for test-retest reliability [42] and to categorize depression severity. The collection of data from these tools ensured internal validity through triangulation in evaluation of data and findings while external validity was obtained to the extent that these study findings can be generalized to other populations. During assessments, we targeted participants whose gestation period was 4 months and above and sought clarification on the duration of somatic symptoms of depression from normal pregnancy related symptoms. Participants who scored above > = 15+ on PHQ-9 (i.e. from moderately severe category onwards) were considered to have symptoms of depression and were therefore referred for specialized care.

Statistical analysis

SPSS version 22 [43] was used in data analysis. The association between depression and its psychosocial correlates was determined in two ways. Firstly, we divided our sample into two groups (depressed and non-depressed according to PHQ-9 cut-off score 15+ or more) and compared these groups using *chi-square* test. Secondly, we assessed each potential correlates with the PHQ-9 score using independent samples *t-test* and ANOVA. Hierarchical multivariate linear regression analyses were performed to determine the independent predictors of depression from the psychosocial factors that were significantly associated with depression at the univariate analyses. We ran regression analysis by entering the participants' socio-demographical variables into Block 1, followed by other characteristics/ conditions in Block 2. There were no missing data for all the independent and dependent variables. Prior to running the analysis, all assumptions were checked including univariate/multivariate normality, linearity, homoscedasticity and diagnostic testing for multicollinearity and independence of errors. After checking for univariate normality, the PHQ depression scores was transformed by a two-step approach using inverse distribution function (IDF) using maximum likelihood estimator (MLE) in which we retained the original series mean and standard deviation to improve the interpretation of results. The level of statistical significance was kept at $P < 0.05$, all tests were two sided.

Results

Sample characteristics

The socio-demographic characteristics associated with depression in our sample can be found in Table 1. Over half of our sample was 18 years of age, most had had primary but not secondary level of education and about half were married. A quarter was gainfully employed and just under half reported their family income to be less than 10,000 Kenyan shillings per month (less than 100 USD per month). A quarter lived in temporary shelters or houses and a large majority (91.5%) attended the antenatal clinic as scheduled. Approximately a quarter of participants reported that they had not received any support from their partner or family members but just over half said they had received a positive response from their partners or parents once pregnancy was disclosed. A large number of our participants had experienced a recent traumatic event such as bereavement, loss of parent or close family member, abuse or feuds in their lives. A third had experienced domestic abuse and about 8 % of our participants were adolescent living with HIV.

Depression prevalence

The EPDS scale was used to screen the risk of depression in our pregnant adolescent sample and we found 58% falling under the category of a likelihood of depression. This was confirmed with the PHQ-9 diagnostic and severity assessment tool when a total of 33% (n = 58) tested positive for clinical depression. Out of 176 participants, 38 (21.6%) had no depression, 42 (23.9%) had mild depression, 38 (21.6%) had moderate depression, 30 (17%) had moderate severe depression while 28 participants (15.9%) were found to have severe depression (see Fig. 1).

Associations between socio-demographic factors and adolescent depression

We used PHQ-9 continuous scores as our main outcome to test associations with socio-demographic factors. On *chi-square* test of association, the age of the participants was significantly associated with their depression status, $\chi^2_{(1, N = 176)} = 8.84$; $P = 0.012$. All of the 27 younger participants (ages 15-16) were depressed, as were the majority of older participants. Of the 176 pregnant adolescents of ages 15-18 years sampled in the study, 32.9% (n = 58) tested positive for a depression diagnosis using PHQ-9 cut-off of 15+. We detected a significant difference those who were depressed and not depressed using PHQ-9 cut off on educational level, marital status, living with parents, monthly income (where we found an inverse relationship, adolescents who were in households earning more than 15,000 kes/per month had higher depression, $\chi^2_{(1, N = 176)} = 27.59$; $P < 0.001$), housing type, receiving social support, experienced stressful event or substance abuse, attending ANC clinic, experiencing domestic violence and having a HIV positive status (see Table 1).

Univariate analyses (see, Tables 1 and 2) findings indicated that *younger age* ($F(2, 173) = 18.63$; $P < 0.001$), *unemployed* ($F\ (1, 174) = 5.49$; $P = 0.020$), single status $t_{(174)} = 8.4$; $P < 0.001$, *living with parents* $t_{(174)} = -8.1$; $P < 0.001$, *higher monthly income* ($F\ (2, 173) = 3.42$; $P = 0.035$), *temporary housing* $t_{(174)} = 4.7$; $P < 0.001$, *not receiving social support* $t_{(174)} = 8.0$; $P < 0.001$, *ambivalent to negative reaction to pregnancy* ($F\ (2, 173) = 40.85$; $P < 0.001$), *having children* from before $t_{(174)} = 3.7$; $P < 0.001$, *experiencing a stressful event* $t_{(174)} = -8.2$; $P < 0.001$, *those experiencing substance abuse* $t_{(174)} = -2.4$; $P = 0.019$, *not attending clinic regularly* $t_{(174)} = 5.2$; $P < 0.001$, *those experiencing domestic violence* $t_{(174)} = -7.8$; $P < 0.001$ and *HIV positive diagnosis* $t_{(174)} = -4.0$; $P < 0.001$ were significantly associated with higher depressive scores.

Overall psychosocial risk factors model using multivariate linear regression

The results of multivariate linear regression using PHQ-9 scores as the dependent variable and 14 predictors in two blocks are shown in Table 2. The overall model with all the predictors were statistically significant and explained 55.4% of the variance in depression among the participants with $F\ (17, 157) = 11.46$, $P < 0.01$. In Block 1, the

Table 1 Demographic and Psychosocial Risk Factors Associated with Depression amongst respondents

Variable	Category	Overall (*N* = 176)	Non-Depressed[1] (*N* = 118)	Depressed[2] (*N* = 58)	Mean(SD) PHQ-Score	95% C.I.	Group Differences
Age in years	15-16 Years	27(15.3)	7(25.9)	20(74.1)	17.2(4.0)	(15.6-18.8)	$(F(2, 173) = 18.63;$ $\mathbf{P < 0.001})^{\dagger}$
	17 Years	41(23.3)	25(61.0)	16(39.0)	11.3(7.0)	(9.0-13.5)	
	18 Years	108(61.4)	86(79.6)	22(20.4)	9.5(5.7)	(8.5-10.6)	
Occupation	Unemployed	133(75.6)	84(63.2)	49(36.8)	11.8(6.4)	(10.7-12.9)	$t_{(174)} = 2.3;$ $\mathbf{P = 0.020}$
	Actively employed	43(24.4)	34(79.1)	9(20.9)	9.2(5.9)	(7.3-11.0)	
Education level	Primary and below	141(80.1)	89(63.1)	52(36.9)	11.5(6.6)	(10.4-12.6)	$t_{(174)} = 1.7; P = 0.091$
	Secondary and above	35(19.9)	29(82.9)	6(17.1)	9.5(5.3)	(7.7-11.3)	
Marital status	Unmarried	85(48.3)	40(47.1)	45(52.9)	14.7(5.1)	(13.6-15.8)	$t_{(174)} = 8.4;$ $\mathbf{P < 0.001}$
	Married	91(51.7)	78(85.7)	13(14.3)	7.8(5.7)	(6.6-9.0)	
Living arrangements	Living with other	113(64.2)	48(58.5)	34(41.5)	8.6(5.9)	(7.5-9.7)	$t_{(174)} = -8.1;$ $\mathbf{P < 0.001}$
	Living with parents	63(35.8)	42(67.7)	20(32.3)	15.6(4.6)	(14.4-16.8)	
Monthly income	< 10,000Ksh.	82(46.6)	28(87.5)	4(12.5)	12.4(6.2)	(11.0-13.7)	$(F (2, 173) = 3.42;$ $\mathbf{P = 0.035})^{\dagger}$
	10,000-14,999Ksh	62(35.2)	12(31.6)	26(68.4)	10.5(6.9)	(8.7-12.2)	
	>= 15,000Ksh	32(18.2)	106(76.8)	32(23.2)	9.2(5.0)	(7.4-11.0)	
Type of housing	Temporary	38(21.6)	93(82.3)	20(17.7)	15.2(6.1)	(13.2-17.2)	$t_{(174)} = 4.7;$ $\mathbf{P < 0.001}$
	Permanent	138(78.4)	25(39.7)	38(60.3)	10.0(6.0)	(9.0-11.0)	
Receiving social support	No	40(22.7)	10(25.0)	30(75.0)	17.2(4.5)	(15.8-18.6)	$t_{(174)} = 8.0;$ $\mathbf{P < 0.001}$
	Yes	136(77.3)	108(79.4)	28(20.6)	9.3(5.7)	(8.4-10.3)	
Partner/ parent reaction	Positive	101(57.4)	87(86.1)	14(13.9)	8.0(5.4)	(7.0-9.1)	$(F (2, 173) = 40.85;$ $\mathbf{P < 0.001})^{\dagger}$
	Negative	36(20.5)	14(38.9)	22(61.1)	15.6(5.1)	(13.9-17.3)	
	Ambivalent	39(22.2)	17(43.6)	22(56.4)	15.0(5.2)	(13.3-16.7)	
Has other children	No	138(78.4)	88(63.8)	50(36.2)	12.0(6.2)	(11.0-13.1)	$t_{(174)} = 3.7;$ $\mathbf{P < 0.001}$
	Yes	38(21.6)	30(78.9)	8(21.1)	7.8(6.1)	(5.8-9.8)	
Experienced a stressful life event	No	53(30.1)	51(96.2)	2(3.8)	6.0(4.1)	(4.9-7.1)	$t_{(174)} = -8.2;$ $\mathbf{P < 0.001}$
	Yes	123(69.9)	67(54.5)	56(45.5)	13.3(5.9)	(12.3-14.4)	
Experience substance abuse	No	161(91.5)	112(69.6)	49(30.4)	10.8(6.3)	(9.8-11.8)	$t_{(174)} = -2.4;$ $\mathbf{P = 0.019}$
	Yes	15(8.5)	6(40.0)	9(60.0)	14.8(6.2)	(11.4-18.2)	
Attending clinic as scheduled	No	15(8.5)	1(6.7)	14(93.3)	18.7(3.4)	(16.8-20.6)	$t_{(174)} = 5.2;$ $\mathbf{P < 0.001}$
	Yes	161(91.5)	117(72.7)	44(27.3)	10.4(6.1)	(9.5-11.4)	
Experience domestic violence	No	108(61.4)	90(83.3)	18(16.7)	8.6(5.9)	(7.4-9.7)	$t_{(174)} = -7.8;$ $\mathbf{P < 0.001}$
	Yes	68(38.6)	28(41.2)	40(58.8)	15.2(4.8)	(14.0-16.3)	
Currently diagnosed with HIV/AIDS	No	162(92.0)	117(72.2)	45(27.8)	10.6(6.3)	(9.6-11.5)	$t_{(174)} = -4.0;$ $\mathbf{P < 0.001}$
	Yes	14(8.0)	1(7.1)	13(92.9)	17.4(3.3)	(15.5-19.4)	

Note: **†One way Analysis of Variance (ANOVA); t-Independent samples t-test (Higher PHQ-9 mean scores translates to higher depression levels)**
Not *Depressed*[1] *and Depressed*[2] is based on PHQ classification of 0-14 and 15 onwards. Mean scores and 95% CI are based on scores of depressed participants

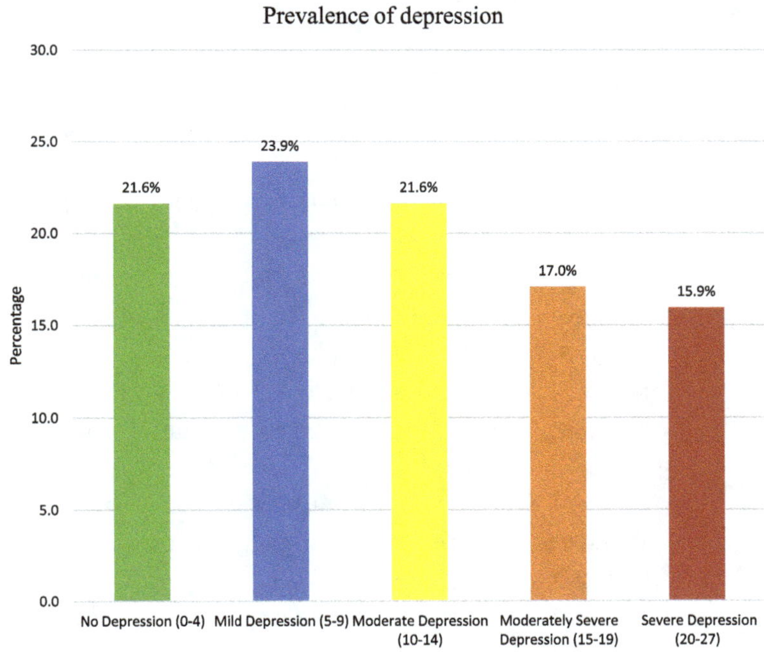

Fig. 1 Depression Severity on PHQ-9. The figures in brackets denote PHQ-9 severity bands

respondents socio-demographic characteristics i.e. age, occupation, marital status, living arrangements and income explained 37.2% of the variance in depression scores, which was statistically significant with F (8, 166) = 12.31, $P < 0.01$), in which age, type of housing and marital status were statistically significant $P < 0.05$. In Block 2, other participants characteristics uniquely explained a statistically significant amount 18.1%, of the variance of the of participants depression after controlling for socio-demographical factors in Block 1, with F (9, 157) =7.10, $P < 0.01$. Therefore, the two blocks of variables significantly contributed to the prediction of the participant's depression. After various iterations, when individual predictors using standardized beta scores were examined, *having experienced a stressful life event* (B = 3.27, P = 0.001, β =0.25), *the absence of social support for pregnant adolescents* (B = – 2.76, P = 0.008, β = – 0.19), *being diagnosed of HIV/AIDS* (B = 3. 81, P = 0.004, β =0.17) and *being of younger age* (B = 2.46, P = 0.038, β =0.14) were the independent correlates of depression.

Discussion

Our study findings that 32.5% of adolescents reported clinically elevated depression symptoms and that 15.9% of our sample had severe depressive features are in line with other SSA studies where prevalence of severe depression in pregnant adolescents is to be between 11 and 18% [9, 18, 43]. Our study identified four critical risk factors for depression such as *having experienced an adverse event or extremely stressful life context, living with HIV/AIDS, absence of support from the partner or the family* and *being a younger adolescent.* We found that 15.3% (n = 27) of pregnant adolescents were of ages 15-16 years indicative of a fairly early sexual initiation in our participants. The early sexual exposure with a concomitant lack of information/ knowledge or freedom to exercise sound sexual protection and contraception is a widely discussed issue in Kenya and in SSA in general. Doyle et al. (2012) in a study addressing the sexual behavior of adolescents in SSA reported that up to 25% of 15-19 years old's across SSA are having sex before the age of 15 years [44]. Recent evidence suggests that young women are less likely to initiate sex if they are currently in school, with at least a secondary education and never married [9] and it is likely that pregnancy has resulted in dropping out of school for these adolescent girls who were between 15 and 16 years of age.

Other studies carried out in Kenya, Uganda and Ghana have pointed to an interplay of various social determinants associated with sexual and reproductive health such as poor education, high poverty and food insecurity, rigid social norms, and under-resourced health systems [9, 33, 45–48]. Given that our study was carried out in a health facility that caters to a large number of families based in informal settlements, each of these environmental factors play a mediating role that needs to be examined further.

We identified HIV positive status to be another risk factor in our study. We know that depression and stigma may impede linkage to HIV care, and to adherence to antiretroviral therapy (ART), additionally literature also suggests that ARVs and HIV positive status increases both HIV-related internalized stigma and depression

Table 2 Results of hierarchical multiple regression analysis on depression

Variable	Category	Beta(S.E)	95%C.I Beta	β	*P*-Value	R^2 change	*F*- ratio R^2 change
Age in years	15 to 16 Years	2.46	(0.1-4.8)	0.14	*0.038*	0.372	12.3[a]
	17 Years	0.32	(−1.3-1.9)	0.02	0.701		
	18 years	*Reference*					
Occupation	Employed	0.11	(−1.7-1.9)	0.01	0.903		
	Unemployed	*Reference*					
Marital status	Married	0.00	(−2.6-2.6)	0. 00	0.999		
	Unmarried	*Reference*					
Living with parents	Yes	1.11	(−1.5-3.7)	0.09	0.403		
	No	*Reference*					
Type of housing	Permanent	−0.27	(−2.2-1.6)	−0.02	0.782		
	Temporary	*Reference*					
Income	< 10,000Ksh	0.27	(−1.7-2.3)	0.02	0.788		
	10,000-14,999	−1.04	(−3.0-0.9)	−0.08	0.286		
	> = 15,000Ksh	*Reference*					
Receiving social support	Yes	−2.76	(−4.8−0.7)	−0.19	*0.008*	0.181	7.1[a]
	No	*Reference*					
Partner reaction	Negative	1.46	(−1.2-4.1)	0.10	0.272		
	Ambivalent	0.96	(−1.4-3.4)	0.06	0.429		
	Positive	*Reference*					
Have other children	Yes	−1.58	(−3.4-0.2)	−0.11	0.089		
	No	*Reference*					
Experience a stressful life event	Yes	3.27	(1.4-5.1)	0.25	*0.001*		
	No	*Reference*					
Substance abuse	Yes	1.44	(−1.0-3.9)	0.07	0.246		
	No	*Reference*					
Experience domestic violence	Yes	0.99	(−0.9-2.8)	0.08	0.292		
	No	*Reference*					
Diagnosed with HIV/AIDS	Yes	3.81	(1.3-6.3)	0.17	*0.004*		
	No	*Reference*					
Whether attending clinic as scheduled	Yes	−2.55	(−5.2-0.1)	−0.11	0.059		
	No	*Reference*					
R^2						0.554	

Note: [a]Correlation is significant at the 0.01 level (2-tailed)
Beta –Unstandardized coefficient; β- Standardized coefficient

[49–52]. We need adolescents to understand sexual and reproductive health decision-making much more clearly. Both HIV prevention and HIV treatment require basic skills in comprehending and digesting information (such as modes of transmission safe practices to avoid infection) and actioning it (learning life skills to negotiate safe sex practices with partners, avoiding sex to get material gains, and adhering to medication). We know that depression can impede that decision-making process [53] thus making adolescents more susceptible to high risk practices and behaviors.

The pathogenesis of depression is further magnified in the context of developing pregnancy in adolescents. A recent study on adverse life events and delinquent behaviors in adolescents from informal settlements on Kenya found that more than half of the adolescents lived in households characterized by either food insecurity or recent parental unemployment, and almost a fifth had dealt with multiple adverse events in their lives [54]. In such an environment where adolescent pregnancy means addition of another mouth to feed, the emotional, economic and social pressures multiply in the family leading to more internal conflicts and poor interpersonal relationships.

We found a negative correlation between presence of social support and depression status. Family and social support is a known protective mechanism in mitigating depression and mental health problems [23, 28]. However, given the research design we are unable to tease out the degree of dependence of these two variables.

Our study contributes to an understanding of how vulnerable pregnant adolescents living with HIV are to depression, social isolation consequently leading to poor utilization of health care and PMTCT services. We also interviewed a select group of participants and our survey findings tally with the lived experience of our participants mapped through the depression and psychosocial risk factors survey reported here [37]. Our findings suggest that the indicators for social support need to be multidimensional – covering parental, partner, educational and health contexts to assess the quality of support available to the young girls. Each one of these girls has unique familial, social and health realities that need to be accounted for in any psychosocial intervention development.

The strength of our work lies in the use of a robust depression diagnostic tool such as PHQ-9 to assess depression symptomatology further. Being a cross-sectional study carried out at a community health center in Nairobi, the study portrays a picture of depression, indicates severity and the association of probable major depressive disorder with psychosocial risk factors in the adolescent antenatal period. Despite addressing a gap in the literature around depression prevalence estimates for this sub-group of adolescents, our data is limited by design and cannot capture the causal directions of associations between the factors we studied and the same applies to the temporal sequence of development of depression in our adolescent participants. On hindsight, we would have liked to use more formal measures of social support, HIV related stigma, trauma and stress experience to identify the impact of these factors on our participants' depression. Using a clinical interview to formalize the diagnoses of depression would have added greater strength to the study. A larger sample size would minimize any type 1 and 2 errors in estimating depression in this vulnerable population. Another limitation of study is that we collected data in a peri-urban health facility context and that may not sufficiently map onto the constraints and specific circumstances of pregnant adolescents in the rural or other remote settings in Kenya.

Conclusion

Most evidence-based perinatal depression interventions in LMICs are focused on adults and there exists very limited understanding of depression related risk factors in depressed pregnant or parenting adolescents. Although a body of epidemiological research in adolescent pregnancies in LMIC context have established mental health problems to be dominant, for good intervention research vulnerable population specific risk factors need to be ascertained [4, 55, 56] and our study fills in that gap in depression prevalence estimate and associated risk factors in pregnant adolescents. We hope our study would provide pointers to critical factors that a depression intervention could encompass.

WHO's Mental Health Treatment Gap Action Program (known as WHO mhGAP) [57, 58] argues for adoption of greater task-shifting models, low intensity and culturally adapted psychosocial models that would seek to inform mental health services implementation in resource constraint contexts. For pregnant adolescents in Kenya, we urgently need these components to be integrated in primary health care settings where we are likely to find young girls struggling with enormous social adversities and mental health challenges.

Abbreviations

ANC: Antenatal clinic; ANOVA: Analysis of Variance; ART: Anti-retroviral therapy; EPDS: Edinburgh Postnatal Depression Score; ERC: Ethics and Review Committee; KNH: Kenyatta National Hospital; LMICs: Lower and Middle income Countries; MCH: Maternal and child health; PHQ-9: Patient Health Questionnaire-9; SD: Standard Deviation; SRH: Sexual and reproductive health; SSA: Sub-Saharan Africa; STIs: Sexually transmitted Infections; UoN: University of Nairobi; YLD: Years lived with disability

Acknowledgements

We would like to thank our study participants, numerous MCH nurses and personnel who supported data collection as well as MEPI's continuous learning programs that helped all the authors to think further about this study. We also acknowledge contribution of Prof Francis Creed in mentoring Ms. Osok during a manuscript writing workshop held at the University of Stellenbosch in South Africa in 2016. We also duly acknowledge Albert Tele for his statistical support.

Funding

This research was part of MEPI's Mental Health Linked Award supported by National Institutes of Health/National Institute of Mental Health grant R25-MH099132 where MK and AVK were co-investigators and JO was granted a fellowship under this award. MK and HKY are currently co-investigators in the NIMH funded U19 MH110001-01.

Authors' contributions

The study was carried out by JO who was awarded a fellowship under a Medical Education Partnership Initiative (MEPI) mental health linked student fellowship. JO collected data and carried out initial analyses of her survey, MK was her primary mentor and helped in conceptualization, writing up and conducting multivariate analysis. PK was her second supervisor who assisted during planning of the research concept and reviewed the manuscript. AVS assisted in designing the study and reviewing the paper for submission. KYH assisted in reviewing the manuscript and addressing the statistical comments. All authors read and approved the final manuscript.

Competing interests

The authors declare that they have no competing interests.

Author details

[1]Department of Psychiatry, School of Medicine, College of Health Sciences, University of Nairobi, P. O. Box 20386, 00100 Nairobi, Kenya. [2]Department of Psychiatry, School of Medicine, College of Health Sciences, University of Nairobi, P. O. Box 19676 (00202), Nairobi, Kenya. [3]Psychiatry & Behavioral Sciences and Epidemiology, Child Health Institute, University of Washington, 6200 NE 74th Street, Suite 210, Seattle, WA 88115-1538, USA. [4]Department of Public Health and Child and Adolescent Psychiatry, New York University, New York, NY 10016, USA. [5]Department of Psychiatry, College of Health Sciences, University of Nairobi, Nairobi 00100 (47074), Kenya. [6]Research Department of Clinical Health and Educational Psychology, University College London, London WC1E 7BT, UK.

References

1. Adolescent health and development. WHO Available from http://www.searo.who.int/entity/child_adolescent/topics/adolescent_health/en/. Accessed 10th Mar, 2018.
2. UNICEF. (2014). Adolescents and youth; Kenya country Programme. https://www.unicef.org/kenya/children_3793.html. Accessed on 10th Mar 2018.
3. Patton G, Sawyer SM, Santenelli JS, Ross DA, Afifi R, Allen NB, et al. Lancet commission on adolescent health and wellbeing. The Lancet. 2016; 387(10036):2423–78.
4. Fisher J, Cabral de Mello M, Patel V, Rahman A, Tran T, Holton S, et al. Prevalence and determinants of common perinatal mental disorders in women in low- and lower-middle-income countries: a systematic review. Bull World Health Organ. 2012;90:139–49G. https://doi.org/10.2471/BLT.11.091850.
5. Sawyer RM, Afifi RA, Bearinger LH, Blakemore SJ, Dick B, Ezeh AC, Patton GC. Adolescence: a foundation for future health. Lancet. 2012;379(9826):1630–40.
6. Ki-moon B (2015). The Global Strategy for Women's and Children's Adolescent Health (2016-2030); Survive Thrive Transform. Every Woman Every Child. p. 4-6. https://www.unicef.org/earlychildhood/files/WHO_EWEC_Supplement-bmj.pdf. Accessed 7 May 2018.
7. UN Habitat (2018). https://unhabitat.org/urban-initiatives/initiatives-programmes/africa-urban-agenda-programme/ Accessed 10th Mar, 2018.
8. UNICEF (2014); Kenya Situation Analysis of Children and Adolescents in Kenya 2014 Our Children, our Future. https://www.unicef.org/kenya/SITAN_2014_Web.pdf. Accessed 10th Mar, 2018.
9. Beguy D, Mumah J, Gottschalk L. Unintended Pregnancies among Young Women Living in Urban Slums; evidence from a prospective study in Nairobi City, Kenya. PLoS One. 2014;9(7):e101034. https://doi.org/10.1371/journal.pone.0101034.
10. Beguy D, Kabiru C, Zulu E, Ezeh A. Timing and sequencing of events marking the transition to adulthood in two informal settlements in Nairobi, Kenya. Journal of Urban Health. 2011;88:318–40.
11. Liran D, Vardi IS, Sergienko R, Sheiner E. Adverse perinatal outcome in teenage pregnancies; is it all due to lack of prenatal care and ethnicity? J Matern Fetal Neonatal Med. 2012;0:1–4.
12. World Health Organization (WHO) (2014). Adolescent Pregnancy. http://www.who.int/maternal_child_adolescent/topics/maternal/adolescent_pregnancy/en. Accessed 12th Mar, 2018.
13. Atuyambe L, Mirembe F, Tumwesigye N, Annika J, Kirumira E, Faxelid E. Adolescent and adult first time mothers' health seeking practices during pregnancy and early motherhood in Wakiso District, Central Uganda. Reprod Health. 2008;5:13.
14. United Nation Population Fund [UNFPA]. (2013). Motherhood in Childhood; Facing the challenge of Adolescent Pregnancy. https://www.unfpa.org/publications/state-world-population-2013. Accessed 7 May 2018.
15. Mumah J, Kabiru CW, Mukiira C, Brinton J, Mutua M, Izugbara C, Birungi H, Askew I. Unintended Pregnancies in Kenya: A Country Profile: STEP UP research report. Nairobi: African Population and Health Research Center; 2014. p. 1–200.
16. Alipour Z, Lamyian M, Hajizadeh E. Anxiety and fear of childbirth as predictors of postnatal depression in nulliparous women. Women Birth. 2012:e37–43.
17. Zachariah R. Social support, life stress and anxiety as predictors of pregnancy complications in low-income women. Res Nurs Health. 2009; 32(4):391–404.
18. Odeljimi O, Fuller P, Bellingham-Young D. Determinants of teenage pregnancy in Africa: implication for public health policy and practice. American Economic Journal: Applied Economics. 2011;3:1–34.
19. Howard LM, Piot P, Stein A. No health without mental health. Lancet. 2014; 384(9956):1723–4. https://doi.org/10.1016/S0140-6736(14)62040-7.
20. Whiteford HA, Degenhardt L, Rehm J, Baxter AJ, Ferrari AJ, et al. Global burden of disease attributable to mental and substance use disorders: findings from the global burden of disease study, 2010. Lancet. 2013;382: 1575–86.
21. World Health Organization (2011). Mental Health Atlas. Geneva, Switzerland www.who.int/mental_health/publications/mental_health_atlas_2011/en/. Accessed 12th Mar, 2018.
22. Grote NK, Bridge JA, Gavin AR, Melville JL, Iyengar S, Katon WJA. Meta-analysis of depression during pregnancy and the risk of preterm birth, low birth weight, and intrauterine growth restriction. Arch Gen Psychiatry. 2010; 67(10):1012–24.
23. Rahman A, Iqbal Z, Harrington R. Life events, social support and depression in childbirth: perspectives from a rural community in the developing world. Psychol med. 2003;33(7):1161–7.
24. Bindt C, Appiah-Poku J, Te Bonle M, Schoppen S, Feldt T, Barkmann C, Guo N. Antepartum depression and anxiety associated with disability in African women: cross-sectional results from the CDS study in Ghana and Côte d'Ivoire. PLoS One. 2012;7(10):e48396.
25. Biratu A, Demewoz H. Prevalence of antenatal depression and associated factors among pregnant women in Addis Ababa, Ethiopia: A cross-sectional study. Reproductive Health. 2015;12(1):1.
26. Kaaya SF, Mbwambo JK, Kilonzo GP, Van Den Borne H, Leshabari MT, Fawzi MC, et al. Socio-economic and partner relationship factors associated with antenatal depressive morbidity among pregnant women in Dar es Salaam, Tanzania. Tanzan J health res. 2010;12(1):23–35.
27. Ongeri L, Otieno P, Mbui J, Juma E, Mathai M. Antepartum risk factors for postpartum depression: a follow up study among urban women living in Nairobi, Kenya. J Preg Child Health. 2016;3:288. https://doi.org/10.4172/2376-127X.1000288.
28. van Heyningen T, Myer L, Onah M, Tomlinson M, Field S, Honikman S. Antenatal depression and adversity in urban South Africa. J Affect Disord. 2016; 203:121–9.
29. Merikangas KR, He J, Burstein M, Swanson SA, Avenevoli S, Cui L, Swendsen J. Lifetime prevalence of mental disorders in US adolescents: results from the National Comorbidity Study- Adolescent Supplement (NCS-A). J Am Acad Child Adolesc Psychiatry. 2010;49(10):980–9. https://doi.org/10.1016/j.jaac.2010.05.017.
30. Centers for Disease Control and Prevention. About the CDC-Kaiser ACE Study. https://www.cdc.gov/violenceprevention/acestudy/about.html. Accessed 12th Mar, 2018.
31. Hodgkinson SC, Colantuoni E, Roberts D, Berg-Cross L, Belcher HM. Depressive symptoms and birth outcomes among pregnant teenagers. J. Pediatr. Adol. 2010; https://doi.org/10.1016/j.jpag.2009.04.006.
32. Salazar-Pousada D, Arroyo D, Hidalgo L, Pérez-López FR, Chedraui P.(2010) Depressive Symptoms and Resilience among Pregnant Adolescents: A Case-Control Study. Obstetrics and Gynecology International, vol. 2010, 952493. https://doi.org/10.1155/2010/952493.
33. Juma M, Alaii J, Bartholomew LK, Askew I, Van den Born B. Understanding orphan and non-orphan adolescents' sexual risks in the context of poverty: a qualitative study in Nyanza Province, Kenya. BMC International Health and Human Rights. 2013;13:32. https://doi.org/10.1186/1472-698X-13-32.
34. Balogan O, Koyanagi A, Sticklay A, Gilmour S, Shibuya A. Alcohol Consumption and Psychological Distress in Adolescents: A Multi-Country Study. Journal of adolescent health. 2014;54(2):228–34.
35. Khasakhala LI, Ndetei DM, Mathai M. Suicidal behaviour among youths associated with psychopathology in both parents and youths attending outpatient psychiatric clinic in Kenya. Ann General Psychiatry. 2013; https://doi.org/10.1186/1744-859X-12-13
36. Cochran WG. Sampling techniques. 3rd ed. New York: John Wiley & Sons; 1977.
37. Osok J, Kigamwa P, Vander Stoep A, Grote N, Huang K-Y, Kumar M. (2018). Adversities and Mental Health Needs of Pregnant Adolescents in Kenya: Identifying interpersonal, practical and cultural barriers to care. BMC Women's health; special issue on structural violence and inequalities (under revision).
38. Cox JL, Holden JM, Sagovsky R. Detection of postnatal depression; Development of the 10-item Edinburgh Postnatal Depression Scale. British Journal of psychiatry. 1987;150:782–6.

39. Kumar M, Ongeri L, Mathai M, Mbwayo A. Translation of EPDS Questionnaire into Kiswahili: Understanding the Cross-Cultural and Translation Issues in Mental Health Research. J Preg child Health. 2015;2:134.
40. Manea L, Gilbody S, McMillan D. Optimal cut-off scores for diagnosing depression with the patient health questionnaire (PHQ-9): a meta-analysis. CMAJ : Canadian Medical Association Journal. 2012;184(3):E191–6. https://doi.org/10.1503/cmaj.110829.
41. Sidebottom AC, Harrison PA, Godecker A, Kim H. Validation of the patient health questionnaire (PHQ)-9 for prenatal depression screening. Arch Womens Ment Health. 2012;15(5):367–74.
42. Corp IBM. IBM SPSS Statistics for Windows, version 22.0. Armonk, NY: IBM Corp; 2013.
43. Santos IS, Tavares BF, Munhoz TN, Manzolli P, De Ávila GB, Jannke E, Matijasevich A. Patient health questionnaire-9 versus Edinburgh postnatal depression scale in screening for major depressive episodes: a cross-sectional population-based study. BMC Research Notes. 2016;9:453. https://doi.org/10.1186/s13104-016-2259-0.
44. Alvarado-Esquivel C, Sifuentes-Alvarez A, Salas-Martinez C. Depression in teenager pregnant women in a public hospital in a northern mexican city: prevalence and correlates. J Clin Med Res. 2015;7:525–33.
45. Doyle AM, Mavedzenge SN, Plummer ML, Ross DA. The sexual behaviour of adolescents in sub-Saharan Africa: patterns and trends from national surveys. Tropical Med Int Health. 2012;17(7):796–807.
46. Atuyambe L, Mirembe F, Johansson A, Kirumira EK, Faxelid E. Experiences of pregnant adolescents - voices from Wakiso district, Uganda. Afr Health Sci. 2005;5(4):304–9.
47. Kaye DK. Negotiating the transition from adolescence to motherhood: Coping with prenatal and parenting stress in teenage mothers in Mulago hospital, Uganda. BMC Public Health. 2008;8:83. https://bmcpublichealth.biomedcentral.com/articles/10.1186/1471-2458-8-83. Accessed 12th Mar, 2018
48. Gyesaw NYK, Ankomah A. Experiences of pregnancy and motherhood among teenage mothers in a suburb of Accra, Ghana: a qualitative study. International Journal of Women's Health. 2013;5:773–80. https://doi.org/10.2147/IJWH.S51528.
49. Turan B, Stringer KL, Onono M, Bukusi EA, Weiser SD, Cohen CR, Turan JM. Linkage to HIV care, postpartum depression and HIV-related stigma in newly diagnosed pregnant women living with HIV in Kenya: a longitudinal observational study. BMC Pregnancy and Childbirth. 2014;14:400. https://doi.org/10.1186/s12884-014-0400-4
50. Yator O, Mathai M, Van der Stoep A, Rao D, Kumar M. Depression and associated risk factors in women attending PMTCT clinic at KNH, Nairobi, Kenya. AIDS Care. 2016;28(7):884–9. https://doi.org/10.1080/09540121.2016.1160026
51. Aziato L, Hindin MJ, Maya ET, Manu A, Amuasi SA, Lawerh RM, Ankomah A. Adolescents' responses to an unintended pregnancy in Ghana: a qualitative study. J Pediatr Adolesc Gynecol. 2016; https://doi.org/10.1016/j.jpag.2016.06.005.
52. Kumar M, Vander Stoep A, Grote N, Madaghe B, Yator O, Ongeri L, Polkonikova-Wamoto A, Osok J, Mochache K. Our journey to build capacity to implement and study an intervention to reduce depression among pregnant, Kenyan adolescents. Solving the grand challenges in mental health meeting held in Toronto, Canada from 2-5th June 2015. 2015. https://doi.org/10.13140/RG.2.1.1284.3685. Accessed 7 May 2018.
53. Kumar M, Huang K-Y, Otieno CJ, Wamalwa D, Madeghe B, Osok J, Njuguna Kahonge S, Nato J, McKay MM. Adolescent pregnancy and challenges in Kenyan context; perspectives of multiple community stakeholders. Global social welfare journal. 2017; https://link.springer.com/article/10.1007/s40609-017-0102-8. Accessed 12th Mar, 2018
54. Vreeman RC, Scanlon ML, Marete I, Mwangi A, Inui TS, McAteer CI, Nyandiko WM. Characteristics of HIV-infected adolescents enrolled in a disclosure intervention trial in western Kenya. AIDS Care. 2015;27(sup1):6–17. https://doi.org/10.1080/09540121.2015.1026307. Accessed on 10th Mar, 2018
55. Kabiru CW., Elung'ata P., Mojola S. A., & Beguy D. (2014). Adverse life events and delinquent behavior among Kenyan adolescents: a cross-sectional study on the protective role of parental monitoring, religiosity, and self-esteem. Child and Adolescent Psychiatry and Mental Health, 8, 24. https://doi.org/10.1186/1753-2000-8-24.
56. UNAIDS UNFPA, WHO (2004). Seen but not heard: Very Young Adolescents Aged 10–14 Years. Geneva: UNAIDS https://www.unicef.org/Seen_but_not_heard-Draft.pdf. Accessed 12th Mar, 2018.
57. Murray LK, Dorsey S, Bolton P, Jordans MJ, Rahman A, Bass J, Verdeli H. Building capacity in mental health interventions in low resource countries: An apprenticeship model for training local providers. International Journal of Mental Health Systems. 2011;5(1):30. https://www.ncbi.nlm.nih.gov/pubmed/22099582. Accessed 12th Mar, 2018
58. mhGAP version 2.0. http://apps.who.int/iris/bitstream/10665/250239/1/9789241549790-eng.pdf?ua=1. Accessed 12th Mar, 2018.

17

Prevalence of depression and associated factors among older adults at Ambo town, Oromia region, Ethiopia

Yohannes Mirkena[1], Mebratu Mitiku Reta[2*], Kibrom Haile[3], Zebiba Nassir[3] and Malede Mequanent Sisay[4]

Abstract

Background: Depression is an important public health concern due to its devastating morbidity and mortality among older adults. The aim of this study was to assess the prevalence of depression and associated factors among older adults (age ≥ 60 years) in Ambo Town, Ethiopia, 2016.

Methods: A community-based cross-sectional study was conducted among older adults in Ambo town from May to June 2016. Geriatric depression scale item 15 (GDS 15) was used to conduct face-to-face interviews with 800 study participants. Data were entered into Epi Info version 7 and analyzed using SPSS version 20. Descriptive statistics and multivariable logistic regression analysis were employed. Adjusted odds ratio (AOR) with a 95% confidence interval was used to calculate significance.

Results: The prevalence of depression was found to be 41.8% [CI = 38.5%, 45.5%]. The multivariable logistic regression model revealed that female sex (AOR = 1.72; 95% CI = 1.12, 2.66), trading (AOR = 2.44; 95% CI =1.32, 4.57), living with children (AOR = 3.19, 95% CI =1.14, 8.93) and retirement (AOR = 3.94, 95% CI = 2.11, 7.35) were associated with depression among older adults.

Conclusion: The prevalence of depression among older adult was found to be high. Due emphasis needs to be given to screening and treating depression, especially among older females, retired individuals, adults living with children and merchants.

Keywords: Prevalence, Depression, Older adults, Ethiopia

Background

Depression is a common mental health disorder in late-life and an important public health problem because of its devastating consequences at any given time in a community. Its recent global prevalence was 4.4% [1, 2]. Among all mentally ill individuals, 40% were diagnosed to have a depressive disorder [3]. Depression was the second global disease burden in 2010 and it is projected to be the first cause of years lived with disability (YLD) in 2020 [4]. It has been increasing in terms of both disability and mortality rates around the world. People with the depressive disorder have a 40% greater chance of premature death than their counterparts. The World Health Organization (WHO) estimated that the global depressive disorder among older adults ranged between 10 and 20%, depending on cultural situations; it affected nearly 300 million people in 2015 [5–8].

A community-based study done on an elderly population reported that depression was the most common mental health disorder in later life [9]. Although old age is not necessarily a time of sadness and depression, some elderly people face challenges that can be difficult to cope with effectively and experience distress, anxiety, demoralization, and loneliness. Most of the time, the clinical picture of depression in old age is masked by memory difficulties with distress and anxiety symptoms; however, these problems are actually secondary to depression [10–12]. Moreover, more older adults commit suicide, often through such indirect means as self-induced starvation or dehydration or failure to take medications prescribed for different reasons

* Correspondence: mebratumitiku@yahoo.com; mebretann16@gmail.com
[2]Department of Internal Medicine, School of Medicine, College of Medicine and Health Sciences, University of Gondar, Gondar, Ethiopia
Full list of author information is available at the end of the article

in the community [13, 14]. A population-based study showed that depression amplifies the functional disabilities caused by physical illness, interferes with treatment and rehabilitation and further contributes to a decline in physical and cognitive functioning of a person [15, 16]. It also has an economic impact on older adults due to its significant contribution to the rise of direct annual livelihood cost [17].

Several community-based studies showed that older adults experienced depression related complications, especially in low-income countries like Ethiopia [1, 18–21]. In addition, compared with other health services, evidence of depressive disorders tends to be relatively poor. Thus, the level of its burden among older adults is not well addressed in Ethiopia. Lack of adequate evidence about depression in older adults may be a factor that contributes to poor or inconsistent mental health care at community level [8, 22]. Therefore, the aim of this study was to investigate the prevalence of depression and associated factors among older adults in Ambo town, Oromia Region, Ethiopia.

Methods

Study design and setting

A community-based cross-sectional study was conducted in Ambo town, Oromia region, Ethiopia. The estimated number of households and the total number of the population in the town were 16,471 and 79,059 respectively, of which 39,553 (50.03%) were males. The town had one government hospital with a psychiatry clinic, which serves as an outpatient department. In addition, the town has 2 health centers, 3 health posts, 13 mediums, and 6 junior private clinics. However, none of these provides mental health care to the community. Older adults aged 60 years and above who were present at a time of data collection participated in the study. The United Nations uses 60 years to define old age and recommends the age range of 50 to 65 years to be used as cut off point by countries; additionally, the settings and contexts of countries play roles in determining old age [23]. In Ethiopia, old age starts at 60 the retirement age [24]. Householders from the selected zones who lived in the town for at least 6 months were eligible to participate. Those who were unable to communicate due to severe illness (individuals with hearing loss and aphasia, or difficulty to respond due to illness) were excluded from the study.

Sample size and sampling procedure

The sample size was determined by using the single population proportion formula with the assumption prevalence (P) of depression, 47.5% of a study in Sudan [25], a 95% confidence interval and a 5% margin of error. The minimum sample size (n) required for the study was calculated by using a design effect of 2 and a 10% non-response rate. With this, the total sample size was found to be 844. The multi-stage sampling technique was used to select participants with the assumption of a homogenous population. The town had three sub-cities, each composed of different zones. Two sub-cities were selected by the lottery method and clustered into 18 zones. Forty percent of the zones and their households were also selected by the lottery method and every household in the selected zones was visited to interview participants.

Data collection tools and procedures

Socio-demographic characteristics, substance use, clinical and psychosocial characteristics of older adults were collected through interviews. Substance use was assessed if the participant used substances like alcohol, khat, cigarettes and/or hashish in the preceding last 3 months. We also assessed clinical conditions that might contribute to depressions such as hypertension, diabetes and heart diseases. Geriatric Depression Scale item 15 (GDS-15) was used to assess the presence of depression among older adults. GDS item 15 has been extensively tested and validated in low and middle-income countries such as India, Nepal and other Asian countries [26–28]. This geriatric depression scale has been suggested by the Royal College of Physicians, the British Geriatric Society and the Royal College of general practitioners; the scale was recommended for screening depression in older people [29]. Depression was considered using a cutoff point greater than or equal to five. The Oslo-3 Social Support Scale (OSS-3) was used to collect social support characteristics. By adding the three items, those with 3–8 values were considered to have poor social support, while those with 9–11 and 12–14 values were considered to have intermediate and strong social support respectively. For this study, two different language experts translated the questionnaire from English into Afan Oromo and back to English to ensure consistency. A one day training was given to data collectors and the supervisor on basic data collection and interviewing techniques.

Data processing and analysis

The completed questionnaire was manually checked for completeness. Then, it was coded and entered into Epi-Info version 7 and exported to SPSS version 20 for further analysis. Descriptive and summary statistics were used to explain the population with respect to the relevant variables. Variables with less than 0.2 *p*-value in the bivariate analysis were fitted to the multivariable logistic regression. Odds ratio with 95% CI were calculated and statistical significance was considered at *P*-values < 0.05 in the multivariable logistic regression.

Results

Socio-demographic characteristics of participants

A total of 800 participants were involved with a response rate of 94.8%. More than half (55%) were male. The mean age of the participants was 66.69 (SD ± 6. 18) years. Nearly half, 359 (44.9%) were married and living with their spouses, while 174 (21.8%) were living only with their children. More than half, 437 (54.6%) of the participants had a secondary or higher level of education. Among the respondents, 569 (71.1%) were Orthodox Christians. One-third of the respondents were daily laborers. Of the respondents, 103 (12.9%) and 102 (12.8%) were merchants and retired people, respectively (Table 1).

The majority, 743 (92.9%) of the respondents had no known self or family history of mental illness. Four hundred forty-nine (56.1%) had a history of other medical illnesses, of which 171 (38%) were diabetic. Less than half of the participants, 356 (44.5%) had strong social support, while 223 (27.9%) had poor help (Table 2). The prevalence of depression among older adults was found to be 41.8% [95% CI (38.5, 45.5)].

Factors associated with depression

This study showed that retirement, living with children, trading and female sex were significantly and independently associated with depression. However, depression

Table 1 Socio-demographic characteristics of older adults at Ambo Town, Oromia region, Ethiopia, 2016 ($n = 800$)

Variables	Categories	Prevalence	Depression		Frequency	Percent
			Yes	No		
Sex	Female	0.46	167	193	360	45.0
	Male	0.38	167	273	440	55.0
Age	60–64	0.28	*103*	*271*	374	46.8
	65–69	0.44	*95*	*119*	214	26.8
	70–74	0.59	*68*	*47*	115	14.4
	75+	0.70	*68*	*29*	97	12.0
Ethnicity	Oromo	0.39	*266*	*413*	679	84.9
	Amhara	0.55	*57*	*46*	103	12.9
	Others[a]	0.61	*11*	*7*	18	2.2
Educational Status	Secondary & above	0.37	162	275	437	54.6
	Primary	0.55	128	105	233	29.1
	Not Educated	0.42	44	86	130	16.3
Marital Status	Married	0.36	128	231	359	44.9
	Widowed	0.39	129	201	330	41.2
	Single	0.64	7	4	11	1.4
	Separated/ divorced	0.70	70	30	100	12.5
Religion	Orthodox	0.34	*196*	*373*	569	71.1
	Protestant	0.59	*99*	*68*	167	20.9
	Others[b]	0.61	*39*	*25*	64	8.0
Occupation	Employed (Government & private organizations)	0.32	38	79	117	14.5
	Retired	0.71	72	30	102	12.8
	merchant (self-employed)	0.59	61	42	103	12.9
	Housewife	0.43	91	123	214	26.8
	Jobless and Daily laborer	0.27	72	192	264	33.0
Income (EBR)	<735	0.41	*70*	*101*	171	21.4
	735–1176	0.43	*209*	*281*	490	61.2
	>1176	0.40	*55*	*84*	139	17.4
Living arrangement	Spouse	0.35	125	230	355	44.4
	Children	0.75	130	44	174	21.8
	Alone	0.37	56	94	150	18.8
	Others[c]	0.19	23	98	121	15.1

[a]Tigre, Gurage [b]Muslim, Catholic, Wakefata, [c]relatives

Table 2 Clinical, social support and substance use of the study participants at Ambo Town, Oromia region, Ethiopia, 2016 ($n = 800$)

Variables		Frequency (n)	Percentages (%)
Mental illness	Yes	57	7.1
	No	743	92.9
Family history of mental illness	Yes	61	7.6
	No	739	92.4
Medical illness	Yes	449	56.1
	No	351	43.9
Social support	poor	223	27.9
	Intermediate	221	27.6
	Strong	356	44.5
Substance use (current)	Yes	134	16.8
	No	666	83.2

had no significant association with income, substance use, clinical and psychosocial characteristics. Elderly female were 1.7 times more likely to have depression compared to males [AOR = 1.72, 95% CI (1.12, 2.66)]. Retired older individuals were almost four times more likely to have depression than their counterparts [AOR = 3.94, 95% CI (2.11, 7.35)]. Older merchants were 2.4 times more likely to be depressed than employees [AOR = 2.44, 95% CI (1.32, 4.57)]. Older individuals living with children were 3.2 times more likely to have depression than those living with their spouses [AOR = 3.19, 95% CI (1.14, 8.93)] (Table 3).

Discussion

In this study, the prevalence of depression among older adults was 41.8% [95% CI: 38.5%, 45.5%]. The finding was in line with that of a community based cross-sectional study done in Sudan (41.1%) [25], Saudi Arabia (39%) [30] and India (42.7%) [31]. However, this finding was higher than the finding of a systematic review in a Caucasian population, where 1 to 16% of the older adults had depression according to both community and institution based study [32]. This variation may be due to the difference in study areas and socioeconomic status of participants. Conversely, our finding is in line with the finding of a systematic review done on a hospitalized Caucasian population, where 14–42% had depression. The finding of this study is also higher than the finding of a community-based survey in Thailand, where a 12-item questionnaire of Thai validated Euro-Depressions scale was used and a 28.5% depression prevalence was noted in old age [33]. The difference could be due to variations in the tools used to screen depression. This result is also higher than that of a meta-analysis conducted in nine European countries, where a pooled prevalence of depression was 12.3% in older adults [34]. This disparity may be due to social-cultural and economic difference. Again, the finding is also higher than that of a community-based survey conducted in Singapore (13.4%) [35]. The variation may be due to differences in tools, since the study in Singapore used the Geriatric Mental State (GMS) to screen depression. Moreover, compared to an institution based study in

Table 3 Multiple Logistic regression analysis of depressive disorder among older adults at Ambo Town, Ethiopia, 2016 ($n = 800$)

Variables	Categories	Depression ($n = 800$)		COR (95% CI)	AOR (95% CI)	*P* value
		Yes	No			
Sex	Female	167	193	1.41 (1.07,1.88)	1.72 (1.12,2.66)	0.013
	Male	167	273	1	1	
Marital status	Married	128	231	1	1	
	Widowed	129	201	1.16 (0.85,1.58)	1.28 (0.45,3.63)	0.52
	Single	77	34	3.16 (0.91,10.00)	4.78 (0.95,23.99)	0.049
	Separated/divorced	70	30	4.21 (2.61,6.80)	2.75 (0.92,8.24)	0.29
Education	Secondary and above	162	275	1	1	
	Primary	128	105	2.07 (1.50,2.86)	1.24 (0.80,1.92)	0.15
	Not educated	44	86	0.87 (0.58,1.31)	0.69 (0.39,1.21)	0.209
Occupation	Employed (Government & Private Organization)	38	79	1	1	
	Retired	72	30	4.99 (2.81,8.87)	3.94 (2.11,7.35)	<0.001
	Merchant (Self-employed)	61	42	3.02 (1.74,5.24)	2.44 (1.32,4.57)	0.009
	Housewife	91	123	1.54 (0.96,2.47)	0.86 (0.44,1.67)	0.712
	Others[a]	72	192	0.78 (0.49,1.25)	0.92 (0.50,1.69)	0.701
Living arrangement	Spouse	125	230	1	1	
	Children	130	44	5.44 (3.63,8.15)	3.19 (1.14,8.93)	0.028
	Others[b]	79	192	0.76 (0.54,1.06)	0.57 (0.20,1.64)	0.281

[a]jobless, daily laborer, [b]alone, relatives

Saudi (17%), our finding is higher [36]. This discrepancy may be due to the difference in the tool they used, the study setup and socio-cultural variations among the study participants. This finding is also higher than that of a community-based study in India (12.7%) and Mexico (23.7%) [37, 38]. Again, this variation may be due to differences in tools used to measure depression. Geriatric depression (ICD-10) and the seven-item version of the Center for Epidemiologic Studies Depression Scale (CES-D) were used in India and Mexico, respectively, beside the socio-cultural and economic differences. The finding of our study was also higher than the finding in the Netherlands (14.9%) [39]. The possible reason may be the difference in the tool they used and socioeconomic variations. In addition, ages 55–85 were included in the Netherland study, whereas age 60 and above were used as a cutoff point in our study. Our finding was higher than the finding of a community-based study conducted among South African older adults 4% [40]. This variation may be due to differences in age of participants in addition to the socio-cultural variations. In the South African study, ages 50 and older were included. The finding of our study was lower than those of other institutions based cross-sectional studies done in Brazil, India, Portugal, and elderly Japanese which reported 49.76%, 53.75%, 61.40% and 57.2%) respectively [41–43]. This variation may be due to the differences in the study setups. The elderly people living in institutions could be more depressing due to changes in the environment after living in private dwelling for a long time. Like our study, research in low and middle income countries (Sudan, Saudi Arabia, India) showed a higher prevalence of depression among the elderly than among the upper-middle and high income countries such as South Africa, Thailand, Singapore, Mexico, and the Netherlands [25, 30, 33, 35, 38–40]. This variation may be due to the impact of socioeconomic status; additionally, people in developed countries may have more access to mental health care and support before they develop problems. Previous studies also revealed that the associations between socio-demographic characteristics and depression among older adults were based on gender, marital status, and occupation [25, 44, 45]. The finding of this study also indicates supports that the same socio-demographic characteristics are significantly and independently associated with depression. Elderly female adults were 1.7 times more likely to have depression than males (AOR = 1.72, 95% CI: 1.12, 2.66). This was in line with the finding in Sudan, Saudi Arabia and India, where females were more affected by depression than males [25, 30, 36, 42, 46]. In addition, this finding was also supported by a systematic review and meta-analysis conducted in 2003 [47]. This finding was also supported by that of another cross-sectional study conducted in Italy [48]. This may be because women bear the burden of household responsibilities in addition to their economic dependency on men, especially in low-income countries.

Retirement was significantly associated with depression in older adults. Retired older adults were 4 times more likely to have depression compared to elderly working individuals [AOR = 3.94, 95% CI (2.11, 7.35)]. This is in line with the finding of a household survey in Sudan, Khartoum [49]. The result was also supported by the finding of a Korean Longitudinal Study of Aging [50]. This may be because retired individuals may not have adequate opportunity to interact with other people to share ideas and feelings. Elderly people may feel like they are isolated and have no support. Furthermore, such feelings might contribute to the development of depression.

Merchant older adults were 2.4 times more likely to develop depression than government employees [AOR = 2.44, 95% CI (1.32, 4.57)]. This was in line with a finding in Malaysia [51]. This may be due to the nature of the work, which involves economic uncertainty. Additionally, depression may visit the elderly when they try to manage their businesses based on their own and work to sustain their business even after they no more able to do so. This study also found that older adults who were living with their children were 3.2 times more likely to develop depression compared to those living with spouse [AOR = 3.19, 95% CI (1.14, 8.93)]. This is supported by another study conducted in India [42] showing that feelings of dependency may lead to the development depression. In previous studies, self and family history of mental illness, the absence of formal education and low income were significantly associated with older adult depression [44, 52, 53]. In this study, however, these variables had no significant association with such depression. Other studies also showed that being single, separation and divorce were significantly associated with older adult depression, but in our study, these variables had no statistically significant association [25, 54]. The disparity could be due to differences in sampling techniques, sample size, measurement tools and other socio-cultural variations among participants.

Conclusion

The finding of this study showed that the prevalence of depression among older adults was high. Retirements, merchant in occupation, living with children and female sex were significantly associated with depression. Greater emphasis has to be given in identifying and treating depression, especially the retired adults, merchants, adults living with children and females. Further studies with solid study design and other important variables need to be considered.

Abbreviations

ADLs: Activities of Daily Living; AOR: Adjusted Odds Ratio; COR: Crude Odds Ratio; CTIDHM: Clinical Tropical Infectious Disease and HIV Medicine; DALYs: Disability Adjusted Life Years; GDS: Geriatric Depression Scale; ICCMH: Integrated Clinical and Community Mental Health; LAMIC: Low and Middle-Income Countries; MDD: Major Depressive Disorder; SPSS: Statistical Package for Social Science; UAE: United Arab Emirates; UK: United Kingdome; UN: United Nation; WHO: World Health Organization; YLD: Years Lived with Disability

Acknowledgments

We acknowledge all staff of Amanuel Mental Specialized Hospital and College of Medicine and Health Sciences, University of Gondar. In addition, Ambo town Administrative Office, data collectors, and all the study participants are highly acknowledged.

Funding

This research received no specific grant from any funding agency in the public, commercial or not-for-profit sectors. Nevertheless, Amanuel Mental Specialized Hospital and the University of Gondar as a grant for staff provided financial backing. The funder has no role in the publication process.

Authors' contributions

YM and MMR wrote the proposal, participated in data collection, did the analysis and wrote the manuscript. KH, ZN, and MMS approved the proposal with some revisions, participated in data analysis, revised subsequent drafts of the paper and participated in manuscript preparation. All authors read and approved the final manuscript.

Consent for publication

Not applicable.

Competing interests

The authors declare that they have no competing interests.

Author details

[1]University of Gondar Teaching and Referral Hospital, Gondar, Ethiopia. [2]Department of Internal Medicine, School of Medicine, College of Medicine and Health Sciences, University of Gondar, Gondar, Ethiopia. [3]Amanuel Specialized Mental Health Hospital, Addis Ababa, Ethiopia. [4]Department of Epidemiology and Biostatistics, Institute of Public Health College of Medicine and Health Sciences, University of Gondar, Gondar, Ethiopia.

References

1. Saxena S, Funk M, Chisholm D. World health assembly adopts comprehensive mental health action plan 2013-2020. Lancet. 2013; 381(9882):1970–1.
2. Organization WH. Depression and other common mental disorders: Global Health estimates. 2017.
3. Patel V, Saxena S. Transforming lives, enhancing communities—innovations in global mental health. N Engl J Med. 2014;370(6):498–501.
4. Becker AE, Kleinman A. Mental health and the global agenda. N Engl J Med. 2013;369(1):66–73.
5. Raviola G, Eustache E, Oswald C, Belkin GS. Mental health response in Haiti in the aftermath of the 2010 earthquake: a case study for building long-term solutions. Harv Rev Psychiatry. 2012;20(1):68–77.
6. Mitchell A, Subramaniam H. Prognosis of depression in old age compared to middle age: a systematic review of comparative studies. Am J of Psychiatry. 2005;162:1588–601.
7. World Health Organization. Mental health of older adults: Fact sheet accessed at http://www.who.int/mediacentre/factsheets/fs381/en/. 2017.
8. Steel Z, Marnane C, Iranpour C, Chey T, Jackson JW, Patel V, et al. The global prevalence of common mental disorders: a systematic review and meta-analysis 1980–2013. Int J Epidemiol. 2014;43(2):476–93.
9. Sivertsen H, Bjørkløf GH, Engedal K, Selbæk G, Helvik A-S. Depression and quality of life in older persons: a review. Dement Geriatr Cogn Disord. 2015; 40:311–39.
10. Loo H, Gallarda T, Fabre I, Olie JP. Depression and aging. Bull Acad Natl Med. 2004;188(6):999–1007.
11. Hasin DS, Goodwin RD, Stinson FS, Grant BF. Epidemiology of major depressive disorder: results from the National Epidemiologic Survey on alcoholism and related conditions. Arch Gen Psychiatry. 2005;62(10):1097–106.
12. Blazer DG. Depression in late life: review and commentary. J Gerontol A Biol Sci Med Sci. 2003;58(3):249–65.
13. Ormel J, Oldehinkel AJ, Brilman EI. The interplay and etiological continuity of neuroticism, difficulties, and life events in the etiology of major and subsyndromal, first and recurrent depressive episodes in later life. Am J Psychiatry. 2001;158(6):885–91.
14. Blackburn P, Wilkins-Ho M, Wiese BS. Depression in older adults: Diagnosis and management. BC Med J. 2017;59(3):171–177.
15. Nicholson IR. New technology, old issues: demonstrating the relevance of the Canadian code of ethics for psychologists to the ever-sharper cutting edge of technology. Canadian Psychology/Psychologie Canadienne. 2011; 52(3):215.
16. Mogga S, Ince MP, Alem A, Kebede D, Stewart R, Glozier N, et al. Outcome of major depression in Ethiopia Outcome of major depression in Ethiopia. Br J Psychiatry. 2006;189:241–6.
17. Luppa M, Heinrich S, Matschinger H, Sandholzer H, Angermeyer MC, Konig HH, et al. Direct costs associated with depression in old age in Germany. J Affect Disord. 2008;105(1–3):195–204.
18. World Health Organization. Global Health Risks: Mortality and burden of disease attributable to selec ted major risks. 2009.
19. Andreasen P, Lonnroos E, MCv E-C. Prevalence of depression among older adults with dementia living in low- and middle-income countries: a cross-sectional study. Eur J Public Health. 2013;24(1):40–4.
20. Padayachey U, Ramlall S, Chipps J. Depression in older adults: prevalence and risk factors in a primary health care sample. S Afr Fam Pract. 2017;59(2): 61–6.
21. Ferrari AJ, Somerville AJ, Baxter AJ, Norman R, Patten SB, Vos T, et al. Global variation in the prevalence and incidence of major depressive disorder: a systematic review of the epidemiological literature. Psychol Med. 2013;43: 471–81.
22. Bitew T. Prevalence and risk factors of depression in Ethiopia: a review. Ethiop J Health Sci 2014;24(2):161–169.
23. Kowal P, Dowd JE. Definition of an older person. Proposed working definition of an older person in Africa for the MDS project. Geneva: World Health Organization; 2001.
24. Federal Negarit Gazeta. A proclamation to provide for the public servants' pension, proclamation No. 714/2011. Addis Ababa: Federal Democratic Republic Ethiopia; 2011.
25. Assil S, Zeidan Z. Prevalence of depression and associated factors among elderly Sudanese: a household survey in Khartoum State/Prévalence de la dépression et des facteurs associés chez des Soudanais âgés: enquête auprès des ménages dans l'État de Khartoum. East Mediterr Health J. 2013; 19(5):435.
26. Sarkar S, Kattimani S, Roy G, Premarajan KC. Validation of the Tamil version of short form geriatric depression Scale-15. J Neurosci Rural Pract. 2015;6(3): 442–6.
27. Gautam R, Houde S. Geriatric depression scale for community-dwelling older adults in Nepal. Asian J Gerontol Geriatr. 2011;6:93–9.
28. Nyunt MSZ, Fones C, Niti M, Ng T-P. Criterion-based validity and reliability of the geriatric depression screening scale (GDS-15) in a large validation sample of community-living Asian older adults. Aging Ment Health. 2009; 13(3):376–82.
29. Yesavage JA, Brink TL, Rose TL, Lum O, Huang V, Adey M, et al. Development and validation of a geriatric depression screening scale: a preliminary report. J Psychiatr Res. 1982;17(1):37–49.
30. Al-Shammari SA, Al-Subaie A. Prevalence and correlates of depression among Saudi elderly. Int J Geriatr Psychiatry. 1999;14(9):739–47.
31. Sinha SP, Shrivastava SR, Ramasamy J. Depression in an older adult rural population in India. MEDICC Rev. 2013;15(4):41–4.
32. Djernes JK. Prevalence and predictors of depression in populations of elderly: a review. Acta Psychiatr Scand. 2006;113(5):372–87.

33. Haseen F, Prasartkul P. Predictors of depression among older people living in rural areas of Thailand. Bangladesh Med Res Counc Bull. 2011;37(2):51–6.
34. Copeland JR, Beekman AT, Dewey ME, Hooijer C, Jordan A, Lawlor BA, et al. Depression in Europe. Geographical distribution among older people. Br J Psychiatry. 1999;174:312–21.
35. Subramaniam M, Abdin E, Sambasivam R, Vaingankar JA, Picco L, Pang S, et al. Prevalence of depression among older adults-results from the well-being of the Singapore elderly study. Ann Acad Med Singap. 2016;45(4):123–33.
36. Alamri SH, Bari AI, Ali AT. Depression and associated factors in hospitalized elderly: a cross-sectional study in a Saudi teaching hospital. Ann Saudi Med. 2017;37(2):122–9.
37. Rajkumar AP, Thangadurai P, Senthilkumar P, Gayathri K, Prince M, Jacob KS. Nature, prevalence and factors associated with depression among the elderly in a rural south Indian community. Int Psychogeriatr. 2009;21(2):372–8.
38. Fernández-Niño JA, Manrique-Espinoza BS, Bojorquez-Chapela I, Salinas-Rodríguez A. Income inequality, socioeconomic deprivation and depressive symptoms among older adults in Mexico. PLoS One. 2014;9(9):e108127.
39. Beekman AT, Deeg DJ, van Tilburg T, Smit JH, Hooijer C, van Tilburg W. Major and minor depression in later life: a study of prevalence and risk factors. J Affect Disord. 1995;36(1–2):65–75.
40. Peltzer K, Phaswana-Mafuya N. Depression and associated factors in older adults in South Africa. Glob Health Action. 2013;6. https://doi.org/10.3402/gha.v6i0.18871.
41. Leal MCC, Apóstolo JLA. Mendes AMdOC, marques APdO. Prevalence of depressive symptoms and associated factors among institutionalized elderly. Acta Paulista de Enfermagem. 2014;27(3):208–14.
42. Goud AA, Nikhade NS. Prevalence of depression in older adults living in old age home. International Archives of Integrated Medicine. 2015;2(11):1–5.
43. Kuzuya M, Masuda Y, Hirakawa Y, Iwata M, Enoki H, Hasegawa J, et al. high prevalence rate of depression among community-dwelling frail elderly Japanese. Nihon Ronen Igakkai Zasshi. 2006;43(4):512–7.
44. Chui P, Chan M. Prevalence of depressive symptoms and associated factors in patients attending a geriatric day hospital. Asian J Gerontol Geriatr. 2006; 1(2):73–7.
45. Rashid A, Manan A, Rohana S. Depression among the elderly Malays living in rural Malaysia. Internet J Public Health. 2011;1(2):128–36.
46. Najim H, Omer AA. Sociodemographic and clinical features of patients with depressive disorder in Khartoum. Sudan Psychiatr Danub. 2015;27(1):S240–2.
47. Cole MG, Dendukuri N. Risk factors for depression among elderly community subjects: a systematic review and meta-analysis. Am J Psychiatry. 2003;160(6):1147–56.
48. Vaccaro R, Borrelli P, Abbondanza S, Davin A, Polito L, Colombo M, et al. Subthreshold depression and clinically significant depression in an Italian population of 70-74-year-olds: prevalence and association with perceptions of self. Biomed Res Int. 2017;3592359(10):14.
49. Assil SM, Zeidan ZA. Prevalence of depression and associated factors among elderly sudanese: a household survey in Khartoum state. East Mediterr Health J. 2013;19(5):435–40.
50. Park H, Kang MY. Effects of voluntary/involuntary retirement on their own and spouses' depressive symptoms. Compr Psychiatry. 2016;66:1–8.
51. Sherina M, Rampal L, Mustaqim A. The prevalence of depression among the elderly in Sepang. Selangor Med J Malaysia. 2004;59(1):45–9.
52. Alexopoulos GS. Depression in the elderly. Lancet. 2005;365(9475):1961–70.
53. Mohd sidik S, Zulkefli M, Afiah N, Shah SA. Factors associated with depression among elderly patients in a primary health care clinic in Malaysia. Asia Pacific Family Medicine. 2003;2(3):148–52.
54. Imran A, Azidah A, Asrenee A, Rosediani M. Prevalence of depression and its associated factors among elderly patients in outpatient clinic of Universiti Sains Malaysia Hospital. Med J Malaysia. 2009;64(2):134–9.

18

Why do I have to suffer? Symptom management, views and experiences of persons with a CPTSD: a grounded theory approach

Manuel P. Stadtmann[1,3*], Andreas Maercker[2], Jochen Binder[3] and Wilfried Schnepp[1]

Abstract

Background: For the 11th version of the International Classification of Diseases, a new stress related diagnosis has been proposed: complex post-traumatic stress disorder (CPTSD). It is described as a chronic condition with several severe and concurrent symptoms. In the literature, these symptoms are discussed as a common reason for seeking psychiatric treatment as they can influence and impair the quality of life not only for affected persons but also for their social and familial system.

Aim: This research studies symptom management in everyday life by exploring and reconstructing the views, perceptions, experiences, facilitators and barriers of adults with CPTSD.

Methods: A theoretical sampling was used to recruit 18 to 65 years old patients diagnosed with CPTSD from an inpatient setting. The 17 semi-structured interviews were audio recorded and transcribed verbatim. The transcriptions were uploaded into MAXQDA, and a Grounded Theory method based on Corbin and Strauss was used to analyse the data.

Results: We provide a process model with 5 interacting phases: trauma experience, emotional ignorance, overcompensation, paroxysm, and perspectives. Each phase is specified with subcategories.

Conclusions: The participants did not recognise their symptoms as such and were unaware of their diagnosis for many years. Nevertheless, they used various resources and were able to develop skills and techniques to deal with their symptoms and to function on a day-to-day basis. Overall, the process of symptom management was extremely exhausting for the participants and they felt left alone with it. The participants were eager to gain support from healthcare professionals and, when necessary, financial support from the government. Thus, these results indicate an essential need to develop support and tailored interventions for the symptom management of persons with a CPTSD.

Keywords: Complex post-traumatic stress disorder, CPTSD, ICD-11, Psychiatry, Symptoms, Mental health, Grounded theory, Experience, View

* Correspondence: manuel.stadtmann@ipw.zh.ch
[1]Department of Health, University of Witten/Herdecke, Alfred-Herrhausen-Straße 50, 58448 Witten, Germany
[3]Centre for Trauma Disorders, Integrierte Psychiatrie Winterthur, Technikumstrasse 81, Winterthur, Switzerland
Full list of author information is available at the end of the article

Background

Over the past decades, there have been approaches to integrating the diagnosis of complex posttraumatic stress disorder (CPTSD) as first proposed by Herman [1]. In 2018, the World Health Organization (WHO) is expected to approve the 11th edition of the International Classification of Diseases (ICD-11) as the official latest version [2], and it will contain the new diagnosis of CPTSD.

Research has proposed using core PTSD (post-traumatic stress disorder) criteria to diagnose CPTSD [2–7]. The prerequisite for PTSD is that the affected person develops the symptoms after a stressful situation of exceptional threat or catastrophic extent. This situation can be, for example, abuse of physical or mental nature, a natural catastrophe, accidents or war experience. Further two symptoms from the following three symptom domains must be identified: re-experiencing (RE), avoidance (AV), and sense of threat (TH) [2, 3, 5, 7, 8]. Re-experiencing describes symptoms where the affected person suffers, for instance, from uncontrollable memories of the traumatic event. The domain avoidance describes symptoms where those affected cannot be exposed to situations that could recall the traumatic event. Sense of threat describes symptoms such as perceptions of heightened current threat, hypervigilance, and feeling keyed-up [4, 9–12].

In addition to the above PTSD criteria, a diagnosis of CPTSD requires the presence of symptoms from the following three domains: a negative self-concept (NSC), disturbances in relationships (DR), symptoms of affective dysregulation (AD) [2–7]. A negative self-concept comprises low self-esteem, negative beliefs due to traumatic experiences and feelings of guilt and shame [4, 9, 12, 13]. The same authors described disturbances in relationships as being based on the lack of skills to build and maintain close social relationships. Also, they defined the domain affective dysregulation involving symptoms such as self-harming behaviour, dissociation, emotional numbness, anger outbursts, irritability, excessive crying, or anhedonia. The traumatic event does not necessarily cause immediate distress [2], the symptom onset can be delayed more than six months post trauma [2]. In a previous study, we have provided first results for the symptom burden in psychiatric inpatients with a CPTSD [14]. We could identify several adverse factors, for instance a high prevalence of unemployment, a single status, and living alone with no social support. The results were in adherence with the findings from other studies [4, 12, 15, 16]. Further we have provided results concerning the high educational level of the affected persons, comorbidity in form of several additional diagnoses, multiple trauma experiences, diverse types of trauma experience, and a high level of symptom burden measured by different validated assessment instruments [14].

Symptoms are discussed in the literature as a common reason for seeking treatment, and patients rarely describe one single symptom to their clinicians [17–20]. A symptom is described as a subjective sensation that may vary over time, has antecedents, influences outcomes, and may be influenced by an intervention [20–23]. The same authors describe symptom clusters as having the same characteristics as a symptom. In addition, these clusters consist of three or more concurrent symptoms, are a stable group of symptoms, have a temporal dimension, and are independent of other clusters [21–24]. During the trajectory of illness, affected individuals often experience multiple co-occurring and contradicting symptoms (e.g. flashbacks, hyperarousal, fatigue, sleep disturbance) [19, 21, 24]. These symptoms can strongly influence and alter life quality and daily life itself [24, 25]. Additionally, when symptoms remain underdiagnosed and undertreated, they have a negative impact on patient-reported outcomes including functional performance, cognitive status, and quality of life [20–22].

Recent research shows that handling symptoms and the resulting difficulties are often left to the responsibility of patients and their relatives, and decisions are necessary on how to deal with symptoms, such as when to contact healthcare providers [19, 24, 26, 27]. There is a need for paths to manage symptoms and improve quality of life and overall functioning, especially for individuals and families living with chronic conditions [21–23]. Nonetheless, symptom cluster research is limited, and science is only beginning to understand how to investigate symptom clusters by developing frameworks and new methods and approaches [20, 22]. Further research to identify the mechanisms and processes that underlie symptom clusters is essential in order to develop targeted interventions [21, 23, 28].

For individuals affected by CPTSD, there are two further issues that need to be addressed. There is currently little information on the treatment regimen for patients with CPTSD, and no statement can be made on the differential effect of individual trauma-focused procedures in CPTSD [3–5, 29, 30]. Processing traumatic experiences appears not to be possible without symptom management for the patients [31, 32]. However, no study has been found that dealt with symptom management in the everyday life of adult patients with CPTSD. This study therefore focuses on adult patients with CPTSD and explores and reconstructs their views, perceptions, experiences and the facilitators and barriers as well as the processes involved in symptom management in everyday life. The results can be used to generate more detailed research questions, which could, at best, result in improved patient treatment. These results could also serve as a basis for further research into developing interventions to improve symptom management in everyday life.

Aims

This study aimed to explore and reconstruct the views, perceptions, experiences, facilitators and barriers of adults with CPTSD in symptom management in everyday life.

Methods

Study design

This study is part of larger mixed-method research to investigate symptom management and the social process of adult inpatients with CPTSD [33]. The literature [34, 35] recommends Grounded Theory as a suitable method to investigate phenomena with little scientific evidence. This is the case with CPTSD and symptom management. The Grounded Theory approach was based on the form proposed by Corbin and Strauss [34]. This form claims to outline a more linear and structured approach, in which rules rather than interpretations play a significant role, with the intention to make the analysis understandable, comprehensible and verifiable [35].

Framework

The study is based on a systemic approach. Chronic illness affects many daily activities [23, 36–39]. It not only affects the person in need but also the surrounding social and familial system [23, 37, 38]. Coping with CPTSD in the social network cannot be adequately understood without being sensitive to the specific kind of relationship between those who are ill and their relatives [23, 29, 37]. Our primary perspective is systemic in that we see the affected individual as part of a system, a member of an interactional group of people who act and react to each other. We also subscribe to a central position of symptom management research that places the experience with the illness and the individual coping strategies at the very centre of attention [19, 23] and addresses the affected person as an expert.

Setting

This study was conducted at the psychiatric institution Integrierte Psychiatrie Winterthur, Zürcher Unterland (IPW). IPW is a large, non-profit, community-based organization that provides psychiatric services in the city of Winterthur in the canton of Zurich, Switzerland. It provides a full continuum of clinical and community-based mental health services for individuals with several mental health issues. The current study was conducted at a specialized inpatient mental health ward for psycho-traumatology. The ward treats approximately 200 patients per year. It provides treatment for a diverse adult population from the German-speaking region of Switzerland. The ward has a capacity for 17 patients and has a 24-h shift organization for nurses.

Sampling and recruitment

Over a six-month period, the participants were chosen from a larger sample of adult inpatients ($n = 133$) who had participated in a previous quantitative study [14]. The Zürcher Cantonal Ethics Review Board approved the study. In order to provide a description of CPTSD sufferers with regard to their symptom management, we aimed at a heterogenous and diverse group of participants using theoretical sampling, with the aim of enabling a rich illustration of relevant aspects of the phenomenon. Inclusion criteria comprised: It was the participants' first inpatient treatment on the psycho-traumatology ward. They had to be between 18 and 65 years of age. A CPTSD based on the International Trauma Questionnaire (ITQ) must have been diagnosed. A good knowledge of German was required. Also, a relative must have been willing to participate. Relatives were defined as individuals who were self-defined relatives, who may or may not have been bound by blood ties, law, friendship or declared commitment and who shared deep personal connections to the participant and provided various forms of support [40, 41]. Exclusion criteria included acute or latent suicidality of the patient and a main diagnosis other than CPTSD. Patients who might endanger themselves or others were also excluded. Written informed consent was given prior to the interviews. Informed consent was obtained from patients as well as from relatives. In this study we report exclusively patient participants' experiences and views. The names contained in this manuscript are pseudonyms and have been changed to ensure the anonymity of study participants. The pseudonyms were introduced after the participants were audio recorded and are solely known to the first author of the study.

Data collection and analyses

The first author, with experience in treating and caring for patients with PTSD, was responsible for the qualitative collection of data with semi-structured interviews. First questions were developed based on the results of the first quantitative phase relating to the level of symptom burden [14]. For instance, asking the sufferers with different levels of symptom burden how they perceived their condition in daily life, or which symptoms they perceived the most impairing or the most difficult. Similarly the domains of the symptom management model [24] were used to develop further questions. For example, what did they do to improve their symptom burden? When did they initiate their strategies? Who delivered support and help? Further questions were also posed, such as how they perceived their quality of life, or how the sufferers perceived their functional status in daily life. The clinician's internal code allowed the identification of patients, after they were asked for an interview.

To create the largest possible contrast between the interview partners, the participants were chosen using theoretical sampling [42]. After the descriptive analyses and results of the first quantitative study ($n = 133$), the first three participants were specifically identified based on their numeric level of symptom burden (low, middle and high) [14]. Further selection and identification of participants was based on the questions arising during the process and performed during the analyses. For instance, in a second step we identified participants with different trauma experiences. In a third step, we identified participants with no diploma or apprenticeship and contrasted the results in a fourth step selecting participants, who were still employed. The descriptive results of the quantitative study allowed us to identify and choose participants with the characteristics of interest.

The interviews took place after the inpatient treatment. The data collection took place between 1st March 2017 and 31st August 2017 within the psychiatric institution IPW in Winterthur, Switzerland. The semi-structured interviews lasted between 45 and 85 min; an additional 30 min after the interviews were available for questions and explanations. If any psychological crises had arisen due to the interviews, these could have been intercepted by a mental health nurse on the ward. The shift organization on the ward is guaranteed 24 h a day by the nursing team.

The interviews were audio recorded and subsequently transcribed verbatim. To comply with data protection, all names were anonymized. The semi-structured interviews were analysed based on grounded theory as proposed by Corbin and Strauss [34]. In a first step we conducted a line-by-line coding, within a group of Ph.D. students. Second, after using analytical techniques in open coding, the set of categories were reduced and clustered during an axial coding phase. The third coding level consisted of selecting and integrating the categories into a final theory [34, 35, 43]. MAXQDA 12 software was used for this process. To ensure the quality of data analysis, the process itself and the results were regularly discussed in a peer group of Ph.D. students led by an experienced qualitative researcher. Based on the discussions and constant comparative analysis process within this research group, data saturation was achieved after the 15th interview when no new data emerged, and all concepts of the theory were well developed. To ensure no new data emerged, we conducted two further interviews, resulting in a total of 17 interviews. This procedure adheres to current literature, which states approximately 15 participants are needed for data saturation to be achieved [44–46]. We also conducted a member check of our final model with the participants to determine the accuracy of the reported data. All patient participants confirmed having been or still being in one of those phases. The data analysis was undertaken in German, the language in which the interviews were conducted. The final report of the findings was written in English.

Results

Data saturation occurred after the 15th interview. To ensure no new categories arose from the data, we conducted two additional interviews. We aimed to select a diverse sample to possibly include a multitude of relevant views and experiences and to strengthen the credibility of the findings. Hence our final sample of 17 participants showed heterogeneous sociodemographic characteristics and different levels of symptom burden (Table 1). The data analysis resulted in a process with five categories or themes that were sorted into an explanatory framework that sequenced the progression and experiences of the participants through their life of coping with symptoms of CPTSD. This framework (Fig. 1) is separated into five phases: 1.) Trauma experience, 2.) Emotional ignorance, 3). Overcompensation, 4.) Paroxysm and 5.) Perspectives. These sections describe each of the characteristic categories and subcategories. We additionally provide participant quotes as examples.

Trauma experience

This phase describes the **Causal Condition**. A more specific description is in the sub-categories of different forms of abuse in childhood and the participants' cumulative trauma experience. All the participants had a story of early childhood trauma and at least two of the following types of traumatic experience: sexual abuse, physical abuse, domestic violence, school violence, neglect, or war.

> *"I got the information about soldiers' illness from the American media... But I didn't know that it can also develop after physical or sexual abuse" Max, 34*

> *"It started in my childhood and then many terrible things happened in my life. I don't know why I still have to suffer." Paul, 46*

Emotional ignorance

This phase describes the main **Phenomena,** and the participants' experience of not recognising their symptoms as such. Participants identified their symptoms as part of their personality and their being: something natural and given, based on the circumstances they mostly grew up with. They sometimes thought their very self was not strong enough, weak, or just odd compared to other humans. In addition to unawareness of symptoms, the participants also struggled with an inability to regulate themselves and to cope with their condition.

> *"I thought it was my personality and I was just weak and useless. Now I know my symptoms were the cause of so many reactions" Sonja, 48*

> *"It's like being a ping pong ball blown by a hair dryer. It does with me what it wants; it shoots me to the right, to the left or up or down and I can't do anything to stop it." Mary, 40*

Table 1 Participants (pseudonyms)

NAME	Gender	Age	Occupation	Trauma experience
Mary	f	40	former nurse	1, 2, 3, 6
Celia	f	60	former teacher	1, 2, 3, 6
Paula	f	22	former teacher	1, 2, 3, 6
Max	m	34	former military	1, 2, 3
Susanne	f	58	former nurse	1, 2, 6
Peter	m	30	economics student	1, 2, 5
Marta	f	48	former smith	1, 2, 6
Sonja	f	48	former airport employee	1, 3, 4
Paul	m	46	no diploma or apprenticeship	1, 2, 6
Yuki	f	47	no diploma or apprenticeship	1, 2, 4
Laura	f	38	bank employee	1, 2, 3, 4
Tim	m	58	former manager	1,3,5,6
Clara	f	19	retail sales person	1,2,3
Laura	f	33	former hairdresser	1,3
Nicole	f	45	self employed	1,2,4
Astrid	f	26	student natural science	1,3,4
Jana	f	62	former branch manager	1,2

Legend: Early Childhood Trauma = 1, Sexual abuse = 2, Physical abuse = 3, Domestic violence = 4, School Violence = 5, Neglect = 6

Further, the results elaborate the struggle of those trying to suppress and control the unknown and, for them, latent dangerous feelings.

> *"Sometimes it was so intense, I was really desperate. I knew there was something else ... Something that makes me react differently from others. I do my best to ignore it." Celia, 60*

The **Context** identifies critical issues such as frequency of symptoms, intensity of symptoms, duration, and social situation. Participants retrospectively experienced a high frequency of symptoms, e.g. every day since their childhood, while the intensity varies. For instance, dissociation had a high impact and intensity in their daily life, while their feeling of worthlessness was described as latent and an almost omnipresent symptom, which eventually was identified as part of their very self. Another important category was the social situation. Participants with an income described a lower level of uncertainty and stress regarding their future. They could also afford to spend money on activities, e.g. movies or inviting their children for lunch in a restaurant, which distracted them, improved their social interactions and helped to release the inner tension. Contrastingly, participants with no secure income or financial support described the feeling of not being a part of society. This situation was described as a context factor that made it difficult for them to cope with their daily life, to manage bills, to manage their administrative tasks, and as a factor that increased symptoms such as rumination and inner tension.

> *" I've had symptoms almost every day since childhood. In school, the others thought I was mad, and I must admit I thought so too. Four years ago, I finally realized that I'm not crazy." Max, 34*

The **Intervening Conditions** describe facilitators and barriers of the patients for symptom management in everyday life, for instance, supportive and caring relatives, with participants describing in diverse ways how relatives play a key role in their life. Individuals related by blood or not were described as a life anchor. Highly important was being able to learn to trust again. Participants who shared some of their traumatic experience with their relatives described talking for the first time: they felt ashamed, unsure, and feared their relatives' reactions. Experiencing comprehension and compassion helped them afterwards to trust a person and improved their level of symptom burden.

> *"But I think it's nice to have such a good friend. It makes it easier... Just to know there is someone around makes me feel less lonely." Paula 22*

Otherwise, not sharing the cause of their condition with their relatives also generated feelings of shame and guilt.

> *"I can't... I just can't. I am too ashamed to tell him (husband). He doesn't understand many things; I think he might if I told him. Then, I feel guilty about our situation." Celia 60*

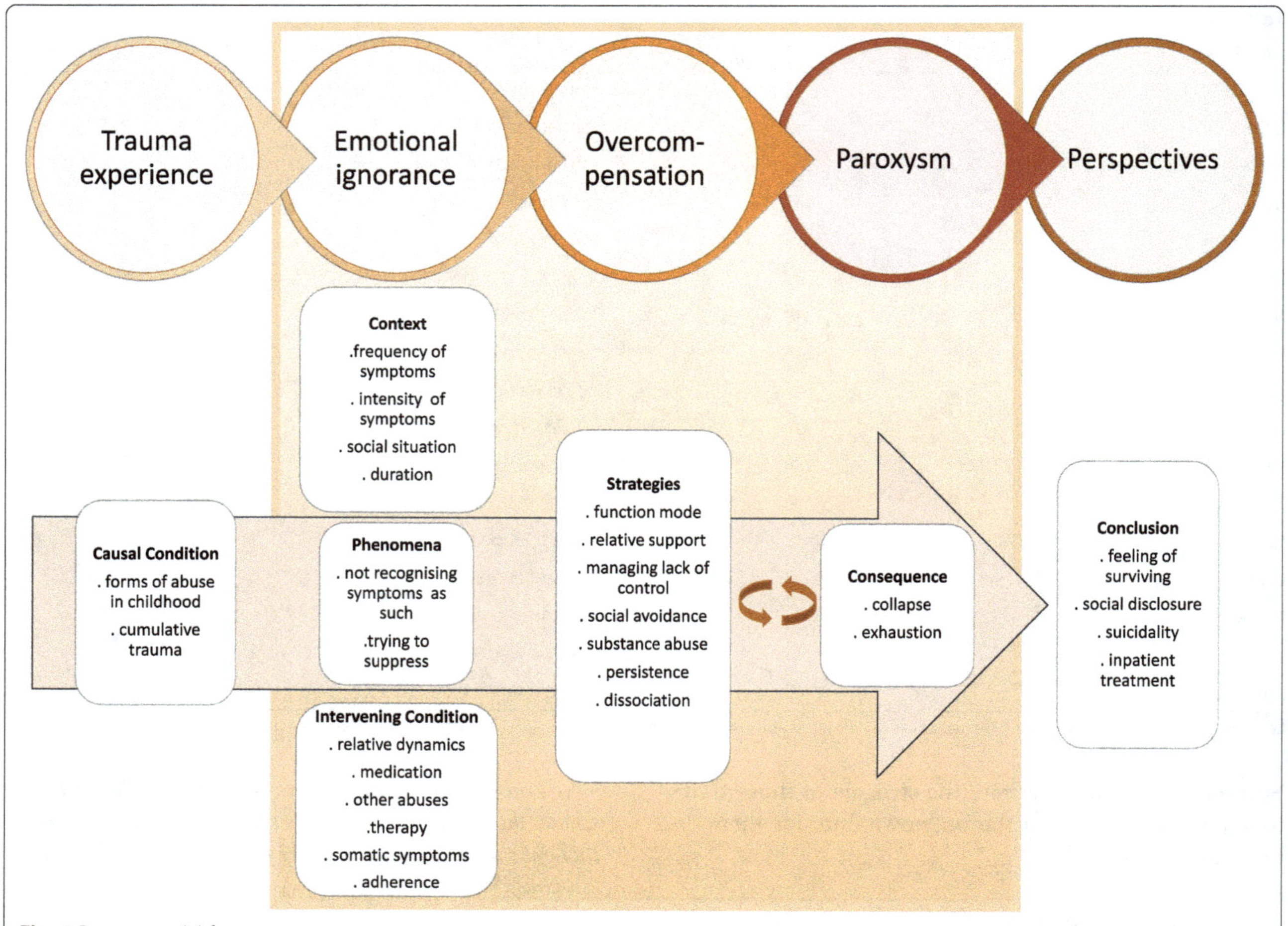

Fig. 1 Process model for symptom management in persons with CPTSD

For the participants, support in activities of daily life through their relatives was of great importance. They learned to accept their lower level of performance and to realize they were not alone. Further, during that time, participants could re-vitalize.

> *"I couldn't even get up and do the dishes, but he was there. He also helped a lot in raising the children. He really is a good husband. I wouldn't be here without him" Marta, 48*

For some, medication was an important facilitator. With the help of different substances, the participants were able to manage their daily life. Where medication was not prescribed, some of the participants tried unknowingly to suppress their symptoms and emotions with substance abuse such as with alcohol, cocaine, or cannabis. This reaction resulted in a barrier, making it more difficult for them to understand and handle their situation. Experiencing multiple abuses during their life was described as a major barrier, due to not being able to give a meaning to the pain and suffering provoked by the traumatic experience.

> *"Not only in my childhood, even afterwards many things happened. I always asked myself, why me? I still don't know why me. Vodka and my joint often helped me to forget." Clara, 19*

Being able to make use of the right therapy and avoid unnecessary medical interventions was a major facilitator. Then again, being treated for another condition, for instance depression or schizophrenia, instead of for PTSD was a major barrier.

> *"I'm angry and sad. I took medication because they thought I had schizophrenia. For many years. Mmm I guess 16 years later I know I have a PTSD and that fits." Yuki, 47*

Several participants described somatic symptoms such as back pain, headache, stomach ache as being a barrier, which also meant it was not easy for medical professionals to handle and identify the symptoms as possible consequences of trauma.

> *"The body sensations are awful. Suddenly my hands are sweaty, or the soles of my feet are wet, bah! The tension in my back is also a nuisance. These body things make it more difficult to deal with" Sonja, 48*

Adherence to diagnosis was also described as a major facilitator in diverse ways. For example, being able to identify the diagnosis and accept it improved the feeling of having a kind of control over the disorder and decreased the feeling of stigma.

> *"I now accept the diagnosis, I no longer feel ashamed, because it was not my fault." Jana, 62*

Overcompensation

In this phase, the category **Strategies** illustrates participants' efforts to cope subconsciously with their symptoms, or to compensate for them, for instance with dissociation or persistence.

> *"I didn't know what it was at the time... that tension. I was just not here... often... I didn't feel my body at all" Mary, 40*

An important sub-category was described as function mode. Mostly participants had a very high level of functioning. They had mostly a higher level of education and, while working, performed efficiently. The reasons for that mode were as follows: The legitimation to be alive based on their school or work performance, the justification as a member of society based on their performance, not having any uncomfortable feelings based on the overcompensation through their workload and seeking confirmation from their professional environment through their performance and qualifications.

> *"Distraction I think, and later at 18 sort of functioning. At 16 I started to work in a hospital. Shift work was a great distraction. For many years I had just two days a month off. Yeah..." Susanne, 58*

Other categories such as "caring relatives" were mostly considered important. Sufferers described that having a helpful and supportive relative ameliorated their symptom burden. Hereby different subcategories could be identified, for instance, managing the activities of daily living, such as cooking, doing the dishes or the laundry, shopping, administrative issues, or support with occurring symptoms, such as providing help after being instructed how to deal with dissociation. Another subcategory was emotional support, for example being there for the affected person when needed, being available when the affected person needed someone to talk to. This subcategory also included not questioning whether the experiences of the affected person were real or not, motivating the affected person to keep in contact with others by taking them out for dinner, a walk, or on vacation.

> *"Don't give up and again and again two or three days without sleep and then work again. My wife had to take over many things. That was helpful" Peter, 30*

Managing the lack of control characterized further participant strategies, mostly based on feelings of anxiety and fear.

> *"I just scratched myself to the bone, just to calm me down. My parents... They thought it was a skin disease, they thought I had chronic eczema." Marta, 48*

When the described strategies no longer functioned, the affected people often struggled with social avoidance and substance abuse to reduce their psychological tension. Being mostly at home for years, just going out when necessary and having no social interactions was one method of feeling in control over their situation.

> *"But yeah, but yeah somehow, I had nothing, so I went through addiction, I started with alcohol and other drugs. I also preferred to be alone, to make the whole thing better." Sonja, 48*

Paroxysm

This phase indicates the possible **Consequence** when overcompensation is no longer working. Paroxysm is described as an uncontrollable outburst, sudden increase, or recurrence of symptoms [47]. That definition complies with the condition described by people affected by CPTSD. In the subcategory collapse, the symptoms can no longer be suppressed and those affected undergo impressions of collapsing and feeling exhausted after strategies used no longer work. Also, feelings of being worthless and of shame and guilt at not being able to perform as they could previously were described. In the subcategory feeling exhausted, the participants described how using their strategies for years consumed most of their energy. Further there was mostly a trigger situation, for example losing their job, a divorce, or an accident. After the event, they felt exhausted and without energy and therefore completely defenceless against and overwhelmed by their symptoms. Additionally, they could not explain to themselves why, apparently, a single event caused such immense reactions and drain of energy.

"I was totally incapable of working and couldn't manage my life" Peter, 30

"For a long time, I did not think I was ill. For me it was as though I could still do everything. Until I noticed nothing worked anymore, because it's all so exhausting." Paula, 22

Perspectives

This phase specifies the **Conclusion** of the process. For instance, the subcategory a feeling of surviving has been described as a possible outcome. Participants experienced the development of perspectives, in which they felt they had new goals, a better understanding of their condition, feelings of control, and they had hope again.

"Because yeaah it's difficult to describe. In a way it's liberating. Because yeah, I now know where the problems lie, and I can work on them." Yuki, 47

The subcategory social disclosure is a possible result of experiencing different recurrent situations of collapsing and not being able to perform as before. The feeling of disappointment in themselves was also described in this subcategory. Furthermore, feelings of shame and disclosure based on not being able to handle social interactions could be identified. If the affected person was aware of the possibility and had access to a health care provider, a possible result was also inpatient treatment. If there was a lack of support either from the social environment or the health care system, those affected also developed suicidal thoughts.

"From the age of 22 to 33 it just didn't exist. It worked unconsciously through nightmares, I suspect. When I was 33 it broke out again and I had a nervous breakdown and nearly killed myself." Susanne, 58

Discussion

This is the first known study that highlights symptom management of those affected by CPTSD. Using the data collected through interviews, we developed a conceptual model (Fig. 1) that identifies five major phases experienced by affected individuals: trauma experience, emotional ignorance, overcompensation, paroxysm and perspectives. Those affected described a situation in which they felt something was different in comparison to others. They mostly interpreted this condition as a deficiency in their personality. Therefore, the phenomenon of not recognising their symptoms as such and trying to suppress these as well as emotions is an important result.

Persons suffering from CPTSD also tried to function over a prolonged period. They achieved, sometimes over decades, an elevated level of performance. For instance, at their workplace they focused on doing an excellent job to satisfy customers and superiors. Nevertheless, there were capacity limits. When these were exceeded, support was an urgently needed. The participants in this study criticised a lack of support from the health care system. Some of the participants were either treated based on another diagnosis or they were not treated at all. These findings raise questions about CPTSD awareness in the public health sector.

The individuals considered it extremely important to organize their daily life (e.g. cooking, doing the dishes, cleaning the apartment, administrative issues). Literature also describes relatives as an important and supportive part in the lives of patients with a chronic condition [27, 39, 48]. Our results are consistent with that evidence. On the one hand, support from relatives in the daily life of those affected by CPTSD was described as a major facilitator, for instance, in managing housework, managing administrative tasks and settling payments. Further, emotional support was a vital element during their process of symptom management. It was an important experience for the participants to be able to trust a person again and to realise that they were not alone, to feel respected as a person even though they could not perform as before. On the other hand, relatives could also function as a barrier, for instance, when the affected person felt guilt and shame for not reporting the causes of their illness or when they recognized that their condition caused elevated stress level in their relatives. Another example was when the relatives were overprotective and those affected avoided speaking out to prevent distress. This raises the question of whether specialized educational and support services could be a possible effective intervention for both parties and whether greater family involvement is required. Recent literature suggests this for patients with PTSD [49–51]. Our results indicate that it is also needed for patients with CPTSD.

An important intervening factor was social support in the form of financial support while being unable to work. Those affected by no financial support either from relatives or the welfare state e.g. a disability pension, experienced considerably more difficulties in handling their daily life, and they did not feel part of society. The financial worries often impeded the participants in overcoming their anxiety. This result highlights the importance of support in this field. This result is also consistent with the findings of another study describing a correlation between high rates of unemployment and CPTSD [4, 14].

Retrospectively, some participants described having experienced various phases of collapse through their lives, as illustrated in our model (Fig. 1). After experiencing feelings of exhaustion, difficulties with rising emotions (such as feelings of loss, worthless and shame), and memories, the participants returned to strategies they knew would work. Those strategies gave them the feeling of being in control of their lives. These results are consistent with recent evidence from Karatzias and colleges [52], reporting negative trauma-related cognitions about the self as a most important factor in CPTSD. Likewise, retrospectively, the participants felt regret and anger for not being able to address the real issues causing their condition. Knowledge about their condition gave them feelings of hope and new perspectives. Understanding interactions and reactions to their symptoms gave them a sense of security. Thus, these results indicate an essential need to develop, support and tailor interventions for symptom management of persons suffering from a CPTSD.

This trial also has limitations that should be considered in evaluating the results. The first author designed the questions; it can be assumed he is not value-free and that he inadvertently influenced the results due to his own personal and professional beliefs. These values may influence the conduction and reporting of the research. Other researchers may have generated different results. The nature of qualitative research implies there is no possibility to generalize the results. Based on our study design, our sampling was selective and targeted, focused on participants with different socio-demographics, distinct levels of symptom burden from an inpatient setting and identified during the ongoing analyses. Additionally, contextual influences were not considered in this research. For instance, we do not know if our results apply to other settings in our health care system, to other countries or to other cultures. We realize that the conceptual model does not represent the unique symptom experiences of those with CPTSD. We do not claim causal inferences based on our data and framework. Further, quantitative research required to test our results to determine possible cause and effect or correlations. Research is also needed to expand the conceptual model and to discover attributes specific to each phase. Moreover, the diagnosis of CPTSD was based on self-report with the ITQ. The instrument we applied was the German test version 1.4 which was still under development. Therefore, diagnosis criteria may differ from the conditions for CPTSD as reformulated by the WHO in the new ICD-11. Despite these limitations, our study contributes first results with regard to symptom management of adults with CPTSD and contributes to the growing literature related to CPTSD.

Conclusion

This study focused on the unique experiences of symptom management of participants with CPTSD. They did not recognise their symptoms as such and did not know their diagnosis for many years. Nevertheless, participants used various resources and were able to develop skills and techniques to deal with their symptoms and to function on a day-to-day basis. Overall, the process of symptom management was extremely exhausting for the participants and they felt left alone with it. The participants were eager to gain support from healthcare professionals and, when necessary, financial support from the government. The results serve to gain a better understanding of the condition. Further, these results could be focal points to developing and researching new interventions, thus improving symptom management and quality of life.

Abbreviations

CPTSD: Complex post-traumatic stress disorder; DGPPN: German Association for Psychiatry, Psychotherapy and Psychosomatics; DRKS: German Clinical Trial Register; Fig: Figure; ICD-11: International Classification of Disease, 11th version; IPW: Integrierte Psychiatrie Winterthur, Zürcher Unterland; ITQ: International Trauma Questionnaire; PTSD: Posttraumatic stress disorder; WHO: World Health Organization

Acknowledgements

Special thanks to Ms. Anne Wegner and Ms. Elaine Melliger for proofreading and editing this paper.

Funding

The costs incurred from the ethic submission were paid by IPW. There is no conflict of interest between IPW and the research team. Additional funding was provided by the German Association for Psychiatry, Psychotherapy and Psychosomatics (DGPPN). DGPPN-Prize for health care professionals in psychiatry, psychotherapy and psychosomatic medicine, 2016. No funding body had a role in the development, design, analysis, interpretation and in the decision to submit the article for publication.

Authors' contributions

MS participated in designing the trial and took primary responsibility for drafting this manuscript. JB participated in managing data collection and participated in drafting this manuscript. AM, WS participated in designing the study, drafting the manuscript and in managing and analysing data. All authors have read and approved the final manuscript.

Authors' information

Correspondence concerning this article should be addressed to Manuel P. Stadtmann, Centre for Trauma Disorders, Integrierte Psychiatrie Winterthur, Winterthur, Switzerland Email: manuel.stadtmann@ipw.zh.ch. Research reported in this publication is supported by the Integrierte Psychiatrie Winterthur. The content is solely the responsibility of the authors and does not necessarily represent the official views.

Consent for publication

Written informed consent, to publish the information contained in this manuscript, was obtained from the participants. Thus, we obtained consent for the publication of potentially identifying information.

Competing interests

The authors declare that they have no competing interests.

Author details

[1]Department of Health, University of Witten/Herdecke, Alfred-Herrhausen-Straße 50, 58448 Witten, Germany. [2]Department of Psychology, Psychopathology and Clinical Intervention, University of Zurich, Binzmühlestrasse 14/17, 8050 Zürich, Switzerland. [3]Centre for Trauma Disorders, Integrierte Psychiatrie Winterthur, Technikumstrasse 81, Winterthur, Switzerland.

References

1. Herman JL. Complex PTSD: A syndrome in survivors of prolonged and repeated trauma. J Trauma Stress. 1992;5(3):377–91.
2. Maercker A, Brewin CR, Bryant RA, Cloitre M, Reed GM, van Ommeren M, Humayun A, Jones LM, Kagee A, Llosa AE. Proposals for mental disorders specifically associated with stress in the international classification of Diseases-11. Lancet. 2013;381(9878):1683.
3. Cloitre M, Garvert DW, Brewin CR, Bryant RA, Maercker A. Evidence for proposed ICD-11 PTSD and complex PTSD: A latent profile analysis. Eur J Psychotraumatol. 2013;4(1):20706.
4. Hyland P, Murphy J, Shevlin M, Vallières F, McElroy E, Elklit A, Christoffersen M, Cloitre M. Variation in post-traumatic response: the role of trauma type in predicting ICD-11 PTSD and CPTSD symptoms. Soc Psychiatry Psychiatr Epidemiol. 2017:1–10.
5. Karatzias T, Shevlin M, Fyvie C, Hyland P, Efthymiadou E, Wilson D, Roberts N, Bisson JI, Brewin CR, Cloitre M. An initial psychometric assessment of an ICD-11 based measure of PTSD and complex PTSD (ICD-TQ): Evidence of construct validity. J Anxiety Disord. 2016;44:73–79.
6. Knefel M, Garvert DW, Cloitre M, Lueger-Schuster B. Update to an evaluation of ICD-11 PTSD and complex PTSD criteria in a sample of adult survivors of childhood institutional abuse by Knefel & Lueger-Schuster (2013): A latent profile analysis. Eur J Psychotraumatol. 2015;6(1):25290.
7. Maercker A: AS13-03 - Trauma- and stress-related disorders: developments for ICD 11. Eur Psychiatry. 2012;27:1.
8. Krammer S, Simmen-Janevska K, Maercker A. Towards' complex PTSD': German translation of the trauma symptom inventory (TSI) for the assessment of complex trauma sequelae. Psychother Psychosom Med Psychol. 2013;63(8):318–26.
9. Karatzias T, Shevlin M, Fyvie C, Hyland P, Efthymiadou E, Wilson D, Roberts N, Bisson JI, Brewin CR, Cloitre M. Evidence of distinct profiles of posttraumatic stress disorder (PTSD) and complex posttraumatic stress disorder (CPTSD) based on the new ICD-11 trauma questionnaire (ICD-TQ). J Affect Disord. 2017;207:181–7.
10. Knefel M, Lueger-Schuster B. An evaluation of ICD-11 PTSD and complex PTSD criteria in a sample of adult survivors of childhood institutional abuse. Eur J Psychotraumatol. 2013;4(1):22608.
11. McDonnell M, Robjant K, Katona C. Complex posttraumatic stress disorder and survivors of human rights violations. Current opinion in psychiatry. 2013;26(1):1–6.
12. Palic S, Zerach G, Shevlin M, Zeligman Z, Elklit A, Solomon Z. Evidence of complex posttraumatic stress disorder (CPTSD) across populations with prolonged trauma of varying interpersonal intensity and ages of exposure. Psychiatry Res. 2016;246:692–9.
13. Hyland P, Shevlin M, Elklit A, Murphy J, Vallieres F, Garvert DW, Cloitre M. An assessment of the construct validity of the ICD-11 proposal for complex posttraumatic stress disorder. Psychol Trauma. 2017;9(1):1–9.
14. Stadtmann MP, Maercker A, Binder J, Schnepp W. Proposed ICD-11 complex posttraumatic stress disorder, characteristics and symptoms of adults in an inpatient psychiatric setting: A descriptive study. J Clin Investig Stud. 2018; 1(2):1–8.
15. Maercker A, Brewin CR, Bryant RA, Cloitre M, Ommeren M, Jones LM, Humayan A, Kagee A, Llosa A, Rousseau C. Diagnosis and classification of disorders specifically associated with stress: proposals for ICD-11. World Psychiatry. 2013;12(3):198–206.
16. Elklit A, Hyland P, Shevlin M. Evidence of symptom profiles consistent with posttraumatic stress disorder and complex posttraumatic stress disorder in different trauma samples. Eur J Psychotraumatol. 2014;5(1):24221.
17. Lehavot K, O'Hara R, Washington DL, Yano EM, Simpson TL. Posttraumatic stress disorder symptom severity and socioeconomic factors associated with veterans health administration use among women veterans. Womens Health Issues. 2015;25(5):535–41.
18. Cloitre M, Koenen KC, Cohen LR, Han H. Skills training in affective and interpersonal regulation followed by exposure: a phase-based treatment for PTSD related to childhood abuse. J Consult Clin Psychol. 2002;70(5):1067–74.
19. Dodd M, Miaskowski C, Lee KA. Occurrence of symptom clusters. Monogr Natl Cancer Inst. 2004;(32):76–8.
20. Redeker NS, Anderson R, Bakken S, Corwin E, Docherty S, Dorsey SG, Heitkemper M, McCloskey DJ, Moore S, Pullen C. Advancing symptom science through use of common data elements. J Nurs Scholarsh. 2015;47(5):379–88.
21. Brant JM, Beck S, Miaskowski C. Building dynamic models and theories to advance the science of symptom management research. J Adv Nurs. 2010;66(1):228–40.
22. Miaskowski C, Barsevick A, Berger A, Casagrande R, Grady PA, Jacobsen P, Kutner J, Patrick D, Zimmerman L, Xiao C. Advancing symptom science through symptom cluster research: expert panel proceedings and recommendations. JNCI: J Natl Cancer Inst. 2017;109(4):djw253. https://doi.org/10.1093/jnci/djw253.
23. Miaskowski C, Dodd M, Lee K. Symptom clusters: the new frontier in symptom management research. JNCI Monographs. 2004;2004(32):17–21.
24. Dodd M, Janson S, Facione N, Faucett J, Froelicher ES, Humphreys J, Lee K, Miaskowski C, Puntillo K, Rankin S. Advancing the science of symptom management. J Adv Nurs. 2001;33(5):668–76.
25. Engel CC, Litz B, Magruder KM, Harper E, Gore K, Stein N, Yeager D, Liu X, Coe TR. Delivery of self training and education for stressful situations (DESTRESS-PC): A randomized trial of nurse assisted online self-management for PTSD in primary care. Gen Hosp Psychiatry. 2015;37(4):323–8.
26. Young-McCaughan S, Bingham MO, Vriend CA, Inman AW, Gaylord KM, Miaskowski C. The impact of symptom burden on the health status of service members with extremity trauma. Nurs Outlook. 2017;65(5):S61–70.
27. Bodenheimer T, Wagner EH, Grumbach K. Improving primary care for patients with chronic illness, part 1. JAMA. 2002;228(14):1775–9.
28. Brant JM. Evolution of the dynamic symptoms model. In: Oncology nursing forum; 2016. p. 2016.
29. Cloitre M, Courtois CA, Charuvastra A, Carapezza R, Stolbach BC, Green BL. Treatment of complex PTSD: results of the ISTSS expert clinician survey on best practices. J Trauma Stress. 2011;24(6):615.
30. Jongh A, Resick PA, Zoellner LA, Minnen A, Lee CW, Monson CM, Foa EB, Wheeler K, Broeke E, Feeny N. Critical analysis of the current treatment guidelines for complex PTSD in adults. Depression and Anxiety. 2016;33(5):359–69.
31. Huber M. Trauma und die Folgen: Trauma und Traumabehandlung: Junfermann Verlag GmbH; 2012.
32. Huber M. Trauma und Traumabehandlung. 2. Wege der Traumabehandlung: Junfermann Verlag GmbH; 2003.
33. Stadtmann MP, Maercker A, Binder J, Schnepp W. Symptom management in complex post-traumatic stress disorder (ICD-11), view and experience of patients and their relatives: a mixed methods approach (research proposal). BMC Res Notes. 2017;10(1):461.
34. Strauss AL, Corbin JM, Niewiarra S. Grounded theory: Grundlagen qualitativer sozialforschung. Beltz: Psychologie-Verlag-Union; 1996.
35. Strauss AL, Corbin JM. Grounded theory methodology. Handbook Qual Res. 1994;17:273–85.
36. Wagner EH, Austin BT, Davis C, Hindmarsh M, Schaefer J, Bonomi A. Improving chronic illness care: translating evidence into action. Health Aff. 2001;20(6):64–78.
37. Wright LM, Leahey M. How to conclude or terminate with families. J Fam Nurs. 2004;10(3):379–401.
38. Corbin JM, Strauss AL: Weiterleben lernen. Verlauf und Bewältigung chronischer Krankheit, 2. vollständig überarbeitete und erweiterte Ausgabe edn. Bern: Huber. In.: Göttingen. Toronto. Seattle: Hans Huber Verlag; 2004.
39. Wagner EH. Academia, chronic care, and the future of primary care. J Gen Intern Med. 2010;25(Suppl 4):S636–8.
40. Whall AL. The family as the unit of care in nursing: A historical review. Public Health Nurs. 1986;3(4):240–9.
41. Wright LM, Leahey M. Nurses and families: A guide to family assessment and intervention: FA Davis; 2012.
42. Draucker CB, Martsolf DS, Ross R, Rusk TB. Theoretical sampling and category development in grounded theory. Qual Health Res. 2007;17(8):1137–48.
43. Metzing-Blau S, Schnepp W. Young carers in Germany: to live on as normal as possible–a grounded theory study. BMC Nurs. 2008;7(1):15.
44. Francis JJ, Johnston M, Robertson C, Glidewell L, Entwistle V, Eccles MP, Grimshaw JM. What is an adequate sample size? Operationalising data saturation for theory-based interview studies. Psychol Health. 2010;25(10):1229–45.
45. Guest G, Bunce A, Johnson L. How many interviews are enough? An experiment with data saturation and variability. Field methods. 2006;18(1):59–82.
46. Mason M. Sample size and saturation in PhD studies using qualitative interviews. In: Forum qualitative Sozialforschung/Forum: qualitative social research, vol. 2010; 2010.

47. Collins English Dictionary – Complete and Unabridged, 12th Edition 2014 [https://www.thefreedictionary.com/paroxysm].
48. Busch A-K, Schnepp W, Spirig R. Psychosoziale Interventionen für Paare, die mit einer Krebserkrankung leben. Eine Literaturübersicht. Pflege. 2009;22(4):254–65.
49. Batten SV, Drapalski AL, Decker ML, DeViva JC, Morris LJ, Mann MA, Dixon LB. Veteran interest in family involvement in PTSD treatment. Psychol Serv. 2009;6(3):184.
50. Meis LA, Schaaf KW, Erbes CR, Polusny MA, Miron LR, Schmitz TM, Nugent SM. Interest in partner-involved services among veterans seeking mental health care from a VA PTSD clinic. Psychol Trauma Theory Res Pract Policy. 2013;5(4):334.
51. Khaylis A, Polusny MA, Erbes CR, Gewirtz A, Rath M. Posttraumatic stress, family adjustment, and treatment preferences among National Guard soldiers deployed to OEF/OIF. Mil Med. 2011;176(2):126–31.
52. Karatzias T, Shevlin M, Hyland P, Brewin CR, Cloitre M, Bradley A, Kitchiner NJ, Jumbe S, Bisson JI, Roberts NP. The role of negative cognitions, emotion regulation strategies, and attachment style in complex post-traumatic stress disorder: implications for new and existing therapies. Br J Clin Psychol. 2018; 57(2):177–85.

Validation of the posttraumatic stress disorder checklist – 5 (PCL-5) in a primary care population with high HIV prevalence in Zimbabwe

Ruth Verhey[1*], Dixon Chibanda[2], Lorna Gibson[3], Jonathan Brakarsh[4] and Soraya Seedat[5]

Abstract

Background: There is a dearth of validated tools measuring posttraumatic stress disorder (PTSD) in low and middle-income countries in sub-Saharan Africa. We validated the Shona version of the PTSD Checklist for DSM-5 (PCL-5) in a primary health care clinic in Harare, Zimbabwe.

Method: Adults aged 18 and above attending the clinic were enrolled over a two-week period in June 2016. After obtaining written consent, trained research assistants administered the tool to eligible participants. Study participants were then interviewed independently using the Clinician Administered PTSD Scale (CAPS-5) as the gold standard by one of five doctors with training in mental health.

Result: A total of 204 participants were assessed. Of these, 91 (44.6%) were HIV positive, 100 (49%) were HIV negative, while 13 (6.4%) did not know their HIV status. PTSD was diagnosed in 40 (19.6%) participants using the gold standard procedure. Using the PCL-5 cut-off of ≥33, sensitivity and specificity were 74.5% (95%CI: 60.4–85.7); 70.6% (95%CI: 62.7–77.7), respectively. The area under the ROC curve was 0.78 (95%CI: 0.72–0.83). The Shona version of the PCL-5 demonstrated good internal consistency (Cronbach's alpha = 0.92).

Conclusion: The PCL-5 performed well in this population with a high prevalence of HIV. There is need to explore ways of integrating screening tools for PTSD in interventions delivered by lay health workers in low and middle-income countries (LMIC).

Keywords: Validation, Posttraumatic stress disorder Checklist-5, PTSD, Trauma, HIV, Low and middle income countries

Background

In sub-Saharan Africa, people living with HIV (PLWH) have a high rate of post-traumatic stress disorder (PTSD) [1, 2]. The negative experience of being HIV positive is cumulative with PLWH exposed to multiple HIV-related stressors and losses [3] which can lead to PTSD symptomatology.

Stressors, both acute and chronic, that people in LMIC are exposed to often occur on a daily basis. Political and economic instability, including poverty and disparity with its consequences of food scarcity and lack of access to medical care are some of the stressors. Furthermore, lack of education, interpersonal violence (IPV), and exposure to weather phenomena due to climate change can contribute to poor mental health outcomes including stress related disorders [4].

Women are reported to be at greater risk of developing symptoms of PTSD [5] with cumulative effects of multiple traumas being common and associated with worse psychiatric and other chronic medical comorbidity [6–8].

In South Africa, PLWH have been found to have high prevalence of persisting psychiatric disorders with PTSD rates at follow-up of 20% being associated with a longer duration of infection and low baseline functionality [9]. The incidence of HIV-related PTSD in a cross-sectional study in the Western Cape, South Africa, was found to

* Correspondence: ruth.verhey@zol.co.zw
[1]Zimbabwe Aids Prevention Project, 92 Prince Edward Road, Milton Park, Harare, Zimbabwe
Full list of author information is available at the end of the article

be at 40% [10]. Receiving an HIV-diagnosis was experienced as a traumatic index event for 36.4% in a population of recently diagnosed persons [9, 11].

The use of different PTSD assessment tools as well as the diversity with which traumatic events have been defined have contributed to varying outcomes in studies of PTSD [12]. Receiving a life-threatening diagnosis meets the threshold for consideration as a traumatic event for the development of PTSD [13] and was included in the Diagnostic and Statistical Manual of Mental Disorders DSM-IV (4th ed.; DSM-IV; American Psychiatric Association, 1994).

In general, too little is known about the prevalence of PTSD and PTSD related to HIV infection and its impact on health outcomes such as, health seeking behavior, treatment adherence and quality of life in sub-Saharan Africa. Furthermore, validated tools are scarce. For Zimbabwe, efforts have been made to validate screening tools for common mental disorders such as depression and anxiety for use in primary health care settings but none have been validated for PTSD [14] therefore this study seeks to address this deficit. The most appropriate current screening tool which based on DSM-5 is the Posttraumatic Stress Disorder Checklist (PCL-5) [15] which has not been validated in Africa. The Posttraumatic Stress Disorder Checklist (PCL) was developed at the National Center for PTSD [15]. It is a self-report measure that is widely used in western contexts and has been found to have very good psychometric properties in various settings [16–20].

Methods

The validation exercise was carried out as a cross-sectional study at the largest clinic in the suburb of Mbare near the central business district of Harare, Zimbabwe.

Adults aged 18 and above attending the clinic were enrolled over a two-week period in June 2016. Pregnant women in their last trimester and women within the 3-month postnatal period were excluded to exempt postnatal depression [21], as were those who were unable to understand the purpose of the study.

After having obtained written consent, research assistants trained in the use of tablet computer facilitated data collection, administered the tool. Study participants were then clinically assessed by one of five doctors trained in mental health using the CAPS-5 (Clinician administered PTSD scale – 5) as the gold standard.

The study was approved by the medical research council of Zimbabwe (MRCZ, reference MRCZ/A/1732) and by the Health Research Ethics Committee at Stellenbosch University (reference S14/05/102).

Sample size

We aimed to recruit a representative sample of $n = 150$ patients from a primary care clinic. We calculated that a minimum of 75 participants who scored positive on the reference standard for PTSD (CAPS-5) and 75 who scored negative would provide good precision for performance indicators for the PCL-5 achieving a sensitivity of 74.5% (95%CI:60.4–85.7%); specificity of 70.6% (95%CI:62.7–77.7%), positive predictive value (PPV) of 45.8% (95%CI:34.8–57.1%) and negative predictive value (NPV) of 89.3% (95%CI:82.3–94.2%).

Translation of tools

The PCL-5, the LEC-5 (Life Events Checklist - 5) and the clinician administered PTSD scale for DSM-5 (CAPS-5) were translated from English into the local language Shona by a bilingual clinical social worker, and a bilingual psychiatrist (DC).

This draft Shona version was reviewed by a team of five lay health workers (LHW) working in a primary care mental health program called the Friendship Bench [22], five nurses working in the psychiatric ward of Harare Central Hospital together with a psychologist.

This phase focused on ensuring contextual equivalence to the original versions based on their understanding and use of local terms for trauma symptomatology.

An independent language expert back-translated the Shona version into English. The first author together with the social worker and the psychiatrist examined both original and back-translated versions and resolved any discrepancies by consensus. Translation and back-translation were carried out using a standard approach [23].

The PCL-5

The PCL was revised to match the adapted DSM-5 criteria for PTSD. The PCL-5 features an adapted answer scale ranging from 0 = not at all to 4 = extremely, thus making the theoretical lowest score 0. It measures 4 symptom clusters; the original clusters intrusion, avoidance and hyper-arousal and the added cluster of negative alterations in cognition and mood with three items (blame, negative emotions, and reckless or self-destructive behavior). Item scores can be summed for an overall severity score as well as for individual symptom cluster sums. A PTSD diagnosis can be made provisionally considering items rated 2 = moderately or higher as according to the DSM-5 diagnostic rule (at least one B, one C, two D, and two E symptoms present). In an empirical calibration, Blevins et al. (2015) found the psychometric properties for the PCL-5 for a US American college convenience sample with subjects who self-identified as having PTSD as follows: internal consistency $\alpha = 0.94$ and test-retest reliability $r = 0.82$, 95% CI [0.71, 0.89] [16].

Clinician administered PTSD scale (CAPS-5)

The Clinician-administered PTSD scale CAPS-5 for DSM-5 [24] was used as the gold standard. It was derived from the CAPS for DSM-IV [25] and adjusted for the changes of the PTSD diagnosis in DSM-5 (American Psychiatric Association, 2013). The CAPS-5 is a structured clinical interview which allows the clinician to make a diagnosis of PTSD according to the criteria described in the DSM-5. Furthermore, overall symptom severity as well as global, social, occupational and personal impairment are assessed. The main Criterion (A), the traumatic event, is assessed with the added Life Events Checklist for the DSM-5 (LEC-5) [26].

The life events checklist for DSM-5 (LEC-5)

The LEC-5 is a self-report questionnaire asking for the prevalence of 16 potentially traumatic life-time events plus an added open category ("any other very stressful event or experience") with five answer categories [26]. We used the LEC-5 in combination with the PCL-5.

SSQ-14

The Shona Symptom Questionnaire (SSQ-14) [27] was developed and recently re-validated in Zimbabwe in a HIV-population [14]. Most of the items are common to those found in tools for depression worldwide such as sleep disturbance and suicidal thoughts; others are local idioms of emotional distress including 'thinking too much'. Participants are asked if they have experienced a list of common mental health symptoms in the past week. Each of the 14 items is scored dichotomously as yes (1) or no (0). With the optimal cut-off of ≥9, the sensitivity and specificity for the SSQ-14 against a diagnosis of depression and/or general anxiety were 84% (95% CI: 78–89) and 73% (95%CI:63–81), respectively. Internal reliability was high (Cronbach α=0.74) [14].

Training procedure

Study personnel (four research assistants, six LHWs and five medical doctors) working in the psychiatric unit of Harare Central hospital attended a two-week training using a guide initially developed by the authors (RV and DC). The research assistants were trained in data collection methods using the socio-demographic forms and the screening tools. The medical doctors were trained in the use of the CAPS-5 through a discussion forum led by RV which involved going through the diagnostic criteria, building consensus on how to manage clinically severe cases during the validation, and procedures for ensuring fidelity. RV and DC observed the doctors during role-play using the tool.

All raters were involved in a pilot study with patients visiting the psychiatric outpatient unit. Cohen's Kappa was found to be high (k = 0.91) using a random sample size of n = 26. Participants in the pilot study were different from the participants of the validation exercise. The referral pathways for participants meeting criteria for PTSD and other acute medical conditions were determined as that they should be seen by the medical officer first, for assessment, before being referred to a tertiary psychiatric facility if needed.

Data collection

Stage 1: Every morning during the study period, an appointed research assistant obtained the register of all adult patients waiting to be seen. The research assistant randomly selected clinic attendees based on a computer-generated random number sequence. Fifteen randomly selected participants were invited at one time to a quiet and private space where eligibility was determined. Informed written consent was sought from all those eligible. The four research assistants administered the SSQ and the PCL-5 to participants in randomly assigned alternating questionnaire order and also collected socio-demographic information such as age, gender, HIV status, marital and employment status. The interviews took 20–30 min and were conducted in a quiet space designated for the study team. Although the PCL-5 including the LEC and the SSQ are self-report tools, we chose to have them administered by trained research assistants as it was found in prior validation exercises using the same approach that tablet computer-use was not familiar to most of the clinic attendees [21].

Stage 2: Following administration of the screening tools, participants were referred to one of five medical doctors who conducted the CAPS-5. The doctors were blinded to the screening data. Each doctor asked the participant to recall the index event that was chosen, or the worst event if several were indicated, from the LEC-5 for the subsequent clinical interview. The CAPS-5 interview lasted 30–60 min in a private and quiet room. In case of a participant not reporting any event, the interview was not carried out.

All those needing acute psychiatric care were further assessed for treatment and referral to the psychiatric hospital.

Data management

All data was double entered onto a password-protected database using Stata (version 13). No participant identifiable information was entered into the database. Ethical considerations and confidentiality for all participants were respected in accordance with Medical Research Council of Zimbabwe guidelines.

Analysis

The performance of the PCL-5 was measured against the CAPS-5 as the gold standard. We estimated the sensitivity, specificity, positive predictive value (PPV) and negative predictive value (NPV) for different cut-points. The optimal cut-point was chosen to deliver a good balance between sensitivity and specificity. Results were presented in the form of a ROC curve which plots the true positive rate (sensitivity) against the false positive rate (specificity) [28]. The area under a ROC curve (AUC) quantifies the overall ability of the test to discriminate between those individuals with the outcome and those without the outcome.

Internal reliability was estimated using Cronbachs' α. All analyses were conducted using Stata (version 13).

Results

Sample description

A total of the 204 (74.1%) participants were recruited during a 2-week period from a total of 275 who had been invited to take part. Seventy one were not illegible or declined participation. Of the final participants, 163 (85.3%) were female, 133 (69.6%) were married, and 139 (59%) had completed secondary education (Table 1). Overall sample mean age was 34 years. There were 108 (65.5%) participants who were unemployed. HIV serostatus was known for 191 (93.6%) participants, of whom 91 were HIV positive (44.6%). 13 (6.4%) did not know or refused to reveal their HIV status. Out of the 91 participants who were HIV positive, 79.1% were female. Being aged 40 and above (OR 15.03 CI6.35–35.57), being widowed (OR CI8.41 2.75–25.70) and having a SSQ 9 and above (OR 2.15 CI1.19–3.87) were associated with HIV positive status, respectively (Table 1).

Forty-two (46.2%) of the HIV positive participants (n = 91) scored equal or above the cut-off score for PTSD. On the measure of depression (SSQ-14), 45 (49.5%) of this group scored above cut-off.

Amongst all 191 participants for whom the HIV status was known, 76 (39.7%) scored equal or above cut-off for PTSD as measured by the PCL-5.

Traumatic events reported using LEC-5

On the self-experienced answer category, participants (n = 204) were asked to indicate all the events that happened to them in their entire life. The following five index events were reported as most common: physical assault [reported by 132 participants (64.7%)], the open category any other very stressful event or experience [130 participants (63.7%)], sudden, unexpected death of someone who was close to the participant (113 participants, 55.4%), life-threatening illness or injury (89 participants, 43.6%), as well as severe human suffering (86 participants, 42.2%).

Traumatic events reported in the CAPS-5

In the clinical interview participants reported a similar distribution of events as the LEC-5. A total of 40 (19.6%) cases of PTSD were identified using our gold standard procedure. Qualifying traumatic events reported were categorized as follows: victim of physical, often combined with sexual assault (18 cases, 45%), being diagnosed with HIV as a life-threatening illness in 13 cases (32.5%) and having experienced sudden death of a person close to the participant in 9 cases (22.5%).

Performance of the PCL-5 against the CAPS-5

A cut-off of ≥33 provided the highest proportion of participants correctly diagnosed compared with the CAPS-5 instrument. With this cut-off, sensitivity was 74.5% (95% CI: 60.4–85.7) and specificity was 70.6% (95% CI: 62.7–77.7) (Table 2).

The PPV was 45.8% (95% CI: 34.8–57.1) and the NPV 89.3% (95% CI: 82.3–94.2) with Cronbach's α = 0.92.

After stratification by HIV status the sensitivity for PLWH was 78.6% (59.0–91.7), and the specificity was 68.3% (55.3–79.4). The PPV was 52.4% (36.4–68.0), the NPV 87.8% (75.2–95.4) using the cut of ≥33.

The ROC curve for the performance of the PCL-5 gave an AUC of 0.78 (95% CI: 0.72–0.83) (Fig. 1).

Discussion

The primary goal of this study was to validate the PCL-5 as the most current, DSM-5 keyed, PTSD measure (5th ed.; DSM-5; American Psychiatric Association, 2013) and to determine its utility and applicability in our context. We have validated other relevant tools for our work in CMD [14] but none for PTSD specifically.

The PCL-5 has not been validated within a comparable setting before, focusing on a population with high HIV prevalence.

The optimum cut-off score was found to be ≥33, a value which gave us a sensitivity of 74.5% (95%CI 60.4–85.7) and a specificity of 70.6% (95%CI 62.7–77.7). There was a difference after stratification according to HIV status [sensitivity = 78.6% (95%CI 59.0–91.7) and specificity = 68.3% (95%CI 55.3–79.4)]. This suggests the tool is more sensitive and less specific for PLWH compared to the results for the whole sample. This is further supported by the positive and negative predictive values which were 45.8% (34.0–57.1) and 89.3% (82.3–94.2) respectively for all participants (n = 204). The ROC curve (Fig. 1) gave an area under the curve (AUC) of 0.78 (95% CI0.716–0.834). The sensitivity of the tool being higher amongst PLWH was also the case in our earlier validation of tools for CMD [14]. There was good internal consistency (Cronbach's α = 0.92).

Our results show that it is feasible to validate PTSD tools in a low resource setting using locally trained researchers. Although the PCL-5 is originally developed in a high-income setting where the context is different, we have shown that using cross-cultural methods as in earlier validation studies [21] is possible for PTSD tool validation. The inclusion of LHWs who are the delivering

Table 1 Socio-demographic characteristics of all participants by HIV status ($n = 191$)[b]

Characteristic	HIV positive ($n = 91$)		HIV negative ($n = 100$)		Logistic regression[a]		
	N	%	N	%	OR	95% CI	*p*-value
Gender							0.02
Male	19	20.9	9	9.0	1	–	
Female	72	79.1	91	91.0	0.37	(0.16–0.88)	
Age group							< 0.001
< 30	16	17.6	63	63.0	1	–	
30–39	33	36.3	26	26.0	5	(2.36–10.60)	
40+	42	46.2	11	11.0	15.03	(6.35–35.57)	
Marital status							< 0.001
Married	54	59.3	79	79.0	1	–	
Single	14	15.4	17	17.0	1.2	(0.55–2.65)	
Widowed	23	25.3	4	4.0	8.41	(2.75–25.70)	
Education							0.009
Less than 'O' level	45	49.5	31	31.0	1	–	
O' level or more	43	50.6	69	69.0	0.46	(0.25–0.83)	
Current employment status							0.11
Unemployed	46	50.5	62	62.0	1	–	
Permanent FT or PT	8	8.8	3	3.0	3.59	(0.90–14.30)	
Casual/self-employed	37	40.7	35	35.0	1.42	(0.78–2.59)	
Main income source							< 0.001
Own business/salary	58	65.2	40	40.4	1	–	
Partner/family	22	24.7	51	51.5	0.3	(0.16–0.57)	
No income	9	10.1	8	8.1	0.78	(0.28–2.18)	
Suffer from chronic illness							< 0.001
No	10	11.0	66	66.0	1	–	
Yes	81	89.0	34	34.0	15.72	(7.23–34.18)	
Reason for clinic visit							< 0.001
HIV-related	37	40.7	1	1.0	1		
Routine/family/antenatal	34	37.4	54	54.0	0.02	(0.00–0.13)	
Other reason	20	22.0	45	45.0	0.01	(0.00–0.09)	
Negative life events in last 6 months							0.21
No	20	22.0	30	30.0	1	–	
Yes	71	78.0	70	70.0	1.52	(0.79–2.93)	
SSQ ≥ 9							0.01
No	46	50.6	68	68.7	1		
Yes	45	49.5	31	31.3	2.15	(1.19–3.87)	
PCL ≥ 33							0.09
No	49	53.8	66	66.0	1		
Yes	42	46.2	34	34.0	1.66	(0.93–2.98)	

[a]univariate logistic regression for outcome HIV+
[b]Participants who did not know or reveal their HIV status excluded ($n = 13$)

agent of the Friendship Bench intervention also makes the eventual use of the PCL-5 tool in their work at primary care level further possible. Including staff at all levels of the health system is important when developing interventions as this contributes to a stronger buy-in and increases the chances of the tool being used by all [29]. The results of this validation study will enable local researchers working on epidemiological and intervention

Table 2 Sensitivity, specificity, PPV & NPV for PCL-5 cut-off ≥33 for whole sample and for PLWH only

	Sensitivity (95%CI)	Specificity (95%CI)	PPV (95%CI)	NPV (95%CI)
N = 204	74.5% (60.4–85.7)	70.6% (62.7–77.7)	45.8%(34.8–57.1)	89.3% (82.3–94.2)
N = 91 PLWH only	78.6% (59.0–91.7)	68.3% (55.3–79.4)	52.4% (36.4–68.0)	87.8% (75.2–95.4)

studies with a focus on PTSD to work with a tool validated using an evidence based approach.

The PTSD prevalence of 46% amongst seropositive participants highlights the close link between HIV-status and PTSD prevalence, therefore it may be necessary to include screening for PTSD in the expanding HIV clinics in the country. Currently PLWH are screened using the SSQ-14 [27] which shows some overlap of symptomatology with PTSD (Table 1), however, there is need for PTSD specific screening in view of the high prevalence of PTSD. The prevalence of PTSD for all participants (n = 204) according to the gold standard measure CAPS-5 was 19.6%. Community studies have shown that trauma exposure is higher, often multiple, and associated with several chronic physical conditions [30].

A positive HIV sero-status is described as a traumatic event [31, 32]. In our study, one third (32.5%) of the PTSD cases identified by the gold standard clinical interview were found to have HIV infection as the qualifying traumatic event.

Being found out to be HIV positive is often met with interpersonal violence by partners or family members [33] with anticipatory fear often leading to non-testing or non-following up of treatment seeking behavior [34].

Whereas HIV can arguably be managed effectively in Western countries, the situation is different for the developing world. Poverty and unemployment, lack of access to medication and medical care, unavailability of adequate food, housing, risk of exposure to illnesses and to being re-infected due to lack of awareness and risky sexual practices as well as exposure to stigma and stigma-related interpersonal violence all comprise daily traumatic events for the HIV population in Zimbabwe.

The cumulative effect of these stressors is seen in the high prevalence of CMD of 49.5% amongst seropositive participants.

The Friendship Bench Program has had a successful, targeted approach to CMD [35], however we realize that PTSD identification could contribute towards adequately addressing the needs of primary care patients.

The use of psychological interventions to address common mental disorders (CMD) in PLWH in sub-Saharan Africa, their scaling-up, as well as their monitoring and evaluation underscores the importance of

Obs	ROC Area	Std. Err.	-- Binomial Exact -- [95% Conf.	Interval]
204	0.7803	0.0386	0.71620	0.83432

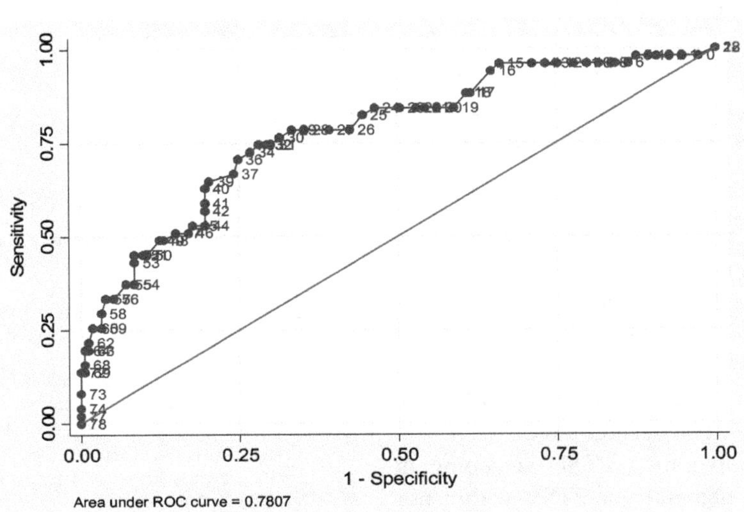

Fig. 1 ROC curve for PCL-5 against CAPS 5 (n = 204)

administering validated tools in rigorously conducted clinical trials [36, 37].

The PCL-5 has been developed in a western setting, as have most other psychological tools. Traumatic events according to the DSM-5 are defined as events that are linked to actual or threat of death, serious injury, or sexual violence experienced by self or close others, witnessed as well as heard of. Given the living situation for the majority of the population in LMIC, in our view the definition of a traumatic event has to be broadened. In LMIC, a wider range of circumstances hold a potential life threat for the population, as seen in the burden of disease studies [38]. Furthermore, people in LMIC are often exposed to multiple traumas [39] and have therefore a pronounced need for adequate, accessible and evidence-based care.

Limitations

The gold standard interviews were carried out by medical doctors who all had a minimum of 2 years of work experience in psychiatry but no formal training in psychiatry. They were trained and supervised in the use of the tool by the first author together with the second author. The duration of training was less in comparison to other settings [16].

Study participants were urban dwellers visiting primary care clinics, therefore generalization beyond primary care settings is not possible. Furthermore, most of the study participants were female (85% females in our sample) which is common in this setting as shown in previous work [35, 40, 41], therefore, our finding may not be gender-sensitive.

PCL-5 and SSQ were administered in interview format despite them being designed for self-administration. Interviews were conducted by trained research assistants as study participants were not familiar with self-administration on tablet computers which were used for the data collection. A limitation of this approach is that participants might have displayed a social desirability bias [42] and therefore decreased the validity of the responses.

We did not investigate aspects of trauma attribution, resilience and vulnerability of individuals in this study nor did we discuss possible co-morbidities, all these are seen as associated with the development of PTSD [43, 44].

Conclusion

It is possible to validate screening tools for PTSD in a low resourced setting with a high HIV prevalence.. We found the PCl-5 to have a good internal consistency with Cronbach's α = 0.92, and with a cut-off score of 33 it showed good performance. Furthermore, our cut-off score is in line with what is suggested by the authors of the PCL-5 in its revised civilian version [16].

There is a need for integrating PTSD screening in primary care due to the high rate of PTSD within our study populations (45% for HIV positive and 34.3% for HIV negative participants, respectively).

Abbreviations

AIDS: Acquired immune deficiency syndrome; ART: Anti-retroviral Therapy; CAPS-5: Clinician administered PTSD scale – 5; CI: Confidence interval; CMD: Common mental disorders; DMS-5: Diagnostic and Statistical Manual of Mental Disorders 5th edition; HIV: Human immunodeficiency virus; IPV: Interpersonal violence; LEC-5: Life Events Checklist – 5; LMIC: Low and middle income countries; MRCZ: Medical research council of Zimbabwe; NPV: Negative predictive value; PCL-5: Posttraumatic Stress Disorder Checklist – 5; PLWH: People living with HIV; PPV: Positive predictive value; PTSD: Posttraumatic Stress Disorder; ROC: Receiver operator curve

Acknowledgements

We thank our research team and all participants.

Authors' contributions

RV and DC conceived and designed the study. DC and RV gained funding for the study. RV and DC carried out the study. LG was responsible for all statistical analysis. RV drafted the first manuscript. DC, JB, SS revised the manuscript. All authors read and approved the manuscript.

Consent for publication

All participants gave written consent to publish all data reported in this and other publications arising from study.

Competing interests

The authors declare that they have no competing interests except for DC who is supported through the DELTAS Africa Initiative [DEL-15-01]. The DELTAS Africa Initiative is an independent funding scheme of the African Academy of Sciences (AAS)'s Alliance for Accelerating Excellence in Science in Africa (AESA) and supported by the New Partnership for Africa's Development Planning and Coordinating Agency (NEPAD Agency) with funding from the Wellcome Trust [DEL-15-01] and the UK government. The views expressed in this publication are those of the author(s) and not necessarily those of AAS, NEPAD Agency, WellcomeTrust or the UK government.

Author details

[1]Zimbabwe Aids Prevention Project, 92 Prince Edward Road, Milton Park, Harare, Zimbabwe. [2]Zimbabwe Aids Prevention Project, Harare, Zimbabwe. [3]London School of Tropical Medicine and Hygiene, London, UK. [4]Say and Play Therapy Centre, Harare, Zimbabwe. [5]College of Health Sciences, Stellenbosch University, Stellenbosch, South Africa.

References

1. Adewuya AO, Afolabi MO, Ola BA, Ogundele OA, Ajibare AO, Oladipo BF, Fakande I. Post-traumatic stress disorder (PTSD) after stigma related events in HIV infected individuals in Nigeria. Soc Psychiatry Psychiatr Epidemiol. 2009;44(9):761–6.
2. Seedat S. Interventions to improve psychological functioning and health outcomes of HIV-infected individuals with a history of trauma or PTSD. Curr HIV/AIDS Reports. 2012;9(4):344–50.
3. Hosegood V, Preston-Whyte E, Busza J, Moitse S, Timaeus IM. Revealing the full extent of households' experiences of HIV and AIDS in rural South Africa. Soc Sci Med. 2007;65(6):1249–59.
4. Lund C, Breen A, Flisher AJ, Kakuma R, Corrigall J, Joska JA, Swartz L, Patel V. Poverty and common mental disorders in low and middle income countries: a systematic review. Soc Sci Med. 2010;71(3):517–28.
5. Galovski TE, Blain LM, Chappuis C, Fletcher T. Sex differences in recovery from PTSD in male and female interpersonal assault survivors. Behav Res Ther. 2013;51(6):247–55.
6. Green BL, Goodman LA, Krupnick JL, Corcoran CB, Petty RM, Stockton P, Stern NM. Outcomes of single versus multiple trauma exposure in a screening sample. J Trauma Stress. 2000;13(2):271–86.

7. Suliman S, Mkabile SG, Fincham DS, Ahmed R, Stein DJ, Seedat S. Cumulative effect of multiple trauma on symptoms of posttraumatic stress disorder, anxiety, and depression in adolescents. Compr Psychiatry. 2009;50(2):121–7.
8. Sledjeski EM, Speisman B, Dierker LC. Does number of lifetime traumas explain the relationship between PTSD and chronic medical conditions? Answers from the National Comorbidity Survey-Replication (NCS-R). J Behav Med. 2008;31(4):341–9.
9. Olley BO, Seedat S, Stein DJ. Persistence of psychiatric disorders in a cohort of HIV/AIDS patients in South Africa: a 6-month follow-up study. J Psychosom Res. 2006;61(4):479–84.
10. Martin L, Kagee A. Lifetime and HIV-related PTSD among persons recently diagnosed with HIV. AIDS Behav. 2011;15(1):125–31.
11. Olley B, Zeier M, Seedat S, Stein D. Post-traumatic stress disorder among recently diagnosed patients with HIV/AIDS in South Africa. AIDS Care. 2005; 17(5):550–7.
12. Breslau N. Outcomes of posttraumatic stress disorder. J Clin Psychiatry. 2001; 62(Suppl 17):55–59.
13. Breslau N, Kessler RC. The stressor criterion in DSM-IV posttraumatic stress disorder: an empirical investigation. Biol Psychiatry. 2001;50(9):699–704.
14. Chibanda D, Verhey R, Gibson LJ, Munetsi E, Machando D, Rusakaniko S, Munjoma R, Araya R, Weiss HA, Abas M. Validation of screening tools for depression and anxiety disorders in a primary care population with high HIV prevalence in Zimbabwe. J Affect Disord. 2016;198:50–5.
15. Weathers F, Litz B, Herman D, Huska J, Keane T. The PTSD checklist-civilian version (PCL-C). Boston: National Center for PTSD; 1994.
16. Blevins CA, Weathers FW, Davis MT, Witte TK, Domino JL. The posttraumatic stress disorder checklist for DSM-5 (PCL-5): development and initial psychometric evaluation. J Trauma Stress. 2015;28(6):489–98.
17. Bovin MJ, Marx BP, Weathers FW, Gallagher MW, Rodriguez P, Schnurr PP, Keane TM. Psychometric properties of the PTSD checklist for diagnostic and statistical manual of mental disorders–fifth edition (PCL-5) in veterans. Psychol Assess. 2016;28(11):1379.
18. Wortmann JH, Jordan AH, Weathers FW, Resick PA, Dondanville KA, Hall-Clark B, Foa EB, Young-McCaughan S, Yarvis JS, Hembree EA. Psychometric analysis of the PTSD Checklist-5 (PCL-5) among treatment-seeking military service members. Psychol Assess. 2016;28(11):1392.
19. Vera-Villarroel P, Celis-Atenas K, Córdova-Rubio N, Zych I, Buela-Casal G. Chilean validation of the posttraumatic stress disorder checklist–civilian version (PCL–C) after the earthquake on February 27, 2010. Psychol Rep. 2011;109(1):47–58.
20. Ashbaugh AR, Houle-Johnson S, Herbert C, El-Hage W, Brunet A. Psychometric validation of the English and French versions of the posttraumatic stress disorder checklist for DSM-5 (PCL-5). PLoS One. 2016; 11(10):e0161645.
21. Chibanda D, Mangezi W, Tshimanga M, Woelk G, Rusakaniko P, Stranix-Chibanda L, Midzi S, Maldonado Y, Shetty AK. Validation of the Edinburgh postnatal depression scale among women in a high HIV prevalence area in urban Zimbabwe. Arch Womens Mental Health. 2010;13(3):201–6.
22. Chibanda D, Mesu P, Kajawu L, Cowan F, Araya R, Abas MA. Problem-solving therapy for depression and common mental disorders in Zimbabwe: piloting a task-shifting primary mental health care intervention in a population with a high prevalence of people living with HIV. BMC Public Health. 2011;11:828.
23. Bontempo R. Translation Fidelity of psychological scales an item response theory analysis of an individualism-collectivism scale. J Cross-Cult Psychol. 1993;24(2):149–66.
24. Weathers F, Blake D, Schnurr P, Kaloupek D, Marx B, Keane T: The clinician-administered PTSD scale for DSM-5 (CAPS-5). Interview available from the National Center for PTSD at www.ptsd.va.gov 2013.
25. Blake DD, Weathers FW, Nagy LM, Kaloupek DG, Gusman FD, Charney DS, Keane TM. The development of a clinician-administered PTSD scale. J Trauma Stress. 1995;8(1):75–90.
26. Weathers F, Blake D, Schnurr P, Kaloupek D, Marx B, Keane T: The life events checklist for DSM-5 (LEC-5). Instrument available from the National Center for PTSD at www.ptsd.va.gov 2013.
27. Patel V, Simunyu E, Gwanzura F, Lewis G, Mann A. The Shona symptom questionnaire: the development of an indigenous measure of common mental disorders in Harare. Acta Psychiatr Scand. 1997;95(6):469–75.
28 Pepe MS. The statistical evaluation of medical tests for classification and prediction. USA: Oxford University Press; 2003.
29. Chibanda D, Verhey R, Munetsi E, Rusakaniko S, Cowan F, Lund C. Scaling up interventions for depression in sub-Saharan Africa: lessons from Zimbabwe. Glob Ment Health (Camb). 2016;3:e13.
30. Atwoli L, Stein DJ, Koenen KC, McLaughlin KA. Epidemiology of posttraumatic stress disorder: prevalence, correlates and consequences. Curr Opin Psychiatry. 2015;28(4):307.
31. Withell B. A study of the experiences of women living with HIV/AIDS in Uganda. Int J Palliat Nurs. 2000;6(5):234–44.
32. Martinez A, Israelski D, Walker C, Koopman C. Posttraumatic stress disorder in women attending human immunodeficiency virus outpatient clinics. AIDS Patient Care STDs. 2002;16(6):283–91.
33. Davis KB. Understanding and addressing stigma and attachment insecurity in HIV-positive women who experience intimate partner violence: a model of medical and psychosocial care. Soc Work Health Care. 2012;51(3):213–31.
34. Turan JM, Bukusi EA, Onono M, Holzemer WL, Miller S, Cohen CR. HIV/AIDS stigma and refusal of HIV testing among pregnant women in rural Kenya: results from the MAMAS study. AIDS Behav. 2011;15(6):1111–20.
35. Chibanda D, Weiss HA, Verhey R, Simms V, Munjoma R, Rusakaniko S, Chingono A, Munetsi E, Bere T, Manda E. Effect of a primary care–based psychological intervention on symptoms of common mental disorders in Zimbabwe: a randomized clinical trial. JAMA. 2016;316(24):2618–26.
36. Abas M, Ali GC, Nakimuli-Mpungu E, Chibanda D. Depression in people living with HIV in sub-Saharan Africa: time to act. Tropical Med Int Health. 2014;19(12):1392–6.
37. Chibanda D, Cowan FM, Healy JL, Abas M, Lund C. Psychological interventions for common mental disorders for people living with HIV in low-and middle-income countries: systematic review. Tropical Med Int Health. 2015;20(7):830–9.
38. Lopez AD, Mathers CD, Ezzati M, Jamison DT, Murray CJ. Global and regional burden of disease and risk factors, 2001: systematic analysis of population health data. Lancet. 2006;367(9524):1747–57.
39. Williams SL, Williams DR, Stein DJ, Seedat S, Jackson PB, Moomal H. Multiple traumatic events and psychological distress: the South Africa stress and health study. J Trauma Stress. 2007;20(5):845–55.
40. Bertakis KD, Azari R, Helms LJ, Callahan EJ, Robbins JA. Gender differences in the utilization of health care services. J Fam Pract. 2000;49(2):147.
41. Carey PD, Stein DJ, Zungu-Dirwayi N, Seedat S. Trauma and posttraumatic stress disorder in an urban Xhosa primary care population: prevalence, comorbidity, and service use patterns. J Nerv Ment Dis. 2003;191(4):230–6.
42. Grimm P: Social desirability bias. Wiley International Encyclopedia of Marketing 2010.
43. Gray MJ, Pumphrey JE, Lombardo TW. The relationship between dispositional pessimistic attributional style versus trauma-specific attributions and PTSD symptoms. J Anxiety Disord. 2003;17(3):289–303.
44. Elwood LS, Hahn KS, Olatunji BO, Williams NL. Cognitive vulnerabilities to the development of PTSD: a review of four vulnerabilities and the proposal of an integrative vulnerability model. Clin Psychol Rev. 2009;29(1):87–100.

The relationship between childhood adversity, recent stressors, and depression in college students attending a South African university

Sumaya Mall[1,2*], Philippe Mortier[3], Lian Taljaard[4,5], Janine Roos[5], Dan J. Stein[1,4] and Christine Lochner[4]

Abstract

Background: College students are at risk of depression. This risk may be increased by the experience of childhood adversity and/or recent stressors. This study examined the association between reported experiences of childhood adversity, recent stressors and depression during the last 12 months in a cohort of South African university students.

Methods: Six hundred and eighty-six first year students at Stellenbosch University in South Africa completed a health-focused e-survey that included items on childhood adversity, recent stressors and mood. Individual and population attributable risk proportions (PARP) between experiences of childhood adversity and 12-month stressful experiences and 12-month depression were estimated using multivariate binomial logistic regression analysis.

Results: About one in six students reported depression during the last 12 months. Being a victim of bullying and emotional abuse or emotional neglect during childhood were the strongest predictors of depression in the past year at both individual and population level. With regard to recent stressors, a romantic partner being unfaithful, serious ongoing arguments or break-ups with some other close friend or family member and a sexual or gender identity crisis were the strongest predictors of depression. The predictor effect of recent stressors was significantly reduced in the final model that adjusted for the type and number of childhood traumatic experiences. At a population level, academic stress, serious ongoing arguments or break-ups with a close friend or family member, and serious betrayal by someone close were the variables that yielded the highest PARP.

Conclusions: Our findings suggest a significant relationship between early adversity, recent stressors, and depression here and throughout, consistent with the broader literature on predictors of depression. This study contributes to the limited data on college students' mental health in low and middle income countries including on the African continent. The findings provide information on the population level effect sizes of trauma as a risk factor for depression, as well as on the relationship between specific recent stressors and depression in college students.

Keywords: College students, Depression, Childhood adversity, Recent Stressors, South Africa

* Correspondence: Sumaya.mall@gmail.com
[1]Department of Psychiatry and Mental Health, University of Cape Town, Cape Town, South Africa
[2]Division of Epidemiology and Biostatistics, School of Public Health, University of the Witwatersrand, Johannesburg, South Africa
Full list of author information is available at the end of the article

Background

Several studies suggest that exposure to early childhood adversity or recent stressors (i.e. experiences during adulthood) are associated with increased risk of depression during adolescence or adulthood [1–4]. Not only could specific experiences of such adversity during childhood (e.g. physical abuse) increase the risk of depression in adulthood more significantly than others [5–8], but repeated trauma exposure may result in more severe symptoms of psychopathology [9, 10]. Further, research has suggested that cumulative stressful experiences, i.e. experience of childhood adversity and recent stressors may interact to increase the risk of depression in adulthood [11, 12].

Although research suggests that depression is common among college students [13, 14] and that childhood adversity may be associated with psychopathology (e.g. depression or alcoholism) in this group [15, 16], several gaps remain in the field. First, a recent meta-analysis of mental health interventions for college students suggests that previous studies of this group have been restricted to higher income countries suggesting a need to conduct studies in low and middle income countries including on the African continent [17]. Second, to our knowledge, no studies have examined population level effect sizes of trauma as risk factor of depression in college students. These population effects can be calculated with population attributable risk proportions (PARP). Assuming a causal relationship between risk factors and outcome, PARPs provide an estimate of the potential reduction in depression prevalence should a particular risk factor be removed from the population [18, 19]. They take into account that highly prevalent risk factors carrying low individual-level risk may be as important to consider as low prevalent risk factors carrying high risk for the affected individuals. Third, while previous studies suggest that a summary score of recent stressors may well be predictive of depression, particularly among adolescents, there is less research on whether specific recent stressors are stronger predictors of depression than others [20, 21].

Here we address these gaps in the literature in a study of a cohort of undergraduate students in South Africa. We hypothesized that in this group, 1) there would be a positive association between depression (i.e. in the last 12 months) and the number of childhood adverse and recent stressors experienced, 2) that different types of childhood trauma and recent stressors may be more significant in terms of their role in depression than others, 3) having any childhood adversity or any recent stressor has a significant role in predicting depression (i.e. in the last 12 months). Finally, we also aimed to calculate PARP, the rationale for which has been provided above [22].

Methods

Aims

This study, conducted at one university in South Africa, is embedded in an international, multi-site investigation into the wellness of undergraduate students known as the World Health Organization (WHO) World Mental Health Initiative Surveys International College Student Project (WMH-ICS). This parent study is an epidemiological study that aims to determine the prevalence and correlates of psychiatric disorders among college students in several participating nations. The WMH-ICS also aims to investigate and highlight paths to mental healthcare undertaken by students, and to encourage and promote treatment-seeking behavior [23].

Study design, setting and participants

The study was conducted at Stellenbosch University (SU), a public research university 40 km from Cape Town. In 2015, when data collection took place, more than half the students were white and females.

The data presented are cross-sectional data. All first year students who entered SU for the first time in 2015 received an email in March of that year, inviting them to participate in this study. A link to the e-survey with questions about lifetime history of risk and protective factors for negative outcomes, such as academic, mental and physical health problems (including past experience of those outcomes) were included. Students received monthly reminders of the survey between March 2015 and November 2015. Data collection ceased in November 2015.

Only students aged 18 or older, who provided informed consent (see below for more details), were allowed to progress into the survey.

All first year students at SU in 2015 ($n = 5338$) were invited to participate in this study. Our sample consisted of 686 participants (12.9% of the original invited sample). Of these 377 were female (54.9%) and 309 were male (45.1%). With regard to ancestry, 66.3% of participating students were white, 18.9% 'coloured'[1], 12.1% were black and 2.7% of Indian descent (See Table 1 below for percentages weighted by gender and race).

Materials and measures

Several measures were employed in the survey. Those relating specifically to trauma, recent stressors and depression are described below:

Childhood adversity

Selected items from validated instruments including: the CIDI-3.0 childhood section [24], The Adverse Childhood Experiences International Questionnaire (ACE-IQ) [25]

Table 1 Sociodemographic characteristics of the sample

Covariate	n(w)[a]	%(w)[a]	SE
Gender			
Male	309	45.1	1.9
Female	377	54.9	1.9
Race			
White	455	66.3	1.7
Coloured	129	18.9	1.5
Black	83	12.1	1.1
Indian	18	2.7	0.5

[a]weighted for gender and race

and the Bully Survey [26], were employed to measure adverse experiences prior to the age of 17. The domains that were extracted from the (ACE-IQ) explore several different experiences of childhood adversity including a) parental psychopathology (e.g. *'One of your parents (or the people who raised you) had a serious emotional or mental health problem',* b) intimate partner violence during adolescence (e.g. *How often were you in a romantic relationship where your partner repeatedly said hurtful or insulting things to you?*, c) sexual assault (e.g. *'You were sexually abused at home'*) and physical assault, ('e.g. *You were physically abused at home*') d) emotional abuse (e.g. *You felt loved and cared for by your family*), e) bullying (e.g. *How often were you bullied at school verbally (*i.e., *teased, called names*)? and f) emotional and physical neglect (e.g. *'You had to do chores too hard and dangerous for someone your own age'*). For the most part, our measures specifically ask about family-related adversity (e.g. physical assault perpetrated by a family member). Questions about sexual assault are not restricted to assault by family members, but include questions about assault by any perpetrator. All experiences are measured on a Likert scale of 1–5 where 1 indicates 'never', 2 indicates 'rarely', '3 indicates sometimes' 4 indicates 'often' and '5' indicates 'very often'. For meaningful comparisons between exposed and unexposed groups at both individual level and PARP analysis, the dichotomously coded variables were set at *"rarely"* for all items, except for bullying for which the cut-off value was set at *"sometimes"*. These scores were consistent with previous WMHS studies [27, 28].

Recent stressful experiences

Questions about recent stressors were adapted from the Life Events Questionnaire (LEQ) [29], which has been shown to possess sound psychometric properties [30]. The LEQ dichotomously assesses the experience of threatening events that occurred during the previous 12 months. Recent stressors or stressful experiences were defined as the occurrence of a stressful event in the last 12 months. Twenty recent stressors were measured in the questionnaire. These included, but were not limited to, serious illness, death of a friend, romantic relationship difficulties, academic stress, sexual and gender identity crisis, unwanted pregnancy, HIV diagnosis, legal difficulties or being involved in crime.

Depression occurring in the past year

We selected three items to measure depression and (from sub-syndromal depression to major depressive disorder) to carefully estimate the burden of this disorder among college students. These criteria are based on the DSM-5 criteria and take into account that depression symptoms lie on a spectrum from symptoms to minor depression to the full disorder [31–34]. This broad concept of depression refers to individuals who have two or more (but less than five) symptoms of depression that have endured for at least two weeks and that are associated with impairment [35]. Respondents were asked to report the experience or frequency of the following symptoms in the past year: depressed mood ('how often did you feel sad or depressed'), low interest ('how often did you take little or no interest and pleasure in things') and interference in their daily activities ('how often did you feel so low that it interfered with your work or personal life?') on a Likert scale of 1–5, ranging from "None of the time" (1) to "All or almost all of the time" (5). If they reported two core symptoms and interference in their work or daily lives 'sometimes' or more, they were categorized as having 'broad depression' [36]. We extracted reports of depression in the past year to associate more closely in time with recent stressful experiences. As described above, the recent stressful experiences had been reported as occurrences during the past year.

Ethical issues

After permission for conducting the study was obtained from the Institutional Review Board of SU and the University's Institutional Research and Planning Division, an email using the students' university email addresses, was sent to all first year students with a description of the study and a link to the e-survey.

In the invitation, students were informed that their participation in the survey was completely voluntary and that their responses would be treated as confidential. They were also informed that the survey results would be anonymous, that there may be potential discomforts (i.e. fatigue, inconvenience) and that there may also be benefits (i.e. contribution to generalizable knowledge). It was also emphasized that the students can withdraw from participation, with no negative consequences. However, due to the anonymity of the survey, they were notified that they will not be able to withdraw from the survey once they had submitted their responses.

Students were also made aware that they will be contacted in subsequent (pre-graduate) years for a follow-up survey.

A phone number to a general study helpdesk was included in the informed consent for students who had questions or concerns. Students who were distressed or requiring urgent assistance were provided with contact details of the 24 h Crisis Line of the local Centre for Student Counselling and Development (CDSC) and the Mental Health Information Centre of Southern Africa. Participants were not able to complete the survey more than once.

Students were not paid to complete the survey. There was however an incentive to compete for a cash prize of 1000 South African rand (approximately 72,8 US dollars).

Data analysis

All analyses were conducted with SAS (version 9.4).

Nonresponse propensity weighting [37] was employed to account for nonresponse bias (i.e. potential differences in prevalence of depression between survey respondents and non-respondents) [38]. Nonresponse propensity weights were calculated using socio-demographic variables available for the full student population (i.e. race and gender of first year students). A logistic model was developed to predict survey response (vs. nonresponse), with gender and race as predictors. There is little variation in age of first year students so we did not include age as a predictor in these models. Based on this multivariable regression equation, predicted probabilities were calculated. Final non-response propensity weights were obtained by taking the inverse of the predicted probabilities, followed by a normalization procedure to reassure that the sum of the final weights matches the actual sample size. Prevalence estimates are reported as weighted numbers, weighted proportions, and associated standard errors. Logistic regression procedures were used to explore the individual-level associations between predictors (i.e., childhood-adolescent traumatic experiences, and 12-month recent stressors) and the outcome variable (i.e., having depression in the last 12 months). Parameter estimates are reported as odds ratios (OR) and associated 95% confidence intervals. Apart from the specific type of traumatic or stressful experience, we also investigated the association between the presence of *any* experience in each risk domain under study, and 12-month depressive symptoms, as well as the *number* of specific experiences (categorized into having 1, 2, or 3 or more experiences with zero as the reference category) in each risk, and depression over the last 12 months. All analyses were (additionally) adjusted for gender and race as suggested by previous research examining mental health of college students [39, 40]. To estimate population-level risk for 12-month depression, PARP proportions [22] were calculated for each predictor under study, using as a summary predictor the probabilities resulting from the logistic regression equations [41, 42]. PARP provides an estimate of how many outcome cases (i.e., students with depression) are associated with a particular predictor variable under study. As such, assuming a causal relationship between predictor

Table 2 Childhood-adolescent adversity as bivariate predictors for the onset of depression during the past year

	prevalence							Chi-square test			Odds Ratio[e]			PARP[e]
Predictor	n(w)	%(w)[a]	SE	%(w)[b]	SE	%(w)[c]	SE	X_2	df	*P*-value[d]	OR	95%-	95%+	%(w)
Parental psychopathology	308	47.6	1.9	44.7	2.1	60.8	4.4	9.03	1	**0.002**	**2.1**	1.3	3.2	**26.7**
Physical abuse	134	20.4	1.5	19.1	1.7	25.5	4.0	2.22	1	0.139	1.8	1.1	3.1	9.3
Emotional abuse	240	37.2	1.8	31.9	2.0	57.0	4.5	23.63	1	**<0.001**	**3.2**	2.0	5.0	**34.3**
Sexual abuse	28	4.4	0.7	3.3	0.7	9.0	2.4	7.06	1	**0.006**	**3.0**	1.3	7.1	**5.2**
Neglect	84	12.9	1.3	10.6	1.3	22.6	3.8	11.39	1	**0.001**	**3.4**	1.9	6.0	**13.0**
Bullying victimization	324	50.0	1.9	45.2	2.1	70.7	4.1	22.36	1	**<0.001**	**3.0**	1.9	4.8	**41.3**
Dating violence	102	15.7	1.3	13.8	1.4	24.6	3.8	7.75	1	**0.005**	**1.9**	1.2	3.3	**9.8**
Any adverse experience	484	79.4	1.6	76.4	1.8	93.6	2.4	14.52	1	**<0.001**	**4.6**	2.0	10.4	**67.9**
No adverse experience	126	20.6	1.6	23.6	1.8	6.4	2.4	–	–	–	(ref)	(ref)	(ref)	(ref)
Exactly one adverse experience	165	27.1	1.7	28.5	1.9	23.4	3.9	–	–	–	**2.9**	1.2	7.0	**14.1**
Exactly two adverse experiences	126	20.6	1.6	21.2	1.8	18.5	3.6	–	–	–	**3.5**	1.4	9.0	**12.1**
Three or more adverse experiences	194	31.7	1.8	26.7	1.9	51.7	4.6	28.98	3	**<0.001**	**8.0**	3.4	18.8	**42.3**

All OR and PARP estimates are adjusted for gender and race. Significant *P*-values, OR and PARP are indicated in bold (α = 0.05); OR = odds ratio; PARP = population-attributable risk proportion

[a]The prevalence of the predictor in the full sample

[b]The prevalence of the predictor among those without 12-month depressive symptoms

[c]The prevalence of the predictor among those with 12-month depressive symptoms

[d]Unadjusted for multiple comparison. For multiple test adjusted *P*-values, see Additional file 1: Table S1

[e]Adjusted for gender and race

and outcome, PARP can be considered as an estimate of the proportion of 12-month depression that could be potentially alleviated if (the impact of) a particular predictor variable was removed from the population. It should be pointed out, however, that similar to individual-level estimates of risk (OR), PARP estimates in our cross-sectional research design are flawed by the inability to establishing temporality between predictor and outcome, and by the inability to take into account potentially important confounder variables. As with OR, all PARP estimates were adjusted for gender and population group. Finally, a series of multivariable models were estimated. Predictors were entered in blocks, beginning with recent stressors, and followed by childhood-adolescent traumatic experiences, giving us the opportunity to look at the cumulative effect of childhood trauma and recent stressful experiences. Our initial objective was to include all predictor variables under study in the final multivariate models. However, due to estimation problems related to data sparseness, low-prevalent predictor variables ($n < 30$; prevalence <5%) were eliminated. Nagelkerke pseudo-R^2 was used as a measure of total effect size, and Area-under-the-Curve as measure of prediction accuracy [43]. Firth's penalized likelihood estimation was consistently applied to avoid inconsistent estimators due to data sparseness [44].

Results

Prevalence estimates of socio-demographic variables

The prevalence of depression over the last 12 months was estimated at 16.1% with an associated standard error (SE)

Table 3 Recent stressors as bivariate predictors for the onset of depression during the past year, adjusted for gender and race

	prevalence							Chi-square test			Odds Ratio[e]			PARP[e]
Predictor	n(w)	%(w)[a]	SE	%(w)[b]	SE	%(w)[c]	SE	X_2	df	*P*-value[d]	OR	95%-	95%+	%(w)
A life-threatening illness or injury of a very close friend or family member	161	24.2	1.6	24.7	1.8	22.5	3.7	0.24	1	0.622	0.8	0.5	1.4	−3.3
Death of a close friend or family member	179	26.8	1.6	28.1	1.9	21.5	3.7	1.89	1	0.165	0.7	0.4	1.2	−6.2
Break-up with a romantic partner	202	30.5	1.7	29.0	1.9	37.7	4.4	3.11	1	0.074	1.5	1.0	2.3	10.1
You discovered that a romantic partner cheated on you	73	11.0	1.2	9.6	1.2	19.7	3.6	8.97	1	**0.003**	**2.4**	1.3	4.3	**9.1**
Serious betrayal by someone else close to you	141	21.2	1.5	18.7	1.6	34.7	4.2	13.43	1	**<0.001**	**2.1**	1.3	3.4	**15.1**
Serious ongoing arguments or break-ups with some other close friend or family member	136	20.6	1.5	17.1	1.6	35.2	4.3	17.85	1	**<0.001**	**2.5**	1.6	4.1	**18.0**
Academic stress	525	78.6	1.5	76.4	1.8	88.2	2.9	7.12	1	**0.007**	**2.1**	1.1	3.9	**39.6**
Sexual/Gender Identity Crisis	47	7.0	1.0	6.0	1.0	14.0	3.1	8.29	1	**0.004**	**3.3**	1.7	6.7	**7.6**
Hospitalization	65	9.8	1.1	9.2	1.2	14.6	3.2	2.83	1	0.092	1.7	0.9	3.2	4.7
You were involved in a life-threatening accident	28	4.2	0.8	4.2	0.8	4.1	1.9	0.01	1	0.941	1.1	0.4	3.1	0.2
You were seriously physically assaulted	25	3.7	0.7	3.3	0.8	4.5	2.1	0.38	1	0.569	2.2	0.7	6.3	2.0
You were sexually assaulted or raped	3	0.5	0.2	0.3	0.2	0.8	0.8	f	–	0.126	2.0	0.2	25.0	0.5
You had trouble with the police	14	2.2	0.6	2.2	0.6	1.1	1.0	0.52	–	0.497	1.1	0.2	6.5	0.2
You spent time in jail	2	0.4	0.2	0.4	0.3	–	–	f	–	1.000	1.7	0.0	62.7	0.1
Serious legal problem	9	1.4	0.5	1.5	0.5	–	–	f	–	0.612	0.4	0.0	8.7	−0.5
You had a pregnancy	2	0.3	0.2	–		1.6	1.1	f	–	**0.032**	14.5	0.3	699.7	1.0
You were diagnosed with a sexually transmitted infection	2	0.3	0.2	0.2	0.1	1.2	1.1	f	–	0.323	8.6	0.5	144.5	0.7
You were diagnosed with HIV	0	0.0	–	–	–	–	–	–	–	–	–	–	–	–
Any other recent experience	70	10.6	1.2	8.7	1.2	17.9	3.5	7.90	1	**0.005**	**2.4**	1.3	4.4	**8.8**
Any recent experience	552	90.7	1.2	89.2	1.4	96.1	1.8	4.34	1	**0.037**	2.4	0.9	6.6	49.6
No recent experience	57	9.3	1.2	10.8	1.4	3.9	1.8	–	–	–	(ref)	(ref)	(ref)	(ref)
Exactly one recent experience	133	21.9	1.6	23.5	1.8	13.1	3.0	–	–	–	1.2	0.4	3.9	2.4
Exactly two recent experiences	147	24.2	1.7	24.4	1.9	25.0	4.1	–	–	–	2.3	0.8	6.7	12.4
Three or more recent experiences	271	44.6	1.9	41.3	2.1	57.9	4.6	13.00	3	**0.004**	**3.1**	1.1	8.8	**35.1**

Significant *P*-values, OR and PARP are indicated in bold (α = 0.05); *OR* Odds ratio, *PARP* Population- attributable risk proportion
[a]The prevalence of the predictor in the full sample
[b]The prevalence of the predictor among those without 12-month depressive symptoms
[c]The prevalence of the predictor among those with 12-month depressive symptoms
[d]Unadjusted for multiple comparison. For multiple test adjusted *P*-values, see Additional file 1: Table S1
[e]Adjusted for gender and race
[f]Fisher-Exact test

Table 4 Multivariable Model adjusted for type and number of childhood-adolescent traumatic experiences

	MODEL 1					MODEL 2				
Predictor	OR	95%-	95%+	PARP	*P*-value[a]	OR	95%-	95%+	PARP	*P*-value[a]
A life-threatening illness or injury of a very close friend or family member	1.0	0.5	1.8	−0.6	0.913	0.9	0.5	1.7	−2.4	0.688
Death of a close friend or family member	0.7	0.4	1.3	−6.5	0.267	0.8	0.4	1.6	−3.2	0.588
Break-up with a romantic partner	1.0	0.6	1.8	0.2	0.974	1.1	0.6	2.0	1.7	0.819
You discovered that a romantic partner cheated on you	**2.1**	1.0	4.3	**7.7**	0.048	1.9	0.8	4.2	5.9	0.137
Serious betrayal by someone else close to you	1.2	0.7	2.2	4.2	0.499	0.9	0.5	1.7	−2.1	0.731
Serious ongoing arguments or break-ups with some other close friend or family member	**2.0**	1.1	3.6	**13.0**	0.023	1.7	0.9	3.3	9.2	0.113
Academic stress	1.5	0.8	3.1	24.3	0.235	1.3	0.6	2.8	14.3	0.493
Sexual/Gender Identity Crisis	**3.0**	1.3	6.8	**6.9**	0.008	2.0	0.7	5.2	3.4	0.168
Hospitalization	1.7	0.8	3.4	4.3	0.154	2.0	0.9	4.5	5.1	0.076
Any other stressful event	2.0	1.0	4.0	6.0	0.061	1.5	0.6	3.4	3.1	0.356
Exactly two recent stressful experiences	1.4	0.7	3.0	6.1	0.359	1.3	0.6	2.9	4.2	0.541
Three or more recent stressful experiences	1.0	0.4	2.9	0.3	0.987	0.8	0.3	2.6	−6.2	0.764
Parental psychopathology						**2.4**	1.2	4.8	**27.1**	0.016
Physical abuse						0.8	0.4	1.7	−3.8	0.502
Emotional abuse						**3.3**	1.5	7.1	31.2	0.003
Sexual abuse						0.8	0.2	2.8	−0.8	0.762
Neglect						**3.1**	1.4	7.1	**10.6**	0.006
Bullying victimization						**3.2**	1.6	6.2	**37.4**	0.001
Dating violence						**2.5**	1.1	5.5	**11.0**	0.028
Exactly two childhood adverse experiences						0.5	0.2	1.4	−10.3	0.194
Three or more childhood adverse experiences						0.3	0.1	1.3	−35.8	0.116

All analyses are adjusted for gender and race. Significant OR and PARP are indicated in bold (α = 0.05); OR = odds ratio; PARP = population- attributable risk proportion. Nagelkerke pseudo R-square for the first model was 9.48%; for the second model this was 15.02%. Area under the Curve for the first model was 0.722; for the second model this was 0.790

[a]unadjusted for multiple comparison. For multiple test adjusted P-values, see Additional file 1: Table S2

of 1.3. Examining the prevalence of adverse events prior to the age of 17 suggested that 79.4% of respondents of the full sample (i.e. with or without depression) reported experiencing at least one childhood adverse event. The three most commonly reported childhood adverse events across the whole sample were bullying (50.0%), emotional abuse (37.2%) and parental psychopathology (47.6%). With regard to recent recent stressors, almost all (90.7%) participants in the whole sample reported experiencing at least one recent stressor. Academic stress was most common, with 78.6% of the students reporting this experience. Other recent stressors, albeit less common, include breaking up with a romantic partner (30.5%) or the death of a close friend or family member (26.8%).

Bivariate correlates of 12-month depressive symptoms

The following experiences of childhood adversity prior to the age of 17 were significantly associated with depression in the past year: parental psychopathology (OR = 2.1; 95% CI = 1.3–3.2), emotional abuse (OR = 3.2; 95% CI = 2.0–5.0), sexual abuse (OR = 3.0; 95% CI = 1.3–7.1), neglect (OR = 3.4; 95% CI = 1.9–6.0), bullying (OR = 3.0; 95% CI = 1.9–4.8) and dating violence (OR = 1.9; 95% CI = 1.2–3.3). There was a clear dose-response relationship between childhood adversity and depression. Having any adverse experience was associated with a 4.6 increased risk of depression (OR = 4.6; 95% CI = 2.0–10.4) with gender and race adjusted ORs ranging from 4.6 to 8.0 for three or more types of adversity (95% CI = 3.4–18.8). Having an experience of any adversity, three or more adversities and bullying yielded the highest PARP (ranging from 41.3% to 67.9%) (See Table 2).

With regard to recent stressors, the following stressors were significantly associated with depression in the past year: discovery that a romantic partner had cheated (OR = 2.4; 95% CI = 1.3–4.3), serious betrayal by someone close to you (OR = 2.1; 95% CI = 1.3–3.4), serious ongoing arguments or breakups with a close friend or family member (OR = 2.5; 95% CI =1.6–4.1], academic stress

(OR = 2.1; 95% CI = 1.1–3.9), sexual or gender identity crisis (OR = 3.3; 95% CI = 1.7–6.7) and 'other' recent experience (OR = 2.4; 95% CI = 1.5–4.4). After disaggregation for the specific number of stressful experiences, we found evidence for an effect of three or more recent stressor (OR = 3.1; 95% CI = 1.1–8.8). From a population-level perspective, academic stress, three or more stressors and serious ongoing arguments were the variables that yielded the highest PARPs ranging from 18.0–39.6%.

Multivariable correlates of 12-month depression

Finally, a series of multivariable models were estimated giving us the opportunity to look at childhood adversity and recent stressors cumulatively (See Table 3). A first model found that, when adjusting for both type and number of 12-month recent stressors, three 12-month recent stressors remained significantly associated with depressive symptoms, i.e., a romantic partner being unfaithful, serious ongoing arguments or break-ups with a close friend or family member and a sexual or gender identity crisis, with ORs ranging from 2.1–3.0, and PARPs ranging from 6.9–13.0%. The effect of 12-month stressful events became non-significant in the final model (Nagelkerke pseudo-R^2 = 15.0%; AUC = 0.79) that additionally adjusted for type and number of childhood traumatic experiences, though it is worth noting that the OR decrease was minimal (see Table 4).

Discussion

Our multivariable logistic regression model indicated that childhood adversity and three recent stressors were significantly associated with current depression in this cohort. Students reporting adverse events during childhood, which included neglect, emotional abuse and being bullied specifically, were about three times more likely to report current depression. From an individual- and population level perspective, emotional abuse and being bullied prior to the age of 17 were significantly associated to current depressive symptoms: The data indicate that roughly 32–38% of the reported depression in this cohort were attributable to these two types of adversities. With regard to recent stressors, the multivariable logistic regression model suggested that a romantic partner being unfaithful, serious ongoing arguments or break-ups with a close friend or family member and a sexual or gender identity crisis were the strongest predictors of depression during the past year.

These data are consistent with a broad range of studies indicating that experiences of childhood adversity like bullying [45] are associated with subsequent onset of psychopathology [46, 47]. Previous studies have also suggested that there is a dose-response relationship between childhood adversity and psychopathology [2, 48]. Similarly, the role of recent stressors in depression has been well explored in the literature [49, 50], with some evidence for the cumulative effect of childhood adversity and recent stressors [11, 51]. While several recent stressors have been found to be associated with depression, our adjusted multivariable model specifically found that gender identity crisis, a romantic partner being unfaithful and arguments within a family to be associated with depression. With regard to a gender identity crisis, a recent review by Turban and Ehrensaft [52] suggest that youth who experience gender identity crisis may be at risk of depression among other comorbid conditions. Similarly, terminating a romantic relationship has been found to be significantly linked to depression in several studies [53]. Reyes-Rodriguez and colleagues [54], who examined depression among a similar sample of college students in Puerto Rico, found that depression was associated with ending a romantic relationship [54]. Studies, albeit of adolescents and not college students, have suggested a plausible association between family arguments and depression [55, 56].

A number of important study limitations must be noted. First, the study was restricted to one university in South Africa, and we are not certain that the results do necessarily extrapolate to others. Second, a minority of the invitees completed the survey (12.9%). However, the use of sophisticated weighting techniques adjusted for the missing data. Third, our data are cross-sectional, and attempts to derive causal relationships are tentative. Fourth, despite our attempts to establish a closer temporal link between recent stressors and depression in the last year, we still cannot be entirely sure if the event (e.g. family arguments) preceded the onset of depressive symptoms. Family arguments could be an antecedent or a consequence of depression, as suggested by previous studies [57, 58]. Fifth, self-reports of childhood adversity may be subject to recall bias. Our survey was designed as a self-report and was completed without the assistance of an interviewer in an attempt to limit recall bias and to collect information that was as accurate as possible [59]. Sixth, our measures of childhood adversity and recent stressors may not however adequately capture the severity or duration of traumatic experiences [60]. Seventh, due to limited statistical power, we were unable to examine associations for sub-syndromal depression and major depressive disorder separately, and to include low-prevalent predictor variables in the final multivariate models. Larger sample sizes are needed to address these objectives in the future. Lastly, this is an exploratory study in which multiple analyses were undertaken without correction. Future confirmatory research should formally test the information this study generated. These phenomena deserve future study.

Despite these limitations, our findings suggest that a history of some childhood adverse events and recent stressors are associated with depression in students attending a tertiary institution for the first time. This association may be particularly pronounced during the transitional period of adolescence to early adulthood, characteristic of the university/college years. Further retrospective and prospective studies with larger samples are needed to examine the interaction between trauma, stress and depression.

Conclusions

In conclusion, the college years are associated with increased risk of depression [61, 62]. Our findings suggest a significant relationship between early adversity, specific recent stressors, and depression in our student cohort, consistent with the broader literature on predictors of depression. Future research should address the impact of childhood trauma and recent stressors on wellbeing, quality of life, academic performance and choices after graduation. While this cross-sectional study underlines a number of variables that are associated with depression, longitudinal research is needed to fully delineate the relevant causal relationships. Universities could be natural sites of awareness campaigns of mental health related issues and intervention strategies and options, both at the prevention and treatment level [63]. First year students should be made aware of, and encouraged to make use of locally available mental health services for psycho-social support and to improve coping strategies.

Endnotes

[1]The South African Apartheid system created population categories including White, Black African, Indian and Coloured. The term 'Indian' refers to individuals whose ancestors are from India. The term 'Coloured' broadly refers to individuals of mixed ancestry. These categories are still used in census and statistical data; we use them here not in order to reify these sociocultural categories, but rather because we are interested in exploring potential health disparities between population groups.

Acknowledgements

We wish to acknowledge the contributions of Professors Ronny Bruffaerts, KU Leuven, Belgium and Martin Kidd, Stellenbosch University, South Africa to the manuscript.

The first author (SM) has received post-doctoral research funding from the Harry Crossley Foundation and the National Research Foundation of South Africa while enrolled in a post-doctoral fellowship at the University of Cape Town.

We gratefully acknowledge the support of the Ithemba Foundation.

Role of the sponsor

The funding sources had no role in the design and conduct of the study; collection, management, analysis, interpretation of the data; preparation, review, or approval of the manuscript; and decision to submit the manuscript for publication. The views reflected in the manuscript are not necessarily the views of the funders.

Authors' contributions

All authors contributed to and have approved the final manuscript. SM, LT & PM had full access to all of the data in this study and take responsibility for the integrity of the data, and the accuracy of the data analysis. *Study concept and design:* SM, LT, JR, DJS, PM & CL. *Acquisition, analysis, or interpretation of data:* SM, LT, PM & CL. *Drafting of the manuscript:* SM. *Critical revision of the manuscript for important intellectual content:* SM, LT, JR, DJS, PM & CL. *Statistical analysis:* PM. *Administrative, technical, or material support:* SM, LT, JR, DJS, PM & CL. *Study supervision:* LT, JR & CL.

Consent for publication

Consent for publication is not applicable in this study.

Competing interests

The authors declare that they have no competing interests.

Author details

[1]Department of Psychiatry and Mental Health, University of Cape Town, Cape Town, South Africa. [2]Division of Epidemiology and Biostatistics, School of Public Health, University of the Witwatersrand, Johannesburg, South Africa. [3]Research Group Psychiatry, Department of Neurosciences, KU, Leuven, Belgium. [4]MRC Unit on Risk and Resilience in Mental Disorders, Department of Psychiatry, Stellenbosch University, Stellenbosch, South Africa. [5]Mental Health Information Centre of Southern Africa, Stellenbosch, South Africa.

References

1. Heim C, Newport DJ, Mletzko T, et al. The link between childhood trauma and depression: Insights from HPA axis studies in humans. Psychoneuroendocrinology. 2008;33:693–710. https://doi.org/10.1016/j.psyneuen.2008.03.008.
2. McLaughlin KA, Green JG, Gruber MJ, et al. Childhood adversities and adult psychiatric disorders in the national comorbidity survey replication II: associations with persistence of DSM-IV disorders. Arch Gen Psychiatry. 2010;67:124–32. https://doi.org/10.1001/archgenpsychiatry.2009.187.
3. Bruwer B, Govender R, Bishop M, et al. Association between childhood adversities and long-term suicidality among south Africans from the results of the south African stress and health study: a cross-sectional study. BMJ Open. 2014;4:–e004644. https://doi.org/10.1136/bmjopen-2013-004644.
4. Nanni V, Uher R, Danese A (2012) Childhood maltreatment predicts unfavorable course of illness and treatment outcome in depression: a meta-analysis. Am J psychiatry 169:141–151. https://doi.org/10.1176/Appi.Ajp.2011.11020335.
5. Lindert J, Von Ehrenstein OS, Grashow R, et al. Sexual and physical abuse in childhood is associated with depression and anxiety over the life course: systematic review and meta-analysis. Int J Public Health. 2014;59:359–72. https://doi.org/10.1007/s00038-013-0519-5.
6. Plaza A, Garcia-Esteve L, Torres A, et al. Childhood physical abuse as a common risk factor for depression and thyroid dysfunction in the earlier postpartum. Psychiatry Res. 2012;200:329–35. https://doi.org/10.1016/j.psychres.2012.06.032.
7. Levitan RD, Parikh SV, Lesage AD, et al. Major depression in individuals with a history of childhood physical or sexual abuse: relationship to neurovegetative features, mania, and gender. Am J Psychiatry. 1998;155:1746–52. https://doi.org/10.1176/ajp.155.12.1746.
8. Infurna MR, Reichl C, Parzer P, et al. Associations between depression and specific childhood experiences of abuse and neglect: a meta-analysis. J Affect Disord. 2016;190:47–55. https://doi.org/10.1016/j.jad.2015.09.006.

9. Solomon Z, Bromet E. The role of social factors in affective disorder: an assessment of the vulnerability model of Brown and this colleagues. Psychol Med. 1982;12:123–30. https://doi.org/10.1017/S0033291700043361.
10. Park SC, Kim D, Jang EY. Prevalence and symptomatic correlates of interpersonal trauma in south Korean outpatients with major depressive disorder. Compr Psychiatry. 2016;66:46–52. https://doi.org/10.1016/j.comppsych.2015.12.006.
11. Suliman S, Mkabile SG, Fincham DS, et al. Cumulative effect of multiple trauma on symptoms of posttraumatic stress disorder, anxiety, and depression in adolescents. Compr Psychiatry. 2009;50:121–7. https://doi.org/10.1016/j.comppsych.2008.06.006.
12. Karam EG, Friedman MJ, Hill ED, et al. Cumulative traumas and risk thresholds: 12-month ptsd in the world mental health (WMH) surveys. Depress Anxiety. 2014;31:130–42. https://doi.org/10.1002/da.22169.
13. Mortier P, Demyttenaere K, Auerbach RP, et al. The impact of lifetime suicidality on academic performance in college freshmen. J Affect Disord. 2015;186:254–60. https://doi.org/10.1016/j.jad.2015.07.030.
14. Beiter R, Nash R, McCrady M, et al. The prevalence and correlates of depression, anxiety, and stress in a sample of college students. J Affect Disord. 2015;173:90–6. https://doi.org/10.1016/j.jad.2014.10.054.
15. Goldstein AL, Flett GL, Wekerle C. Child maltreatment, alcohol use and drinking consequences among male and female college students: an examination of drinking motives as mediators. Addict Behav. 2010;35:636–9. https://doi.org/10.1016/j.addbeh.2010.02.002.
16. Curran TA, Gawley E, Casey P, et al. Depression, suicidality and alcohol abuse among medical and business students. Ir Med J. 2009;102
17. Regehr C, Glancy D, Pitts A. Interventions to reduce stress in university students: a review and meta-analysis. J Affect Disord. 2013;148:1–11. https://doi.org/10.1016/j.jad.2012.11.026.
18. Booth KVP, Paunesku D, Msall M, et al. Using population attributable risk to help target preventive interventions for adolescent depression. Int J Adolesc Med Health. 2008;20:307–19.
19. Patel V, Maj M, Flisher AJ, et al. Reducing the treatment gap for mental disorders: a WPA survey. World Psychiatry. 2010;9:169–76. https://doi.org/10.1002/j.2051-5545.2010.tb00305.x.
20. Schuler KL, Ruggero CJ, Goldstein BL, et al. Diurnal cortisol interacts with stressful events to prospectively predict depressive symptoms in adolescent girls. J Adolesc Health. 2017; https://doi.org/10.1016/j.jadohealth.2017.06.005.
21. LeMoult J, Ordaz SJ, Kircanski K, et al. Predicting first onset of depression in young girls: interaction of diurnal cortisol and negative life events. J Abnorm Psychol. 2015;124:850–9. https://doi.org/10.1037/abn0000087.
22. Krysinska K, Martin G. The struggle to prevent and evaluate: application of population attributable risk and preventive fraction to suicide prevention research. Suicide Life Threat Behav. 2009;39:548–57. https://doi.org/10.1521/suli.2009.39.5.548.
23. Auerbach RP, Alonso J, Axinn WG, et al. Mental disorders among college students in the World Health Organization world mental health surveys. Psychol Med. 2016:1–16. https://doi.org/10.1017/S0033291716001665.
24. Kessler RC, Üstün BB. The world mental health (WMH) survey initiative version of the World Health Organization (WHO) composite international diagnostic interview (CIDI). Int J Methods Psychiatr Res. 2004;13:93–117. https://doi.org/10.1002/mpr.168.
25. Felitti VJ, Anda RF, Nordenberg D, et al. Relationship of childhood abuse and household dysfunction to many of the leading causes of death in adults - impact on children. Am J Prev Med. 1998;14:14. https://doi.org/10.1016/S0749-3797(98)00017-8.
26. Swearer SM, Cary PT. Perceptions and attitudes toward bullying in middle school youth. J Appl Sch Psychol. 2003;19:63–79. https://doi.org/10.1300/J008v19n02_05.
27. Mortier P, Kiekens G, Auerbach RP, et al. A risk algorithm for the persistence of suicidal thoughts and behaviors during college. J Clin Psychiatry. 2017;78: e828–36. https://doi.org/10.4088/JCP.17m11485.
28. Nansel TR, Overpeck M, Pilla RS, et al. Bullying behaviors among US youth: prevalence and association with psychosocial adjustment. JAMA. 2001;285: 2094–100. https://doi.org/10.1001/jama.285.16.2094.
29. Brugha TS, Cragg D. The list of threatening experiences: the reliability and validity of a brief life events questionnaire. Acta Psychiatr Scand. 1990;82: 77–81. https://doi.org/10.1111/j.1600-0447.1990.tb01360.x.
30. Gray MJ, Litz BT, Hsu JL, Lombardo TW. Psychometric properties of the life events checklist. Assessment. 2004;11:330–41. https://doi.org/10.1177/1073191104269954.
31. Angst J, Sellar R, Merikangas KR. Depressive spectrum diagnoses. Compr Psychiatry. 2000;41:39–47. https://doi.org/10.1016/S0010-440X(00)80007-3.
32. Judd LL, Akiskal HS. Delineating the longitudinal structure of depressive illness: beyond clinical subtypes and duration thresholds. Pharmacopsychiatry. 2000;33:3–7. https://doi.org/10.1055/s-2000-7967.
33. Andrews G, Brugha T, Thase ME, et al. Dimensionality and the category of major depressive episode. Int J Methods Psychiatr Res. 2007; https://doi.org/10.1002/mpr.216.
34. Ayuso-Mateos JL, Nuevo R, Verdes E, et al. From depressive symptoms to depressive disorders: the relevance of thresholds. Br J Psychiatry. 2010;196: 365–71. https://doi.org/10.1192/bjp.bp.109.071191.
35. Karsten J, Hartman CA, Ormel J, et al. Subthreshold depression based on functional impairment better defined by symptom severity than by number of DSM-IV symptoms. J Affect Disord. 2010;123:230–7. https://doi.org/10.1016/j.jad.2009.10.013.
36. Sadek N, Bona J. Subsyndromal symptomatic depression: a new concept. Depress Anxiety. 2000;12:30–9. https://doi.org/10.1002/1520-6394(2000)12:1<30::AID-DA4>3.0.CO;2-P.
37. Rosenbaum PR, Rubin DB (1983) a. "The central role of the propensity score in observational studies for causal effects" Biometrika. Biometrika 70 SRC-: 41–55. https://doi.org/10.1093/biomet/70.1.41.
38. Kiekens G, Claes L, Demyttenaere K, et al. Lifetime and 12-month nonsuicidal self-injury and academic performance in college freshmen. Suicide Life-Threatening Behav. 2016;46:563–76. https://doi.org/10.1111/sltb.12237.
39. Forke CM, Myers RK, Catallozzi M, Schwarz DF. Relationship violence among female and male college undergraduate students. Arch Pediatr Adolesc Med. 2008;162:634–41. https://doi.org/10.1001/archpedi.162.7.634.
40. Krupnick JL, Green BL, Stockton P, et al. Mental health effects of adolescent trauma exposure in a female college sample: exploring differential outcomes based on experiences of unique trauma types and dimensions. Psychiatry. 2004;67:264–79. https://doi.org/10.1521/psyc.67.3.264.48986.
41. Bruffaerts R, Demyttenaere K, Borges G, et al. Childhood adversities as risk factors for onset and persistence of suicidal behaviour. Br J Psychiatry. 2010; 197:20–7. https://doi.org/10.1192/bjp.bp.109.074716.
42. Nock MK, Borges G, Bromet EJ, et al. Suicide and suicidal behavior. Epidemiol Rev. 2008;30:133–54. https://doi.org/10.1093/epirev/mxn002.
43. Hu B, Shao J, Palta M. Pseudo-R2 in Logistic Regression Model. Stat Sin. 2006;16:847–60.
44. Firth D. Bias reduction of maximum likelihood estimates. Biometrika. 1993; 80:27–38. https://doi.org/10.1093/biomet/80.1.27.
45. Ttofi MM, Farrington DP. Risk and protective factors, longitudinal research, and bullying prevention. New Dir Youth Dev. 2012;2012:85–98. https://doi.org/10.1002/yd.20009.
46. Clark C, Caldwell T, Power C, Stansfeld S. Does the influence of childhood adversity on psychopathology persist across the lifecourse? A 45-year prospective epidemiologic study. Ann Epidemiol. 2010;20:385–94. https://doi.org/10.1016/j.annepidem.2010.02.008.
47. Turner HA, Butler MJC-D. Direct and indirect effects of childhood adversity on depressive symptoms in young adults. J youth Adolesc. 2003;32:89–103. ST–direct and indirect effects of childh
48. Green JG, McLaughlin KA, Berglund PA, et al. Childhood adversities and adult psychiatric disorders in the national comorbidity survey replication I: associations with first onset of DSM-IV disorders. Arch Gen Psychiatry. 2010; 67:113–23. https://doi.org/10.1001/archgenpsychiatry.2009.186.
49. Kendler KS, Thornton LM, Gardner CO. Stressful life events and previous episodes in the etiology of major depression in women: an evaluation of the "kindling" hypothesis. Am J Psychiatry. 2000;157:1243–51. https://doi.org/10.1176/appi.ajp.157.8.1243.
50. Kendler KS, Karkowski LM, Prescott CA. Causal relationship between stressful life events and the onset of major depression. Psychiatry Interpers Biol Process. 1999;156:837–41. https://doi.org/10.1176/ajp.156.6.837.
51. Comijs HC, Beekman ATF, Smit F, et al. Childhood adversity, recent life events and depression in late life. J Affect Disord. 2007;103:243–6. https://doi.org/10.1016/j.jad.2007.01.012.
52. Turban JL, Ehrensaft D. Research review: gender identity in youth: treatment paradigms and controversies. J Child Psychol Psychiatry. 2017; https://doi.org/10.1111/jcpp.12833.
53. Tao M, Li Y, Xie D, et al. Examining the relationship between lifetime stressful life events and the onset of major depression in Chinese women. J Affect Disord. 2011;135:95–9. https://doi.org/10.1016/j.jad.2011.06.054.
54. Reyes-Rodríguez ML, Rivera-Medina CL, Cámara-Fuentes L, et al. Depression symptoms and stressful life events among college students in Puerto Rico.

J Affect Disord. 2013;145:324–30. https://doi.org/10.1016/j.jad.2012.08.010.
55. Lin FG, Chou YC, CH W, Lin JD. Short-term and long-term influences of family arguments and gender difference on developing psychological well-being in Taiwanese adolescents. Res Dev Disabil. 2014;35:2735–43. https://doi.org/10.1016/j.ridd.2014.07.018.
56. Paradis AD, Reinherz HZ, Giaconia RM, et al. Long-term impact of family arguments and physical violence on adult functioning at age 30 years: findings from the Simmons longitudinal study. J Am Acad Child Adolesc Psychiatry. 2009;48:290–8. https://doi.org/10.1097/CHI.0b013e3181948fdd.
57. Sheeber LB, Davis B, Leve C, et al. Adolescents' relationships with their mothers and fathers: associations with depressive disorder and subdiagnostic symptomatology. J Abnorm Psychol. 2007;116:144–54. https://doi.org/10.1037/0021-843X.116.1.144.
58. Dmitrieva J, Chen C, Greenberger E, Gil-Rivas V. Family relationships and adolescent psychosocial outcomes: converging findings from eastern and western cultures. J Res Adolesc. 2004;14:425–47. https://doi.org/10.1111/j.1532-7795.2004.00081.x.
59. Susser E, Widom CS. Still searching for lost truths about the bitter sorrows of childhood. Schizophr Bull. 2012;38:672–5. https://doi.org/10.1093/schbul/sbs074.
60. Kelleher I, Keeley H, Corcoran P, et al. Childhood trauma and psychosis in a prospective cohort study: cause, effect, and directionality. Am J Psychiatry. 2013;170:734–41. https://doi.org/10.1176/appi.ajp.2012.12091169.
61. Zivin K, Eisenberg D, Gollust SE, Golberstein E. Persistence of mental health problems and needs in a college student population. J Affect Disord. 2009;117:180–5. https://doi.org/10.1016/j.jad.2009.01.001.
62. Ibrahim AK, Kelly SJ, Adams CE, Glazebrook C. A systematic review of studies of depression prevalence in university students. J Psychiatr Res. 2013;47:391–400. https://doi.org/10.1016/j.jpsychires.2012.11.015.
63. Cuijpers P, Cristea IA, Ebert DD, et al. PSYCHOLOGICAL TREATMENT of DEPRESSION in COLLEGE STUDENTS: a METAANALYSIS. Depress Anxiety. 2016;33:400–14. https://doi.org/10.1002/da.22461.

Coping strategies of women with postpartum depression symptoms in rural Ethiopia

Telake Azale[1,2], Abebaw Fekadu[2,3], Girmay Medhin[4] and Charlotte Hanlon[2,5*]

Abstract

Background: Most women with postpartum depression (PPD) in low- and middle-income countries remain undiagnosed and untreated, despite evidence for adverse effects on the woman and her child. The aim of this study was to identify the coping strategies used by women with PPD symptoms in rural Ethiopia to inform the development of socio-culturally appropriate interventions.

Methods: A population-based, cross-sectional study was conducted in a predominantly rural district in southern Ethiopia. All women with live infants between one and 12 months post-partum ($n = 3147$) were screened for depression symptoms using the validated Patient Health Questionnaire, 9 item version (PHQ-9). Those scoring five or more, 'high PPD symptoms', ($n = 385$) were included in this study. The Brief Coping with Problems Experienced (COPE-28) scale was used to assess coping strategies. Construct validity of the brief COPE was evaluated using confirmatory factor analysis.

Results: Confirmatory factor analysis of the brief COPE scale supported the previously hypothesized three dimensions of coping (problem-focused, emotion-focused, and dysfunctional). Emotion-focused coping was the most commonly employed coping strategy by women with PPD symptoms. Urban residence was associated positively with all three dimensions of coping. Women who had attended formal education and who attributed their symptoms to a physical cause were more likely to use both problem-focused and emotion-focused coping strategies. Women with better subjective wealth and those who perceived that their husband drank too much alcohol were more likely to use emotion-focused coping. Dysfunctional coping strategies were reported by women who had a poor relationship with their husbands.

Conclusions: As in high-income countries, women with PPD symptoms were most likely to use emotion-focused and dysfunctional coping strategies. Poverty and the low level of awareness of depression as an illness may additionally impede problem-solving attempts to cope. Prospective studies are needed to understand the prognostic significance of coping styles in this setting and to inform psychosocial intervention development.

Background

Postpartum depression (PPD) is a major public health concern in low and middle income countries (LMICs) [1]. PPD is the most common mental health problem in the perinatal period, with a weighted mean prevalence estimate of 19.8% (95% confidence interval 19.5 to 20.0%) in community studies from LMICs [2]. Risk factors for PPD in LMICs are mostly social stressors, including poverty, poor social support, intimate partner violence, history of pregnancy loss and unintended pregnancy, all of which tend to be common in LMICs [2]. Evidence for a negative impact of PPD in LMICs is accumulating [3]. Many studies have shown that the children of depressed mothers are more likely to be undernourished [4], although evidence from sub-Saharan Africa is conflicting [5–7]. Increased risk of infant diarrheal episodes has been found in Ethiopia [8] and Pakistan [9], and increased infant mortality associated with maternal depression has been shown in Ethiopia [10] and Ghana [11]. Adverse effects of maternal depression on child development have been found in India [12] and Bangladesh [13], with conflicting reports from Ethiopia [5, 14]. Despite

* Correspondence: charlotte.hanlon@kcl.ac.uk
[2]Addis Ababa University, Department of Psychiatry, School of Medicine, College of Health Sciences, 9086 Addis Ababa, PO, Ethiopia
[5]King's College London, Institute of Psychiatry, Psychology and Neuroscience, Centre for Global Mental Health, London, UK
Full list of author information is available at the end of the article

these adverse effects, PPD in women in LMICs mostly remains undetected and untreated.

There is a global initiative to integrate mental health services into maternal health care [15]. The World Health Organization has identified evidence-based packages of care for depression and other priority mental disorders which can be delivered by general health workers [16]. Given the challenges associated with safety and acceptability of psychotropic medicines in the perinatal period, there is a need for contextually appropriate psychosocial interventions [17, 18]. There is burgeoning evidence for effective psychosocial interventions for PPD that can be provided by non-mental health professionals in middle-income countries [19–21], but little from rural, low income country settings. Adaptation and successful implementation of a psychosocial intervention requires an understanding of women's existing coping mechanisms within that context.

Coping is described as the cognitive and behavioral processes that a person uses to deal with stressful circumstances that are judged to be demanding, challenging, threatening and/or have a potential for harm or loss [22]. Coping styles have been categorized into three dimensions: problem-focused, emotion-focused and dysfunctional or avoidance coping [22, 23]. Problem-focused coping involves dealing with the source of stress, while emotion focused-coping is when the person attempts to handle thoughts and feelings associated with the stressor [22]. Avoidance or dysfunctional coping refers to strategies which avoid dealing with either the problem or the associated emotions [23]. The choice of coping strategies also depends on the nature of the stressor, the person's perception of the seriousness of the experience and his/her evaluation of the resources available for coping and the likely effectiveness of a given strategy [22]. The negative cognitive biases and self-concept seen in individuals with depression may weaken their use of adaptive coping strategies and thereby influence outcome [24]. In support of this, associations have been found between coping strategies and the onset, course and outcome of depression in high-income countries [25]. People with depression are more likely to use avoidance coping strategies [25, 26]. Problem solving and emotion-focused coping are associated with less severe symptoms, while venting emotions (a dysfunctional strategy) has been associated with more impairment in functioning [27].

Coping strategies vary across cultures [28, 29]. There have been few studies examining the association between perinatal depression and coping strategies. Perinatal depression has been associated with emotion-focused coping in Greece [30] and with avoidance or dysfunctional coping in Belgium [31], Spain [32] and Greece [33]. In a study from a middle-income country, Brazil, an association was found between PPD and avoidance coping [34]. A study of coping among Ethiopians displaced from Eritrea found that both women and those who experienced traumatic events used emotion-focused coping more frequently, although female sex and better social support were associated with problem-focused coping [35].

The lack of evidence on coping strategies employed by women with PPD in a rural, low-income country setting, like Ethiopia, is a barrier to scaling up appropriate care. In Ethiopia and four other LMICs, the PRogramme for Improving Mental health carE (PRIME) is working to integrate maternal mental health services into primary health care. The aim of the current study was to assess the specific coping strategies used by women with symptoms of PPD in a rural Ethiopian setting with a view to informing development of appropriate interventions.

Methods

Study design

A population-based cross-sectional survey.

Study area

The study was conducted in Sodo district, Gurage Zone, Southern Nations, Nationalities and Peoples' Region (SNNPR) of Ethiopia. Sodo is located about 100 km south of the capital city, Addis Ababa. In the most recent census, the population was estimated to be 161,097 (79,896 male and 81,201 female) [36]. About 85% of the population lives in a rural setting. Amharic is the official language of the region but is the second language for the majority of inhabitants. Within Sodo district, there are eight primary care health centers, each linked to health posts which are staffed by community-based health extension workers.

The nearest psychiatric out-patient service is located in Butajira town, 30 to 50 km away. At the time of the study there was no specialist mental health professional located within the district. As part of the PRogramme for Improving Mental health carE (PRIME) [37], health centre staff, including midwives, were given brief in-service training to deliver mental health care in the primary care setting, supported by periodic supervision by a psychiatric nurse. At the time of data collection, the new service was not yet operational.

Sampling

A population census was conducted by the PRIME project. The census was used to identify women with infant children (< 1 year of age). To augment this strategy, a list of immunized infants was obtained from a registry maintained by the health extension workers. As a further strategy, data collectors, who had been recruited from the local community, went house to house to identify any additional eligible women. A total of 3147 eligible women were identified. As part of an interview assessment (described below), all women were screened for PPD symptoms using the Patient Health Questionnaire (PHQ-9). Those scoring above the validated cut-off indicating depression ('high PPD symptoms') were included in the study. The eligibility criteria were as follows:

women between one and 12 months postpartum, able to converse in Amharic (the official language of the region) and not acutely unwell.

Data collection

Data were collected using a structured questionnaire that included socio-demographic, obstetric, psychosocial and behavioral variables. Data collectors ($n = 36$) were trained for nine days and interviewed women in their homes. Four supervisors were also trained and assisted by the investigators. The data collectors were recruited from the district and the sub-districts or, in cases where eligible persons were not available at the specific sub-district, from the neighboring sub-districts. A pretest was conducted in three sub-districts of another district near the study area.

Each household containing an eligible woman was visited by a data collector who then explained the purpose of the research and gave the woman an information sheet or read the information aloud for those who were unable to read. Women who consented to participate were interviewed at a time and place that was convenient for them. Following screening with PHQ-9, those women scoring 5 or more were administered additional questionnaires. Data were collected between April and June 2014.

Measures

Coping strategies

In this study we used the Brief COPE Scale [38] to measure coping strategies. The brief COPE is a shortened version of the COPE scale, and has been used widely, including in LMICs.

In validation studies, the Brief COPE Scale was found to have reasonable reliability and validity [39–46]. Although the brief COPE has been used in more than 400 studies, it has rarely been used to assess coping in people with depression. For example, a systematic review of 80 studies that used the Brief COPE revealed that none of the studies was on people with depression [47].

The Brief COPE was originally developed to measure coping with any stressor [38]. The scale has 28 items that assess the degree to which a respondent utilizes a specific coping strategy. The 28 items have been categorized into 14 coping strategies named as: active coping, planning, positive reframing, acceptance, humor, religion, using emotional support, using instrumental support, self-distraction, denial, venting, substance use, behavioral disengagement and self-blame [38] and three higher order categories known as problem-focused, emotion-focused [22, 23], and avoidance or dysfunctional coping [23]. Alternatively, the brief COPE items have been categorized into "adaptive" and "maladaptive" coping. The development of these sub-scales was conceptually driven, and the theoretical grouping of the items to their sub-scales was largely established using principal components analysis [23]. Respondents rate items on a 4-point Likert scale, ranging from 1 *"I haven't been doing this at all"* to 4 *"I've been doing this a lot"*. As most of the participants were not literate, the items were rephrased into questions so that the questionnaire became interviewer administered. For example, *"have you been turning to work or other activities to take your mind off things?"* for I have been turning to work or other activities to take my mind of things.

PPD was measured using the Patient Health Questionnaire (PHQ-9) [48]. This instrument was developed to measure depression in the Primary Health Care (PHC) setting. The PHQ-9 has been culturally validated for use in several African country settings [49–53], including postpartum women in a rural setting in Ghana [54], and in the primary health care context in rural Ethiopia [55]. In Ethiopia, a score of five or more was found to have a sensitivity of 83% and specificity of 75% for the detection of major depressive disorder.

Explanatory models for PPD symptoms were measured with the Short Explanatory Model Interview (SEMI) [56]. The woman's perception of causes, severity, treatment need and options for symptoms of PPD were assessed by asking open-ended questions and coding the responses using pre-specified categories which had been adapted for the socio-cultural context in Ethiopia. Perceived severity of the condition was coded using the following categories: unable to say, not at all serious, mildly serious, moderately serious or very serious.

Disability was measured using the World Health Organization Disability Assessment Schedule (WHODAS) [57]. Disability was measured in six domains of functional impairment, including understanding and communicating, getting around, self-care, getting along with people, life activities, and participation in society. Scores were from 1 (no difficulty) to 5 (extreme or cannot do). The instrument has been used previously in perinatal women in a rural Ethiopian setting and found to have convergent validity with depressive symptoms [58].

Social support was measured using the Oslo Social Support Scale (OSSS-3) [59], which measures strength of social support. Scores from 3 to 8 indicate poor support, scores from 9 to 11 intermediate support, and a score between 12 and 14 is considered indicative of strong social support. The OSSS-3 has been used in community studies in Ethiopia previously [60].

The following potential confounders were measured using questions which have been used previously in postnatal women in the neighboring district: educational level, perceived relative wealth and hunger due to lack of resources in the past month (socio-economic status), quality of marital relationship, perception that the husband drank too much alcohol or chewed too much khat, and rural or urban residence.

Data management and analysis

Data were double entered using EpiData version 3.1 and then exported to SPSS version 20, cleaned, coded and analyzed. Descriptive analyses were carried out, including frequencies, mean and standard deviation and correlations among the items and sub-scales of the Brief COPE. Frequencies of the 28 items of the Brief COPE scale were calculated into the four Likert categories. The internal consistencies of the higher order scales were calculated with Cronbach's alpha. Confirmatory factor analysis was carried out to confirm the recommended three dimensions of coping namely, problem-focused, emotion-focused, and dysfunctional or avoidant coping [22, 61] using STATA 12 and AMOS-23 software. The most frequently used model fit indices include chi-square, root mean square error of approximation (RMSREA), comparative fit index (CFI), and Tucker-Lewis Index (TLI). Although there is no agreement as to the acceptable values of the indices, values closer to 1 are considered good fit if TFI and CLI. A value closer to zero is better for RMSEA. The chi-square test is frequently used as an index of model fit. A smaller chi-square value which is insignificant at $p = 0.05$ is considered to be a good fit. However, the value of chi-square is affected by several factors, such as sample size, the number of variables, and distribution of variables. Hence it is said to not be a good index practically. This is the reason for the use of alternative indices [62].

The 28 items of the Brief COPE scale were summed into 14 subscales after confirmatory factor analyses. Simple and multiple linear regression analyses were then carried out to examine factors associated with each of the three dimensions of coping. A priori confounders were included in the model, as described above. Other items of exploratory interest, e.g. from the SEMI, were included in the multivariable model if the univariate association with coping strategies had $p < 0.2$).

Ethical considerations

Ethical approval was obtained from the Institutional Review Board (IRB) of the College of Health Sciences, Addis Ababa University. Permission letters were received from the district health and administrative offices. Eligible women were given information sheets and those who agreed to participate signed or gave their finger prints before they were interviewed. Women who expressed suicidal ideation were put in contact with mental health care.

Results

There was a 100% response rate in the women screened for PPD symptoms. A total of 385 women with a PHQ-9 score of 5 or more were included in the analyses. The percentage of women with high PPD symptoms was, therefore, 12.2% (385/3147). One woman was excluded due to probable psychotic symptoms.

Socio-demographic and psychosocial characteristics

The mean PHQ score of the participants was 7.8 (Standard Deviation (SD): 3.03). The mean age of the respondents was 28.8 years with 5.23) standard deviation. More than half (n = 232; 60.3%) of the respondents were between 25 and 34 years of age. Almost all, (n = 374; 97.1%) were married. Three hundred and sixty-three women (94.3%) were rural residents. More than two-thirds, (n = 271; 70.4%) were unable to read and write. The vast majority, (n = 365; 94.8%) of the respondents were followers of Orthodox Christianity and 353 (91.7%) were Gurage by ethnicity. See Table 1.

Coping strategies

Religious coping was the most frequently used strategy. The two items: *"I have been praying or meditating"* and *"I have been trying to find comfort in my religion or spiritual beliefs"* were reported to be used 'a lot' by 49.9% (n = 192) and 36.4% (n = 140) respondents, respectively. The least frequently used coping strategies were substance use (n = 8; 2.1%) and humor 4.2% (n = 16). See Table 2.

Scores on the problem-focused coping sub-scale ranged from six to 24, with a mean of 14.6 (SD 3.95). The emotion-focused coping score ranged from 10 to 40, with a mean of 21.4 (SD 5.41). Dysfunctional coping scores ranged from 12 to 48 with a mean of 22.6 (SD 6.07).

Construct validity of the brief COPE

The internal consistency of each sub-scale was good, with Cronbach's alpha between 0.72 and 0.74. In the confirmatory factor analysis, the coefficients for items loading onto the three dimensions of coping ranged from 0.38 for substance use (*I have been using alcohol or other drugs to help me get through it*) to 0.82 for self-blame (*I have been blaming myself for things that happened*) and religion (*I have been trying to find comfort in my religion or spiritual beliefs*). The inter-item correlations were all significant except for the religion and humor items. The three higher order categories (problem-focused, emotion-focused and dysfunctional coping) were highly correlated. The CFA model fit indices were as follows: CMIN/DF 3.58, root mean squared error of approximation (RMSEA) 0.02, the comparative fit index 0.72, and Tucker Lewis Index 0.65. Removing the items with low coefficients did not improve the model fit. Therefore, all items were retained for further analysis. (See Additional file 1).

Factors associated with problem-focused coping

In the univariate analysis, urban residence, formal education, better relative wealth and attribution of symptoms to a physical cause were all associated significantly with higher scores on the problem-focused coping sub-scale. Not knowing the cause of the illness was associated with significantly lower problem-focused coping scores.

Table 1 Socio-demographic and psychosocial characteristics of women with symptoms of postpartum depression, Sodo district, 2014 ($n = 385$)

Socio-demographic characteristic	Frequency (%)
Age (in years)	
Less than 20	28 (7.3)
20–29	174 (45.2)
30–39	175 (45.5)
40 or above	8 (2.1)
Marital status	
Married	374 (97.1)
Single/widowed/divorced	11 (2.9)
Residence	
Rural	363 (94.3)
Urban	22 (5.7)
Education	
No formal education	308 (80.0)
Formal education	77 (20.0)
Religion	
Orthodox	365 (94.8)
Protestant	12 (3.1)
Muslim	6 (1.6)
Other	2 (0.6)
Ethnicity	
Gurage	353 (91.7)
Oromo	26 (6.8)
Amhara	5 (1.3)
Other	1 (0.3)
Psychosocial characteristics	
Hunger in the past one month	
No	259 (67.3)
Yes	126 (32.7)
Relative wealth	
Less	171 (44.4)
Same	198 (51.4)
Better	16 (4.2)
Social support	
Poor	104 (27.0)
Intermediate	187 (48.6)
Strong	94 (24.4)
Husband drinks too much	
No	290 (75.3)
Yes	95 (24.3)
Quality of marital relationship	
Bad	80 (20.8)
Good	305 (79.2)
Perceived cause of postpartum depression symptoms	
Psychosocial	231 (60.0)
Physical	89 (23.1)
Supernatural	16 (4.2)
Don't know	49 (12.8)
Perceived severity of PPD symptoms	
Mild	81 (21.0)
Moderate	151 (39.2)
Severe	153 (39.8)
WHODAS score (Disability)	
None	28 (7.3)
Mild	212 (55.1)
Moderate	126 (32.7)
Severe	18 (4.7)
Extreme or cannot do	1 (0.3)

All except relative wealth remained significantly associated in the multivariable model. See Table 3.

Factors associated with emotion-focused coping

Urban residence, formal education, better wealth, perception that her husband drank too much alcohol, and perceived physical cause for the symptoms were associated positively with emotion-focused coping in both the simple and multivariable linear regression analyses. Not knowing the cause of the illness and WHODAS score were negatively associated with emotion-focused coping. See Table 4.

Factors associated with avoidance/dysfunctional coping

Urban residence, better wealth, perception that her husband drank too much alcohol and bad marital relationship were positively associated with dysfunctional coping. Not knowing the cause of illness, and WHODAS score were negatively associated with dysfunctional coping in the simple linear regression. Relative wealth and perception that the husband drank too much alcohol were no longer significant in the multivariate analysis. See Table 5.

Discussion

In this community-based study from a rural, low-income country setting, women with PPD were found to be most likely to use religious and emotion-based coping strategies. Higher scores on emotion- and problem-based coping were associated with higher educational level, socio-economic status, urban residence and physical attribution to the symptoms. Dysfunctional coping was associated with marital problems. Emotion-based

Table 2 Frequency of use of coping strategies by women with symptoms of PPD (n = 385)

Coping strategies	Mean(SD)	Not at all or a little bit	A medium amount	A lot
Emotion-focused coping strategies				
I've been praying or meditating.	2.24 (0.83)	96 (24.9)	97 (25.2)	192 (49.9)
I've been trying to find comfort in my religion or spiritual beliefs.	1.95 (0.87)	156 (40.5)	89 (23.1)	140 (36.4)
I've been getting comfort and understanding from someone.	1.84 (0.84)	171 (44.4)	102 (26.5)	112 (29.1)
I've been accepting the reality of the fact that it has happened.	1.48 (0.76)	261 (67.8)	61 (15.8)	63 (16.4)
I've been looking for something good in what is happening.	1.46 (0.75)	269 (69.9)	54 (14)	62 (16.1)
I've been trying to see it in a different light, to make it seem more positive.	1.44 (0.74)	273 (70.9)	53 (13.8)	59 (15.3)
I've been learning to live with it.	1.37 (0.67)	284 (73.8)	59 (15.3)	42 (10.9)
I've been making jokes about it.	1.10 (0.42)	361(93.8)	8(2.1)	16(4.2)
I've been making fun of the situation.	1.12 (0.42)	359(93.2)	10(2.6)	16(4.2)
Problem-focused coping strategies				
I've been taking action to try to make the situation better.	1.79 (0.82)	178 (46.2)	109 (28.3)	98 (25.5)
I've been trying to get advice or help from other people about what to do.	1.65 (0.82)	219 (56.9)	78 (20.3)	88 (22.9)
I've been concentrating my efforts on doing something about the situation I'm in.	1.63 (0.80)	222 (57.7)	82 (21.3)	81 (21)
I've been thinking hard about what steps to take.	1.67 (0.79)	206 (53.5)	100 (26)	79 (20.5)
I've been trying to come up with a strategy about what to do.	1.62 (0.79)	221 (57.4)	88 (22.9)	76 (19.7)
I've been getting help and advice from other people.	1.41 (0.71)	276 (71.7)	58 (15.1)	51 (13.2)
I've been getting emotional support from others.	1.48 (0.78)	269 (69.9)	47 (12.2)	69 (17.9)
Avoidance/ dysfunctional coping strategies				
I've been turning to work or other activities to take my mind off things.	1.68 (0.87)	288 (59.2)	50 (13)	107 (27.8)
I've been doing something to think about it less, such as going to movies, watching TV, reading, daydreaming, sleeping, or shopping.	1.73 (0.86)	207 (53.5)	73 (19)	105 (27.3)
I've been saying things to let my unpleasant feelings escape.	1.52 (0.77)	250 (64.9)	68 (17.7)	67 (17.4)
I've been blaming myself for things that happened.	1.54 (0.77)	242 (62.9)	76 (19.7)	67 (17.4)
I've been criticizing myself.	1.51 (0.76)	253 (65.7)	67 (17.4)	65 (16.9)
I've been saying to myself "this isn't real".	1.38 (0.70)	287 (74.5)	47 (12.2)	51 (13.2)
I've been expressing my negative feelings.	1.37 (0.69	291 (75.6)	45 (11.7)	49 (12.7)
I've been refusing to believe that it has happened.	1.34 (0.69)	300 (77.9)	37 (9.6)	48 (12.5)
I've been giving up trying to deal with it.	1.26 (0.60)	316(82.1)	37(9.6)	32(8.3)
I've been giving up the attempt to cope.	1.21 (0.55)	329(85.5)	30(7.8)	26(6.8)
I've been using alcohol or other drugs to make myself feel better.	1.08 (0.37)	366(95.1)	6(1.6)	13(3.4)
I've been using alcohol or other drugs to help me get through it.	1.06 (0.31)	369(95.8)	8(2.1)	8(2.1)

functioning was also increased in women who perceived their husbands to drink too much alcohol.

Religious coping has been found to be among the most frequently used coping strategy by people with depression and other stressors [47, 63–65]. In Ethiopia, most people affiliate themselves with a religion and, thus, it is consistent that religion emerged as the main resource for coping with symptoms of distress and stressful experiences in this study. Emotional coping, of which religious coping is an example, is usually understood to be employed when a person perceives the problem to be beyond their control [22]. However, religious coping has been conceptualized as either a mediator or a buffer for depressive symptoms, depending on how it is used by the individual [64–66]. An example of positive religious coping could be looking to God for strength, support or guidance. Negative religious coping on the other hand might involve feeling abandoned or being punished by God [67]. Negative religious coping has been found to be a strong predictor of worsening symptoms of depression [68]. In studies from Poland and Greece, women with symptoms of PPD were found to more often use emotion-focused coping [30, 33].

Table 3 Simple and multiple linear regression analysis of factors associated with problem focused coping among women with symptoms of postpartum depression, ($n = 385$)

	Mean (SD)	Crude β (95% CI)	Adjusted β (95% CI)
Age, mean (SD), 28.8(5.2)		−0.00 (− 0.08, 0.07)	0.02 (− 0.04, 0 .10)
Residence			
Rural	14.4 (0.2)	Ref	Ref
Urban	17.3 (0.7)	**2.96 (1.28, 4.65)**	**2.39 (0.67, 4.11)**
Educational Status			
No formal education	14.2 (0.2)	Ref	Ref
Formal education	15.8 (0.4)	**1.53 (0.55, 2.51)**	**1.50 (0.44, 2.56)**
Hunger in the preceding month			
No	14.7 (0.2)	Ref	Ref
Yes	14.1 (0.3)	−0.63 (− 1.48, 0.20)	−0.47 (− 1.46, 0.50)
Subjective relative wealth			
Less	14.0 (4.2)	Ref	Ref
Same	14.8 (3.5)	**0.84 (0.04, 1.65)**	0.80 (−0.14, 1.75)
Better	16.5 (4.5)	**2.53 (0.52, 4.55)**	1.62 (−0.36, 3.61)
Social support			
Poor	14.8 (3.9)	Ref	Ref
Intermediate	14.0 (3.6)	−0.76 (−1.71, 0.18)	− 0.91 (− 1.86, 0.04)
Strong	15.2 (4.5)	0.32 (−0.77, 1.42)	− 0.18 (− 1.33, 0 .95)
Husband drinks too much alcohol			
No	14.3 (0.2)	Ref	Ref
Yes	15.1 (0.4)	0.80 (−0.11, 1.71)	0.90 (0.00, 1.81)
Marital relationship			
Bad	14.9 (0.4)	Ref	Ref
Good	14.4 (0.2)	−0.45 (−1.43, 0.52)	− 0.45 (− 1.44, 0.53)
PHQ score		0.11 (− 0.02, 0.24)	0.12 (− 0.00, 0.25)
Perceived cause			
Psychosocial	14.5 (3.8)	Ref	Ref
Physical	15.6 (4.3)	**1.13 (0.18, 2.08)**	**1.12 (0.17, 2.07)**
Supernatural	13.8 (3.6)	−0.71 (− 2.69, 1.26)	−0.95 (− 2.94, 1.04)
Unable to say	12.9 (3.4)	**−1.54 (− 2.75, − 0.34)**	**−1.41 (− 2.62, − 0.21)**
Perceived severity			
Mild	14.8 (3.7)	Ref	Ref
Moderate	14.0 (3.8)	−0.75 (−1.82, − 0.31)	−0.61 (− 1.69, 0.46)
Severe	14.9 (4.2)	0.08 (−0.98, 1.14)	0.36 (− 0.74, 1.47)
WHODAS Score		−0.05 (− 0.16, 0.04)	−0.09 (− 0.20, 0.01)

bold type signifies statistical significance at $p < 0.05$

The least frequently used coping strategies by women with symptoms of PPD in this study were substance use or humor. This is in keeping with the high endorsement of religious coping strategies [69]. Moreover, the participants of this study are women who are less likely to be frequent alcohol users for socio-cultural reasons. The low levels of humor-related coping strategies- may reflect cultural norms, but also that this sample of women had high levels of depressive symptoms.

The brief COPE scale and its construct validity

Confirmatory factor analysis supported the three dimensions of coping, with high loading values for most of the

Table 4 Simple and multiple linear regression analysis of factors associated with emotion focused coping among women with symptoms of postpartum depression, (n = 385)

Characteristics	Mean(SD)	Crude β(95% CI)	Adjusted β(95% CI)
Age		0.00 (− 0.09, 0.10)	0.04 (− 0.05, 0.15)
Residence			
Rural	21.2 (0.2)	ref	ref
Urban	24.4 (1.1)	**3.18 (0.86, 5.50)**	**2.60 (0.28, 4.93)**
Educational Status			
No formal education	21.0 (0.3)	ref	ref
Formal education	22.9 (0.6)	**1.91 (0.56, 3.25)**	**2.02 (0.59, 3.46)**
Hunger			
No	21.6 (0.3)	ref	ref
Yes	20.8 (0.4)	−0.75 (−1.91, 0.40)	−0.34 (−1.69,1.00)
Relative wealth			
Less	20.8 (5.4)	Ref	ref
Same	21.5 (5.2)	0.72 (−0.37, 1.82)	0.74 (−0.54, 2.03)
Better	25.3 (6.5)	**4.53 (1.77, 7.28)**	**3.22 (0.53, 5.92)**
Social support			
Poor	21.4 (4.4)	Ref	ref
Intermediate	20.8 (4.9)	−0.56 (−1.85, 0.73)	−0.56 (−1.85, 0.72)
Strong	22.4 (6.9)	1.04 (−0.46, 2.55)	0.41 (−1.13, 1.95)
Husband drinks too much alcohol			
No	20.9 (0.3	ref	ref
Yes	22.8 (0.6)	**1.89 (0.64, 3.14)**	**(0.69, 3.14)**
Marital relationship			
Bad	21.8 (0.6)	ref	ref
Good	21.3 (0.3)	−0.59 (−1.93, 0.74)	− 0.52 (− 1.86, 0.81)
PHQscore (Mean:7.83, SD: 3.03)		0.11 (− 0.06, 0.29)	0.15 (− 0.02, 0.33)
Perceived cause			
Psychosocial	21.2 (4.9)	ref	ref
Physical	23.4 (6.2)	**2.21 (0.91, 3.50)**	**2.35 (1.06, 3.63)**
Supernatural	21.0 (6.2)	−0.18 (−2.86, 2.50	−0.61 (−3.31, 2.08)
Unable to say	18.9(4.6)	**−2.20 (−3.83, − 0.56)**	**−1.96 (−3.59, − 0.33)**
Perceived severity			
Mild	21.3 (4.9)	ref	ref
Moderate	21.1 (5.6)	−0.15 (−1.62, 1.31)	0.09 (−1.37, 1.55)
Severe	21.7 (5.4)	0.42 (−1.04,1.88)	0.65 (−0.85,2.15)
WHODAS Score		−0.13 (− 0.27, 0.00)	**−0.16 (− 0.30, − 0.02)**

bold type signifies statistical significance at $p < 0.05$

items except the substance use and venting items. The model fit was also fairly good, but fell short of the conventional cut-offs on the indices of model fit. It is possible that some aspects of coping which are relevant in this context were not captured fully by the scale. The Brief COPE scale has been validated in different cultures among women with breast cancer in Malaysia [39] and caregivers of people with dementia in the UK [40]. In both of these studies, the Brief COPE was reported to be valid and reliable. In the first validation study, sensitivity of the scale to change was also indicated, with the Effect Size Index (ESI) ranging from 0 to 0.53. In the second study, high internal consistency and test-retest reliability over a year were demonstrated for emotion-focused, problem-focused, and dysfunctional subscales.

Table 5 Simple and multiple linear regression analysis of factors associated with dysfunctional coping among women with symptoms of postpartum depression, ($n = 385$)

Characteristics	Mean (SD)	Crude β (95% CI)	Adjusted β (95% CI)
Age		0.02 (– 0.09, 0.13)	0.07 (– 0.04, 0.19)
Residence			
Rural	22.4 (0.3)	Ref	Ref
Urban	26.0 (1.3)	**3.63 (1.03, 6.23)**	**4.13 (1.50, 6.76)**
Educational Status			
No formal education	22.5 (0.3)	Ref	Ref
Formal education	22.8 (0.7)	0.23 (−1.28, 1.75)	0.60 (– 1.02, 2.22)
Hunger			
No	22.9 (0.4)	Ref	Ref
Yes	21.9 (0.5)	−0.94 (−2.23, 0.35)	−0.92 (−2.45,0.60)
Relative wealth			
Less	22.2 (5.9)	Ref	Ref
Same	22.6 (5.8)	0.38 (−0.85,1.62)	0.28 (−1.17, 1.73)
Better	25.6 (9.5)	**3.34 (0.23, 6.45)**	1.72 (−1.32, 4.77)
Social support			
Poor	22.1 (5.5)	Ref	Ref
intermediate	22.4 (5.3)	0.30 (−1.15, 1.76)	−0.15 (– 1.61, 1.30)
Strong	23.4 (7.7)	1.25 (−0.44, 2.95)	0.11 (−1.63, 1.30)
Husband drinks too much alcohol			
No	22.2 (0.3)	Ref	Ref
Yes	23.8 (0.7)	**1.65 (0.24, 3.05)**	1.23 (−0.14, 2.62)
Marital relationship			
Bad	24.6 (0.6)	**2.54 (1.06, 4.02)**	**2.94 (1.44, 4.43)**
Good	22.0 (0.3)	**Ref**	**Ref**
PHQ score		0.09 (−0.10, 0.30)	0.11 (– 0.09, 0.31)
Perceived cause			
Psychosocial	22.6 (5.7)	Ref	Ref
Physical	23.7 (7.3)	1.03 (−0.44, 2.51)	1.39 (−0.05,2.84)
Supernatural	21.7 (5.0)	−0.92 (−3.99, 2.13)	– 0.56 (−3.61, 2.49)
Unable to say	20.6 (5.0)	**−2.02 (−3.88, – 0.15)**	**−1.97 (– 3.82, – 0.13)**
Perceived severity			
Mild	23.4 (5.8)	Ref	Ref
Moderate	22.2 (6.1)	−1.25 (−2.90, 0.38)	−0.66 (– 2.31, 0.99)
Severe	22.5 (6.1)	−0.86 (−2.50,0.77)	0.08 (−1.62, 1.78)
WHODAS Score		**−0.32 (– 0.48, – 0.17)**	**−0.36 (– 0.53, – 0.20)**

bold type signifies statistical significance at $p < 0.05$

Factors associated with coping styles

There were very high correlations among the sub-scales of the COPE in this study, for example 0.98 between problem-focused and emotion-focused coping. The scores on all of the COPE sub-scales, problem-focused, emotion-focused and dysfunctional, were significantly higher for urban residents. Women with formal education were more likely to use both problem- and emotion-focused coping. Urban women may differ from rural women in characteristics such as their access to resources and information, and the way in which they express their feelings, all of which will influence coping styles. Women living in rural areas in Ethiopia are often less empowered than their urban counterparts, for example, more likely to live in a non-consenting marriage [70]. They are likely to have fewer resources for problem-focused coping, less propensity to express their private feelings for emotion-focused coping, and may have less personal freedom for dysfunctional coping. Women who perceived that their wealth was better than their neighbors were more likely to use emotion-focused, but not problem-focused, coping. In this rural Ethiopian context, social support is closely linked to a person's capacity to reciprocate; therefore, poverty may undermine the possibility of obtaining emotional support and reframing of women's difficulties [71].

Attribution of the symptoms of postpartum depression to a physical cause was associated with significantly higher scores for both problem and emotion-focused coping. However, being unable to identify a cause for the PPD symptoms was negatively associated with all three dimensions of coping. It follows that if a person does not know what caused their problem, this is likely to be a barrier to effective coping. One possible explanation is that women may not consider their PPD symptoms to be the result of an illness (and, therefore, to be a 'problem'), but rather a part of life experience that they have to accept and live with. Women in LMICs attribute PPD to financial difficulties and marital conflict [72]. Similarly, in Ethiopia, although symptoms of PPD are recognized, they are attributed to social adversity or to failure of carrying out cultural chores that could expose to supernatural attacks which they believe cause the symptoms [73]. The implication of this may be that resources such as knowledge about depression and increasing social support might promote more problem-focused coping and contribute to improving symptoms.

Dysfunctional coping was increased in women who said that their relationship with their husbands was poor. Dysfunctional coping has been reported to be commonly used by people with high emotional distress, for example in the context of marital discord [74, 75]. The perception that their husbands drink too much alcohol was positively associated with emotion-focused coping. Thinking that one's husband drinks too much alcohol may mean it is difficult to modify that behavior. This may lead to the perception of the problem as unsolvable. Those individuals who perceive that their stressor is uncontrollable tend to use either emotion-focused or dysfunctional coping strategies [22]. Women in Ethiopia especially in the rural parts get married at early age without their consent and are economically dependent on their husbands. They are expected to stoically tolerate marital problems and maintain their marriage at all costs. Women who are married at young age are unlikely to have been to school and less likely to have known about the marriage beforehand and more likely to have experienced forced first marital sex and subsequent intimate partner violence [70].

Women who reported more functional impairment (scoring higher on the WHODAS) were less likely to use emotion-focused and dysfunctional coping compared to those with less functional impairment. Furthermore, no association was seen between functional impairment and problem-focused coping. This finding was unexpected as more apparent disability would be expected to motivate women to engage in more overt coping actions. The WHODAS is a measure of disability linked to any health condition, not specific to mental health problems. However, we have shown previously in this context that postpartum depressive symptoms are independent of physical health status indicators, such as low hemoglobin or low body mass index [76], and are strongly associated with functional impairment [58]. It is possible that aspects of problem-solving coping in this context were not captured adequately with the COPE scale; however, further studies are required to better understand this association.

Limitations

A limitation of this study is that we had not undertaken a formal cultural validation of the brief COPE for the local context. Nonetheless, the COPE was found to have reasonable construct validity in this sample. A further limitation is that it was not possible to elucidate the cause-effect relationship between depression and the coping strategies due to the cross-sectional nature of the study. A prospective study could help to elucidate whether coping strategies predispose women to depression or are a consequence of depression. The prognostic significance of particular coping strategies could also be investigated with a prospective design and would be an important evaluation of the predictive validity of the Brief COPE scale in this setting.

Conclusion

Religious coping was the most commonly used coping strategy by women with symptoms of postpartum depression in this rural Ethiopian community. Although it is not possible to know whether coping strategies lead to depression or vice versa, interventions can be developed that build on existing coping strategies and enhance the capacity of women to use more adaptive coping. The Brief COPE scale has fair internal consistency and acceptable construct validity but further cultural validation is needed.

Abbreviations

AMOS: Analysis of Moment Structure; CFI: Comparative Fit Index; COPE: Coping Orientation for Problems Experienced; IRB: Institutional Review Board; LMIC: Low and Middle-Income Country; OSSS: Oslo Social Support Scale; PHC: Primary Health Care; PHQ: Patient Health Questionnaire; PPD: Postpartum Depression; PRIME: Program for Improving Mental Health care; RMSEA: Root Mean Square Error of Approximation; SEMI: Short Explanatory Model Interview,; SNNPR: South Nations Nationalities and Peoples Region; TLI: Tucker Lewis Index; WHODAS: World Health Organization Disability Assessment Schedule

Acknowledgements
We are grateful to the study participants for giving their time and energy to respond to the interview questions. The authors acknowledge the PRIME project for funding the research. The district health office, administrative office and the respective sub-districts are highly acknowledged for their cooperation in the process of the research. We also thank the data collectors, supervisors, and other members of the research team for their commitment to the study.

Funding
This study is an output of the PRogramme for Improving Mental health carE (PRIME). This work was supported by the UK Department for International Development [201446]. The views expressed do not necessarily reflect the UK Government's official policies.

Authors' contributions
TA developed the proposal, supervised the data collection process, developed the data entry template, checked the data entry periodically, analyzed the data, and prepared the draft manuscript. CH: supported development of the proposal, analyzed the data and contributed to interpretation of the findings, as well as commenting on the manuscript. AF: contributed to the development of the proposal including the translation of the instruments, helped in interpretation of the results and commented on the manuscript. GM: contributed to data analysis and commented on the manuscript. All of the authors proofread and approved the final manuscript.

Consent for publication
N/A

Competing interests
The authors declare that they have no competing interests.

Author details
[1]University of Gondar, College of Medicine and Health Sciences, Department of Health Education and Behavioral Sciences, Gondar, Ethiopia. [2]Addis Ababa University, Department of Psychiatry, School of Medicine, College of Health Sciences, 9086 Addis Ababa, PO, Ethiopia. [3]King's College London, Institute of Psychiatry, Psychology and Neuroscience, Department of Psychological Medicine, Centre for Affective Disorders, London, UK. [4]Addis Ababa University, Aklilu Lemma Institute of Pathobiology, Addis Ababa, Ethiopia. [5]King's College London, Institute of Psychiatry, Psychology and Neuroscience, Centre for Global Mental Health, London, UK.

References
1. Shidhaye P, Giri P. Maternal depression: a hidden burden in developing countries. Ann Med Health Sci Res. 2014;4(4):463–5.
2. Fisher J, Cabral de Mello M, Patel V, Rahman A, Tran T, Holton S, Holmes W. Prevalence and determinants of common perinatal mental disorders in women in low- and lower-middle-income countries: a systematic review. Bull World Health Organ. 2012;90(2):139G–49G.
3. Parsons CE, Young KS, Rochat TJ, Kringelbach ML, Stein A. Postnatal depression and its effects on child development: a review of evidence from low- and middle-income countries. Br Med Bull. 2012;101:57–79.
4. Surkan PJ, Kennedy CE, Hurley KM, Black MM. Maternal depression and early childhood growth in developing countries: systematic review and meta-analysis. Bull World Health Organ. 2011;89:608–15.
5. Medhin G, Hanlon C, Dewey M, Alem A, Tesfaye F, Lakew Z, Worku B, Aray M, Abdulahi A, Tomlinson M, et al. The effect of maternal common mental disorders on infant undernutrition in Butajira, Ethiopia: the P-MaMiE study. BMC psychiatry. 2010;10:32.
6. Stewart RC. Maternal depression and infant growth: a review of recent evidence. Maternal & child nutrition. 2007;3(2):94–107.
7. Tomlinson M, Cooper PJ, Stein A. Post-partum depression and infant growth in a south African peri-urban settlement. Child Care Health Dev. 2006;32:81–6.
8. Ross J, Hanlon C, Medhin G, Alem A, Tesfaye F, Worku B, Dewey M, Patel V, Prince M. Perinatal mental distress and infant morbidity in Ethiopia: a cohort study. Arch Dis Child Fetal Neonatal Ed. 2011;96(1):F59–64.
9. Rahman A, Iqbal Z, Bunn J, Lovel H, Harrington R. Impact of maternal depression on infant nutritional status and illness: a cohort study. Arch Gen Psychiatry. 2004;61(9):946–52.
10. Deyessa N, Berhane Y, Emmelin M, Ellsberg MC, Kullgren G, Hogberg U. Joint effect of maternal depression and intimate partner violence on increased risk of child death in rural Ethiopia. Arch Dis Child. 2010;95(10):771–5.
11. Weobong B, Asbroek AH, Soremekun S, Gram L, Amenga-Etego S, Danso S, Owusu-Agyei S, Prince M, Kirkwood BR. Association between probable postnatal depression and increased infant mortality and morbidity: findings from the DON population-based cohort study in rural Ghana. BMJ. 2015;5
12. Patel V, DeSouza N, Rodrigues M. Postnatal depression and infant growth and development in low income countries: a cohort study from Goa, India. Arch Dis Child. 2003;88(1):34–7.
13. Black MM, Baqui AH, Zaman K, McNary SW, Le K, Arifeen SE, Hamadani JD, Parveen M, Yunus M, Black RE. Depressive symptoms among rural Bangladeshi mothers: implications for infant development. Journal of child psychology and psychiatry, and allied disciplines. 2007;48(8):764–72.
14. Hadley C, Tegegn A, Tessema F, Asefa M, Galea S. Parental symptoms of common mental disorders and children's social, motor and language development in sub- Saharan Africa. Ann Hum Biol. 2008;35(3):259–75.
15. WHO: Integrating mental health into primary care: a global perspective. In. Geneva World Health Organization / World Organization of Family Doctors; 2008: 206.
16. WHO: mhGAP Mental Health Gap Action Programme: Scaling up care for mental, neurological, and substance use disorders. In.; 2008.
17. Misri S, Kostaras X, Milis L. The use of antidepressants in pregnancy and lactation. BCMJ. 2005;47(3):139–42.
18. Misri S, Kendrick K. Treatment of perinatal mood and anxiety disorders: a review. Can J Psychiatry. 2007;52(8):489–98.
19. Chowdhary N, Sikander S, Atif N, Singh N, Ahmad I, Fuhr DC, Rahman A, Patel V. The content and delivery of psychological interventions for perinatal depression by non-specialist health workers in low and middle income countries: a systematic review. Best practice & research Clinical obstetrics & gynaecology. 2014;28(1):113–33.
20. Clarke K, King M, Prost A. Psychosocial interventions for perinatal common mental disorders delivered by providers who are not mental health specialists in low- and middle-income countries: a systematic review and meta-analysis. PLoS Med. 2013;10(10):e1001541.
21. Rahman A, Fisher J, Bower P, Luchters S, Tran T, Yasamy MT, Saxena S, Waheed W. Interventions for common perinatal mental disorders in women in low- and middle-income countries: a systematic review and meta-analysis. Bull World Health Organ. 2013;91(8):593–601I.
22. Folkman S. Personal control and stress and coping processes: a theoretical analysis. J Pers Soc Psychol. 1984;46:839–52.
23. Carver CS, Scheier MF, Weintraub JK. Assessing coping strategies: a theoretically based approach. J Pers Soc Psychol. 1989;56(2):267–83.
24. Scheier MF, Matthews KA, Owens J, Magovern GJS, Lefebvre RC. Dispositional optimism and recovery from coronary artery bypass surgery: the beneficial effects on physical and psychological well-being. J Pers Soc Psychol. 1989;57:1024–40.
25. Bjorklof GH, Engedal K, Selbaek G, Kouwenhoven SE, Helvik AS. Coping and depression in old age: a literature review. Dement Geriatr Cogn Disord. 2013;35(3–4):121–54.
26. Orzechowska A, Zajaczkowska M, Talarowska M, Galecki P. Depression and ways of coping with stress: a preliminary study. Medical science monitor : international medical journal of experimental and clinical research. 2013;19:1050–6.
27. Billings AG, Moos RH. Coping, stress, and social resources among adults with unipolar depression. J Pers Soc Psychol. 1984;46(4):877–91.
28. Wong DF. Stage-specific and culture-specific coping strategies used by mainland Chinese immigrants during resettlement in Hong Kong: a qualitative analysis. Soc Work Health Care. 2002;35(1–2):479–99.
29. See CM, Essau CA: Coping strategies in cross-cultural comparison. In: Psychologie-Kulter-Gesellschaft VS Verlag für Sozialwissenschaften; 2010.

30. Podolska MZ, Majkowicz M, Sipak-Szmigiel O, Ronin-Walknowska E. Ways of coping in stressful situations and anxiety-state or anxiety-trait among women with symptoms of perinatal depression. Ginekol Pol. 2009;80(3):201–6.
31. Demyttenaere K, Bonte L, Gheldof M, Vervaeke M, Meuleman C, Vanderschuerem D, D'Hooghe T. Coping style and depression level influence outcome in in vitro fertilization. Fertil Steril. 1998;69(6):1026–33.
32. Gutierrez-Zotes A, Labad J, Martin-Santos R, Garcia-Esteve L, Gelabert E, Jover M, Guillamat R, Mayoral F, Gornemann I, Canellas F, et al. Coping strategies for postpartum depression: a multi-centric study of 1626 women. Archives of women's mental health. 2015;
33. Gourounti K, Anagnostopoulos F, Lykeridou K. Coping strategies as psychological risk factor for antenatal anxiety, worries, and depression among Greek women. Archives of women's mental health. 2013;16:353–61.
34. Faisal-Cury A, Tedesco JJ, Kahhale S, Menezes PR, Zugaib M. Postpartum depression: in relation to life events and patterns of coping. Archives of women's mental health. 2004;7(2):123–31.
35. Araya M, Chotai J, Komproe IH, Joop TV, de Jong M. Gender differences in traumatic life events, coping strategies, perceived social support and sociodemographics among postconflict displaced persons in Ethiopia. Soc Psychiatry Psychiatr Epidemiol. 2007;42:307–15.
36. CSA: Population Projection of Ethiopia for All Regions At Wereda Level from 2014–2017. In Edited by Agency CS Addis Ababa: Central Statistical Agency; 2013.
37. Lund C, Tomlinson M, De Silva M, Fekadu A, Shidhaye R. PRIME: a Programme to reduce the treatment gap for mental disorders in five low- and middle-income countries. PLoS Med. 2012;9(12)
38. Carver CS. You want to measure coping but your protocol's too long: consider the brief COPE. International journal of behavioral medicine. 1997; 4(1):92–100.
39. Yusoff N, Low WY, Yip CH. Reliability and validity of the brief COPE scale (English version) among women with breast cancer undergoing treatment of adjuvant chemotherapy: a Malaysian study. Med J Malaysia. 2010;65(1):41–4.
40. Cooper C, Katona C, Livingston G. Validity and reliability of the brief COPE in carers of people with dementia: the LASER-AD study. J Nerv Ment Dis. 2008; 196(11):838–43.
41. BACANLI H, SÜRÜCÜ M, İLHAN T: An Investigation of Psychometric Properties of Coping Styles Scale Brief Form: A Study of Validity and Reliability. Educational Sciences: Theory & Practice 2013, 13(1).
42. Snell DL, Siegert RJ, Hay-Smith EJ, Surgenor LJ. Factor structure of the brief COPE in people with mild traumatic brain injury. J Head Trauma Rehabil. 2011;26(6):468–77.
43. Muller L, Spitz E. Multidimensional assessment of coping: validation of the brief COPE among French population. L'Encephale. 2003;29(6):507–18.
44. Doron J, Trouillet R, Gana K, Boiche J, Neveu D, Ninot G. Examination of the hierarchical structure of the brief COPE in a French sample: empirical and theoretical convergences. J Pers Assess. 2014;96(5):567–75.
45. Mohanraj R, Jeyaseelan V, Kumar S, Mani T, Rao D, Murray KR, Manhart LE. Cultural adaptation of the brief COPE for persons living with HIV/AIDS in southern India. AIDS Behav. 2015;19(2):341–51.
46. Kapsou M, Panayiotou G, Kokkinos CM, Demetriou AG. Dimensionality of coping: an empirical contribution to the construct validation of the brief-COPE with a Greek-speaking sample. J Health Psychol. 2010;15(2):215–29.
47. Krägeloh CU. A systematic review of studies using the brief COPE: religious coping in factor analyses. Religions. 2011;2:216–46.
48. Kroenke K, Spitzer RL, Williams JB. The PHQ-9: validity of a brief depression severity measure. J Gen Intern Med. 2001;16(9):606–13.
49. Adewuya AO, Ola BA, Afolabi OO. Validity of the patient health questionnaire (PHQ-9) as a screening tool for depression amongst Nigerian university students. J Affect Disord. 2006;96(1–2):89–93.
50. Chen S, Chiu H, Xu B, Ma Y, Jin T, Wu M, Conwell Y. Reliability and validity of the PHQ-9 for screening late-life depression in Chinese primary care. International journal of geriatric psychiatry. 2010;25(11):1127–33.
51. de Lima Osorio F, Vilela Mendes A, Crippa JA, Loureiro SR. Study of the discriminative validity of the PHQ-9 and PHQ-2 in a sample of Brazilian women in the context of primary health care. Perspectives in psychiatric care. 2009;45(3):216–27.
52. Gjerdingen D, Crow S, McGovern P, Miner M, Center B. Postpartum depression screening at well-child visits: validity of a 2-question screen and the PHQ-9. Ann Fam Med. 2009;7(1):63–70.
53. Zhong Q, Gelaye B, Fann JR, Sanchez SE, Williams MA. Cross-cultural validity of the Spanish version of PHQ-9 among pregnant Peruvian women: a Rasch item response theory analysis. J Affect Disord. 2014;158:148–53.
54. Weobong B, Akpalu B, Doku V, Owusu-Agyei S, Hurt L, Kirkwood B, Prince M. The comparative validity of screening scales for postnatal common mental disorder in Kintampo, Ghana. J Affect Disord. 2009; 113(1–2):109–17.
55. Hanlon C, Medhin G, Selamu M, Breuer E, Worku B, Hailemariam M, Lund C, Prince M, Fekadu A. Validity of brief screening questionnaires to detect depression in primary care in Ethiopia. J Affect Disord. 2015;186:32–9.
56. Lloyd KR, Jacob KS, Patel V, St Louis L, Bhugra D, Mann AH. The development of the short explanatory model interview (SEMI) and its use among primary-care attenders with common mental disorders. Psychol Med. 1998;28(5):1231–7.
57. WHO: WORLD HEALTH ORGANIZATION DISABILITY ASSESSMENT SCHEDULE (WHODAS-II). In. Switzerland: World health Organization; 2000.
58. Senturk V, Hanlon C, Medhin G, Dewey M, Araya M, Alem A, Prince M, Stewart R. Impact of perinatal somatic and common mental disorder symptoms on functioning in Ethiopian women: the P-MaMiE population-based cohort study. J Affect Disord. 2012;136(3):340–9.
59. Dalgard OS, Dowrick C, Lehtinen V, Vazquez-Barquero JL, Casey P, Wilkinson G. Negative life events, social support and gender difference in depression: a multinational community survey with data from the ODIN study. Soc Psychiatry Psychiatr Epidemiol. 2006;41:444–51.
60. Fekadu A, Medhin G, Selamu M, Hailemariam M, Alem A, Giorgis TW, Breuer E, Lund C, Prince M, Hanlon C. Population level mental distress in rural Ethiopia. BMC psychiatry. 2014;14:194.
61. Skinner EA, Edge K, Altman J, Sherwood H. Searching for the structure of coping: a review and critique of category Systems for Classifying Ways of coping. Psychol Bull. 2003;129(2):216–69.
62. Hooper D, Coughlan J, Mullen MR. Structural equation modelling: guidelines for determining model fit. The Electronic Journal of Business Research Methods. 2008;6(1):53–60.
63. Kasi PM, Naqvi HA, Afghan AK, Khawar T, Khan FH, Khan UZ, Khuwaja UB, Kiani J, Khan HM. Coping styles in patients with anxiety and depression. ISRN Psychiatry. 2012;2012:128672.
64. Abernethy AD, Chang HT, Seidlitz L, Evinger JS, Duberstein PR. Religious coping and depression among spouses of people with lung cancer. Psychosomatics. 2002;43(6):456–63.
65. Rahnama P, Javidan AN, Saberi H, Montazeri A, Tavakkoli S, Pakpour AH, Hajiaghababaei M. Does religious coping and spirituality have a moderating role on depression and anxiety in patients with spinal cord injury? A study from Iran. Spinal Cord. 2015;
66. Carpenter TP, Laney T, Mezulis A: Religious coping, stress, and depressive symptoms among adolescents: a prospective study. Psychology of Religion and Spirituality 2011.
67. Pargament KI, Koenig HG, Perez LM. The many methods of religious coping: development and initial validation of the RCOPE. J Clin Psychol. 2000;56:519–43.
68. Hebert R, Zdaniuk B, Schulz R, Scheier M. Positive and negative religious coping and well-being in women with breast cancer. J Palliat Med. 2009;12(6):537–45.
69. Koenig HG, Cohen HJ, Blazer DG, Pieper C, Meador KG, Shelp F, Goli V, DiPasquale B. Religious coping and depression among elderly, hospitalized medically ill men. Am J Psychiatry. 1992;149(12):1693–700.
70. Erulkar A. Early marriage, marital relations and intimate partner violence in Ethiopia. Int Perspect Sex Reprod Health. 2013;39(1):6–13.
71. Hailemariam M, Fekadu A, Prince M, Hanlon C. Engaging and staying engaged: a phenomenological study of barriers to equitable access to mental healthcare for people with severe mental disorders in a rural African setting. Int J Equity Health. 2017;16(1):156.
72. Rodriguesa M, Patel V, Jaswal S, de Souza N. Listening to mothers: qualitative studies on motherhood and depression from Goa, India. Soc Sci Med. 2003;57:1797–806.
73. Hanlon C, Whitley R, Wondimagegn D, Alem A, Prince M. Postnatal mental distress in relation to the sociocultural practices of childbirth: an exploratory qualitative study from Ethiopia. Soc Sci Med. 2009;69:1211–9.
74. Lee H, Yoon JY, Kim I, Jeong YH. The effects of personal resources and coping strategies on depression and anxiety in patients with chronic obstructive pulmonary disease. Heart & lung : the journal of critical care. 2013;42(6):473–9.

22

Yoga for posttraumatic stress disorder

Holger Cramer*, Dennis Anheyer, Felix J. Saha and Gustav Dobos

Abstract

Background: Yoga is increasingly used as a therapeutic treatment and seems to improve psychiatric conditions such as anxiety disorders and depression. The aim of this systematic review was to assess the evidence of yoga for reducing symptoms of posttraumatic stress disorder (PTSD).

Methods: The Cochrane Library, Medline/PubMed, PsycINFO, Scopus, and IndMED were searched through July 2017 for randomized controlled trials (RCTs) assessing the effects of yoga on symptoms of PTSD. Mean differences (MD) and standardized mean differences (SMD) with 95% confidence intervals (CI) were computed. The quality of evidence and the strength of recommendation were graded according to the GRADE recommendations.

Results: Seven RCTs ($N = 284$) were included. Meta-analysis revealed low quality evidence for clinically relevant effects of yoga on PTSD symptoms compared to no treatment (SMD = − 1.10, 95% CI [− 1.72, − 0.47], $p < .001$, $I^2 = 72\%$; MD = − 13.11, 95% CI [− 17.95, − 8.27]); and very low evidence for comparable effects of yoga and attention control interventions (SMD = − 0.31, 95%CI = [− 0.84, 0.22], $p = .25$; $I^2 = 43\%$). Very low evidence was found for comparable retention of patients in the trial for yoga and no treatment (OR = 0.68, 95%CI [0.06, 7.72]) or attention control interventions (OR = 0.66, 95%CI [0.10, 4.46]). No serious adverse events were reported.

Limitations: Few RCTs with only limited sample size were available.

Conclusions: Only a weak recommendation for yoga as an adjunctive intervention for PTSD can be made. More high quality research is needed to confirm or disconfirm these findings.

Keywords: Posttraumatic stress disorder, PTSD, Yoga, Meta-analysis

Background

With a lifetime prevalence of up to 6.1% worldwide, posttraumatic stress disorder (PTSD) is a major public health problem [1]. PTSD often results from substantial traumatic experiences and is thus far more common among veterans, survivors of wars or natural disasters, and victims of violence. The syndrome is associated with re-experiencing, avoidance, arousal, cognition, and mood symptoms [2].

A wide range of pharmacological and psychotherapeutic approaches are used in the treatment of PTSD [3]. Recent meta-analyses demonstrated that differences between most pharmacological treatments for PTSD and placebo are small at best [4, 5]. While phenelzine seems to be most effective, the paucity of available studies hindered definite conclusions [5]. The strong placebo effect in pharmacological treatment of PTSD might be a main reason for their perceived efficacy [4]. Psychotherapy, especially trauma-focused psychotherapy, seems to be superior to medication as a first-line treatment [6]. While psychotherapy thus seems to be the most promising first-line treatment for PTSD [3], a recent Cochrane Review rated the quality of evidence to be very low even for trauma-focused psychotherapy; and a considerable number of patients terminated the included psychotherapeutic trials early during the treatment period [7]. The latter might hint to a limited tolerability of these treatment approaches in some patients. In recent years, complementary therapy approaches for individuals with PTSD and other trauma-related disorders have received increasing interest [8]. Specifically mind-body approaches might

* Correspondence: h.cramer@kliniken-essen-mitte.de
Department of Internal and Integrative Medicine, Kliniken Essen-Mitte, Faculty of Medicine, University of Duisburg-Essen, Essen, Germany

be able to decrease trauma-related symptoms and emotion dysregulation [9]; and could thus be offered when patients are not able to tolerate psychotherapeutic treatment.

The most commonly used mind-body approach is yoga, a traditional Indian philosophical and spiritual school, as well as a health care practice which originated more than 3000 year ago and combines physical activity, mindfulness, relaxation, and breathing exercises [10]. Beside physical aspects, traditional yoga comprises ethical and spiritual perspectives. Modern yoga forms mostly comprise physical poses, breathing exercises, and meditation. Therefore, yoga is a holistic approach, which is thought to help uniting body, mind and spirit [10]. Thus, yoga is increasingly used to foster physical and mental well-being [10]. The efficacy of yoga in improving comorbid mental symptoms could be shown for different health conditions such as pain [11] and cancer [12]. There also is emerging evidence of efficacy of yoga as an ancillary treatment for psychiatric conditions such as depression [13–15], anxiety disorders [16, 17], and perhaps psychosis [18–20]. Yoga has become one of the most commonly used complementary therapy approaches in Northern America [21]. With respect to potential mechanisms of action, physical activity is a major element in yoga and this physical activity alone already seems to improve PTSD symptoms [22]. It has however been argued that by reducing stress-induced allostatic load and increasing parasympathic activity, yoga can directly reduce amygdala hyperactivation and elevated cortisol levels in patients with PTSD and thereby reduce symptoms [23]. This shift in autonomic balance to the parasympathic branch of the autonomic nervous system seems to be mainly triggered by breathing, relaxation, and meditation which are specific to yoga interventions [24]. Beyond biological mechanisms, yoga might potentially impact PTSD via different psychological pathways. Two major mechanisms of the paradox that patients feel anxious about the future although the traumatic event lies in the past were identified: negative appraisals of the trauma or its sequelae and the nature of the trauma memory itself [25]. Negative appraisals include overgeneralization, negative appraisal of own actions, negative reactions by other people and life prospects. These different types of appraisals can trigger the different emotional experiences by patients with PTSD [25]. Yoga often involves aspects of mindfulness, ie, a non-judgmental mindful attention to and acknowledgment of even unpleasant emotions or memories [26]. This is thought to increase emotion regulation rather than avoidance. The mindful awareness of the transitory nature of one's momentary physical, sensory, and emotional experience during yoga practice is thought to lead to a change in self-appraisal [27] and to also induce positive effects on PTSD symptoms [28]. Furthermore, even unspecific relaxation has been shown to contribute to an amelioration of PTSD symptoms although to a much smaller extent than more specific psychotherapeutic approaches [29]. Physical activity in yoga is mainly associated with an increased attentional focus to bodily perceptions and sensations. This can increase body awareness and potentially accurate identification of the triggered emotional response [30]. Beyond that, the social support in yoga classes might positively influence negative cognitive appraisals [31].

This systematic review aimed to investigate and meta-analyze the evidence of yoga for symptoms of PTSD.

Method

In conducting and reporting of this review, the Preferred Reporting Items for Systematic Reviews and Meta-Analyses (PRISMA) [32] statement and the Cochrane Collaboration's recommendations [33] were applied. The protocol was not published a priori.

Eligibility criteria

Types of studies: Randomized controlled trials (RCTs) were eligible. Studies were eligible regardless of the language they were published in, their country of origin or sample size.

Types of participants: Studies on adults with PTSD diagnosed by an established clinician-administered instrument and/or using a validated self-report instrument were eligible. Studies involving participants with comorbid physical or mental disorders were eligible for inclusion. Studies also including participants without PTSD were excluded unless outcomes for patients with PTSD were reported separately.

Types of interventions: RCTs on yoga were eligible. Studies were eligible regardless of the specific yoga style, the frequency or length of the intervention program or the duration of yoga sessions.

Types of control interventions: RCTs comparing yoga to no treatment, attention control ('placebo' interventions controlling for therapists' attention without a presumed specific therapeutic component) or other comparators were eligible. Meta-analyses were conducted separately for the different control conditions.

Studies allowing participants to use individual co-interventions (such as pharmacotherapy) were eligible as long as all participants in all group received the same co-interventions.

Types of outcome measures: Studies assessing symptoms of PTSD by at least one validated instrument were eligible. Where multiple instruments for PTSD symptoms were used in a single study, primacy was given to the instrument used in most of the other studies to increase comparability and homogeneity. If instruments were only used in a single study, primacy was given to clinician-assessed instruments over self-report measures.

Retention of patients in the trial and safety were assessed as secondary outcomes. Retention in the trial was defined as the number of patients who did not terminate the trial early during the treatment period; safety was defined as the number of patients who experienced adverse events.

Search methods

The electronic databases the Cochrane Library, Medline/PubMed, PsycINFO, Scopus, and IndMED were searched from their inception until July 31, 2017. The complete search strategy for all databases is shown in Additional file 1. Our own extensive database [34] was searched manually, as were the reference lists of articles identified during literature search and the tables of contents of the the Journal of Yoga & Physical Therapy, International Journal of Yoga Therapy, and the International Scientific Yoga Journal SENSE. The PILOTS database was additionally searched. Two reviewers independently assessed abstracts and potentially eligible articles identified during literature search. Discrepancies were resolved by discussion; if necessary a third reviewer was involved.

Data extraction and management

Data on participants, methods, interventions, control interventions, outcomes, and results were extracted by two review authors independently. An a priori developed data extraction form was used. Discrepancies were resolved by discussion; if necessary a third reviewer was involved.

The same two reviewers independently assessed risk of bias using the Cochrane tool [33]. Using this tool, risk of bias is assessed on seven domains including random sequence generation, allocation concealment, blinding of participants and personnel, blinding of outcome assessment, incomplete outcome data, selective reporting, and other bias. All domains were scored as low risk of bias, unclear risk of bias, or high risk of bias. No summary score is computed but all domains are assessed individually. Discrepancies were resolved by discussion; if necessary a third reviewer was involved.

Data analysis

For PTSD symptoms, meta-analyses were computed using standardized mean differences (SMD) and their respective 95% confidence intervals (CI) by a random-effects inverse variance model [33]. Using Hedges' correction for studies with small sample size, SMDs were computed as the between-group difference in means which is divided by the pooled standard deviation. When the original studies reported no standard deviations, they were calculated from standard errors, CIs or t-values. In line with the approach used by the Cochrane Collaboration, a negative SMD was regarded to indicate fewer PTSD symptoms in the yoga group compared to the control group [33]. Cohen's categories were used to estimate the size of the overall effect: SMDs ranging from 0.2 to 0.5 were defined as small effects; SMDs ranging from 0.5 to 0.8 were defined as medium size effects and SMDs beyond 0.8 were defined as large effect sizes [33, 35]. Where the same assessment instrument was used in multiple studies, mean differences and their 95% CI were further calculated as the absolute difference between mean values in the two groups [33]. For retention of patients in the trial, odds ratios (OR) with 95% confidence intervals (CIs) were calculated [33]. We originally planned to also calculate OR for safety; due to the paucity of studies reporting adequate safety-related data, this could not be done.

All analyses were computed using Review Manager 5 software (Version 5.3, The Nordic Cochrane Centre, Copenhagen).

As a measure of heterogeneity between studies, the I^2 statistics and Chi^2 test were used. Given the low power of this test, when only few studies or studies with low sample sizes are included in a meta-analysis, a p-value ≤ 0.10 was regarded as indicating significant heterogeneity [33].

Taking the quality of the respective studies as well as the confidence in the results into account, we graded the quality of evidence and the strength of recommendation. The recommendations of the Grading of Recommendations Assessment, Development and Evaluation (GRADE) working group were used. The quality of evidence was graded as high quality, moderate quality, low quality or very low quality based on the limitations of the respective studies, the inconsistency between the results of the respective, the indirectness of the evidence, the imprecision of the findings, the risk of publication bias, as well as the risk of other bias [36]. A body of evidence obtained from RCTs is initially graded as high quality, this rating can be downgraded due to risk of methodological bias, heterogeneity, differences in study characteristics between studies, wide confidence intervals, and risk of publication bias. Importantly, GRADE does not evaluate the quality of single studies but the quality of the complete body of evidence; e.g. the evidence for effects of yoga compared to a specific comparator on PTSD symptoms is rated [36]. A high quality of evidence indicates a high confidence that the effect found in the meta-analysis is a relatively good estimator for the true. A moderate quality indicates that the effect found in the meta-analysis is likely to be a good estimator for the true effect, however the true effect might also differ substantially from it. A low quality indicates that the effect found in the meta-analysis may differ substantially from the true effect. A very low quality indicates that the effect found in the meta-analysis will likely substantially differ from the true effect [37]. Finally, the strength of recommendation for or against yoga as an intervention for PTSD was judged as either strong or weak according to the GRADE recommendations. This judgement was based on the direction of the evidence (in favor of yoga or in favor of the control interventions), the quality of the evidence (see above) and the risk of adverse events of the interventions [36].

We conducted subgroup analyses to assess effects for different types of interventions (yoga using physical poses or yoga using no physical poses).

Risk of bias across studies

We had planned to investigate risk of publication bias by visual judgement of funnel plot asymmetry using Review Manager Software [33, 38]. As this approach requires at least 10 studies to be include in a respective meta-analysis, and all analyses included less than 10 studies, this could not be done.

Results

Literature search

Out of 282 records identified (143 after duplicates removed), 9 full-texts were assessed [39–47]. Two full-texts were excluded because they were additional publications on already included RCTs reporting additional outcomes [46] or follow-up assessments [47]. Seven RCTs on 284 patients were included in the qualitative and quantitative review [40–45] (Fig. 1).

Study characteristics

Five of the included RCTs originated from North America [40, 41, 43–45], one from South America [42], and one from Australia [39]. The included patients in three RCTs were diagnosed by the self-report Posttraumatic Stress Disorder Checklist [40, 42, 44] while four RCTs used clinician-assessed instruments [39, 41, 43, 45]. The majority of included patients were male (median = 73%), mean age ranged from 28.7 to 58.0 years (median = 43.6 years) (Table 1). Four RCTs included only military personnel and/or veterans [39, 42–44]. RCTs were roughly comparable regarding duration (median = 9.5 weeks) and intensity of the intervention (median = 1.75 sessions per week). Only one RCT used a staged intervention starting with daily, then weekly, then monthly sessions [39]. A variety of yoga styles was used, only one of them (applied in two RCTs) was specifically designed for patients with an experience of trauma [41, 45]. All but one yoga intervention [44] included physical postures. Four RCTs used waitlist control groups without any specific treatment; two RCTs used attention control interventions

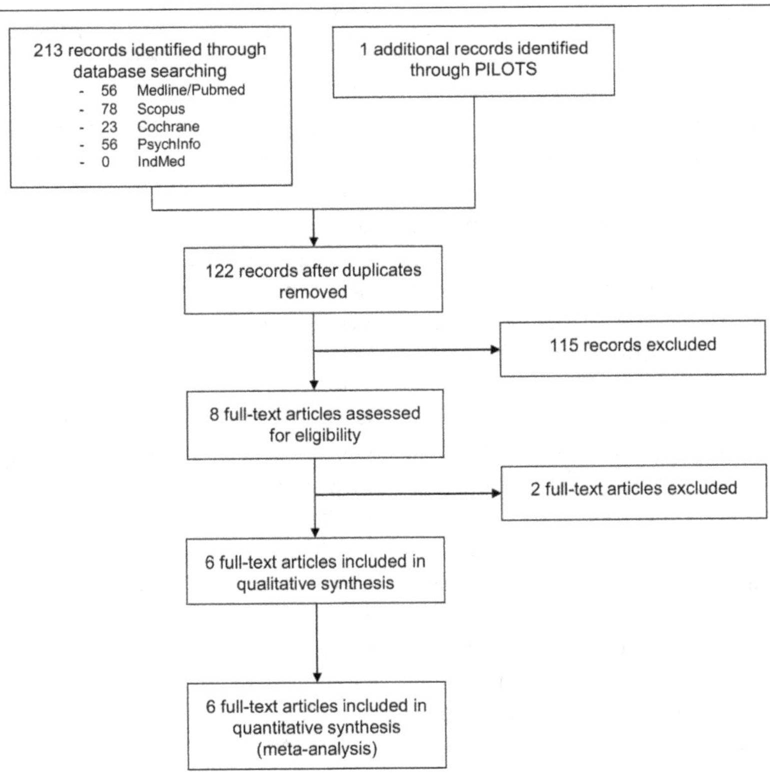

Fig. 1 Study flow diagram

Table 1 Characteristics of included studies

Author, year	Participants and setting	*N*	Diagnostic instrument	Mean age	% female	Treatment group	Control group	Outcome measures
Carter et al., 2013 [36]	Australian veterans recruited from private psychiatry clinic and through advertisements	31	CAPS	58.5 years	0%	Sudarshan Kriya Yoga: 22 h within 5 days, then once weekly for one month, then once monthly for 5 months, 120 min each	Waitlist: 6 weeks	CAPS, PCL-M
Jindani et al., 2015 [40]	Canadan community-dwelling adults recruited through advertisements	80	PCL-17	41.00 years	89%	Kundalini Yoga: 8 weeks, once weekly, 90 min each	Waitlist: 8 weeks	PCL-17
Mitchell et al., 2014 [41]	Veterans and civilians recruited from a US Veteran Affairs medical center	38	PSS-I	44.37 years	100%	Kripalu-based Yoga: 6 or 12 weeks, once or twice weekly, 75 min	Assessment control: 12 weeks, once weekly, duration not reported	PCL-C, TLEQ
Quinones et al., 2015 [42]	Colombian reintegrating PTSD patients recruited through the Agencia Colombiana para la Reintegración	100	PCL-C	Not reported	27%	Satvananda Yoga: 16 weeks, twice weekly, 60 min	Waitlist: 16 weeks	PCL-C
Reinhardt et al., 2017 [43]	US active duty military personnel and veterans recruited by flyers and advertisement	51	SCID-CT	46.74 years	8%	Kripalu Yoga: 10 weeks, twice weekly, 90 min	Assessment control: 10 weeks, three times in total, duration not reported	PCL-M, PCL-C, CAPS, IES
Seppälä et al., 2014 [44]	US veterans recruited through flyers and veteran and military organizations	21	PCL-M	28.65 years	0%	Sudarshan Kriya Yoga: 7 days, once daily, 180 min	Waitlist: 7 days	PCL-M
Van der Kolk et al., 2014 [45]	US women recruited through advertisements and mental health professionals	64	CAPS	42.9 years	100%	Trauma-informed Yoga: 10 weeks, once weekly, 60 min	Women's health education: 10 weeks, once weekly, 60 min	CAPS, DES, DTS

CAPS Clinician-Administered Posttraumatic Stress Disorder Scale, *DES* Dissociative Experience Scale, *DTS* Davidson Trauma Scale, *IES* Impact of Events Scale, *PCL-17* Posttraumatic Stress Disorder Checklist, *PCL-C* Posttraumatic Stress Disorder Checklist-Civilian, *PCL-M* Posttraumatic Stress Disorder Checklist-Military, *PSS-I* PTSD Symptom Scale-Interview, *SCID-CT* Structured Clinical Interview for DSM-IV-TR Axis I Disorders, clinical trials version, *TLEQ* Trauma Life Events Questionnaire

which controlled for therapists' time and attention but without a specific therapeutic component, i.e., an unspecific women's health education program and a weekly assessment group session without a therapeutic component [41, 45] (Table 1). A further study used a so-called assessment-only control, but while it used a group-assessment session, this session only took place once before and after the intervention while the intervention group met twice weekly over 10 weeks, so we classified this control condition as no treatment [43].

Risk of bias was mixed (Fig. 2). While five RCTs used adequate methods of random sequence generation [40, 41, 43–45], none adequately concealed allocation and only three RCTs blinded outcome assessors [39, 42, 43]. Five RCTs explicitly reported to not have blinded patients to treatment allocation [39–41, 43, 44]; the remaining RCTs did not report on blinding of participants and personnel. Given the difficulties of blinding behavioral interventions, participants and personnel were most likely not blinded to the allocated intervention in these trials. Attrition was high and not well balanced between groups in three RCTs and no adequate intention-to-treat analysis was used [40, 42, 43]. Finally, one study was rated as having high risk of other bias because it offered a substantial financial compensation to control participants but not to participants in the yoga group [42]. This methodologic approach most likely resulted in the strong imbalance in dropouts between groups.

Outcomes

Meta-analysis revealed evidence for statistically significant effects of yoga on PTSD symptoms compared to no treatment (SMD = – 1.10, 95% CI [– 1.72, – 0.47], $p < .001$; Fig. 3), with significant heterogeneity ($I^2 = 72\%$, $p = .007$). All studies used the PTSD checklist. The mean difference (MD = – 13.11, 95% CI [– 17.95, – 827]) was above the defined threshold of 10 points indicating clinical relevance [48], while the confidence interval also included values below the threshold for clinical relevance. The quality of evidence was downgraded to low due to high likelihood of bias, imprecision of results and the unclear risk of publication bias. The results did not change substantially when only

	Random sequence generation (selection bias)	Allocation concealment (selection bias)	Blinding of participants and personnel (performance bias)	Blinding of outcome assessment (detection bias)	Incomplete outcome data (attrition bias)	Selective reporting (reporting bias)	Other bias
Carter 2013	?	?	−	+	+	+	+
Jinandi 2015	+	?	−	?	−	−	+
Mitchell 2014	+	?	−	?	+	−	+
Quinones 2015	+	?	?	+	−	+	+
Reinhardt 2017	+	?	−	+	−	+	−
Seppälä 2014	+	−	−	?	+	+	+
van der Kolk 2014	?	?	?	?	+	?	?

Fig. 2 Risk of bias assessment for each included study. +, low risk of bias; −, high risk of bias; ?, unclear risk of bias

those RCTs were considered whose yoga intervention included physical postures (SMD = − 1.24, 95% CI [− 1.99, − 0.48], $p < .001$; heterogeneity: $I^2 = 78\%$, $p = .004$). The effects were however no longer present when the single RCT was considered that did not include physical postures (SMD = − 0.53, 95% CI [− 1.43, 0.36], $p = .24$).

Meta-analysis found no group differences of yoga compared to attention control interventions (SMD = − 0.31, 95%CI = [− 0.84, 0.22], $p = .25$; Fig. 3), without significant heterogeneity ($I^2 = 43\%$, $p = .19$). The quality of evidence for this lack of effects was downgraded to very low because of high likelihood of bias, unexplained heterogeneity, imprecision of results, and unclear risk of publication bias. Effects did not differ between the comparisons of yoga versus no treatment and yoga versus attention control ($Chi^2 = 3.53$, $P = 0.06$, $I^2 = 71.1\%$).

Retention of patients in the trial was comparable between yoga and no treatment (OR = 0.68, 95%CI = [0.06, 7.72], $p = 0.75$) and between yoga and attention control (OR = 0.66, 95%CI = [0.10, 4.46], $p = 0.67$) (Fig. 4). The quality of evidence for this lack of differences was downgraded to very low because of high likelihood of bias, unexplained heterogeneity, imprecision of results, and unclear publication bias. Retention did not differ between the comparisons of yoga versus no treatment and yoga versus attention control ($Chi^2 = .00$, $p = .99$, $I^2 = 0\%$).

The exported data and analyses of the meta-analyses are provided in Additional file 2.

Only three RCTs reported any safety-related data; and reported that no adverse reactions [41], no serious adverse events occurred [42], or reported two exacerbations of preexisting breathing problems in the yoga group while not reporting on adverse events in the control group [39].

Discussion

This meta-analysis found low quality evidence for statistically significant and potentially clinically relevant effects of yoga on symptoms of PTSD. While yoga was not superior to attention control interventions, the true effect is likely to be substantially different from the estimated effect [37]. Retention of patients in the trial differed widely between studies, but overall, dropouts were comparable between yoga and the control interventions. The evidence for this non-significant group difference was very low. It should however be noted that low and very low quality of evidence is a common finding when using GRADE methodology in meta-analyses of non-pharmacological interventions for PTSD [e.g. 7]. While safety was insufficiently reported, yoga did not seem to be associated with serious adverse events. The RCTs included veterans and civilians, a wide age range and patients of both genders. The applicability of the findings however is limited by the fact that all but one study were conducted in North America. Regarding intervention types, the effects seem to be only applicable to yoga interventions which include physical postures but not to mainly breathing-based yoga intervention without physical postures.

The findings of this meta-analysis are partly in line with that of a recent meta-analysis demonstrating a small to medium-size effect of yoga and meditation on PTSD symptoms [49]. While the analysis found no significant effects when only so called yoga based approaches were considered, it included one non-yoga study in their analysis [50]. It moreover pooled a variety of control conditions in a single analysis, rendering interpretation of their findings difficult and hindering direct comparison to our analysis. The findings of our meta-analysis are further in line with that of a recent

Study or Subgroup	Experimental Mean	Experimental SD	Experimental Total	Control Mean	Control SD	Control Total	Weight	Std. Mean Difference IV, Random, 95% CI
1.1.1 Yoga versus no treatment								
Carter 2013	32.1	6.8	16	50.8	6.9	15	16.8%	-2.66 [-3.66, -1.66]
Jinandi 2015	41.8	12	29	55.4	13.5	21	23.2%	-1.06 [-1.66, -0.46]
Quinones 2015	38.84	14.91	48	48.26	14.1	42	26.0%	-0.64 [-1.07, -0.22]
Reinhardt 2017	43	14.28	8	58	17.7	7	15.7%	-0.89 [-1.96, 0.19]
Seppälä 2014	26	6.91	10	32.5	15.01	10	18.4%	-0.53 [-1.43, 0.36]
Subtotal (95% CI)			**111**			**95**	**100.0%**	**-1.10 [-1.72, -0.47]**
Heterogeneity: Tau² = 0.34; Chi² = 14.20, df = 4 (P = 0.007); I² = 72%								
Test for overall effect: Z = 3.44 (P = 0.0006)								
1.1.2 Yoga versus attention control								
Mitchell 2014	39.07	16.01	20	39.09	12.65	18	43.2%	-0.00 [-0.64, 0.64]
van der Kolk 2014	49.48	25.16	32	63.49	25.48	32	56.8%	-0.55 [-1.05, -0.05]
Subtotal (95% CI)			**52**			**50**	**100.0%**	**-0.31 [-0.84, 0.22]**
Heterogeneity: Tau² = 0.06; Chi² = 1.74, df = 1 (P = 0.19); I² = 43%								
Test for overall effect: Z = 1.15 (P = 0.25)								
Test for subgroup differences: Chi² = 3.53, df = 1 (P = 0.06), I² = 71.7%								

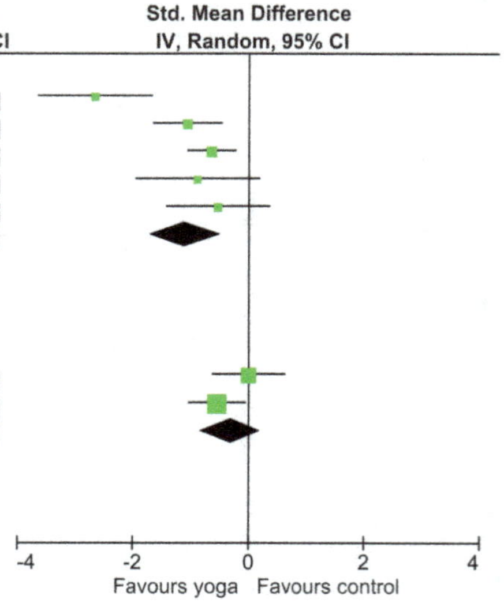

Fig. 3 Effects of yoga versus no treatment or attention control interventions on PTSD symptoms. CI, confidence interval; IV, inverse variance; SD; standard deviation

meta-analysis on meditation that found evidence for positive effects across different meditation types including yoga [51]. In line with our findings, a recent qualitative review on emerging PTSD interventions found moderate quality evidence for positive effects of yoga on PTSD symptoms [52]. Further narrative non-systematic reviews found comparable results [53, 54].

A limitation of this review is the diagnosis method used in the included studies. Only four trials used an established clinician-administered instrument [39, 41, 43, 45] while the others relied on potentially less precise self-report measures. Future studies should ensure adequate diagnostic criteria. The small number of studies included in this systematic review, the mixed risk of bias and the inadequate reporting of safety-related data further limit the validity of the findings. Future studies of yoga for PTSD should ensure rigorous trial design and reporting, mainly adequate allocation concealment

Study or Subgroup	Experimental Events	Experimental Total	Control Events	Control Total	Weight	Odds Ratio M-H, Random, 95% CI
2.1.1 Yoga versus no treatment						
Carter 2013	14	16	11	15	27.7%	2.55 [0.39, 16.55]
Jinandi 2015	29	59	21	21	22.8%	0.02 [0.00, 0.39]
Quinones 2015	48	50	42	50	29.0%	4.57 [0.92, 22.73]
Seppälä 2014	10	11	10	10	20.5%	0.33 [0.01, 9.16]
Subtotal (95% CI)		**136**		**96**	**100.0%**	**0.68 [0.06, 7.72]**
Total events	101		84			
Heterogeneity: Tau² = 4.66; Chi² = 13.75, df = 3 (P = 0.003); I² = 78%						
Test for overall effect: Z = 0.32 (P = 0.75)						
2.1.2 Yoga versus attention control						
Mitchell 2014	14	20	12	18	36.3%	1.17 [0.30, 4.59]
Reinhardt 2017	10	26	21	25	36.7%	0.12 [0.03, 0.45]
van der Kolk 2014	31	32	29	32	26.9%	3.21 [0.32, 32.60]
Subtotal (95% CI)		**78**		**75**	**100.0%**	**0.66 [0.10, 4.46]**
Total events	55		62			
Heterogeneity: Tau² = 2.12; Chi² = 8.41, df = 2 (P = 0.01); I² = 76%						
Test for overall effect: Z = 0.42 (P = 0.67)						
Test for subgroup differences: Chi² = 0.00, df = 1 (P = 0.99), I² = 0%						

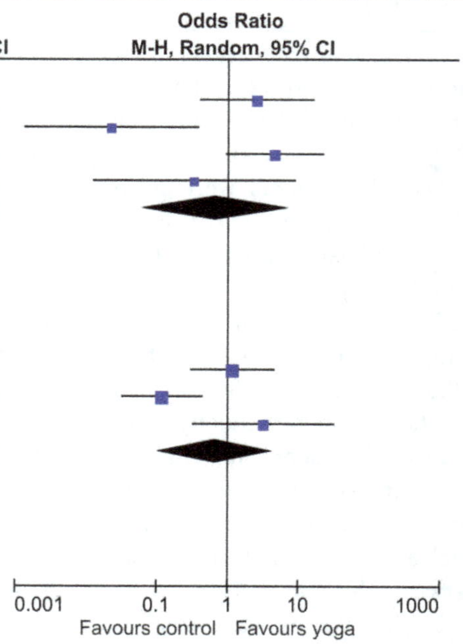

Fig. 4 Retention of patients in the trial for yoga versus no treatment or attention control interventions. CI, confidence interval; IV, inverse variance; SD; standard deviation

and blinding of at least outcome assessors [55]. At the moment, yoga can only be considered as an adjunct to other established treatments such as exposure therapy. If yoga is thought to be considered as a stand-alone intervention for PTSD, it should be empirically tested to an equal degree as established therapies [56]. Future studies should then further compare yoga to established therapies for PTSD to assess their comparative effectiveness. Standardization is an important question in yoga intervention and as shown in this meta-analysis, not all yoga styles can be considered equally effective for PTSD. In line with this, the active components of yoga interventions remain unclear; dismantling studies would be needed to assess the individual effects of yoga postures, breathing exercises and meditation/relaxation. An essential question for future studies on yoga for PTSD is the development of adequate control conditions. As shown, the two included studies found no difference between yoga and attention control. While this might also be due to a lack of power, more studies using adequately designed attention-control interventions are needed to conclusively address this issue. Comparing yoga to relaxation, exercise or support groups might further test the particular contributions of these intervention components to the overall effect of yoga [56].

Conclusions

There is low quality evidence that yoga interventions including physical postures could be an effective, acceptable and safe intervention for PTSD. According to the GRADE guidelines, only a weak recommendation for the use of yoga as an adjunctive intervention for PTSD can be made because the true effect may be substantially different from the effect estimated in this analysis [37]. Therefore, more high quality studies are needed to confirm or disconfirm these findings.

Abbreviations

CAPS: Clinician-administered posttraumatic stress disorder scale; CI: Confidence interval; DES: Dissociative experience scale; DTS: Davidson trauma scale; IES, impact of events scale; GRADE: Grading of recommendations assessment, development and evaluation; MD: Mean differences; PCL-17: Posttraumatic stress disorder checklist; PCL-C: Posttraumatic stress disorder checklist-civilian; PCL-M: Posttraumatic stress disorder checklist-military; PRISMA: Preferred reporting items for systematic reviews and meta-analyses; PSS-I: PTSD Symptom Scale-Interview; PTSD: Posttraumatic stress disorder; RCT: Randomized controlled trial; SCID-CT: Structured Clinical Interview for DSM-IV-TR Axis I Disorders, clinical trials version; SMD: Standardized mean differences; TLEQ: Trauma life events questionnaire

Acknowledgements

Not applicable.

Funding

No external funding was received for this meta-analysis.

Authors' contributions

HC conceived and designed of the review, performed the literature search, extracted and analyzed the data, assessed risk of bias, and drafted the manuscript. DA extracted the data, assessed risk of bias, and critically revised the manuscript. FJS and GD critically revised the manuscript. All authors read and approved the final manuscript.

Consent for publication

Not applicable.

Competing interests

The authors declare that they have no competing interests.

References

1. Kessler RC, Ustun TB. The WHO world mental health surveys: global perspectives on the epidemiology of mental disorders. New York: Cambridge University Press; 2008.
2. American Psychiatric Association. Diagnostic and statistical manual of mental disorders, 5 edn. Washington, DC: American Psychiatric Association; 2013.
3. NICE. Post-traumatic stress disorder: management [https://www.nice.org.uk/guidance/cg26/chapter/1-Guidance#the-treatment-of-ptsd]. Accessed 20 Aug 2017.
4. Hoskins M, Pearce J, Bethell A, Dankova L, Barbui C, Tol WA, van Ommeren M, de Jong J, Seedat S, Chen H, et al. Pharmacotherapy for post-traumatic stress disorder: systematic review and meta-analysis. Br J Psychiatry. 2015; 206(2):93–100.
5. Cipriani A, Williams T, Nikolakopoulou A, Salanti G, Chaimani A, Ipser J, Cowen PJ, Geddes JR, Stein DJ. Comparative efficacy and acceptability of pharmacological treatments for post-traumatic stress disorder in adults: a network meta-analysis. Psychol Med. 2017:1–10.
6. Lee DJ, Schnitzlein CW, Wolf JP, Vythilingam M, Rasmusson AM, Hoge CW. Psychotherapy versus pharmacotherapy for posttraumatic stress disorder: systematic review and meta-analysis to dtermine first-line treatment. Depress Anxiety. 2016;33(9):792–806.
7. Bisson JI, Roberts NP, Andrew M, Cooper R, Lewis C. Psychological therapies for chronic post-traumatic stress disorder (PTSD) in adults. Cochrane Database Syst Rev. 2013;12:CD003388.
8. Wynn GH. Complementary and alternative medicine approaches in the treatment of PTSD. Curr Psychiatry Rep. 2015;17(8):600.
9. Kim SH, Schneider SM, Kravitz L, Mermier C, Burge MR. Mind-body practices for posttraumatic stress disorder. J Investig Med. 2013;61(5):827–34.
10. Iyengar BKS. Light on yoga. New York: Schocken Books; 1966.
11. Bussing A, Ostermann T, Ludtke R, Michalsen A. Effects of yoga interventions on pain and pain-associated disability: a meta-analysis. J Pain. 2012;13(1):1–9.
12. Cramer H, Lauche R, Klose P, Lange S, Langhorst J, Dobos GJ. Yoga for improving health-related quality of life, mental health and cancer-related symptoms in women diagnosed with breast cancer. Cochrane Database Syst Rev. 2017;1:CD010802.
13. Cramer H, Lauche R, Langhorst J, Dobos G. Yoga for depression: a systematic review and meta-analysis. Depress Anxiety. 2013;30(11):1068–83.
14. Cramer H, Anheyer D, Lauche R, Dobos G. A systematic review of yoga for major depressive disorder. J Affect Disord. 2017;213:70–7.
15. Sharma A, Barrett MS, Cucchiara AJ, Gooneratne NS, Thase ME. A breathing-based meditation intervention for patients with major depressive disorder following inadequate response to antidepressants: a randomized pilot study. J Clin Psychiatry. 2017;78(1):e59–63.
16. Kirkwood G, Rampes H, Tuffrey V, Richardson J, Pilkington K. Yoga for anxiety: a systematic review of the research evidence. Br J Sports Med. 2005; 39(12):884–91.
17. Doria S, de Vuono A, Sanlorenzo R, Irtelli F, Mencacci C. Anti-anxiety efficacy of Sudarshan Kriya yoga in general anxiety disorder: a multicomponent, yoga based, breath intervention program for patients suffering from generalized anxiety disorder with or without comorbidities. J Affect Disord. 2015;184:310–7.
18. Vancampfort D, Vansteelandt K, Scheewe T, Probst M, Knapen J, De Herdt A,

De Hert M. Yoga in schizophrenia: a systematic review of randomised controlled trials. Acta Psychiatr Scand. 2012;126(1):12–20.
19. Broderick J, Knowles A, Chadwick J, Vancampfort D. Yoga versus standard care for schizophrenia. Cochrane Database Syst Rev. 2015;10:CD010554.
20. Cramer H, Lauche R, Klose P, Langhorst J, Dobos G. Yoga for schizophrenia: a systematic review and meta-analysis. BMC Psychiatry. 2013;13:32.
21. Cramer H, Ward L, Steel A, Lauche R, Dobos G, Zhang Y. Prevalence, patterns, and predictors of yoga use: results of a U.S. nationally representative survey. Am J Prev Med. 2016;50(2):230–5.
22. Rosenbaum S, Vancampfort D, Steel Z, Newby J, Ward PB, Stubbs B. Physical activity in the treatment of post-traumatic stress disorder: a systematic review and meta-analysis. Psychiatry Res. 2015;230(2):130–6.
23. Streeter CC, Gerbarg PL, Saper RB, Ciraulo DA, Brown RP. Effects of yoga on the autonomic nervous system, gamma-aminobutyric-acid, and allostasis in epilepsy, depression, and post-traumatic stress disorder. Med Hypotheses. 2012;78(5):571–9.
24. Cramer H. The efficacy and safety of yoga in managing hypertension. Exp Clin Endocrinol Diabetes. 2016;124(2):65–70.
25. Brewin CR, Holmes EA. Psychological theories of posttraumatic stress disorder. Clin Psychol Rev. 2003;23(3):339–76.
26. Bishop SR, Lau M, Shapiro S, Carlson L, Anderson ND, Carmody J, Segal ZV, Abbey S, Speca M, Velting D, et al. Mindfulness: a proposed Oerational definition. Clin Psychology. 2004;11:230–41.
27. Descilo T, Vedamurtachar A, Gerbarg PL, Nagaraja D, Gangadhar BN, Damodaran B, Adelson B, Braslow LH, Marcus S, Brown RP. Effects of a yoga breath intervention alone and in combination with an exposure therapy for post-traumatic stress disorder and depression in survivors of the 2004 South-East Asia tsunami. Acta Psychiatr Scand. 2010;121(4):289–300.
28. Emerson D, Hopper E, Levine PA, Cope S, van der Kolk B. Overcoming trauma through yoga: reclaiming your body. Berkeley: North Atlantic Books; 2011.
29. Bradley R, Greene J, Russ E, Dutra L, Westen D. A multidimensional meta-analysis of psychotherapy for PTSD. Am J Psychiatry. 2005;162(2):214–27.
30. Daubenmier JJ. The relationship of yoga, body awareness, and body responsiveness to self-objectification and disordered eating. Psychol Women Q. 2005;29:207–19.
31. Hitchcock C, Ellis AA, Williamson P, Nixon RD. The prospective role of cognitive appraisals and social support in predicting Children's posttraumatic stress. J Abnorm Child Psychol. 2015;43(8):1485–92.
32. Moher D, Liberati A, Tetzlaff J, Altman DG. Preferred reporting items for systematic reviews and meta-analyses: the PRISMA statement. Int J Surg. 2010;8(5):336–41.
33. Higgins JPT, Green S. Cochrane handbook for systematic reviews of interventions. West Sussex: Wiley; 2008.
34. Cramer H, Lauche R, Dobos G. Characteristics of randomized controlled trials of yoga: a bibliometric analysis. BMC Complement Altern Med. 2014;14:328.
35. Cohen J. Statistical power analysis for the behavioral sciences. New York, London: Lawrence Erlbaum Associates; 1988.
36. Guyatt G, Oxman AD, Akl EA, Kunz R, Vist G, Brozek J, Norris S, Falck-Ytter Y, Glasziou P, DeBeer H, et al. GRADE guidelines: 1. Introduction-GRADE evidence profiles and summary of findings tables. J Clin Epidemiol. 2011;64(4):383–94.
37. Balshem H, Helfand M, Schunemann HJ, Oxman AD, Kunz R, Brozek J, Vist GE, Falck-Ytter Y, Meerpohl J, Norris S, et al. GRADE guidelines: 3. Rating the quality of evidence. J Clin Epidemiol. 2011;64(4):401–6.
38. Higgins JP, Thompson SG, Deeks JJ, Altman DG. Measuring inconsistency in meta-analyses. BMJ. 2003;327(7414):557–60.
39. Carter JJ, Gebarg PL, Brown RP, Ware RS, D'Ambrosio C, Anand L, Dirlea M, Vermani M, Katzman MA. Multi-component yoga breath program for Vietnam veteran post traumatic stress disorder: randomized controlled trial. J Trauma Stress Disor Treat. 2013;2:3.
40. Jindani F, Turner N, Khalsa SB. A yoga intervention for posttraumatic stress: a preliminary randomized control trial. Evid Based Complement Alternat Med. 2015;2015:351746.
41. Mitchell KS, Dick AM, DiMartino DM, Smith BN, Niles B, Koenen KC, Street A. A pilot study of a randomized controlled trial of yoga as an intervention for PTSD symptoms in women. J Trauma Stress. 2014;27(2):121–8.
42. Quinones N, Maquet YG, Velez DM, Lopez MA. Efficacy of a Satyananda yoga intervention for reintegrating adults diagnosed with posttraumatic stress disorder. Int J Yoga Therap. 2015;25(1):89–99.
43. Reinhardt KM, Noggle Taylor JJ, Johnston J, Zameer A, Cheema S, Khalsa SBS. Kripalu yoga for military veterans with PTSD: a randomized trial. J Clin Psychol. 2017;74(1):93-108.
44. Seppala EM, Nitschke JB, Tudorascu DL, Hayes A, Goldstein MR, Nguyen DT, Perlman D, Davidson RJ. Breathing-based meditation decreases posttraumatic stress disorder symptoms in U.S. military veterans: a randomized controlled longitudinal study. J Trauma Stress. 2014;27(4):397–405.
45. van der Kolk BA, Stone L, West J, Rhodes A, Emerson D, Suvak M, Spinazzola J. Yoga as an adjunctive treatment for posttraumatic stress disorder: a randomized controlled trial. J Clin Psychiatry. 2014;75(6):e559–65.
46. Reddy S, Dick AM, Gerber MR, Mitchell K. The effect of a yoga intervention on alcohol and drug abuse risk in veteran and civilian women with posttraumatic stress disorder. J Altern Complement Med. 2014;20(10):750–6.
47. Rhodes A, Spinazzola J, van der Kolk B. Yoga for adult women with chronic PTSD: a long-term follow-up study. J Altern Complement Med. 2016;22(3):189–96.
48. Monson CM, Gradus JL, Young-Xu Y, Schnurr PP, Price JL, Schumm JA. Change in posttraumatic stress disorder symptoms: do clinicians and patients agree? Psychol Assess. 2008;20(2):131–8.
49. Gallegos AM, Crean HF, Pigeon WR, Heffner KL. Meditation and yoga for posttraumatic stress disorder: a meta-analytic review of randomized controlled trials. Clin Psychol Rev. 2017;58:115–24.
50. Kim SH, Schneider SM, Bevans M, Kravitz L, Mermier C, Qualls C, Burge MR. PTSD symptom reduction with mindfulness-based stretching and deep breathing exercise: randomized controlled clinical trial of efficacy. J Clin Endocrinol Metab. 2013;98(7):2984–92.
51. Hilton L, Maher AR, Colaiaco B, Apaydin E, Sorbero ME, Booth M, Shanman RM, Hempel S. Meditation for posttraumatic stress: systematic review and meta-analysis. Psychol Trauma. 2017;9(4):453–60.
52. Metcalf O, Varker T, Forbes D, Phelps A, Dell L, DiBattista A, Ralph N, O'Donnell M. Efficacy of fifteen emerging interventions for the treatment of posttraumatic stress disorder: a systematic review. J Trauma Stress. 2016;29(1):88–92.
53. Longacre M, Silver-Highfield E, Lama P, Grodin M. Complementary and alternative medicine in the treatment of refugees and survivors of torture: a review and proposal for action. Torture. 2012;22(1):38–57.
54. Telles S, Singh N, Balkrishna A. Managing mental health disorders resulting from trauma through yoga: a review. Depress Res Treat. 2012;2012:401513.
55. Schulz KF, Altman DG, Moher D. CONSORT 2010 statement: updated guidelines for reporting parallel group randomised trials. J Clin Epidemiol. 2010;63(8):834–40.
56. Siddaway AP, Wood AM. Recommendations for conducting mindfulness based cognitive therapy trials. Psychiatry Res. 2013;207(3):229–31.

Permissions

All chapters in this book were first published in PSYCHIATRY, by BioMed Central; hereby published with permission under the Creative Commons Attribution License or equivalent. Every chapter published in this book has been scrutinized by our experts. Their significance has been extensively debated. The topics covered herein carry significant findings which will fuel the growth of the discipline. They may even be implemented as practical applications or may be referred to as a beginning point for another development.

The contributors of this book come from diverse backgrounds, making this book a truly international effort. This book will bring forth new frontiers with its revolutionizing research information and detailed analysis of the nascent developments around the world.

We would like to thank all the contributing authors for lending their expertise to make the book truly unique. They have played a crucial role in the development of this book. Without their invaluable contributions this book wouldn't have been possible. They have made vital efforts to compile up to date information on the varied aspects of this subject to make this book a valuable addition to the collection of many professionals and students.

This book was conceptualized with the vision of imparting up-to-date information and advanced data in this field. To ensure the same, a matchless editorial board was set up. Every individual on the board went through rigorous rounds of assessment to prove their worth. After which they invested a large part of their time researching and compiling the most relevant data for our readers.

The editorial board has been involved in producing this book since its inception. They have spent rigorous hours researching and exploring the diverse topics which have resulted in the successful publishing of this book. They have passed on their knowledge of decades through this book. To expedite this challenging task, the publisher supported the team at every step. A small team of assistant editors was also appointed to further simplify the editing procedure and attain best results for the readers.

Apart from the editorial board, the designing team has also invested a significant amount of their time in understanding the subject and creating the most relevant covers. They scrutinized every image to scout for the most suitable representation of the subject and create an appropriate cover for the book.

The publishing team has been an ardent support to the editorial, designing and production team. Their endless efforts to recruit the best for this project, has resulted in the accomplishment of this book. They are a veteran in the field of academics and their pool of knowledge is as vast as their experience in printing. Their expertise and guidance has proved useful at every step. Their uncompromising quality standards have made this book an exceptional effort. Their encouragement from time to time has been an inspiration for everyone.

The publisher and the editorial board hope that this book will prove to be a valuable piece of knowledge for researchers, students, practitioners and scholars across the globe.

List of Contributors

Tobias Teismann and Jürgen Margraf
Mental Health Research and Treatment Center, Ruhr-Universität Bochum, Massenbergstraße 11, 44787 Bochum, Germany

Karoline Lukaschek
Institute of General Practice and Family Medicine, University Hospital of Ludwig-Maximilians-University Munich, Pettenkoferstr. 10, D-80336 Munich, Germany
Institute of Epidemiology, Helmholtz Zentrum München, German Research Center for Environmental Health, Ingolstädter Landstraße 1, D-85764 Neuherberg, Germany

Jochen Gensichen
Institute of General Practice and Family Medicine, University Hospital of Ludwig-Maximilians-University Munich, Pettenkoferstr. 10, D-80336 Munich, Germany
Institute of General Practice and Family Medicine, Jena University Hospital, Friedrich-Schiller-Universität, Bachstr. 18, D-07743 Jena, Germany

Thomas S. Hiller and Jörg Breitbart
Institute of General Practice and Family Medicine, Jena University Hospital, Friedrich-Schiller-Universität, Bachstr. 18, D-07743 Jena, Germany

Christian Brettschneider
Department of Health Economics and Health Services Research, Hamburg Center for Health Economics, University Medical Center Hamburg-Eppendorf, Martinistr. 52, D-20246 Hamburg, Germany

Ulrike Schumacher
Centre for Clinical Studies, Jena University Hospital, Salvador-Allende-Platz 27, D-07747 Jena, Germany

Dixon Chibanda
Zimbabwe Aids Prevention Project, Harare, Zimbabwe

Lorna Gibson
London School of Tropical Medicine and Hygiene, London, UK

Jonathan Brakarsh
Say and Play Therapy Centre, Harare, Zimbabwe

Soraya Seedat
College of Health Sciences, Stellenbosch University, Stellenbosch, South Africa

Isabelle Dibu Mulango
District Hospital Kumba, Kumba, South West Region, Cameroon

Julius Atashili
Medicine Programme, Faculty of Health Sciences, University of Buea, Buea, Cameroon

Bradley N. Gaynes
Department of Psychiatry, University of North Carolina School of Medicine, Chapel Hill, North Carolina, USA

Tsi Njim
Health and Human Development Research Group, Douala, Littoral Region, Cameroon
Nuffield Department of Health, Centre for Global Health and Tropical Medicine, University of Oxford, Oxfordshire, UK

Gunilla Sydsjö, Marie Bladh and Ann Josefsson
Department of Obstetrics and Gynaecology and Department of Clinical and Experimental Medicine, Linköping University, SE-581 85 Linköping, Sweden

Sara Agnafors
Department of Child and Adolescent Psychiatry and Department of Clinical and Experimental Medicine, Linköping University, Linköping, Sweden

Zhifeng Gu
Department of Rheumatology, Affliated Hospital of Nantong University, 20th Xisi road, 226001 Nantong, People's Republic of China

Yafei Cui
Department of Rheumatology, Affliated Hospital of Nantong University, 20th Xisi road, 226001 Nantong, People's Republic of China
School of Nursing, Nantong University, 19th Qixiu Road, 226001 Nantong, People's Republic of China

Lin li, Qian Zhao and Shengnan Chen
School of Nursing, Nantong University, 19th Qixiu Road, 226001 Nantong, People's Republic of China

Ling Xia
Department of Nursing, Affliated Hospital of Nantong University, 20th Xisi road, Nantong 226001, China

Tingting Wang, Hanlin Fu, Lizhang Chen and Qiongxuan Li
Department of Epidemiology and Health Statistics, Xiangya School of Public Health, Central South University, Changsha, Hunan Province, China

Atipatsa Chiwanda Kaminga
Department of Epidemiology and Health Statistics, Xiangya School of Public Health, Central South University, Changsha, Hunan Province, China
Department of Mathematics, Mzuzu University, Mzuzu 2, Malawi

Zhanzhan Li
Department of Oncology, Xiangya Hospital, Central South University, Changsha, Hunan Province, China

Guiping Guo
Department of Medical Psychology, The Second Xiangya Hospital of Central South University, Changsha, Hunan Province, China

Jurate Butnoriene
Institute of Endocrinology, Lithuanian University of Health Sciences, Eiveniu str

Vesta Steibliene
LT-50161 Kaunas, Lithuania
Psychiatry Clinic, Lithuanian University of Health Sciences, Kaunas, Lithuania

Ausra Saudargiene
Lithuanian University of Health Sciences, Kaunas, Lithuania
Neuroscience Institute, Lithuanian University of Health Sciences, Kaunas, Lithuania

Adomas Bunevicius
Neuroscience Institute, Lithuanian University of Health Sciences, Kaunas, Lithuania

Tian Xiao, Na Wang and Chaowei Fu
Department of Epidemiology, School of Public Health; Key Laboratory of Public Health Safety; Pudong Institute of Prevention Medicine, Fudan University, Shanghai 200032, China

Hua Qiu, Xianfeng Zhou, Kang Wu and Xiaonan Ruan
Department of Chronic Disease, Pudong New Area Center for Disease Control and Prevention, Shanghai 200136, China

Yue Chen
School of Epidemiology and Public Health, Faculty of Medicine, University of Ottawa, Ottawa, ON K1G 5Z3, Canada

Ruth Verhey
Zimbabwe Aids Prevention Project, 92 Prince Edward Road, Milton Park, Harare, Zimbabwe

Sanne J. E. Bruijniks
Department of Clinical Psychology, VU Amsterdam, Van der Boechorststraat 1, 1081, BT, Amsterdam, the Netherlands

Marcus J. H. Huibers
Department of Clinical Psychology, VU Amsterdam, Van der Boechorststraat 1, 1081, BT, Amsterdam, the Netherlands
Department of Psychology, University of Pennsylvania, Philadelphia, USA

Gerdien Franx
113 Zelfmoordpreventie, Amsterdam, the Netherlands

Jing Deng and Aizhong Liu
Department of Epidemiology and Health Statistics, Xiangya School of Public Health, Central South University, Changsha, Hunan, China

Atipatsa C. Kaminga
Department of Epidemiology and Health Statistics, Xiangya School of Public Health, Central South University, Changsha, Hunan, China
Department of Mathematics, Mzuzu University, Mzuzu, Malawi

Wenjie Dai and Shi Wu Wen
Department of Epidemiology and Health Statistics, Xiangya School of Public Health, Central South University, Changsha, Hunan, China
OMNI Research Group, Department of Obstetrics and Gynecology, Faculty of Medicine, University of Ottawa, Ottawa, ON, Canada
Ottawa Hospital Research Institute, Clinical Epidemiology Program, Ottawa, ON, Canada
School of Epidemiology, Public Health, and Preventive Medicine, Faculty of Medicine, University of Ottawa, Ottawa, ON, Canada

Zhiwei Lai
Immunization Programme Department, Hunan Provincial Center for Disease Control and Prevention, Changsha, Hunan, China

Jianzhou Yang
Department of Preventive Medicine, Changzhi Medical College, Changzhi, Shanxi, China

Hashima E. Nasreen, Jamalludin Ab Rahman and Razman Mohd Rus
Faculty of Medicine, International Islamic University Malaysia, Jalan Sultan Ahmad Shah, 25200 Kuantan, Pahang, Malaysia

Mira Kartiwi
Faculty of Information and Communication Technology, International Islamic University Malaysia, Jalan Gombak, 53100 Kuala Lumpur, Malaysia

Rosnah Sutan
Community Health Department, Universiti Kebangsaan Malaysia, Bandar Tun Razak Cheras, 56000 Kuala Lumpur, Malaysia

Maigun Edhborg
Department of Neurobiology, Care Sciences and Society, Karolinska Institute, SE-141 83 Huddinge, Stockholm, Sweden

Philip Held, Brian J. Klassen, Ashton M. Lofgreen, Patricia S. Normand, Michael B. Brennan, Thad S. Rydberg, Randy A. Boley, Mark H. Pollack and Niranjan S. Karnik
Rush University Medical Center, Chicago, IL 60612, USA

Alyson K. Zalta
Rush University Medical Center, Chicago, IL 60612, USA
University of California, Irvine, Irvine, CA 92697, USA

Dale L. Smith
Olivet Nazarene University, Bourbonnais, IL 60914, USA

Ahmad Hajebi
Research Center for Addiction and Risky Behavior (ReCARB), Iran University of Medical Sciences, Tehran, Iran
Department of Psychiatry, School of Medicine, Iran University of Medical Sciences, Tehran, Iran

Seyed Abbas Motevalian
Research Center for Addiction and Risky Behavior (ReCARB), Iran University of Medical Sciences, Tehran, Iran
Department of Epidemiology, School of Public Health, Iran University of Medical Sciences, Crossroads of Hemmat and Chamran Highways, Tehran, Iran

Afarin Rahimi-Movaghar, Masoumeh Amin-Esmaeili, Reza Radgoodarzi and Mitra Hefazi
Iranian National Center for Addiction Studies (INCAS), Tehran University of Medical Sciences, Tehran, Iran

Vandad Sharifi
Psychiatry and Psychology Research Center, Tehran University of Medical Sciences, Tehran, Iran
Department of Psychiatry, School of Medicine, Tehran University of Medical Sciences, Tehran, Iran

Yohannes Mirkena
University of Gondar Teaching and Referral Hospital, Gondar, Ethiopia

Mebratu Mitiku Reta
Department of Internal Medicine, School of Medicine, College of Medicine and Health Sciences, University of Gondar, Gondar, Ethiopia

Kibrom Haile and Zebiba Nassir
Amanuel Specialized Mental Health Hospital, Addis Ababa, Ethiopia

Malede Mequanent Sisay
Department of Epidemiology and Biostatistics, Institute of Public Health College of Medicine and Health Sciences, University of Gondar, Gondar, Ethiopia

Yingying Gu
Department of Psychiatry, the First Affiliated Hospital of Wenzhou Medical University, Wenzhou 325000, Zhejiang Province, China

Xiaoqian Luan, Wenwei Ren and Jincai He
Department of Neurology, the First Affiliated Hospital of Wenzhou Medical University, Wenzhou 325000, Zhejiang Province, China

Lin Zhu
Department of Pediatrics, the First Affiliated Hospital of Wenzhou Medical University, Wenzhou 325000, Zhejiang Province, China

Johanne Smith-Nielsen and Mette Skovgaard Væver
Centre for Early Intervention and Family Studies, Department of Psychology, University of Copenhagen, Oester Farimagsgade

Stephen Matthey
A, DK-1353 Copenhagen, Denmark
South West Sydney Local Health District, Liverpool Hospital, University of Sydney, Sydney, Australia

Theis Lange
Department of Public Health, Section of Biostatistics, University of Copenhagen, Copenhagen, Denmark

Wilfried Schnepp
Department of Health, University of Witten/Herdecke, Alfred-Herrhausen-Straße 50, 58448 Witten, Germany

Manuel P. Stadtmann
Department of Health, University of Witten/Herdecke, Alfred-Herrhausen-Straße 50, 58448 Witten, Germany
Centre for Trauma Disorders, Integrierte Psychiatrie Winterthur, Technikumstrasse 81, Winterthur, Switzerland

Andreas Maercker
Department of Psychology, Psychopathology and Clinical Intervention, University of Zurich, Binzmühlestrasse 14/17, 8050 Zürich, Switzerland

Jochen Binder
Centre for Trauma Disorders, Integrierte Psychiatrie Winterthur, Technikumstrasse 81, Winterthur, Switzerland

Julia Bretschneider, Silke Janitza, Julia Thom, Ulfert Hapke and Ulrike E. Maske
Unit 26 Mental Health, Department of Epidemiology and Health Monitoring, Robert Koch-Institute, Berlin, Germany

Frank Jacobi
Psychologische Hochschule Berlin, Berlin, Germany

Tobias Kurth
Institute of Public Health, Charité – Universitätsmedizin Berlin, Berlin, Germany

Judith Osok
Department of Psychiatry, School of Medicine, College of Health Sciences, University of Nairobi, 00100 Nairobi, Kenya

Pius Kigamwa
Department of Psychiatry, School of Medicine, College of Health Sciences, University of Nairobi, Nairobi, Kenya

Ann Vander Stoep
Psychiatry & Behavioral Sciences and Epidemiology, Child Health Institute, University of Washington, 6200 NE 74th Street, Suite 210, Seattle, WA 88115-1538, USA

Keng-Yen Huang
Department of Public Health and Child and Adolescent Psychiatry, New York University, New York, NY 10016, USA

Manasi Kumar
Department of Psychiatry, College of Health Sciences, University of Nairobi, Nairobi 00100 (47074), Kenya
Research Department of Clinical Health and Educational Psychology, University College London, London WC1E 7BT, UK

Lian Taljaard
MRC Unit on Risk and Resilience in Mental Disorders, Department of Psychiatry, Stellenbosch University, Stellenbosch, South Africa
Mental Health Information Centre of Southern Africa, Stellenbosch, South Africa

Telake Azale
University of Gondar, College of Medicine and Health Sciences, Department of Health Education and Behavioral Sciences, Gondar, Ethiopia
Addis Ababa University, Department of Psychiatry, School of Medicine, College of Health Sciences, 9086 Addis Ababa, PO, Ethiopia

Abebaw Fekadu
Addis Ababa University, Department of Psychiatry, School of Medicine, College of Health Sciences, 9086 Addis Ababa, PO, Ethiopia
King's College London, Institute of Psychiatry, Psychology and Neuroscience, Department of Psychological Medicine, Centre for Affective Disorders, London, UK

Charlotte Hanlon
Addis Ababa University, Department of Psychiatry, School of Medicine, College of Health Sciences, 9086 Addis Ababa, PO, Ethiopia
King's College London, Institute of Psychiatry, Psychology and Neuroscience, Centre for Global Mental Health, London, UK

Girmay Medhin
Addis Ababa University, Aklilu Lemma Institute of Pathobiology, Addis Ababa, Ethiopia

Sumaya Mall
Department of Psychiatry and Mental Health, University of Cape Town, Cape Town, South Africa
Division of Epidemiology and Biostatistics, School of Public Health, University of the Witwatersrand, Johannesburg, South Africa

Dan J. Stein
Department of Psychiatry and Mental Health, University of Cape Town, Cape Town, South Africa
MRC Unit on Risk and Resilience in Mental Disorders, Department of Psychiatry, Stellenbosch University, Stellenbosch, South Africa

Philippe Mortier
Research Group Psychiatry, Department of Neurosciences, KU, Leuven, Belgium

Christine Lochner
MRC Unit on Risk and Resilience in Mental Disorders, Department of Psychiatry, Stellenbosch University, Stellenbosch, South Africa

Janine Roos
Mental Health Information Centre of Southern Africa, Stellenbosch, South Africa

Holger Cramer, Dennis Anheyer, Felix J. Saha and Gustav Dobos
Department of Internal and Integrative Medicine, Kliniken Essen-Mitte, Faculty of Medicine, University of Duisburg-Essen, Essen, Germany

Index

www.ingramcontent.com/pod-product-compliance
Lightning Source LLC
LaVergne TN
LVHW080709210926
848485LV00003B/437